THE   DIRECTORY   OF

# Jobs and Careers Abroad

# THE DIRECTORY OF

# Jobs and
# Careers Abroad

*Editor*
## JONATHAN PACKER

*Distributed in the U.S.A. by*
**PETERSON'S GUIDES, INC**
202 Carnegie Center
Princeton, N.J. 08543-2123

*Published by*
**VACATION WORK**
9 Park End Street, Oxford

First published in 1971
edited by Alison Garthwaite
Second edition 1975
Third edition 1977
Second Impression 1978
Fourth edition 1979
edited by Roger Brown
Fifth edition 1982
edited by Philip Dodd
Sixth edition 1985
edited by David Leppard
Seventh edition 1989
edited by Alex Lipinski
Eighth edition 1993
edited by André de Vries
Ninth edition 1997
edited by Jonathan Packer

## THE DIRECTORY OF JOBS & CAREERS ABROAD

Copyright © Vacation Work 1997
ISBN 1 85458 167-8 (hardback)
ISBN 1 85458 166-X (softback)
ISSN 0143 — 3482

Cover Design by
Miller Craig & Cocking Design Partnership

Printed by Unwin Bros, The Gresham Press, Old Woking, Surrey, England

# Contents

# The General Approach

# Specific Careers

# Worldwide Employment

**Asia**

**Middle East and North Africa**

**Africa**

# Appendices

# Introduction

The world of work is changing; and interest in working abroad is at an all-time high. Educational qualifications and linguistic competence are two key requirements for the international jobseeker. Flexibility, and a new conception of career 'ownership' — which brings the responsibilty for pursuing and developing a career much closer to the individual — are also important consider-ations, whether you are a high-flyer in banking or engineering, a voluntary worker, or a graduate still searching for your first step on the employment ladder.

Your own decisions will affect, as never before, the outcome of your job search, and your future career. This spirit of self-reliance — and a readiness to accept new challenges and experiences — are also key requirements for those considering working abroad. Less hampered by rigid corporate structures of promotion and career advancement, we can use these changes in the world of work to our own advantage.

One of these changes is 'dejobbing'. Jobs are no longer fixed, but in an efficient organisation are flexible according ot the work that needs to be done; and they are not as easily organised into careers as they once were. Another trend is globalisation. The last decade of the twentieth century has seen the growth of an international market in many fields of employment, especially within certain specialised areas like information technology. Developments like the Internet — and the relative ease of modern communications — have helped in this process.

All of which can be good news for the creative jobseeker. Where there are few opportunities in your own country, there may be many abroad, where the same qualifications and experience may be in short supply. Voluntary work is one area where the market — if this is the right term — is increasingly international and 'global'; and a spell as a volunteer or intern abroad may also lead to more permanent employment in a related field.

In this brave new world of work, CV's are now said to be 'functional' — which means that the individual components of your work and experience are important, not just a chronology of the jobs you have done. Careers are now 'targeted'; and organisational structures are 'flatter'. Recruitment agencies are still looking for the same thing — the right person for the right vacancy, and to do this as efficiently as possible — but increasingly they are doing so in new ways. Scanning technology for analysing CV's and shortlisting candidates is now widely used, for instance, which means that a portfolio of individual attributes — the right 'profile' — is favoured over a more conventional account of your career to date.

This new market for jobs is global. But it is not necessarily free. There are the restrictions of language; and all the difficulties of relocating to another country — often with your partner and children. And there are many immigration restric-tions which mean that the qualified jobseeker will always be favoured over others wishing to work in unskilled areas of employment. You should consider education, and what you will learn which will aid you in your future career; and the experience you will gain. These should all be factors in your decision to move abroad (and not just your prospects within one company or organisation).

There is the phenomenon of large-scale unemployment; which is one problem even the most 'advanced' societies still seem unable to solve. The recent experi-ence of the relatively prosperous countries — like Germany and Japan — is a sign that economic success and full employment do not always go together. This is why there is a permanent pressure on governments to keep barriers to international employment up, even when other trading restrictions have been lifted. The same pressures are pushing even more workers to market their skills abroad, in the expectation of enhanced career prospects, higher earnings, or a better lifestyle.

## Jobs and Careers Abroad

Those who use the information in this book will fall into every possible category, from students on a working holiday to a company executive looking for an overseas posting. However long you are intending to stay, doing some homework in advance is advisable, if not essential, if you are to make the most of your experience of living and working abroad.

Life in another country can be fascinating or frustrating by turns — or more usually a mixture of the two. *The Directory of Jobs and Careers Abroad* is specifically designed to emphasise the former, by giving its readers the essential information they need to find their way to suitable employment. So, to address a very broad readership, it covers an extensive vocational and geographical spectrum — from two-month contracts as an au pair in France, to five-year engineering contracts in Saudi Arabia, or permanent emigration to New Zealand, Australia or Canada. If you already work for an international company, or if you are taking a more informal career path, if you are a new graduate and are taking time out to travel, or a consultant in a specialised field, there will be a range of information to help.

This ninth edition takes into account the many rapid changes in working abroad which the Directory itself chronicles over its history. It includes a new chapter on Russia and former CIS or Soviet Union countries; updated information about South Africa; a revised and expanded chapter on the environment; an introduction to jobseeking on the Internet; and a revision and updating of the specific information about jobs in different sectors; as well as of the cultural and economic information which gives the general background to life and work in many different countries. This Directory continues to look forward, as the international labour market has changed and continues to change.

## International Employment

The rapid transformation of the economies of Central and Eastern Europe — and former CIS — is perhaps the major recent change in the world economy, opening up a whole new range of employment possibilities for consultants and skilled workers. Free market ideas also seem to have won the day in all but a few countries — like North Korea or Cuba — where the future also looks likely to be one of one of slow or sudden integration into the global economy.

In the English-speaking world, the emergence of a multi-racial democracy in South Africa has had its own effect on job opportunities. In these countries, slow growth and unemployment still place some practical limits on the prospects for total labour mobility, despite an upturn in the American economy. So, in the USA, Canada, New Zealand, Australia, and the UK, strict controls on immigration continue to apply, which is encouraged only in certain areas of labour or skills shortage.

In Asia, the handover of Hong Kong to China could mean fewer opportunities there, at least in the short term. But China itself, with its huge economic potential, could emerge (alongside countries like Burma and Vietnam) as a major force in the 'second wave' of Asian economies to modernise (as the economies of Malaysia, the Philippines, Singapore, South Korea, Taiwan, and Thailand have done before them). These latter continue to grow, but at a slower pace. Japan seems likely to continue as the strongest economy in the region.

Within the European Union (EU) countries (which have adopted policies to favour the free movement of labour within their borders) working abroad is far less of a novelty than it used to be. In the federal European Union envisaged for the next century — for some if not all of its member states — the only real barriers to labour mobility will be cultural and linguistic.

In Latin America, too, one of the major disincentives for UK or US citizens seeking employment is linguistic. There are stronger historical ties in this region with Spain and Portugal, and greater employment and trading links to the USA than to Britain. In Africa, on the other hand, where there are still relatively few opportunities, the main barrier is economic. Voluntary and consultancy work in the field of development are the likeliest sources of employment in these underdeveloped or developing countries.

The oil-producing countries of North Africa and especially the Middle East are an exception to this rule. Some — like Libya — tend to award large-scale contracts to individual companies, which will then advertise the vacancies themselves, or work with recruitment agencies. Sanctions against some states may also act against those looking for work. But the market for jobs in development, construction, engineering, and the petrochemical industry, is strong.

**Using this Directory**
Generally, this edition retains the format of previous editions. The first and introductory section is practical, with chapters on *Discovering Your Employment Potential; Getting the Job; The Creative Job Search; Rules and Regulations; Learning the Language;* and *Preparation and Follow-up.* If you want to find out about rules governing employment in the EU, for instance, or about a creative approach to jobseeking, social security or taxation issues, or how to prepare for your stay in another country, you will find the relevant information here, and some pointers to future research and steps to take. This introductory section is called *The General Approach.*

If a particular career or category of work is your starting-point, the second section on *Specific Careers* is arranged to help. There are contacts for recruitment agencies and potential employers; and an introduction to each chapter on a particular sector of the employment market. A revised chapter on *Agriculture and the Environment* reflects the importance of environmental issues, in employment as in other areas.

The focus is on opportunities for a broad spectrum of jobseekers. A career in diplomacy, for instance, could take you to postings on several continents, from some of the most remote areas of the world to its major cities. Other areas include: banking and accountancy; computer services and information technology; engineering; education; journalism; the law; medicine; secretarial and interpreting work; transport; hospitality; teaching; and tourism.

International organisations are separately treated, as are the armed forces and the police. There is also a separate chapter on voluntary work.

The third section is called *Worldwide Employment.* Here there is a general introduction to the country or region; some facts and figures; a guide to conditions of work and work available; and specific contacts for jobseekers. Most people who consider emigrating — for very practical reasons — still choose one of the more affluent countries of western Europe, the Middle East, Asia, North America or Australasia. So, the amount of space devoted to these countries reflects the greater prospects — for mainly British and North American readers — of finding work there. Some countries which are in the process of transformation into developed economies, such as Russia, are given greater space, reflecting the potential for opportunities, and their growing importance in the international jobs market.

As in previous editions, in each of these three main sections there is specific information for North American as well as British citizens, reflecting the readership of this book in these countries. The approach is open-ended; and each address or specific contact — or suggestion for further research — should not be considered as the end of the story, but is an invitation to action, one link in the chain of opportunity which could lead to a job or career abroad.

## The Creative Job Search

The section entitled *The General Approach* also includes a technique for finding work which will be unfamiliar to many readers, and may require a preliminary remark here. The method is called 'the creative job search'. This begins with the idea that there are a large number of 'invisible' vacancies and opportunities for employment which jobseekers using the more conventional approaches may be unaware of.

It has been estimated that up to 75% of vacancies in the USA, and about 65% of those in the UK, fall into this category; and these 'invisible' vacancies are not publicly advertised through Jobcentres, employment agencies, or in the press. The reality of recruitment is often more about more informal arrangements like word-of-mouth, or a network of 'contacts' who are closely connected with the particular field of employment.

New jobseekers may wish to use the careers advice service or business library in their locality as a useful starting-point for information and advice. But you should remember all the other possible ways of finding work. You can establish contacts in your chosen field, by visiting the relevant trade fairs, for instance, or working on a job placement or as a volunteer. Then there are all the informal meetings you have: the contacts you can make when travelling abroad, for instance, or on the Internet.

This 'creative approach' will be more suitable in some areas than others. Many vacancies are classified by recruitment professionals as 'low-risk', and these are more likely to be dealt with by the more familiar methods of a job application and an interview or interviews. Middle management positions are usually 'medium-risk' (or more 'creative'). Then there are the 'high-risk' appointments, which are for high-flyers or short-term workers. These are often in smaller companies where other considerations will predominate — shortage of time or a deadline to be met. In these 'high-risk' areas, a more creative approach is certainly called for. Incidentally, workers in each of these different gradations of employment risk often know little about conditions for working in the others. For many, the experience of living and working abroad — in a different environment and culture – is one way they find out!

Nowadays it is said that employees even of large companies should regard themselves as 'self-employed' (which may be how their company itself sees them); and they should actively market their expertise and ability, even when in employment. This is the frame of mind which will aid all international jobseekers. A positive and enthusiastic approach to career development is the reverse side of the trend towards 'downsizing' and job insecurity which are features of the jobs market today.

This is why a 'creative approach' is called for. Those who don't move on in their career may be moved on, or sideways, or back into unemployment. The widespread interest in working abroad itself may be a response to the more temporary and uncertain nature of work in a competitive global economy.

The aim of this job search, for those who are willing to take a more creative and positive approach (which will usually run alongside the more conventional methods), is to become as much as possible a link in the 'chain of informal vacancy notification' (which is discussed more fully in the chapter on *The Creative Job Search*). Consistent preparation and perseverance are also necessary ingredients of your success (as they are also the preconditions for living and working in a country where the way of life and living conditions may be very different).

So, more than ever, individuals themselves are having to take responsibility for their career choices. This applies most of all to jobs and careers abroad.

13

**Vacation Work**

For over twenty-five years, Vacation Work has been broadening its range of publications for international jobseekers, in different countries and fields of employment (and not just on vacation). Your next port of call for more about life in different countries may be one of the *'Live and Work in...'* series (on 'Australia and New Zealand'; 'Belgium, The Netherlands and Luxembourg'; 'France'; 'Germany'; 'Italy'; 'Scandinavia'; 'Spain and Portugal'; and 'the USA and Canada'). *Work Your Way Around the World* or *The Directory of Summer Jobs Abroad* are the invaluable companions of those seeking shorter-term jobs in other countries.

Then there are more specialist publications — *Teaching English Abroad; Working in Tourism; Health Professionals Abroad; The Au Pair & Nannies Guide to Working Abroad; The International Directory of Voluntary Work*; and *Working with the Environment* — which will help you in your chosen field. You will find a list of these titles on the inside back page.

*Jonathan Packer*
Oxford, December 1996

# Acknowledgements

Of those who have contributed to the making of this book, I would like to thank Ros Tallett for help with research, the index and the bibliography; David Woodworth, Victoria Pybus and Tim Ryder at Vacation Work for their help and advice generally and with specific chapters; Alison Jones for revealing the possibilities of the Internet; Lynne Jackson of the University of London Careers Service for her comments; and those organisations and individuals, too numerous to mention, who have given time to help with information and research material.

Note: While every effort has been made to ensure that the information contained in this book was accurate at the time of going to press, some details are bound to change within the lifetime of this edition. Wages, exchange rates, telephone numbers, government policies and political situations are all particularly susceptible to change/fluctuations, so the ones quoted here are intended as a guide. Readers are strongly advised to check facts and the credentials of organisations included in this edition for themselves.

If you have any updated or new information which you feel might be of interest to readers of the next edition, or notice any errors or omissions please write to the Editor of Jobs and Careers Abroad, Vacation Work, 9 Park End Street, Oxford OX1 1HJ or fax 01865-790885. All those whose contributions are used will receive a complimentary copy of the next edition.

# The General Approach

# Discovering Your Employment Potential

Discovering your employment potential is the first step on the road to job-hunting success. Whether you are still at school or university; have left school or graduated, but have not yet decided which job to do — or if you are considering a change of employment, or are thinking about working abroad for the first time — in all these cases it is important for you to take some time out to consider your own aims and objectives.

Some jobs may suit you, and others will not. Simply working and surviving in another country may be your goal. But the subject certainly requires some deeper thought than this! However much you may love the culture and way of life, an ideal can quickly fade when you are faced with the everyday and often mundane reality of making ends meet.

Or your aim may be more practical. You may have a longer-term career in mind. In either case, your own perception of your achievements will be your yardstick of success. So you will have to think clearly and realistically about your goals. What do you hope to get out of your stay abroad? What kind of work really appeals to you? How will you match up to its requirements?

A more basic question – which careers advisers often ask – is: what do you consider of importance or value? You can look back on your experiences to date — in work or education — and ask what you have been most proud of. Which achievements gave you most satisfaction? These are questions for all those embarking on a career or a change in their lives. But they can apply equally to those considering living and working abroad.

Some useful reference books which can be found in larger bookshops or libraries are: *Careers Encyclopaedia* edited by A. Segal; *Equal Opportunities: A Career Guide* by Anna Alston (which contains some advice aimed specifically at women); *What Color is your Parachute?* by Richard Nelson Bolles — a 'how to' book giving techniques to help find a suitable career — which is published both in the UK and the USA; and *Build Your own Rainbow, a Workbook for Career and Life Management* by Barrie Hopson and Mike Scally (Mercury Books), which explores many of the same issues.

The *Association of Graduate Careers Advisory Services (AGCAS)* publishes a wide range of reasonably-priced booklets on all kinds of occupations and careers, from jobseeking after graduation to working abroad. For a catalogue, write to: CSU (Publications) Ltd., Armstrong House, Oxford Road, Manchester M1 7ED; or telephone 0161-236 9816. CSU also publishes *Where Next*, a self-help pack with a 50-minute video on career planning and making career choices. The *CEPEC Recruitment Guide* contains some useful articles on topics like 'Career Planning for the Individual' as well as a list of UK recruitment agencies; and will tell you about the selection methods they use. See the list of 'Management Recruitment Agencies' in the chapter *Getting the Job* for more on these.

Some background reading is one way for you to define your goals, and choice of career (as well as some reflection on your own previous life-experiences). Universities and colleges in the USA and Britain also offer advice and infor-mation centres and libraries for new jobseekers. A leader in this field, which is certainly worth contacting, is the *University of London Careers Service*, 50

Gordon Square, London WC1H 0PQ, Tel 0171-387 8221. It is one of the sponsors of the annual London Graduate Recruitment Fair.

If you find that you are still uncertain about your choice of future employment — or if you want to find out more about working abroad — a visit to the careers advice service in your university or locality is the recommended next step.

## CAREERS ADVISORY SERVICES

In Britain, Local Education Authorities (LEAs) — which will generally be your local authority or council — are required by law to provide a careers service to schools and some colleges; and to young people who are no longer in full-time education. Universities have their own careers advisory services as well. Students at these institutions also have the option of consulting their local Careers Advisory Service.

Vocational interest guides are widely used by higher education and LEA Careers Services. They are frequently linked with one of the growing number of computer databases providing occupational information. Training and Enterprise Councils (TECS) — known as LECS in Scotland — often maintain a similar information centre, with publications about careers, qualifications and overseas working; and a careers guidance service where the accent is on self-employment.

Access to a careers advisory service — both in Britain and the USA — usually follows a consultation with a careers adviser or guidance practitioner. The easiest way to find this Careers Service — or your nearest TEC — or LEC — is to consult your local telephone directory or one of the business telephone directories.

### Careers Europe

Careers Europe is the UK centre for Careers Information in Europe. It is based in Bradford, and provides careers information on education, employment and training opportunities for each of the EU member states to Careers Services. If you need more general information about employment prospects in the EU, or have an enquiry about the specific career you wish to follow, then this local Careers Sevice is the place to start. They may then contact Careers Europe in response to your enquiry.

Careers Europe has also produced a wide range of general Eurofact information sheets (which are generally available in Careers Service centres, and also TECS and public libraries). They cover different aspects of working, training and studying in particular EU countries. (There is more about these under the different country headings in the *Wordwide Employment* section of this book. And other fact-sheets about specific careers are available in your TEC or careers library — see *Rules and Regulations*).

Their resource centre is also based at the address below; and Careers Europe also publishes a magazine *EuroExpress* aimed at professionals in the recruitment and advisory field, and also those seeking work. *Careers Europe,* Fourth Floor, Midland House, 14 Cheapside, Bradford, West Yorkshire BD1 4JA, tel 01274-829600, fax 01274-829610.

## CAREER COUNSELLORS

As well as publicly funded careers advice facilities, private career counsellors are also available to those able and willing to pay for them. Career counsellors are similar to management recruitment consultants in that they tend to deal with more senior managers or executives. But their service is aimed at the individual who is considering the whole course of his career, and will usually combine an analysis of his or her capabilities with a prognosis for future action.

Career counsellors do not place people in specific jobs, but merely provide general guidelines based on the applicant's personality, achievements, qualifications, ambitions, and personal circumstances, making use of personality profiles; 'psychometric testing'; work style questionnaires; and other methods of assessment. One positive outcome of such counselling is a re-evaluation by the individual of his or her employment potential. Obviously, this could include advice on the applicant's suitability for work abroad.

As well as providing advice on the applicant's future career, much emphasis is laid on matters which should interest all jobseekers: how best to present oneself when applying for vacancies; submitting job applications and CV's; and interview and selection techniques. Fees for this service vary widely, even within the different companies. The following is a list of those that offer career counselling:

*Career Analysts,* Career House, 90 Gloucester Place, London W1H 4BL, tel 0171-935 5452, fax 0171-486 9922 — is a professional group of consultant psychologists offering career assessments and advice to applicants of all ages, and in particular on GAP year activities overseas. The service provides a complete career 'check-up' and all assessments include completion of a personal history form, tests of aptitude, interests, personality and needs, an in-depth consultation, followed by a full report and continuing contact. The services range from young people aged 15 and upwards to senior executives. Advice given on career direction, courses and qualifications, as well as on the best career opportunities abroad. Free brochure available on request.

*CareerSense,* 4 Farriers Close, Codicote, Hitchin, Hertfordshire SG4 8DU, tel 01438-821469, fax 01438-821897 — offers vocational and training advice on an individual basis. Agreed programme may include self-assessment exercises; careers audit; skills change strategy; training needs analysis; and personal effectiveness training. For career changers and those returning to the labour market, and those in need of an in-depth personal approach. Fluent Italian spoken.

*Fokkina McDonnell Associates,* 6th Floor, World Trade Centre, 8 Exchange Quay, Salford, Greater Manchester M5 3EQ, tel 0161-932 1120, fax 0161-932 1100 — career consultancy, psychometric testing and mid-career reviews targeted at the public, finance, and human resources sectors. Jobsearch, CV, and coaching for interviews, presentation and interpersonal skills, are provided. Also information about jobs in Europe.

*InterExec Career Management (ICM),* 1 Warwick Row, Off Bressenden Place, London SW1 5ER, tel 0171-630 0155, fax 0171-630 0117 — is a Human Resource Management Consultancy specialising in career management and outplacement for senior managers and board level executives; and salary and career change advice for graduates up to the age of 28.

*New Careers,* 2 Blake House, Admiral's Way, London E14 9UJ — CV preparation, psychometric testing and computerised jobsearch. Interview training and other counselling services for redundancy and franchise evaluation. Library facilities and resource centres available nationally: targeted at all levels of office personnel, factory staff, junior, middle and senior management, with services available in French.

*Working with Words,* 99 West Street, Warminster, Wiltshire BA12 8JZ, tel/fax 01985-214670 — CV and letter format and production following an in-depth interview. Additional services can include briefing before your interview; strategic mailshots in Britain and abroad; advice on career and training; and appraisal of current approach and CV or resumé style.

# Getting the Job

## Overview

There are probably almost as many possible ways of getting a job abroad as there are individual jobseekers. In general terms, speaking the local language will be an advantage if you are considering moving abroad. So are 'cultural awareness' (see the chapter *Preparation and Follow Up*); and also an understanding of the application procedures which are used in different countries.

Some have already entered a profession which is known to offer potential for working abroad — for example accountancy, or journalism — or are already working for an international company or organisation; or in a field with international links. Surprisingly, many companies do not like to publicise opportunities for a posting overseas in their recruitment activities. Be aware of this! It means they will see your suitability for the job as such — and not your interest in foreign travel — as the main reason for giving you the job.

For the new graduate, your suitability for the job — and not your 'international outlook' — will be your strongest point (although this does not apply in quite the same way in voluntary work, travel and tourism, or English language teaching, for instance, where a service to a 'customer' is involved. Here your readiness to adapt to another culture matters in a quite direct way).

For many international jobseekers, this will be a way to start a new career, or to take advantage of opportunities that are not available at home. For some the impulse will be entrepreneurial (and those economies which are in the process of transformation, in Eastern Europe and elsewhere, are likely destinations for this more adventurous category of jobseeker). A temporary job in a foreign country may also end in a more permanent stay, which is another point to consider before you make this important career and life choice.

At the 'lower' end of the jobs market — for those with a desire to travel and see the world — you will be doing the same jobs the locals are unwilling to do (working as an au pair for example, or doing seasonal work). *Work Your Way Around the World* is a very useful source here (and see some of the other Vacation Work publications).

In most cases, qualifications are at a premium. But the less qualified may be using a stay abroad to gain wider experience and qualifications. There may be a shortage of skilled tradespeople in some countries, which can make working abroad a suitable option, in building and construction for example. But it is the skilled engineers, the electronics and IT professionals, consultants, and those with a specialist knowledge or training, who are most in demand.

Some will carry out their job search independently, by using the contact addresses in this directory, or publications such as *Overseas Jobs Express*; or may even look for a job from their chosen destination or country. Sometimes your company or organisation will take the decision to send you on an overseas posting (in which case you can 'fast-forward' to some of the specific country information later in this book, and the chapters on *Rules and Regulations, Learning the Language*, and *Preparation and Follow up*).

In other cases this decision comes about simply because of an opportunity which is 'too good to miss' – although you can work to maximise these 'unexpected' opportunities by adopting a more creative approach to your job search.

It is a general rule of jobseeking — as well as for recruiters — that you should endeavour to minimise the element of luck, to maximise the predictability of the outcome.

## Where to Start

The pages of 'jobs abroad' publications and trade magazines, at home and abroad, are literally crammed with vacancies. English-language advertisments regularly appear in the main newspapers which carry recruitment advertising in even the non-English-speaking countries (see the individual country chapters for these). These are all good starting-points. The development of the Internet and World Wide Web means that some specialised jobs are are becoming more directly available to applicants everywhere in the world. This unprecedented expansion of job availability is leading to greater specialisation in the types of job which are on offer — and the applicants which are required — a point to bear in mind when you send off that all-important application and CV.

Learning another language is another option which may aid you in your job search. Major companies in the UK and North America are often looking for qualified staff who have one or more foreign languages, or a multicultural background, whether or not there is an immediate opening abroad. Companies in other countries (which have their own language deficit in English) are also now looking to the UK and the English-speaking world as an important source of recruitment — which can be seen in the advertising they take out in the UK and USA, either directly or through recruitment agencies.

Whatever your intended career path, doing some homework and preparation beforehand is recommended. And given that many Britons and North Americans do find employment, and successfully make the transition to living and working abroad, it is self-evident the challenge is not too great. There is every reason to feel optimistic!

## International Vacancies

Unemployment is a worldwide problem. But the number of vacancies and job opportunities around the world is still enormous. Taking the UK scene as an example, although there are officially more than two million people unemployed and seeking work, there are still over 25 million others who are in employment at present. This means there are some 25 million jobs on the domestic market alone, of which up to 20% will be changing occupants every year.

Also, the number of vacancies being publicly advertised continues to run at a high rate. In just one month, for example, the UK Department of Employment noted more than 200,000 new vacancies registered at local UK Jobcentres. The estimates say that they are notified of one-third of all jobs advertised publicly. So, allowing for a percentage of jobs which are readvertised, this suggests a jobs market of at least 5 million vacancies advertised every year, in Jobcentres, newspapers and magazines, or through recruitment agencies.

If we apply the same method to calculating overseas vacancies, we can begin to see just how extensive the international availability of work really is; and as will become clear in the following sections, publicly advertised vacancies are by no means the only source available to those seeking work, at home or in another country.

Of course, while no one can doubt the existence of so many job opportunities, finding the right one for you requires energy, initiative, and sometimes a willingness to take risks. Competition for work through the whole spectrum of careers is greater than ever before, so great that a reappraisal of traditional methods of job hunting seems necessary. The most successful applicants today are actively marketing their expertise, and continually updating their skills and knowledge. Even those in employment are constantly looking for work — even 'pieces of work' in the current jargon — and finding success in 'unusual places or collocations of interest' as one commentator put it. (1)

Everybody who has at some time been unemployed will be familiar with the cliché that looking for work is a job in itself. Certainly, in a more fragmented jobs market, this holds true for many categories of jobseeker. It is no longer enough simply to rely solely on the time-honoured methods of replying to job advertisements, or sending off hundreds of speculative applications. Some imagination and even some 'lateral thinking' is called for.

### Finding the Job

Apart from answering publicly advertised vacancies and making direct applications, there are two main methods of finding a long-term job. You can rely on an organisation or search consultancy ; or you can use your own initiative and enterprise, and set about finding the job yourself.

Using a recruitment consultant or jobs database is reasonable when you have the appropriate qualifications (and there are certainly enough jobs available). But you should remember that it is not the main function of recruitment agencies — or even careers consellors — to find specific jobs for individuals. Their role is to find the right applicant for the job, and to fill available vacancies. They are more suited to 'low-risk' areas of employment (see the *Preface* above).

There are many international jobseekers who expect organisations like foreign embassies to help them find them work in a another country. Unfortunately, this is usually not how it works (with a few exceptions — see the embassies mentioned below). In fact, very few foreign embassies are actively involved in recruitment, although they may be able to send useful information and advice on immigration and employment conditions in that country.

So, a more dynamic approach is called for; and it is far better to show the initiative and self-reliance which employers themselves are looking for, and the job itself may call for, in your initial contact, which is your way of presenting yourself. So, for example, in your covering letter, you should include something about why you are applying for that particular job; and why the employer — or recruitment agency — should consider you for this particular position rather than someone else.

There are 'conventional' and 'creative' approaches to finding a job; and the combination of these two approaches, combining thoroughness and imagination, consistency and some lateral thinking, will be most successful.

### Interviews and CVs

There is a plethora of advice available on interview technique and CV preparation. It can suffice here to repeat the advice of an earlier edition of *Jobs and Careers Abroad*, that the the CV should be carefully spaced and laid out, including details about yourself, your employment history, and education, and beginning with your most recent or most relevant experience; and do not forget to say *which* vacancy it is that you are applying for. Large firms, of course, deal with many.

Also try to state your qualifications clearly. You may know what your particular qualification means; but the employer who deals with applicants from many countries may not; and may need some help from you in understanding it, that your qualification is at degree level for instance.

Including a self-addressed envelope or International Reply Coupons to the correct value is a good idea. If a fax or e-mail number is given, then this can be another option — or a telephone call for an application form — but an initial letter is usually the best approach, and sometimes this is specified even in ads for international jobs. Many careers counsellors and consultants offer help with CV preparation. One specialist is: *Working with Words* (see *Career Counsellors* above). At the *University of London Careers Service,* they recommend the following books which contain information about preparation, applications and interviews: *And A Good Job Too,* by David Mackintosh (Orion); *How to Write a Curriculum Vitae* (ULCS); *How to Complete a Job Application Form* (ULCS);

*Succeed at your job interview,* by George Heariside (BBC Books); *Great Answers to Tough Interview Questions,* by Martin John Yate (Kogan Page); and *Test Your Own Aptitude,* by J. Barrett and G. Williams (Kogan Page).

Your initial research should also include: finding out more about recruitment opportunities in your chosen country or area of work; learning the language; using your existing contacts and knowledge; increasing your employability, for example through education or training; and generally improving your knowledge and understanding of the country and its culture.(2)

This is just a short checklist for the international jobseeker. But if you are serious in your ambition to find employment in another country, you will already be making a start.

# The Conventional Job Search

The conventional job search forms the basis of the traditional approach to jobseeking. Since it is the traditional method, the vast majority of applicants will be following the same path. You should put some time and effort into this approach, and also combine it with some more creative ways of seeking work, to create a competitive advantage for yourself. And you should identify your own strengths and weaknesses; and take actions accordingly, to remedy your areas of inexperience or lack of knowledge, and build on your strengths.

## ADVERTISEMENTS

Advertisements in the press can work in two ways. There will certainly be 'situations vacant' and 'situations wanted' columns in the newspaper you read every day (and its equivalent in the country where you are seeking work). For specialist trades and professions, you will find a greater concentration of suitable vacancies in the more specialist journals and magazines. You should also be interested in the foreign language equivalents of these specialist publications in the country or countries you are considering. Sometimes foreign-language newspapers will carry English-language advertising. A full list of general and specialist newspapers and magazines published in he UK is given in *British Rates and Data* (known as 'BRAD'), available in public reference libraries.

The major US newspapers carrying international recruitment advertising are: the *Chicago Tribune*, 435 North Michigan Avenue, Chicago, Il 60611; the *Los Angeles Times,* Times Mirror Square, Los Angeles, California, CA 90053; and the *New York Times,* 229 West 43rd Street, New York, NY 10036. The *International Herald Tribune,* 181 Avenue Charles de Gaulle, 92521 Neuilly-sur-Seine, France, also contains some high-flying vacancies; as does the *Financial Times,* Number One, Southwark Bridge, London SE1 9HL.

*Canada Employment Weekly*, 15 Madison Avenue, Toronto, Canada M5R 2ST, offers professional jobs vacancies in that country. In Britain, *Outbound Newspapers,* 1 Commercial Road, Eastbourne, East Sussex BN21 3XQ, publishes newspapers for jobseekers whose intended destinations are New Zealand, Australia, Canada, South Africa, or the USA, with useful news and information about emigration to these countries. There is more about the various national newspapers in the relevant country section in *Worldwide Employment. Johsearch,*

(1) Dr Lewis Rushbrook in the introduction to the CEPEC Recruitment Guide, 1995, p.2
(2) See the various Vacation Work publications. Lonely Planet (PO Box 617, Hawthorn, Victoria 3122, Australia) and Rough Guides (1 Mercer Street, London WC2H 8QJ) also publish some excellent guides which are primarily for travellers but have general background cultural information. Other guide publishers are Let's Go, Michelin, Fodor's, and Blue Guides.

at Bradley Pavillions, Bradley Stoke North, Bristol BS12 0BQ, contains international recruitment advertising. And *Overseas Jobs Express — OJE*, Premier House, Shoreham Airport, West Sussex BN43 5FF, tel 01273-440220/540, fax 01273-440229, http://www.ahoy.com/oje/ — has a wide range of vacancies and the latest news on international work and jobseeking worldwide. On the Internet, you can send a blank e-mail to OJE@zoom.com, for subscription information and answers to frequently asked questions (FAQs).

The main UK magazines carrying overseas recruitment advertising are: *Architects' Journal; Caterer and Hotelkeeper; Certified Accountant; Computing* and *Computing Weekly; Construction News* and *Contract Journal* (for the building and construction trades); *The Engineer; Flight International; The Lancet* (medical); *Nature* (science); *New Scientist; Nursery World; Nursing Times; The Stage; Surveyor*; and *Press Gazette*.

The 'in-house' publications of foreign trade and professional associations produced for circulation among their members can be another useful source. The vacancy list produced by the union BECTU for entertainment and broadcast staff is one of many examples. Your own national trade association or union may also have other international contacts as well.

In many ways the best and most direct contacts are offered by the foreign press, especially if your focus is on a particular place or country. The better-known foreign papers are available in most newsagents or libraries. One useful contact is *Reuters Business Briefing,* an on-line service giving access both to news and 2,000 business publications from around the world, including newspapers and trade journals. Information can be retrieved by word search or selection lists for companies, countries and topics (Reuters Business Information; tel 0171-250 1122; e-mail paul.waddington@reuters.com Etweedie@firefly.-co.uk).

There are an increasing number of publications internationally — like *The Times* and *The Financial Times* in the UK — which also have on-line access. Embassies and cultural organisations also have their reading rooms. You may also consider a 'situation wanted' ad in one of the many publications for expatriates in the various countries, like *The Union Jack* for Britons in the United States; or *The American* for Americans in Britain.

An excellent selection of international newspapers is to be found in the *City Business Library*, 1 Brewers Hall Garden, London EC2V 5BX; tel 0171-638 8215. Or you can arrange a subscription through their UK or US agents (see the various countries in *Worldwide Employment*).

Single copies of foreign newspapers are most easily obtained by contacting the head office — and usually the advertising department — of the paper concerned. In Europe, the *European Media Directory* covers 26 countries with lists of specialist publications organised by category and country. In the USA, the *Magazines and Internal Publications Directory* (National Register Publishing, 121 Chanlon Road, New Providence, New Jersey 07974) details newsletters and magazines organised by subject. Situations wanted ads can also be placed indirectly through agencies, who will assist you in your choice of paper, and help with the wording if this is necessary, the most practical reference source in this respect being *Benn's Media* directory (Europe and World volumes). It gives the addresses of the main newspapers and a classified list of periodicals and specialist journals with cross-coded references to the UK agents; or to the UK branch office of the newspaper itself.

*Willings Press Guide* gives much the same worldwide information. The 'overseas' volume lists each country's papers in straightforward alphabetical order (along with any relevant agents), but the lists themselves are more detailed than Benn's. Addresses of major foreign newspapers and UK agents can also be obtained from the *Advertisers' Annual* (Reed Information Services), which details some international recruiters. All three of these books should be available in public or business libraries. American readers can consult *Newspaper International* (National Register Publishing Company) or *Ulrich's International Periodicals Directory* (R.R. Bowker, New York).

The representatives in the UK and USA of the most important newspapers are listed under some of the separate chapters of *Worldwide Employment*. It has to be stressed that these newspaper agents do not arrange jobs abroad, and that they require advance payment. In addition, there are also a number of advertising consultancies that act independently of the papers and can therefore offer free advice on your choice of medium, as well as helping you with the ad, and placing it on your behalf. These consultancies are listed separately in the *Advertisers' Annual*.

## DIRECT APPLICATION

An initial approach is to write directly to companies or organisations abroad. The best results are obtained by targeting your letters, including full details of the type of work you are looking for. The main challenge is finding the right names and addresses of contacts and companies. Use a library or information centre as a starting point — and the other information which may be available to you — and your own personal contacts (see *The Creative Job Search*). You can also consult the international trade yearbooks which list companies worldwide. Such yearbooks include the *Advertisers' Annual, Bankers' Almanac and Yearbook, Flight International Directory, Insurance Directory and Yearbook, Oil and Gas World*, and others in the same vein.

Other publications with contact addresses include: the *Europa Yearbook*, which lists international organisations and each country's principal banks, universities, radio and TV stations, and trade associations; and *The World of Learning* (also published by Europa), with learned societies, research institutes and universities. And there are the country or regional tourist guides (which will have useful addresses for those wishing to work in hotels and restaurants, or tourism).

Foreign telephone directories and 'yellow pages' offer the widest range of contacts. Embassies stock their own national directories; and an appointment is usually necessary for access. A large selection is available at the *City Business Library* (see above). It does not hold every directory, as some are impossible to obtain, so always telephone in advance. And international telephone directories are usually available at major reference libraries, such as *Westminster Reference Library*, St Martin Street, London WC2H 7HP, tel 0171-798 2036, open 10am-7pm Monday to Friday, 10am-5pm on Saturday, or those situated in the major cities. In the US, these major libraries include: the *Library of Congress Information Office*, LM-103, Washington, DC, tel 202-287-5108 (open 8.30am-9.30pm Monday to Friday, 8.30am-5pm Saturday, 1pm-5pm Sunday); which provides a reference service on subjects including business, economics, and employment; and the *Federal Trade Commission Library*, 6th Street and Pennsylvania Avenue, NW, Washington, DC 20580, tel 202-236-2395 (open 8.30am-5pm Monday to Friday); which also contains many trade and commercial directories. The *Los Angeles Public Library*, 630 West 5th Street, Los Angeles, CA9007, tel 213-612-3320, has a large business and economics section, and an on-line computer search service. For researchers who cannot visit, the *Westminster Reference Library* has an 'Information for Business' service (tel 0171-976 1285).

Many reference and business libraries also hold a selection of the *Kompass Registers*, containing lists of the major commercial enterprises across the world. They are classified by country and type of product. Another valuable collection of international trade and telephone directories is held at the *Export Market Information Centre (EMIC)*, Kingsgate House, 66-74 Victoria Street, London

SW1E 6SW, tel 0171-215 5444-5, fax 0171-215 4231, e-mail EMI@Cash001.
ots.dti.gov.uk. It is open from 9am-8pm Monday to Friday, 9am-5.30pm on
Saturday; and also has market research reports, trade fair catalogues, and country
profiles. Students require an appointment. It is also worth visiting — if you can —
the *British Library Business Information Service*, 25 Southampton Buildings,
Chancery Lane, London WC2A 1AW, tel 0171-215 5444, open 9.30am-9pm
Monday to Friday, 10am-1pm Saturday. (It is due to move to new premises in
1999). This library has a service for researchers — usually companies — the
British Library/Lloyds Bank Business Line: tel 0171-412 7454 or 412 7977.

## OVERSEAS SUBSIDIARIES

### British Subsidiaries
The overseas branches or subsidiaries of British firms are able to provide work
in one of two ways. Direct application is one method. The other, more usual
way is to begin with a job in Britain and then ask to be transferred abroad. In
some cases, it may be possible to discuss overseas work experience at the
interview stage; and some companies take on workers because they have some
foreign language or cultural aptitude in addition to other qualifications. Of
course, being sent on a posting abroad will usually depend on how successful
you have been in your home country, and is not an automatic next step.

Lists of the major British enterprises in European countries are included at
the end of their respective chapters in *Worldwide Employment*, but more
complete and up-to-date information can sometimes be obtained from the British
Chambers of Commerce there. The *British Chambers of Commerce Directory* has
details of 150 such organisations around the world as well as trade associations in
the UK (which often have links abroad); it is available for £25 from: *The
Association of British Chambers of Commerce*, 9 Tufton Street, London SW1P
3QB; fax 0171-799 2202. Where such lists of affiliates or subsidiaries of UK or
US companies exist separately, or as part of Chamber of Commerce yearbooks,
details are also given at the end of the individual chapters of *Worldwide
Employment*.

If you are unwilling to part with your money for all these lists and information
services, consult *Who Owns Whom*, which is available in many reference or
business libraries. Chambers of Commerce yearbooks are also sometimes found
on general reference library shelves.

### American Subsidiaries
The overseas subsidiaries of American parent companies can also offer work.
UK jobseekers can begin with those with a large presence in the UK. In some
areas, only those trained in the USA are likely to be considered. Because of the
vast scale of US business enterprise abroad, subsidiaries have not been listed,
but some American Chambers of Commerce publish lists, about which details
are given in *Worldwide Employment* where relevant. Directories of American
parent and subsidiary companies are also available from *Uniworld Business
Publications,* 342 East 51st Street, New York, NY 10022-7847, tel 212-752-
0329, which publishes the 1,700-page *Directory of American Firms Operating in
Foreign Countries*, 14th edition, $220 — an extensive list for each country and
a short description of the main areas of operation of each company — and also
the *Directory of Foreign Firms Operating in the United States*, 8th edition, at
$150. Their pricelist gives latest prices and postage charges. Addresses of
American parent and subsidiary companies are also included in *Who Owns
Whom* (see above).

### International Companies
There are other international companies which may be contacted by jobseekers
with a specialist skill or suitable experience. The *European Handbook* (Financial

Times Information, Fitzroy House, 13-17 Epworth Street, London EC2A 4DC) lists leading companies across Europe, with detailed information on each, and its area of operation; and is regularly updated. These directories are expensive. A single copy is £120 in the UK, and £140 elsewhere. And *European Market Guide* published by Dunn & Bradstreet features around 250,000 companies across Europe. The *Directory of Corporate Affiliations* (National Register Publishing, New Providence, NJ) is a listing of international companies, subsidiaries, and non-US holdings, classified according to the sectors in which they operate; and a good source for companies in a particular area or industry. For multinational companies, there is *Worldwide Branch Locations of Multinational Companies* edited by David S. Hooper (Gale Research). A directory with profiles of major international companies which can be found in most business libraries is *Hoover's Handbook of World Business*, edited by Patrick J. Spavin and James R. Talbot; it has a comprehensive country-by-country guide.

### Foreign Subsidiaries in Britain

The British branches, subsidiaries and affiliates of foreign-based firms may also be worth approaching. Addresses of these British-based foreign firms are available through the Commercial Section of the relevant Embassy in London, or through the relevant foreign Trade Centres and Associations, whose addresses may be found in the Central London Yellow Pages.

## TRADE UNIONS AND PROFESSIONAL ASSOCIATIONS

Most unions will be able to advise their members on employment prospects and conditions abroad; and in some cases they may put you in touch with foreign employers, international associations of trade unions, or sister unions in other countries.

Similarly, most professional associations can offer some kind of help in the search for work internationally. Such help may include an appointments service that includes vacancies abroad; advice on foreign registration requirements, or further examinations that have to be passed; an 'in-house' publication that contains advertisements for overseas jobs; an information service on working conditions; or providing introductory letters to sister associations; or even direct introductions to potential employers abroad. Most professional associations will offer some of these services to their members.

For a comprehensive list of British professional associations, readers can consult the book *Trade Associations and Professional Bodies of the United Kingdom,* edited by Patricia Millard. An equally useful source is *Professional Organisations in the Commonwealth,* edited by A. Tett and J. Chadwick. In Europe, the *European Directory of Trade and Business Associations* is a directory of professional and trade associations. The *Business Organisations, Agencies, and Publications Directory* edited by Holly M. Selden (Gale Research) details trade and business associations in the US — and internationally — with a listing of boards of trade and American chambers of commerce worldwide. These books are available in the larger public reference libraries. Information on some of the relevant professional associations appears at the end of the relevant chapter in the *Specific Careers* section.

## EMPLOYMENT SERVICE: EURES

The Overseas Placing Unit (OPU) co-ordinates all dealings with overseas/ EU/EEA vacancies for the Employment Service in the UK. These vacancies, distributed to Jobcentres via a computerised system called Labour Market System (LMS), can be short or long term and for a wide range of skills from hotel work to management. (1)

The EU/EEA employment services co-operate in the exchange of vacancies, usually for hard-to-fill posts, or where knowledge of other EU/EEA languages is required, via a system known as EURES, which operates a fully computerised system to facilitate the exchange of vacancies and information within the EU/EAA. Under the EURES project, applicants with knowledge of another European language and good qualifications in their line of work can complete an application form in that language to be sent to the relevant employment service for linking with suitable posts. This is known as a speculative application. You should contact your local Jobcentre for further details.

OPU can also provide advice and guidance about working abroad. A series of booklets is available at Jobcentres, including *Working Abroad*, 17 booklets on the EU/EAA countries and several other countries. These give practical help on finding work and outline the main things to be considered when seeking work abroad. The similar *Eurofacts* series of leaflets (also available in Jobcentres and most TECS — see above) covers the general background and work in specific fields in the European countries.

It is noteworthy that the Employment Service in the UK occasionally advertises vacancies itself, in the national or overseas recruitment press. And prospective applicants interested in particular towns or regions within the EU or EAA should contact the relevant National Employment Agency administrative head offices, which will supply lists of local employment centres. Addresses of these head offices are listed in the specific country chapters in the section *Worldwide Employment*.

*(1) For more about the European Union (EU) and European Economic Area (EEA) see Rules and Regulations.*

## GOVERNMENT AGENCIES

Given that many countries are experiencing high levels of unemployment within their own workforce, it is hardly surprising that few governments wish to promote migrant labour. So, most embassies and diplomatic missions in the UK and USA can do no more than give some general background information on their respective countries. However, some of these do act as intermediaries between employers and potential emigrants, or at least run information services and occasional recruitment drives. These include the Canadian, Australian and New Zealand High Commissions. For details, see these countries' separate chapters. But most vacancies for the consultants and specialists required by individual states, and the programmes run by them, are advertised through the relevant US, EU, or UK agency. Also, the embassies of some Commonwealth states occasionally place advertisements in the national and trade press. Below are some active missions in the field of recruitment in Britain:

*Brunei High Commission (Recruitment Unit)*
    19 Belgrave Square, London SW1X 8PG, tel 0171-581 0521.
*The Gambia High Commission*
    57 Kensington Court, London W8 5DG, tel 0171-937 6316.
*Ghana High Commission*
    102 Park Street, London W1Y 3RJ, tel 0171-493 4901.
*Nigeria High Commission*
    Nigeria House, 9 Northumberland Avenue, London WC2N 5BX, tel 0171-839 1244.
*Sierra Leone High Commission*
    33 Portland Place, London W1N 3AG, tel 0171-636 6483.
*Zambian High Commission*
    Zambia House, 2 Palace Gate, London W8 5NG, tel 0171-589 6655.

Although needs obviously change from year to year, the most common personnel requirements are for experienced professionals for administrative and advisory positions in government departments, and in the various nationally or locally run industries, like railways or the public utilities.

Other governments that promote imported expertise are almost exclusively those of the developing and former communist countries (where the need is for expertise in restructuring or privatisation). The work is usually on fixed-term contracts; and the ultimate goal will be to train local staff to administer and carry on the project. Much of this recruitment activity is therefore in the training and consultancy fields, and usually channelled through suitable third parties or agencies. Apart from the organisations listed below, there are other UK and US bodies — concerned mainly with teaching and voluntary work — which also work with foreign governments. You should refer to these *Specific Careers* chapters.

Those staff who are chosen for consultancy positions or assignments abroad by their government — or its agencies — are usually assured adequate terms and employment conditions through arrangements for financial supplementation which are a usual part of these contracts.

*Overseas Development Administration (ODA)*, 94 Victoria Street, London SW1E 5JL, tel 0171-917 0286, fax 0171-917 0523 — runs the British Government's programme of aid to developing countries. Vacancies occur on an ad hoc basis and are normally advertised in the national press, professional journals, and overseas. Particular skills are usually required, in professions such as law, sociology and accountancy, as well as more familiar areas like agriculture, engineering and economics. You can write off for the *ODA Guide to Working Overseas for the Aid Programme* booklet for more details and a 'skills list'. The ODA also keeps a register of people interested in working for the aid programme. And study awards are offered under the APOS (Associate Professional Officers Scheme) to those less qualified, giving academic training to masters degree level, followed by a period of practical training overseas. EEA and Commonwealth citizens with an established right to work in the UK are eligible. Application forms can be obtained by writing to ODA, 94 Victoria Street, London SW1E 5JL, tel. 0171-917 7000,31 January being the annual closing date. These APOS awards are presently in the agriculture, agricultural engineering, animal health/animal production, biodiversity preservation, biometrics, environment, engineering, physical planning, forestry, agro-forestry, fisheries, health and population, institutional development, natural resources economics, small enterprise development, and social development sectors.

The Recruitment and Personnel Management Branch (RPMB) looks after recruitment matters, and preparation for moving abroad. The ODA also assists in the recruitment of specialists for the field programmes of the United Nations and its specialised agencies e.g. UNHCR, FAO, and the International Labour Office (see the *International Organisations* chapter). A number of useful free booklets, such as *Action for the Environment, Action on Health and Population, Women in Development,* and *British Overseas Development,* a bimonthly magazine on development topics, are available on request from the ODA Information Department, Room V523, 94 Victoria Street, London SW1E 5JL, tel 0171-917 0503.

*Crown Agents for Overseas Governments and Administration,* St Nicholas House, St Nicholas Road, Sutton, Surrey SM1 1EL, tel 0181-643 3311, fax 0181-643 8232 — is a long-established and nowadays self-funding body providing a recruitment service to over 100 governments, public authorities, and international aid agencies. Overseas positions are either direct with a client government or on an aid-funded project managed by Crown Agents. Personnel-related activities are greatest in the Middle East and the emerging economies of eastern Europe and former Soviet Union, with some programmes in Africa. All overseas opportunities are for senior level, experienced staff, educated to degree standard and holding relevant professional qualifications) Recent assignments include human resources development and training, oil/gas industry engineering, development economists, government financial management, and logisticians. Vacancies are filled as far as possible from the large CV database held by Crown Agents, for which applications are always welcome. Vacancies may also be advertised in the national, technical, or overseas recruitment press.

*The Overseas Development Institute,* Regent's College, Inner Circle, Regent's Park, London NW1 4NS, tel 0171-487 7413, fax 0171-487 7590 — runs the ODI Fellowship Scheme where recent young economists and those in related fields, from Britain and the EU countries, and on occasions the United States, can work for two years in the public sectors of developing countries in Africa, the Caribbean and the Pacific. Candidates must have (or be studying for) a postgraduate qualification. It provides some practical work experience in developing countries. About 20 Fellowships are awarded annually. Otherwise, it should be noted that the ODI does not place graduates in international employment. Application forms are available each September from ODI or from University Careers Advisory Offices, and a booklet, the *ODI Fellowship Scheme*, is also published.

*The Natural Resources Institute,* Central Avenue, Chatham Maritime, Kent ME4 4TE — was formerly a government agency but is now a part of the University of Greenwich. Its principal aim is to alleviate poverty and hardship in developing countries by increasing sustainable productivity of their renewable natural resources. The operational staff cover a range of specialisms, the main ones being agriculture, forestry, entomology, food technology, engineering and economics. Recruitment enquiries can be made to the Establishment Secretary at the above address.

## CONSULTANTS AND AGENCIES

The process of applying for long-term overseas work through management recruitment consultants (MRCs) and employment agencies provides a better chance of success than any of the other methods of the conventional job search mentioned so far, for those who are experienced and qualified, although applying to companies direct may have a greater success rate in many parts of the world.

There is much discussion as to what constitutes a management recruitment consultancy, as opposed to a simple employment agency. In some cases, the dividing line is hard to draw; but the difference lies mainly in the types of personnel they are interested in. Management recruitment consultants target 'high-flyers' — executives, management, and professional staff, particularly engineers and those with specialised job skills and professional qualifications. Recruitment or employment agencies, on the other hand, find work for a wide range of staff, at the 'low-risk' and 'medium-risk' levels, as well as temporary employment. Personal assistants, domestic staff and au pairs, as well as clerical staff, translators, and workers across commerce and industry can use the services of this kind of employment agency. The current trend towards more flexible working in many industries has also eroded the distinction between temporary and permanent work; and qualifications and training are increasingly important at all levels of employment.

There is an important difference in their methods of recruitment. It is appropriate for management consultants to spend much more time finding exactly the right person for the right job, for instance, to match the supply with the more specialised demand at the 'high-risk' end of the market. Employment agencies as a rule deal with more general applications.

These agencies and consultancies in the UK are brought together under the

Employment Agencies Act (which came into effect in 1976, and is said at the time of writing to be due for some revision). What this means in practice (with some exceptions, see the *Au Pair and Domestic* chapter) is that agencies and consultants may not charge a fee for finding you a job. This law does not apply to agencies which are based abroad; and there are regular complaints about some international recruitment agencies — in construction for instance — which charge a fee and then do not provide the service offered. Of course, all agencies are allowed to obtain money from their client companies for their recruitment services.

Most recruitment agencies around the world are governed by similar rules. But this has affected UK agencies in some fields of recruitment in those countries where the laws are different. In Germany, it is illegal for agencies which are not in possession of a German Labour Leasing Licence, or companies not registered there, to offer work to British or American jobseekers, and workers must be employed directly by the German company, which will then deduct the individual's tax and insurance. In some other countries the rules are less strict. Generally speaking, prospective employees should be vigilant, particularly when a foreign employment agency offers jobs in a third country.

## MANAGEMENT RECRUITMENT CONSULTANTS

Included below is a selection of those management recruitment consultants which cover a broad range of opportunities, and cannot therefore be easily placed under the relevant chapter in *Specific Careers*. Many employment agencies tend to be more career-specific, and will therefore be found in such chapters as *Au Pair and Domestic, Medicine and Nursing*, and *Secretarial, Translating and Interpreting*. Also, some of the more helpful foreign-based agencies and consultants are located under the individual country chapters in the section *Worldwide Employment*, along with some relevant British and US employment agencies and consultancies.

Some of them offer a general, international 'headhunting' service. Others concentrate on a particular area of recruitment, for example in information technology or sales. Since consultants have a steady stream of job offers on their books, many also have a permanent register of job applicants for them to match up the applicants on file with new vacancies as they arise.

Apart from these databases, and some services like a 'portfolio of clients' or 'access to unadvertised vacancies', it is a general rule that very few MRCs operate actively on behalf of the applicant to find them a job. This is because, like all employment agencies, their main task is to find people for the jobs and not the other way around. In a typical case, some 70% of their business is jobsearch or headhunting, the remainder being advertised positions; and most will already have a large number of applicants already on their books. For this reason, candidates should target their applications and CVs as far as possible at those consultancies which are really suited to their qualifications and experience.

The *Institute of Management Consultants*, 5th Floor, 32/33 Hatton Garden, London EC1N 8DL, tel 0171-242 2140, fax 0171-831 4597, provides clients with guidance regarding their consultancy needs, and will draw up a short-list of appropriate consultants among its members. Its client support service freephone number is 0800-318030. The *Management Consultancies Association*, 11 West Halkin Street, London SW1X 8JL, is another trade association in Britain. In addition, the *CEPEC Recruitment Guide*, produced by *CEPEC Ltd.*, Lilly House, 13 Hanover Square, London W1R 9HD, tel 0171-629 2266, fax 0171-629 7066, whose fifth edition was published in 1996, lists over 400 recruitment agencies and search consultants in the UK, about half of whom will undertake assignments abroad. The guide also includes valuable advice on how to get the most out of recruitment agencies, and on job-search techniques generally, and is available from the address above. More useful advice on effective job-seeking is contained in their Job Search Guide which is available in two versions, one aimed at executive and professional staff, and the other for supervisory and support staff. Internationally, The International Directory of Executive Recruitment Consultants (Executive Grapevine International) has UK consultants in its first volume and profiles more consultants from more than 50 countries in the second.

The MRCs below may accept applications for a broad range of overseas management or professional positions. Consultancies regularly advertising in the national or trade press in your own field or specialisation could also be contacted, and those in your local telephone or business directory.

*Antal International Executive Recruitment,* 8 Alice Court, 116 Putney Bridge Road, London SW15 2NQ, tel 0181-874 2744, fax 0181-871 2211 — deals with middle and senior managers in all disciplines, and has three regional offices in Warsaw, Budapest, and Moscow. It specialises in eastern European recruitment, and is expanding to cover the Asia-Pacific region.

*Anthony Moss & Associates,* 173/175 Drummond Street, London NW1 3JD — recruits international experts in banking, training, transportation, water, waste, agriculture, construction, oil and gas and manufacturing, at middle and senior management level in Europe, the Middle East and Africa. Candidates must be experienced and qualified to degree or chartered level. *Malla Recruitment* (same address) recruits technical, middle and senior management and sales staff in nursing/medical, construction, engineering, computer sectors, etc. for one year/ permanent/interim management positions.

*Barton Executive Search/Barton Interim Management,* Bere Barton, Bere Ferrers, Yelverton, Devon PL20 7JL, tel 01822-840220, fax 01822-841134 — is a research-driven senior executive consultancy which seeks to identify qualified candidates wherever they may be. Middle and senior management and board level assignments in all sectors of business and industry in the UK, USA, and Europe are dealt with. Minimum length of contract: three years (executive search), 3-6 months (interim management). CVs are held against client requirements.

*Berenschot Euro Management,* PO Box 8039, NL-3503 RA Utrecht, The Netherlands, fax 291-6827 — is involved in managing and implementing large international projects, and European affairs and public procurement consulting and recruits professional consultants and experts from all disciplines, with an emphasis on administration reform, privatisation and regional development for the European Commission and other international agencies. Requirements are experience of project work in Central and Eastern Europe, the former Soviet Union, and/or the Mediterranean countries. Applicants should also have a knowledge of the process of European integration and the accession of those countries to the EU.

*Butler Service Group UK Ltd.,* Kings Mill, Kings Mill Lane, South Nutfield, Redhill, Surrey RH1 5NE, tel 01737-822000, fax 01737-823031 — is one of the world's leading providers of technical specialists and managers in all areas of industry. Appointments in most parts of the world. Butler Service Group, Inc. has 50 offices throughout North America (Corporate offices: 110 Summit Avenue, PO Box 460, Montvale, NJ 07645, USA). The majority of personnel are highly qualified in their field of expertise. UK enquiries to the Recruitment Department, Operations and Recruitment Manager.

*GMZ*, PO Box 5180, D-65726 Eschborn, Germany, fax 6196-797-302 — recruits worldwide on behalf of the German government and other donor countries in the development field, with openings for consultants in finance, small enterprise development, and management in consultancy. Qualifications, several years' experience, as well as proven management ability are required.

*Grafton Recruitment Ltd.*, 35-37 Queens Square, Belfast BT1 3FG, tel 01232-242824, fax 01232-242897, http://www.msldb.com/grafton, e-mail Recruitment-@Grafton.com — with offices in Northern Ireland, Dublin, Prague, Budapest and Kuala Lumpur (see individual country guides for these) is Ireland's leading consultancy group. The International Division recruits experienced and qualified personnel mainly for the Czech Republic, Germany, Hungary, Malaysia, Saudi Arabia, and the USA. Sectors handled include accountancy, catering, construction, electronics, IT, nursing, and sales and management; the 'necessary skills and experience' are required. A CV, passport photos, references and copies of qualifications/memberships should be forwarded to the relevant office. The other Irish and overseas addresses can be obtained from the Queens Square office.

*JCR Executive Search, Selection, and Graduate Careers*, 1 Cromwell Place, London SW7 2JF, tel 0171-581 2977, fax 0171-581 1766 — promises 'care and attention to its clients and candidates' in areas like marketing and the media, general and product management, professional services, management consulting, professional services, retail, the public sector, trade associations, and market research, mainly in the UK but also in Europe (which accounts for 20% of its business). As a guide, £20,000 to £50,000 is its main salary range.

*Miller, Brand & Co. Ltd.,* 36 Spital Square, London E1 6DY, tel 0171-377 5661, fax 0171-377 5437 — places middle and senior management and other professional staff in the EU and Norway, eastern Europe, and Hong Kong, across the whole range of commercial and industrial enterprises, with departments for 'advertising', 'healthcare', and 'travel and conference'. There are associated offices in Belgium, Denmark, France, Germany, the Netherlands, Italy, Norway, Spain (see the individual country guides), and in Ireland: *Orion Search & Selection Ltd.,* 121 Lower Baggott Street, Dublin 2, Ireland, tel (0)1-676-4755. All positions are permanent.

*Mottet & Associates,* 25 rue Vlasendael, B-1070 Brussels, Belgium, tel 2-527-03-09, fax 2-527-16-99 — are management consultants for top and middle management positions in all types of industry and business in mainly central and western Europe. Suitable experience is required; and speakers of other languages are particularly welcome. *Mottet Selection* is their department for middle management; *MBA Transfer* is for MBA graduates.

*Opta,* Cockayne House, 126-128 Crockhamwell Road, Woodley RG5 3JH, tel 01734-695600, fax 01734-691412 — is primarily a management consultancy specialising in the telecommunications market. They also provide sub-contracted resources to companies across Europe (through *Opta Resources* at the above address) especially in France and Germany, and further afield in Indonesia.

*Scott Neale & Partners*, Scott House, Basing View, Basingstoke, Hampshire RG21 4JG, fax 01256-460582 — places institutional development experts in areas such as asset sales, business appraisal and planning, marketing, healthcare management, and management development in Europe and Africa. Experience in public administration, manufacturing, and transportation is an advantage. You should specify your specialism and sector and write to the Chief Executive at the above address.

*Systematic Management Search (SMS),* Bahnhofstrasse 69, CH-8001 Zürich, tel 01-211-27-50 — also with offices in Düsseldorf, Frankfurt and Berlin, specialises in headhunting top and senior executives on an international basis. They have associated partner companies in Paris, London and New York.

*Transtec SA,* Ave. de Tyras 75, B-1120 Brussels, Belgium, tel 2-266-49-50, fax 2-266-49-65, compuserve 100571,2403, e-mail TRANSTEC@TRANSTEC.be — recruits high-level consultants to governments and other international bodies in the areas of transport, tourism, urban and rural development, irrigation and export promotion. Only those with a minimum of 10 years' experience of high-level consultancy, advanced degrees and fluency in foreign languages can be considered.

Further information on UK recruitment consultants and agencies dealing with overseas recruitment can be obtained from the *Federation of Recruitment and Employment Services,* 36-38, Mortimer Street, London W1N 7RB 'by post only'. It publishes an annual *Yearbook of Recruitment and Employment Services,* and represents both management consultancies and employment agencies.

## STUDENT WORKING EXCHANGES

Generally, student exchange schemes are either cultural or vocational in nature, although this is not a hard-and-fast distinction as cultural exchanges can often lead to educational, employment and career opportunities as well.

The following section deals with a number of vocation-orientated student exchange schemes, giving an opportunity for interested students to gain practical experience of living and working abroad. Details of the *British Universities North America Club (BUNAC), Camp America* and other voluntary exchange schemes are given in the *Voluntary Work* chapter. Details of farming work exchange schemes appear in the chapter on *Agriculture and the Environment.*

*AIESEC* (French acronym for *International Association for Students of Economics and Management),* 29-31 Cowper Street, London EC2A 4AP, tel 0171-336 7939, fax 0171-336 7971 — offers students and recent graduates within accountancy, business administration, computing, marketing, economics, and finance the opportunity to take placements in diverse working environments through its Work Abroad programmes. Placements last between six and seventy-two weeks in any one of its 87 member countries — including the USA, where it has an office in New York — at any time of the year. These are for students or recent graduates (one to two years) in a business-related degree course, with languages if they wish to work outside the English-speaking world. AIESEC US is listed below. The headquarters of AIESEC International is in Brussels. Applications to the *Work Abroad* programme at the address above. AIESEC wishes to stress that very few placements will be available, because of an imbalance in the numbers of outgoing and incoming students.

*AIESEC US,* 135 West 35th Street, 20th Floor, New York, NY 10020, tel 212-757-3774 — operates a similar scheme in the USA. Again, the main precondition for an overseas placing is membership of an AIESEC chapter in an American university, and the need to ensure an equal number of work exchange positions for foreign students in the US, which limits numbers.

*American-Scandinavian Foundation,* 725 Park Avenue, New York, NY 10021, tel 212-879-9779 — arranges work exchanges with Scandinavia, mostly for technical students; the largest number of placements are in Finland. Traineeships are generally two-three months in the summer (June-August). Contact above for application procedures and deadline.

*Association for International Practical Training (AIPT),* 10400 Little Patuxent Parkway, Suite 250, Columbia, MD 21044-3510, tel 410-997-2200, fax 410-992-3924, e-mail aip@taipt.org, http://www.aipt.org — conducts 'high-quality experiential exchanges which enhance the ability of individual participants, employers and host organizations.' It helps around 250 US citizens in exchanges with 25 or so other countries every year, and 2,000 people from 70 countries to train with US employers. Around half of these exchange schemes are with other member countries of IAESTE, of which it is the American branch (like the *Central Bureau* in Britain, see below). AIPT's major scheme is the *Career Development Exchanges Program* for recent graduates, young professionals, and businesses in many career fields which offers opportunities in Austria, Finland, France, Germany, Ireland, Japan, Malaysia, Switzerland, the Slovak Republic, Hungary, and other countries (including the UK). Most vocations and professions can be catered for, as long as the foreign placement includes some practical training. Training periods range from eight weeks to 18 months. AIPT's other major scheme is the *Hospitality/Tourism Exchange Program* dealt with in the chapter, *Transport, Tourism and Hospitality.*

*The Central Bureau for Educational Visits and Exchanges,* 10 Spring Gardens, London SW1A 2BN, tel 0171-389 4004, fax 0171-389 4426, Campus 2000 01:YNK330 — runs the Language Assistant Scheme which enables modern language students from Britain and over 30 other countries to spend a year working in a school or college where their target language is spoken. Appointments as Junior Language Assistants are also available in France and Germany for school leavers intending to study French and German at an institution of higher education. The Central Bureau arranges numerous other exchange programmes which are covered in individual chapters, administers the various European Union Socrates programmes (see below), and provides useful information on exchanges.
There are also offices at: 3 Bruntsfield Crescent, Edinburgh EH10 4HD, tel 0131-447 8024, fax 0171-452 8569; and 1 Chlorine Gardens, Belfast BT9 5DJ, tel 01232-664418, fax 01232-661275.

*Council on International Educational Exchange (CIEE),* 205 East 42nd Street, New York, NY 10071-5706, USA, tel 212-822-2695, fax 212-822-2689, http://www.ciee.org/ — sponsors 2-4 week volunteer projects in the USA and abroad during the summer months. Choosing from over 600 projects worldwide, participants join an international team of 10-20 volunteers to work on an environmental or community service project alongside local residents. Volunteers (aged 18 and over) have planted grass and trees to protect endangered coastlines and forests, restored historical sites, renovated low-income housing and cared for the disabled while learning the benefits of international cooperation. The cost of participating is $250-$750 plus travel to and from the project site. Room and board is provided. The Council recruits only US residents directly and receives international volunteers on projects in the USA through its partner organisations in other countries. For further country-by-country details write to the above address. Also see the country chapters in this book.

*GAP Activity Projects,* Gap House, 44 Queen's Road, Reading, Berkshire RG1 4BB, tel 01734-594914, fax 01734-576634 — arranges voluntary work placements in over 34 countries around the world for young people in their 'gap' year between school and further education (aged 18-19 only). Volunteers pay a GAP fee on selection, £390 in 1997, and all travelling costs, but once at their placement, board and lodging are provided, and sometimes pocket money. Jobs include teaching English in Hungary, the Czech and Slovak Republics, and Bulgaria; social work in India; conservation work in Australia; and assisting in a hospital in Japan. Those interested should apply from September in the year before final examinations.

*International Association for the Exchange of Students for Technical Experience (IAESTE UK)*, The Central Bureau, 10 Spring Gardens, London SW1A 2BN, tel 0171-389 4774, fax 0171-389 4426 — arranges an exchange scheme whereby penultimate year students from scientific and technical backgrounds can spend 8-12 weeks mainly in the summer vacation in more than 60 countries worldwide gaining practical experience abroad. Students should apply to the programme in the autumn for placements beginning the following summer.

*SOCRATES*, coordinated in the UK by the Central Bureau for Educational Visits and Exchanges (see above), is the general name for the European Union Actions on languages, education (at pre-university level), and study visits. Action 1 is called *Lingua*, and provides for exchanges and in-service training in other EU and EEA countries (see *Teaching*). Action 2 is *Comenius*, for education at pre-university level and projects organised between schools. It makes provisions for preparatory visits, and exchange or study-visits for teachers/managers. Action 3, known as *Arion*, involves more specialist visits and exchanges for education professionals. A leaflet produced by the Central Bureau, *Making Sense of Socrates*, gives more details. The similar *Leonardo da Vinci Programme* is at the university and vocational level, and has some 'strands' which will support short and longer-term work placements for young people of up to three years, as well as student exchange programmes, vocational training, and language study for work purposes. An information leaflet about 'Leonardo' is also available from the Central Bureau. The *Erasmus* programme or action covers transnational cooperation and projects between universities. More information about this is available from: *UK Erasmus Students Grants Council*, The University, Canterbury, Kent CT2 7PD, tel 01227-762712, fax 01227-762711. These EU education and training programmes are scheduled to run in their present form until 1999. Information on contact details for exchange schemes and education within the EU is available in a useful booklet called *The European Union — A Guide for Students and Teachers*, available from the *European Parliament Office (UK)*, 2 Queen Anne's Gate, London SW1H 9AA.

Students interested in gaining short-term practical experience in a wide range of employment categories in the USA should consult *Internships,* a comprehensive directory published annually by Peterson's (and available in Europe through Vacation Work). It provides listings of over 35,000 career-orientated internship positions in everything from business to the theatre, communications to science; see the bibliography for details.

## OTHER OPPORTUNITIES

*Jobs Abroad,* Worldwide House, Broad Street, Ramsgate, Kent CT11 8NQ — publishes an employment manual which has 'full information including addresses) on employment opportunities, work permits, visas, and emigration,' and information on skilled and unskilled jobs. A copy is £25/$40.

*International Employment Gazette,* 220 North Main Street, Suite 100, Greenville, SC 29601, tel 803-235-444 — is an international recruitment newspaper. For details of subscriptions, contact IEG at the above address.

*International Jobs Report,* 500 Newport Center Drive, Suite 300, Newport Beach, California 92660, USA, tel 714-721-7990, fax 714-721-799, e-mail iscincusa@aol.com — is a weekly research and advertising clipping service for international jobseekers. You can receive the 'help wanted' advertisments for USA or international careers. A trial subscription is £19.95 ($32) for six weeks outside the USA, or $24 in the USA. This service is run by *International Staffing Consultants Inc.* at the same address.

Also see *Overseas Jobs Express* under *Direct Application* above.

# The Creative Job Search

The 'creative job search' is a phrase for an extremely effective way of getting a job. It is an approach which requires a lot of skill, daring and panache. The technique originated in North America, and is particularly productive for those who are prepared to use it in the search for work abroad.

The success of the creative job search depends on understanding that there are thousands of jobs available which are not advertised or made public. Recruitment for these jobs takes place on an informal basis, through a network of contacts passing information to each other by word of mouth. The objective, for the creative jobseeker, is to make the most of existing contacts, while simultaneously building up a network of new ones, through which he or she may be able to get work. Of course, the method is not a new one, but it is the difference of approach and emphasis which is important.

You should also aim to become more knowledgeable about yourself, and your own aptitudes and interests. Analysing your own employment potential is the necessary first step (see *Discovering your Employment Potential*). This requires an 'introspective realism' that most of us shy away from. But the goals you are seeking are worth it.

You should also be very well-informed about a particular job area; and if you intend to concentrate your search on a particular country, you should find out more about its politics, economy, and culture, with the same aim in mind. And in particular, you need to know what the overseas work you are seeking involves, about the experience and qualifications needed, and how recruitment in that field takes place. Also, who is responsible for recruitment in a particular company or organisation? Who are the decision-makers? You have to place yourself within this network of contacts in which most of this 'invisible' (or not advertised) recruiting takes place. As you are seeking a job abroad, this will be an international network. Your contacts should also be persuaded that you understand the special abilities or experience which that particular kind of work needs. These are the general objectives of the creative job search.

It is true that these objectives are not easy to achieve (but then, living and working abroad is also a challenge). You should certainly not assume that all the jobs which are available are already public knowledge. The idea that all such vacancies are given, and cannot consequently be created, does not correspond with the complexities of the jobs market; and your creative approach means being practical. The golden rule is that publicly advertised vacancies (including positions circulated through consultants and agencies) are just the tip of the jobs market iceberg

It is the way you go about your job search — and your frame of mind — which is most important. If you carry out this task effectively, your chances of finding the right job abroad will be greatly increased. Discovering your own employment potential, and acquiring detailed knowledge about the particular field of work which interests you, are the first steps on the road to getting the job.

## JOBS WHICH ARE NOT PUBLICLY ADVERTISED

Every month, thousands of job opportunities are never made public, or notified to employment services and recruitment agencies. Some of these vacancies may appear in newsletters, or on the noticeboards of the organisations which sponsor them. Examples are the vacancy lists of trade unions, or promotions within companies — and in organisations like the United Nations — which are advertised on lists which are circulated internally.

Many vacancies are not publicised even on this restricted basis; but are circulated instead through a system of well-established (and therefore more reliable) contacts known to the employer. In many small and medium-sized companies, advertising is seen — rightly or wrongly — as an unnecessary procedure taking time and money. 'Word-of-mouth' represents a quicker and more cost-effective approach.

This is how it sometimes seems to the employer at least. Even the standard job interview itself is seen by many organisations as be a somewhat haphazard and ineffective means of recruiting new staff. These employers will therefore tend to by-pass the 'conventional' methods of selection, especially where they already have in mind someone who they have met — or know of — and who is enthusiastic about working for them. The creative job search is a way for you to be considered for these jobs which are not made public, or advertised through the press or other means.

### Jobs which are Created

It is a feature of much recruitment within companies that many of these jobs are 'created'. They do not actually exist before they are filled. Some employers or managers are prepared to consider constructive ideas, and then take on someone to carry them out, provided they can be persuaded that they have the right person for the job. The potential here for the creative jobseeker is enormous. The question is, how to proceed.

A good example of one way is to convince an employer of the great advantages of taking on an English-speaker to deal with their relations and contacts with the English-speaking world. English is already a widely spoken language, but in many countries there are not enough linguists of the right calibre. This kind of opportunity exists throughout Europe, and in the entire non-English-speaking world. Even your British or American accent could be a decisive factor. An advertising firm in the USA might be persuaded of the value of having someone with an English accent to deal with clients, for example; alternatively, a satellite television station in Europe might decide that it is better to have an announcer who speaks American English. Also, schools and universities, where the regulations allow, can sometimes be persuaded to take on a native British or American teacher of English. Companies which trade with others abroad may also see the advantage of having an English-speaker on the staff. In fact, there are few which do not wish to expand their sales or trading activities in a world which increasingly speaks this international language.

There are many areas where these opportunities exist, in journalism, commerce, public relations, marketing, personnel management, and so on. A knowledge of the local language and culture, as well as the work experience which you already have, will also set you apart from the competition. This model corresponds more closely, too, with people's actual experience of finding work abroad. For many case histories where a creative approach actually led to a job, sometimes in a surprising or unusual way, see *Work Your Way Around the World* (Vacation Work). Some ways of doing it include: joining a club with international connections; writing off to all the names and addresses you know in a particular country; meeting fellow travellers; or even 'being nosey and talkative'.

Nowadays, creative jobseekers have another powerful ally to aid them in their search, a club which is truly international: the Internet.

## THE INTERNET AND THE WORLD WIDE WEB

The Internet is more than simply a worldwide communication system. Internet communications can be with anyone, anywhere in the world, and can be used relatively cheaply to make the same information available to thousands of other users. The advantage for recruiters is obvious, especially in high-tech industries and universities, where access to computers is already commonplace. This can be the most effective way of advertising vacancies which call for this kind of specialist knowledge; and more and more individuals who have no such expertise are also taking advantage of the many packages which are available, installing a modem, and plugging in to the Internet, with consequences, for recruitment and other global activities like tourism, whose implications have not yet properly been assessed. One of the main service providers which offers access to the Internet is CompuServe, with toll-free membership support services in Australia (1-800-025240); the United Kingdom (0800-289458); and the United States (800-848-8990).

Electronic mail (e-mail) is one of the uses of the Internet that can aid your creative job search. There are thousands of discussion groups, forums and 'newsgroups'. Many of them can bring you into contact with potential employers or sources of employment, either directly or indirectly. With so many choices, it is as well to be precise about the goal, which should be to extend your network of decision-makers to aid you in your job search, even if this will not always be the topic of your discussions. Participating in a newsgroup is simply like talking to others who share the same interest. The way to start is to search for some frequently asked questions (FAQs) which will tell you more about the newsgroup and its interests; and remember you should offer information, and your own point of view, as well as ask for advice.

Bulletin boards (BBSes) are another way to network on-line. These are usually run by individuals, not organisations — and may not offer the same access to employment as Internet or World Wide Web services — but do cater for the local community. They are the equivalent of local newsletters; and mean you can have instant access to people who live in the country or locality which may be your eventual destination (see *Preparation and Follow-up*). Some BBS systems offer jobs, nationally and internationally, as well as business or company listings, and can also provide the equivalent of a 'situation wanted' ad, the chance to post your own CV. Some of these deal with specific sectors like computing, construction, or insurance. Others have detailed information about particular countries. An example is the *S.A. Jobweb Home Page* maintained by Jack McKenzie — 'for reasons I do not fully understand,' he says — which offers links to the *S.A. Jobweb Vacancy Page*; the *S.A. Jobweb Agency Page*; the *S.A. Jobweb CV Database*; the jobs listing run by the 'Mail and Guardian' newspaper; *Computer Week Jobs On-line*; *Niche On-line Employment*; and other services. This gives just a flavour of the opportunities on bulletin boards (and the World Wide Web) for the international jobseeker.

The Internet itself can be a source of direct employment opportunities, and information about countries and potential recruiters, as well as mailing lists, and education and travel information. Many jobs-orientated pages also have searchable databases of current vacancies, which can be accessed using keywords or by employment category. Of course, many of these will be aimed at the locals (and are in the local language). But if you are persistent and creative in your search, others could lead to a more conventional meeting or interview; and there are also an increasing number of resources on the Internet which are aimed specifically at international jobseekers: for example, the site at *http://snow-mass.zdv.gov:8080/jobs.html* run by Jeff Allen. This can lead you to information on finding a job in over 30 countries and regions, to sites in Canada offering jobs, recruitment, and immigration news for instance; to vacancies in Sweden; or an IT job in France. One commercial organisation which offers an employment service on the Internet is *NetJobs*, http://www.netjobs.com/, tel 905-5429484 ext. 231, fax 905-5429479. A job site in the USA which offers career assistance and a searchable database of vacancies, careers fairs and events in the United

States, and also the opportunity to post your CV, is the *Online Career Center,* http://www.occ.com/. Another site, run by Fishnet NewMedia, is at http:// www.overseas jobs.com, which enables jobseekers to surf quickly and easily to 500 employment links in over 35 countries and regions.

Your route to all of this will usually be through the World Wide Web, which information services like *CompuServe, America Online, The Microsoft Network, Europe Online,* or *UK Online,* enable you to access. These World Wide Web addresses start with 'http:'. An e-mail address with the letters 'co' means that this is a company; 'edu' or 'ac' means an academic institution; 'gov' is a government organisation; and 'org' refers to other organisations such as charities. *How to Get Your Dream Job Using the Internet* by Shannon Bounds and Arthur Karl (Coriolis Group Books, 7339 E. Acoma Drive, Suite 7, Scottsdale, AZ 85260, USA, tel 0800-410-0192, fax 602-483-0192, http://www.coriolis.com, $29.99) has more about using the Internet to find employment, a guide to Internet recruiters and companies on-line, and chapters on 'getting connected' and creating your own Home Page.

## JOINING THE NETWORK

The Internet can be an invaluable research tool; and aid you in your creative jobsearch; it is also one way of establishing contacts in your prospective area of employment or country, and joining the recruitment network. Of course, it will be very difficult, if you are looking for a real job in Sweden, Italy, or South Korea, to find employment by using the Internet alone; and the process of cultivating contacts is always slow. See the chapter 'Schmoozing Online' in *How to Get Your Dream Job on the Internet* for the right approach here. However you go about it, your search for international employment will usually end up with a face-to-face interview (even if your initial contact is by letter, fax, telephone, or on-line).

There are probably as many ways of 'joining the network' and finding a job as there are individual jobseekers. But the process of widening your range of contacts and meeting the decision-makers always involves three general stages. First, you have to develop a network of intermediaries or 'referees' who can put you in touch with your target contacts; then you must arrange to go and see these contacts (or to contact them on-line). Eventually, you will have to know how to handle the face-to-face meeting (or 'creative job search interview') and how to follow it up most effectively.

### Intermediaries and Referees
Draw up a select list of the people or the kinds of people, you wish to contact, and the 'referees' you can go through, people who are known both you and those you wish to contact. When you call — or write, or e-mail — your request for information or a meeting will carry more authority. The age of letters of recommendation may be over, but the principle remains the same. You are meeting your contact on more equal terms, if you can say 'your name was given me by so-and-so...' You should observe the normal rules of politeness and courtesy (and on the Net, your 'netiquette'); and remember, too, that your contact can be a source of future contacts, even if he or she does not offer you a job straightaway. The creative job search is also about planning for the future.

Which is all no more than practical common sense. But how do you find referees or intermediaries for jobs overseas? More conventional jobseekers will not know how to do this. This is because the limits of any job search are really creative: the limits of your own imagination and initiative. Creative jobseekers will realise the potential, and actively exploit their existing connections to find new ones; and discover — often by a process of lateral thinking — the best course of action to take.

You may wish to draw up a general list of suitable newsgroups on the Internet; of others in your profession who can help; or those in your situation who have useful leads and contacts; or people who already live where you wish to work. There are several newsgroups for expatriates on the Internet, for example. Possible intermediaries who are already known to you are:

* parents and relations
* friends and their parents and relations
* past or present school or university teachers
* past or present school or university friends and acquaintance
* members of your church, political party, club, or society
* your family doctor or solicitor
* your bank or building society manager
* work colleagues
* people you have met through your work

Some questions you can ask are: 'Can you help me get advice about working abroad?'; 'Do you know anybody who lives in X or Y country or city?'; 'Do you know anyone who works in this particular profession or field?'; 'Do you know anyone who knows anyone who does?'. There will be some blind alleys, of course, but also some valuable leads; and in the end, these intermediaries may be able to put you in touch with those who can provide you with work. Some other intermediaries who can help you in your creative job search are:

* members of foreign trade associations
* members of your local Chamber of Commerce who have contacts abroad. Many local Chambers of Commerce in the UK are members of the Franco-British Chamber of Commerce and Industry in Paris for instance
* members of foreign nationals' associations in your country, or the equivalent expatriate associations in the place you wish to work
* managers and employees of international companies, or British or US-based firms with branches abroad
* those working for firms in your chosen field in your own country
* those you have met while travelling abroad

**Visits and Contacts**
The first thing to say about arranging visits to potential employers or contacts (whose organisations do not advertise the vacancies you are ultimately seeking) is that you should not sell yourself too much (except maybe in a field where selling is important). There is no reason at this stage to ask for a job. These are visits mainly to find out what the jobs you are interested in involves, or what jobs are available. You may, in turn, be able to help your contact, which can lead to other useful contacts of course. Your eventual aim should be to obtain an interview with someone who can offer you work, or knows someone who can.

If you are asking simply for advice, then you are more likely to be able to arrange a meeting; and it is easier to refuse a specific request than a general one. The same kind of etiquette applies to the newsgroups you participate in on the Internet, where employment may be of more interest to you than the other participants. If you can't arrange a suitable meeting straightaway, then there will normally be somebody else your contact will be able to put you in touch with, if he or she feels you are a person worth helping.

Another rule for the creative jobseeker is that just getting in touch is not the aim of the exercise. You have to get that job! So the all-important personal visit is the logical next step; and if, as is often the case, your letter of enquiry is not answered in a reasonable time, telephoning to arrange a visit is another alternative.. Or you can begin with a phone call or e-mail — but it is always advisable to follow this up with a letter. If you follow up your enquiry, then the potential contact is not so likely to have forgotten who your are when you arrive on the doorstep.

### The Creative Job Search Interview

Unlike a simple application for a job, the creative job search interview should be seen more as a discussion about the general possibilities of getting work. You may see your meetings with your target contacts as a means of showing that you are a professional and serious-minded person; and it is certainly reasonable to discuss employment possibilities (in a field which after all is of interest to you both); or to find out more about your chosen career or destination. This initial approach is of the greatest importance. All the time you are working towards achieving your goal, which is a job abroad.

Some persistence will be needed. The job you can just walk into is probably not the one you need; and you need confidence in your own ability and aims to be able to demonstrate this to your potential employer. You could ask him or her about practical details: how they got their job; and what kind of qualifications or expertise would help. What do you need to do to integrate into an international environment, and how do you deal with colleagues? What is living in that country like? Remember that your contact needs to see your approach in a positive light, as an opportunity, not a problem.

The right approach will depend on the person. But the message you are trying to get across is always the same; it has to do with the seriousness of your enquiry; and your genuine interest in the job. Only when you have made this impression, or got this message across, is it worth asking a more direct question. If someone from your background and with your experience were to apply for a job with this organisation, how would it be be viewed? From the answer to this question, you may be able to gather how closely you should keep in touch with this contact in future.

It is also a good idea to find out all you can about other target contacts in your field of interest. From these, you will quickly create the network of contacts which will give you the greatest chance of success.

If you follow these general principles, you will soon know — and become known by — a large number of key people; and this applies to your participation in newsgroups too. If you are working effectively, you will have managed in a very short time what takes most people years to achieve: and become a link in the chain of notification through which non-publicly advertised or 'invisible' vacancies are circulated.

This approach represents the formalisation of the many informal methods of finding work which are actually used by jobseekers. More detailed information about the methods of the creative job search is available in the book *What Color is Your Parachute?* — see the bibliography for details.

## SHORT-TERM WORK ABROAD

The really determined jobseeker will be able to exploit the methods outlined above in both a 'conventional' and a 'creative' sense. There is no creative job search which does not have specific goals and objectives in mind, and vice versa: no conventional methods which should not also involve some creativity and imagination. And there is a third, 'high-risk' way of finding work abroad, for those who enjoy travel, and are prepared to spend some time in their chosen country. This is to apply the techniques of both conventional and creative job searches on the spot, and look for work in the country concerned.

This will naturally be more suited to some careers and professions than others, for example English teaching, agricultural work, or tourism. One way of doing it may be to take on short-term work in the country you are interested in to support yourself, while you continue your search for a longer-term career. Just being there can be an advantage in many ways; and employers may prefer to take on someone who is based locally, and is already familiar with the country and its customs.

Doing a temporary job in another country can bring you closer to the more permanent career you are looking for. This kind of jobseeking, for British and Irish citizens, can be easier in the EU than in other countries (and not so easy for Americans) because of the directive allowing them to stay for three months in any European Union member state and look for work. Very few other countries permit this; and you need to be entitled to residence for other reasons. Even a holiday in your chosen destination can be a good idea — a way of checking out job opportunities and familiarising yourself with the local environment; and you can find out how to get a work permit, which is more often a practical than a legal matter. Educational or exchange visits to another country are another way into the world of work. (See *Working Exchanges* above).

You should make friends, meet people, and keep an eye on vacancies in newspapers and visit a few employment agencies or companies. It is better to go armed with a potential list of contacts, and to make the right preparations before you go . Time will be at a premium. And you will also be able to improve your understanding of the local way of life and language. You can also find out something about yourself, and how you would cope with living there for a longer time.

Most of the short-term jobs available to foreigners anywhere do not require any specific qualifications, except some willingness to work at the bottom end of the jobs market (and an understanding of the language).This sort of work is largely to do with agriculture, the tourist industry, labouring, or voluntary work. There are many areas which call for large numbers of unskilled workers for a short time each year, jobs which exist because of a local labour shortage, or a need for English-speaking people. In practice, there is no such thing as total labour mobility, and enthusiastic workers from abroad may be more adaptable (and exploitable) than many of the locals.

You need some pointers to find even temporary work (which are covered more fully in many Vacation Work publications). This Directory gives brief details of the opportunities to be found in each country, and mentions the main organisations that can help you to find work.The *Specific Careers* section covers those approaches to finding work that are applicable to several countries, such as writing to national tourist offices to obtain lists of hotels, or reading guide-books (in the *Transport, Tourism and Hospitality* chapter). The chapters in *Worldwide Employment* section cover those aspects of temporary work that are unique to that country, and what and where the opportunities are.

# Rules and Regulations

## IMMIGRATION REQUIREMENTS

There are only a few countries around the world which actively encourage immigration, and most have very strict entry regulations which have to be dealt with in advance. Common requirements are that you have a positive job offer, be able to speak the language, and have pre-arranged accommodation. Anyone seeking work abroad is advised to request up-to-date information from the appropriate embassy as to these requirements. Addresses of embassies and high commissions are given in the country chapters of this book. If you are working in a sponsored programme or for an international company, the immigration requirements will usually be taken care of for you. If not, the usual requirement is for an employer to apply on your behalf to the immigration authorities some months in advance. And those travelling on holiday or for business will have different requirements to fulfil.

## THE EUROPEAN UNION

The Treaty of Rome which established the European Economic Community (EEC) was signed by its original six members — France, West Germany, Italy, the Netherlands, Belgium and Luxembourg — in 1957. In 1967, this was merged with the European Coal and Steel Community (ECSC) — which was the forerunner of the EEC — to form the European Community (EC). The Maastricht Treaty changed the name and vocation of the EC when it came into force in 1993; and it is now more accurately known as the European Union (EU). The EC is one of the constituent parts or 'pillars' of the EU, which has a common European citizenship and a timetable for European Monetary Union. The UK, Ireland, and Denmark joined in January 1973; Greece entered in January 1981; Spain and Portugal in January 1986; and the former East Germany became a part of the EU when Germany was reunified in 1990; Austria, Finland, and Sweden (from the 'rival' European Free Trade Area) joined the EU in 1995. Poland, Hungary, Romania, Bulgaria, the Czech Republic, the Slovak Republic, Estonia, Latvia, Lithuania, and Slovenia have all signed agreements which could eventually lead to their membership; as well as Malta, Cyprus, and Turkey, which have association agreements (and have previously tried and failed to join). Partnership agreements which exclude membership have been signed with Ukraine, Russia, Moldova, Kyrgyzstan, and Belarus.

The EU is expanding 'horizontally' but also 'vertically'; there is a timetable which should lead to a European Central Bank and a single currency. In addition, there is close cooperation between the EU and those European Free Trade Area (EFTA) countries which have not become members  (which are, at the time of writing, Iceland, Liechtenstein, Norway, and Switzerland). EFTA was originally a free trade area which was set up in response to the creation of the EEC. This joint grouping is known as the European Economic Area (EEA).

The aims of the EU are varied. Its remit runs to areas like education, culture, and the law, as well as economics. The most dominant of these is the creation of a 'federal' or decentralised union of all member states, in effect a single state, or 'union'. This is of great importance for businesses wishing to operate in a the European market as well as for international companies investing in EU countries. Most important for the purposes of this book, however, is the policy of free movement of labour, which makes travel for work easier within its borders; the abolition of work permits (which are no longer required); and European Monetary Union and the creation of a single currency. A federal union is the logical consequence of these common European institutions which have been created, the harmonisation of tax and labour law, progress towards a level playing-field for competition between EU companies, and the establishment of a common European citizenship.

At present, it seems likely that a 'core' group of European countries, notably France, Germany, and the Benelux countries, and Italy, will lead the way to the creation of a federal Europe, with later entry for countries such as Britain. The abolition of work permits — and a single or common currency — does not necessarily create new jobs, of course; and employers will always tend to recruit local labour on purely practical grounds. But it will create more favourable conditions for international jobseekers in some areas, such as teaching, where restrictions to mobility between EU countries will in the course of time be lifted; and the removal of passport and frontier controls between the countries covered by the 1995 Schengen Agreement (currently France, Germany, Belgium, Luxembourg, the Netherlands, Spain, Portugal, Austria, Italy, Greece, Denmark, Finland, and Sweden) makes travel between these countries a lot easier for everyone.

**European Monetary Union**
In December 1991, the Treaty of European Union was signed in Maastricht in the Netherlands. The Maastricht Treaty sets out the plans to work towards ultimate European economic, monetary and political union. It established a European Union composed of the previously existing European Community and all its laws; the European Political Co-operation framework, dealing with foreign and security policy; and justice and interior affairs, including immigration and conditions of entry.

Despite opposition in some countries, and the reservations of many economists, progress towards EMU is not likely to be reversed, although it may be delayed. Already, EU businesses have unrestricted access to a market which is larger than that of the United States or Japan. The Single Market — which came into being in 1 January 1993 — was meant to create jobs. But the need to bring the widely differing economies of member states together — which is known as 'convergence', has led to a slowdown in economic growth and job losses in some cases.

**Immigration and Residence**
As far as the British jobseeker is concerned, EMU should make it easier to live and work in other European countries. The EURES scheme (see *Rules and Regulations*) already allows well-qualified and multilingual applicants in Britain to visit any Jobcentre and fill in a form (ES13) which can be sent to the relevant Employment Service in other EU countries for linking with suitable posts. The Single Market means that you are already entitled to exactly the same rights, rates of pay, healthcare, and unemployment provision, as others in the EU country where you are working (leading to the anomaly of greater employment rights in some countries than exist for workers who stay in the UK, which presently has secured an 'opt-out' from some EU labour law). You must also pay the same taxes and Social Security contributions as nationals of that country. You may also claim the local equivalent of Unemployment Benefit (or 'Jobseeker's Allowance') on the same basis is the nationals of that country (see *Social Security* below).

Those who are not working have some greater rights. After the Maastricht Treaty, it became possible for students, pensioners, and persons of independent means, to move to another EU country without applying for a residence permit in their home country; they can instead make their application once they have arrived. This means that UK or Irish citizens can always apply for a residence permit after they have arrived in another EU country, provided that they have found a job, are actually or potentially self-employed, or are looking for work (although evidence of this may be required, job applications being one example). You do not require a work permit for any EU country, but will need a residence permit which goes with some form of identity card. This will itself be enough to travel between many EU countries (without a passport) and is granted automatically to those who fulfil the criteria above; it lasts for five years and is automatically renewable. But the authorities in other EU countries can still deport an EU citizen who has no means of support.

These changes do not benefit US citizens, or those from the US and Commonwealth countries who do not have a right to UK or EU citizenship: for example — in Britain and Ireland — 'patriality', a grandparent born in one of these countries.

Immigration regulations for EU and US citizens are given in the *Immigration* section under each country covered in the *Worldwide Employment* section of this book. The current regulations for EU members can be summarised as follows. If you arrive in an EU country with the intention of looking for work, you should report to the local town hall or police station (depending on the rules in that country), within a few days of arrival. Those working for less than three months in an EU country will not automatically be issued with a residence permit. They still have to bring a valid passport/identity card (a British Visitor's Passport is not enough) and produce a letter from their employer for the authorities. A temporary residence permit is issued if the contract of employment lasts for between three months and a year. Where employment is expected to exceed one year, they will receive a five-year residence permit. Completing these formalities means you will have some protection and rights. It is generally not advisable to work for employers who cut corners, and are not willing to provide you with a suitable letter or contract.

The abolition of internal frontier controls between the signatories to the Schengen Agreement (see above) means in practice, for British and Irish citizens, that this applies to them, too, when they move between these countries. An ID card or residence permit in one is enough to obtain entry to another. And so — and this applies to some extent to other travellers — it is more difficult for the authorities in each country to know how long you have been on their territory, since your passport is unlikely to be checked, or only at your first point of arrival.

## The European Economic Area

Of great significance to EU workers is the implementation of the European Economic Area (EEA) Treaty in January 1993. Agreement on the EEA Treaty was reached in April 1992 between the EC member states and the then seven members of the European Free Trade Association (EFTA). In broad terms it guarantees the free movement of labour, goods, services and capital within the EU countries and those which are still in EFTA, meaning that the abolition of work permits for EU citizens also applies in Iceland, Norway, Liechtenstein, and Switzerland. The need for residence permits remains.

## Recognition of Qualifications

Many EU directives have appeared over the years concerning mutual recognition of professional qualifications, for instance those of doctors, veterinarians and nurses. In many different professions, EU citizens are eligible to join a counterpart professional association in another EU country without having to retrain. Some professions, such as teaching, have aptitude tests or exams in the language of the country concerned, although many of these discriminatory restrictions are being challenged at present (with the consequence for English language teachers that they should more easily be able to work in schools and universities in the EU in future if they are qualified as teachers in Britain or Ireland).

The basic directive on training and qualifications (89/48/EEC) which recognised three-year training courses, has been expanded so that qualifications gained through any post-secondary course of more than one year, as well as work experience, must be taken into account where entry to a job is regulated on the basis of specific national qualifications. This means that National and Scottish Vocational Qualifications (NVQs/SVQs) and GNVQs and their equivalents are now recognized in the EU. For those wishing to check on the acceptability of UK qualifications, you can contact the Comparability Coordinator at the Employment Department, QSI, Room E454, Moorfoot, Sheffield S1 4PQ, tel 0114-259 4144.

If you have experience but no formal qualifications in a job, it is also possible to obtain a European Community Certificate of Experience. For EU citizens in the UK this is issued by the Department of Trade and Industry (DTI). You should first make sure that your type of work experience is covered by an EU directive by asking your trade union or professional organisation. If you are in doubt, the DTI will send you a copy of the relevant directive. You can write to them at: Department of Trade and Industry, European Division, Ashdown House, 6th Floor, 123 Victoria Street, London SW1E 6RB. The DTI also supplies the application form for a Certificate of Experience with explanations attached.

Further useful information on qualifications, and other aspects of working in the EU, can be found in the 'Eurofacts' leaflets published by EUROPPS to be found in Careers Advice Offices and TECS (or write to: The Institute of Careers Officers, 27a Lower High Street, Stourbridge, West Midlands DY8 1TA). *First Steps to Working in Europe* (CSU Publications, Armstrong House, Oxford Road, Manchester M1 7ED, tel 0161-2375409, http://www.prospects.csu.man.as.uk) is a guide for higher education students and recent graduates in Britain and Ireland who wish to work in another European country. (Others in their 'special interest series' include *Using Languages* and *Work and Study Abroad*). *The European Commission (UK)*, 8 Storey's Gate, London SW1P 3AT, tel 0171-973 1992, can give useful information about the EU and its institutions. *Comparability of Vocational Training Qualifications*, published by the Office for Official Publications of the European Communities, is a directory of EU qualifications and their equivalents. This office also publishes *Working in the European Union: a Guide for Graduate Recruiters and Job-seekers*, by W. H. Archer and J. C. Raban.

### Self-employment
Many work contracts, especially in the construction industry, are on a self-employed basis. A prospective employee must normally be self-employed in the United Kingdom before he or she can apply for the certificate E101, issued by the International Services Contributions Agency of the DSS, Benton Park Road, Newcastle-upon-Tyne NE98 1YX, tel 06451-54811. The E101 exempts the holder from paying social security contributions in another EU country for up to 12 months. It can only be issued on the basis of a definite job offer from a named employer and can take several weeks to process. This can lead to problems, as many employers will not offer you a job unless you already have an E101. The DSS issues a leaflet, SA 29, which gives more about the position of the self-employed in Europe.

Anyone thinking of setting up in the EU in a non-salaried or independent profession (e.g. carpenter, plumber, plasterer, restaurateur, etc.) will have to register their qualifications or a Certificate of Experience with the relevant local regulatory body. Proof of ability to manage one's own business is also needed. This is not a discriminatory practice — rather a requirement to conform to the same regulations that govern local people who provide services to the public.

### British citizenship
The 1981 British Nationality Act complicated this issue somewhat by replacing the old category of 'citizen of the United Kingdom and colonies' with three new categories of citizenship:

1. *British Citizenship*, for people closely connected (i.e. by birth, registration/naturalisation, or descent) with the United Kingdom, the Channel Islands and the Isle of Man.

2. *British Dependent Territories Citizenship*, for people connected with the dependencies.

3. *British Overseas Citizenship*, for those citizens of the United Kingdom and Colonies who do not have these connections with either the United Kingdom or the dependencies.

The Home Office advises that free movement of labour within the EU and the EEA is granted only to those with British Citizenship (Class 1); who have the right of abode in the UK. The only exception to this is for British Dependent Territories Citizens (Class 2) connected with Gibraltar.

In order to work within the EU or EEA you must have a valid British passport passport. This must be either endorsed *Holder has the right of abode in the United Kingdom* or show the holder's national status as a British citizen.

Any queries on nationality from people living in the United Kingdom should be addressed to the *Nationality Division,* 3rd floor, India Buildings, Water Street, Liverpool L2 0QN. People resident abroad should contact their nearest British consulate or embassy.

Among the entitlements of a UK citizen in Europe is the right for his or her spouse and dependants to join him or her and enjoy the same privileges, including the right to take up employment.

## SOCIAL SECURITY

Working in a foreign country normally means joining that country's social security scheme. There are many exceptions to this rule, however, and in certain cases contributions are still payable in Britain. Claims for national insurance benefits can also be complicated where more than one country's scheme is involved. The Department of Social Security publishes a series of leaflets (described below) which are available from the Contributions Agency of the DSS International Services, Newcastle upon Tyne NE98 1YX. Leaflets CH 5 and CH 6, however, are obtainable from local DSS offices, which may also be able to provide copies of leaflet NI 38.

This leaflet, *Social Security Abroad,* explains in general terms about cases where there are no reciprocal agreements involved. If you are claiming child benefit, ask for leaflets CH 5 *Child benefit for people entering Britain,* and CH 6 *Child benefit for people leaving Britain.* However, child benefit is only affected if the child goes abroad for more than eight weeks.

### European Union Regulations

The rules concerning the EU Social Security Regulations are complex. Get advice from the Contributions Agency of the DSS International Services should you decide to live or work in another EU country. Leaflet SA 29 explains your social security, insurance benefits, and health-care rights in the EU, and Iceland, Liechtenstein and Norway. The European Commission also issues a useful guide which explain in basic terms the Social Security arrangements of each EU country: *The Community Provisions on Social Security.* Copies are available on application to the Contributions Agency, International Servicess (EU), address above.

### Other Reciprocal Agreements

In addition to the leaflets mentioned above, the following leaflets outline social security agreements between Britain and: *Australia* (SA 5); *Barbados* (SA 43);

*Bermuda* (SA 23); *Canada* (SA 20); *Cyprus* (SA 12); *Israel* (SA 14); *Jamaica* (SA 27); *Jersey and Guernsey* (SA 4); *Malta* (SA 11); *Mauritius* (SA 38); *New Zealand* (SA 8); *The Philippines* (SA 42); *Turkey* (SA 22); *USA* (SA 33); and the states of the former *Yugoslavia* (SA 17).


## HEALTH CARE

The Department of Health produces the leaflet T5, *Health Advice for Travellers anywhere in the world,* giving a country-by-country explanation on how British citizens can obtain free or reduced-cost treatment and refunds for medical treatment and medicines paid for in the EU countries. This leaflet also includes advice on what health care is available outside the EU and general advice on health risks abroad, along with the form E111 *Certificate of Entitlement to Benefits in Kind during a Stay in a Member State* and the form CM1 *Application for Form E111.* Leaflet T5 is available at post offices and can be processed by a post office. Anyone planning to live and work in another EU country should write to the International Services Contributions Agency, Benton Park Road, Newcastle-upon-Tyne NE98 1YX, tel 06451-54811, before they leave. The E111 is only valid for temporary visits. Even with the E111 it is still likely that you will have to pay for some of your costs and so you are advised to look into taking out private health insurance wherever you will be working. Amongst the leading providers of medical cover is BUPA International: tel 01273-208181; fax 01273-866583.


## UNEMPLOYMENT BENEFIT IN EU COUNTRIES

Those who have been registered unemployed in Britain for four weeks can go abroad to other EU countries to look for work, and still receive the UK benefit. See Leaflet UBL22 *Unemployment Benefit for people going abroad or coming from abroad.* There is an application form for transferring benefit: E303. This should be done before your departure. It should be noted that this is only possible in the case of benefit paid for with National Insurance contributions; and not in the case of income support.

Those wishing to transfer their unemployment benefit abroad should first select the town where they intend to look for work, and notify the local unemployment benefit office in this country of their plans. The unemployment benefit office will inform the Pensions and Overseas Benefits Directorate of the Department of Social Security who will consider the issuing of form E303. This form authorises the other state to pay your UK unemployment benefit/ Jobseeker's Allowance. It may be issued to you before departure from the UK if enough time exists, and you are going to Austria, Belgium, Finland, France, Germany, Greece, Iceland, Italy, Norway, Portugal, Spain, or Sweden. Otherwise, the E303 form will be sent to a liaison officer in the country concerned and your unemployment benefit office can supply you with a letter of introduction to the foreign employment service. (What this means in practice is that you should make these arrangements before you go).

This system involves, in effect, the exporting of UK unemployment benefit, and works in the other direction too. Benefit is paid at the standard UK rate, which may not go far in a country like Sweden which has a high cost of living. But it is also possible for people who have worked in another EU country, and have paid contributions into its unemployment benefit insurance scheme, to claim unemployment benefit there at that country's rate, which is likely to be higher than in Britain. The exact details, such as who administers the system and the length of time for which contributions must have been paid, vary from country to country.

Time spent working, and paying contributions, in one EU country can be

If you live and work abroad, it's important to have medical cover. As the world's leading health care specialists, BUPA International provides help and advice on medical treatment worldwide, with members in over 180 countries. Membership provides you with a 24 hour helpline, open 365 days a year. For more details on how BUPA can cover you and your family wherever you are in the world phone 01273 208181 or fax 01273 866583.

credited towards your entitlement to unemployment benefit if you move on to another EU country too — as long as you have worked and paid contributions in the country you are leaving. Thus, someone may work first in Britain and then in Germany, where he may lose his job and begin claiming German unemployment benefit; his UK insurance may be used first to satisfy the rules for payment of German unemployment benefit; and if he then moves on to France he can continue to claim unemployment benefit there for up to three months, but at the German rate. If these scheme seems attractive to unemployed readers of this Directory, remember that the cost of living — as well as the levels of unemployment benefit — is higher in most European countries too.

## TAXATION

The extent of the liability to United Kingdom tax of a person who is temporarily abroad depends on several factors, the principal one being whether the person is classed as resident in the UK for tax purposes. In the simplest of cases, where a UK citizen works abroad full-time during an entire tax year (i.e. 6 April to 5 April), there will be no liability for UK tax, as long as that person does not spend more than 91 days in the UK on average in one tax year. An outline of residence and its effect on tax liability is given in the Inland Revenue's leaflet IR 20, *Residents' and Non-Residents' Liability to Tax in the United Kingdom.*

Where a person who is abroad remains resident in the UK for tax purposes, he may in some circumstances be liable to tax both in the UK and in the country he is visiting. If this happens, however, he or she can normally claim relief under a Double Taxation Agreement made between the two countries from either one tax or the other. Details are given in the Inland Revenue's leaflet IR 58 *Going to Work Abroad.*

A person who is abroad but remains liable to UK tax may be able to claim certain expenses for travelling. Details of the rules can be obtained from any local office of the Inspector of Taxes (to find the address of your local office, look in the Telephone Directory under 'Inland Revenue'). Inland Revenue leaflets are available from any local office of the Inspector of Taxes. Other general enquiries, claims and problems should be addressed to the *Inland Revenue Financial Intermediaries and Claims Office (FICO)*, Non-residents Section, St John's House, Merton Road, Bootle, Merseyside L69 9BB.

Enquiries about claims to exemption under a Double Taxation Agreement should be addressed to *FICO (Nottingham)*, Fitzroy House, Nottingham NG2 1BD. And many EU countries operate a 'pay as you earn' system similar to that in Britain. This means you are taxed on the assumption that your monthly income is representative of your annual income. If your job is seasonal, or temporary, or varies from month to month, it often isn't. Hence your right to claim back tax. It doesn't mean you can get around the system by moving from country to country, though. This is the reason for the 'double taxation' agreements mentioned above. It is also a good idea — especially when you work abroad — to keep all payslips and other financial information in case you need to plead your case at a later date; and you should be careful when your employer sets out your tax position at the beginning of your employment. There are rules which vary from country to country, but generally you do not want to end up on the local equivalent of 'emergency' or higher-rate tax.

## US CITIZENS IN THE EU

Economic and Monetary Union will not improve the chances of Americans wishing to work in EU countries. Those which have previously been willing to tolerate some illegal non-EU workers are taking more steps to stop such practices. It is also important to bear in mind that the EU and EEA also have to deal with large numbers of migrant workers, many from eastern Europe, where political change has also opened up a new source of potential labour.

US citizens can, of course, be legally employed where no suitable EU worker can be found and a work permit has been issued. There is no equivalent of the Green Card though. A letter or authorisation is required for this permit from the company which will employ you; and it should be noted that you must have the relevant documentation with you when you arrive to take up employment.

Details of programmes which allow American citizens to work abroad legally are given in many of the chapters in *Specific Careers*, in particular under *Agriculture and the Environment; Au Pair and Domestic; Transport, Tourism and Hospitality;* and *Voluntary Work.* Further information is also given under separate country chapters.

As regards taxation, US citizens need to inform themselves before going abroad as to their liability on overseas earnings. Even where overseas residence is established, there is a ceiling on the amount which can be earned free of US tax. The Inland Revenue Service issues a helpful leaflet, *Tax Guide for US Citizens Abroad (Publication 54),* which is available from the *Forms Distribution Centre,* PO Box 25866, Richmond, Virginia 23260. As far as social security is concerned, US citizens working for US companies abroad can continue to pay US social security contributions for several years — and claim exemption from local social security payments so long as a reciprocal agreement exists with the other country. A great deal of helpful information on the financial implications of working abroad is contained in *Evaluating an Overseas Job Opportunity,* by John Williams (Pilot Books, 103 Cooper Street, Babylon, New York 11702).

# Learning the Language

Living and working abroad usually means learning another language. In your job search, and any international career, speaking other languages can be a decisive advantage, as well as one of the opportunities which this can bring. Our (often negative) attitudes to language-learning in the USA and Britain are often as much cultural as linguistic. The other 'world' languages, like French or Spanish, are by far the most popular with English-speakers; and German is becoming an important second language in eastern Europe too. It is reasonable for all international jobseekers to aim to perfect the second language they may have learnt at school, and to start learning another, maybe more exotic or minority language, something which will set you apart from the competition. How serious are you in your desire to live and work another country? Your commitment to learning its language, and making a start before you go, is one way you — and your potential employer — will find out.

Speakers of 'minority' languages, like Finnish or Flemish, understand very well the importance of mastering other languages; and we can learn something from their attitudes to language-learning. A second, third, or even fourth foreign language is simply no big deal in the Netherlands, a country which itself has started exporting English language teachers around the world. It is understood that language-learning is not a difficult or academic subject, but simply a skill, one which involves mastering the phonology — or system of sounds — of the language in question, as well as its grammar and written form. There is nothing haphazard about this. There are rules for producing the right sounds which will enable you to speak and understand a foreign language to a reasonable level, and these can be learned.

Even if you do not wish to learn languages for their own sake, there are the economic factors which themselves may lead to a transformation of attitudes to language-learning in the English-speaking countries, even as English is becoming a global language, the language of science and computing, business and commerce. As the other barriers to the free movement of labour come down in Europe, those with a good knowledge of other languages will have the widest range of job opportunities open to them, in translation and interpreting for instance, but also administration, sales and marketing, and a wide variety of other fields. If Britons and Americans do not learn French, or Russian, or Japanese, then we can be sure that many speakers of these other languages are already busy learning ours, some 150 million or so in China at the last count.

In your daily life abroad, even if English is used in your work environment and in your dealings with other expatriates, you can be sure that not speaking the language of your host country will put you at a disadvantage, not least in your abilty to recognise further job opportunities. Learning the language of that country helps you to integrate into the local community, as well as leading to other career and life choices; and could be a decisive factor in the success or otherwise of your stay. The British and Irish still lag behind the other EU nations where language-learning is concerned; but economic necessity, and some greater emphasis on language-learning in schools, means that this is already changing.

The question is, where to start — and it should certainly be with the idea that learning another language is not some kind of grim necessity, but a positive opportunity which you should welcome. Then, readers of this Directory may choose to visit their local library or bookshop to find courses like the *Teach Yourself...* books (Hodder & Stoughton, London, usually under £20) which each come with a cassette (and which should be used ideally with other, more basic courses or a teacher). *Colloquial...* is a similar and slightly more expensive 'interactive' series (Routledge, 11 New Fetter Lane, London EC 4P 4EE; 29 West 35th Street, New York, NY 10001). A long-standing and popular series is *Teach Yourself...* (Hugo, generally priced at around £35). The well-known *Linguaphone* courses can be ordered by telephoning 0800-282417. These are suitable for beginners, and are organised around useful vocabulary and phrases, as well as grammar.

You should remember when you learn in this way that simple repetition of phrases — which may of course be useful in themselves — is not be-all and end-all of your study. You are endeavouring to discover, in a practical way, how the individual sounds of the language are made, and how they relate to each other, as well as its basic structures. A useful companion book which explains some of these issues (and an indispensible referencee for all those who will teach English as a foreign language) is *A Mouthful of Air* by Anthony Burgess (Hutchinson). This can tell you why we should learn foreign languages, and how these can be studied in a practical way.

There are many phrase-books on the market, but these are generally less useful as many try to transcribe the phrases into the English (really the Roman) alphabet, without enough explanation of how these sounds are made. In fact, there is an International Phonetic Alphabet which would much more helpful to those who really have to use these phrases. *Berlitz* publishes some phrase-books (Berlitz Publishing Co. Ltd., Peterley Road, Cowley, Oxford OX4 2TX); as do *Lonely Planet* (PO Box 617, Hawthorn, Victoria 3122, Australia, tel 03-9819-1877, fax 03-9819-6459) and *Rough Guides* (1 Mercer Street, London WC2H 8QJ). The *Cortina Institute of Languages* (19 Newton Turnpike, Westport, CT 06880) publishes a series of *Traveler's Dictionaries* at around $5.95, as well as interactive courses with a cassette which are available only in the USA and Canada.

Private or home tuition, or study in your local college or university, are other options — or some combination of these. Contact with native speakers of the language will also help (and could be a part of your creative job search and preparation too). Some countries, like Norway and Belgium, provide special classes for foreign workers and their families; and some companies in the USA and UK include language courses as part of their training programmes. In many countries, language courses for the locals are even subsidised by the state, and may lead to employment for English language teachers (see *Teaching*). Also, there will be many language schools and colleges 'on the spot' which can provide general or specialist courses after your arrival (see below).

However you learn, it is advisable to make a start before you go. Here are some ideas on where to begin.

## LOCAL COURSES

Most universities and colleges of further education, as well as workers' educational associations and adult education centres, run part-time or evening classes in a number of foreign languages. These are often very good value. You may wish to combine them with some more intensive study, private tuition, a home-study or 'distance-learning' course, or a short intensive or 'immersion' course abroad.

## THE OPEN UNIVERSITY

The *Open University (OU)*, Walton Hall, Milton Keynes MK7 6AA, tel 01908-274066, fax 01908-653744, with offices in the UK and many overseas, has distance or 'open-learning' courses in French and German (with a new one for Spanish scheduled for 1999). Those who have learnt these languages informally, or have no formal qualifications, are encouraged to apply. There are books, videos, and audio-tapes, with centres where students can 'drop in' for tuition, and 18 hours of face-to-face tuition over 32 weeks. The course can lead towards a degree-level qualification in this or other subjects. The level you need is about GCSE to start off with; and by the third year the student should have 'a level approximately equal to a first-year undergraduate course.' A *Language Learner's Good Study Guide* has also been produced which is recommended reading for anyone considering learning another language.

## CILT

The *Centre for Information on Language Teaching and Research (CILT)*, Regent's College, Inner Circle, Regent's Park, London NW1 4NS, is the organisation in the UK which provides information on the available range of resources for the study of many languages, including some of the more out-of-the-way ones for which information is difficult to obtain. If you want to study one of these, the *CILT Library* (tel 0171-379 5110) has a certain amount of documentation on courses, especially in London. A list of their publications can be obtained by sending an SAE to the above address.

## PRIVATE LANGUAGE SCHOOLS

There are many private language schools offering anything from correspondence courses with cassettes to intensive stays in the country of the language concerned, with private tuition or classes in the school. The following list of some of these language travel organisations, and is certainly not comprehensive. *The Earls Guide to Language Schools in Europe* (Cassell, Wellington House, 125 Strand, London WC2R 0BB; 387 Park Avenue South, New York, NY 10016-8810) details over 1,000 schools in Europe from Poland to Portugal, with many in France, Germany, Italy and Spain. There is cross-referencing by subject specialism and some useful information on many of the schools listed.

*Berlitz (U.K.) Ltd.*, 9-13 Grosvenor Street, London W1A 3BZ, tel 0171-9150 909, fax 0171-915 0222 (also in many cities across Europe and the USA)) — has native-speakers to teach almost any language. The Berlitz method was one of the first to combine the study of grammar with speaking, and will be suited to those who prefer a rather more formal approach to learning. It is what all their schools have in common. Courses range from group tuition (of up to eight students) to the 'total immersion' course. Private tuition can be arranged at times and schedules to suit the student; or given in the form of a crash course of six hours a day, five days a week. In-company language training can be given to groups of up to 12 people in the same firm; or executive crash courses can be arranged. Some other schools are at: 29 rue de la Michodière, Paris F-75002, France, tel 1-47 42 46 54, fax 1-47 42 44 05; Gerhard-von-Are-Strasse 4-6, D-53111 Bonn, Germany, tel 228-655005, fax 228-636238; Via Largo 8, I-20122 Milano, Italy; Gran Via 80/4, E-28013 Madrid, Spain. Applications should be direct to individual schools.

*Bénédict Business and Language Schools*, rue des Terraux 29, c.p.270, CH-1000, Lausanne 9, Switzerland, tel 021-323-66-55, fax 021-311-02-29 — asks you to write directly to its many schools in Europe, Africa, and America, which are run independently. A list is available from the address above.

*Castrum, lenguas, culturas y turismo, Eat, Sleep, and Study Español, C.* Doctor Fleming, 4, Bjos, 2a, E-08960 Sant Just Desvern, Barcelona, Spain, tel/fax 3-371-8725 — specialises in one-to-one tuition, and living, learning, and socialising with the tutor; and recommends this as the 'best way to learn a language.'

*ENFOREX Spanish Language School,* Alberto Aguilera 26, E-28015 Madrid, Spain, tel 15 94 37 76, fax 15 94 51 59, e-mail enforex@mad.servicom.es, http:// www.servicom.es/enforex — is a widely recognised language school with a series of courses adapted to each need: general Spanish, business and legal Spanish, teaching Spanish, study tours, and one-to-one lessons. Family, residential and hotel accommodation can be provided. Classes are small; and excursions are organised.

*Euro-Academy Outbound,* 77a George Street, Croydon CRO 1LD, tel 0181-686 2363, fax 0181-681 8850 — offers a number of courses for French, German, Italian, Portuguese, and Spanish, in attractive locations across Europe (and one in Ecuador). These will suit both young people and adults. Intensive executive courses are also available at all levels (beginning on any Monday of the year). Enquiries and requests for their brochures 'Learn the Language on Location' and 'Business Class' can be sent marked 'freepost' to the address above; telephone enquiries are welcome.

*Eurocentres,* 56 Eccleston Square, London SW1V 1PQ, tel 0171-834 4155, fax 0171-834 1866 — is a non profit-making organisation which provides language courses in various European countries for periods of up to six months. The minimum age is 16. There are centres for French in Paris, La Rochelle, Amboise, and Lausanne; for German in Cologne; for Spanish in Madrid and Barcelona; for Italian in Florence; and some other schools. All teaching is conducted in the language concerned, with extensive use of language laboratories, computer-assisted language learning, and audio-visual materials. Excursions are organised. All schools have facilities for independent study to complement classwork. Accommodation is arranged in private households.

*The Eurolingua Institute,* Eurolingua House, 2 Nelson Street, Congleton CW12 4BS, tel/fax 01260-271685 (with offices in the UK, France and Spain) — is the largest pan-European organisation of its kind, providing unique opportunities for people of all ages and from all walks of life to learn languages in the countries where they are spoken. Combined language learning, study, activity and holiday programmes are offered in the UK, France, Germany, Italy, Russia, Spain, Canada, Mexico and the USA. You may live and learn on a one-to-one homestay basis with your personal tutor, participate in a group programme, or attend one of their institutes: *Eurolingua Espace Langues,* in Montpellier, France; or *Eurolingua España,* in Sevilla, Spain.

*The Goethe Institute,* Postfach 190419, D-80604 München, Germany, tel 089-1592-1200, fax 089-1592-1202, http://www.goethe.de — has initiated a series of intensive business and commercial German courses for the international business community. It has 17 in-country locations; and is the state-owned non-profit and cultural institution in Germany which corresponds to the British Council in Britain. Additionally, these centres provide specialised courses in medical, hotel trade and tourism German.

*inlingua School of Languages,* 28 Rotton Park Road, Edgebaston, Birmingham BI6 9JL, fax 0121-456 8264 — can offer a wide variety of courses in all the major western European languages — and many rarer ones — at centres in Austria, France, Germany, Italy, and Spain, as well as schools in Bangkok, São Paolo, and Tokyo. There is an extensive range of possible courses, and prospective participants should, in the first instance, write to the Information Centre at the above address.

*McGill Centre for Continuing Education,* 770 Sherbrooke Street West, Montreal QC H3A 1G1, tel 398-6160, fax 398-2650 — offers intensive language programmes in both English and French. Available at levels ranging from beginners to advanced intermediates. Special Intensive Programs run for nine weeks, five days a week. Small classes of about 15 students work with highly qualified and dedicated lecturers. An emphasis on the communicative approach and the personal attention of caring, experienced lecturers, and all the facilities needed combine to make gaining confidence in either English or French a natural process. Students who complete level five of the Certificate of Proficiency in French may go on to take an advanced 30-credit programme for people wishing to practise in an entirely or partially French-speaking professional environment; and there are a variety of other professional and business programmes.

*SOUFFLE* (contact: Jean Petrissans, B.P. 133, F-83957 La Garde Cedex, France) — is an association of language centres in France which (like AEEA in Spain, ARELS in Britain, RELSEA in Ireland and ASILS in Italy) offers a charter of quality and may send you a list of its member schools (currently 18) which can offer a variety of French business and vacation courses.

*Unilangues,* La Grande Arche, Pario Nord-1, le Parvis, F-92044 Paris-la-Défense Cedex 41, tel 1-47 78 45 80, fax 1-49 00 03 16 — is a language school in Paris la Défense, one of the most modern business districts in Europe, teaching all languages and specialising in teaching French as a foreign language. Method and approach are tailored to all levels and objectives. 'Our aim is to help you succeed in a world of international communication.' Private tuition, group or mini-group classes, and intensive or extensive courses available; and accommodation with family, residential, or hotel can be provided on request.

# Preparation and Follow up

Generalisations abound about other countries, and their way of life, people, and customs. This is one of the ways we understand another country or culture; and many people have an interest in another country which is based on one of these stereotypes, the French and food, the Italians and culture, or fast cars, or fashion, the list should stop here before it takes up the rest of this chapter!

Many of these stereotypes are negative, but the positive ones can be misleading, too. Sometimes the negative ones also contain a grain of truth. With an idea of the fun-loving and pleasure-seeking French, you may be disappointed to find yourself working in the serious-minded and hierarchical atmosphere of a French company. You may be surpised to discover that the Japanese are not quite as devoted to their work as you expect, and find time to enjoy themselves and have fun; and that these attributes are quite highly valued. You may have an idea — even subconsciously — of the superiority of your own country and way of life. This is actually part of the culture of countries such as Britain or the United States, although we may not admit it - and it is also a mistake. In the place you are visiting they may also have an idea — which you are unaware of — of their superiority in relation to you!

As well as learning the language, it will also be worthwhile finding out something about the culture of the country in which you will be working. This is obviously most important if your destination is a country whose culture and social climate are very different from your own, particularly if you intend to stay a long time, and where contact with local people is an important part of the work you will be doing, as it usually is. But even if you work and socialise mainly with other expatriates, some understanding of the cultural background will help you along the way, to settle down, and feel 'at home'; and perform more effectively in your job. Many companies and government bodies feel that it is worthwhile investing in briefings for workers who are about to serve terms overseas, in the expectation that these employees can then operate more efficiently and acclimatise themselves more rapidly to the new environment.

## GETTING THERE

The arrangements for your trip should be made as far as possible in advance. Shopping around, whether this be for a removal company or your ticket, will minimise expense, rather than taking the first deal which is offered. Specialist removal companies advertise in the international employment press. Air ticket and travel agencies advertise in the travel sections of most major newspapers. Amongst those worth contacting for a quote is *Campus Travel*, with 44 branches around the UK including London (52, Grosvenor Gardens, London SW1W OAG; tel 0171-730 3402 for Europe; 0171-730 2101 for the USA or 0171-730 8111.worldwide; web site www.campustravel.co.uk/). For those on a tight budget *Eurolines* has an extensive European coach network. Tickets are available through Campus Travel. *Fregata Travel* (13 Regent Street, London SW1 4LR; tel 0171-451 7000; fax 0171-451 7017), which with Eurolines is part of the National Express Group, offers an extensive range of business and travel packages to central and eastern Europe. The Channel Tunnel has made communications with western Europe easier. *Eurostar* operates direct services to Paris, Brussels and Lille and can be contacted at Unit 18, Royce Road, Crawley, West Sussex RH10 2NX; tel 01293-527222): tickets are also available from Campus Travel branches nationwide.

## CULTURE SHOCK

Everyone who moves to another country will experience, to a greater or lesser extent, a phenomenon known to psychologists as 'culture shock'. It is as well to be aware of this before you go, and to be prepared for its effects ranging from elation to disappointment, according to the person, the environment, and the experiences he or she has. You should understand that living abroad has its highs and lows; and that this is entirely to be expected.

There are several stages in this process which you can expect to go through, beginning with what is known as the 'honeymoon stage', when you 'do not let small irritations spoil your enjoyment and admiration of your new environment;' the next is 'crisis and disintegration', as you become more aware of differences in values and behaviour: isolation and a search for comfort and security are its consequences. It is quite normal to go through this stage. Indeed, the time to worry is when you don't!

Then there is a period of readjustment or 'reintegration', which begins with a return to your own values and beliefs, and a rejection of the new culture. You keep company with people from your own, or other similar countries. American expatriates start finding things in common with their British colleagues, and so on. You may cling to stereotypes about your own country which you find reassuring; and your negative stereotypes are reinforced. But all this is not entirely negative. You are beginning to assert yourself, even in a rather limited way; and to find your own space in this new and unfamiliar world. With time, and growing self-esteen, you move — if your integration is successful — towards a state of 'autonomy'. You can then enjoy the positive aspects of the new culture; and are less concerned about the negative differences. You accept them for what they are. There are some other theories about the different stages of culture shock, but they all share this same general pattern.

It will depend on your own self-image and personality. The more self-confident and well-travelled individuals, those who enjoy meeting people and finding out about themselves, are likely to make the easiest transition to life in a new country; with the same ones being more prepared for their their eventual return to their own.

Some strategies for beating culture shock are as follows: being aware of the symptoms, which can include physical and psychological effects ranging from headaches and tiredness to sleep problems and irritability; also good preparation is important, for example contacts with people from that country before your departure, and finding out about the way of life there; it is a good idea to avoid mixing only with expatriates and other foreigners; and you should also try to reduce stress during the 'crisis' stage by keeping fit and healthy; or even writing down some things you like and do not like about your new life, and seeing if you can change the bad things, or find a way to live with them.

And some of these symptoms of culture shock can be repeated after your return home, during your reintegration into this 'new' way of life which is now not so familiar. You should be aware of this on your return.

## PREPARATION

There are some practical steps to take which will make it easier to settle in. There is no space in this directory for an exhaustive account of these, but you do need a check-list, of all the things you need to do before your departure. You can consult *The Equitable Guide to Working Abroad*, by William Essex (Bloomsbury, 2 Soho Square, London W1V 6HB). This has good chapters on financial planning for UK citizens, and making arrangements for your family.

Some companies brief their staff extensively before they go abroad. Other jobseekers will travel more independently. Either way, the organisations listed here will be useful in your preparation for life abroad. There is a need, too, for organisations offering follow-up and 'rehabilitation' services to workers returning from abroad, as well as preparation. The following is a list of organisations involved in these fields, and may be able to help. None of them is in any way involved in recruitment or finding work.

*The Centre for International Briefing,* Farnham Castle, Farnham, Surrey GU9 0AG, tel 01252-721194, fax 01252-711283, e-mail cib.farnham@dial.-pipex.com — runs about 100 residential courses per year to help people going overseas or coming to the UK to work more effectively in their new environment. Programmes are provided on any country. Each programme includes lectures and discussions about its history, geography, politics and economics, as well as the people and their culture. Visiting speakers discuss the business environment; and many include intensive courses on international negotiation skills. For those going to live overseas, social and domestic conditions are discussed. The Centre is an independent non-profit organisation, founded in 1953. A briefing is published on forthcoming programmes and issues around culture shock and international working.

*The Centre for Professional Employment Counselling (CEPEC),* Lilly House, 13 Hanover Square, London W1R 9HD, tel 0171-629 2266, fax 0171-629 7066 — provides a careers counselling and resettlement service for corporate-sponsored

professional expatriates returning to the UK. Their counselling service covers career, personal and financial matters to determine the client's career direction and options. Enquiries to the Client Services Manager.

*Corona Worldwide (The Women's Corona Society),* The Commonwealth Institute, Kensington High Street, London W8 6NQ, tel 0171-610 4407, fax 0171-602 7374 — is a voluntary organisation with branches in the UK and overseas providing, among other services, either postal or personal briefing for women and men about to live or work abroad. The postal briefing is in the form of a series of booklets containing all the practical and domestic details needed to prepare for setting up home in a new country, including climate, clothing, educational and medical facilities, housing, household requirements, food, leisure activities etc. Publications includes this 'Notes for Newcomers' series (£5) and 'Living in a Muslim Country'.

The society also runs day-long or telephone briefings on how to adapt to a new lifestyle and culture. Also included are lectures, medical advice, and a chance to meet a 'briefer' who has recently returned from that country, giving participants information on health, security, tax, finance, and preparation for the life ahead. 'Living Overseas' courses cost £100+. Membership of the society is £10 per annum, or is free to any woman who has attended a meeting. Men can be associate members. Details of these services are available on request. Also available is a Children's Escort Service to assist overseas parents with transport from schools in this country to airports and vice versa. Their annual magazine lists contacts and addresses as well as some reports from people who are already working abroad.

*Expatriate Management Ltd.*, St Clements House, 2 St Clements Lane, London EC4N 7AP, tel/fax 0171-280 7732 — handles the administration of expatriate employees for companies, but also organises orientation and training courses. Prospective expatriates should enquire about a briefing.

*Going Places*, 84 Coombe Road, New Malden, Surrey KT3 4QS, tel 0181-949 8811, fax 0181-949 6237 — was formerly part of 'Employment Conditions Abroad', and provides half-day, one-day, and two-day training courses for individuals, couples and company delegates, varying from country to country and meeting specific requirements. It costs around £1,000 for a one-day course. The scheduled company-specific briefings can bring you useful contacts with other professionals who will be moving to the same country.

*Returned Volunteer Action,* 1 Amwell Street, London EC1R 1UL — does not send people to work abroad but does give advice and information to those considering working overseas. It is an independent organisation of individuals who have worked overseas as project workers or volunteers in development projects, and works to ensure that the experience of volunteers is put to good use after their return, both through contacts with British community groups and through feedback to overseas development agencies and sending societies information regarding the appropriateness of their programmes and methods.

There is an RVA network of local groups and contacts across the country who organise events for recently returned project workers, as well as providing a focus for those who want to participate in relevant activities at a local level. They also publish an Introductory Pack *Thinking about Volunteering Overseas* and a *Guide to Opportunities* (send £3.50 and a large stamped SAE).

**Sources of Information**
*BBC World Service,* Bush House, London WC2B 4PH, e-mail worldservice.letters@bbc.co.uk — recommends a short-wave radio which covers the frequency ranges 5950-6200, 7100-7600, 9400-9900, 11500-12100, 13600-13900, 15000-156000, 17700-17900, 21400-21800 kHz, to receive its programmes anywhere in the world. It also publishes a monthly listings magazine *BBC On Air* with comprehensive programme information, background information, and advice on how to listen. A subscription is £18 per year; you can telephone 0171-257 2211. Radio programmes are also relayed through many local stations; and there is also a worldwide television sevrvice available by satellite or cable.

*First Point International,* York House, 17 Great Cumberland Place, London W1H 7LA, tel 0171-724 9009, fax 0171-724 7997 — along with 'International Jobsearch' have 'a service for obtaining the correct visa and achieving your new job offer' and can send an order form for their International Appraisal Pack.

*Foreign & Commonwealth Office,* Consular Department (room CL 605), Clive House, Petty France, London SW1H 9HD, tel 0171-270 4137 or 0171-270 4142 — can send copies of Consular Department publications with details of those services which consuls abroad can and cannot provide.

*Resident Abroad,* FT Magazines, Greystoke Place, Fetter Place, London EC4A 1ND, tel 0171-405 6969, fax 0171-831 9136 — is an expatriate magazine with general interest articles and a focus on tax and financial planning issues. It also publishes, for £10, an 'Expatriate Survival Kit' containing information on preparation for living and working overseas.

*Transitions Abroad,* 18 Hulst Road, PO Box 1300, Amherst, Massachusetts 01004, tel 413-247-3300, fax 413-256-0373 — is a bimonthly magazine with excellent articles on living and working in foreign countries and letters from readers abroad. It also contains contact addresses for organisations which can arrange work abroad and promotes 'active involvement as a guest in the host community rather than as a tourist'. A subscription presently costs $19.95 for one year in the US, $26 in Canada, and $38 in other countries). Order from Transitions Abroad Subscriber Services, Dept. TRA, PO Box 3000, Denville, NJ 07834, USA, tel 800-293-0373. They also publish the *Alternative Travel Directory* with country-by-country listings including study programmes and volunteer opportunities; and can send back issues and planning guides on a single subject or country.

# Specific Careers

# Agriculture and the Environment

Agriculture has always been a traditional source of seasonal work abroad. There are more long-term opportunities for those with the right experience and qualifications, and in the allied area of forestry. This chapter also deals with work in an area that no one can fail to be aware of: conservation and the environment. While many developing countries have made great progress towards self-sufficiency in food, much of the developed world is struggling with problems caused by over-production and damage to the environment. Intensive farming methods and over-reliance on monoculture in Third World countries (and former Soviet economies like the 'new' republics of Central Asia) have had disastrous environmental consequences. Here, the emphasis is on diversification and self-sufficiency, and helping communities and countries to develop more stable production and distribution systems. Technological progress has already enabled many countries to be free from food shortages. The need now is to implement the right, often small-scale technologies — and the larger-scale infrastructure — to eliminate this threat everywhere.

Poverty is itself another source of environmental degradation; and unsuitable forms of agriculture are often a threat to wildlife and its habitats, from the rainforests of Amazonia to central Africa. This is a consequence of underdevelopment. Planning in the more developed economies is more about dealing with the effects of economic success and protecting what remains of wildlife habitats which have often been extensively damaged. All the the progress which has been made in environmental engineering, in plant-breeding and biotechnology, could come to nothing if these larger issues are not addressed; and the changes in global climate caused by global warming are not brought under control.

So, the protection of the environment is often allied with the areas of agriculture and voluntary work. Disasters like Chernobyl have focused attention on the truly international scale of the problem; and the interconnectedness of the solutions. The same companies which are involved in large-scale 'clear-cutting' and permanent degradation of the forests in Siberia may also be operating in the same way in Cambodia or Zaire. The habitats of widely differing species can come under the same threat: and a global agreement is needed to preserve species as diverse as the Siberian tiger or Asian orang-utans.

It is widely recognised that action in the environmental field must be international (which is why this is a growing field for international workers who may often pursue a career in many countries). There are several international organisations like Friends of the Earth and Greenpeace which exist to promote conservation and sustainable development, in the 'developing' and the 'developed' worlds, the South and the North. It is true to say that conservationists and ecologists are probably most concerned with helping the developing countries preserve their varied wildlife and habitats. But the same issues apply in the developed economies of Europe and North America too. The question which faces agriculturalists, economists, and environmentalists, is how to develop systems for sustainable development.

## AGRICULTURE AND FORESTRY

Agriculturists and foresters with recognised professional qualifications and experience are in steady demand in the South in positions centred on research and development, education, or rural administration and economy. Appointments will vary from consultancy appointments of only a few weeks to contracts for several years. A degree in agriculture or forestry is usually the minimum requirement; applicants will be preferred who have post-graduate training and experience in a specialised field relevant to the work being offered.

Most of this type of work is handled by foreign governments, whose recruitment programmes are often administered in collaboration with voluntary organisations (see the chapter on *Voluntary Work*); the United Nations specialised agencies and development programmes (see *United Nations*); other official and international bodies (see *International Organisations* later in this *Specific Careers* section, and also *Working Exchanges* in the chapter *Getting the Job*); as well as some management recruitment consultants (see the section *The Conventional Job Search*).

Opportunities in the industrialised nations are more limited, not so much because agriculture and forestry are problem-free areas but because most of the industrialised nations have enough of their own workers with suitable qualifications.

*Future Farmers of America,* National FFA Center, Student Services – International, PO Box 15160, Alexandria, VA 22309-0160 — runs the *Work Experience Abroad Program,* which allows young US agriculturalists to gain hands-on experience of farming abroad. The WEA programme lasts from 1-12 months and costs from $1,500 upwards. Participants receive international transportation, as well as board and lodging with their host family. Most programmes begin during the summer, from June to August. Countries covered include: Australia; Austria; Belgium; Brazil; Bulgaria; Costa Rica; the Czech and Slovak Republics; Denmark; Finland; France; Germany; Greece; Honduras; Hungary; Ireland; Italy; Japan; Luxembourg; Netherlands; New Zealand; Norway; Poland; Sweden; and the UK.

*Hendrikson Associiierte Consultants GmbH,* Mergenthalerallee 51-59, Postfach 5480, Badsoden-am-Taunus, D-6236 Eschborn 1, Germany — accepts applications for overseas employment from well-qualified and experienced livestock specialists, range specialists, agricultural economists, agricultural development banking specialists and financial controllers, for assignments mainly in African and Asian countries of short and long term duration.

*Hunting Technical Services Ltd.,* Thamesfield House, Boundary Way, Hemel Hempstead, Herts HP2 7SR — recruits a number of professionals to work on its development projects in the Third World, including agriculturalists, agronomists, livestock specialists, foresters, agricultural engineers and others with relevant skills. HTS staff are predominantly permanent employees with a minority of personnel on contract terms (6-36 months). HTS currently have teams operating in Bangladesh; Belgium; Bhutan; Bulgaria; China; Ghana; Ethiopia; Egypt; Jordan; Indonesia; Italy; Malawi; Malaysia; Pakistan; Romania; Spain; Sudan; Swaziland; Tanzania; Yemen; Zambia; and Zimbabwe.

Vacancies generally do not exceed ten a year. All candidates must be graduates or possess equivalent professional qualifications. Most HTS clients require that they have 4-5 years' postgraduate overseas experience. Applicants must be in good health and aged under 60. There are no nationality restrictions. Applications to the Administrative Manager at the above address.

The *International Agricultural Exchange Association IAEA,* YFC Centre, National Agricultural Centre, Kenilworth, Warwickshire CV8 2LG, tel 01203-696584, fax 01203-696559 — arranges working visits to Australia, New Zealand,

Canada, the USA and many other countries for those with a background in farming. Internationally about 1,000 such visits are arranged every year. Applicants must be single, between 19 and 30 years with at least one year's practical farming/horticulture experience. Participants receive a wage in accordance with local rates. The IAEA arranges group air travel, full insurance cover, and work permits, There is an information meeting before leaving, and an orientation seminar and supervision in the host country.

It also has 'servicing offices' in Australia, Canada, Denmark, New Zealand, and the USA, which arrange placements and exchanges from these countries (conditions of acceptance are the same as above): *IAEA Servicing Office Australia*, 50 Oxford Street, Paddington, Sydney, N.S.W. 2021, tel 02-332-4699; *IAEA Servicing Office Canada*, No. 206, 1505-17 Ave S.W., Calgary, Alberta T2T 0E2, Canada, tel 403-244-1814; *IAEA Servicing Office New Zealand,* Park Lane Arcade, The Strand, Box 328, Whakatane, tel 07-307-0086; *IAEA Servicing Office USA*, 1000 1st Ave. South, Great Falls, Montana 59401, USA, tel 406-727-1999. Its member countries include: Austria; Belgium; Denmark; Finland; France; Germany; Iceland; Ireland; Luxembourg; Netherlands; Norway; Sweden; Switzerland; United Kingdom; Japan; Canada; USA; Australia; and New Zealand.

The *International Farm Experience Programme*, NFYFC, YFC Centre, National Agricultural Centre, Kenilworth, Warwickshire CV8 2LG, tel 01203-696584, fax 01203-696559 — arranges for young people who are making a career in agriculture and horticulture and have worked in the industry for at least two years (minimum age 18) to obtain placements on farms overseas to broaden their experience. Work for three or six months is available in many countries (see above); and work training can also be offered in the USA. They may also send a list of partner organisations around the world.

## CONSERVATION AND THE ENVIRONMENT

The field of conservation is one which includes agriculture and forestry, and and encompasses the whole area of ecology and the environment. Opportunities range from research work to more practical participation in international projects. While agriculture and forestry are traditionally aimed at the most practical and economical use of land resources, the purpose of conservation also includes protecting and improving habitats and the protection of the environment. In many countries around the world, ecological or 'green' movements are also having a considerable influence on governments; but it remains to be seen whether citizens of the developed and developing world are willing to sacrifice their increasingly affluent lifestyles for the sake of the environment.

Many developing countries reasonably demand that environmental programmes should be paid for by the wealthy industrialised nations who were often responsible for these problems in the first place; but the tendency is for countries in the South to take more responsibility themselves; and their principle demand is for a more equitable economic order. The pressures of population growth and industrialisation still make environmental protection a low priority for the very poorest nations.

Numbers of vacancies — and the scope for an international career in conservation and the environment — continue to increase as more major programmes are undertaken and international agreements implemented. A substantial amount of international consultancy work is now being funded by the European Union,for example, through its LIFE programme, and other funds which aim to implement habitat directives, and the PHARE and TACIS programmes of aid to Central and Eastern Europe and the former CIS. Generally speaking, the intervention of outside agencies is seen as a means of promoting more sustainable development, or preserving widlife habitats; and the help of outside 'experts' in the short or medium term is often needed. Schemes need to be set up; and local staff trained. Working for an international organisation or pressure group is one way into a career in conservation. Qualifications in agriculture and forestry, biology, or allied areas, are also generally needed by those who wish to work — as opposed to volunteering, or carrying out paying volunteer work — in another country. Knowledge of at least one other language is also a 'must'.

The *Asian Development Bank*, PO Box 789, 0980 Manila, Philippines, fax 2-636-2550 — administers a portfolio of forestry loans, and occasionally seeks staff in the forestry and forestry economics fields with post-graduate qualifications and experience (at least part of which should have been in Asia). Knowledge of the concepts and practices relating to sustainable forestry management is required.

The *Australian Trust for Conservation Volunteers*. PO Box 423, Ballarat VIC 3353, Australia, tel 053-331-483, fax 053-332-290, e-mail atcv@peg.apc.org, web page http://peg.apc.org/mca/atcv.html — offers opportunities for international volunteers in Australia. Typical projects include: tree-planting; erosion and salinity control; collecting native seed; restoring damaged habitats; monitoring endangered fauna; creating wetlands; and constructing walking-tracks. Volunteers must be at least 18 years old. Experience and qualifications relating to the environment are welcome, but not essential. A contribution of $20 per day is made to the Trust.

*BTCV International Working Holidays*, Room IWH, 36 St Mary's Street, Wallingford, Oxfordshire OX10 0EU, tel 01491-839766, fax 01491-839646 — is a department of the British Trust for Conservation Volunteers dealing with working conservation holidays in 18 countries around the world; and focuses on supporting and developing its partner organisations, and enabling local people to improve their environment. The costs of these holidays do not usually include transport to the pick-up point, and can vary from around £200 to £1,000. It is not necessary to have done conservation work before; but some more experienced volunteers are always needed.

*International Primate Protection League*, PO Box 766, Summerville, SC 29484 — provides for sanctuaries and other measures to protect endangered primates. Long-term volunteers are taken on for general administration and animal care. There are also opportunities to assist on some field projects, but demand for these positions far exceeds the limited number available. Suitable practical experience and a proven commitment to animal welfare are required. The UK office is at: 116 Judd Street, London WC1H 9NS, tel 0171-278 7227, fax 0171-278 3317.

The *National Wildlife Federation*, 1400 Sixteenth Street, NW, Washington DC 20036 — publishes the annual *Conservation Directory*, which concentrates on listing American and Canadian organisations concerned with conservation, and also gives the addresses of some conservation and environment departments of foreign governments.

The *Overseas Development Organisation*, Information Department, Room V523, 94 Victoria Street, London SW1E 5JL, tel 0171-917 0503 — publishes a helpful information booklet entitled *Action for the Environment*. Horticulturalists, agronomists, livestock managers, botanists, ecologists, geneticists, and veterinarians are some of the skilled professionals they recruit. More information about recruitment can be obtained by writing to *ODA Resource Development Group*, at the address above.

The *Rainforest Foundation International*, 270 Lafayette Street, New York, NY10012, fax 212-431-9197 — works to conserve the world's rainforests and protect the rights of indigenous people. Environmental and human rights campaigning, multicultural management and communications skills, as well as at least one other language, are the attributes they look for in potential volunteers and recruits.

*Traveler's Earth Repair Network (TERN),* Friends of the Trees Society, PO Box 4469, Bellingham, WA 98227 — is a networking service for travellers wishing to make a positive contribution to the environment. It links them with hosts and contacts involved in reforestation, sustainable agriculture and other areas, with visits ranging from a short stay to seasonal apprenticeships. There may be a nominal further charge. The cost is $50 ($35 for students) for twenty references.

*Willing Workers on Organic Farms (WWOOF),* W Tree, Buchan, Victoria 3885, Australia — is a worldwide non-profit-making organisation providing voluntary help to organic farmers and smallholders. There are WWOOF groups in many countries; and it publishes a list of work opportunities including farmwork in some 48 others which is presently £8.

*World Wide Fund for Nature (WWF),* Avenue du Mont-Blanc, CH-1196 Gland, Switzerland, tel 022-364-91-11, fax 022-364-42-38 — is one of the largest independent conservation organisations, supporting programmes and campaigns around the world. Staff directly employed in conservation work are generally qualified to post-graduate level in areas such as biology, ecology, and natural resources mangement; and will have several years experience of working in these fields. The international office above does not take on volunteers or interns. National offices are: *WWF UK,* Panda House, Weyside Park, Godalming, Surrey GU7 1XR, tel 01483-426444, fax 01483-426409; *WWF USA,* 1250 24th Street, NW, Washington, DC 20037-1175, tel 202-293-4800, fax 202-293-9211 or 202-293-9345. In the US, their *Jobline* provides information on internships and summer jobs (tel 202-861-8350). There are other offices in Australia, Canada, and New Zealand.

**Sources of Information**

A list of other opportunities in conservation work appears in *Internships USA* (Peterson's), a directory of training and work placement opportunities for college students and adults (see bibliography), and in the chapters on *Transport, Tourism and Hospitality* and *Voluntary Work.* Positions are available on a short-term basis in America for students and other qualified individuals.

*Agraria Press Ltd,* Yew Tree House, Horne, Horley, Surrey RH6 9JP, publishes a monthly four-page newsletter *Opportunities in agriculture, development, and biologically related arts and sciences* which includes both situations vacant and situations wanted sections. Also see the Vacation Work publication *Working with the Environment* by Tim Ryder for UK and international opportunities.

On the World Wide Web, the *British Trust for Conservation Volunteers* site, http://www.demon.co.uk/dobx/btcv/, details projects for conservation in the UK. See *CIEE International Volunteer Projects,* http://www.ciee.org/vol/ivpho-me.htm, for some of their international workcamps devoted to environmental and conservation projects (the application deadline is May 1); and also *Earthwatch,* http://gaia. earthwatch.org, for opportunities for paying volunteers as well as scientists on a wide range of projects in the animal behaviour, ecology, marine biology, and other fields: *Earthwatch Headquarters,* 680 Mount Auburn Street, PO Box 403, Watertown, MA 02272-9924, tel 617-926-8200, fax 617-926-8532; *Earthwatch Europe,* Belsyre Court, 57 Woodstock Road, Oxford OX2 6HU, tel 01865-311600, fax 01865-311383.

# Au Pair and Domestic

The main source of recruitment for au pairs, mother's helps and nannies abroad are the many employment agencies which specialise in this area. This chapter has a list of some of these. The advertising columns of the UK-based magazine *The Lady* are a good source for agencies and many international vacancies, even if you are looking for work from the US or another country (The Lady, 39-40, Bedford Street, London WC2E 9ER, tel 0171-379 4717, fax 0171-497 2137); and there is an 'overseas situations vacant' section. *Overseas Jobs Express* carries ads for nanny and au pair agencies; and the other national newspapers provide a useful supplementary source for these organisations. *The Federation of Recruitment and Employment Agencies*, 36-38 Mortimer Street, London W1N 7RB, publishes a list of their member agencies which offer this kind of work. This can be obtained by sending them a large SAE.

It should be noted that some au pair agencies are entitled to charge a fee of up to £40 (plus VAT) to au pairs for finding them overseas posts, when a placement has been verified. Prospective au pairs are advised to check with the agency concerned before registration; and also to sound them out about the realistic chances of finding a suitable job.

Au pairs, mother's helps and nannies are not the same thing. An au pair, according to the Council of Europe definition, is a young person who goes to another country to improve their language skills while living with a family. Au pairs work for no more than 30 hours a week over six days, plus up to three evenings of babysitting, and receive pocket money or living expenses. They are (or should be) treated more like a member of the family; and in theory an au pair has less responsibility for the welfare of the children than a nanny. This is a good way to live and work in — and sometimes gain entry to — another country; but the financial rewards are not great. If you respond to a private ad you are taking 'pot luck'. Sometimes conditions will be good; and this can be a good way to learn the language and find out more about another country and its way of life. Sometimes you will not be so lucky; and the back-up and support of family and friends is important in these more difficult situations; as well as a knowledge and understanding of the country you are visiting. The normal minimum age for au pair and other private domestic work is 18; but in some countries — like Italy, Spain, and Belgium — responsible girls of 17 are accepted.

Mother's helps often work full-time around the house in exchange for a wage, which should be correspondingly greater; nannies are concerned with children; and usually need some qualification in this field, such as the NNEB (Nursery Nurses Examination Board) Diploma or an NVQ (National Vocational Qualification) in Child Care and Education. Further information may be obtained from the *Council for Awards in Children's Care and Education (CACHE)* (which incorporates the old NNEB and Council for Early Years or CEYA awards): 8 Chequers Street, St. Albans, Hertfordshire AL1 3XZ, tel 01727-847636, fax 01727-867609. Like governesses, who are usually engaged to teach children, nannies should expect a salary. Private domestic positions for men are nowadays quite rare (although there are some opportunities for authentically British butlers in the United States or Japan). Male au pairs definitely need to have childcare experience and relevant qualifications. In addition, some of the agencies below can occasionally offer work for male as well as female staff, for example in British embassies abroad.

The idea of professionally trained nannies has been slow to catch on in the US and there is no qualification comparable to the NNEB Diploma. The National Association of Nannies in the USA (7413 Six Fork Road, Suite 317, Raleigh, North Carolina 27615) works to promote the interests of nannies and their employers. It publishes the *National Nanny Newsletter* six times a year, which has good advice on looking after children and how to obtain jobs.

**Immigration procedures**
A word of warning concerning immigration regulations. While work permits are unnecessary for EU citizens going to another EU country, in most other cases residence and work permits will be needed; and there may be special immigration arrangements which govern this kind of work. It is also important to have adequate health insurance (especially if you are applying direct, and not through an agency). These arrangements need to be checked before you go.

As stated above, au pairs are officially associated with language-learning, at least in Europe; and some European countries require non-EU au pairs to be registered on language courses, or to show basic proficiency in the language before a work-permit is granted. It is possible for au pairs to go to the USA on a one-year approved au pair scheme or exchange programme available through agencies such as *Au Pair in America* (see below). They are given a J-1 Exchange Visitor visa. You need to be between 18 and 25, have UK or other western European nationality, and at least be learning to drive! It may also be possible to work on a Q Visa, a new category created under the 1990 US Immigration Act for foreign trainees.

Those interested in opportunities in North America should note that the Canadian Immigration authorities have introduced measures enabling people to apply for permanent residence after the completion of two years as a nanny or mother's help. A work permit must be obtained before taking up employment; and there are a number of rules to follow. Under the 'Live-In Caregiver Program', candidates must have at least six months' training in some aspect of caregiving, such as childhood education, geriatric care, paediatric nursing, first aid, etc., or one year's employment, full-time, with at least six months with the same employer. There is also a stringent medical examination. A leaflet may be obtained from the Canadian High Commission, although agencies dealing with that country should be well-informed about these regulations. On completion of your second year, you will be free to undertake any type of employment in Canada for which you are qualified. Further information is also available from agencies such as *Childcare in Canada* (see below). Americans seeking work in Europe may contact such organisations as *AIFS* (see below).

More detailed information on au pair and nanny work can be found in *The Au Pair and Nanny's Guide to Working Abroad,* edited by Susan Griffith (Vacation Work), which contains a country-by-country guide to au pair and nanny regulations as well as listing the names and addresses of many other employment agencies.

**Opportunities for US citizens**
Private au pair and nanny agencies are not so quite common in the USA. The major scheme for Americans going to Europe as au pairs is the Au Pair/Homestay Abroad Program, run by *World Learning Inc.* (formerly the *Experiment in International Living*), details of which are given below. As an alternative, prospective American au pairs can approach local agencies. Information on immigration procedures and agencies is given under separate country chapters.

# AGENCIES

When making enquiries to agencies it is advisable to enclose a large Stamped Addressed Envelope (SAE), or International Reply Coupons to the correct value;

normally this is approximately the same as the cost of postage to the country in question.

*Academy Au Pair Agency Ltd.*, 'Glenlea', Dulwich Common, Dulwich, London SE21 7ES — accepts applications for au pair positions in the EU (mainly) for at least six months. A few short-term stays in the summer are available, but nothing shorter than two months. Positions in Canada and the USA are also arranged.

*The Agency for Nannies,* 2097 Glenforest Crescent, Oakville, Ontario L6J 2G5, Canada — arranges one-year live-in positions for nannies, mother's helps and housekeepers from overseas in Canada. There are no fees for applicants, but they must be qualified and committed to completing their assignment.

*AIFS (American Institute for Foreign Study Foundation),* 102 Greenwich Avenue, Greenwich, CT 06830, tel 203-869-9090, fax 203-869-1173 — receives approximately 3,000 young Europeans who live with American families and assist wih child care. This one-year programme is carefully supervised by local Community Counsellors who provide advise and arrange social and cultural activities for the au pairs. Its subsidiary in Germany *GIJK* offers au pair and other stays for Americans in Germany, and recruits for the Au Pair in America programmes.

*Alliances Abroad,* 2525 Arapahoe Ave., Suite E4-288, Boulder, Colorado 80302, tel 303-494-4164 — au pairs placed in Britain; Canada; Finland; France; Germany; Ireland; Italy; the Netherlands; Spain; and Switzerland.

*America AuPairCare,* One Post Street, 7th Floor, San Francisco, California 94104 — offers the opportunity to spend a year with an American family, the services of a Community Counsellor, a four-day orientation and training programme, return flight, weekly payment of $115, insurance, tuition allowance, and two weeks paid vacation, to British or Irish citizens. See *AuPairCare* below.

*The Au Pair Centre,* 25 Kings Road, London SW3 4RP — has positions for au pairs, mother's helps and nannies in most European countries. The minimum stay is six months, although most jobs are for a year.

*Au Pair/Homestay Abroad,* 1015 15th Street NW, Suite 750, Washington DC 20005, tel 301-431-1613 — is a programme of World Learning Inc. (founded in 1932 as the US Experiment in International Living). Applicants should usually be 18-26 (placements sometimes made up to age 35), single, high school graduates, have experience of babysitting/child care, and a commitment to cross-cultural learning. Countries include: Britain; France; Germany; the Netherlands; Norway; Spain; and Switzerland. A basic knowledge of French, German or Spanish will be expected depending on the country. Fees are $1,200-$1,400 including full insurance. An average monthly wage of $250-$300 is paid in local currency. Summer stays are three months; otherwise six to 12 months with possible extensions.

*Au Pair in America,* 37 Queens Gate, London SW7 5HR, tel 0171-581 7322, fax 0171-581 7345/7355 — sends au pairs to the USA for 12 months. Au pairs receive $125 weekly payment ($115 if caring for children over 2); free medical insurance; free return flights between major European cities and New York; 4-day orientation course near New York City; year-long local Counsellor support; $500 tuition allowance; and an optional 13th month to travel throughout the USA. Applicants should be between 18-26, have practical childcare experience (e.g. babysitting); a full driver's licence; and be able to commit for the full twelve months. A $500 'good faith' deposit is required which is refunded after successful completion of the programme. Their Freephone number is 0800-413116.

*Au Pair in Europe,* PO Box 68056 Blakely Postal Outlet, Hamilton, Ontario,

Canada, tel 800-665-6305 or 545-6305, also PO Box 2647, Niagara Falls, NY 14302-2647 — places au pairs in 18 countries including many in western Europe; Australia; Bermuda; Israel; and South Africa. The fee is C$300. Enquiries to the Directors.

*AuPairCare Cultural Exchange,* 101 Lorna Road, Hove, Sussex BN3 3EL — places au pairs in America with the support of the American authorities. One-year scheme open to those aged 18-26 with driver's licence (or who have taken a driving test before departure), and some practical child care experience. Visa, return flight, medical insurance, pocket money, two weeks' paid holiday, etc. are all provided and no placement fee is charged.

*Childcare in Canada,* 40 Kingsley Court, Welwyn Garden City, Herts AL7 4HZ — arranges nanny and mother's help positions in Canada for EU and Commonwealth citizens age 18-50 through contact agencies all over Canada. Work permits are for one year, extendable for a second year. Wages up to $850 a month for a standard 44-hour working week, with overtime possible.

*Childcare Europe,* Trafalgar House, Grenville Place, London NW7 3SA — deals with au pairs/mother's helps/nannies wanting to work in Austria, Belgium, France, Germany, Greece, Holland, Italy, Spain, and Switzerland. Length of contract 6-12 months starting at any time of the year. Also short-term summer placements and winter ski au pair positions.

*Delaney International,* Larchwood, Snowdenham Links Road, Bramley, Surrey GU5 0BX — places British au pairs in France, Germany, Italy and Norway. Babysitting or child care references are required. Nannies with NNEB Diploma or equivalent are also placed.

*England and Overseas Au Pair Bureau,* 87 Regent Street, Piccadilly, London W1R 7HF, tel 0171-494 2929, fax 0171-494 2922 — is one of the largest in the field. It also has vacancies for nannies, mother's helps, and domestic positions and 28 overseas agency representatives.

*Euro Employment Centre,* 14 Chadderton Drive, Bury BL9 8NL, tel 01617-68399, fax 01617-962249 — has vacancies for au pairs and mother's helps in Austria; France; Germany; Greece; Holland; Israel; Italy, Spain; and Switzerland; and some UK positions.

*Galentinas Nannies & Childcare Consultancy,* PO Box 51181, GR-14510 Kiffissia, Greece, tel/fax 1-8081005 — provides screened families and 24-hour agency support, airport pickup, arrival orientation, and introductions to other candidates presently working in Greece. Specialises in placing fluent English, French or German-speakers (20-45), mother's helps, au pairs, silver service domestic maids, and couples placements to high profile clients. EU and non-EU candidates accepted. One month paid vacation for 18 months. Three month summer placements and long-term placements also available with no fee. All enquiries must be accompanied by a photo, CV, and four postage coupons.

*The Helping Hand,* 24 Stoirvale Gardens, Chandlers Ford, Hampshire SO53 3NE, tel 01703-254287, fax 01703-570441, e-mail helphand@tcp.co.uk — places au pairs in Austria; Belgium; Denmark; France; Germany; and Spain. It offers 'a friendly, personal and professional service'. SAE to be enclosed when applying.

*International Catholic Society for Girls,* St. Patrick's International Youth Centre, 24 Great Chapel Street, London W1V 3AF — has au pair posts (not restricted to Catholics) in Europe for a minimum of nine months. Applicants must be aged at least 18, have some relevant experience of child care and household tasks, and some knowledge of the native language. Include an SAE.

*Inter Sejours*, 179 rue de Courcelles, F-75017 Paris, France — places EU girls aged between 18 and 25 for a minimum stay of 6 to 18 months in several EU countries. Full board, pocket money, and the opportunity to study the language are included.

*Kiddie Care Nanny Agency Services Ltd.*, tel 01708-478179, fax 01708-500008, international line +44-1708-500777 – has vacancies for nannies, nursery and maternity nurses, mother's helps, au pairs, and domestic staff in Australia; France; the Far East; Greece; Italy; South Africa; Spain; Switzerland; and the UK.

*Knightsbridge Nannies*, PO Box 7772, London SW6 2YN, tel 0171-610 9232, fax 0171-731 5792 — offers positions in the UK and overseas.

*Mondial Agency*, 32 Links Road, West Wickham, Kent BR4 0QW — au pair posts available in Austria and France for a minimum period of six months. During the summer months a three-month period is possible. Age limit 18-27.

*Relations Internationales*, 20 rue de l'Exposition, F-75007 Paris, France — handles six-month au pair positions throughout France, as well as Italy, Spain, Greece and Germany; also 12-month mother's help positions in Canada and USA. Age limit 18-28 years.

*The Nanny Service*, 9 Paddington Street, London W1M 3LA — places NNEB-qualified and experienced nannies in European countries outside the UK. Age limit 19-35. Only female nannies.

*Solihull Au Pair and Nanny Agency*, 87 Warwick Road, Olton, Solihull, West Midlands B92 7HP — is a sister agency of *Edgware Au Pair Agency* (19 Manor Park Crescent, Edgware, Middx HA8 7NH). Places au pairs in all major European countries, and can also arrange work for non-UK European citizens within Europe. Nannies and mother's help positions in Europe also arranged. Also one-year posts for au pairs/nannies in America — EU members, aged 18-25, with child care experience (e.g. baby-sitting references) and a valid driving licence. Conditions: $100 a week pocket money, two weeks' paid holiday, and maximum 45-hour working week. Male applicants with excellent child care experience also considered. Regional organisers for Au Pair in America.

*Universal Aunts Ltd.*, P.O. Box 304, London SW4 0NN — offers places for nannies, mother's helps, housekeepers and companions in European Union countries.

*Tarooki Au Pair and Catering Agency*, 1 Turnpike Close, Darlington DL1 3SH, tel/fax 01325-483342 — places all European au pairs in Belgium, Britain and Ireland, Czech Republic, France, Italy, Sardinia, Spain, Tenerife, and Turkey. EU citizens are also placed in hotel work in the UK (with a good level of English, and able to stay six months).

# Banking and Accountancy

The field of finance offers scope for careers in four main areas:

**commercial banking** — private and company bank accounts
**merchant banking** — large-scale company investments
**accountancy** — auditing and managing company finances
**actuarial science** — managing pension, insurance and investment funds

Most of the recruitment for personnel is carried out by the banks and companies themselves. Recruitment consultants specialising in banking and accountancy positions are also active in this field. The international banking organisations, such as the World Bank and International Monetary Fund can be found in the chapter *United Nations*.

## COMMERCIAL BANKING

The commercial banking which is familiar to us all is concerned with handling our personal bank accounts, arranging loans and generally helping with all financial matters. But the average High Street bank is also engaged in some of the same activities as the merchant bankers — handling company profits, investments and credit facilities and offering advisory services on taxation, insurance and unit trusts. International commercial banking is also largely involved with money transfers and exchanges.

Commercial banks are the largest recruiters of banking personnel; but in most cases overseas opportunities will be limited, as the foreign branches of the major banks tend to be run and staffed by local workers and managers. Monetary Union in Europe and the general globalisation of banking services, on the other hand, mean that banking trainees who want to spend some time abroad have a better chance of doing so than before, despite the development of direct banking services which have meant widespread redundancies in the USA and UK in the banking sector. There are still opportunities, though, and the major banks continue to be active in the recruitment of new graduates; and there are openings in the financial services sector for consultants and staff of the rapidly developing eastern European economies and Russia. The best chances of working abroad early on in one's career still lie with the merchant banks (see below). Language skills will aid all those wishing to work in international banking or financial services.

### The Clearing Banks

The major 'clearing' banks in the UK — especially Barclays, Lloyds, and Midland — are most likely to offer overseas positions. The recruitment activities of their respective international divisions are detailed below.

*Barclays Plc.*, 54 Lombard Street, London EC3P 3AN — is one of the largest international banking organisations in the world, operating in more than 70 countries. The Management Development Programme recruits about 50 to 70 graduates annually for a four-year programme, which commences in the UK and may include at least one year abroad. There follows a series of assignments, some overseas and some in the UK throughout their career. Enquiries to 'Graduate Recruitment' at the address above.

*Lloyds Bank,* 46-48 Park Street, London SE1 9EQ — runs comprehensive training programmes for graduates, focusing on key managerial qualities. Enquiries to the 'Graduate Recruitment Office'.

*Midland Bank Plc.,* Graduate Recruitment Manager, 1st Floor, St Magnus House, 3 Lower Thames Street, London EC3R 6HA — Midland Bank is a diverse banking and financial services organisation offering a wide range of career opportunities in the UK and in a network of offices across continental Europe. It is a principal member of HSBC Group which has a wider banking presence in North America and the Asia Pacific region. A good honours degree in any discipline is required. Trainees are recruited to the Midland Executive Training Programme. The majority are initially based within their branch network, but there is scope to move to other business areas such as Midland Corporate Banking, Risk Management, Cards and Electronic Banking, Private Banking, Financial Services, and First Direct. In 1996, there were 40-50 vacancies. Opportunities in coming years are likely to be the same. The closing date for applications is mid-March; and the method of application involves completing the Employer's Application Form.

*Midland Executive Trainee Programme:* This is the training programme which prepares graduates to take on their first management role within two years of joining. It combines technical training with practical experience and is kick-started by a ten week fully residential course at the Midland Bank training centre in Hertfordshire. Participants gain a broad introduction to key business areas and are offered a choice of area in which to specialise during their second year. There are also other specialist training programmes.

**Other British and Commonwealth Banks**
In addition, there are a number of banks with close connections to the UK that are less well known in this country because they operate mainly overseas. Staff recruitment tends to be carried out locally. These banks include:

Australia and New Zealand Banking Group Ltd., (including Grindlays Bank Plc), Minerva House, Montague Close, London SE1 9DH.
The Hong Kong and Shanghai Bank, P.O. Box 199, 99 Bishopsgate, London EC2P 2LA.
Standard Chartered Bank, 1 Aldermanbury Square, London EC2V 7SB.

**Foreign Banks**
Those who have already gained several years' banking experience at home, and who have the necessary languages and cultural adaptability, may wish to consider working abroad for a foreign bank. Working in the London or New York branch of a foreign bank can offer the possibility of an eventual transfer abroad. A more direct approach, for experienced staff, is to apply direct to banks abroad, to use the services of a recruitment consultant, or to use the methods of the creative job search to keep in touch with international vacancies.

Apart from the City of London, the main financial centres of the world are Zurich, New York and Tokyo, with the development of other centres such as Paris. Because of the current Swiss immigration laws, the opportunities for working in that country are restricted only to the most senior personnel. In recent years there has been a strong growth in the number of Japanese banks represented internationally, and a scaling down of the presence of American banks abroad. Eight out of ten of the world's largest banks, in terms of capital, are now Japanese, while American banks are not represented in the top ten at all.

There is some demand for English-speakers in the major Japanese banks; these are the addresses of the London branches of some of them.

*Bank of Tokyo,* 12-15 Finsbury Circus, Finsbury Circus House, London EC2M 7BP.

*Daiwa Bank*, 5th Floor, 4 Broadgate, London EC2M 2QS.
*Mitsubishi Bank Ltd*, 6 Broadgate, London EC2M 2SX.
*Sakura Bank Ltd.*, 6 Broadgate, London EC2M 2RQ.
*Sumitomo Bank*, Temple Court, 11 Queen Victoria Street, London EC4N 4TA.

The *Japan Information and Cultural Centre,* Embassy of Japan, London W1V9FN, can provide a comprehensive list of Japanese banks in the UK.

## MERCHANT BANKING

The merchant bankers originated as merchants, trading in goods, usually on an international scale. Gradually, they began to provide financial services to other traders, and this is the essence of their work today. Their services are offered not merely to traders, but also to industry, insurance companies, transport companies, in short to anyone with large financing needs. Increasingly in the UK, the term investment bank is replacing the term merchant bank as many of the large international Houses from other countries have opened offices in the City.

The services they provide may be conveniently grouped into banking, corporate finance, and investment management or trading in securities; they include project finance, advisory services to governments and international corporations, and dealing in financial derivatives. The merchant banks all have offices in the City of London (on Wall Street they are known as investment banks) and, being international businesses, they are strongly represented overseas through subsidiaries, affiliates and representative offices.

In terms of numbers employed, the merchant banks are small in comparison with clearing banks. The best opportunities are for graduates, preferably though not necessarily with degrees in economics, law or business studies. Apart from the actual banking activities, there are also occasional vacancies for experienced and well-qualified specialist staff, such as accountants.

Recruitment is carried out by the banks themselves, all of which offer graduate training programmes lasting from six months to two years, and sometimes including a posting overseas. The number of vacancies per year is low and competition stiff. Following the training course, the early part of a career may well be spent in London (or New York); but at the senior level opportunities should arise for promotion, secondment or transfer to branches or agents abroad.

The most prominent merchant banks are the main members of the Securities and Futures Authority. UK firms, now often foreign owned, include:

Brown, Shipley & Co. Ltd., Founders Court, Lothbury, EC2R 7HE.
Charterhouse Bank Ltd., 1 Paternoster Row, St. Paul's, EC4M 7DH.
Deutsche Morgan Grenfell, 23 Great Winchester Street, EC2P 2AX.
Robert Fleming Holdings Ltd., 25 Copthall Avenue, EC2R 7DR.
Guinness Mahon & Co. Ltd., 32 St. Mary At Hill, EC3P 3AJ.
Hambros Bank Ltd., 41 Tower Hill, EC3N 4HA.
HSBC Investment Bank Plc., 10 Lower Thames Street, EC3R 6AE.
Kleinwort Benson Group Plc., PO Box 560, 20 Fenchurch Street, EC3P 3DB.
Lazard Brothers & Co. Ltd., PO Box 516, 21 Moorfields, EC2P 2HT.
Rea Brothers Ltd., Alderman's House, Alderman's Walk, EC2M 3XR.
J. Henry Schroder & Co. Ltd., 120 Cheapside, EC2V 6DS.
Singer & Friedlander Holdings Ltd., 21 New Street, Bishopsgate, EC2M 4HR.
SBC Warburg, 1 High Timber Street, EC4V 3SB.

Further information regarding career prospects in merchant banking can be obtained from the *London Investment Banking Association (LIBA)*, 6 Frederick's Place, London EC2R 8BT.

# ACCOUNTANCY

Accountancy is a relatively secure profession with prospects for an international career which are growing as financial markets and companies themselves become more global; British and US accountants are highly respected and in demand in many countries throughout the world. School leavers and, more particularly, graduates intending to take up accountancy as a career are faced with a sometimes confusing array of qualifications in Britain to aim for; and some preparatory research — for example reading one of the many magazines published by the various associations — is a good first step, and some examination of the entrance syllabuses. The *Institute of Company Accountants* publishes *Company Accountant* and a *Student Digest*; the *Chartered Association of Certified Accountants* publishes *Certified Accountant*; in Canada, *CGA Magazine* is published by the *Certified General Accountants' Association of Canada*. These associations also generally publish vacancies updates or lists. Each qualification generally involves a period of practical experience (usually a minimum of three years); a preliminary or foundation exam (for non-graduates); and then a professional examination. In particular, you should ask the various professional associations about the advice or help they offer once you have qualified in finding international vacancies.

These qualifications in the UK, and the associations offering them are listed below:

*ACA* — *the Institute of Chartered Accountants in England and Wales*, PO Box 433, Chartered Accountants' Hall, Moorgate Place, London EC2P 2BJ, tel 0171-920 8100, fax 0171-920 0547.

*ACCA* — *the Chartered Association of Certified Accountants*, 29 Lincoln's Inn Fields, London WC2A 3EE, tel 0171-242 6855, fax 0171-396 5757.

*AIA* — *the Association of International Accountants*, South Bank Building, Kingsway, Team Valley, Newcastle upon Tyne NE11 OJS, tel 0191-4824409, fax 0191-4825578, e-mail aia@i-a.org.uk, http://www.a-i-a.org.uk.

*ASCA* — *The Institute of Company Accountants*, 40 Tyndalls Park Road, Bristol BS8 1PL, tel 0117-9738261, fax 0117-9238292.

*CA* — *the Institute of Chartered Accountants of Scotland*, 27 Queen Street, Edinburgh EH2 1LA, tel 0131-2255673.

*CIMA* — *the Chartered Institute of Management Accountants*, 63 Portland Place, London W1N 4AB, tel 0171-637 2311, fax 0171-631 5309.

To qualify as a Chartered Accountant, training must be undertaken in an authorised training office. The majority of students train with firms of chartered accountants; but training is now also available in a growing number of industrial, commercial and public sector organisations under the Training Outside Public Practice (TOPP) scheme. The training contract combines work experience with preparation for the Professional Examinations and students train for three or four years depending on educational background. Chartered Management Accountants, Certified Accountants, and Company Accountants train within a specific company and are able to determine their own time frame with respect to obtaining their professional qualifications.

On qualification there are many openings abroad for Chartered Accountants; Certified Management Accountants are slightly more restricted as their qualifications are considered to be more UK based. It is now becoming common practice for young accountants to go abroad on a two-year assignment immediately after qualifying. An international posting is now seen as a way to make rapid progress to the top of the profession in the major international accountancy firms, and Australasia and the Far East are popular destinations. There are also postings in the EU and Eastern Europe. Other areas where British accountants are in demand are Canada, South Africa and the Middle East. The largest British firms with overseas associated offices are:

*Arthur Andersen,* 1 Surrey Street, London WC2R 2PS.
*Coopers & Lybrand,* 1 Embankment Place, London WC2N 6NN.
*Deloitte & Touche,* Hill House, Little New Street, London EC4A 3TR.
They have offices in many cities throughout Britain.
*Ernst & Young,* Becket House, 1 Lambeth Palace Road, London SE1 7EU.
*KPMG,* 1 Salisbury Square, London EC4Y 8BB.
*Price Waterhouse,* No.1 London Bridge, London SE1 3TR.

**Accountants in the Single European Market**
The implementation of the Single European Market means that EU member countries should already be working towards harmonisation of auditing practices. Accountancy organisations in each country are now obliged to have schemes whereby accountants can transfer their skills abroad. In order to deal with this requirement, it has been generally decided that accountants will have to pass an aptitude test in the relevant language of the country where they want to practise.

While European accountants tend to concern themselves with auditing a firm's books once a year (an auditor is known as a *commissaire aux comptes* in French and a *Wirtschaftsprüfer* in German), British accountants are more likely to become involved in advising firms on how best to manage their finances from day to day (management accountancy). British qualifications are highly respected in Europe, and there is considerable scope for Britons to work abroad independently advising UK, US and European businesses. The EU countries most open to foreign accountants are Belgium, the Netherlands and France.

**Accountancy in the USA and Canada**
Accountancy in the US is regulated by 54 *State Boards of Accountancy* (the 50 States plus Washington DC, Guam, Puerto Rico and the US Virgin Islands), the *American Institute of Certified Public Accountants (AICPA)* and the 54 *State Societies of Certified Public Accountants.* The AICPA is responsible for the Uniform Final Examination which is the accepted final qualifying examination throughout the USA. Only 35 State Boards will consider applications from those holding overseas qualifications. Most British accountants are to be found in New York, New Jersey, Connecticut and California. The AICPA's address is: 1211 Avenue of the Americas, New York, NY 10036.

The situation for certified accountants is easier. There are no restrictions on them working in industry and commerce, but they can improve their chances by holding local qualifications. The *Institute of Management Accountants* (IMA, 10 Paragon Drive, Montvale, NJ 07645-1760) administers the Certified Management Accountant and Certified in Financial Management examinations.

Canada is more accessible to British accountants than the USA, but they are still strongly advised to gain Canadian qualifications. The three main associations listed below can give information on qualifications:

*Certified General Accountants' Association of Canada (CGA),* 700-1188 West Georgia Street, Vancouver, B.C. V6E 4A2, tel 604-669-3555, http://www.cga-canada.org.
*Society of Management Accountants (SMA)* — 154 Main Street East, PO Box 176, Hamilton, ONT L8N 3C3.
*Canadian Institute of Chartered Accountants (CICA)* — 150 Bloor Street West, Avenue Road, Toronto, ONT M5S 2Y2.

# ACTUARIES

Actuaries are responsible for managing the sums invested in insurance policies and pension funds. Over half work in insurance companies. Others work as partners in firms of consulting actuaries or for firms of employee benefit consultants where they deal mainly with pension funds. A high standard in mathematics is a prerequisite of your training as an actuary. There are openings for actuaries both in the EU and North America. The *Careers Department, Institute of Actuaries*, Napier House, 4 Worcester Street, Oxford OX1 2AW, tel 01865-794144, fax 01865-794094, can provide a *List of Actuarial Employers*, including opportunities overseas. They can also supply a useful pamphlet *Information for those considering an Actuarial Career*. with information on international actuarial science degrees and diplomas. The relevant Scottish body is the *Faculty of Actuaries*, 40-44 Thistle Street, Edinburgh EH2 1EN, tel 0131-220 4555, fax 0131-220 2280. There are a number of associations in the USA, including the *American Academy of Actuaries*, 1100 17th Street NW, 7th Floor, Washington DC 20036, which can provide information about training.

## RECRUITMENT CONSULTANTS

The activities of the recruitment consultant below are mainly in the field of finance. Other consultants with a wider scope to be found under the heading *Consultants and Agencies.*

*ASA International,* 63 George Street, Edinburgh EH2 2JG, tel 0131-226 6222, fax 0131-226 5110 — specialises in the recruitment of accountancy staff and financial management for overseas clients, both in the profession and in industry and commerce. Suitable applications are kept on file for matching with appropriate vacancies as and when they rise. Offices also in Aberdeen, Glasgow, London, Prague, and Warsaw.

*Davies Kidd,* Hamilton House, 1 Temple Avenue, London EC4Y 0HA, tel 0171-353 4212, fax 0171-353 0612 — specialises in the recruitment of staff for the Chartered Accountancy Profession. Liaising with the London offices of the 'Top 6' firms they recruit newly and recently qualified ACA's for a number of overseas opportunities, the majority of which will require relevant language skills. Successful applicants are likely to be aged under 30 with a first time exam record and good audit exience gained in a large firm. Locations include Hong Kong, China, Middle East, USA, Caribbean, South Africa, Germany, France, Poland, Russia, Hungary, and the Czech Republic.

*Sherry Sherratt Technical Recruitment Ltd.,* PO Box 4529, London SW18 3SX, tel 0181-875 1849, fax 0181-875 1894, has occasional vacancies for qualified accountants (ACA, ACCA, CIMA, or MBA finance stream) with appropriate language skills to work in central and eastern Europe and Russia. Fluent German may be relevant for some vacancies.

## PROFESSIONAL ASSOCIATIONS

### Banking

Career prospects in commercial banking — domestic and international — are greatly enhanced by passing the Chartered Institute of Banker's examinations, which include papers on law, accountancy, economic and monetary theory and practice of banking. Successful candidates also receive a BSc (Hons) from Manchester University. The qualification is an integral part of special management trainee programmes offered by the major British banks. Details of the qualification — the Associateship of the Chartered Institute of Bankers (ACIB) — are available from *The Chartered Institute of Bankers,* 10 Lombard Street, London EC3V 9AS.

The *American Bankers Association*, 1120 Connecticut Avenue, NW, Washington DC 20036, runs various programmes to encourage high school and college graduates to train for careers in banking. It does not have specific information on working abroad.

**Accountancy**
*The Institute of Chartered Accountants in England and Wales,* PO Box 433,
Chartered Accountants' Hall, Moorgate Place, London EC2P 2BJ, runs a recruitment service for its members which covers all countries.

# Computer Services

## THE COMPUTER INDUSTRY

Information technology and computing has become an integral part of modern society. Its role in our lives has grown as personal computers have become widely available for home and business use. The hardware is the computer and all the associated technology. Software is everything that a computer is programmed to do. Networking is the increasingly commercialised field of the the Internet and its services. Software systems are now used in ways that are too numerous too mention — throughout industry, commerce, the media, science and medicine, administration, management, distribution, manufacturing, sales, human resources, and a host of other applications. These functions can be carried out with greater efficiency than ever before: banking transactions, ticket reservations, research and international communications through the Internet, the development of the Intranet for 'in-company' use, home shopping, financial services, academic and scientific work; or even medical diagnosis, can all now be carried out more effectively as computers have come to play an increasingly important role in our everyday lives.

This global revolution in information processing and communications has made whole new industries possible; and is changing the nature of work itself, which can be 'international' even as you work from home. Great corporations have grown up, like Microsoft, which mediate between the potentialities of home computing and all their applications; at present, new companies are springing up which offer a wide variety of Internet services. The easy-to-operate software which is available meets the needs of this new market for home computers — presently 4 million households in the UK; and it can be operated by those who may have no particular technical expertise or understanding. Increasingly, it is said, we live in an 'information' or 'post-industrial' society which has changed the relationship between producer and consumer. This society is knowledge-based; and it is this 'software', the way this information is used and understood, and not the computing power itself, which is most important; the term *Information Technology (IT),* stands for the use of computers and computer software for this wider information processing and communication.

It is inevitable that some jobs are lost, as computers 'replace' people in many sectors of industry. But whole new industries and areas of work have grown up. New staff are required in many companies and organisations to design the software, and to operate these systems. The recruitment market for IT specialists has become truly international, with a wide range of jobs directly available on the Internet. It is still a 'buyer's market', and job opportunities are everywhere; but it is the Middle East, the USA, EU countries like Germany, Holland, Belgium, and France, and the countries of East Asia, that offer highly paid short and long-term jobs. The Central and Eastern European region has become a new and expanding market for IT specialists, with some technical, training, and specialist openings in Russia and neighbouring states. Computer skills are rather easily transferable, as their general principles, the computer languages for instance, can be understood internationally. A knowledge of a foreign language (especially French or German) will open many doors. A degree is sometimes called for but is not always required.

## Careers in IT

The rapid growth in applications for information technology means that there are good prospects for advancement for suitably qualified people. To work in information technology, the basic requirement is not so much a background in mathematics or science, as the possession of a flexible mind and a certain level of analytical intelligence. The interests of employers are practical. According to one consultant, "If you ask a manager to describe the best employee they have ever had, they rarely say, 'Oh yes, John had a degree in computer science, two years' experience as an analyst and was 28 years old, but rather, 'John was really good at meeting deadlines and always did what he said he'd do'."

Working professionally with computers in a particular field or application requires mainly a knowledge of that field or application; and is more a practical than a theoretical matter. The complexity of the software systems themselves will often not be an issue, as most applications involve adapting an existing system or software package to a particular use. Someone already experienced in that field will be best placed to carry this out. A methodical approach must be combined with a knowledge of the application. This, and a good track record, together with an appropriate qualification, up to degree level — and some of the methods of the *Creative Job Search* — will help you to get a job in one of the areas covered by the terms 'computer services' or 'information technology'. Some of these are:

1 — *Systems design/analysis.* The systems designer is called in to examine the way a company or a particular function is operating, and decides how best a system could improve the situation. From this initial analysis, suitable methods must be devised for developing such a system. An analyst ensures that systems run smoothly, and finds ways to match existing systems to a customer's requirements. For this sort of job, prospective employees would either have qualifications up to a degree standard, or previous programming experience.

2 — *Programming.* The programmer is responsible for preparing sequenced instructions in the particular computer language in use, in other words the program, according to the design drawn up by the systems analyst. An applications programmer develops programs for specific tasks, using the language and instructions of an existing applications package, such as a database or spreadsheet; the systems programmer works on the basic functions allowing a program to be obeyed. Minimum qualifications here are usually secondary level for applications programming, while the systems programmer is usually a graduate, and highly experienced.

3 — *Operations.* Operators handle the day-to-day running of computers, acting as a link between user and computer. Within the operations field come a range of different activities: data preparation (turning data into an acceptable form for the computer); data control; operating (loading tapes etc); keyboard operators; right up to senior posts such as operations manager. Suitable qualifications in this area would be typing and office procedure experience, plus (for school leavers in Britain) five GCSE passes including English and mathematics.

4 — *Hardware Design.* Hardware is the actual machinery and electronics operating the computer, so this area applies to electronic and mechanical engineers, with knowledge of logic electronics a benefit. There are also posts for computer engineers who look after the maintenance and repair of computers.

5 — *Sales and Support.* To convince a prospective buyer or user of the worth of a new system, sales staff need a good knowledge of computers and their uses. Customers need support both before and after installing new equipment. Large software and hardware companies also offer telephone support to enable clients to get the most from their computer systems.

6 — *Documentation.* There is always a need for technical writers who can write manuals for computer software in a style which can be easily understood by computer users. Technical writers do not have to be programmers, but a certain amount of computer literacy is necessary.

To work abroad, it should be emphasised that it is essential to have relevant experience in one of the above or related areas. Qualifications alone count for little, and applicants for any job should have an absolute minimum of two years' experience in their field before they even consider applying. That said, because of the high level of job mobility in the industry, those suitably experienced should have little difficulty finding work overseas, as is borne out by the large number of computer recruitment agencies and ads in the trade press.

A valuable reference book available in reference or business libraries is the *Computer User's Year Book* which contains useful lists and addresses of recruitment agencies throughout Britain, in addition to extensive lists of the various training courses available at all levels, plus salary surveys for each job area. In Britain, the weekly journals *Computing,* 32-34 Broadwick Street, London W1A 2HG, tel 0171-316 9818 (for general queries — also on-line at http://www.vnu.co.uk/bc/ctg — and *Computer Weekly,* Quadrant House, The Quadrant, Sutton, Surrey SM2 5AS, tel 0181-652 8080, e-mail Computer.Weekly.Recruitment@rbp.co.uk, http://www.computerweekly.co.uk, are the reference point for vacancies in the computer industry, including many vacancies abroad.

## COMPUTER RECRUITMENT AGENCIES

The following organisations are particularly involved in recruiting staff for overseas jobs; it must again be strongly emphasised that only those with relevant experience should apply for work through these agencies. In addition, other opportunities are listed under *Consultants and Agencies* in *The General Approach* section.

*Austin Knight Ltd.,* Knightway House, 20 Soho Square, London W1A 1DS — offers positions to marketing executives, customer support engineers, computer engineers and field service engineers in Saudi Arabia and the Middle East generally.

*Bower and Company,* 36 Essenden Road, Sanderstead, Surrey CR2 0BU, tel 0181-657 3564, fax 0181-651 4754 — specialises in the use of IT in banking, and recruits staff for the North America, Eastern Europe, EU and Scandinavia regions.

*Cerco Ltd.,* Yeoman's Gate, 60 Stow Road, Spaldwick, Huntingdon, Cambs PE18 0TE, tel 01480-891514 — specialise in recruitment and consultancy in the computer hardware maintenance sector. All levels of engineer, support and logistics, project management, sales and marketing, administration and management staff within the computer maintenance, to work in Europe and North America. Both permanent positions and contract work.

*Computer Futures,* SAP Division, 2 Fouberts Place, Regent Street, London W1V 2AD, tel 0171-446 6644, fax 0171-446 0099, e-mail permanent@compfutures.co.uk — are market leaders in the provision of SAP Personnel and IT managers internationally with many opportunities in the UK, United States, Australia, and Europe; and arranges visa, accommodation, and flights.

*Computer People International,* Piccadilly House, 33 Regent Street, London SW1Y 4NB, tel 0171-440 2000, fax 0171-440 2026, e-mail 100633.2312@compuserve.com — places staff with at least one year's experience in computer systems or software in the USA, UK, Germany, Japan, the EU, Norway and Australia. Contracts are for 12 months plus, and at all levels within operations, systems and programming, and management. Computer People has offices throughout the UK and the USA (head office: Computer People Inc., 2049 Century Park East, Suite 3390, Los Angeles, CA 90067). There is also a German office: Computer People (Deutschland) Ltd., Mainzer Landstrasse 97, D-6000 Frankfurt am Main 1, Germany.

*Comtex Solutions*, Kingswood House, Woburn Road, Leighton Buzzard, Bedfordshire LU7 0AP, tel 01525-379111 — handles work in Germany and the Benelux countries in all areas of the IT industry including computer operators, analysts, programmers, data and voice communications specialists and software engineers. Education to degree level preferred; all candidates must have at least 2-3 years' practical experience.

*Dalroth and Partners Ltd.*, The Centre, 68 High Street, Weybridge, Surrey KT13 8BL, tel 01372-726299, fax 01372-744020 — is a well-established agency specialising in computing and Information Technology appointments. Deals mainly with Europe and the Middle East, and occasionaly other countries. Recruits from shift leaders up to IT consultants and directors; minimum of 5 years' practical experience is usually required. Contracts are from 6 months to 2 years.

*Digitext*, 15 High Street, Thame, Oxon OX9 2BZ, tel 01844-214690, fax 01844-213434, e-mail admin@digitext.co.uk, http://www.digitext.co.uk — specialises in placing IT documentation and training professionals in all EU countries. Must have proven skills.

*Eagling Computerserv Ltd.*, 4 Cromwell Road, Stevenage, Herts SG2 9HT, tel 01438-353262 or 365545, fax 01438-314619 — serves all sectors of industry and business. Posts range from operators and programmers, to analysts and IT directors. Candidates for overseas assignments should have at least 5 years' experience and preferably foreign language ability; contracts are 3-36 months. Applicants should be based in the UK.

*Focal Point Consultancy & Recruitment Ltd.*, Stuart House, 43-47 Crown Street, Reading, Berks RG1 2SN — supplies contract and permanent placings within the Data Processing industry around the world.

*Grafton Recruitment Ltd.* recruits in IT and electronics for Czech Republic, Hungary, Malaysia, USA, Germany, and Saudi Arabia. See under *Management Recruitment Consultants* in *Getting the Job.*

*Harvey Nash Plc.*, 13 Bruton Street, London W1X 7AH, tel 0171-333 0033, fax 0171-333 0032, http://taps.com/Harvey – Nash — offers wide range of senior and other IT appointments in most areas for international companies.

*Hexagon Computer Services*, Hexagon House, 145 Wardour Street, London W1V 3TB, tel 0171-439 3671, fax 0171-734 0503, e-mail 100627.2214@Compuserve — has a steady supply of contract staff to Europe, and occasional openings in the Middle East and the USA. Contracts vary between three months and a year, and cover most areas of computer activities, particularly real time and database analysts, systems designers and programmers. Applicants with 2-3 years' full-time commercial experience can contact the External Resources Division.

*InterConnect Communications Ltd.*, Merlin House, Station Road, Chepstow, Gwent NP6 5PH, tel 01291-620425 — is an independent telecommunications and postal consulting company requiring skilled consultants to work throughout western, central and eastern Europe for short periods of time across a broad range of technical and commercial activities including network application/ software, interactive service with emphasis on multimedia, information systems, financial, personnel and network management, and broadband networking.

*International Staffing Consultants, Europe,* PO Box 124, Eastleigh, Hampshire SO50 8ZE, tel 01703-651281, fax 01703-620877 — is the European Office of *International Staffing Consultants Inc.,* 500 Newport Center Drive, Newport Beach, California 92660, and a member of NPA, the largest and oldest network of employment agencies in the world. With over 1,000 recruiters in 400 offices, their association with their affiliates means they can network their openings and candidates to provide one of the most comprehensive services available. Affiliates are located throughout the USA, Canada, Europe, the Far East and Middle East. Specialists for recruiting European staff for North American assignments and US staff for assignments worldwide. Recruitment is usually for experienced and qualified Engineers, Managers, Sales and Marketing, and IT professionals for USA, Europe and the Middle East. All fees paid by clients; there is never a charge for candidates for the services of ISC or any affiliated company.

*James Baker Associates,* 46 Queens Road, Reading, Berkshire RG1 4BD, tel 01734-505022, fax 01734-505056 — recruits specialists and managers into the IT and high technology industries, covering all levels from juniors to directors. Also recruit HR/personnel specialists. Posts in Europe (including Scandinavia), USA, Middle East, Australia, etc. Mainly permanent in Europe, and for one year or more in USA and Middle East. Graduates are preferred, with at least three years' relevant experience, plus a foreign language for Europe.

*James Duncan & Associates,* Seabridge House, 8 St. John's Road, Tunbridge Wells, Kent, TN4 9NP, tel 01892-513344, fax 01892-547273 — formed in 1976 is a proven supplier of contract computer personnel to both the United Kingdom and Benelux countries offering opportunities ranging from programmers through to senior management roles across a variety of hardware and software platforms. Contracts range from 3 to 12 months' duration.

*LA International Computer Consultants Ltd.,* Ridge House, Ridge House Drive, Festival Park, Stoke-on-Trent, ST1 5SJ, tel 01782-279099, fax 01782-273919 — has opportunities for EU citizens to work in the UK, mainland Europe, Scandinavia and Hong Kong, in most sectors of industry and commerce. Assignment areas include operator, programmer/analyst, systems/business/designer analyst, systems developer, software engineer, technical writer and database specialist. Five years' experience and in some cases a degree are required.

*Lexstra International Inc.,* 240 West 44th Street, NY 10036 USA, tel 212-575-2799, fax 212-575-2820 — has openings in the United States for degreed candidates with 3 to 10 years experience in MVS, COBOL, CICS, DB2, IMS, INIX, C, C++, Windows, NT, Oracle, Informix, Sybase, Information Engineering, and other areas offering competitive salaries, and paid air-fare and relocation.

*Modus International,* Kingswood House, Heath and Reach, Leighton Buzzard, Bedford LU7 0AP — recruits all types of computer personnel, from programmers and technical authors to systems analysts and software engineers, for positions in Europe and the USA. Permanent and short term contracts are available. Applicants should be graduates with at least three years' experience.

*PKS Information Services Inc.,* c/o Head Hunter International, 68 Harcourt Street, Dublin 2, Ireland, fax 1-478-1663 — has opportunities in the United States; and provides total IS solutions for customers, including outsourcing mainframe operations, developing state-of-the-art client server systems, and solving the century conversion date problem solutions, and provides assistance with visa applications and relocation.

*SBS Ltd.,* 22 Bloomsbury Square, London WC1A 2NS, tel 0171-580 2355, fax 0171-636 9170 — has temporary and permanent assignments worldwide in computing/data processing and IT. Associated offices are: *SBS (Benelux) BV,*

5th Floor, Stadhouderskade 14E, NL-1054 ES Amsterdam, Holland, tel 20-607-7119, fax 20-607-7200; *SBS Inc.*, 2 Park Avenue, Suite 2011A, New York, NY 10016, tel 212-481-1310, fax 212-481-1319; *Euro Systems Inc.*, 3335 Main Street, Stratford, Connecticut 06497, tel 203-381-0352, fax 203-386-0175.

*Stanlake Search,* 61 Stanlake Road, London W12 7HG, tel 0181-749 4786, fax 0181-248 7436 — is an executive search agency specialising in IT with overseas assignments in the EU and Eastern Europe.

## PROFESSIONAL ASSOCIATIONS

*Association for Computing Machinery,* 11 West 42nd Street, New York NY 10036, USA — sets qualifying examinations for the computer industry in the USA, and can also supply information on careers in computing.

*The British Computer Society,* 1 Sanford Street, Swindon SN1 1HJ — produces a useful booklet dealing with careers in computing and sets qualifying examinations.

*Canadian Information Processing Society,* 430 King Street West, Suite 205, Toronto, Ontario M5V 1L5 — performs the same functions as the above in Canada.

*The Institution of Analysts and Programmers,* Charles House, 36 Culmington Road, London W13 9NH, tel 0181-567 2118 — can help members and potential members with general advice on careers in computer programming and systems analysis.

*International Computer Professional Association (ICPA),* 2261 Market St., Suite 309, San Francisco, CA 94114, tel 415-252-7467, fax 415-252-5769 — offers a number of membership services to software professionals in all countries looking for work abroad, including a two-weekly newsletter with job-listings and articles, *The Network.* Further information is available from the above address. ICPA also has an e-mail address — icpa@holonet.net.

# Journalism

In comparison with the numbers of freelance journalists, more permanent openings are few and therefore fiercely contested. Promotion and advancement can slow procedures, so journalists usually have to spend several years working on a regional newspaper or specialist magazine at home before becoming eligible for a posting abroad.

As a rule, journalism is a difficult profession to enter. Apart from having some relevant training, qualities required of journalists in any of the media include a wide knowledge of current affairs, a lively interest in people, places and events, the ability to write well and concisely, and a willingness to work under pressure to meet deadlines. Potential employers like to see evidence of a commitment to journalism in the form of a file of published work as well as a CV or resumé; reporting and interview skills can be acquired initially through writing for publications like college magazines — which do not pay. In freelance journalism, a great deal of work is found by word of mouth and through a network of personal contacts; but this is of course only possible if you are already on the inside track. To get there, you may submit articles on spec (with covering letter and SAE) in your chosen area or specialisation; and more and more English-language articles are being accepted by foreign language magazines and newspapers.

## THE PRESS

### British Press

Working for a UK newspaper will only bring an overseas appointment if you are employed by one of the national daily or Sunday papers. Several years' experience on a national paper are usually necessary before you will be sent abroad; and full-time staff positions are few and far between. There are few full-time staff who are posted permanently abroad, and these will generally be specialists. This is also true of the major newspapers in the US and other countries.

If you have local knowledge (in particular of the language) and are sufficiently determined, it is possible to work at least part-time as a freelance foreign correspondent, although it is advisable to have some solid journalistic experience before you start, and to develop your contacts among editors and commissioning editors. The section on *Stringers*, below, discusses this in more detail.

It is common for journalists to gain experience on local newspapers or specialist or trade magazines, before moving on to a national or international career. But this is by no means the only way. It is also true that many journalists have a recognised qualification such as the National Certificate, a National Vocational Qualification in Newspaper Journalism (Writing), or equivalent. Details of training programmes are available from: *The Newspaper Society,* Bloomsbury House, Bloomsbury Square, 74-77 Great Russell Street, London WC1B 3DA. But for most international jobseekers a more creative approach will be required, which will involve identifying a market for your articles, finding out what editors want, and then working to supply it. The UK or US newspapers can be interested in your articles on a wide variety of subjects if you live abroad. There are also many local English-language publications which you should approach.

Journalists who wish to write for UK newspapers should apply to the appropriate editors, including a strong reason or unique selling-point which will encourage them to consider your work.

Daily Express/Daily Star/Sunday Express, Ludgate House, 245 Blackfriars Road, London SE1 9UX; tel 0171-928 8000.

Daily Mail/Mail on Sunday, Northcliffe House, 2 Derry Street, London W8 5TT; tel 0171-938 6000.

Daily Mirror/Sunday Mirror/The People, Holborn Circus, London EC1P 1DQ; tel 0171-293 3000.

Daily Telegraph/Sunday Telegraph, 1 Canada Square, Canary Wharf, London E14 5DT; tel 0171-538 5000.

The European, Orbit House, 5 New Fetter Lane, London EC4 1AP; tel 0171-418 7777.

Financial Times, Number One, Southwark Bridge, London SE1 9HL; tel 0171-873 3000.

Guardian/Observer, 119 Farringdon Road, London EC1R 3ER; tel 0171-278 2332.

Independent, 1 Canada Square, London E14 5DC; tel 0171-293 2000.

Sun/News of the World, 1 Virginia Street, London EC1 9XR; tel 0171-782 4600.

Times/Sunday Times, 1 Pennington Street, London EC1 9XN; tel 0171-782 5000.

**American Press**

The path to becoming a foreign correspondent for an American newspaper is not essentially different from that described above. Editors tend to consider a wide knowledge of politics, international affairs and history as more important than a degree in journalism. Taking a course in journalism is of course always useful. Practical experience as well as useful contacts are usually acquired through internships on newspapers. The major American papers employ numerous foreign correspondents — *The New York Times* and *The Washington Post* have the most. Some addresses are given below:

*Christian Science Monitor,* PO Box 125, Astor Station, Boston, MA 02123.

*Los Angeles Times,* Times Mirror Square, Los Angeles, CA 90053.

*New York Times,* 229 West 43rd Street, New York, NY 10036.

*Newsweek, Inc.,* 444 Madison Avenue, New York, NY 10022.

*Time, Inc.,* Time and Life Building, Rockefeller Centre, New York, NY 10020.

*Wall Street Journal,* Dow Jones and Co., 206 Liberty Street, New York, NY 10281.

*Washington Post,* 1150 15th Street NW, Washington DC 20071.

**English-language Press**

The Commonwealth countries have a well-established English-language press and there are opportunities not only for field reporters and photographers, but also for editorial and management staff. Needless to say, a high level of professionalism and training is expected.

The most practical way of finding work on a foreign paper is direct application. Addresses of newspapers will be found in *Willings Press Guide,* the international volume of *Benn's Media Directory,* or the blue pages of the *Advertisers' Annual.* All three directories should be obtainable in local reference libraries. In addition, *Writers' and Artists' Yearbook* (A&C Black, 35 Bedford Road, London WC1R 4JH) lists the addresses of newspapers and magazines in the English-speaking world (excluding the USA).

If you already live abroad, or are intending to move, there is always a possibility of finding work on a local English-language newspaper or magazine where enthusiasm and a direct approach may count more than experience; a personal visit to these publications should be on your itinerary; or you could even start your own small newspaper or magazine. Such publications are found in most countries where there are English-speaking expatriates, for example in Europe, the Middle East and East Asia, as well as Eastern Europe, where there are often magazines for local people and the expatriate community in English. Large multinationals with overseas offices also usually have in-house magazines, and these are another way of gaining experience in the world of journalism.

## RADIO AND TELEVISION

### British Radio and Television

The BBC is one major producer of television and radio programmes in the UK; nowdays there are also many smaller independent production companies. The range of jobs in the BBC is wide; equally the skills and experience required are broad.

All jobs open to external applicants are advertised in the UK national press. The right skills and experience are required, and competition is fierce. Applicants must watch the job vacancy pages and match their skills to those outlined in the advertisement. There are limited opportunities to work abroad. When such opportunities arise, the department, whether it is production or news, or the World Service, wants people who have the job skills to begin work immediately wherever they are sent. It is rare that such responsibility would be given immediately to a newcomer. Trainee jobs, when advertised, require enthusiasm and involvement in activities relevant to the job.

For more information contact:

*BBC Corporate Recruitment Services*, PO Box 7000, London W5 2WY.
*BBC Engineering & Technical Operations Recruitment*, Villiers House, The Broadway, Ealing W5 2PA.
*BBC World Service*, PO Box 76, Bush House, Strand, London WC2B 4PH.

The BBC also has overseas offices in New York, Washington, Cairo, Singapore, Buenos Aires, Sydney, New Delhi, Paris, Berlin, and Brussels.

Employment in independent television is handled by the individual companies whose addresses can be obtained from the *Independent Television Commission (ITC)*, 33 Foley Street, London W1P 7LB, tel 0171-255 3000. Information on independent radio is available from *The Radio Authority,* Holbrook House, 14 Great Queen Street, London W2 5SH, tel 0171-727 2646.

### American Radio and Television

The US broadcasting media maintain considerable numbers of staff overseas. Such jobs are not easy to come by, especially in what are seen as the more desirable foreign locations, i.e. European capital cities. One of the major companies is CNN (Cable News Network), whose offices can be found throughout the world. Some addresses are given below:

*ABC News,* 7 West 66th Street, New York, NY 10023.
*Cable News Network*, 1050 Techwood Drive, NW, Atlanta, GA 30318.
*CBS Inc.,* 51 W. 52nd Avenue, New York, NY 10019.
*NBC,* 30 Rockefeller Plaza, New York, NY 10020.
*Turner Broadcasting System,* One CNN Center, Box 105366, Atlanta, GA 30305.

### Overseas Radio and Television

Vacancies are even rarer in overseas broadcasting companies than in the foreign press. The major companies in the English-speaking world can usually fill their own needs internally; other specialised vacancies are sometimes advertised in the British or American press. Addresses of individual companies are to be found in the *World Radio and Television Handbook,* available in public reference libraries or through bookshops.

There are many non-English speaking countries that have English language broadcasts, usually as part of their external services, rather like the BBC World Service or Voice of America. Naturally, there are a few openings for native English-speaking personnel to produce, direct and broadcast these services. Full details of English language broadcasts are also given in the *World Radio and Television Handbook.*

## STRINGERS

The international news system is so structured that most of the foreign news in the British/American press and media originates either from news agencies or from individual 'stringers', and not from permanently based expatriate reporters. Stringers tend to be people already based overseas who, for a retainer and/or commission, will feed stories from their part of the world back to Britain. Stringers thus function on a part-time, freelance basis; and their work — while providing a valuable source of extra income — is usually secondary to a full-time career (often as a reporter or editor for a locally-based paper). If you have journalistic experience and are going abroad to another job, you should consider offering your services as a stringer to one of the national papers.

There are considerable opportunities for the dedicated foreign stringer which do not fall into any of the conventional categories discussed so far. A stringer need not be restricted to finding the occasional news story for the national and international press. If he or she really knows the market, opportunities for writing travel, sociological, and current affairs features for national and specialist magazines and newspapers abound. You should contact likely sources of publication, if possible, before setting off, to ensure the best chances of success. *Writers' and Artists' Yearbook* contains useful information on newspapers and magazines across the world, while the *UK Press Gazette,* the weekly newspaper for journalists, sometimes contains advertisements from sources looking for foreign freelance contributions. Prospective foreign stringers will also do well to advertise their availability for occasional or one-off contributions in those columns.

## NEWS AGENCIES

The many news agencies (also known as 'wire services') offer good opportunities for journalists based abroad. In recent times, international news-gathering has come to be dominated by European companies, particularly Reuters and Agence France Presse. Reuters' main competitor in supplying global news services is now the American-owned Associated Press (AP).

A list of the news agencies in Britain, and the services they provide, is given in *Benn's Media Directory,* under the heading *Agencies and Services for the Media Industry.* As many of these agencies operate mainly within the UK or USA, a career in one of the larger agencies is unlikely to include more than the occasional trip or tour of duty overseas. The major exception is Reuters.

*Reuters Ltd.,* 85 Fleet Street, London EC4 — an international news organisation which supplies news of political, economic, financial, general and sports interest to the media and business communities in most countries of the world. It also produces a wide range of computerised data retrieval services, combining both news and statistical data, using the latest technology to supply banks, brokers, financial institutions and major corporations worldwide with up to the minute information on international money rates, securities, commodities and all factors affecting these markets.

Reuters has one of the largest private communication systems in the world and is a major user of minicomputers to service over 25,000 subscribers in some 150 countries. Its extensive real-time data retrieval networks are among the most sophisticated and reliable in operation, interfacing with high-speed communication links and making use of satellites, cables and high-frequency radio.

They employ a number of graduates each year for training in a wide range of disciplines, including marketing, finance and information technology. Successful candidates will be expected to have at least a Second Class Honours Degree. In addition, applicants for the journalist training scheme will be required to speak two languages, one of which should be English. All four schemes offer opportunities for posts at home and abroad.

Applications in writing to the Graduate Recruitment Officer at the above address before 30 December each year.

*Associated Press (AP)*, 50 Rockefeller Plaza, New York, NY 10020 — provides many of the same services as Reuters, but is less heavily involved in supplying financial data. AP employs 200 correspondents around the world. A conventional route to an overseas posting would be to work in one of AP's smaller offices in the USA, and then on a foreign desk in New York, before being sent abroad. In some cases, however, AP will hire locally based reporters when the need arises.

# The Law

Like banking and accountancy, the law is a highly reputable and well-established profession; and opportunities exist for qualified British lawyers in many countries throughout the world.

## SOLICITORS

Despite the wide differences between legal systems in countries across the world, which might seem to restrict opportunities to move from one to another, a variety of opportunities exists for solicitors to practise abroad. Many of the larger London solicitors' firms have offices abroad, particularly in Europe, the USA and the Middle East. It is now a common practice to send trainees abroad for six months to gain overseas experience in Paris or Brussels, or another European city.

International commercial law is not in itself a separate category of law — rather it refers to the practice of law across national boundaries. Only those already expert in the laws of their own country can expect to move into this area. Linguistic skills are essential; and the ability to function in another culture is also an asset. Cases involving the laws of other countries are generally handled by the most experienced partners in any firm — trainees are sent abroad to enhance their training while doing low-level support work.

A number of UK solicitors hold posts with local lawyers' firms abroad or as legal advisers employed by the in-house legal departments of industrial and commercial concerns. Needless to say, mastering a legal system in a foreign language is intellectually highly demanding. Because of the common law roots of their legal systems, and their common language, many UK solicitors seek admission to the United States, Canada, Australia and New Zealand, although immigration restrictions and the need for further training are major barriers.

There are solicitors on the staffs of various international organisations such as the institutions of the European Union, the European Patent Office, the Council of Europe and the United Nations, undertaking legal and administrative work or acting as translators and interpreters. Others work as legal draftsmen or in other capacities in Commonwealth countries under schemes run by the Commonwealth Fund for Technical Co-operation or by other Commonwealth institutions.

Finally, there are a number of opportunities for professional exchanges for those solicitors interested in gaining practical experience of other legal systems for short periods. Details of the Young Lawyers' International Associations Scheme and of national schemes are available from The Law Society's International Relations Department (address below).

The training to become a solicitor is lengthy and exacting. A would-be solicitor must normally either obtain a qualifying law degree (details of these are available from the Law Society) or a degree in a subject other than law, and subsequently take the course leading to the Common Professional Examination or equivalent (details available from the Law Society). They must then successfully complete the Legal Practice Course at a validated institution. This will enable the candidate to obtain the necessary skills and abilities as well as the legal knowledge required in the solicitors' profession. Full details of how to qualify, including information about the non-graduate route into the profession, are included in the booklet *Careers in the International Legal Field* available from the Law Society's Careers Office, 227/228 Strand, London WC2R 1BA. The head office address is below.

## BARRISTERS

The *General Council of the Bar,* 3 Bedford Row, London WC1R 4DB, tel 0171-242 0934, fax 0171-831 9217, advises that, in many overseas countries, the distinction between the work done by a barrister and that performed by a solicitor does not exist, since the professions are merged. It follows that much of the information describing opportunities for solicitors also applies to working prospects for barristers. The main exception is that there are no official professional exchange schemes for barristers.

The Bar Council also advises that overseas vacancies for British barristers are more common in the Commonwealth and North America than in most other countries. Intending overseas barristers are advised to contact the Bar Association of the country in which they are interested, addresses available on request from The General Council of the Bar or from the information offices of the relevant embassy in London.

There are three stages in the process of becoming a barrister in Britain. A student must (1) be admitted to an Inn of Court, (2) satisfy the educational and training requirements of the Bar Council and, finally (3) be called to the Bar. He or she should also hold a degree from a British or Irish university. Full details appear in *Bar into the Nineties,* available from the *Bar Council Education and Training Department,* 213 Cursitor Street, London EC4A 1NE. Please enclose a large SAE.

## US LAWYERS

American lawyers generally find it difficult to practise abroad, except when they are employed by an American company where they are still mainly dealing with US law. Otherwise it is necessary to pass the examinations of the country you wish to practise in after a recognised course of study. As stated above, international law tends to be the preserve of the most experienced partners of any firm. Some law schools offer courses in international law and also have international law societies for students. Further information can be obtained from the following:

*American Bar Association,* Section on International Law and Practice, 1800 M St. NW, Washington DC 20036.

*Association of Student International Law Societies (ASILS),* American Society of International Law, 2223 Massachusetts Ave. NW, Washington DC 20008.

**Recruitment Consultants**
The following recruitment consultants deal with legal and accountancy appointments abroad:

*City Financial Recruitment Group,* 72 Waterloo Street, Glasgow G2 7DA, tel 0141-221 0900, fax 0141-221 1252 — specialises in accountancy, financial services and insurance and posts are usually filled from its own register of applicants. The main focus is Scotland; but there are also overseas assignments in the EU, Scandinavia, Indonesia, Malaysia and Singapore.

*Pepper, Hamilton & Scheetz*, 9 Haywards Place, London EC1R 0EE — is one of the most experienced firms in Russia and former CIS with offices in this region, and a varied, interesting and challenging practice. At least four years' experience is required and fluent Russian is preferred.

*Quarry Dougall Recruitment*, 37-41 Bedford Row, London WC1R 4JH, tel 0171-405 6062, fax 0171-831 6394 — recruits at all levels from trainee solicitors up to and including partners and teams, and senior legal advisers, for law firms and in-house legal departments in commerce and industry, in the UK, Hong Kong, Australia, New Zealand, the USA, and all EU countries. Associated offices in Leeds, Hong Kong, Australia, New Zealand, New York and Boston.

*Sheffield International Ltd.*, 10-15 Quarry Street, London EC4N 1TJ — specialises in top-flight banking, financial and legal services, including investment analysts and economists throughout the world, including Eastern Europe and East Asia.

See also the section on *Consultants and Agencies* in the chapter *Getting the Job.*

**Professional Association**
The Professional Association for solicitors in England and Wales is the *Law Society*, 113 Chancery Lane, London WC2A 1PL; tel 0171-242 1222; fax 0171-831 0344.

The Law Society's *Careers and Recruitment Service* does not have vacancies for solicitors abroad and can only give some general advice in this area.

# Medicine and Nursing

There is always a demand for people with medical, paramedical and nursing qualifications willing to work abroad. British and US qualifications are highly respected around the world, and it is now far easier for UK and Irish personnel to work in other EU countries than in the past because of the mutual recognition of qualifications between member states. The UK, North America, Australia, New Zealand and the Middle East are popular destinations for travelling health professionals, although the demand is uneven and it is advisable to research where the opportunities currently are before departure. In countries such as Saudi Arabia and the USA, for example, there are generous salaries and benefits packages available, especially through some of the recruitment agencies listed below. Although there is an urgent need for doctors and nurses in Eastern Europe, most of the work is done on a voluntary basis and usually involves training local personnel. See *Eastern European Partnership* in the chapter *Voluntary Work*.

English-speaking medical personnel, in particular doctors and dentists, tend to restrict themselves to working in hospitals and other situations overseas where they can use English. Those who can speak other languages will find a great many more opportunities open to them. For more information, *Nursing Standard*, which is on sale through newsagents weekly, carries international vacancies, as does *Nursing Standard Online*, accessible on the Internet at http://www.nursing-standard.co.uk.

This chapter sets out the major employment possibilities in a wide range of medical and hospital careers. Further substantial references to this type of work will be found in many of the chapters in *Worldwide Employment*, and also in the chapters on *Voluntary Work*, *United Nations* and *Military Service*.

Agencies dealing with nannies and nursery staff for domestic positions are dealt with in the chapter *Au Pair and Domestic*. Other employers and recruitment agencies can also be found in the chapter *Getting the Job*.


## AGENCIES

There are a huge number of recruitment agencies dealing with international employment opportunities for doctors, nurses, dentists, occupational and physiotherapists, pharmacists and many other categories of health professional. The following list includes a selection offering a range of appointments.

*Action Medical International*, 3 Raby Place, Bath BA2 4EH, tel 01225-447445, fax 01225-446161, e-mail 100413.510@compuserve.com — provides an employment and relocation service to physiotherapists, occupational therapists and speech therapists who wish to work in the USA.

*BNA International*, The Colonnades, Beaconsfield Close, Hatfield, Hertfordshire AL10 8YD — has vacancies for qualified nurses in many countries around the world. Registration and language requirements vary with location. Specialist nurses are particularly welcome. Appointments are available for short and long-term contracts in Europe, the Middle East and the USA. Also see *Worldwide Healthcare Exchange* below.

*DSI Staff RX Inc*, 1940 Drew Street, Clearwater, Florida 34625-3040, tel 813-461-9642/800-345-9642, fax 813-446-4609 — concentrates on the fields of diagnostic imaging and radiation therapy, and places staff in these fields throughout the USA.

*GMZ* — recruits worldwide on behalf of the German government and others in the development field. See under *Management Recruitment Consultants* in the *Getting the Job* chapter.

*Grafton Recruitment Ltd*, 35-37 Queens Square, Belfast BT1 3FG, tel 01232-242824, fax 01232-242897, http://www.msldb.com/grafton, e-mail recruitment@ grafton.com — recruits qualified and experienced medical personnel at all levels in Europe and the Middle East through its International Division. Also management, administration, engineering and other staff. Associated offices in Northern Ireland, Dublin, Prague, Budapest, Kuala Lumpur. Also see under *Management Recruitment Consultants* in *Getting the Job*.

*Grant Thornton Management Consultants*, 1 Melton Street, London NW1 2EP, tel 0171-383 5100, fax 0171-387 5356 — has assignments worldwide in the health care and other sectors at senior level. Also at: St John's Centre, 110 Albion Street, Leeds LS2 8LA, tel 0113-245 5514, fax 0113-246 5055.

*IMS Recruitment*, 20a Eden Street, Kingston-upon-Thames, Surrey KT1 1BB — recruits all grades and specialities of nurses, support services, administration, and all specialities of senior registrar and consultant doctors for the Middle East. Nurses need 2 to 3 years' post-basic experience, and doctors should have a minimum of 3 years' post-FRCS/MRCP experience. Contracts are from 1 to 3 years.

*Nightingale Nursing Bureau Ltd*, 2 Tavistock Place, London WC1H 9RA, tel 0171-833 3952/2045, fax 0171-278 4067 — places nurses, midwives, auxiliary nurses and care assistants from New Zealand, Australia and South Africa in nursing placements in the UK. Work is available in both National Health Service and independent hospitals, and in private homes.

*Rand Medical Recruitment International*, 3 Blandford Close, London N2 0DH, tel/fax 0181-905 5163 — places all types of medical staff in English-speaking hospitals overseas, mainly in the Middle East, especially medical consultants. Most vacancies are for contracts of 1 year or longer.

*Scott Neale & Partners* — places institutional development experts in areas such as healthcare. See under *Management Recruitment Consultants* in *Getting the Job*.

*Supplemental Health Care*, 2829 Sheridan Drive, Buffalo, New York 14150, USA — offers assignments lasting from 3 months to 1 year or more for physicians, nurses and allied health technicians in acute care general hospitals. Countries include USA, Canada, Saudi Arabia, United Arab Emirates and Qatar. Applications to the Director, International Division. Associated office: *Supplemental Health Care International*, PO Box 628, Coogee Beach, Sydney, NSW 2034, Australia.

*Worldwide Healthcare Exchange*, The Colonnades, Beaconsfield Close, Hatfield, Hertfordshire AL10 8YD, tel 01707-258233, fax 01701-259233 — recruits RGNs, physiotherapists, occupational therapists and other health care professionals for hospitals in Australia, Hong Kong, South Africa, New Zealand, The Netherlands and Canada. Support with work permit applications, travel arrangements, and accommodation are often available, 'a free and professional service to make travelling and working overseas as easy as possible.' CVs may be mailed or faxed to the above address.

# HOSPITAL MANAGEMENT ORGANISATIONS

A number of organisations are responsible for the entire management and staffing of hospitals or chains of hospitals. This is often done in the Middle East, for example, and qualified medical and health care staff are then recruited from overseas, often through agencies specifically set up to meet a particular hospital's (or group of hospitals') needs. Engineering and maintenance personnel may also be found in this way, where they cannot be recruited locally.

*Arabian Careers Ltd*, 115 Shaftesbury Avenue, Cambridge Circus, London WC2H 8AD, tel 0171-379 7877, fax 0171-379 0885 — has vacancies in Middle Eastern hospitals for qualified and experienced applicants.

*GAMA International Limited*, 2nd Floor, Moreau House, 116 Brompton Road, London SW3 1JJ, tel 0171-581 5544; 'E' Floor, West Corridor, Milburn House, Dean Street, Newcastle upon Tyne NE1 1LE — is a Saudi Arabian company that provides health care management and related services within the Kingdom of Saudi Arabia. It recruits all types of qualified, experienced hospital staff to work in its general, psychiatric and other specialist hospitals. Positions are for one-year contracts, although renewal on a yearly basis is usually possible. Occasionally there are vacancies for highly specialist medical and nursing locum staff with contracts of 3-4 months.

*Gulf Link*, PO Box 15331, Manama, Bahrain, tel 973-240090, fax 973-240040 — recruits a wide variety of management, technical and medical staff for hospitals in Bahrain and Saudi Arabia.

*HCA International Ltd*, Southgate Office Village, Ground Floor, 284 Chase Road, Southgate, London N14 6HF, tel 0181-882 6363, fax 0181-882 5266 — recruits a wide variety of staff for the King Faisal Specialist Hospital & Research Centre in Riyadh, Saudi Arabia, including consultants, nurses, radiographers, physiotherapists, medical secretaries, CSSD technicians and laboratory technologists. Most positions are for 2 years.

*International Hospitals Group (IHG)*, Stoke Poges, Slough, Bucks SL2 4NS — is a UK-owned and based group specialising in consultancy, management and operation of hospitals worldwide.

*Professional Management Resources Limited (PMR)*, — PO Box 23, Wadhurst, East Sussex TN5 6XL, tel 01892-784226, fax 01892-784228 — is involved through its *Medical Resources* company in the co-ordination and design, construction and staffing of hospital projects, especially primary health care clinics, in developing areas.

# PROFESSIONAL ASSOCIATIONS

Professional associations are most useful for their advisory and information services, which in some cases are also available to non-members. Some associations are also active in helping their members to find work abroad. The associations below rank among the most helpful.

The *Society of Chiropodists and Podiatrists*, 53 Welbeck Street, London W1M 7HE, tel 0171-486 3381, fax 0171-935 6359 — can advise state-registered chiropodists about the prospects of working in Europe under the EU Directives on the Mutual Recognition of Qualifications, and about working elsewhere overseas.

The *International Dental Federation*, 64 Wimpole Street, London W1M 8AL — publishes *FDI Basic Facts – Dentistry Around The World*, which lists manpower statistics, education, licensing and legislation information on oral health care systems.

The *British Medical Association*, Tavistock Square, London WC1H 9JP, tel 0171-387 4499, fax 0171-383 6400 — has an International Department that can give advice and information to members wishing to work abroad.

The *Medical Women's Federation*, Tavistock House North, Tavistock Square, London WC1H 9HX — has an Appointments Service that can circulate to interested members any information on vacancies in Britain and overseas. They warn, however, that they hear of very few vacancies.

The *International Confederation of Midwives* 10 Barley Mow Passage, Chiswick, London W4 4PH, tel 0181-991 6177, fax 0181-995 1332 — works with midwifery associations abroad and will put midwives in touch with local associations overseas. It is compiling a database of information from its extensive library resource; and produces a newsletter three times a year (£20 p.a. or £55 for a three-year subscription).

The *Royal College of Midwives*, International Section, 15 Mansfield Street, London W1M 0BE — is able to advise members who are interested in practising midwifery overseas or making study visits for short periods. It also welcomes applications from overseas for its courses and will design a specific programme for an individual or group of midwives visiting the UK.

The *Royal College of Nursing*, 20 Cavendish Square, London W1M 0AB, tel 0171-409 3333, fax 0171-495 0961 — has an international office that provides an advisory service for members seeking employment overseas or planning electives or professional visits outside the UK. The International Office does not arrange employment but can provide information and contacts for most countries.

The *British Association of Occupational Therapists*, 6-8 Marshalsea Road, Southwark, London SE1 1HO — can refer members to the national professional associations in the other 34 countries belonging to the World Federation of Occupational Therapists.

The *College of Optometrists*, 10 Knaresborough Place, London SW5 0TG, tel 0171-373 7765, fax 0171-373 1143 — can offer advice and assistance to members.

The *Royal Pharmaceutical Society of Great Britain*, 1 Lambeth High Street, London SE1 7JN, tel 0171-735 9141, fax 0171-735 7629 — cannot help in finding employment, but overseas vacancies are advertised in their publication, the weekly *Pharmaceutical Journal*. Registered pharmaceutical chemists applying for a position abroad are advised to contact the Society for information on pharmaceutical practice in the country concerned. This is particularly important for those seeking work in countries where no reciprocal recognition of qualifications exists.

The *College of Radiographers*, 2 Carriage Row, 183 Eversholt Street, London NW1 1BU, tel 0171-391 4500, fax 0171-391 4504 — offers advice to qualified, state-registered radiographers seeking employment overseas. The College can also refer radiographers to the national professional associations in other countries belonging to the International Society of Radiographers and Radiologic Technologists (ISRRT).

The *British Association of Social Workers*, 16 Kent Street, Birmingham B5 6RD — can put its members in touch with other member associations of the International Federation of Social Workers.

## FURTHER INFORMATION

The best sources of information on work prospects abroad are the professional associations (see above), which will also be able to give advice on the acceptability of British qualifications in foreign countries. Specific advertisements for posts abroad as well as background information can be found in the *British Medical Journal, Nursing Standard* and other professional journals.

Information on training and careers in nursing and midwifery is offered by *ENB Careers*, PO Box 2EN, London W1A 2EN, tel 0171-391 6200/6205 (10am-4pm, Mon-Fri), fax 0171-391 6207, e-mail enb.careers@easynet.co.uk, http://www.enb.org.uk/.

## DEVELOPMENT

*Action Health*, The Gate House, 22 Gwydir Street, Cambridge CB1 2LG, tel 01223-460853, fax 01223-461787 — is concerned with the promotion of appropriate health care in developing countries and operates in India, Tanzania and Uganda. It recruits fully qualified health professionals, doctors, physiotherapists, midwives and health visitors, occupational therapists, dentists, and speech and language therapists with a minimum of 2 years' post-qualification experience. Contracts range from 6 months to 2 years.

*British Red Cross (BRC)*, 9 Grosvenor Crescent, London SW1X 7EJ, tel 0171-235 5454, fax 0171-245 6315 — works as part of the International Red Cross and Red Crescent Movement, protecting and assisting victims of conflicts and natural disasters, with neutrality and impartiality, in the UK and overseas. BRC volunteers not only provide a trained and skilled response to emergencies, but also care for people in crisis, by offering vital services in the local community. The BRC maintains a register of suitably qualified doctors and nurses who are available to work overseas.

*CARE International UK*, 36-38 Southampton Street, London WC2E 7AF, tel 0171-379 5247, fax 0171-379 0543 — is one of the world's largest relief and development charities, working in Africa, Asia, Latin America and eastern Europe. It employs health professionals with extensive experience in their field, preferably gained with an organisation similar to CARE.

*Christian Outreach*, 1 New Street, Leamington Spa, Warwickshire CV31 1JL, tel 01926-315301, fax 01926-885786, e-mail 100656.1612@Compuserve.com — recruits managers of projects, local staff and/or expatriate teams, for community development projects for health and other areas in Cambodia, Mozambique, Tanzania, Rwanda, for one-year minimum contracts usually renewable for another year. Minimum age 23; and must have relevant qualifications and be committed and practising Christians. Apply to the Personnel Officer.

*International Healthcare Exchange (IHE)*, 8-10 Dryden Street, London WC2E 9NA, tel 0171-836 5883, fax 0171-379 1239 — is a registered charity that helps provide health workers to developing countries. IHE acts as a clearing house for information on posts with UK and international aid agencies, runs a register of health professionals, and provides short training courses and workshops. IHE also publishes *The Health Exchange* magazine, which lists job vacancies in international health.

*Medical Missionary Association (MMA)*, 157 Waterloo Road, London SE1 8XN, tel 0171-928 4694, fax 0171-620 2453 — exists to mobilise health professionals to serve in mission and church-related hospitals overseas. They advise on student elective training periods and overseas and long-term service and publish a magazine *Saving Health* 3-4 times a year, which includes a list of service opportunities with many UK-based mission societies.

*Médecins Sans Frontières*, International Office, Rue de la Tourelle 39, 1040 Brussels, Belgium, tel 02-280 1881, fax 02-280 0173 — sends 2,000 volunteers every year to 70 countries throughout the world affected by war, famine or natural disaster. Volunteers are contracted for a minimum of 9 months, but some take on longer assignments. MSF needs qualified doctors, nurses (RGNs), anaesthetists, midwives, laboratory technicians and surgeons with 2 years' post-qualification experience. For all categories of staff previous travel and work experience in developing countries is highly valuable.

*MERLIN (Medical Emergency Relief International)*, 14 David Mews, London W1M 1HW, tel 0171-487 2505, fax 0171-487 4042, e-mail merlin@gn.apc.org — is a British charity providing emergency medical care in disaster situations around the world. Contracts are for 6-12 months. Doctors, nurses, logisticians and administrators are needed, as well as some specialists, and must be flexible, motivated and committed, have stamina and enthusiasm, and be receptive and responsive to local cultures.

*Overseas Development Administration*, ODA Information Department, Room V523, 94 Victoria Street, London SW1E 5JL, tel 0171-917 0503 — publishes a booklet *Action on Health and Population* and a *List of Useful Addresses* for the development field.

*Tear Fund*, 100 Church Road, Teddington, Middlesex TW11 8QE, tel 0181-943 7888, fax 0181-943 3594 — is an evangelical Christian and relief organisation providing personnel for church and Christian groups. Skilled and experienced personnel are needed for community development programmes, including doctors, nurses, midwives, community health advisors and physiotherapists. Projects are generally for 4 years. Contact the *Overseas Service Advisor*.

Many other charitable organisations with a medical or nursing brief are cited in the chapter *Voluntary Work*.

# Oil, Mining and Engineering

A career in engineering offers a great deal in terms of security and mobility between different areas of work, and the chance to be involved in major projects abroad. The term engineering covers a great variety of disciplines. It would hardly be possible to go into each area in detail in a chapter of this length. In most cases, people wishing to work in engineering, whether it be civil, mechanical, electrical, petrochemical, marine, or some other branch of engineering, will have directly relevant degrees or other post-school training.

Many major construction projects around the world are in the hands of British and North American companies, who need engineers both for project management and to supervise the day-to-day work on the ground. The recession of the early 1990s hit the engineering industry less hard than most. In particular, there are major projects under way in the shape of the Hong Kong Airport (nearing completion at the time of writing) and in Kuwait. There are other major infrastructure projects in Eastern Europe and the countries of the former Soviet Union, as well as many opportunities for qualified engineers in the oil and petrochemical industries, two thirds of whose annual intake is of qualified engineers and scientists. Most opportunities are for chemical, electrical, and mechanical engineers. In particular, those experienced in the use of information technology, and who can exploit new technologies to solve problems, are most in demand across every sector of industry.

The 'Jobs' columns of *Overseas Jobs Express*, Premier House, Shoreham Airport, BN43 5RL, are a good source of engineering vacancies in the automotive, aviation, electronics, marine, oil & gas, operations & maintenance, science & technology, environmental engineering, transport engineering, and other sectors, as well as under the 'engineering' heading. A database of CVs in engineering, construction, electronics. computers/IT, telecommunications, as well as oil & gas, is offered by *Recruitment Database International Limited*, tel 01624-861638/862661, e-mail recruitmentdb@enterprise.net, http://www.enterprise.net/recruitmentdb.

*Adderley Featherstone Plc.*, Lisbon Square, Leeds, West Yorkshire LS1 4LY, tel 0113-244 4074, fax 0113-245 1578 — recruits engineers across all business sectors with overseas assignments in Southern Africa, North America, South America, Australasia/Pacific, Caribbean, Eastern Europe, the EU, Scandinavia, China, Indonesia, Japan, Malaysia, Philippines, Singapore, the Indian Subcontinent, Sri Lanka, and the Middle East. There is a branch office in London, 12 Harley Street, W1N1ED, also in Bristol, Glasgow, and Newcastle. The Dublin office is at: Europa House, Harcourt Street, Dublin 2, tel 01-475-1714, fax 01-475-4778.

*Alasdair Graham Associates*, 97 Ayr Road, Newton Mearns, Glasgow G77 6RA, tel 0141-639 3345, fax 0141-639 291 — is a specialist energy engineering recruitment agency with oil/gas and other vacancies in the Middle and Far East. vacancies for civil, electrical, instrument, mechanical, and project engineers worldwide.

*Beechwood Recruitment Ltd.*, 221 High Street, London W3 9BY, tel 0181-992 8647, fax 0181-992 5658 — recruits professional and technical staff in the chemical, civil, electrical/electronic, instrument, management, and project engineering fields, specialising in defence engineers, electrical/electronic engineers, mechanical engineers, and computing. Assignments worldwide.

*Daulton Construction Personnel*, 2 Greycoat Place, London SW1P 1SB, tel 0171-222 0817-8, fax 0171-233 0734 — specialises in architecture, construction and engineering with vacancies for civil, mechanical, and project engineers worldwide.

*Fairway Associates*, 3 Grooms Court, Parbrook, Billingshurst, West Sussex RH14 9EU, tel 01403-786079, fax 01403-784847 — specialises in engineering, as well as computing and information technology, with overseas assignments in the European Union. Their office in France is c/o *Adesia*, 21 Boulevard Vauban, BP-701, F-62031 Arras Cedex.

## OIL AND GAS COMPANIES

Oil and gas companies require a wide variety of scientists, engineers and other types of personnel, from the exploration stage (pilots, aerial photographers, divers, geologists, geophysicists and cartographers) through to production (drilling engineers, geochemists, petrochemists), refining and manufacturing (making oil usable), research and development, marketing and distribution, and other commercial services (for example, financial management, trading, logistics, marketing, and human resources). A general breakdown might be: engineers — 30%; geologists, geophysicists — 25%; computer programmers — 10%; accountants — 10%; administrators, researchers, analysts — 20%; lawyers, doctors, nurses and others — 5%.

Graduate recruitment is increasing in the oil industry; and there is a growth in international careers. Increased specialisation means that graduates are called on to use their expertise throughout the world, rather than carrying out a more general role in a single location. Many major oil companies have developed relations with universities in the UK and USA, and have recruitment programmes with their own application forms and brochures. Closing dates tend to be in December or January. Those who have studied arts and languages are likely to do the more business and commercial work, along with some other engineers and scientists. Oil companies also employ many less highly qualified workers, in particular on oil-rigs, where there is a definite hierarchy, starting from roustabout, through roughneck and derrickman, to drillers and toolpushers. In the first instance, it is necessary to take an 'Offshore Survival Course', and then to be available for work in one of the main centres of offshore drilling activity, which in the UK means Yarmouth/Lowestoft and Aberdeen. Experience of onshore operations is also a plus. UK companies expect workers to have at least two years' experience on North Sea oil rigs before they will be considered for overseas assignments. Working conditions on oil rigs are not easy, but the work is highly paid; workers under the age of 21 are rarely taken on. Applicants over 28 are not likely to be successful unless they have transferable skills.

The main overseas opportunities are in the Middle East, North Africa, North America, Venezuela, Mexico, Brazil, Australia, Brunei, Indonesia, Russia, and several European countries. It should be noted that the Netherlands has recently become a major producer of natural gas; and that former Soviet Union has now opened up to the major foreign companies. China has also signed agreements with several foreign companies to develop its petrochemicals industry.

The large international oil companies usually recruit local staff where they can; and posts abroad are often filled by internal transfer or promotion. Vacancies are therefore highly competitive and only those with the right scientific, engineering, mathematics, or other qualifications will be considered. Some will continue to specialise in their chosen skill, while others may branch out into activities relating to buying or selling, information technology, or distribution. There are trainee opportunities straight from school for those with three suitable GCSE passes, or equivalent GNVQs. Employment in the petrochemical industry is often handled by management recruitment consultants, some of which are listed under *Consultants and Agencies* in the chapter *Getting the Job.*

Details of the world's oil and gas companies and their activities are given in the *Oil and Gas International Yearbook,* available in public reference and business libraries. *The UK Offshore Oil and Gas Yearbook* has detailed information on the production and exploration licensees in the British, Norwegian, German and Dutch sectors of the North Sea, as well as lists of the contractors and companies actively involved in providing services to the North Sea oil and gas industries. For the latest information it is worth consulting the weekly *Oil & Gas Journal* (PennWell Publishing, PO Box 1260, 1421 South Sheridan Road, Tulsa, Oklahoma 74101). *World Oil*, PO Box 2608, 3301 Allen Parkway, Houston, TX 77252-2608; tel 617-848-9306; fax 713-520-443: UK representative, Roger Kingswell, 36 Ashford Road, Bearsted, Kent ME14 4LP; tel 01622-631636; fax 01622-631637), is a specialist 'downhole' magazine, dealing with the stages of exploration, drilling and production that come before refining. *Hydrocarbon Processing* (same address) concentrates on the problems facing management and technical personnel in the worldwide Hydrocarbon Processing Industry (HPI): refining, gas processing, synfuels, and chemical/petrochemical manufacturing, the stages which are 'downstream' of the well-head.

The personnel or human resources departments of major national and multinational oil companies are worth contacting to obtain details of their current recruitment programmes. The UK offices of some of the principal operating companies are:

*BP Exploration Operating Company Ltd.,* Farburn Industrial Estate, Dyce, Aberdeen AB2 0PB; tel 01224-832000; fax 01224-834010.

*Chevron (UK) Ltd.,* 2 Portman Street, London W1H 0AN; tel 0171-487 8100; fax 0171-487 8905.

*British Petroleum,* Britannic House, 1 Finsbury Circus, London EC2M 7BA; tel 0171-496 4000; fax 0171-496 5656.

*Conoco (UK) Ltd.,* Park House, 116 Park Street, London W1Y 4NN; tel 0171-408 6000; fax 0171-408 6660.

*Elf Enterprise Caledonia Ltd.,* 1 Claymore Drive, Bridge of Don, Aberdeen AB23 8GB; tel 01224-233000; fax 01224-233838.

*Elf Petroleum UK Plc.,* 30 Buckingham Gate, London SW1E 6NN; tel 0171-963 5000; fax 0171-957 5197.

*Enterprise Oil Plc.,* Grand Buildings, Trafalgar Square, London WC2N 5EJ, tel 0171-925 4000; fax 0171-925 4321.

*Esso,* Esso House, Victoria Street, London SW1E 5JW; tel 0171-834 6677; fax 0171-245 2982.

*Mobil North Sea Ltd.,* Mobil Court, 3 Clement's Inn, London WC2A 2EB; tel 0171-412 4000; fax 0171-412 4084.

*Phillips Petroleum (UK),* Phillips Quadrant, 35 Guildford Road, Woking, Surrey GU22 7QT; tel 01483-756666; fax 01483-752309.

*Shell International* (see *Shell (UK) Exploration and Production* below).

*Texaco Ltd.,* 1 Westferry Circus, Canary Wharf, London E14 4HA; tel 0171-719 3000; fax 0171-719 5145.

*Total Oil Marine Plc.,* Crawpeel Road, Altens, Aberdeen AB9 2AG, tel 01224-858000; fax 01224-858999.

*Union Texas Petroleum Ltd.,* 5th Floor, Bowater House, 68-114 Knightsbridge, London SW1X 7LR; tel 0171-581 5122; fax 0171-584 7785.

Offices of major US oil firms:

*Ashland Oil Inc.,* Box 391, Ashland, KY 41114; tel 606-329-3333.

*BP America Inc.,* 200 Public Square, Cleveland, OH 44114-2375; tel 216-586-4141.

*Conoco Inc.,* Box 2197, Houston, TX 77252; tel 713-293-100.

*Exxon Corporation,* 225 E. John W. Carpenter Frwy., Irving, TX 75062-2298.

*Marathon Oil Company,* Box 3128, Houston, TX 77253; tel 713-629-6600.

*Mobil Corporation,* 3225 Gallows Road, Fairfax, VA 22037-0001; tel 703-846-3000.

*Occidental Petroleum Corporation,* 10889 Wilshire Boulevard, Los Angeles, CA 90024; tel 213-879-1700.

*Phillips Petroleum Company,* 16 Phillips Building, Bartlesville, OK 74004; tel 918-661-6600.

*Texaco Inc.,* 2000 Westchester Avenue, White Plains, NY 10650; tel 914-253-4000.

The companies listed below are representative of the type of recruitment being carried out in the petrochemical field, and include the companies most interested in employing British and North American staff:

*Al Wazan,* PO Box 3994, Abu Dhabi, United Arab Emirates, tel +9712-223-200, fax +9712-223-335, e-mail alwazan@emirates.net.ae — is one of the leading recruitment agencies in the Gulf Countries (Abu Dhabi, Dubai, Bahrain, Saudi Arabia, Qatar, Oman, and other Middle East countries) for various oilfield-related positions (for ADNOC, ADCO, ADMA-OPCO, ADGAS, ADNOC-FOD, GASCO, ZADCO, NDC, FERTIL) and is the official representative throughout GCC countries for 'The Search' (Overseas Job Search magazine), as well as recruiting through the Internet.

*Anthony Moss and Associates Ltd.,* 173-175 Drummond Street, London NW1 3JD, tel 0171-388 0918, fax 0171-387 4973, e-mail anthony@moss5814.sonnet.co.uk — specialises in the recruitment of a wide range of senior management and professionals worldwide in Europe, Africa, Middle, and Far East, specifically with up-stream Oil and Gas Companies.

*Contracts Consultancy Ltd.(CCL),* 162-164 Upper Richmond Road, London SW15 2SL, tel 0181-871 2994, fax 0181-871 9461 — requires high calibre, well-qualified engineers and professionals with recent experience of offshore and onshore oil, gas, power, and infrastructure projects in the UK, Europe, Africa, the Middle and Far East.

*Heston (Middle East) Ltd.,* The Parade, Market Square, Castletown, Isle of Man — recruits engineers and technicians for the oil and gas, petrochemical, engineering and construction industry in the Middle East and Far East. All disciplines are covered, including civil, structural mechanical, electrical and instrumentation, for all categories of engineers, designers, supervision and technical staff. Contracts range from six months to three years. For senior grade positions, degree are essential; however, for intermediate positions HNC/HND will normally suffice.

*Jawaby Oil Service,* Recruitment Department, 15-17 Lodge Road, London NW8 7JA, tel 0171-266 4545, fax 0171-266 2298 — specialises in overseas recruitment for the oil and petrochemical industries.

*D.J.Mills Management Ltd.,* 15-17 Church Street, Epsom, Surrey KT17 4PF, tel 01372-728911, fax 01372-722826 — offer location employees on short or long-term contracts in petro/chemical — instrumentation, piping vessels, steelwork etc. — and mechanical and other engineering fields, including piping, plant layout and process machinery.

*Overseas Technical Service (Harrow) Ltd.,* First Floor, 100 College Road, Harrow

HA1 1BQ — are recruitment consultants specialising in the provision of engineers and technicians for the UK and overseas oil, gas and petrochemical industries.

*Petro-Canada,* PO Box 2844, Calgary, Alberta, Canada T2P 3E3, tel 403-296-8486, fax 403-296-3125 — is one of Canada's major corporations. It explores for and produces crude oil, natural gas and natural gas liquids; and refines, distributes and markets petroleum products. Petro-Canada employs over 5,000 professional, technical, clerical and secretarial staff, and advises that there are permanent opportunities for graduates from time to time.

*Precision Resources,* London House, 100 New Kings Road, London SW6 4LX, e-mail ambit@cix.compulink.co.uk — is a technical recruitment consultancy with vacancies for suitably qualified and experienced staff in oil & gas refinery operations and maintenance and other areas.

*Recruitment Services Ltd.,* Penthouse Suite, Worthing House, 2-6 South Street, Worthing, West Sussex BN11 3AE — specialises in the recruitment of technical personnel for the oil, gas and petrochemical industry and associated heavy engineering, at all levels from field operators to project directors. Opportunities open to British, European and American citizen; temporary and permanent contracts. Relevant qualifications and experience always needed.

*Preng and Associates,* 211 Piccadilly, London W1v 9LD, tel 0171-917 9860, fax 0171-895 1361 — recruits directors and management level staff in the energy and petrol/petrol products fields in Russia and former CIS countries, as well as Europe and the UK. USA office: 2925 Briar Park, Suite 1111, Houston, TX 77042; tel 713-266-2600; fax 713-266-3070.

*Schlumberger Wireline & Testing,* 158 Avenue de Tervuren, B-1150 Brussels, Belgium — is one part of the worldwide Schlumberger oilfield services group. The technique of wireline logging was pioneered by Schlumberger in 1927. This involves lowering measuring instruments on an electrical cable — a wireline — into a borehole and assessing the rock formations and potential for oil and gas as it is brought back up to the surface. Wireline services are used during the whole lifetime of a well. Schlumberger also provides testing services to evaluate the production potential of an oil well, and well maintenance and enhanced oil recovery techniques. The company recruits graduates as Field Engineers. Applicants must have a good degree in engineering, physics, geology or geophysics. They need to be single, physically fit and under 28 years old. British applicants should write to the recruitment department at the above address. American applicants should contact: The Recruiting Coordinator, PO Box 2175, Houston, TX 77252-2175. The UK office is: *Schlumberger Evaluation and Production Services,* Kirkton Industrial Estate, Dyce, Aberdeen AB2 0BF; tel 01224-723671; fax 01224-723497.

*Professional Management Resources (PMR),* PO Box 23, Wadhurst, East Sussex TN5 6XL, tel 01892-784226, fax 01892-784228 — recruits expatriate manpower to clients/projects in the Middle East, Far East and Africa. All engineering disciplines and support personnel to the civil construction, oil, gas, petrochem, telecoms, IT, power and water industries. Also training personnel in all engineering disciplines plus English, maths and science, curriculum development and HRO Training.

*Shell (UK) Exploration and Production,* Shell-Mex House, The Strand, London WC2R 0DX, tel 0171-409 0015, fax 0171-257 3920 — offers career prospects in the Exploration and Production Function for exploration geologists, geophysicists, petroleum engineers and field engineers — all of which will involve a considerable amount of time overseas. Shorter overseas assignments may also be included in a general career pattern in other branches of the company, e.g. manufacturing and refining, marketing or research. Support staff most often recruited in Britain include teachers and nursing sisters to work in staff schools and hospitals in the remoter areas of the operation.

*Simpson Crowden Consultants Ltd.,* 97-99 Park Street, London W1Y 3HA, tel 0171-629 5909, fax 0171-408 0608, specialises in the petrol/products and energy industries with most vacancies for engineers. Overseas assignments worldwide.

## Pipelines

One area where personnel are constantly required is pipeline work: contracts of two to three months require an enormous amount of labour. Although it is better to possess some kind of specialised skill (digger, driver, welder or crane operator), there is also work for the unskilled on fencing, cooking or just general labouring.

Although you could contact the major companies in this field, it is unlikely that this would be the best approach, since you must have prior knowledge of when and where contracts are due to take place. The quickest and simplest way to discover these details is to obtain a copy of *Pipeline Digest,* available from PO Box 1917, Denver, Colorado 80201-1917, USA. This excellent publication contains lists of all the major contracts planned throughout the world, including the name of the main contractor with telephone number, and the start-up and completion dates. With this information, those interested in this kind of work can contact the correct main contractor; and in addition find out from that source the firms involved in sub-contract work. *Pipe Line & Gas* targets personnel engaged in the design, operation, maintenance, management and construction of pipe lines and is a source for industry news, technical information and markets trends: PO Box 2608, 3301 Allen Parkway, Houston TX 77252-2608, tel 713-529-4301; fax 713-520-4433: the UK/Scandinavia representative is Roger Kingswell, 36 Ashford Road, Bearsted, Kent ME14 4LP; tel 01622-631636; fax 01622-631637.

## Professional Associations

*The American Petroleum Institute,* 1220 L Street NW, Washington DC 20005 — is a regulatory and research organisation representing over 200 companies in the oil and gas industry. The institute will be glad to give information on employment prospects in the industry. The Institute runs an annual paid internship programme which lasts for three months for those interested in a career in the petroleum industry. Only 6-10 applicants are accepted each year from abroad.

*The Institute of Petroleum,* 61 New Cavendish Street, London W1M 8AR, tel 0171-467 7116, fax 0171-255 1472, e-mail InstPet@cityscape.co.uk — gives advice to those wanting to work in the oil industry in the UK, upstream and downstream, onshore and offshore. The Institute produces a wide range of useful publications, career information booklets, and oil data sheets which are available to the public. *Careers in Oil* is a booklet outlining careers opportunities for graduates and the different fields of work in the oil industry. One copy is free. *Working Offshore* is a useful publication which is regularly updated, outlining training courses, the jobs available in North Sea operating companies, drilling companies and construction yards, and a list of recruitment agencies for such work. This costs £5 inclusive of postage and packing. Membership of the Institute includes a subscription to the monthly journal, *Petroleum Review.* The head of membership administration can be contacted on 0171-467 7100. There is also a Library and Information Service at the above address.

# MINING

Mining offers employment in many countries; see *Worldwide Employment* for some of these. The main areas for recruitment are former Soviet Union; Canada;

Australia; and South Africa; as well as countries like Brazil, Thailand, Malaysia, and others which employ experienced international workers for training, engineering, as well as administration and other jobs. Geologists, metallurgists and geophysicists are some of the specialist staff employed by all mining companies.

The *Mining Association of Great Britain*, 6 St. James's Square, London SW1Y 4LD — is an association of mining companies recruiting both in Britain and abroad; and can send a list of its member companies. Senior professional staff will find it most worthwhile contacting them; as other staff are more likely to be recruited locally.

*British Columbia and Yukon Chamber of Mines*, 840 West Hastings Street, Vancouver BC, Canada V6C 1C8 — can supply a list of some of the major mining operations in Canada.

*Thomas Mining Associates*, PO Box 2023, Bournemouth, Dorset BH4 8YR, tel 01202-751658, fax 01202-764448 — provides technical back-up to the Mining and Extractive industries in the fields of personnel and management consultancy and, in particular, in the recruitment of mining and quarrying personnel; and is one of the world leaders in recruitment, with a base of international clients from small operators to the largest major mining houses. TMA has an extensive database of mining and quarrying professionals of many nationalities, covering all disciplines and including personnel such as exploration and mining geologists, mining engineers, mineral processors, mechanical/electrical/construction engineers, surveyors, samplers, accountants, administrators, personnel managers, materials managers (stores and purchasing), mine security, and artisans (fitters, electricians, diesel mechanics).

*Woodridge Associates,* see below.


# ENGINEERING

There are many kinds of specialised careers in engineering, which means that many agencies listed under *Management Recruitment Consultants* and the chapters on *International Organisations, Military Services* (among others), and the country chapters in *Worldwide Employment,* may be worth consulting, as well as the information about the petrochemical and mining industries above.

*Mott MacDonald Group,* St. Anne House, 20-26 Wellesley Road, Croydon CR9 2UL, tel 0181-686 5041, fax 0181-681 5706 — is an independent, multi-disciplinary engineering consultancy, with over 4,200 staff operating from offices in nearly 50 countries across Asia and the Pacific, the Middle East, Africa, Europe and the Americas. Over 60% of the firm's business is generated overseas through projects covering transportation, civil engineering, building and infrastructure, power and energy, industrial development, water supply and wastewater, project management, communications, mechanical and electrical engineering, environmental management and rural development. In all these fields staff are recruited at graduate and more senior levels.

*Survey and Development Services Limited,* 3 Hope Street, Bo'ness, West Lothian, EH51 0AA, tel 01506-518000, fax 01506-517777, e-mail webmaster@sds.co.uk — are Land, Engineering and Photogrammetric Surveyors involved in topographical mapping and civil engineering surveying. The Company's surveyors are equipped with the latest state of the art GPS systems. Their overseas involvement is the Arabian peninsula through their sister company Jatco, which is located in Dammam, Saudi Arabia. They also have staff working in France and Germany in conjunction with associate companies. Personnel for overseas tours are either seconded to their associates, or taken on for specific contract periods.

**Recruitment Consultants**
Below is a selection of the many management recruitment consultancies involved principally or on a large scale in engineering recruitment. Those with a broader field of interest are otherwise listed in the *Getting the Job* chapter.

*Anders Glaser Wills,* Capital House, 1 Houndwell Place, Southampton SO14 1HU, tel 01703-223511, fax 01703-227911 — are international recruitment consultants in the construction, engineering, quantity surveying, water and building service sectors. Assigments from Site Engineer to Senior Technical positions, Project manager and Resident Engineer. Countries handled include: Spain; France; Germany; The Netherlands; North America; Botswana; Pakistan; the Middle East; Far East; UK; and others. Degrees/experience and good references required. Offices in Birmingham, Bristol, North London, Twickenham, Newcastle and Manchester, as well as associated offices in Italy, Hong Kong, United Arab Emirates, The Netherlands and California.

*BDC Technical Services Limited,* Slack Lane, Derby DE22 3FL, tel 01332-347123, fax 01332-291464 — places qualified staff up to project management level for European clients. Sectors dealt with include: engineering; power generation; water; petrochemical; transport; information technology; nuclear; and gas.

*Daulton Construction Personnel,* 2 Greycoat Place, London SW1P 1SB, tel 0171-222 0817-8, fax 0171-233 0734 — is a consultancy for worldwide recruitment in the construction industry, including architects, construction personnel, civil, mechanical and project engineering, and facilities management, particularly for Europe, the Middle East and East Asia. Management and technical staff with experience and qualifications are needed (no trades). Contracts are mainly for one year or permanent.

*EMA Partners UK Ltd.,* 150 Regent Street, London W1R 5FA, tel 0171-734 4165, fax 0171-734 4166 — specialises in electrical and electronic engineers, as well as defence and manufacturing positions, in particular in the Franco-British business sector. There are associated offices in Argentina, Australia, Austria, Belgium, France, Germany, Italy, Mexico, The Netherlands, Singapore, Spain, Switzerland, USA and Venezuela.

*International Staffing Consultants, Europe,* PO Box 124, Eastleigh, Hampshire SO50 8ZE, tel 01703-651281, fax 01703-620877 — is the European office of *International Staffing Consultants, Inc.,* 500 Newport Center Drive, Newport Beach, California 92660. They are members of the largest and oldest network of employment agencies in the world, NPA. With over 1,000 recruiters in 400 offices their association with its affiliates offers a unique opportunity to network vacancies and candidates to provide a comprehensive service. Affiliates are located throughout the USA, Canada, Europe and the Middle East. Specialists in recruiting European staff for North America and US staff for assignments worldwide. Recruitment is usually for experienced and qualified engineers, as well as managers, sales & marketing, and IT professionals for USA, Europe and the Middle East. All fees paid by clients; there is never a charge to candidates for the services of ISC or any affiliated company.

*Peter Glaser & Associates,* Bramble Hill, Bramble Lane, Christchurch, Dorset BH23 5NB — recruits British and Amercian staff to work abroad in the contruction, engineering and oil and gas industries. Contracts vary from one week to two years, or permanent.

*Survey Data Services Ltd.,* De Salis Court, Hampton Lovett, Droitwich, Worcestershire WR9 0NX — is a recruitment agency specialising in site engineering staff — site engineers, agents, land surveyors — for the construction industry in the UK and overseas, on long and short term contracts.

*Woodridge Associates,* The Ridge House, The Ridge, Broad Blunsdon, Swindon, SN2 4AD, tel 01977-559215, fax 01977-556869 — maintains an active list of qualified mining and civil engineers, metallurgists, project managers, mechanical, electrical, diesel and mobile plant engineers and exploration and mining geologists for long, medium and/or short-term assignments.

## PROFESSIONAL ASSOCIATIONS

The Appointments Bureau of the *Royal Institute of British Architects,* 66 Portland Place, London W1N 4AD, tel 0171-580 5533, handles UK and overseas appointments (often in the Middle East) for experienced architects and architectural technicians. Its *International Directory of Practices* gives details of British firms with overseas offices.

The *Royal Institution of Chartered Surveyors* has a recruitment consultancy. Over 7,000 of its qualified members are serving in over 100 overseas countries, including the Middle East and North America.

The *Institution of Electrical Engineers,* Michael Faraday House, Six Hills Way, Stevenage, Herts. SG1 2AY, provides a professional brief for its members called *Working Abroad* containing general information on living and working abroad. Its fortnightly newspaper *IEE Recruitment* contains classified advertisements which sometimes include overseas positions, and is included as a supplement with *IEE News* and *IEE Review.*

# Secretarial, Translating & Interpreting

## SECRETARIAL

Opportunities for properly trained secretaries with language skills abound in many countries and organisations abroad. Apart from the employment agencies listed below, those interested in secretarial work should consult the chapters on *International Organisations, United Nations, Voluntary Work* and *British Government Departments.* Agencies which specialise in secretarial vacancies in one specific country may also be found in the relevant country chapters. Branches, affiliates and subsidiaries of British or US-based companies abroad listed in these country chapters may also be worth contacting. Another way for any sufficiently qualified secretary who speaks the local language is to apply successfully for work on the spot. It should be noted that a bilingual secretary is one who is equally capable in both writing and speaking another language.

As well as opportunities with the agencies below, senior secretarial staff are handled by several of the companies listed in the section *Management Recruitment Consultants* above.

*Albemarle Appointments,* 107 New Bond Street, London W1 — can help experienced secretaries with shorthand and typing skills (and where relevant, knowledge of the country's language) to find work in the Middle East, Europe and the Far East.

*Bilingual People,* 14 Hanover Street, London W1R 9HG, tel 0171-491 2400, fax 0171-491 1900 — provides contract and temporary staff, secretaries, PAs, executives, translators and interpreters with two or more languages, and has many years experience in the industry.

*CLC Language Services,* Buckingham House, 6 Buckingham Street, London WC2N 6BU, tel 0171-738 4203 — specialises in placing staff with languages in EU countries in a variety of sectors, including translating and interpreting and secretarial. Opportunities open to EU citizens and North Americans with valid work permits. Relevant experience is preferred.

*Cavell Bilingual Recruitment,* 26 Goodge Street, London W1P 1FG, tel 0171-255 3277, fax 0171-631 1379 — specialises in language appointments across a wide range of industries, with assignments in Eastern Europe, the European Union and Scandinavia.

*Crone Corkill,* Victory House, 99-101 Regent Street, London W1R 7HB — is a secretarial recruitment consultancy. The Multilingual Division recruits bilingual personnel in London, Paris, Brussels and other European capitals. Candidates wishing to work abroad need either a language degree plus a minimum six month secretarial training, or a bilingual secretarial diploma. 50 wpm typing and some word processing knowledge are essential.

*Manpower,* 66 Chiltern Street, London W1M 1PR, tel 0171-224 6688 — is the world's largest temporary office employment agency. Manpower offices throughout Europe offer secretarial work to experienced, linguistically fluent secretaries; work abroad must be arranged locally. Manpower has offices in Ireland, France, Germany, Holland, Denmark, Belgium, Luxembourg, Spain and Portugal, as well as in Israel, Latin America and the Far East. An address list is available from the headquarters at the above address.

*Multilingual Services,* 22 Charing Cross Road, London WC2H 0HR, tel 0171-836 3794 (general), 0171-836 2979 (interpreting), fax 0171-836 4093 — selects experienced bilingual secretaries for permanent positions in EU countries. Candidates must have a secretarial qualification and be fluent in the language of the target country. countries.

*Sheila Burgess International,* 62 rue St Lazare, F-75009 Paris, tel 1-44 63 02 57, fax 1-44 63 02 59, London tel 0171-584 6446 — established in London for over 15 years and in Paris for eight, specialise in the recruitment of bilingual/ secretarial/PA personnel for permanent positions with international companies in Paris, Germany, and Brussels (not London). The clients include prestigious law firms, media, fashion, finance, medical research, property and IT companies as well as EU bodies and international organisations. Interested candidates must be EU nationals — if not, valid, permanent, unlimited working papers are essential. Candidates require an excellent command (degree or equivalent) of English and French/German; confident secretarial skills — 50 wpm WP; knowledge of at least two WP systems; and smart presentation with a professional outlook. Positions range from college leaver secretaries to top level Exec PAs and Office managers. Sheila Burgess do not handle temporary positions.

*TM International Bilingual Secretarial Recruitment,* 36/38 rue des Mathurins, F-75008 Paris, tel 1-47 42 71 00, fax 1-47 42 18 87 — selects and recruits bilingual English/French secretaries and Personal Assistants for permanent positions in international companies. Pre-selection of candidates based on language, aptitude and personality tests, as well as detailed interviews. Secretarial training and/or experience, computer knowledge of basic applications, ie. Word and Excel for Windows and/or DOS, and good French and English language skills, both spoken and written, together with a professional attitude and appearance. Minimum typing speed, 35wpm (English and French). Detailed CVs in both English and French, plus a small photograph, are required.

## TRANSLATING AND INTERPRETING

Overseas work for translators and interpreters is open to properly qualified personnel; work is often assigned to locally available people as the need arises. The world's largest employer of translators and interpreters is probably the European Commission in Brussels, which has over 1,000 (see under *International Organisations*). Apart from fluency in the language or languages, and a university language degree, candidates usually need to have some post-graduate training. Translators and interpreters generally specialise in certain technical, scientific or commercial fields, and may have degrees in other subjects in addition to their linguistic abilities. Advice on which courses to take is available from the *Institute of Translating and Interpreting* or the *Institute of Linguists* (see below).

Staff jobs and freelance work as a translator is far easier to find than as an interpreter. Large organisations, such as the EU and the UN, do have some full-time interpreters, but still recruit freelances as the need arises. Those who wish to work as freelance interpreters will have to prove their ability to potential employers before they can expect a steady flow of work. Most freelances do a considerable amount of written translating work as well. Successful freelances are usually members of a professional association, such as the IL, ITI, AIIC (see below).

Potential employers can be found in the chapters, *International Organisations* and *United Nations*. See also the organisations dealing with international work in the Central London Yellow Pages, under the heading *Translators and Interpreters*, or your local directory.

*Alpnet Interlingua*, Rothschild House, Whitgift Centre, Croydon, Surrey CR9 3QJ, tel 0181-688 3852 — is the world's largest translation network with offices in the US, Switzerland, Hong Kong, Singapore, Spain, France, Germany and Canada. US office at 44 South 700 E., Suite 204, Salt Lake City, Utah 84107-3075.

*Institute of Linguists*, Mangold House, 24A Highbury Grove, London N5 2EA, tel 0171-359 7445 — cannot find employment but does offer general advice on careers with languages, how to make use of qualifications already held, and details of qualifications required for specific jobs connected with languages.

*Institute of Translating and Interpreting (ITI)*, 377 City Road, London EC1V 1NA, tel 0171-713 7600, fax 0171-713 7650, e-mail 101376.1430@compuserve.-com — is a professional association of translators and interpreters. ITI publishes a bi-monthly bulletin and many other useful publications. There are several categories of membership, including a low-cost Student Scheme for those studying to become translators or interpreters.

*International Association of Conference Interpreters (AIIC)*, 10 avenue de Secheron, CH-1202 Geneva, Switzerland — is the only worldwide association of conference interpreters. AIIC negotiates and concludes agreements with intergovernmental organisations and generally fosters high standards in the profession.

**Opportunities for US Citizens**
Major employers of translators and interpreters in the USA include the Federal Government, CIA, FBI, the National Security Agency and Voice of America Radio. American citizens interested in working in this field can obtain a free publication, *Special Career Opportunities for Linguists/Translators/Interpreters* from: US Department of State, Language Services Division, Room 2212, Washington DC 20520.

Most of the main private agencies for translators and interpreters have offices in New York.

# Teaching

There are good opportunities for teachers wishing to work abroad, although this will depend on the subject and your qualifications. In Britain and the USA, there are too few trained teachers in some subjects and too many in others; and the uncertain jobs situation leads many to consider moving to another country, where the salaries can be high and the lifestyle may be less stressful. Teaching overseas provides a realistic opportunity for career development, particularly in higher education and specialist training. In the EU, recent rulings by the European Court mean that member countries can no longer prevent non-nationals working in public-sector jobs, including education, and this should allow UK and Irish teachers greater freedom to move to other European Union countries. In the developing world, there is a general shortage of qualified teachers; and there are plenty of opportunities for volunteers (if you are prepared to work in more difficult conditions than at home). Vacancies are widely advertised in the national press, particularly in *The Times Educational* and *Higher Education Supplements.*

One disadvantage of moving abroad is that you may not have any guarantee of employment when you return; and teachers already in employment should check on this with their Local Education Authority (in Britain) or the relevant body before making any arrangements.

Working abroad might also have an adverse effect on social security (enquire at your DSS office) and your superannuation position (enquiries to the Teachers' Pensions Agency, Staindrop Road, Mowden Hall, Darlington, Co. Durham DL3 9EE). The TPA issues free leaflets which explain the options to those who wish to leave the scheme early. This includes an arrangement which allows teachers to contribute to the scheme in respect of a period of absence, if they pay both the employers and employees contribution available from the Agency (see *The General Approach* section for more about social security issues).

When looking for work abroad, whether in the developing or developed world, some sort of qualification is usually necessary. For those who are unqualified and who wish to teach, a most useful qualification is the Certificate in Language Teaching to Adults (CELTA). In particular, having the certificates or diplomas accredited by the Royal Society of Arts (RSA) with the University of Cambridge Local Examinations Certificate (UCLES) on the one hand, or Trinity College, on the other, will be most important (although not essential in some English language teaching work): UCLES, Syndicate Buildings, 1 Hills Road, Cambridge CB1 2EU, tel 01223-61111; Trinity College London, 16 Park Crescent, London W1N 4AP, tel 0171-323 2328. These organisations will send details of their accredited training centres nationally and internationally.

Among the organisations providing training is inlingua Teacher Training & Recruitment (Rodney Lodge, Rodney Road, Cheltenham GL50 1JF, tel 01242-253171); they offer both 5 week Trinity College TESOL courses and 2 week inlingua Introduction to TEFL courses.

Graduates looking for a more advanced initial qualification can take a one-year Postgraduate Certificate in Education (PGCE) course in teaching English as a Foreign Language.

It should be borne in mind that many English language schools — whether or not they require an initial qualification — are more concerned with practical teaching ability than with very advanced qualifications. Training courses without classroom practice are viewed with scepticism. Far Eastern employers, and those in Russia and neighbouring countries, still attach the traditional importance to degrees; and some of the communicative teaching methods which are currently taught to TEFL trainees may be less appropriate in these countries, although the qualifications are often necessary.

The British Council's *English Language Information Unit (ELIU)*, Medlock Street, Manchester M15 4PR, provides information to the public on all aspects of English language teaching (ELT). ELIU also produces various publications, including a free information pack.

Apart from the prospects outlined on the following pages, teaching posts are also featured in the chapters on *Voluntary Work* and *British Government Departments*, and under the separate country chapters. Teacher recruitment also forms part of the activities of some of the government agencies listed in the chapter *Getting the Job*.

**Training in the United States**
In the USA, the emphasis is on university degree courses in linguistics, although increasingly universities are offering intensive TESL training (the American acronym for Teaching English as a Second Language). For a guide to the academic courses (but not the more 'intensive' ones), there is the *Directory of Professional Placement Programs in TESOL in the US* (TESOL Inc., 1600 Cameron St, Suite 300, Alexandria, Virginia 22314-2751). 'TESOL' stands for Teaching English to Speakers of Other Languages. There are also many community-based programmes where you can obtain practical experience of teaching English as a second or foreign language.

The most popular postgraduate qualification is the one-year MA in TESOL, which requires a considerable financial investment. An alternative is a BA in Education or TESOL/Applied Linguistics. The one-month Cambridge/RSA CELTA (see above) is gaining popularity and credibility in the United States too. Contacts for these Cambridge/RSA courses in the US and around the world, as well as in Britain, and much other useful information, are to be found in Vacation Work's *Teaching English Abroad* (see *Useful Publications* below).

## TEACHER EXCHANGE SCHEMES AND ASSISTANTSHIPS

*The Central Bureau for Educational Visits and Exchanges,* 10 Spring Gardens, London SW1A 2BN, tel 0171-389 4004, fax 0171-389 4426, CAMPUS 2000 01:YNK 330 — arranges assistantships for undergraduates and graduates on an exchange basis. Applications should be made by December of the year preceding appointment. Appointments are for one academic year, and are available in approximately 30 countries worldwide. The emphasis is on foreign languages; and the aim of the Central Bureau is to provide information, advice, and support on all forms of educational visits and exchanges. It also publishes a wide range of information guides and newsletters. The enquiry number for publications is 0171-389 4880, and for information 0171-389 4697. You can send off for its *Guide to Publications and Videos.*

As part of its Schools and Professional Development Programmes, it also administers some of the EU-sponsored exchange and educational development programmes (see *Working Exchanges* in *Getting the Job*), including Arion, Comenius Action 1, and Comenius Action 3, as well as the Lingua language programmes; also European Post-to-Post Teacher Exchanges, for language teachers and teachers of other subjects, lasting from three weeks to one year — countries involved are Austria, Denmark, France, Germany, the Netherlands, Spain, and Switzerland, tel 0171-389 4930 (teachers keep their salary, and their return travel is paid); a UK/US teacher exchange programme (under which teachers of any subject and any phase swap their posts for six months or one year — tel 0171-389 4620); 'headteacher jobshadowing'; the Council of Europe Teacher Bursaries Scheme; the Finnish Hospitality Programme; the German Hospitality Programme; and funding for overseas visits 'having the potential to lead to development work of national significance'.

*Council on International Educational Exchange (CIEE),* 52 Poland Street, London W1V 4JQ, tel 0171-478 2006, fax, 0171-734 7322, e-mail infouk@-ciee.org, — administers the US/UK Career Development Programme to promote transnational training for qualified individuals. The aim of the programme is to gain practical work experience in the US or the UK. This programme is administered in the US by AIPT, 10400 Little Patuxent Parkway, Suite 250, Columbia MD 21044-3510, tel 410-997-2200, fax 410-992-3924.

*The League for the Exchange of Commonwealth Teachers,* Commonwealth House, 7 Lion Yard, Tremadoc Road, Clapham, London SW4 7NQ, tel 0171-498 1101, fax 0171-720 5403 — arranges for British teachers with at least 5 years' teaching experience, aged generally between 25 and 45, to exchange their post for one year with a teacher from another Commonwealth country. Included in the scheme are about 23 overseas Commonwealth countries. Successful candidates will continue to receive their salary together with a travel grant. A short-term programme also exists. Publications include a twice-yearly newsletter for past, present, and future exchangees *The Commonwealth Times* and the annual report *Exchange Teacher* which comes out each May.

*United States Information Agency (USIA),* English Programs Division, E/AL, Room 304, 301 4th Street, SW, Washington, DC 20547, tel 202-619-5869, fax 202-401-1250, e-mail english@usia.gov, http://www.usia.gov/education/engteaching/eal-ndx.htm — recruits American academics in the field of TEFL/TESL and Applied Lingustics for short-term assignments abroad, to work on curriculum projects, teacher training, English for Specialised Purposes, training seminars, materials development and similar short-term projects. Thy may also supply a list of *Opportunities for Teaching English Abroad* with organisations recruiting US citizens for English language teaching positions abroad.

## THE BRITISH COUNCIL

Apart from teaching and other posts within the British Council (see under *British Government Departments),* the BC is also active as a recruiting agency for teaching and educational advisory posts in foreign governments and institutions. Most vacancies are for senior English language positions at all levels of education, so the necessary requirements are usually a degree or diploma in education, or a TEFL qualification at Diploma or PGCE level. Teaching experience is always required, except for lectureships and assistantships in some less 'popular' destinations. The scope of appointments is worldwide, but concentrated mainly in the non-English speaking countries. Contracts are from one to three years; and although terms and conditions are not standardised, all teachers employed through London have their air fares paid and receive a baggage allowance.

Further details can be obtained from the Overseas Educational Appointments Department, *The British Council,* Medlock Street, Manchester M15 4PR, from whom the free booklet *Teaching Overseas* is available. Information on qualifications is available from the British Council Information Unit (see above). Their information sheet on *Employment in TEFL* is also useful. The many BC offices and resource centres around the world (and their noticeboards) can be a useful source of vacancies and contacts for private tutors, and in local language schools and universities.

## PRIVATE SCHOOLS

*The European Council of International Schools (ECIS),* 21 Lavant Street, Peters-field, Hants GU32 3EL, tel 01730-268244, fax 01730-267914, e-mail 100412.242@compuserve. com, http://www.ecis.org — is an organisation of over 420 independent international schools around the world from Japan to the United States. It has associate and affiliate members among other education-related organisations; and assists in staffing member schools and advertises vacancies on the ECIS World Wide Web site. ECIS publishes: the *ECIS International Schools Directory* (which is also accessible at their web-site), enabling global access to information about 800 or so independent and international schools; a newsletter; and the semi-annual *International Schools Journal* concerned specifically with education in international schools. The medium of instruction in the various subjects is usually English. Applications are welcome from candidates who are suitably qualified and have a minimum of two years' recent full-time experience within the age range 3-18. Individual members of ECIS may also make use of the Council's placement service, which matches applications to current vacancies, circulating professional dossiers to appropriate schools; and also be considered for the twice yearly London Recruitment Centres which are attended by school representatives from all over the world.

ECIS North American Office is at: 105 Tuxford Terrace, Basking Ridge, New Jersey 07920, tel 908-903-0552, fax 908-580-9381, e-mail malyecisna@aol.com. Also offices in Madrid, and Victoria, Australia.

*Gabbitas Educational Consultants Ltd.,* 126-130 Regent Street, London W1R 6EE, tel 0171-734 0161 or 439 2071, fax 0171-437 1764 — is concerned with longer-term placements at English-medium schools for candidates with British teaching qualifications, not so much TEFL, and stresses that 'we receive too many enquiries from prospective EFL teachers whom we cannot help.'

*International Schools Service,* PO Box 5910, Princeton, New Jersey 08543, tel 609-452-0990, fax 609-452-2690 — primarily seeks to place state certified teachers in English-medium international schools following an American curriculum. They hold recruitment meetings in February and June attended by approximately 100 schools worldwide.

*Worldwide Education Service (WES),* Canada House, 272 Field End Road, Eastcote, Middlesex HA4 9PE, tel 0181-866 4400, fax 0181-429 4838 — recruits mostly full-time teachers worldwide for international schools. WES maintains a register of qualified teachers. This service works at the nursery, primary and secondary levels of teaching, as well as tutorial organisations and English language schools. WES is a consultancy for the Bell language schools. Include an SAE with your request for information.

## LANGUAGE SCHOOLS

English language teachers (Teachers of English as a Foreign Language, sometimes called TEFL or EFL teachers, or TESOL or ESL teachers in America) can find a useful source of employment in the many language schools abroad, and increasingly in schools and universities. Although methods based on 'role-plays' and communication are widely used — which mean that teaching can be entirely in English — a knowledge of the country's language and the experience of learning it is always an asset, and sometimes a requirement. *A Mouthful of Air* by Anthony Burgess (Hutchinson), about 'language and languages, especially English', provides an introduction to these general principles of language-learning and phonology which will help all English language teachers. It is good to be aware, also, of the general principles of classroom management if you are to teach large groups; many of the wide range of EFL or ELT (English Language

Teaching) textbooks available also have a teacher's book which gives help on these practical matters.

Generally, being on time and courteous, as well as being of a reasonably smart appearance, will count for a lot in the world of Teaching English as a Foreign Language. Many language schools hire native speakers who simply turn up in person at the school, or are known to someone already teaching there. Being an EFL teacher often means, in practice, working freelance, or having several jobs, so the principles of the creative job search certainly apply; and when you have a current job this does not mean you should not be on the lookout for other job opportunities in future.

It is better, of course, for the teacher to be able to arrange employment before setting off; but this often means going through a rather more formal and time-consuming process; so a trip to the country concerned — to visit some language schools yourself — may be a good idea. Some international chains of language schools run four-week or eight-week training courses in the UK and other countries for more formal entry into the profession; and these have become indispensible if you want to pursue a longer-term career or increase your earning power (and will certainly be necessary if you return home to teach English later). The Cambridge/RSA Certificate is the main one, and the equivalent Trinity College course (see above). The more advanced Cambridge/RSA Diploma is becoming popular with those wishing to have an edge over those who only hold the Certificate; and a track-record, experience, and good references are equally important in finding new work. In some cases, teachers are also required to take a short induction course in the school's own teaching methods before they start, in addition to any qualifications they have.

In fact, with this enormous demand for English teachers in many parts of the world, opportunities for EFL teachers wishing to work abroad have never been better. But the profession is becoming more regulated, as well as crowded: the number of English language teachers trained to Certficate level has increased enormously, and there is stiff competition for the more prestigious and better-paid jobs. It can be easy to find work but difficult to develop a longer-term career in TEFL.

The weekly *Times Educational Supplement* published every Friday carries a strong overseas TEFL vacancies section. These jobs generally require qualifications and/or experience. You can contact The *TES,* PO Box 14, Harold Hill, Romford, Essex RM3 8EQ, tel 0178-378379. The minimum subscription is for six months, and is at the time of writing $68.50 in the US and £49.50 in Europe.

*AEON Intercultural USA,* 9301 Wilshire Blvd. Suite 202, Beverly Hills, CA 90210, tel 310-550-0940, fax 310-550-1463 — has the largest chain of English conversation schools in Japan with 230 branch schools, 450 foreign teachers and 2,500 Japanese employees. Aeon hires new teachers year round to fill one-year contracts. A four-year college/university degree in any major is required. They provide a fully furnished apartment at a subsidised rent, full sickness and accident insurance, and return airfare. Teachers are recruited in the United States and Canada. Resumes should be sent to the above office. Also see their Web Site: http://www.aeonet.com. An essay entitled 'Why I want to Live and Work in Japan' is also required. Other recruitment offices are at: 203 N. LaSalle Street 2100, Chicago, IL 60601, tel 312-251-0900; and 230 Park Avenue 1000, New York, NY 101169, tel 212-808-3080.

*ELS Language Centers,* Director of Field Operations, International Division, 5761 Buckingham Parkway, Culver City, CA 90230, USA, tel 213-642-0982, fax 642-410-4688 — has language schools in the following locations: Abu Dhabi, Al Ain, Bangkok, Beijing, Buenos Aires, Cali, Curitiba, Jakarta, Kaohsiung (Taiwan), Kobe, Kuala Lumpur, Kuching, Kuwait City, Lanzhou, London, Osaka, Petaling Jaya, Pusan (Korea), Rio de Janeiro, Riyadh, São Paulo, Sapporo,

Seoul, Sydney, Taegu, Taichung, Taipei, Tokyo, and Wagga Wagga. Further information can be obtained from the above address. Enquiries should be accompanied by your CV. Candidates must have a minimum of a bachelor's degree and a TEFL Certificate and preferably one or two years' experience.

*ILC Recruitment (International Language Centres),* Palace Court, White Rock, Hastings, Esat Sussex TN34 1JY, tel 01424-720109, fax 01424-720323 — recruits for International Language Centres around the world and in the UK, and for non-ILC employers worldwide.

*i to i international projects,* Notre Dame SFC, Saint Mark's Avenue, Leeds LS2 9BL, tel 0113-245 3515 (for information pack), fax 0113-245 3350, e-mail 106144.174@compuserve.com, http://ourworld.compuserve.com/home pages/i-to-i — offers vocational guidance to young people in the North of England (as well as workshops on independent travel). Placements are available in Russia, India, Greece, and Turkey for people age 17-25. Length varies from six weeks to three months. Board and accommodation provided. Local salary in Greece and Turkey. Volunteers must find their own travel and insurance costs, plus the placement fee of £390. All teaching assistants will need to take a twenty-hour TEFL course. Applications two months before travel.

*inlingua Teacher Training & Recruitment* Rodney Lodge, Rodney Road, Cheltenham GL50 1JF, tel 01242-253171 — each year recruits approximately 200 teachers of English as a Foreign Language to work within inlingua and non-inlingua schools abroad. Vacancies occur mainly in Western and Eastern Europe with some vacancies in Far East Asia. Minimum qualifications required are Trinity Cert TESOL or RSA CELTA or inlingua Introduction to TEFL. Degree often required. Also arrange Trinity TESOL courses throughout the year plus two Introduction to TEFL courses. Contact the Administrator for further details.

*International House,* 106 Piccadilly, London W1V 9FL, tel 0171-491 2598, fax 0171-409 0959, e-mail 100733.511@compuserve.com — offers around 300 TEFL posts a year in around 93 affiliated schools in 25 countries in Europe, the Middle East, North Africa, South America and the Far East, from Argentina to Ukraine, and is the largest trainer of Cambridge/RSA Certificate (CELTA) and Diploma (DELTA) candidates in the world. It has around 300 jobs to offer each year. The minimum qualification for an appointment is a CELTA with a Pass Grade B. Most recruiting is carried out in spring or early summer in preparation for the beginning of the next academic year. However some posts are available at other times of the year. Contracts in Europe are normally for 9-12 months, while those further afield tend to be for two years. These are normally renewable by mutual consent. Travelling expenses and settling-in allowances are paid. For further details, contact the Staffing Unit at *International House* which also produces an advice leaflet and handbook of training courses.

*International Language Services,* 36 Fowlers Road, Salisbury, Wiltshire SP1 1ED, tel 01722-331011, fax 01722-328324 — recruits teachers for Sweden. Applicants should be between 22 and 40 with a degree and a recognised TEFL qualification. Single teachers are preferred; exceptionally, married couples who both teach can be considered.

*Language Matters,* 2 Rookery Road, Selly Oak, Birmingham B29 7DQ, tel/fax 0121-477 1988 — places qualified language teachers in posts in Spain, Portugal, Greece, Poland among other European countries and Abu Dhabi and Japan. Contracts are usually for 9 months with full local employment protection. A CV, photographs and references are required.

*Nord-Anglia International,* 10 Eden Place, Cheadle, Cheshire SK8 1AT, tel 0161-491 4191, fax 0161-491 4408 — recruits internationally and for its summer schools in the UK. Cambridge/RSA Certificate or equivalent required.

*Saxoncourt Recruitment,* 59 South Molton Street, London W1Y 1HH, fax 0171-499 9374 — is a specialist EFL recruitment service recruiting over 200 teachers annually for schools in Asia, Western Europe, Eastern Europe, South America, and Africa. Candidates must have either Cambridge/RSA or Trinity College London TEFL Cert. Applicants should send a CV and covering letter to the Recruitment manager at the above address.

## OTHER OPPORTUNITIES

*Berlitz (UK) Limited,* 9-13 Grosvenor Street, London W1A 3BZ, tel 0171-915 0909, fax 0171-915 0222 — does not recruit teachers for schools abroad. 'Each country has its own method of recruitment,' they say. 'School directors normally require applicants to be available for interview in the country concerned.' They do hold a list of a selection of Berlitz schools around the world, though, in many countries from Austria to Venezuela. The headquarters of *Berlitz International* may also be contacted for a full list, at 400 Alexander Park Drive, Princeton, NJ 08540.

*Britain-Vietnam Friendship Society,* Flat 2, 26 Tomlins Grove, London E3 4NX, tel/fax 0181-980 7146 — in co-operation with the Vietnamese NGO Highland Education Development Organisation (HEDO) seeks qualified teachers of English, willing to volunteer for one year, teaching in the highland provinces of Vietnam. Accommodation, food, plus a small allowance are offered. Send an SAE for details.

*CfBT Education Services,* 1 The Chambers, East Street, Reading RG1 4JD, tel 0118-523910, fax 0118-523924 — recruits qualified and experienced teachers of EFL for overseas posts in Brunei, Malaysia, Oman and Turkey.

*Christians Abroad,* 1 Stockwell Green, London SW9 9HP, tel 0171-737 7811, fax 0171-737327 — recruits qualified English teachers on behalf of overseas employers, mainly in sub-Saharan Africa.

The *Council on International Educational Exchange (CIEE),* (see above) runs the Japan Exchange and Teaching programme (JET). This is an official Japanes government programme involving the recruitment of Assistant Language Teachers from Great Britain, Ireland, the USA, Canada, Australia, and New Zealand. See the chapter on *Japan* for further information.

*English Contacts Abroad,* PO Box 126, Oxford OX2 6UB — is an international networking service for English language teachers thinking of going abroad; and will put you in touch with a teacher on the spot or supply lists of local schools currently recruiting teachers. They may also provide useful information and advice about living and working in that country. An administration fee of £48 is charged; and an SAE and CV should be enclosed with your enquiry.

*Teaching Abroad,* 46 Beech View, Angmering, Sussex BN16 4DE, tel 01903-859911, fax 01903-785779, e-mail teaching-abroad@garlands.uk.com, http://www.garlands.uk.com/ta — requires paying teachers to work in Poland, India, Ukraine, Ghana, and Russia. No TEFL or teaching qualifications are required. Dates by arrangement. Summer and long-term work (for up to a year) available. Back-up services for teachers working in each country. Prices (ranging from around £500 to £2,000 include a home and all meals with a local family or in a comfortable hostel for teachers, and may include air fare.

*United States Information Agency (USIA),* English Language Teaching Division, 301 4th Street W, Washington DC 20547 — is roughly the equivalent of the British Council, with many English teaching programmes, especially in developing countries. Most teachers are hired directly by the centre in question. A list of centres is available from the above address. Under the auspices of UISA, the Fulbright Commission administers the *Council for International Exchange of Scholars,* 3007 Tilden St NW, Suite 5M, Washington, DC 20008-3009. A PhD is normally required for high-level teaching vacancies in a variety of countries, particularly in central end eastern Europe. Also see *USIA* entry under *Teacher Exchange Schemes and Assistantships.*

*WorldTeach,* Harvard Institute for International Development, One Eliot Street, Cambridge, Massachusetts 02138-5705 — is a private non-profit organisation sending English-speaking volunteers abroad primarily to teach English. There are programmes in Eastern Europe, Central America and East Asia, including China. A fee of about $3,500 is paid to cover transportation and other costs; and teachers receive a stipend equivalent to local teaching rates.

## HIGHER EDUCATION

*The Association of Commonwealth Universities,* John Foster House, 36 Gordon Square, London WC1H 0PF, tel 0171-387 8572 — provides facilities for any member university (and for certain other Commonwealth institutions) to invite applications and assess candidates from outside its own region for vacancies on its staff. The service is most frequently used by universities in Australia, New Zealand, the South Pacific, Papua New Guinea, Malaysia, Brunei Darussalam, the West Indies, Botswana, Lesotho, Swaziland and Zimbabwe. Vacancies are advertised as they arise in the UK national press, and details are circulated to university registrars and careers advisory services in the UK.

## SOURCES OF INFORMATION

All the organisations above provide brochures and information on their services. If you want to apply direct to schools abroad, local telephone or business directories are a good starting point; and some cultural institutes can provide lists of possible employers. A number of relevant reference sources will be found under *Specific Contacts* in the various chapters in *Worldwide Employment.*

Those who wish to make direct applications to foreign universities, academies, colleges, and research institutes will find a very comprehensive listing of addresses in the book *The World of Learning,* published by Europa and available in public reference libraries.

Detailed information about universities in all Commonwealth countries is contained in the *Commonwealth Universities Yearbook,* which is published by the Association of Commonwealth Universities (see above). They also publish the biennial *Awards for Postgraduate Study at Commonwealth Universities* which gives information about awards open to graduates of Commonwealth universities who wish to undertake postgraduate study or research in another Commonwealth country; and, also biennial, *Awards for University Teachers and Research Workers*, which gives information for university teaching and research staff who wish to research, study or teach in a Commonwealth country other than their own. These books are available for consultation in academic and public reference libraries, and in many British Council offices.

A directory which contains information about higher education and other teaching qualifications and their international comparability is the *International Guide to Qualifications in Education,* published by NARIC (National Academic Recognition Information Centre), Mansell Publishing, Wellington House, 125 Strand, London WC2R 0BB.

**Useful Publications**
*EL Gazette,* 10 Wrights Lane, London W8 6TA, is a monthly newspaper dealing with all aspects of English language teaching. It includes country reports, information on training and qualifications, and some job advertisements. It is available from specialist language-teaching bookshops or by subscription. They publish (in association with EFL Ltd., 9 Hope Street, Douglas, Isle of Man 1M1 1AQ, British Isles) the annual *ELT Guide,* with many useful addresses and contacts including intensive training courses and US university programmes, and ELT specialist bookshops worldwide.

*Teaching Abroad: Opportunities for US Educators Worldwide,* is available from The Institute of International Education, 809 United Nations Plaza, New York, NY 10017.

*Teaching English Abroad,* by Susan Griffith (Vacation Work) has indispensable information on training for TEFL, how to find work abroad, and lists of language schools and agencies in many countries.

*TESOL Placement Bulletin,* published by Teachers of English to Speakers of Other Languages, Inc., 1600 Cameron Street, Suite 300, Alexandria, Virginia 22314-2751, e-mail place@tesol.edu — is a very useful bi-monthly listing of teaching positions, teacher exchanges and grant announcements for English Language Professionals. Annual subscription is presently $21 (USA, Canada and Mexico) and $31 elsewhere. Subscriptions are only available to members of TESOL. Members are also eligible for the TESOL Placement Service. For further information contact the TESOL Membership Department at the above address. TESOL, Inc. also publishes the *Directory of Professional Preparation Programs in TESOL in the US,* at $34 plus postage.

Some booklets on career prospects in teaching overseas are:

*Teaching Overseas,* from The British Council, Medlock Street, Manchester M15 4AA. Also, the British Council Information Unit produces a series of English Studies Information Sheets which list training courses available at a number of levels for EFL.

*Opportunities in Education Overseas,* is published by the Overseas Development Administration, 94 Victoria Street, London SW1E SJL, tel 0171-917 7000.

# Transport, Tourism, and Hospitality

The tourist and transport industries form a vast source of employment for millions of people worldwide. While the jobs described in this chapter may take you travelling around the world, some will mean that you are based at home. If you work as an airline pilot or a long-distance driver, or in the merchant navy, there may be no need to relocate to another country. The seasonal or permanent foreign-based staff of British or US tour operators will spend more time abroad; and working in tourism and hospitality is a good way for you to subsidise your own travels and see the world. See *Work Your Way Around the World* for more ideas on this. Vacation Work also publishes *Working in Tourism* for seasonal and permanent staff in this industry.

## Merchant Navy

Following a period of retrenchment, which has seen a continuing decline in the number of ships in the British Merchant Navy, recruitment is now on the increase again. There are currently vacancies for appropriately qualified applicants for training as deck and engineer officers as well as ratings. Enquiries should be made direct to individual shipping companies, lists of which appears in Lloyds *Register of Ships* and *Register of Shipowners* (Lloyds Register of Shipping, 71 Fenchurch Street, London EC3M 4BS), to be found in reference and business libraries. Addresses can also be found in the Financial Times' *World Shipping Year Book* and the Yellow Pages (or equivalent) of major seaport areas, under *Shipping Companies and Agents.* The Department of Transport runs a scheme to assist in the training of Merchant Navy officers; and further details as well as a list of companies participating in the scheme may be obtained from: The Co-ordinating Agent, Merchant Navy Officer Training, Carthusian Court, 12 Carthusian St, London EC1M 6EB, tel 0171-702 1100.

### OFFICERS

(1) *Junior Deck, Engine-room and Catering Ratings:* (Company sponsorship is essential before enrolment). Pre-sea training takes place at the National Sea Training College, Denton, Gravesend, Kent DA12 2HR, tel 01474-363656. There are no set academic entry qualifications but companies will normally expect candidates to have been successful in mathematics and English at GCSE level. Applicants must be in good health (including good eyesight), and are eligible for training from the age of 16 with a normal maximum of around 18 years.

(2) *Deck and Engineer Cadets:* these officer cadetships involve integrated programmes of college-based education and shipboard training leading to various National and Higher National awards as well as the statutory qualifications issued by the Department of Transport. Minimum entry requirements are the

possession of four GCSE passes (or equivalent), including English, maths, and a science subject, or two A Levels for a shortened cadetship. Again, candidates for the deck department must have excellent eyesight and good physical health. An upper age-limit for entry is 22.

(3) *Radio/Electronic Officers:* candidates are required to complete a course of training for the GMDSS Certificate at a college affiliated to the Association of Marine Electronic Radio Colleges (AMERC) before engagement; and a minimum of six months' experience at sea is needed to validate the Certificate and operate the ship's radio equipment singlehanded. Employment opportunities for sea-going radio officers are restricted. Enquiries should be addressed to one of the colleges listed below.

(4) *Pursers, Purserettes (including Nurses, Stewardesses/Hostesses etc.):* these administration and other posts are normally only found on passenger ships. There is usually a long waiting list. Trainees on board are not accepted for any of these positions. The ability to speak at least one foreign language is desirable, as well as some related experience, and qualifications like a Higher National Diploma (HND) in Hotel Management. Accountants, bookkeepers, and receptionists also work in the Purser's office. The earliest age of acceptance is usually at least 21, to allow for a period of proven experience in a related field of work after training and qualification.

(5) *Adult Entry:* vacancies for adult entrants/re-entrants do occur from time to time, especially for those with specialist skills or with engineering qualifications. Those interested should make periodic enquiries to individual shipping companies.

*Clyde Marine,* 209, Govan Road, Glasgow G51 1HJ, tel 0141-427 6886 — is a firm which can place cadets with these shipping companies.

*Glasgow College of Nautical Studies,* 21 Thistle Street, Glasgow G5 9XB, tel 0141-429 3201; *Liverpool John Moores University,* Byrom Street, Liverpool L3 3AF, tel 0151-231 2294; and *Southampton Institute,* Warsash Campus, Newtown Road, Warsash, Hampshire SO3 9ZL, tel 01489-576161 — are some of those in the UK offering training for deck officers and ratings.

*Trinity House,* Tower Hill, London EC3N 4DH, tel 0171-480 6601 offers awards and scholarships.

## RATINGS

Ratings are non-officer technical, engineering and other staff, and these jobs are often filled by staff from non English-speaking and lower wage countries. Entry as a junior deck or catering rating is generally restricted to young persons aged 16-17½. Able Seaman (AB) certificates are issued to deck ratings who have passed the qualifying exam and complied with regulations regarding periods of service and pre-sea training. Details of the certificates that can be gained by merchant navy ratings are given in the relevant Merchant Shipping Notices (see under *Further Details* below). Deckhands with company sponsorship normally attend a course at the *National Sea Training College* in Kent (see below) leading to the Department of Transport Efficent Deck Hand examination (EDH).

## FURTHER DETAILS

The *Department of Transport,* Marine Directorate, Sunley House, 90 High Holborn, London WC1V 6LP, issues a wide variety of Merchant Shipping Notices, including explanations of the regulations regarding examinations, qualifications, periods of service etc. required for attaining different ranks and information about relevant publications. A list of current Merchant Shipping Notices is available from the Department of Transport.

The *Southampton Institute of Higher Education,* East Park Terrace, Southampton SO14, tel 01703-319335, fax 01703-334441, can supply information, training and examination facilities for the GMDSS General Operator Certificate, which is required to run radio equipment on ships. Enquiries should be addressed to Systems Engineering faculty, which also runs courses in electronics and communications. Enquiries should be addressed to the Information Systems Division, Technology School, which also runs courses in electronics and communications.

The *National Sea Training College,* Denton, Gravesend, Kent DA12 2HR, tel 01474-363656 — is able to provide further information about recruitment opportunities for ratings. Information is also available careers advice services in your university or locality.

## PASSENGER AND CRUISE SHIPS

The openings described above apply equally to both passenger and freight vessels. In addition a variety of vacancies are available on passenger and cruise ships. Competition for these posts is very keen, and there are generally no trainee schemes (other than those in tourism, hospitality and catering) for this kind of work. Direct application should be made to those shipping companies who operate large passenger vessels (lists available in the *Journal of Commerce*) or the major cruise lines (Carnival, Princess Cruises, Royal Caribbean, Cunard, Costa, Holland America Line, Norwegian Cruise Line, Chandris Cruises, P&O Cruises, and latterly Disney); or more usually to the specialist agencies to which these companies will probably refer you. *Caterer and Hotelkeeper* magazine, Quadrant House, The Quadrant, Sutton, Surrey SM2 5AS, has occasional vacancies on cruise ships in its appoinments section; and *Overseas Jobs Express,* Premier House, Shoreham Airport, West Sussex BN43 5FF, also carries some vacancies (under *Cruising*). The following is a guide to some specialist staff areas and their requirements:

(a) *Assistant Purser/Purserette* — secretarial, clerical and reception work. Candidates should be 21-30, with GCSEs in English and maths, shorthand at 120 wpm, typing at 55 wpm, and have a pleasant manner.

(b) *Children's Host/Hostess* — responsible to the purser for children on board (organising games, entertainments etc.). Candidates, aged 25-35, should possess the relevant qualifications and experience for working with the under 12 age range. (Some ships also take on Nursery Stewards/Stewardesses, who may be younger, but must have an NNEB Certificate or equivalent).

(c) *Social Host/Hostess* — plays host to passengers, especially the old and lonely, and organises general passenger entertainment. Candidates, aged 26-34, should combine a high educational standard with a sympathetic manner and good organisational ability.

(d) *Telephonist* — maintains a 24-hour service on a duty rota. Candidates should be aged 24-35 with professional training and experience. Knowledge of at least one continental language is preferable.

(e) *Hairdresser* — must hold a recognised hairdressing diploma, and be fully trained and qualified in styling, beauty culture and manicure. Experience (as with all these posts) is an advantage.

(f) *Retail Assistant* — must have several years retail experience.

There is really a wide range of jobs available on cruise and passenger ships; and a useful guide to the field is *Working on Cruise Ships* by Sandra Bow (Vacation Work) which has a more detailed 'ABC' of these vacancies and useful background information. Some areas where jobs are often advertised are: gift shops/retail; hairdressing/beauty; shore excursions/guides; casino staff; cruise staff/entertainment; technical/engineering; sports/fitness; hotel management/pursers office; medical; and photography.

*Fieldings Worldwide Cruises,* is a guide for cruise line passsengers, published by Fielding Worldwide Inc., 308 South Cataline Avenue, Redondo Beach, CA 90277. which includes lots of information about ships, the lines, and ports of call. The *International Cruise Line Association* can be contacted at: 500 Fifth Avenue, Suite 1407, New York, NY 10110, tel 212-921-0066. Some recruitment agency and cruise line addresses in the UK and USA follow:

*Allders International (Ships) Ltd.,* 84/98 Southampton Road, Eastleigh, Hampshire SO5 5ZF, tel 01703-644599 — recruits experienced retail staff and beauty therapists/hairstylists for their retail concessions on board cruise ships worldwide and also UK ships and ferries. Candidates must be at least 23 years old and are required to work on board for a period of six months, which is followed by one month's leave. Also in the US: 1510 17th St, Fort Lauderdale, FL 33316, tel 305-763-8551.

*Blue Seas International Cruise Services Inc.,* 530 East 84th Street, Suite 5R, New York, NY 10028-7355, tel 212-734-6749 — recruits candidates for shipboard positions worldwide; they charge a consultation fee and then 15% of your gross salary if hired.

*Carnival Cruise Lines,* Walter House, 418-422 Strand, London WC2R 0PT, tel 0171-240 8471; 3655 NW 87th Avenue, Miami, FL 33178, tel 305-599-2600.

*Chandris Cruises,* 17 Old Park Lane, London W1Y 3LH, tel 0171-412 3999; 5200 Blue Lagoon Drive, Miami, FL 33126, tel 305-262-6677.

*Costa Cruise Lines,* Albany House, 45-49 Mortimer Street, London W1N 8JL; World Trade Center, 80 SW 8th St, Miami, FL 33130-3097, tel 305-359-7325; VC 11 San Nicola Alla Dogana 9/32, Napoli, Italy, tel 81-5512483.

*Crewfinders (Marine Placement Agency),* 2 Markham Avenue, Sunderland SR6 7DE; tel 0191-529 4397.

*Cunard Line,* South Western House, Canute Road, Southampton SO9 1ZA, tel 01703-716500; 555 Fifth Avenue, New York NY 10017, tel 212-880-7500.

*Holland America Line,* 300 Elliott Avenue West, Seattle, WA 98119; tel 206-281-3535.

*Logbridge Ltd.,* South Western House, Canute Road, Southampton SO14 3EW, tel 01703-631331 — recruits qualified individuals with at least two years' experience in luxury hotels or restaurants and possessing an excellent command of English at every level, for some of the world's most prestigious liners (QE2, Vistafjord, Sea Goddess I and II, and Royal Viking Sun). Applicants are requested to forward a full CV, references, and passport-sized photo.

*Norwegian Cruise Line,* Brook House, 229 Shepherds Bush Road, Hammersmith, London W6 7NL, tel 0171-4936041; 95 Merrick Way, Coral Gables, FL 33134, tel 305-447-9660.

*Oceanic Associates,* 77 Montem Road, Forest Hill, London SE23 1SH, fax 0171-6907576 — recruits reception and hotel staff, bar staff, photographers, and youth counsellors (NNEB) in the UK for American cruise ships.

*P&O Cruises,* Richmond House, Terminus Terrace, Southampton SO14 3PN, tel 01703-534200.

*Princess Cruises,* 77 New Oxford Street, London WC1A 1PP, tel 0171-8002345; 10100 Santa Monica Blvd, Los Angeles, CA 90067, tel 310-553-1770.

*Royal Caribbean Cruise Line,* Royal Caribbean House, Addlestone Road, Weybridge, Surrey KT15 2UE, tel 01932-820230; 1050 Caribbean Way, Miami, FL 33132-2601, tel 305-539-6000.

*Renaissance Cruises Inc.,* 1800 Eller Drive, Suite 300, PO Box 350307, Fort Lauderdale. FL 33335-0307, tel 305-463-0982, fax 305-463-8121 — is a cruise line operating around the world requiring bar staff, silver service waiters, cruise directors, stewardesses, and cooks. Enquiries to the Fleet Personnel Office.

*Steiner Training Ltd.,* 57-65 The Broadway, Stanmore, Middlesex HA7 4DU — recruit hairdressers, beauty therapists, and aerobic instructors for their health spas on more than 100 cruise ships around the world. They require a CV, copies of certificates, and a photo.

*Viking Recruitment,* Protea House, Marine Parade, Dover, Kent CT17 9BW; tel 01304-240881. For officers only, with relevant technical skills and experience.

# Civil Aviation

Civil Aviation is a constantly expanding industry, which each year offers career possibilities to a growing number of people. Generally, air traffic controllers, airport staff, and other ground crew personnel, with the exception of a few topflight managers and adminstrators, tend to be recruited locally; and foreign airlines prefer to recruit their own nationals in their home country. Even the developing countries, which in the past have relied on experienced personnel from Britain and the USA, are now training their own staff and becoming more self-reliant. Expertise in management and adminstration is required by many airlines in the formerly communist countries — and some others — which are currently upgrading their services and systems, in the fields of aircraft maintenance, telecommunications and information technology. Some vacancies of this sort can be found in under *Aviation* in the 'Jobs' section of *Overseas Jobs Express* (see above).

The information below relates mainly to two careers: pilot and cabin crew, where personnel will mostly be based at home but will travel internationally in the course of their duties, and may be transferred or move abroad in the course of their career.

## PILOTS

The main qualification to fly as an airline pilot in the UK is a Civil Aviation Authority Commercial Pilot's Licence and Instrument Rating, and to fly as an airline captain it is necessary to hold the senior CAA professional pilot's licence, the Airline Transport Pilot's Licence. At present only the major British airlines have any form of sponsorship scheme.

The essential requirements for applicants are as follows (subject to review):-
*Academic:* Five GCSEs at Grade C or above, including English language, mathematics and a science subject, preferably physics. British Airways also require two A levels, preferably in mathematics and physics.
*Age:* When training commences the pilot cadet must be at least 18.
*Medical:* A high standard of physical fitness is required.

The only schools which run CAA approved courses for the Commercial Pilot's Licence and Instrument Rating are:

*Bristow Helicopters,* Redhill Aerodrome, Redhill, Surrey RH1 5JZ
*Cabair College of Air Training,* Cranfield Airfield, Bedford MK43 0AI
*Oxford Air Training School,* Oxford Airport, Kidlington, Oxford OX5 1RA

Further information can be obtained from the Corporate Communications Department, *Civil Aviation Authority,* CAA House, 45-59 Kingsway, London WC2B 6TE, tel 0171-379 7311.

## CABIN CREW

The work of air stewards and air stewardesses (or hostesses) is very demanding: during one flight they can expect to fulfil the roles of receptionist, clerk, nurse, waiter/waitress, nanny, guide and companion. While experience in any of these occupations is obviously an advantage, a more important qualification is the ability to discharge all these duties and retain an unruffled appearance and a pleasant humour throughout.

Although applicants are normally required to have reached a GCSE standard of education, and fluency in at least one foreign language is preferred, the selection procedure is based far more on the applicant's disposition and ability to converse pleasantly, freely and reassuringly in English. An above average intelligence and general awareness are essential.

Good health is another deciding factor; for practical reasons there are also height and weight limitations and an attractive and neat appearance is essential. The minimum entry age is 18, but most successful candidates are in their early to mid-twenties.

## FURTHER DETAILS

Apart from the sponsored pilot training schemes discussed above, applicants for appointments with British airlines, and with private air charter and helicopter services, should contact companies direct; a full list in the UK can be found in the *Directory of British Aviation* (under *Commercial Aviation*) available in most reference and business libraries.

### General Publications

Leaflets on careers in Civil Aviation can also be found in your local careers offices. The Civil Aviation Authority publishes a number of books and pamphlets, including some that are of interest to prospective air and ground crew members. A catalogue is available from the *CAA, Printing and Publication Services,* Greville House, 37 Gratton Road, Cheltenham, Glos GL5 2BN, tel 01242-235151.

# Road Transport

There are opportunities for drivers with relevant HGV licences and several years' experience in the UK, to drive vehicles on international routes, mainly within Europe, although a few companies operate on routes into Asia and North Africa. Knowledge of foreign languages is obviously helpful, although not essential. Most of the international companies prefer to employ drivers for a trial period of several months in Britain before sending them abroad.

Since most only employ a few drivers for their foreign routes, applicants should enquire about prospects for international work with more than one company. A wide variety of companies — removal and freight — are listed in the major cities' Yellow Pages under *Road Haulage,* and other business telephone directories.

If you are employed as an international trucker, or if you are running a haulage firm that operates on international routes, you are advised to obtain the *Guidance Notes — A Guide to Taking Your Lorry Abroad* from the *Department of Transport,* International Road Freight Office, Westgate House, Westgate Road, Newcastle-upon-Tyne NE1 1TW (tel 0191-201 4090).

The road transport trade associations in the UK can help with enquiries about international work. The publication, *ABC Freight Guide* (Centaur Communications, 50 Poland Street, London W1V 4AX) can be consulted in public libraries, along with business directories and Yellow Pages for names of employers.

# Travel and Tourism

## TOUR OPERATORS

The overseas requirements of conventional tour operators are mainly seasonal; and mainly involve couriers and representatives. As tourism becomes more specialised, though, so do the people who are needed. Coach tour operators also need coach drivers. There are guides who may have their own specialised skill or knowledge, campsite couriers and resort representatives, entertainment or administrative staff, and instructors in sports like skiing or windsurfing.

While the coach drivers and couriers work from a home base, representatives are based in towns and resorts abroad, and are sometimes either recruited locally or selected from among the permanent staff at home. The requirements for the different types of work are: a PSV licence and coach driving experience for drivers; fluency in another language or languages for couriers and representatives, who may also take short courses organised by their employers, and must have the ability to organise their tour groups, liaise with hotels, and generally be efficient, organised, and able to put people at their ease. Couriers and guides need to be able to cope with any emergencies that might arise. Like resort representatives, they also need a good knowledge of the place or places where they are located; activity holidays need instructors and supervisors; camping holidays require someone to maintain and clean the tents, as well as to greet clients; skiing holidays need chalet girls; and so on.

Recruitment for the summer season usually takes place any time from the previous September, and is often finished by February. The ads begin to appear in the summer (or even after Easter when the season ends) for skiing and winter holiday representatives and staff. Some ski companies do not advertise, as staff will come to them anyway; so prospective employees should do some research, and see which companies are offering skiing holidays; and make their first contact as early as they can. In fact, planning (including recruitment and training) is really an all-year activity for travel companies. This means your planning, too, should start early. Although the jobs themselves may be short-term, this does not mean you should leave your application to the last minute.

Word of mouth, and the techniques of the creative job search, are also important in an industry which itself involves meeting and getting on with people. This is often how jobs are found. Tourism trade fairs can be a way to find out more; and to meet the people who can employ you. The various national tourist offices are another useful source of information (there is a list of these offices in the UK in *Working in Tourism* — see below — or consult Yellow Pages and the other business directories).

Working in travel and tourism can be a way to travel yourself; or to find out more about the country concerned; and may be combined with other careers and job patterns. Administration in tourism is a good preparation for administration in other fields, for example. It is now estimated that this global industry employs one in every 15 workers worldwide, directly or indirectly; and it is an increasingly popular career choice. Applying on the spot, or in advance from your own country, are both options; but some previous experience, or at least one of the skills mentioned above, will help. A British company, Holiday Solutions (Sinclair House, The Avenue, Ealing, London W13 8NT; tel 0181-577 7400; fax 0181-737 7020) runs one-day courses for potential reps around the UK between September and April. The course aims to give clients a step-by-step guide on how to be successful at landing a rep's job.

The following are mostly general tour operators who carry out regular (but mostly seasonal) recruitment. A more detailed list can be found in *Summer Jobs Abroad, Summer Jobs in Britain, Working in Ski Resorts, and Working in Tourism* (which also has UK, European and US training courses and a guide to some more permanent jobs). These are all published by Vacation Work. It is advisable to enclose a large SAE when writing to the travel and tour companies below; and a letter or CV which shows you have the right experience and outlook.

*Airtours Holidays Ltd.,* Overseas Personnel Department, Wavell House, Holcombe Road, Helmshore, Rossendale, Lancashire BB4 4NB, tel 01706-240033 — needs: Overseas Representatives to work long and unsociable hours to ensure a high standard of customer service to guests on holiday in Europe, meeting sales and customer service targets. Applicants must be a minimum of 21 years of age, well groomed, with good communication and administration skills, and able to work on their own initiative. Experience of working in a customer service or sales environment is a must; Children's Representatives to be responsible for organising and running daily activities for groups of up to 15 children aged from 3-15 years; also to be involved in guiding, evening excursions and accompanying guests to and from the airport. A minimum of 20 years of age and both a strong desire to work with children and previous relevant experience necessary; Suncentre Representatives/Entertainers to be responsible for providing a varied programme of day and night-time activities. For people with strong entertainment skills, this position combines the role of entertainer and overseas representativeApplicants must be a minimum of 21 years of age with relevant entertainments experience.

*American Institute for Foreign Study (AIFS UK Ltd.),* 15-17 Young Street, London W8 5EH, tel 0171-376 0800, fax 0171-376 0789 — is an educational travel company based in the US which needs tour directors with local knowledge and experience to lead groups of North American High School students on their various itineraries in Europe. Tours last for one to three weeks over the summer. Applications should be sent to the Courier Office between October and February. The minimum knowledge is 21, and applicants should be fluent in at least one European language.

*Canvas Holidays Ltd.,* Courier Department, 12 Abbey Park Place, Dunfermline KY12 7PD, Scotland — need residential couriers (graduates and undergraduates) for the summer season in Austria, France, Italy, Spain, Germany and Switzerland.

*Club Cantabrica Holidays Ltd.,* 146-148 London Road, St Albans, Herts. AL1 1PQ — require campsite couriers, resort managers, maintenance staff and childrens' activities couriers (NNEB or equivalent) to work on campsites in France, Italy, Spain and Corfu in the summer. Must be available May to October and be over 21 years old. Knowledge of languages an advantage. Experience preferable. Please send a full CV and SAE before the end of November. Interviews January-February.

*CLUB MED,* 106-110 Brompton Road, London SW3 1JJ, tel 0171-225 1066 —

runs holiday villages in Europe and North Africa. Summer staff needs are for qualified and experienced instructors in golf, scuba-diving, sailing, water-skiing, riding and tennis, as well as hosts/hostesses, cashiers, nurses, physiotherapists, playgroup leaders and restaurant, boutique, and administrative personnel. Ages from 20 to 30. Applications should be submitted from November to February. Basic requirements are fluency in French, and if possible one other language, like German; and availability for work from April to October. Applications from EEA nationals only to the above address.

*Contiki Holidays,* Wells House, 15 Elmfield Road, Bromley BR1 1LS, tel 0181-290 6777 — specialises in touring holidays by coach throughout Europe, Australia, America, New Zealand, and Great Britain and Ireland. Tour managers and drivers are employed on a seasonal basis from March to October. Drivers should be PSV qualified and aged between 23-25. Tour managers should be outgoing and be capable of assisting in the overall organisation of the tour. Applications should be made in writing between September and January. Board, accommodation, medical insurance, and training provided. EEA nationals only.

*EF Educational Tours,* Kensington Cloisters, 5 Kensington Church Street, London W8 4LD, tel 0171-376 9400 — needs Tour Directors to lead groups of North American students around Europe over Easter and in June and July on educational tours. Applicants should be over 23, well-travelled and fluent in English and at least one other European language. Employment is for the duration of the the the tour, which may be from nine to 31 days. Applications from November to February at the above address.

*Eurocamp Summer Jobs,* PO Box 170, Liverpool L70 1ES, tel 01565-650053 — is a leading operator recruiting campsite staff from April to October. Campsite couriers should be over 18 and have a good working knowledge of a European language. Children's couriers organise activities for groups of children and must have experience of this kind of work. Eurocamp has sites in Austria, Belgium, Denmark, France, Germany, Greece, Italy, Luxembourg, Spain, and Switzerland. Interviews start in October.

*Inghams,* 10-18 Putney Hill, London SW15 6AX, tel 0181-780 4444 — well-known for their Chalet Skiing holidays, also have a summer programme. In winter they employ around 300 staff for Switzerland, Austria, Italy, France, Canada, and the States, including Hotel Managers, Chefs, Cooks/Chalet Girls/ Boys, Nannies, and Waitresses/Chambermaids. The summer staff are now employed in the same capacity as the winter staff. Formerly *Bladon Lines.*

*Jobs in the Alps,* 17 High Street, Gretton, Northants, NN17 3DE, tel 01536-771150 — arranges jobs in Alpine resorts in Europe. Winter jobs last from December to April. Summer jobs are generally 3 months, with some 6-month jobs in Germany for non-German speakers. In Switzerland and France knowledge of French and/or German is needed. Jobs include: night-porter; porter; cook; dishwasher; waiter and waitress; chambermaid; and a few barmaids and receptionists. Basic pay is £220 gross/£130 net per week for 9-hour day, 5 days a week. Write with SAE. Closing dates for interview 15 September/15 April.

*Mark Warner Ltd.,* 61-65 Kensington Church Street, London W8 4EP, tel 0171-393 3178 (personnel department) — require club managers, chefs, kitchen porters, watersports instructors, tennis instructors, ski hosts, chambermaids, waitresses, nannies, bar staff, nightwatch, handymen, accountants, and customer services officers for their summer watersports holidays in Turkey, Greece, Sardinia, Corsica, and Italy, and for their winter ski holidays in France, Switzerland, Austria, and Italy. Mark Warner also require staff for their Summer in the Alps programme.

*PGL Adventure,* Alton Court, Penyard Lane (874), Ross-on-Wye, Herefordshire HR9 5NR, tel 01989-764211 — run adventure holidays in France. They require canoe and sailing instructors, couriers/group leaders, kitchen, site and store assistants, drivers, fibreglassers, nurses and administrative assistants from May to September.

*PGL Young Adventure Ltd.,* at the same address, operates barge holidays in the Netherlands and need couriers/groups leaders to accompany groups on each departure from London for eight to 12 days mainly during July and August.

*Ski Peak Ltd.,* The Old Bakery, Dockenfield, Nr Farnham, Surrey GU10 4HX, tel 01252-794941 — are specialists to Vaujanay, Alpe D'Huez, France, and recruit for a small team of 16 from mid-December to end of April. Jobs available are resort and hotel reps, hotel chefs, hotel waitresses/chambermaids, barman, chalet girls, and nanny. Fluency in French is necessary for the first two jobs and useful with some of the others. Relevant experience in all cases is essential. Applicants must have friendly, outgoing personalities and be hardworking. Remuneration according to the job and includes free lift pass, medical insurance, board and lodging.

*Skiworld Ltd.,* 41 North End Road, West Kensington, London W14 8SZ, tel 0171-602 4826 — with its sister companies *Chalet World* and *Ski Val* recruits overseas staff for the winter season. Vacancies exist in top resorts within France, Switzerland, the USA and Canada. They require Resort Managers and Resort Representatives who have relevant language experience, related experience, and a good skiing ability; Head Chefs to run the kitchens of chalet hotels (50-70 heads); Chalet Girls/Boys/Couples to run their chalets, catering for up to 12 people; and Nannies (NNEB or equivalent) to run crèche facilities. All applicants need to have a friendly, outgoing personality; and there is a minimum age of 21 years. All staff have a weekly wage and accommodation; ski equipment and a lift pass will be provided; and applicants need to be available from early December to mid/end April. Please apply with CV and covering letter.

*Thomson Holidays,* Overseas Personnel Department, Greater London House, Hampstead Road, London NW1 7SD, tel 0171-383 1324 — is Britain's largest tour operator operating throughout the world. Meeting guests, organising social events, and giving advice and information on hotel and resort facilities, they will 'need to remain flexible on duties and location at all times'. Ages 22-35. Applicants should be fluent in English and at least one of the following: Spanish, German, Greek, Italian, French, Portuguese; and must have at least one year's experience working with the public in a Customer Service or quality sales role; be in good health and particularly well-groomed. Salary paid monthly in UK with commission on excursion sales.

Children's representatives also required to organise a varied programme of activities for children aged 4-11. Aged 19-30, applicants must have a childcare, infant teaching or nursing qualification, with a minimum of six months' practical experience working independently with large groups of children. Accommodation, meals and uniform provided. For all jobs, applicants must have a friendly, outgoing nature, lots of enthusiasm, tact, diplomacy, and a strong sense of purpose. Applicants must be available to work beginning April-end October and hold a UK or EU passport.

*Travelsphere Ltd.,* Compass House, Rockingham Road, Market Harborough, Leicestershire LE16 7QD, fax 01858-434323 — require tour escorts/couriers (20-30) to accompany groups of 40-50 people on European tours giving commentaries on places of interest and looking after the general well-being of the group. £25 per day plus commission on the sale of excursions. Hours are variable but may involve 6-day weeks. Minimum period of work 6 weeks between April and

October. Board and accommodation free of charge. Applicants must have a friendly outgoing personality, be hardworking and have a thorough knowledge of a European language, preferably German, Italian or French. Applications to the above address from January to March. Please enclose a full CV and a recent photograph.

*Vigvatten Natur Klubb,* Apartado Numero 3253, E-01002 Vitoria-Gasteiz, Spain, tel/fax 945-281794 — organises camps which run in sessions of two weeks over the summer to help Spanish children and teenagers (aged 8-18) to improve their knowledge of the English language, and to provide a balanced programme of leisure activities and adventure holidays. The first language of the camps is English. Monitors, support staff, cooks, and nurses are required; and all staff are required to take part in a training programme a few days before the start of each summer camp. Send off for an application form to the address above.

*Village Camps, Inc.,* CH-1854 Leysin, Switzerland, tel 25-342-338, fax 25-343-276 — runs summer activity and winter ski camps throughout Europe. Recruits counsellors and qualified instructors for these camps. Must be over 21, possess a working knowledge of a second European language and have experience in working with children.

## OVERLANDERS AND SPECIALIST OPERATORS

The overland tour companies differ from the regular operators and travel agencies in two main ways; in the places they go and how they do it — travelling through more difficult terrain to reach some of the most remote regions which have not yet been developed as destinations for mass tourism. Some organise these trips all year round; others operate just in the summer. This is not an expedition as such; an overland tour is promoted and marketed in much the same way as other forms of tourism. This is one kind of special interest tour where the main motivation is more than just a holiday. Overland tours or 'expeditions' involve adventure and self-discovery. There are also health and spa holidays; holidays for the disabled; holidays in leisure complexes; campsite holidays; senior citizen travel; ski and other sporting holidays (see above); language and youth travel; the cruise industry (see above); cultural tourism; and environmental tourism (eco-tourism — see *Agriculture and the Environment*).

In all of these areas tourism is becoming more 'realistic' and specialised; and the experience and qualifications called for will also be of a more specialised nature; your background outside the tourist industry in everything from sales and marketing to vehicle maintenance can be an advantage. On overland tours the type of work involved is very rigorous; but one of the main aims is participation on the part of all the travellers. So, many tours are run by one leader/driver, who is in charge of route planning, itinerary, driving, mechanical problems and any other difficulties which can arise on a long-distance trip in unfamiliar surroundings, of a legal or medical nature for instance. For insurance purposes, drivers must be aged 25 or over and have an HGV or PCV licence, depending on the type of vehicle used. They also need linguistic, mechanical and organisational abilities. Most companies prefer their drivers to work for two years (or two summers) as a minimum. Training of one form or another is always given; and the first tour might be as an unpaid assistant driver. Some of the less rugged tours are staffed by more than one; but three — a driver, a leader and a cook — is perhaps the upper limit.

The list of overland and specialist tour operators given below is by no means exhaustive (the number of companies in this category probably runs into hundreds), but is intended to give an idea of the scope of operations and recruitment policies. Other companies will be found by looking through the advertisements in *Trailfinder,* published three times yearly by Trailfinders Ltd.,

42-48 Earls Court Road, London W8 6EJ. *TNT Magazine,* 14-15 Child's Place, Earls Court, London, tel 0171-373 3377, contains advertisements for some of the main companies in Britain and is distributed free in London.

*Dragoman Adventure Travel,* 4 Camp Green, Debenham, Stowmarket IP14 6LA, tel 0171-370 1930 — needs drivers and leaders to conduct expeditions across Asia, Africa and South America. Applicants should be aged 25-30, and preferably have a PCV driving licence. Positions are available throughout the year for at least 18 months. Applications to the Operations Manager at the above address.

*Encounter Overland Ltd.,* 267 Old Brompton Road, London SW5 9JA — operates treks, safaris, expeditions in Africa, Asia and South America. Vehicles used are safari trucks. Groups of 20 people from around the world participate between the ages of 18 and 50. Employment is for leader drivers. Full-time job for about 3 years. Applicants 24-32; should have leadership abilities and mechanical aptitude. PCV is required but can be obtained during training.

*Explore Worldwide Ltd.,* 1 Frederick Street, Aldershot, Hampshire GU11 1LQ, tel 01252-333031 — annually recruit leaders for a comprehensive worldwide programme of small group adventure/exploratory holidays. Applicants should be over 23 and either already qualified first-aiders or prepared to undertake qualification. Preference will be given to those who can demonstrate previous travel experience — particularly in the Third World — linguistic ability and experience of working with groups. For some trekking tours, mountain leadership qualifications are essential.

*Guerba Expeditions Ltd.,* 101 Eden Vale Road, Westbury, Wiltshire BA13 3QX, tel 01373-826611 or 826689 — employs a number of expedition leaders for overland tours in Africa: applicants should have an HGV or PCV licence, be over 25, have experience of organisation and of handling groups of people, some basic ability in French, an aptitude for mechanics, a cool head and some knowledge and interest in Africa. US office: *Adventure Center,* 1311 63rd St, Suite 200, Emeryville, CA 94608, tel 510-654-1879.

*The Imaginative Traveller,* 14 Barley Mow Passage, Chiswick, London W4 4PH, tel 0181-742 3113 — is a leading adventure travel specialist to the Middle East, Turkey, India, Nepal, Britain and Ireland, South East Asia, and the Americas and employs tour leaders for their small groups who live in the various destinations for a minimum of 9 months. No specific skills are required, although the company emphasises sound experience in people management, and having the capacity to handle any crises. They also need to be knowledgeable about the destinations. Successful applicants go through an extensive training period.

*Journey Latin America Ltd.,* 14-16 Devonshire Road, Chiswick, London W4 2HD, tel 0181-747 8315 — is a large Latin American travel specialist operating tours in Latin America throughout the year, ranging from Mexico to Tierra del Fuego. The main requirements for tour leaders are a good working knowledge of Spanish or Portuguese, experience of the region and experience with groups or organising people (e.g. teachers). Tour leaders do not need to be drivers, since transport is organised locally. Journey Latin America regrets it is unable to offer general advice on employment in Latin America.

*Sundowners International,* 267 Old Brompton Road, London SW5 9JA — operates coach trips between London and Kathmandu. Couriers and drivers. Drivers must have PSV and mechanical aptitude. Couriers need leadership and organisation skills. Their Australian head office is: *Sundowners,* 151 Dorcas Street, Melbourne 3205, tel 03-690-2499.

*Tracks Africa* and *Tracks Europe,* 12 Abingdon Road, London W8 6AF, tel 0171-937 3028 — need drivers/couriers and cooks for their extensive range of camping tours in Europe. Drivers must hold English PSV licences; minimum age for all positions is 25. Driver/leaders are also required for overland safaris and expeditions in Africa. Drivers require HGV licences for the four-wheel drive expedition vehicles.

*Truck Africa,* 37 Ranelagh Gardens Mansions, Fulham, London SW6 3UQ, tel 0171-731 6142, fax 0171-371 7445 — is an overland tour operator requiring drivers and couriers. Drivers must be diesel mechanics with HGV licence and first-hand knowledge of travel in Africa or be prepared to train for at least 3 months with no subsequent guarantee of work.

*World Challenge Expeditions,* Black Arrow House, 2 Chandos Road, London NW10 6NF, tel 0181-961 1122, fax 0181-961 1155 — requires Expedition Leaders to supervise school expeditions to the developing countries. Fees depend on experience and qualifications. Applicants must have relevant experience of travel in developing countries and have appropriate qualifications in hill-walking, mountaineering, and first aid. For some countries knowledge of Spanish and French may be required. Board and lodging are free and costs and expenses are covered. Periods of work are 5 weeks between late June and August.

## EXPEDITIONS

Expeditions are one way to travel abroad and gain the experience and understanding which may lead to a job in another country. It may seem misleading to include these in a directory of jobs and careers, as almost without exception, participation in expeditions involves no financial reward and no employer-employee relationship. But travel experience is important if you are considering living and working abroad; and really there is a continuum of opportunities in tourism, as in voluntary work, some of which are paid and some which you pay for. These can be considered as somewhere on the fringes of work and education, like work placements or some volunteer work. Taking part in an expedition can be a valuable life experience; but is also good training for some of the jobs covered in this and the following chapters. It may be taken as a positive recommendation by many employers who are seeking leadership and planning skills. Most important of all, however, it is a way of learning more about yourself.

Mentioned below are a few organisations that run or sponsor expeditions, and the self-help organisatons that offer advice, assistance or even financial aid for independent expeditions.

These are generally organised, often at very irregular intervals, by schools, universities and associations or clubs, with leaders and crew members generally belonging to the organisation involved. Most have a scientific, educational, or environmental bias; the staffing needs for paid employment being for science graduates with relevant degrees in geology, biology, or conservation (depending on the expedition), as well as the photographers and leaders who will also be required. Having a wide range of skills, or being willing to learn, is an asset: cooking, driving, etc., will often be shared duties. The aim is often educational; and on school expeditions, the staff and leaders will include teaching among their other roles.

It should be stressed that the organisations below do not offer employment in any normal sense of the word. Most offer an interchange of ideas and information which will be useful for those thinking of planning or participating in an expedition.

*British Schools Exploring Society,* at the Royal Geographical Society, 1 Kensington Gore, London SW7 2AR, tel 0171-581 2057 — organises annual expeditions (about 6 weeks in duration) to arctic, sub-arctic or tropical regions, between July and September. Expeditions of up to one hundred people (16-20) from schools and colleges are led by experts in the field from universities, the services and industry, preferably with past expedition experience, and for this a register of personnel is maintained. Other 3-4 month expeditions are also mounted for those between school and universiy. Applications should be made in September of the previous year to the Executive Director.

The *Expedition Advisory Centre,* at the Royal Geographical Society (address above) — aims to advise and assist individuals and groups in planning expeditions overseas. The Centre provides information on all aspects such as planning, and organises an annual seminar which is the starting-point for many hundreds of projects. In addition, a number of publications are available, including *The Expedition Planners' Handbook*; and it publishes a booklet: *Joining an Expedition.* While the Centre does keep a list of all planned expeditions, it is not in a position to place individuals on these. Those who do have a particular skill to offer, and wish to be included on the register of personnel mentioned above should send an SAE to the Centre for the appropriate form.

*The Globetrotters Club,* BCM/Roving, London WC1N 3XX — is a club for international travellers. The principal benefit of its modestly priced membership is an interchange of information, ideas and hospitality through its directory of worldwide members. The bi-monthly newsletter *Globe* (circulated free to its members) includes a 'Mutual Aid' section in which free advertisements can be placed for travelling companions, expedition members, or contacts abroad.

*Raleigh International,* Raleigh House, 27 Parsons Green Lane, London SW6 4HZ, tel 0171-371 8585 — aims to develop the potential of young people by sending them on environmental and community projects around the world. Also see the *Voluntary Work* chapter.

*Servas International,* 11 St John St, Room 407, New York, NY 10038-4009, tel 212-267-0252 — runs a worldwide programme of free hospitality exchanges for travellers, to further world peace and understanding. Normally you don't stay with one host family for more than a couple of days, they advise. There is a joining fee of $55 and a refundable deposit of $25 for host lists which may be requested for up to five countries.

*WEXAS (World Expeditionary Association),* 45 Brompton Road, London SW3 1DE — provides members with advice and information through *Traveller,* a magazine which is published quarterly. It offers financial assistance to selected expeditions through its annual award programme administered by the Royal Geographical Society.

# Hospitality

The hospitality industry encompasses hotel and restaurant work, institutional catering, (staff canteens, hospitals, schools, etc.) and work in tourism. In the UK, it is the second largest employer in the country and there are plenty of career opportunities for hospitality staff to work abroad, especially those who speak the language. As an example 10% of the members of the Hotel Catering and Institutional Management Association (HCIMA) work overseas, in more than 90 countries (see below).

Hotel and restaurant work is often seasonal. Many hotels and restaurants need large numbers of extra workers to look after clients at the height of their tourist seasons — perhaps only for a few weeks. Such seasonal workers need not always have previous experience, or even knowledge of the local language, although this will help. These jobs only represent part of the picture; a temporary job can easily become a full-time one; and most restaurants and hotels need staff all the year round.

The work can be short or long-term; and you can begin your job search in your own country, or your chosen destination. The various travel guides are useful sources of names and addresses of potential employers: those published by *Lonely Planet* (PO Box 617, Hawthorn, Victoria 3122, Australia) or *Rough Guides* (1 Mercer Street, London WC2H 8QJ) are particularly recommended, and the many Vacation Work books (particularly *Summer Jobs Abroad*) which touch on hospitality and catering, especially in tourism, for cruise ships or for ski companies, are recommended, as are the international hotel directories, and especially any personal contacts you can make.

Representatives of travel firms in resorts around the world will often know the local hoteliers and restaurateurs, for example. To get a more permanent job, or follow an international career in hospitality (as in tourism), you will need better qualifications, more experience and skills, and especially a knowledge of languages (which in part you can acquire through living and working in the country). Work on cruise ships, in tourist complexes, and in the more up-market hotels is now largely limited to qualified and experienced personnel like this. International vacancies are advertised under *Hotel and Catering* in the 'Jobs' section of *Overseas Jobs Express* (see above) and in the trade journal *Caterer and Hotelkeeper,* Quadrant House, The Quadrant, Sutton, Surrey SM2 5AS, tel 01444-445566 (subscriptions).

For information on career prospects, the *Hotel Catering and Institutional Management Association (HCIMA),* 191 Trinity Road, London SW17 7HN, tel 0181-672 4251, fax 0181-682 1707, can supply various brochures; and can now also be contacted via the Internet at: http://hcima.org.uk/; e-mail: sabine@hcima.org.uk (for general enquiries): membership@hcima.org.uk (for membership details); pds@hcima.org.uk (for professional development services. Some information on worker exchange schemes is given below.

*Association for International Practical Training (AIPT),* Hospitality/Tourism Exchanges, Suite 250, 10400 Little Patuxent Parkway, Columbia, Maryland 21044-3510, tel 410-997-2200, fax 410-992-3924, e-mail aipt@aipt.org, http://www.aipt.org — arranges work experience and exchanges abroad for US citizens in the hospitality industry. The training period varies from six to 18 months, and the age limit from 18 to 35, depending on the country. These countries include Australia, Austria, Finland, France, Germany, Ireland, Japan, Malaysia, The Netherlands, Switzerland and the UK. Applicants should be either students or graduates in Hotel Management or Culinary Arts. Some countries will only accept graduates. In the UK, this scheme is now administered by the Council on International Educational Exchanges (CIEE), tel 0171-478 2006.

*Centre de Liaison Européen et International (CLEI),* 103 Avenue Herriot, F-56000 Vannes, France — can place young professionals in the hospitality industry in suitable hotels and restaurants in France. Placements may be preceded by a probationary period at CLEI's training centre in Vannes, Brittany or a French technical school. Arrangements can be made by individuals or through institutions of higher education.

*Hotel and Culinary Exchange Programme,* is run in Britain by the *Council on International Educational Visits and Exchanges (CIEE)* (see under *AIPT* above). Their US head office is at: 205 East 42nd Street, New York, NY 10071; tel 212-822-2695; fax 212-822-2689; http://www.ciee.org/. Another scheme is the Open Hotel and Culinary Exchange Programme. In this case, applicants supply detailed information on their training and experience which is then circulated to potential placement organisations in the USA. It can take up to six months to find a suitable post.

**Recruitment Agencies**

*FM Recruitment,* Hedges House, 153-155 Regent Street, London W1R 7FD, tel 0171-287 4540, fax 0171-287 5411 — provides a focused specialist service covering accounting, finance systems, and consulting appointments within the hotel, leisure and tourism industries in the hotel and leisure industry, UK and abroad. Positions handled vary from junior accounts trainee to group financial director, although FM Recruitment tends to handle more senior positions. Applicants should have financial or systems exposure within the hospitality and leisure industry.

*International Services (Tour C.I.T),* 3 rue de l'arrivee, F-75749 Paris, France, tel 60 75 95 95, fax 60 75 97 97 — recruits *commis de rang* and *chefs de rang* who speak fluent English throughout the year. Catering qualifications or two years' experience are needed. All nationalities welcome.

*Logbridge Ltd.,* see *Passenger and Cruise Ships* above.

*Sobeir Agency,* Avenue Louise 396, B-1050 Brussels, Belgium, tel 02-640-12-20, fax 02-647-28-97 — handles assignments in hotels and starred restaurants, and other hotel-related industries, at all levels and in all departments in Belgium and France. Relevant experience and language capabilities (French or Dutch) would be an advantage.

*Towngate Personnel Ltd.,* 65 Seamoor Road, Westbourne, Bournemouth, Dorset, tel 01202-752955, fax 01202-752954 — is a recruitment agency specialising in Hotel and Catering. They recruit mainly in the United Kingdom including the Channel Islands and also occasionally have vacancies for qualified and experienced staff in Europe and the Middle East. Vacancies normally include Chefs of all grades, Hotel Receptionists and Restaurant Staff.

*VIP International,* 17 Charing Cross Road, London WC2H 0EP, tel/fax 0171-930 2860, e-mail vip.intl@dial.pipex.com — is a worldwide recruiting agency for the luxury hotel and cruise line industries. Positions for executives and managers in the hotel industry, and service personnel — like silver service waiters, chefs, food and beverage mangers, bartenders, bar waiters — on cruise liners. Ideal candidates are 20-30 with a minimum of 3 years' experience in fine establisments. You should mail a CV, two passport-size photographs and employement references. A good command of English is required.

**Useful Contacts**

For more information about which colleges and universities offer degree courses in travel and tourism in the US, see *Peterson's Four Year Colleges* (Peterson's, 202 Carnegie Center, Princeton, NJ 08543-2123).

For information about which qualifications are recognised in the UK, see *Fact Sheet 3* published by the European Commission in London (Jean Monnet House, 8 Storey's Gate, London SW1P 3AT, tel 0171-973 1992).

*The American Society of Travel Agents* is the largest in the world (ASTA, 1101 King Street, Alexandria, VA 22314); and publishes a list of affiliated travel schools in the USA and worldwide.

*Working in Tourism* (Vacation Work) contains a short directory of UK and international training courses in tourism and hospitality.

Full and part-time Intensive Diploma Courses in business and travel studies are offered in the UK by *Hove College of Travel,* Medina House, Brighton BN3 2RP, tel 01273-731352.

A book on working for US-based cruise line companies is *How to Get a Job with a Cruise Line,* by Mary Fallon Miller, published by *Ticket to Adventure, Inc.,* PO Box 41005, St Petersburg, Florida.

# Voluntary Work

While voluntary work is generally associated with the poorer nations of Africa, Asia and Latin America, there is also a great demand for volunteer labour in more developed countries, and areas like Eastern Europe and Russia. A volunteer is most easily be defined as an unpaid worker, but there is actually a wide variety of relations between voluntary and charitable organisations and their volunteers. In some cases, the worker may pay a contribution to take part in a particular project; and some organisations themselves may be more commercial than charitable. Some are required to raise money for the charity — and more and more include travel and sponsored events abroad as part of their fundraising. There are also many full-time and paid opportunities in fundraising, adminstration, or development. Typically, longer-term volunteers receive free board and accommodation and an adequate local salary or allowance.

A volunteer might be described as someone who works without the primary motive of financial or material gain. Many more enlightened charities and Non-Governmental organisations (NGOs) see voluntary work as a way to educate and inform the volunteer as much as the local people they may be helping; and see the process as an exchange which benefits those carrying out this work — in this respect at least — as much as the recipient of aid. These charity or aid projects are about working with people; and encouraging autonomy and self-reliance. These issues relating to your own motivation and outlook should be considered by anyone thinking of carrying out charitable or voluntary work abroad.

It is reasonable to be sceptical of those voluntary organisations which charge an excessive fee; or are charging another organisation (the one you end up working for) for their services. These are really more like employment agencies; and should be considered as such. As well as volunteers driven by altruism or missionary zeal, this chapter also encompasses those who seek experience and understanding which will help in their future careers and life, through the work itself, or the encounter with a another way of life and a different culture.

# The Developing World

Attitudes to development have changed radically over recent years; and the emphasis in national aid programmes has now shifted to helping developing countries to help themselves through expert guidance, rather than supplying voluntary labour (which itself may be in plentiful supply in that country). The developing countries, as a general rule, need expertise and education, and may not welcome volunteers who work without reference to local people and their own assessment of their needs. Particular importance is now attached to appropriate technologies which can be operated and maintained in the country concerned; the protection of the environment; and economic development which benefits the whole community. So, the demand is for skilled professionals, principally in the fields of administration, agriculture, education, engineering, finance, and medicine. Volunteers are usually recruited for at least a year (with the exception of more short-term emergency relief). This gives them time to come to terms with their new environment; and to make a more meaningful contribution than on more short-term placements or programmes. It is also more cost-effective for the charities to employ longer-term volunteer staff.

It should be emphasised that in the developing world voluntary or professional work needs training, qualifications or skills which are in demand in that country. Even then, the selection process can be rigorous, with no guarantee of a job. There are other obstacles, too, not the least of which is getting a work permit; and restrictions on foreign workers (which are imposed by many governments even in areas where skilled workers are desperately needed).

Recruitment is mainly carried out by organisations based in Europe and North America, and these are classified here under two main headings: religious and secular.

## DENOMINATIONAL CHRISTIAN ORGANISATIONS

There are hundreds of denominational missionary societies in the UK, and many more in the United States; and so a complete listing is not possible in this chapter. A useful booklet is *World Service Enquiry* published by *Christians Abroad* (see below) which lists agencies and organisations (both religious and secular) involved in development and volunteer work, as well as summer placements and exchanges. Below are the main recruiters of personnel in the fields of agriculture, engineering, education, and medicine. Although membership of the religious denomination in question is not always specified, applicants with a Christian background are generally preferred. The minimum that will be required is a positive attitude towards the organisation in question. Regions and countries in which these organisations and societies operate vary, but most are concerned with Africa and Asia — and British charities have strong links with the other Commonwealth countries.

*Associate Missionaries of the Assumption,* 227 North Bowman Avenue, Merion, PA 19066, tel 610-664-1284, fax 610-664-7328 — has projects in Africa, the USA, Japan and Europe requiring 15 volunteers a year, single Catholics aged 23 to 40 with a college degree and speaking the local language; and generally paying their insurance and visa expenses.

*Catholic Medical Mission Board (CMMB),* 10 West 17th Street, New York, NY 10011-5765 USA, tel 212-242-7757, fax 212-807-9161 — places licensed and certified US and Canadian volunteer medical doctors and registered nurses at independently operated Catholic medical mission hospitals and clinics in Africa, the Caribbean, Central and South America, India and Papua New Guinea. The length of service, which varies, is dependent on mission needs. One-month, 6-month, and 1-2 year tours of service may be available. Applicants may contact the Co-ordinator, Program Services at the above address for further information or an application form. UK and non-US/Canada personnel interested in working with one of their affiliated facilities should send a self-addresses envelope and International Reply Coupons; and can receive a listing of appropriate contact people.

*Catholic Network of Volunteer Service,* 4121 Harewood Road NE, Washington, DC 20017 — acts as a coordinating Centre for over 180 voluntary lay mission programmes. Call toll free 1-800-543-5046 for their free *Volunteer Opportunities Directory* with short and long-term, domestic and international volunteer service opportunities (including a list of US Christian organisations which accept volunteers from outside the United States).

*Christians Abroad* is an ecumenical charity which maintains a database of skilled personnel and a monthly listing of vacancies (see *Sources of Information* below).

*Christian Outreach,* 1 New Street, Leamington Spa, Warwickshire CV31 1HP, tel 01926-315301, fax 01926-885786, e-mail 100656.1612@Compuserve.com — welcomes qualified applicants who are committed and practising Christians from a variety of backgrounds: health professionals; mechanics; logisticians; community development workers and managers; and construction and water engineers. Current operations are in Cambodia, Mozambique, Tanzania, and Rwanda. Wherever possible Christian Outreach works alongside existing structures and works to encourage local initiatives and community involvement. Encouraging self-reliance, and giving communities and individuals greater control over their lives, is the objective of its relief and development work. Contracts are for one year, usually renewable for a second. Team members with no previous overseas experience have expenses only paid (except for a small allowance of $150 per month). Those with overseas experience may qualifiy for a UK allowance too.

*Church Mission Society,* Parnership House, 157 Waterloo Road, London SE1 8UU, tel 0171-928 8681, fax 0171-401 3215 — offers opportunities to qualified and experienced people in a range of areas, eg. medical, pastoral, in partnership with churches in Europe, Africa, and Asia. Mission Partner openings are for a minimum of two years. Overseas Experience Placements are available for those aged 21-30. These individual placements provide opportunities for young people to gain experience of the Church in a different culture. Placements are self-financing and vary in length from 6-18 months. Africa, Europe (incl. Britain), Asia, and the Middle East. Project Experience camps give opportunity for a group of people to discover what it means to be a Christian in a different culture. Departures in the summer. Duration 3-5 weeks. Africa, Europe, Asia, and the Middle East. Contact the Personnel Programmes Team. They offer medical, teaching, pastoral and clerical opportunities in partnership with churches in Africa and Asia. *Mission Partner* openings are for a minimum of 2 years. The *Experience Programme* offers camps and placements for people between 18-30.

*Church of Scotland,* Board of World Mission, 121 George Street, Edinburgh EH2 4YN, tel 0131-225 5722, fax 0131-226 6121 — places professionals with a Christian outlook like accountants, administrators, agriculturalists, ministers, teachers, technical staff, and all kinds of medical and para-medical staff in Africa and Asia, usually for a minimum of 4 years. *World Exchange* also offers Scottish Christians the chance to spend up to a year working abroad on church based projects.

*The Council for World Mission,* Livingstone House, 11 Carteret Street, London SW1H 9DL, tel 0171-222 4214, fax 0171-233 1747 — is an international organisation serving different churches which recruit Missionaries for specialised ministries, teaching, medical, and administrative work in Zambia, Papua New Guinea, Samoa, Kiribati, Taiwan and many other countries. Offers of service should be made through the member churches in the United Kingdom: the Congregational Federation; the Congregational Union of Scotland; the Presbyterian Church of Wales; the Union of Welsh Independents; and the United Reformed Church in the United Kingdom.

*Irish Missionary Union,* Orwell Park, Rathgar, Dublin 6, Ireland, tel 1-496-5433 or 497-1770, fax 1-496-5029 — offers voluntary work for Irish citizens in Africa, Asia, and Latin America. Volunteers should be motivated by Christian values, at least 21 years old, and be able to serve a minimum period of two years. They should also have a qualification or experience in one of the following areas: medicine, education, trades, agriculture, accountancy, missionary work, and community development. A monthly allowance, accommodation, resettlement allowance, and insurance while overseas is provided, as is the return airfare.

Further details can be obtained from the Special Projects Officer at the above address.

*Mennonite Central Committee,* 21 South 12th Street, Akron, Pennsylvania 17501, tel 717-859-1151 — is a voluntary relief and development agency that supports about 900 volunteers a year in 50 countries in Asia, Africa, Latin and North America, usually in conjunction with other agencies. Experience and/or qualifications are necessary, relevant to work in the following fields: agriculture, economics, technology, health, education, etc. Applicants must be Christians. Expenses are paid. There is no restriction on nationality. Enquiries and applications to the Personnel Office at the address above.

*Methodist Church, Britain,* 25 Marylebone Road, London NW1 5JR, tel 0171-486 5502, fax 0171 935-1507 — sends Christians who are professionally qualified and experienced teachers, doctors, midwives and nursing tutors to work at the invitation of partner churches in Africa, Asia, Latin America, the Pacific, and Europe. Tours usually last 3 years, and each mission partner is expected to serve for 2 tours.

*Quaker International Social Projects (QISP),* Religious Society of Friends, Friends House, Euston Road, London NW1 2BJ, tel 0171-387 3601 — runs 25-30 short-term (2-4 weeks) residential voluntary work projects in Britain and Northern Ireland each year during spring and summer. QISP also sends volunteers abroad, through exchange agreements with other volunteer organisations in Bulgaria, the Czech Republic, Denmark, France, Germany, Greece, Greenland, Netherlands, Poland, Slovakia, Spain, Turkey, Ukraine, and the USA. There are many types of projects, from manual work to working with children, disabled people, or the elderly. Most run in the summer, and last from 1 to 4 weeks.

Minimum age for projects abroad is 18. Applicants aged 18-24 should have completed a project in the UK, or had similar volunteering experience, or should have lived abroad. Applicants over 24: no requirements. Special skills or qualifications are not necessary. Motivation, enthusiasm, and commitment to living and working in a group are more important! Volunteers work as a team of 8 to 15 people people who come from all walks of life and nationalities. Food and accommodation (usually basic) are provided free of charge. QISP charges a small registration fee (£22 unwaged, £33 student, £44 waged). Volunteers arrange to pay for travel to the project. To receive a programme (for the spring programme before January; for the summer programme before April) send a large (C5) stamped SAE and a cover letter stating age and, if applicable, volunteer experience.

*Short Term Experience Projects (Step) Latin Link,* 325 Kennington Road, London SE11 4QE, fax 0171-207 5885 — sends around 150 young Christians to help with community-based tasks in support of the Latin American Church in Brazil, Peru, Bolivia, Argentina and Nicaragua. Tasks are varied and periods of work ranges from 7 weeks to 6 months. Specific skills are not necessay. Applicants should be 17-35 and committed Christians. Older people will be considered. Travel expenses are not paid.

*WEC International,* Bulstrode, Gerrards Cross, Bucks SL9 8SZ, tel 0173-884631, fax 01753-882470, e-mail Compuserve 100546.1550 — founded in 1913, has over 1,700 full-time workers 'advancing the cause of Christ' in more than 60 countries of the world. Salaries are not paid; workers share in the offerings of supporters of sending bases in Australia, Brazil, Canada, France, Germany, Great Britain, Holland, Hong Kong, New Zealand, Singapore, South Africa, Switzerland, Taiwan and the USA. In addition to evangelical work, there are special ministries, such as medical, educational and rural development programmes where this is deemed to advance the primary objective of evangelisation.

*World Council of Churches,* Ecumenical Youth Action, 150 route de Ferney, PO Box 2100, CH-1211 Geneva 2, Switzerland, tel 791-61-11 — has opportunities for young people to participate as volunteers within its Ecumenical Youth Action programme. Recent workcamps have been held in Africa, Asia, the Caribbean, Europe, and the Middle East. Volunteers assist local groups in manual work such as agriculture, construction, and renovation of buildings.

## OTHER CHRISTIAN ORGANISATIONS

The following societies are non-denominational, but they recruit mainly for overseas churches and Christian institutions, and therefore prefer applicants with a Christian background.

*Eirene, International Christian Service for Peace,* Strasse 74b, D-56564 Neuwied, Germany, tel 2631-8379, fax 2631-31160, e-mail EIRENE-INT@OLN.comlink.-apc.org — organises programmes in Nicaragua, Nigeria and Chad and the 'solidarity and learning' programme in Africa, Latin, America and Asia, as well as a North programme in Europe and the USA. 30 volunteers are required each year, most of them recruited from Germany. Each must know the language of the local country. Costs are paid for; but volunteers are asked to find a support group to give some financial contribution. The minimum duration of service is one year.

*The Medical Missionary Association,* 157 Waterloo Road, London SE1 8XN, tel 0171-928 4694, fax 0171-620 2453 — exists to mobilise healthcare professionals to serve in mission and church-related hospitals overseas. They can advise on student elective training periods and overseas and long-term service. They also publish a magazine *Saving Health* 3-4 times a year, which includes a list of service opportunities associated with many UK based missions. It does not operate its own recruitment programme.

*Tear Fund,* 100 Church Road, Teddington, Middlesex TW11 8QE, tel 0181-943 7888, fax 0181-943 3594 — an evangelical Christian relief and development agency, provides personnel and other assistance to churches and Christian groups throughout the developing world. Skilled and experienced personnel are needed for community development programmes, mainly in the following skill areas: doctors, nurses, midwives, community health advisors, physiotherapists, agriculturalists, technical trainers, programme managers, community development advisors. Appointments are generally for four years. For further details contact the Overseas Service Advisor.

## OTHER ORGANISATIONS

*Action Health 2000,* The Gate House, 25 Gwydir Street, Cambridge CB1 2LG, tel 01223-460853, fax 01223-461787 — is concerned with appropriate health care in developing countries and operates in India, Tanzania, and Uganda. It recruits fully qualified health professionals with a minimum of two years' post qualification experience; and welcomes applications from doctors, physiotherapists, midwives and health visitors, occupational therapists, dentists, and speech and language therapists. Action Health considers applications from individuals, couples, families, mature individuals, and those with no previous experience of working abroad. Contracts range from 6 months to 2 years.

See under *Development* in the *Medicine and Nursing* chapter for more medical charities and voluntary work organisations.

*Amigos de las Americas,* 5618 Star Lane, Houston, Texas 77057, tel 713-782-5290 or 800-2317796, fax 713-782-9267, e-mail info@amigoslink.org, http://www.amigoslink.org — is an international, not-for-profit organisation that, through service, promotes improved community health in Latin America; provides leadership development opportunities for youth; and facilitates better cross-cultural understanding in the Americas. The volunteers, usually high school and college students, serve from 4-8 weeks in Ecuador, Mexico, Paraguay, Costa Rica, Brazil, Honduras, and the Dominican Republic. The programmes include school renovation, community sanitation, home improvement, gardening, human immunisations and rabies vaccinations. The costs range from $2700-3200. Scholarships are awarded on the basis of demonstrated need. Applications to the Correspondent Volunteer Coordinator before April 15. Also see their website for more details.

*The Agency for Personal Services Abroad (APSO),* 29-30 Fitzwilliam Square, Dublin 2, Ireland, tel 1-661-4411, fax 1-661-4202, e-mail apso@iol.ie — is the state-sponsored organisation which recruits, trains and funds Irish development workers for developing countries. Around 1,000 volunteers are recruited every year. Skills and qualifications in areas like health, engineering, administration, socila, technical and other trades. Only Irish citizens are eligible. Its quarterly publication is a *APSO Post.* There is also a comprehensive resource centre. Applications to the above address.

*ATD Fourth World,* 48 Addington Square, London SE5 7LB, tel 0171-703 3231, fax 0171-252 4276 — is an international organisation working in Europe, the USA, Canada, Asia, Africa and Central America involved in long-term projects with the most disadvantaged. These practical projects show 'the will and the capacity of the very poorest individuals and families to fulfill their roles as parents and citizens'. International volunteers undergo a three-month training programme in their country of origin. The minimum age is 18; good health and references required; but not necessarily specific qualifications. For more information, and details of their weekend summer camps in the UK and France for volunteers to find out more about ATD and 'to discover how people can work together to change the situation of these families,' contact the above address.

*Bharat Sevak Samaj,* 22 Sardar Patel Road, Chanakya Puri, New Delhi and *Nehru Seva Kendra,* Gurgaon Bypass Road, Mehrauli, New Delhi, India — BSS is a nationwide voluntary organisation with 10,000 members working on projects at any time. Projects include organising urban community centres, child welfare, night shelters, family planning clinics, disaster relief and housing for untouchables etc. Both skilled and unskilled foreign volunteers are welcome for periods of 2-12 weeks. They must finance their own stay and expect to live like local people. Applications to the General Secretary.

*British Executive Service Overseas (BESO),* 164 Vauxhall Bridge Road, London SW1V 2RB, tel 0171-630 0644 — recruits retired volunteer business executives with professional, technical or specialised management skills to advise on projects overseas. Short-term placements on an expenses only basis.

*Britain-Vietnam Friendship Society* require English teachers for Vietnam. See *Teaching.*

*British Red Cross Society,* 9 Grosvenor Crescent, London SW1X 7EJ, tel 0171-235 5454, fax 0171-245 6315 — keeps a register of doctors, nurses, administrators, mechanics, engineers, agriculturalists, programme managers, telecommunications specialists, development advisers and others with relevant professional experience who are willing to go abroad on short-term assignments to assist victims of disasters. Longer-term development projects are occasionally undertaken. Age group 25; airfares and allowances are provided. There is a one-week residential course for briefing before taking up residence overseas.

*CUSO,* 2255 Carling Avenue, Suite 400, Ottawa, ON, Canada K2B 1A6, tel 613-829-7445, fax 613-829-7996 — is a Canadian non-profit organisation committed to social justice around the globe. CUSO shares specific skills through the placement of Canadian cooperants overseas. It also provides funds for locally-controlled development projects and programmes, promotes awareness of the developing world, and helps forge links between similar groups with common concerns in Canada and overseas. Cooperants are expected to provide specialised technical assistance and administrative and organisational support. The annual intake of volunteers is about 200 and contracts are for two years. recruitment is aimed at Canadian citizens and landed immigrants. Experience and/or qualifications are always required.

*The Institute of Cultural Affairs,* PO Box 505, London N19 3YX — is a registered charity involved with community development projects in many countries worldwide. Volunteers are taken on for a minimum of 9 months. No specific requirements are necessary but experience in health or teaching is an advantage.

*Health Volunteers Overseas (HVO),* c/o Washington Station, PO Box 65157, Washington DC 20035-5157, tel 202-296-0928 — sends over 180 qualified volunteers every year to train local health care providers in seven different areas of medicine including anaesthesia and pediatrics. Most are North American but other nationalities are welcome to apply. Volunteers are sought who are innovative and flexible, and interested primarily in the teaching aspect of the work.

*International Medical Corps,* 5933 West Century Boulevard, Suite 310, Los Angeles, CA 90045 — is a private, non-profit, humanitarian organisation which provides health care and training to devastated areas worldwide, often where few other relief organisations operate. The philosophy behind IMC is not to help people with a hand-out, but to give them the knowledge to rebuild their lives and health care systems. IMC has programmes in Afghanistan, Pakistan, Angola, Somalia and Cambodia; and is developing a project for the United States. Qualified applicants should send a resumé indicating international experience and foreign language skills.

*Joint Assistance Centre,* G-17/3, DLF Qutab Enclave, 1 Gurgaon, Haryana-122022, India — is a voluntary agency working in India for nearly two decades which accepts international volunteers from nearly 25 countries around the world. Around 200 volunteers a year engage in international youth work in different parts of India. The minimum age is 18; and volunteers must pay for at least one month, even if they stay for less. This is £75 per month, with a registration fee of £15. The working environment is safe but challenging: only vegetarian food, simple shared sleeping floor, and no eggs, no alcohol, and no smoking are the rule. This is a unique and flexible way of visiting the country and carrying out voluntary work. Requests for application forms, plus 3 International Reply Coupons, to the above address.

*Peace Corps,* 1990 K Street NW, Washington DC 20526, tel 202-376-2550 — is the official agency for the US government which sends some 60,000 US citizens each year to work on 2-year assignments in Africa, Asia and Latin America. Most opportunities arise in the following areas: teaching, health and nutrition, energy projects, forestry and fisheries, water sanitation, vocational skills and agriculture.

*Project Trust,* Hebridean Centre, Braecachadh Castle, Isle of Coll, Scotland PA76 6TE, tel 01879-230444, fax 01879-230357 — sends between 150 and 200 school leavers every year on one-year voluntary placements overseas. Environmental, social service, or teaching projects take place throughout the world, and volunteers must raise a portion of the total cost (with assistance in training and fundraising). Once abroad, they receive free board and lodging and pocket money. Applications from those in full-time secondary education before they go abroad.

*Save the Children,* 17 Grove Lane, London SE5 8RD, tel 0171-703 5400, fax 0171-703 2278 — is the UK's largest international voluntary agency concerned with child health and welfare. The principal emphasis of overseas work is on long-term programmes concerned with health, nutrition, community development, and welfare; and recruitment is generally within each country (where there is some scope for volunteers). In addition, there are paid posts for qualified and experienced project coordinators, medical officers, nurses, midwives, tutors, health visitors, nutritionists, engineers, social workers, disability specialists, and others.

*Schools Partnership Worldwide,* 17 Dean's Yard, London SW1P 3PB, tel 0171-222 0138, fax 0171-963 1006 — has overseas placements and environmental programmes for young people in Zimbabwe, Tanzania, Uganda, Namibia, India, and Nepal. There are English language teaching and social programmes, and environmental programmes where a group of young people from the North is matched with a group from the country being targeted, and learn about and act upon important environmental issues. These are open to young people aged between 18 and 25. The cost of teaching programmes are about £1,750 including expenses such as travel and insurance and sponsorship which provides a basic living allowance, training etc. The environmental programmes cost about £2,250. More information from the Director. Pre-departure and in-country training programmes are obligatory.

*Skillshare Africa,* 3 Belvoir Street, Leicester LE1 6SL, tel 0116-254 0517 — sends skilled and experienced people (*cooperants*) to work in support of development in Botswana, Lesotho, Mozambique and Swaziland. It is committed to the promotion of self-reliance and so cooperants are placed only where there is a real need for outside help and where the transfer of skills accords with the ideas and ideals of the people of southern Africa. There are about 80 cooperants working at any one time. Recent projects have required building and forestry workers, civil engineers, auto mechanics, metalwork instructors, and EFL teachers.

Applicants should be aged over 21, have relevant qualifications and experience, particularly in training others, and right of residence in the EU. Placements are for two years and the following are provided: flights, national insurance payments, modest living allowance/salary, small home savings allowance, rent-free accommodation, health insurance and equipment grants. Details can be obtained by writing to Recruitment/Selection at the above address.

*United Nations Association International Service (UNAIS),* Suite 3a, Hunter House, 57 Goodramgate, York YO1 2LS, tel 01904-647799 — recruits agricultural, health and engineering professional for two-year placements in West Africa, Latin America, and the Middle East.

*United Nations Volunteers (UNV),* Palais des Nations, CH-1211 Geneva 10, Switzerland, tel 798-58-50 — recruits highly qualified and experienced volunteers from all UN countries work in over 70 developing countries for UN-sponsored development projects for a period of two years (and some shorter-term humanitarian relief work). Travel to and from the country is provided for volunteers and dependants are authorised to accompany them. A modest monthly allowance is provided at either single or dependency rates, along with a settling in grant. Appropriate academic or trade qualifications in a particular profession are required, along with a minimum of 2 years' working experience in that field. UK applicants should contact VSO at the address below for an application form. For more about the UN and its organisations see *International Organisations.*

*Voluntary Service Overseas (VSO),* 317 Putney Bridge Road, London SW15 2PN, tel 0181-780 1331, fax 0181-780 1081, e-mail enquiries@vso.org.uk., http:// www.oneworld.org/vso/ — enables men and women to make a long-term commitment — usually two years — to share their skills with people in a developing country. Placements are offered in a whole range of skill areas including education, technical trades, small business development, health, agriculture, social work/community development and sport. It also offers a number of shorter-term placements (3-18 months) in most skill areas. 900 volunteers are sent overseas each year in 57 countries in Africa, Asia, the Pacific and Caribbean, Latin America, and Eastern Europe. Flights, health insurance, and national insurance contributions, plus grants towards equipment and resettlement are paid. Accommodation and a modest living allowance are provided by the local employer. VSO has a development education programme which encourages volunteers to share their understanding with others when they return home. They must have a qualification and a skill, be aged 20-70, without dependents, and have unrestricted right of re-entry to the UK.

*East European Partnership* is a VSO initiative for around 100 volunteers at any one time in many central and eastern European countries working with local goverment and NGOs involving teachers, health-care workers, and business trainers. Send for application form to: East European Partnership, Carlton House, 27A Carlton Drive, London SW15 2BS; tel 0181-780 2841.

# Projects in the North

## WORKCAMPS

Voluntary work in the more developed countries is as varied as the social and environmental problems of these countries across Europe, North America and East Asia (as well as Australasia) sometimes collectively known as 'the North'. An opportunity for international volunteering is provided by workcamps or summer camps, which accept short-term labour and often unskilled help; and are popular with young people interested in working holidays. The work itself is often demanding, involving physical labour like construction or agriculture; general maintenance and duties like cleaning and cooking; or activities with a more 'social' bias (playschemes for deprived or disabled children, hospital work, development work, teaching, and environmental protection). The financial arrangements vary considerably. In some cases, volunteers are provided with board, lodging and pocket money; in others, volunteers may have to make a substantial contribution towards costs. Travel expenses are usually (although not always) the responsibility of the volunteer.

Applicants should normally apply for workcamps through the representatives or organisations in their own country; but there are some organisations abroad where applications must be made direct, which may suit those who prefer independent travel. An enormous number of associations recruit for workcamps at a local or national level in the UK and USA, so only a selection has been included here. A creative job search will turn up more. Some are included under the country headings of *Worldwide Employment.* Lists of these organisations will also be found in the publications cited under *Sources of Information* below.

Within Western Europe and North America, major efforts have been made to co-ordinate workcamp programmes, so volunteers should contact the appropriate body in their own country where possible; or the international head offices abroad. When writing to an organisation dealing with many countries, or which offers exchange programmes, applicants should state their preferred destinations and preferences as to the type of work, as well as enquiring about the organisation, and including dates for availabilty, and other relevant information (like childcare qualifications or similar experience in the past).

Those wishing to work in the less developed Eastern European or former CIS countries are advised to check with a workcamp organisation in their own country if they are applying direct. Usually this means going through one of the 27 members of Service Civil International (SCI) in countries which send volunteers to workcamps. These include: International Voluntary Service (IVS) in the UK; and SCI-USA or Volunteers for Peace (VFP) in the USA (see below). Also see East European Partnership under *Long-Term Opportunities* below.

*American Hiking Society,* Volunteer Vacations, PO Box 20160, Washington DC 20041-2160, tel 301-565-6704, fax 301-565-6714, e-mail AMHIKER-@aol.com — sends up to thirty teams of 10-12 volunteers to remote yet beautiful locations within the USA to maintain trails and build new ones for one and two-week vacations. Volunteers should be over 18 years of age, able to hike five miles in a day, supply all their own backpacking equipment (backpack, tent, sleeping bag, personal items), arrange transportation to and from the work site, and pay a $50 registration fee to AHS upon application. AHS also annually publishes *Helping Out in the Outdoors,* listing more than 2,000 internship and volunteer opportunities on America's public lands in all 50 states. Possible jobs include fire lookouts, wildlife observers, historical interpreters, backcountry patrollers, and many more: cost $7.00 within USA; add $5.00 from abroad.

*Concordia (Youth Service Volunteers) Ltd.,* 8 Brunswick Place, Hove, Sussex BN3 1ET, tel 01273-772086, fax 01273-327284 — in conjunction with similar foreign organisations, recruits for voluntary work in Western and Eastern European and some North African countries. Applicants must be aged 18-30 (20 or over in Turkey, Tunisia, and Morocco) and a registration fee of £65 is payable. Send SAE for details.

*Council on International Educational Exchange (CIEE),* 205 East 42nd Street, New York, NY 10017, tel 212-822-2695, fax 212-822-2089, http://www.ciee.org/ — sponsors 2-4 week volunteer projects in the USA and abroad during the summer months. Choosing from over 600 projects worldwide, participants join an international team of 10-20 volunteers to work on an environmental or community service project alongside local residents. Volunteers (aged 18 or over) have planted grass and trees to protect endangered coastlines and forests, restored historical sites, renovated low-income housing and cared for the disabled while learning the benefits of international cooperation. The cost of participating is $250-750 plus travel to and from the project site. Room and board is provided. The Council recruits only US residents directly and receives volunteers on projects in the US through its partner organisations in other countries.
The UK address is: 52 Poland Street, London W1V 4JQ, tel 0171-478 2000.

*Crown Agents for Overseas Governments and Administrations,* see under *Government Agencies* in the *Getting the Job* chapter.

*Hostelling International-American Youth Hostels (HI-AYH),* 733 15th Street, NW, Suite 840, Washington, DC 20005, tel 202-738-6161, fax 202-783-6171 — has forty regional offices (councils) in the United States, and offers intern opportunities in Hostel Services, Hostel Development, Marketing, Programs and Education, and Resource Development. Interns receive free housing at the hostel, a bi-weekly stipend, and $200 relocation assistance. The stipend is $100 a week if you are at or working towards undergraduate degree level and $150 a week if you are working towards or have completed a graduate degree. The minimum length is 10 weeks. To apply send a cover letter, current resumé, college transcript, and three letters of recommendation to the Internship Coordinator at the above address. Application deadlines: August 1; December 1; February 1; May 1.

*Internationale Bouworde (International Building Companions),* Tiensesteenweg 145, B-3010 Kessel-Lo, Belgium — runs 2-4 week workcamps to assist in socially useful building projects in many European countries on behalf of the socially underprivileged and mentally disabled. Volunteers work for 8 hours per day, 5 days per week. Free board, accommodation and insurance (approx. £30) are provided. Offices in Europe: Osterreichiser Bauorden, Hörnesgasse 3, $1031 Wien, Austria; Compagnons Bâtisseurs, Secrétariat International, 2 rue Claude-Bertholet, F-81100 Castres, France; Internationaler Bauorden, Liebigstrasse 23, D-67551 Worms-Horchheim; IBO Soci Construttori, via Mazza 48, I-20071 Casalpusterlengo, Italy; Internationale Bouworde, St Annastrat 172, NL-6524 GT Nijmegen; Internationaler Bauorden, Sekretariat Schweiz, CH-9438 Luchingen, Switzerland.

*International Exchange Centre,* 2 Republic Square, LV-1010 Riga, Latvia (tel 3717-027-216, fax 3717-830-257) — seeks camp leaders and sports instructors to look after children in summer camps in Latvia, Lithuania, Russia, and Ukraine; and au pairs. Minimum one month commitment. Enquiries should be made well in advance. There is an application fee of $50. Basic Russian or local language useful.

*International Voluntary Service (IVS) Britain,* Old Hall, East Bergholt, nr Colchester CO7 6TQ — runs a Workcamps Programme which co-ordinates approximately 50 short-term camps a year in Britain, and sends British volunteers to take part in projects in about 25 countries in Europe (west and east), North Africa, and North America. In some countries the projects take place with branches of SCI (*Service Civil International*), the movement of which IVS is a part; in others, IVS cooperates with other workcamp organisations. Most projects last 2-4 weeks and take place between June and September. A list of summer projects abroad is available in April. Send SAE to the above address for information. Applicants must be over 18 and pay a registration fee for membership of IVS and their own costs. The projects are not holidays and the work can be hard and demands commitment.

*Involvement Volunteers Association Inc.,* PO Box 218, Port Melbourne, Victoria 3207, tel 613-646-5504 — gives individual and team volunteers the opportunity to gain experience on practical conservation, environmental research, archaeology, history or social service projects. Volunteers must speak and understand English as well as the local language in some cases. Individual or team placements run for 2-4 weeks, some with free accommodation and food, others needing Aus$5 per day for camp expenses. A fee is charged to cover administration costs including orientation on arrival and paid work introductions for volunteers with suitable work permits. Volunteers pay their own travel and insurance costs. Placements are available in all states of Australia, as well as Austria, Fiji, Germany, India, India, Latvia, New Zealand, Thailand, and the USA.

This includes orientation on arrival and paid work introductions for volunteers with suitable work permits. Associated organisations are *Involvement Corps, Inc.,* 15515 Sunset Blvd., Suite 108, Pacific Palisades, CA 90272, USA; and *Involvement Volunteers Deutschland,* Postfach 110224, D-3400 Göttingen, Germany.

*Overseas Development Institute,* see under *Government Agencies* in the *Getting the Job* chapter.

*SCI International Voluntary Service (SCI-IVS),* 5474 Walnut Level Road, Crozet,

VA 22932, tel 804-823-1826, fax 804-823-5027, internet sciivsuusa@igc.ap-c.org — is the US branch of Service Civil International-International Voluntary Service and one of the major co-ordinating centres for US citizens who wish to organise voluntary work in Europe; there are particularly close links with Eastern European organisations. Volunteers for Europe should be aged at least 18 and may be required to speak a foreign language. The *International Workcamp Directory* with a wide range of opportunities is available each April for $5 and SCI-IVS also publishes a newsletter *Workcamp News.*

*United Nations Association (Wales) International Youth Service (UNAIYS),* Temple of Peace, Cathays Park, Cardiff CF1 3AP — recruits young British people to work for 2-3 weeks on international voluntary projects run by sister organisations in Europe, the USA, some African countries, South East Asia, Latin America, and India.

*Volunteers for Peace (VFP),* 43 Tiffany Road, Belmont, Vermont 05730, tel 802-259-2759, fax 802-259-2922, e-mail vfp@vermontel.com — co-ordinates international workcamps in 60 countries in Europe, North and West Africa, and North and Central America. VFP is strongly represented in the countries of Eastern Europe and the former Soviet Union (the Czech Republic, Slovakia, Poland, Lithuania, Estonia, Ukraine, Belarus, Hungary, Romania, Bulgaria, Armenia, Slovenia, and Croatia). Work involved includes construction, environmental, agricultural and social work. There is an emphasis on learning and recreation. Camps last two to three weeks. Minimum age 18 in most cases; upper age limit variable. Volunteers pay travel expenses as well as $175 per workcamp ($200-500 in Russia). Most applications are taken from mid-April to mid-May. Interested persons should obtain VFP's *International Workcamp Directory* ($12 post-paid in the USA) for precise details. There is also an *International Work-camps* video.

*Youth Action for Peace (YAP),* (formerly *Christian Movement for Peace*), Methold House, North Street, Worthing BN11 1DU, tel 01903-528619, fax 01903-528611 — organises international youth exchanges and sends volunteers to projects in Europe and beyond. Volunteers work in groups for periods of two to three weeks, though longer voluntary placements are possible. The range of projects is varied: from renovation to playscheme activities with children. All of them aim to support local communities and to encourage young people to be more aware of other cultures. A brochure with a complete list of the projects is available in April.

Also see some entries under *Other Organisations* above for long-term volunteering opportunities.

## CAMP COUNSELLING

Looking after a campful of schoolchildren during the summer vacation may not be everybody's idea of fun, but with hundreds of children spending at least part of their summer at a camp, the staff needs are naturally high. Most summer camps are staffed on an international basis by male and female camp counsellors who provide leadership, assist in organisation, and take part in the various activities. This programme of activities is usually varied, and includes all kinds of sports, handicrafts, and artistic and educational pursuits. Sometimes counsellors are chosen for their special skills in these areas, particularly the ability to entertain and motivate children. Many organisations also offer opportunities for travel once the contract has been completed. *British Universities North America Club (BUNAC),* 16 Bowling Green Lane, London EC1R 0BD, operates a variety of programmes in the USA, Canada and Australia for students and other young people.

*BUNACAMP* is a low-cost, non-profit camp counselor programme which places young people aged 19½-35 in US and Canadian summer camps from mid-June to the end of August. Applicants should have some kind of leadership experience with children and/or specialised creative or sporting skills. Nurses and those with secretarial skills are also invited to apply. Students currently studying at degree, HND or 2 year BTEC level can apply to the *KAMP* programme and choose a job in the busy food preparation, maintenance or other support areas using the *KAMP* job directory. Both programmes provide a return flight, work and travel visa (through US sponsors ICCP), salary, board and lodging while at camp and up to six weeks' travel afterwards. Interviews begin in November.

BUNAC also operates a *Work America Programme* (see chapter on USA); and programmes in New Zealand and South Africa.

*Camp America,* 37 Queens Gate, London SW7 5HR — also places students in jobs lasting for 9 weeks in summer camps for children, but will consider applications from teachers, sports coaches and social workers as well. There are also vacancies for nurses. Their minimum age for applicants is 18. In addition, they offer a limited number of places for students who are interested in spending the summer in an American family as a working guest, or 'family companion'. There are also places available working in the camp kitchens or camp maintenance. Applicants can also spend up to 10 weeks after their placement travelling the States. Free return flight London-New York, pocket money, visa sponsorship, and board and lodging at the camp are provided.

*Camp Counsellors USA,* UK Office, 27 Woodside Gardens, Musselburgh, Edinburgh EH21 7LJ — has a high-quality programme placing young people (19-28) as Counsellors at American summer camps. Each year CCUSA staff inspect the camps and interview Counsellors, so that improvements can be made where necessary. CCUSA require people with sports or nursing qualifications, or willing to assist the physically and mentally handicapped. Proficiency in the arts, outdoor pursuits, water sports, etc. is also useful. Patience, a good sense of humour and a high degree of maturity are prerequisites. Counsellors receive a free return flight to the USA, pocket money and the chance to travel after the camp.

## KIBBUTZIM AND MOSHAVIM

Kibbutzim are unique to Israel but have built a reputation throughout the world as centres of hard work. They began in 1909 as agriculturally based collective villages; and today are rural communal settlements where work, income and property are shared by their members. They represent the ultimate in commune life: the means of production are owned by the community as a whole; and working visitors, too, are expected to participate in this 'alternative' lifestyle. The way of life is changing on some and becoming less communal. On their small-scale, the ideals are not unlike those of communism: division of labour is decided according to ability, the division of wealth according to need: working visitors are expected to work hard at whatever job is assigned to them. Long-term members of a Kibbutz must undergo a trial period of a year; but temporary workers from abroad may apply through specialist agencies, and visits are best arranged in advance. There are vacancies throughout the year although these are limited in July and August. Visitors are expected to work eight hours a day, six days a week, with a few days' holiday each month. The minimum period of work is usually one month. Board and lodging is provided, together with other allowances.

Moshavim are the family-based settlements which, like Kibbutzim, were originally agricultural but are now involved in other work as well. Unlike the

Kibbutz, the Moshav allows for private enterprise and members have their own land and property. Volunteers are given accommodation and a small wage by the family for whom they work. Visitors are expected to share in the social and cultural activities of the village; and the wage volunteers receive, the slightly longer working hours, and the greater personal involvement with the family all make life on a Moshav a little different from working in a Kibbutz.

The following organisations offer positions for Kibbutz and/or Moshav visitors. In addition to the registration fees, visitors are also required to pay for their travel to Israel.

*Kibbutz Program Center,* Fourth Floor, 110 East 59th Street, New York, NY 10022, tel 212-318-6130, fax 212-318-6130 — represents all Kibbutzim in Israel. They have information on kibbutz stays, archaeological, Hebrew-study, cultural and other programmes in Israel. Other representatives in North America include: *Kibbutz Aliya Desk,* 6505 Wiltshire Blvd, Suite 816, Los Angeles CA 90048, tel 213-782-0504, fax 213-655-1827; *Kibbutz Aliyah Desk,* 6600 West Maple Road, West Bloomfield, Michigan 48033; *Israel Aliya Center (Kibbutz),* 126 High Street, Boston, MA 12110, tel 617-457-8750, fax 617-988-6256; *Kibbutz Aliya Desk,* Suite 503, 2320 W Peterson, Chicago, Illinois 60659; and *Israel Aliya Center,* 950 West 41st Avenue, Vancouver BC V5Z 2N7.

*Kibbutz Representatives,* 1A Accommodation Road, London NW11 8ED, tel 0181-458 9235 — run regular visitor schemes throughout the year both for groups and individuals. Minimum period two months and the maximum period of stay is six months. Applicants must be in good physical and mental health, and aged between 18 and 32. Due to the popularity of the scheme, the application process is by selection; group or individual travel can be arranged. A typical Kibbutz travel package will cost approximately £312. Insurance is compulsory and will start from £33. An SAE to above address will bring leaflet and application forms by return.

*Project 67 Ltd.,* 10 Hatton Garden, London EC1N 8AH, tel 0171-831 7626 — offers working holidays on Kibbutzim for periods from 5 weeks to 3 months (or up to one year by special arrangement), with travel arranged in groups on pre-set dates; also working holidays on Moshavim where volunteers work with an Israeli family on a commercial farm. Age limit is 18-35. There are departures scheduled for every week of the year. You can or write or call for a brochure, or call in to see an informative video.

## ARCHAEOLOGICAL DIGS

Archaeological work is often hard but can be extremely satisfying for those with an interest in the subject, or are willing to learn. Archaeological digs also tend to be a rather expensive form of voluntary work, as there is rarely an unlimited budget to back up project of this kind. Fares are seldom paid except to qualified specialists but food and accommodation are usually provided on site. Some pay pocket money. The minimum stay required is usually two weeks, but may be longer. Volunteers are advised to gain some experience on one or two digs more locally, before applying for a position abroad.

*Archaeology Abroad,* c/o Institute of Archaeology, 31-34 Gordon Square, London WC1H 0PY — provides information bulletins (available by subscription) about opportunities for archaeological field work and excavations abroad. Information is also supplied to organisers of expeditions who wish to recruit personnel. Information on digs to be carried out in Britain is given in *British Archaeological News,* available from the *Council for British Archaeology,* Bowes Morrell House, 111 Walmgate, York YO2 2UA, tel 01904-671417. (Send an SAE for subscription details). This information is relevant since volunteers are advised to gain experience at least one or two digs locally before applying for positions abroad. In the USA, a list of over 200 digs worldwide needing volunteers is the *Archaeological Fieldwork Opportunities Bulletin*, published by the *Archaeological Institute of America* (fax 617-353-6550) and available from Kendall/Hunt Publishing, 4050 Westmark Drive, PO Box 1840, Dubuque, Iowa 52004-1840.

# CONSERVATION

Unpaid or paying conservation work is an increasingly popular choice for the short and long-term in both the developing and developed countries and many of the voluntary organisations listed above offer programmes to protect the environment, and conserve habitats and ecosystems, for scientists and those with training in biology, zoology, and other environmental disciplines, as well as untrained volunteers (also see the *Agriculture and the Environment* chapter).

*British Trust for Conservation Volunteers (BTCV)*, 36 St. Mary's St, Wallingford, Oxfordshire OX10 0EU, tel 01491-839736, fax 01494-839646 — runs a programme of international projects in most European countries as well as North America. Further details are available from the International Development Unit at the above address.

*Conservation International*, 1015 18th St NW, Suite 1000, Washington, DC 20036, tel 202-429-5660 — recruits volunteers to work for between one and eight weeks to preserve rainforests and their ecosystems in Botswana, Brazil, Costa Rica, and many other countries.

*Concordia (Youth Service Volunteers) Ltd.*, 8 Brunswick Place, Hove BN3 1ET, tel 01273-772086, fax 01273-327284 — can offer work to anyone interested in conservation aged 18-30 on projects throughout Europe. Only British volunteers are accepted.

*Coral Cay Conservation Ltd.*, 154 Clapham Park Road, London SW4 7DE, tel 0171-498 6248, fax 0171-498 8447, e-mail ccc@coralcay.demon.co.uk, http://www.demon.co.uk/coralcay/home.html — recruits paying volunteers to assist with tropical forest and coral reef conservation. Expeditions to the Caribbean and the Indo-Pacific. On arrival volunteers take an intensive training course in tropical marine and/or terrestrial ecology, species identification, and field survey techniques. Expeditions depart monthly and fees range from £750 for 2 weeks to £3,000 for 12 weeks (excluding flights). Qualified staff are also recruited to help manage expeditions.

*Earthwatch Europe*, Belsyre Court, 57 Woodstock Road, Oxford OX2 6HJ, tel 01865-516366, fax 01865-311383 — takes on volunteers to work with scientists around the world conducting research into rainforests, endangered species, archaeology,and restoration. Volunteers pay a share of the costs (from £300-£2,000) to cover food and lodging, as well as a contribution to the research costs. team projects last from 2-3 weeks. For further details contact the address above enclosing an SAE or International Reply Coupons.

*Raleigh International*, 27 Parsons Green Lane, London SW6 4HS — recruits 17-25 year olds who must raise the considerable costs of their expeditions (currently £2,950) to work on community or conservation programmes. You must be able to swim; but no other special qualifications are required. There is also a taxing Assessment Weekend where candidates are selected. Expeditions in the past have been to Guyana, Belize, and Alaska.

# LONG-TERM OPPORTUNITIES

Those doing long-term voluntary work are increasingly required to bring specific skills in areas such as project management and training, besides the physical fitness and enthusiasm and a willingness to learn from your hosts which are feature of all voluntary work in another country. You will need a greater dedication and willingness to adapt, as you are likely to come into closer contact with the local community, as well as a realistic idea of your own expectations and objectives. In-depth preparation (which may include learning another language) will also be required (see the chapter *Preparation and Follow Up*). These postings often involve a complete break from a secure job at home. You will have to be prepared to work with others, and show self-reliance. Culture shock, and all the practical probems involved in living and working abroad, are also issues to be faced before your departure. *The International Directory of Voluntary Work* (Vacation Work) is a guide to all aspects of volunteering abroad, with many useful contacts. *Returned Volunteer Action* (see below) publishes two informative booklets, *Thinking About Volunteering Overseas* and *Volunteering and Overseas Development: A Guide to Opportunities,* and provides a monthly noticeboard of jobs and events.

*Arbeitskreis Freiwillige Soziale Dienste,* Stafflenbergstrasse 76, D-70184 Stuttgart, Germany, tel 0711-2159-266, fax 0711-2159-288 — offers one year's voluntary work on social projects in the Evangelical Church. Applications must be made at least one year ahead and volunteers should be between 18 and 25 years old. The scheme operates throughout Germany, and all participants must be able to speak fluent German. Travel expenses not paid.

*Brethren Volunteer Service,* 1451 Dundee Avenue, Elgin, IL 60120, tel 847-742-5100, fax 847-742-6103 — runs a programme that aims at peacemaking, advocating social justice, meeting human needs and caring for the environment. Volunteers help with counselling, community development and refugee work, etc. Minimum period of work is one year in the USA or two years abroad. Minimum age 20; specific requirements may apply to some placements. The more skills an applicant has, the better; but none are essential. Applicants need not be Christian but must be motivated by values od spiritual and humanitarian concern.

*The Camphill Movement,* Delrow House, Hillfield Lane, Aldenham, Watford WD2 8DJ, tel 01923-856006, fax 01923-858035 — runs schools and communities on Rudolf Steiner principles for mentally disabled adults and children in Austria, Brazil, Finland, France, Germany, The Netherlands, Norway, South Africa, Switzerland and the USA. Volunteers work for a minimum of six months. More details can be obtained from the Secretary.

*East European Partnership* is an initiative of *Voluntary Services Overseas* (see above).

*The Missions to Seamen,* St Michael Paternoster Royal, College Hill, London EC4R 2RL, tel 0171-248 5202 — occasionally requires volunteers to assist port chaplains in their work of caring for seafarers of all nations. The work involves ship and hospital visiting, befriending seafarers and welcoming them to the mission club, organising social events and sharing the general duties of running the club. Opportunities in Europe, the USA, Africa, the Far East and Australia; usual length of service one year. Applicants must be practising members of the Church (any denomination). Applications to the Ministry Secretary at the address above.

# Sources of Information

*Appropriate Health Resources and Technologies Action Group (AHRTAG),* 1 London Bridge Street, London SE1 9SG — is not a sending or recruiting agency but an organisation that disseminates information on primary health care for developing countries. It has a Resource Centre open to the public on Monday, Wednesday and Friday, 9.30am-5.30pm, with a comprehensive selection of materials on primary healthcare, health programmes in different countries, and health organisations worldwide.

*Catholic Network of Volunteer Service,* Harewood Road NE, Washington, DC 20017-1593 — acts as a coordinating centre for over 180 voluntary lay mission programmes. Call toll free 1-800-5435406 in the USA for their free directory of volunteer opportunities, short and long-term, domestic and international.

*The Central Bureau for Educational Visits and Exchanges,* Publication Sales, Seymour Mews House, Seymour Mews, London W1H 9PE, tel 0171-389-4880 — publishes: *Working Holidays,* a guide to short-term paid and voluntary jobs available throughout the UK and abroad; and *Volunteer Work,* a guide to voluntary work and service with information on organisations recruiting volunteers for medium and long-term projects all over the world.

*Christians Abroad,* 1 Stockwell Green, London SW9 9HP, tel 0171-737 7811, fax 0171-737 3237 — is the ecumenical charity mentioned above whose *World Service Enquiry* section provides information and advice to people of any faith or none who are thinking of working overseas, whatever their circumstances. A free information booklet lists a variety of voluntary organisations. For skilled people *Opportunities Abroad,* a monthly listing of vacancies through around 40 voluntary and development agencies, is available; a database of skilled personnel is kept and searched on behalf of agencies needing jobs filled. *World Service Projects* provides an ecumenical recruitment service on behalf of overseas partners, mainly in sub-Saharan Africa.

*Commission on Voluntary Service and Action,* PO Box 117-19, New York, NY 10009, USA — publishes the excellent *Invest Yourself* catalogue which provides a comprehensive list of openings in voluntary work in America and internationally. CVSA also provides additional consultation and services to volunteer organisations, such as producing the quarterly journal *Voluntary Services in Action,* dealing with the non-governmental Voluntary Service Movement.

*The Coordinating Committee for International Voluntary Service,* UNESCO, 1 rue Miollis, F-75015 Paris Cedex 15, tel 1-45 68 27 31, fax 1-42 73 06 21 — issues lists of workcamp/long-term voluntary service organisers by country and publishes on a regular basis directories of short-term and long-term voluntary service throughout the world. A list of CCIVS publications and their costs is also available from the above address, in exchange for four international reply coupons.

*International Health Exchange,* Africa Centre, 38 King Street, London WC2E 8JT, tel 0171-836 5833 — acts as a reference centre for health and management professionals who wish to work in developing countries and coordinator for the agencies it services. IHE also runs training courses and produces a magazine which explores practical approaches to health care in developing countries as well as carrying job and course information.

*The National Council for Voluntary Organisations (NCVO),* Regents Wharf, 8 All Saints Street, London N1 9RL — has information sheets on employment in the voluntary sector, both paid and unpaid. They also have free fact-sheets with addresses of the major voluntary organisations which work in the UK and overseas. These cover (i) Volunteering in the UK; (ii) Volunteering Overseas; (iii) Conservation and Environmental Organisations. Please send an SAE to the Enquiries Team.

*One World Broadcasting Trust,* Hedgerley Wood, Red Lane, Chinnor, Oxon OX9 4BW, tel 01494-481628, fax 01494-481751, e-mail office@oneworld.org — is a forum for the exchange of information on North-South and development issues, especially in relation to broadcasting. The One World Broadcasting Trust bursaries offer a programme of exchange visits for professional broadcasters from South and North; and its jobs home page lists general vacancies in the aid and development fields.

*The Overseas Development Administration (ODA)* issues a useful booklet *The ODA Guide to Working Overseas for the Aid Programme* which is available from the *ODA Information Department,* Room V523, 94 Victoria Street, London SW1E 5JL, tel 0171-917 0503; further information on recruitment is available from: *Resource Development Group,* Overseas Appointments and Contracts Dept., ODA, Abercrombie House, Eaglesham Road, East Kilbride G75 8EA. The ODA web site is http://www.oneworld.org/oda/index.html. (Also see *One World Broadcasting Trust* above).

*Returned Volunteer Action,* 1 Amwell Street, London EC1R 5UL, tel 0171-278-9084, is an independent membership organisation for prospective, serving, and returned overseas development workers, and people interested or active in development work. It does not send people overseas but provides advice and information to people interested in overseas development work and issues; supports returning volunteers in reacclimatising to life back in Britain; supports and encourages returned volunteers in applying their overseas experience in educational or awareness-raising work about development issues; and helps people to critically assess the possibility of working overseas in terms of the implications of their own lives. It publishes a starter pack of two booklets: *Thinking About Volunteering Overseas* and *Volunteering and Overseas Development: A Guide to Opportunities* for £3.50 plus an A5 SAE. They also provide a monthly noticeboard of jobs, events, resources, and campaigns, subscription £4.00 annually.

*Vacation Work Publications,* 9 Park End Street, Oxford OX1 1HJ, publish *The International Directory of Voluntary Work,* a comprehensive, worldwide guide that lists over 600 organisations and covers all types of work; *The Directory of Work and Study in Developing Countries,* which includes information on short and long-term voluntary work in over 100 countries; *The Directory of Summer Jobs Abroad* with details of voluntary projects, from conservation to care of the elderly; and *Kibbutz Volunteer,* with information on 220 individual kibbutzim and kibbutz work.

# International Organisations

Employment opportunities in the United Nations — the largest of all international bodies — are treated separately in the next chapter. The international organisations included in this one recruit on a smaller scale, but have a steady intake of UK and international personnel, particularly the most highly qualified professionals and administrators, and particularly in the EU. It should be noted that British citizens are under-represented in European Union institutions, and that open competitions are organised for the secretarial and clerical grades (see below).

The organisations detailed below provide examples of the scope of work available; this is not intended as a complete list of the international organisations that are recruiting. A fuller list of the world's major international organisations and associations is given in Volume I of the *Europa Yearbook,* available in public reference libraries. The most comprehensive list of all is in the *Yearbook of International Organisations,* published by the Union of International Associations in Brussels, and also available in reference libraries.

## THE EUROPEAN UNION

### Constitution
What sets the European Union apart from more traditional international organisations is its unique institutional structure. In accepting the treaties of Paris, Rome and Maastricht, Member States gave up a measure of their sovereignty, which is invested in some of the institutions below. These complement each other, and are part of the same recruitment procedures. There is more about the history of the European Union and its relation to the European Economic Area in the chapter *Rules and Regulations* of this book. Two useful guides are published by the Office for Official Publications of the European Communities, L-2985 Luxebourg: *Serving the European Union* and *Europe in Ten Points* by Pascal Fontaine, available in the UK from the *European Commission Office,* 8 Storey's Gate, London SW1P 3AT, tel 0171-973 1991.

The *European Commission,* Rue de la Loi 200, B-1049 Brussels, tel 02-299-11-11 — was created for all three original Communities, the EEC (European Economic Community), ECSC (European Coal and Steel Community), and Euratom when these were merged in 1967 creating the forerunner of today's EU. It enjoys a great deal of independence in its duties and represents the Community interest, not that of individual Member States. It is responsible for the implementation of regulations and directives of the European Council; and can bring a case before the European Court of Justice to ensure that Community law is enforced. It is the guardian of the various Treaties which set up the EU and its institutions and can intervene in the legislative process to facilitate agreement between the European Council and Parliament. It also has powers in relation to areas such as research and technology, development aid within the EU and regional cohesion, and the conduct of common policies. The Commission is organised into 26 Directorates-General, each administering different areas of policy, and departments including the Legal Service, Joint Interpretation and Conference Service, Statistical Office, Informatics Directorate, and Translation Service, located mainly in Brussels and Luxembourg. In contrast to many other international organisations it controls its own financial affairs; and is seen by some as the embryo of a future European government accountable to a two-chamber parliament which might evolve from the present European Parliament (see below) and a new organisation along the lines of the present Council.

*Council of the European Union,* Rue de la Loi 175, B-1048 Brussels, tel 02-285-61-11, fax 02-285-73-97 or 285-73-81 — is a body with some of the characteristics of both a supranational and intergovernmental organisation. The heads of state of EU Member Countries meet (along with the President of the European Commission) twice a year; and there are other ministerial meetings in areas such as foreign affairs, agriculture, transport, the environment. This Council legislates for the European Union (along with the Parliament and Commission, whose proposals it must ratify) and generally takes the most important decisions, setting its political and practical objectives. The Council also deals with current international issues through the common foreign and security policy (CFSP) which allows the Member States to align their diplomatic positions. Each state has a national delegation of civil servants, diplomats and administrative staff. The Council is supported by a secretariat of around 2,500 staff based in Brussels, of whom about 300 are adminstrative (A grade) and 550 translation staff (LA grade).

*European Parliament,* General Secretariat of the European Parliament, L-2929 Luxembourg, tel 352-43001 — has a watchdog function and also plays a part in the legislative process. Elections are held every five years and its plenary sessions are normally in Strasbourg. Brussels is the usual venue for meetings of its various committees which prepare the ground for full meetings and the different political groupings. The Maastricht Treaty strengthened its legislative role by extending its powers of co-decision to specific areas such as the free movement of workers, education, research, the environment, health, culture and consumer protection. It also approves the Union's budget each year.

*European Court of Auditors,* 12 Rue Alcide de Gasperi, L-1615 Luxembourg, tel 352-43981, fax 352-439342 — has members appointed by the Member States and oversees the European Union's budget.

*Court of Justice of the European Communities,* L-2925, Luxembourg, tel 352-430-31, fax 352-430-32600 — comprises 15 judges and nine advocates-general. It ensures that Community law is interpreted and implemented in line with the Treaties.

*Economic and Social Committee,* Rue Ravenstein 2, B-1000 Brussels, tel 02-546-90-11, fax 02-523-48-93 — assists the Council and Commission in the administration of Euratom and legislation on a wide range of other matters. Through this committee, trade and industry, and the unions can be involved in the development of EU policy.

*Committee of the Regions,* Rue Belliard 79, B-1040 Brussels, tel 02-282-22-11, fax 02-282-28-96 — was set up by the Maastricht Treaty and is consulted by the Council or the Commission on regional matters.

*European Investment Bank,* 100 Boulevard Konrad Adenauer, L-2950 Luxembourg, tel 352-43791, fax 352-437704 — is the EU's financing institution and provides long-term loans to the transport, telecommunications, and energy transfer sectors (the trans-European networks) as well as industry, the environment and the regions. Along with the European Commission, and other banks, it has also set up the European Investment Fund to support financing in some of these areas, including small and medium-size enterprises (SMEs) for which, at the time of writing, the EIF was recruiting senior staff to originate and negotiate operations in this kind of corporate finance. There were also secretarial vacancies at the EIB. Write to the *Recruitment Division* at the address above, fax 352-437-92545.

**Recruitment**

There are opportunities for British and Irish citizens to work in these institutions at all grades. Personnel grading for all institutions follows the same pattern:

> Grade A — *degree-level administrative staff*
> Grade LA — *degree-level linguists/translators/interpreters*
> Grade B — *secondary education level administrative staff*
> Grade C — *clerical officers, secretaries, shorthand/typists*
> Grade D — *skilled workers*

The Commission, Council, Parliament, Committe of the Regions, and the Economic and Social Committee, all share the same method of recruitment: vacancies are filled by open competition following published notices. These competitions are in three stages and the process may take some months. Advertisements of these notices are published in the national press; and for more detailed information you can see the *Official Journal of the European Communities*, the availability of which is described under *Information* below. Candidates who are selected in the open competitions form a reserve recruitment list and may be offered positions as they become vacant. Success in a competition is not, therefore, a guarantee of getting a job; and it may be several years before a post is offered. Entry level posts are usually restricted to those under 35 years of age. For entry to higher level posts, the usual age limit may be raised to 50 years.

In addition to permanent staff, the Commission sometimes advertises for administrators and specialists for temporary contracts of three to five years, and for short-term posts where recruitment procedures differ from the competition process.

Enquiries concerning competitions should be addressed to the Personnel Division or General Administration of the institution concerned. Or you can subscribe directly to the *Official Journal of the European Communities* by contacting the various national government bookshops (UK addresses below). Also available from the *European Commission Office* in London (see above) and the other representations in other states, is the useful booklet *Career Opportunities in the European Commission*.

Those interested in interpreting and translating for the Commission can obtain further information from the *Joint Interpreting and Conference Service,* Translation Service and Recruitment Unit, European Commission, Commission of the European Communities, 200 rue de la Loi, B-1049 Brussels. Applications to participate in the intensive 6-month training course this service offers should be addressed to: *Head of Training,* SCIC, 200 rue de la Loi, B-1049 Brussels (which is also the contact for freelance interpreters). There are strict eligibility criteria. The Council of Ministers also employs translators, but not interpreters, as they use the Commission's interpreters. Details are published in the *Official Journal of the European Communities* or may be obtained from the *Recruitment Service,* General Secretariat of the Council of the European Union, Rue de la Loi 175, B-1048 Brussels, Belgium.

Information concerning scientific posts can be obtained from the *Directorate-General for Science Research and Development,* Joint Research Centre, European Commission.

Apart from the normal recruitment channels outlined here, some special schemes also exist. The European Parliament has two training schemes: one for holders of Robert Schuman scholarships in research and documentation; the other for linguists, to spend periods of one to five months in the translating and interpreting departments. Attendance on these schemes in no way guarantees permanent employment. Applications for Robert Schuman scholarships should be addressed to the Director General for Research and Documentation at the European Parliament; applications for the translating and interpreting placements should be sent to the Director of Translating and Terminology or the Director of Interpretation.

The European Commission, the Committee of the Regions, and the Economic and Social Committee, run a five-month *stagiaire* training course for graduates which is helpful in preparing for the competitive examinations for Grade A (administrative) posts; enquiries to the *Secretariat General,* Training Office (stages) at the Commission (cited above).

Undergraduates and recent graduates wishing to find out about *stages* (or work placements) for administrative trainees should see the European Commission leaflet *Guidelines on Applying for a Stage* available from the *European Commission Office* in London. The address given for information and an application form for these work placements or *stages* for the *Translation Service* (which coincide with the 5-month schemes outlined above) is: *Translation Service (stagiaires),* Rue de la Loi 200, B-1049 Brussels.

The UK Civil Service operates a fast-track scheme through which graduates (who must hold a second or first class degree) are selected to work in Civil Service departments with a strong European connection; and are given help and preparation to enter EU competitive examinations. Details of this scheme are given in the booklet *European Fast Stream,* available from the *Vacancy Information Service,* European Staffing Division, Cabinet Office (OPS), Room 73/2, Horseguards Road, London SW1P 3AL. The European Staffing Division provides information about vacancies arising in the European Union, and can send an application form for its mailing service detailing current vacancies. Relevant information on Civil Service recruitment is also to be found on the Internet under Fast Stream and European Staffing Division: http://www.open.-gov.uk/co/fsaesd/fsaesd.htm, e-mail fsesd.recruit,co@gtnet.gov.uk

The Court of Justice recruits independently of the other institutions of the European Communities but on a similar basis. All vacant posts are advertised in the national press as and when they arise.

There are also two 'first generation' satellite bodies of the European Community, the *European Centre for Development of International Vocational Training* in Thessaloniki (postal address: POB 27 — Finikas, GR-55102 Thessaloniki, Greece; office: Marinou Antipa 12, GR-57001, Thessaloniki) and the *European Foundation for the Improvement of Living and Working Conditions* in Dublin (Loughlinstown House, Shankill, Co. Dublin) which occasionally have vacancies. Enquiries should be addressed to the Head of Administration in both cases, although prospective applicants should be highly qualified/experienced.

**Information**

The Personnel and Administration Department of the European Commission produces a free booklet entitled *Opportunities in the European Commission,* explaining its recruitment procedures and employment conditions. Detailed information about careers in the Commission may be obtained from the Recruitment Unit — Info Recruitment Office, Commission of the European Communities, 41 rue de la Science, B-1040 Brussels, Belgium.

Apart from the separate institutions themselves, the main sources of information on the EU are the four British offices (or Representations) of the European Commission). These are at:

8 Storey's Gate, London SW1P 3AT, tel 0171-973 1992
9 Alva Street, Edinburgh EH2 4PH, tel 0131-225 2058
4 Cathedral Road, Cardiff CF1 9SG, tel 01222-371631
Windsor House, 9/15 Bedford Street, Belfast, tel 01232-240708

There are also regional *European Information Centres* in many cities which can be contacted for information about funding and regional development. The Irish Representation of the European Commission is at 39 Molesworth Street, Dublin 2, tel 1-671-2244, fax 1-671-2657.

The London office of the European Parliament is at: 2 Queen Anne's Gate, London SW1H 9AA, tel 0171-222 0411, fax 0171-222 2713; and the Irish office address is: Jean Monnet Centre, 39, Molesworth Street, Dublin 2, Ireland, tel 1-671-2244.

As far as notices of competitions are concerned, the *Official Journal of the European Communities* can be consulted at these offices, as can copies of all EU documents and publications. These can also be found at many public, university and specialist libraries (some of which are designated as *European Documentation Centres*); also see the UK Civil Service *European Union Recruitment Competitions* leaflet and their World Wide Web site above. Government bookshops which stock EU and European Union publications in Britain as well as official government publications are: *HMSO Bookshops:* 49 High Holborn, London WC1V 6HB, tel 0171-873 0011, fax 0171-831 1326; 71 Lothian Road, Edinburgh EH3 9AZ, tel 0131-228 4181, fax 0131-229 2734; 16 Arthur Street, Belfast BT1 4GD, tel 01232-238451, fax 01232-235401; 9-21 Princess Street, Albert Square, Manchester M60 8AS, tel 0161-834 7201, fax 0161-833 0634; 68-69 Bull Street, Birmingham B4 6AD, tel 0121-236 9696, fax 0121-236 9699.

## OTHER ORGANISATIONS

*Commonwealth Development Corporation (CDC),* One Bessborough Gardens, London SW1V 2JQ — A public corporation established by Act of Parliament in 1948, CDC's purpose is to assist overseas countries in the development of their economies. Funded substantially by interest-bearing loans from the British government, CDC invests directly in productive and revenue-earning enterprises capable of servicing their capital.

CDC can operate in any territory dependent on Britain and, with Ministerial approval, in any other Commonwealth or developing country; and has investments or commitments in around 50 countries.

CDC recruits a number of staff every year to work on projects which it manages in the developing world. Agricultural positions are offered to candidates with a minimum Honours degree in Agricultural Science, and MSc in Tropical Agriculture and experience of relevant crops: applicants in the engineering field should be qualified to Chartered level, with relevant experience; candidates for financial positions should be graduates with professional qualifications or an MBA and with experience in accounting, banking or economics. There are a limited number of horticultural and aquacultural opportunities for which overseas management experience is essential. Contracts with projects average two years and retirement age is 60.

Application forms and further information are available from the Personnel Manager.

*The Commonwealth Fund for Technical Co-operation (CFTC),* Marlborough House, Pall Mall, London SW1Y 5HX — is a multilateral agency set up in 1971 within the Commonwealth Secretariat to provide technical assistance (advice, experts and training) to Commonwealth developing countries. The Fund's General Technical Assistance Programme provides experts such as accountants, agriculturalists, architects, auditors, bankers, economists, engineers, lawyers, librarians, managing directors, medical officers, quantity surveyors, statisticians, and specialists in broadcasting, education, industrial development, telecommunications and tourism. CFTC also runs a variety of other programmes. A roster is maintained of experts who wish to be considered for field assignments; experts have been drawn from 29 Commonwealth countries.

The *Consultative Group on International Agricultural Research (CGIAR)* is an informal association of 52 members that support a network of 16 international agricultural research centres. The Group, co-sponsored by FAO, UNDP, UNEP, and the World Bank, consists of 37 governments, 11 multilateral development agencies, and four non-government foundations. CGIAR centres conduct research into food crops that provide 75% of food energy ad a similar share of protein requirements in developing countries. For more details contact the *CGIAR Secretariat,* 1818 H St. NW, Washington DC, 20433; tel 202-473-8951; fax 202-473-8110.

The *Council of Europe,* F-67006 Strasbourg, France — 'Europe of the 39' periodically recruits graduates for general administrative posts at the secretariat in Strasbourg, with an initial contract of two years. The essential requirements are a good university degree, excellent drafting ability in English and very good reading knowledge of French. Two years' administrative experience is usually required. Upper age limit normally 35 years. Application forms available from the Human Resources Division at the above address. Recruitment by written examination and interview of shortlisted candidates. Specialist vacancies also occur notably for practising lawyers, subject to the same age limits. In addition, English language secretaries are recruited regularly, with good GCSEs and some A levels (with good grades in English and French) and 50 wpm minimum typing, age limit 35 years. Occasional freelance work for fully-qualified conference interpreters with bilingual English/French, capable of translating from German, Italian, Russian or other major Slavonic languages. Translator competitions: postgraduate translation diploma and experience essential.

The *European Organisation for Nuclear Research (CERN),* CH-1211 Geneva 23, Switzerland — accepts applications from nationals of member states (including the UK) for their fellowships. Most appointments are in the field of experimental and theoretical subnuclear physics; however there are some openings in applied physics, electronics, computing and engineering. One-year fellowships (extending for a second year) are granted to young post-graduates usually having just completed a doctorate or occasionally to more senior scientists (up to age 33) with post-doctoral experience.

Associateships in the fields listed above are available for research scientists of any nationality, who will normally be on leave of absence from their parent institute during the tenancy of the associateship (maximum duration one year). Scientific associateships for collaboration in CERN laboratory work are usually supported financially by parent institutes but there are a number of paid associateships to enable scientists to join an existing project.

Applications should normally be made 6-12 months before the expected starting date. Further information may be obtained from the *Recruitment Service, Personnel Division* at the address above, fax 022-767-27-50.

The *International Organization for Migration (IOM),* 17 route des Morillons, P.O.B. 71, CH-1211 Geneva 19, Switzerland, tel 022-717-92-41-2, fax 022-798-61-50, http://www.iom.ch/who.html (the address for the IOM publication *IOM News* is: The Information Channelling Coordinator, PO Box 71, CH-1211, Geneva 19, tel 022-7179-482, fax 022-7179-446) — has 59 member governments and 42 observer governments, among which are the UK and USA. Since 1951, it has carried out migratory movements of refugees and nationals on a worldwide scale. In 45 years of operations, IOM has processed and moved over 8 million migrants to resettlement countries.

In addition to providing services and assistance to refugees, the Organisation's task is to assist qualified technicians and professionals to ensure transfer of technology in order to promote the economic, social and cultural advancement of developing countries. In this connection IOM carries out Migration for Development programmes such as Return of Talent, Selective Migration, Integrated Experts, and Intraregional Cooperation among Latin American countries, in close cooperation with the national labour authorities.

Although the UK has only observer status with IOM, British (and US) nationals possessing the required professional qualifications are not excluded from the Selective Migration Programme. For details, contact IOM, Geneva Office for Latin America, 17 route des Morillons, CH-1211 Geneva 19, Switzerland, tel 022-717-911, fax 022-798-61-50, e-mail telex@geneva.com.ch.

The *International Telecommunications Satellite Organisation (Intelsat),* 3400 Internat Drive NW, Washington DC 20008, USA — has as its main objective the development of the global satellite system required for international public telecommunications. The staff at Washington has 636 members, including 425 professionals and some 211 general staff members. While the general staff is recruited locally, the professionals are recruited locally and from the member countries on an international scale. Candidates must be highly qualified scientists with experience in space research and/or telecommunications.

The *North Atlantic Treaty Organisation (NATO),* B-1110 Brussels, Belgium, tel 02-7074-111, fax 02-7073-677 — has vacancies for professional and administrative posts, which are filled either by secondment from member nations' civil service and diplomatic service staff or by direct hire. These posts generally require several years' graduate experience together with a good knowledge of the two NATO official languages, English and French. There is also a need for secretarial and linguistic staff; examinations are held regularly for the recruitment of translators and interpreters. NATO employs citizens of all the NATO nations. Candidates wishing to apply should do so via their national authorities or directly to NATO by sending a detailed CV.

The *Organisation for Economic Co-operation and Development (OECD),* 2 rue de André-Pascal, F-75775 Paris 16, France — recruits for administrative jobs at their secretariat in Paris. Applicants must have strong economic qualifications, plus experience in one of the organisation's spheres of activity: social affairs, labour, education, environment, science, industry, agriculture and fisheries, energy, finance and public management. Fluency in one of the official languages of the Organisation (English and French) is required. A good command of both is desirable.

Applications are handled by the Recruitment Branch, *Overseas Development Administration,* 94 Victoria Street, London SW1E SJL.

The *South Pacific Commission,* BP D5 Noumea Cedex, New Caledonia — employs two main categories of staff: specialists and support staff. Most of the latter are recruited, whenever possible, locally. Occasionally, support service vacancies arise which cannot be filled locally.

The South Pacific Commission is a technical and developmental organisation which provides training and assistance in social, economic and cultural fields, with particular emphasis on rural development.

The Commission has staff members based at SPC headquarters in Noumea, New Caledonia, in Suva, Fiji and Honiara, Solomon Islands. The official languages of the Commission are French and English.

Fields of activity include Food and Materials (Agriculture, Plant Protection); Marine Resources (Coastal and Oceanic Fisheries); Community Health Services (Health Education, Nutrition, Disease Prevention and Control), AIDS and STDs, Dental Health, Rural Water Supply and Sanitation, Environmental Health and Food Hygiene); Socio-Economic and Statistical Services (Statistics, Economics, Rural Development, Population and Development Planning, Social Statistics and Rural Technology); Community Education Services (Women's Programmes and Activities, Community Education Training, Regional Media Centre, Youth and Adult Education); and Cultural Conservation and Exchange.

*United Nations Populations Fund (UNFPA),* 220 East 42nd Street, New York, NY 10017, tel 212-297-5000, fax 212-370-0201 — is an initiative funded by the Rockefeller Foundation and the World Bank set up by ten developing countries with the aim of promoting cooperation in the field of reproductive health and family planning. Technical advisers with excellent communications skills (and, in the Middle East, Arabic); a post-graduate degree in public or business administration; social sciences; or health science; and ten years' wide experience in the development field are recruited for asia and the Middle East.

The *Universal Esperanto Association,* Head Office, Nieuwe Binnenweg 176, NL-3015 Rotterdam BJ, The Netherlands — collects and files information on opportunities for paid and voluntary work, mainly clerical, at the head office. Fluent knowledge of Esperanto is essential.

# United Nations

The United Nations Organisation has a variety of agencies; and employment opportunities which are mainly for those who are qualified in their particular field. One growth area is in information technology and the implementation of these systems. Employment of varying types can be found at the UN Secretariat headquarters in New York; at overseas offices and missions directly subordinate to the Secretariat; and in the Specialised Agencies, which are independent in most activities, including personnel recruitment. Vacancies are open to nationals of all member countries, and at the professional level attempts are made to maintain a proportional geographical distribution of personnel. Britain and the USA are members of the UN and its main agencies, however, as both are heavily over-represented, prospects for employment from these countries may be limited.

The main need is for specialised professional staff. Economics and related fields, as well as development, are obviously important career areas. Preference is always given to applicants with a knowledge of both English and French, the official working languages of the UN. A knowledge of one of the other four official languages — Arabic, Chinese, Russian and Spanish — is also an advantage.

A general source of information is the *United Nations Information Centre* at 20 Buckingham Gate, London SW1E 6LB (in the USA: *United Nations Information Centre,* 1889 F Street NW, Washington DC 20006) which can supply a list of addresses of recruitment offices of the United Nations and its specialised agencies, and any other information on request.

An active role in the recruitment of United Nations field personnel in the UK is played by the *Recruitment Branch, Overseas Development Administration,* 94 Victoria Street, London SW1E SJL. A booklet on opportunities in international organisations is available from this address. All those interested in employment with the UN or its associated organisations may also contact *The Director, Division of Recruitment,* Office of Human Resources Management, United Nations, New York 10017, USA; alternatively enquiries may be made to the separate organisations below.


## SECRETARIAT

The United Nations Secretariat includes the United Nations Headquarters in New York, the United Nations Offices in Geneva and Vienna, the United Nations Conference on Trade and Development (UNCTAD) and the Office of the United Nations High Commissioner for Refugees (UNHCR) in Geneva, the United Nations Population Fund (UNFPA) in New York, the peace-keeping missions, the information centres throughout the world and the various economic commissions of the UN.

The United Nations has a steady need for competent staff in various fields. While it is impossible to list in detail the different types of positions for which the Organisation recruits, the major categories are given below. The majority of professional posts in the Secretariat are closely related to the nature of the work required by the resolutions of the General Assembly and its principal bodies. As a result, the need is largely for specialists in the major fields of administration, economics, information technology and science; and in providing technical assistance to developing countries in the areas of economic and social development.

The United Nations is particularly interested in those candidates with international experience in more than one of these major areas which will enable them to follow an integrated and interdisciplinary approach to problems in development planning, econometrics, financial and industrial planning and administration of economic programmes. In statistical work, vacancies may arise in census and demography, industrial labour and trade statistics, national accounts and training of personnel in statistical methodology. In the fields of energy and natural resources, experts are needed in geothermal, petroleum and mineral exploration, energy systems planning, solar energy development and water management. In the field of housing and planning, professionals in construction, environmental planning and urban, rural and regional planning are sought.

There is a continuous need for *stenographic and clerical staff* and for high speed conference typists in the six official languages of the United Nations (Arabic, Chinese, English, French, Russian and Spanish) to serve in large typing pools.

The United Nations *field service staff* is responsible for servicing various United Nations field missions and comprises security officers, vehicle mechanics, radio technicians, radio officers and secretaries.

*Guides* are recruited usually once a year for a period of two years and their service as Guides does not carry any expectation of career employment with the organisation.

Recruitment of *translators/précis-writers* and *interpreters* is by competitive examinations. Apart from their own language, which must be one of the six official languages, candidates should have knowledge of at least two of the other languages.

*Librarians* should have an advanced degree or equivalent professional qualification, and working knowledge of at least two official languages, together with several years' practical library experience.

The United Nations is especially interested in recruiting women with a combination of skills and experiences acquired in an international setting which will enable them to assume administrative responsibilities.

Grade levels correspond to certain age limits, and these are taken into consideration when evaluating candidates for professional posts. Professional requirements include an advanced university degreee and ability to work easily in either English or French. Knowledge of one of the other official languages of the United Nations may also be desirable, as indicated above.

Staff may be expected to work at United Nations Headquarters in New York or in any of its other offices around the world (see below).

Requests for further information about posts in any of the above job areas should be addressed to the *The Director, Division of Recruitment,* Office of Human Resources Management, United Nations, New York 10017, USA.

## OTHER OFFICES AND MISSIONS

The *United Nations Office at Geneva* is the largest United Nations office outside Headquarters in New York. The work done here encompasses primarily conference and other international meetings, specialised economic activities, administrative and related functions. The United Nations at Geneva always gives careful consideration to applications from persons well qualified for employment. Secretarial staff are recruited locally and priority is normally given to candidates who already have familiarity with the function of the Organisation, and to those whose names have been put on a waiting list. Applications for all types of work should be addressed to: the *Secretariat Recruitment Section, Personnel Service, Palais des Nations, CH-1211 Geneva 10, Switzerland, tel 022-917-12-34, fax 022-917-01-23*. However, due to current financial restrictions, vacancies that do arise are in the first instance filled through internal redeployment.

Application forms for internships are obtainable from the applicant's own university or from the United Nations Information Centres in London or Washington.

*The International Trade Centre*: An organisation in the United Nations system that carries out technical cooperation activities with developing countries in trade promotion. ITC recruits approximately 700 consultants each year for its projects in developing countries. Such consultants work in the areas of institutional infrastructure for trade promotion, export marketing, specialised trade promotion services, import techniques and training. Inquiries should be addressed to the Personnel Administration Section, International Trade Centre UNCTAD, Palais des Nations, CH-1211 Geneva 10, Switzerland, tel 022-917-12-34, fax 022-917-01-23.

*United Nations Conference on Trade and Development*: UNCTAD deals with international trade and related issues such as protectionism.

*United Nations Environment Programme:* UNEP, like UNCTAD and UNIDO, is a part of the Secretariat, but carries out its own recruitment. The Programme's work is based on environmental problems, and experts in this field are occasionally needed. Applications should be addressed to *UNEP,* Personnel Service, PO Box 30552, Nairobi, Kenya, tel 2-520-600, fax 2-520-711.

*United Nations Industrial Development Oraganization (UNIDO),* PO Box 300, Wagramerstrasse 5, Vienna, Austria, tel 1-211-310, fax 1-232-156 or 214-0414, http://www.unido.org — is the specialist agency of the United Nations dedicated to promoting sustainable industrial development in countries with developing and transition economies. It harnesses the joint forces of government and the private sector to foster competitive industrial economies, develop international industrial partnerships and promote socially equitable and environmentally friendly industrial development. UNIDO is the only worldwide organisation dealing exclusively with industry from a development perspective. Its services are non-profit, neutral and specialised. UNIDO staff are highly qualified with the widest range and depth of required industrial expertise. The Organisation acts as a catalyst to help generate national economic wealth and raise industrial capacity through its roles as a worldwide form for industrial development and as a provider of technical cooperation services. UNIDO's ultimate goal is to create a better life for people by laying the industrial foundations for long-term prosperity. The recruitment for the headquarters posts is carried out by UNIDO's Recruitment Section, Personnel Services Division, and for technical assistance field assignments by UNIDO'S Project Personnel Recruitment Branch. Applicants interested in technical assistance assignments should contact the *ODA*: 94 Victoria Street, London SW1E 5JL. The main professional need in this area of activity is for highly qualified experts with at least five years' professional experience who have specialised in problems related to industrial development. UNIDO'S secretarial staff are normally recruited locally and candidates who are in Vienna, even on a temporary basis, are allowed to sit for the qualifying tests. Enquiries about these posts should be addressed to UNIDO'S Recruitment Section.

*United Nations Development Programmes*: Financed by the UNDP and in conjunction with overseas offices or specialised agencies, these need technical assistance experts in the ares of finance, transport statistics, electric power, mineral resources, economic development, public administration and social welfare. Candidates should have reached high professional standing in their fields, after long experience — usually at least 15 years. Junior candidates are very rarely accepted. There is also a summer graduate internship programme. UK nationals wishing to apply for these posts should address their enquiries to the Recruitment Branch, *Overseas Development Administration,* 94 Victoria Street, London SW1E 5JL.

*United Nations Economic Commissions*: The UN maintains five regional economic commissions, aimed at the economic and social development of the areas they represent. The five commissions are: the ECE (for Europe) in Geneva (Switzerland); ESCAP (for Asia and the Pacific) in Bangkok (Thailand), with a subregional office in Vanuatu; ECLA (for Latin America and the Caribbean) in Santiago (Chile), with subregional offices in Mexico City (Mexico) and Port of Spain (Trinidad and Tobago); ECA (for Africa) in Addis Ababa (Ethiopia), with subregional offices (Multinational Programming and Operational Centers — MULPOCS) for North Africa in Tangiers (Morocco), for West Africa in Niamey (Niger), for East and Southern Africa in Lusaka (Zambia), for Central Africa I in Yaounde (Cameroon) and for countries of Great Lakes (CEPGL) Central Africa II Rwanda, Burundi, Zaire, in Gisenyi (Rwanda); and ESCWA (for Western Asia) in Amman (Jordan). Staff recruitment in all these offices is primarily for specialists experienced in economics, statistics, sociology, public administration and related fields. Applications should be addressed to the Chief of Professional Recruitment, *Secretariat Recruitment Service,* United Nations, New York, NY 10017, USA.

There are several projects under way in the developing countries, which began under the auspices of the UN or one or more of its agencies, and which are now largely autonomous. Such a project is the Interim Mekong Committee, whose headquarters are in Bangkok. It is partially (5%) funded by UNDP. Positions at the Secretariat in Bangkok, and for field work — mainly for professional engineers and socio-economists — are dealt with by the *Interim Mekong Committee* at the *Mekong Secretariat,* Kasatsuk Bridge, Rama 1 Road, Bangkok 10330, Thailand.

Seminal publications dealing with these areas are: ECE: Economic Bulletin for Europe, Economic Survey of Europe; ESCAP: Economic and Social Survey of Asia and the Pacific, State of the Environment in Asia and the Pacific; ECLAC: Economic Survey of Latin America and the Caribbean, Social Panorama of Latin America; ECA: Economic Report on Africa, Africa Index: Selected Articles on Socio-economic Development, Survey of Economic and Social Conditions in Africa, African Socio-economic Indicators. ESCWA: Survey of Economic and Social Developments in the ESCWA Region, Price and Financial Statistics in the ESCWA Region, Population Bulletin of Africa.

*Information Centres and Field Missions*: The UN maintains 64 small information centres around the world and a number of field missions. These offices have no vacancies to speak of, since administrative posts are filled by internal reassignment, and secretarial staff are recruited locally.

*Military Personnel*: Military observers and UN peace-keeping forces are not recruited by the UN, but are selected from the armed forces of member countries.

*Associated Projects*: There are several projects which are now largely autonomous for recruitment purposes. The varied associated agencies of the UN include: the *United Nations University (UNU),* 53-70 Jingumae 5-chome, Shibuya-ku, Tokyo

150, tel 22-739-8111, fax 22-731-9546; and the *Centro Internacional de Agricultura Tropical (CIAT)*, Apartado Aereo 6713, Cali, Colombia; and see below under *Specialised Agencies*.

*Voluntary Work*: The opportunities for voluntary service under UN schemes are covered in the chapter on *Voluntary Work*.

*Internships*: The *United Nations Internship Programme* is offered to graduate students who may find sponsors or provide financial support themselves. It consists of three 2-month programmes through the year, January to March, May to July, and September to November. Interested candidates should contact: *Internship Programme, Room* S-2575, Recruitment and Placement Division, Office of Human Resources Management, New York, NY 10017, USA.

## SPECIALISED AGENCIES

The United Nations specialised agencies recruit their own staff, both for work in their head offices, and also on projects and development programmes abroad, especially in the developing countries. Secretarial and clerical staff are invariably recruited from local sources, and the only vacancies to be filled internationally are for fully qualified and well experienced professionals in the fields with which the agencies are concerned. Details of only a few agencies are given below, on the understanding that agencies' recruitment programmes differ only in the type of professional staff they employ; further information can always be obtained from the agencies themselves.

In general, unsolicited applications are unlikely to be considered; nor do many agencies maintain files on candidates. Instead, details of vacancies are forwarded to the appropriate departments in member states, who are invited to advertise the vacancies, hold interviews, and return a short list of suitable candidates. Thus, the ICAO will notify vacancies to the British Civil Aviation Authority, for example. These departments in turn are responsible for recruitment; and many of them maintain selective files of candidates already screened, who would be likely to fill the type of vacancies that might arise. Applications from UK citizens for posts in the developing countries under the auspices of UNDP, ILO, FAO, UNIDO, and IMO should be addressed to the Recruitment Branch, *Overseas Development Administration*, 94 Victoria Street, London SW1E 5JL.

*Food and Agriculture Organization (FAO)*, Viale delle Terme di Caracalla, I-00100 Rome, Italy — employs 2,600 staff at headquarters and 1,689 staff in the field, the vast majority in developing countries. At present these numbers are declining. Around 1,500 professional, two-thirds of who work at headquarters, carry out FAO's development mandate in agriculture, fisheries and forestry, and related areas such as soil and water resources, nutrition, economics, marketing, statistics, and project evaluation. Most positions require a minimum of five years' professional experience after university. The more usual way for younger candidates (under 30) to join FAO is as an Associate Professional Officer, a two or three year post that is financed by the officer's national government. Enquiries can be made to one's own Foreign Affairs Ministry, International Organisations Branch or equivalent. Experienced candidates can enquire about vacancies at *Central Recruitment, Personnel Division* at the address above. The work is evenly divided between headquarters and other duty stations, in some 2300 field projects in developing countries. Most is in the fields of agriculture, fisheries and forestry, and related subjects such as soil and water resources, nutrition, economics, marketing, statistics, and project evaluation; and most positions require a minimum of five years' professional experience after university. However, there are a limited number of junior level openings for candidates with less experience. UK citizens should apply to the Overseas Development

Administration. North American candidates should contact the FAO Liaison Office for North America, Suite 300, 1001 22nd Street NW, Washington DC 20437, USA.

*International Atomic Energy Authority (IAEA)*, Wagramerstrasse 5, PO Box 100, A-1400 Vienna, Austria — Recruitment is usually for professionals with experience in nuclear sciences, reactor physics and engineering, spectrometry, and the application of radio-isotopes in agriculture, biology, industry and medicine. Applications direct to IAEA headquarters.

Applications for secretarial and clerical positions in the General Service category should also be submitted direct to the IAEA, and are generally assessed for local recruitment.

*International Bank for Reconstruction and Development (IBRD)*, 1818 H Street NW, Washington DC 20433, USA — operates closely with the *International Development Association (IDA)* and the *International Finance Corporation (IFC)* (both based at the above address). Together they are known as the *World Bank Group;* recruitment is carried out both separately and jointly.

The World Bank Group differs from other agencies in that its professional staff (which numbers 1,800) are usually given an initial assignment to headquarters, from where they may be expected to travel extensively; only 5% of the staff are stationed outside Washington.

Qualified, experienced economists are most in demand, the preferred age being 30-55. Applied experience is required in one of the fields in which the Bank operates, such as development economics, transport, agriculture, industrial problems, commodities, international trade, or fiscal affairs. The Bank's predominant concern with loans and the investigation of schemes put forward for loan approval, leads to the employment of two further categories of staff: those with specialised knowledge or experience of the various aspects of investments and loans; and those experts who can investigate schemes requiring loans — including agriculturalists, agricultural and irrigation engineers; power, telecommunications and water supply engineers; road, port and railway engineers; architects, planners and educationalists. (UK applications to the Overseas Development Administration).

Candidates aged under 30, with a recognised masters degree or equivalent in economics, management, public administration, law, and related fields, can apply for employment under the Junior Professional Officer Programme, which involves 12-18 month tours of duty. Selection is on a competitive basis.

*International Labour Organisation (ILO)*, 4 route des Morillons, CH-1211 Geneva 22, Switzerland, http://www.unicc.org/ilo — The experts employed by ILO need long experience in employment and development (manpower planning, alleviation of poverty, small scale industry development); vocational training; sectoral activities (development of co-operatives); working conditions; and industrial relations. (Applications to the Overseas Development Administration).

*International Monetary Fund (IMF)*, 700 19th Street NW, Washington DC 20431, USA, tel 202-623-7000, fax 202-623-4661 — employs qualified economists, as well as accountants, administrators, computer systems officers, language specialists and lawyers. Nearly all staff members are based in Washington although the Fund also maintains small offices in Paris and Geneva. A few staff members are also stationed for varying periods in member countries as resident representatives. In addition, work assignments frequently require travel to member countries to study economic problems and lend technical assistance. Recruitment·is either through direct appointment to the regular staff (or by appointment for a fixed term, usually 2-3 years), or through the Fund's Economist Programme, which is open to well-educated graduates below 33 years of age, who may not have previous relevant work experience. The Economist Programme operates twice a year, in April and October. Enquiries to the Recruitment Division. For direct or fixed term appointments, applicants usually have significant prior experience in a government department or academic or financial institution.

*International Telecommunication Union (ITU)*, Place des Nations, 1211 Geneva 20, Switzerland, tel 022-730-8111, fax 022-734-2326 — Vacancies at headquarters (which are rare and very competitive) and in the developing countries are advertised internationally through the co-operation of the telecommunications administrations of the member countries. British applicants should address enquiries in the first instance to the *Department of Trade and Industry*, 151 Buckingham Palace Road, London SW1W 9SS. Specialist posts are open to qualified engineers with several years' experience in one of the fields of telecommunications.

*United Nations Development Programme (UNDP)*, One United Nations Plaza, New York, NY 10017, USA, tel 212-906-5000, fax 212-826-2057 — is the largest provider of UN technical cooperation grants and the main coordinator of UN development assistance. the goal is to help countries build capacity for sustainable human development combining economic growth, an equitable distribution of its benefits and careful management of natural resources.

Through a network of 136 offices worldwide, UNDP works with people and governments in 175 countries and territories, focusing on poverty eradication, environmental regeneration, job creation and the advancement of women. In support of these objectives it is frequently asked to assist in promoting sound governance and market developmant, and to help in rebuilding societies in the aftermath of war and humanitarian emergencies.

UNDP's core resources, averaging about $1 billion a year, come from the voluntary contributions of nearly every nation on earth. Eighty-seven per cent of the core programme funds go to countries with an annual per capita GNP of $750 or less. Eighty-three per cent go to 50 countries that are home to three-fourths of the world's extremely poor.

UNDP staff numbers approximately 6,000, eighty per cent of whom spend most of their careers in their fields. Requirements are for people with postgraduate qualifications, preferably in the social sciences (e.g. economics, public administration, sociology). UK applications to the *ODA*. Also see above.

*United Nations Educational, Scientific and Cultural Organization (UNESCO)*, UNESCO House, 7 place de Fontenoy, F-75700 Paris, France, tel 1-45 68 10 00, fax 1-45 67 16 90 — frequently needs specialists to work on projects in the UNESCO Field Programme in the developing countries. Most field appointments are for 1-2 years, but some may be even shorter. The Field Programme requires highly qualified people already established in a specific field of education (particularly in the areas of science, engineering and technology), and with a substantial amount of teaching experience at university, college of education or technical college level. Experience in curriculum development, teacher-training and educational organisation, administration and research are common prerequisites. Occasionally, vacancies also arise for experts in educational broadcasting, audio-visual aids, mass media, librarianship and documentation.

*World Health Organization (WHO)*, 20 Avenue Appia, CH-1211 Geneva 27, Switzerland, tel 022-791-21-11, fax 022-791-07-46 — has main staff requirements which are for highly qualified medical personnel to work on health projects in developing countries. The staff includes: senior medical officers, nursing administrators and sanitary engineers, to act as advisers to governments on broad health programmes; nurse educators, sanitarians, sanitary engineers and other medical personnel to teach or supervise teams of instructors in schools and institutes; specialists in paediatrics and child health, serology, entomology, bacteriology, biochemistry and epidemiology: hospital administrators, radiologists, X-ray technicians and dieticians: and fully qualified doctors with experience in malaria, tuberculosis, nutrition, leprology, venereal diseases and treponematoses. Vacancies at WHO head office are rare, but the Geneva headquarters also recruits on behalf of the regional head offices in Brazzaville (covering Africa), New Delhi (Asia), Copenhagen (Europe), Alexandria (Eastern Mediterranean), Manila (Western Pacific) and Washington DC (Americas).

Other specialised agencies include:

*International Civil Aviation Organization (ICAO),* 1000 Sherbrooke Street West, Suite 400, Montreal, Canada H3A 2R2; tel 514-285-8219; fax 514-288-4772.

*International Fund for Agricultural Development (IFAD),* 107 Via del Serafico, I-00142 Rome, Italy; tel 6-54591; fax 6-504-3463.

*International Maritime Organization (IMO),* 4 Albert Embankment, London SE1 7SR; tel 0171-735 7611; fax 0171-587 3210.

*United Nations Children's Fund (UNICEF),* 866 United Nations Plaza, 6th Floor, New York, NY 10017, USA.

*Universal Postal Union (UPU),* Weltpostrasse, CH-3000 Berne 15, Switzerland; tel 031-43-22-11; fax 031-43-22-10.

*World Intellectual Property Organization (WIPO),* 34 chemin des Colombettes, CH-1211 Geneva 20, Switzerland; tel 022-730-91-91; fax 022-733-54-28.

*World Meteorological Organization (WMO),* Case postale No.2300, Geneva, Switzerland; tel 022-730-81-11; fax 022-734-23-26.

## SUB-CONTRACTS

In many cases, the work of the United Nations and its specialised agencies consists of financial assistance to complete a particular project, rather than carrying out the project alone. The money is then used to procure the relevant services throughout international bidding for contracts. Sometimes a contract is only for supplies and equipment, but there are also cases where a complete project, including personnel, is involved. Of course, the familiar pattern will evolve — all but the most specialised and highly qualified personnel will be recruited locally. But there is still scope — at the upper levels — to work for one of these subcontractors.

Details of contracts being offered are given in the fortnightly newspaper *Development Business*, published by the UN. Information on subscriptions is available from *Development Business,* United Nations, PO Box 5850, GCPO, New York, NY 10163-5850, USA.

# British Government Departments

## HM DIPLOMATIC SERVICE

Members of the Diplomatic Service staff over 222 British Embassies, High Commissions, Consulates, and other missions worldwide. They must serve overseas wherever and whenever they are required. In practice, officers spend half to two thirds of their time in diplomatic missions overseas; and the remainder in the Foreign and Commonwealth Office (FCO) in London. The work is demanding. It calls for adaptability, resourcefulness, resilience, and the ability to mix with all types of people. As for nationality, you must be a British citizen and be able to show a close affiliation with the United Kingdom, taking into account such considerations as upbringing and residence.

### Career Opportunities

New entrants to the Diplomatic Service join at three separate entry points; the *Policy entry point* (formerly known as Fast Stream); the *Operational entry point* (formerly known as Main Stream); or the *Executive Assistant Branch (EAB)*. All these are distinct career options, requiring people with differing skills and ambitions. You should think very carefully about which entry point would best suit your talents and aspirations.

Policy work involves advising the Government on foreign policy; reporting and analysing world events; and putting forward the UK's views overseas. This requires a quick and clear intellect and the ability to master complex issues. In addition, applicants must have a second class honours degree in any discipline.

Operational entrants deal mainly with the practical side of Diplomatic Service work. They work in some or all of the following areas: consular; immigration; management; commercial. They may also have the opportunity to do policy work at some point in their career. There are no set educational qualifications for the operational entry point. A greater emphasis is placed on work experience. Candidates who have had some work experience are more likely to succeed in the selection process, which assesses applicants' ability to handle aspects of operational work on the basis of experience gained in other workplaces.

The Executive Assistant Branch (EAB) is a new branch of the Diplomatic Service replacing the secretarial and clerical grades. Executive Assistants provide support in London and overseas, and their duties vary from registering official papers, administration, secretarial and financial tasks to maintaining the communication links between Posts overseas and the FCO in London. There are no minimum educational requirements; but candidates are expected to have IT, numeracy and literacy skills plus previous work experience. EAB staff can expect to spend over two-thirds of their career overseas. They will not be eligible for promotion within the Service.

The preferred age range for these entry points is 21 to 52.

*Legal Advisers*: There are a small number of legal advisers in the Diplomatic Service, most of whom are based in London, although there are a few opportunities for work abroad. Applicants must be barristers or admitted solicitors. Vacancies are advertised as they occur.

*Research Analysts*: Officers compile information on the history, politics and current affairs of certain foreign countries, and prepare reports. Candidates must have a good honours degree, an aptitude for foreign languages and special qualifications in a relevant field, e.g. history, economics, and political studies. The Department is based in London, although there are occasional opportunities for work abroad. Vacancies are advertised as they occur.

*Information Technology/Technicians*: Further information can be obtained from the Recruitment Officer, Services, Planning and Resources Department, Hanslope Park, Milton Keynes, MK19 7BH.

**Recruitment**
If you would like further details on a career in the Diplomatic Service you should write to: *Recruitment Section, Personnel Management Department,* Foreign and Commonwealth Office, 1 Palace Street, London SW1E 5HE, specifying which area you are interested in. There may also be openings in the *Communications Branch* for those with technical qualifications in telecommunications; and the *Security Officer Branch* for those aged 35-50 with relevant security experience, and prepared to serve only at missions abroad.

Those wishing to join the Diplomatic Service at either the the Policy Entry Point ('Fast Stream') or Operational Entry Point levels should apply to *Recruitment and Assessment Services,* Alençon Link, Basingstoke, Hampshire RG21 1JB, tel 01256-29222, from whom they will receive an application form described by one recent applicant as extremely comprehensive. Full details of the recruitment regulations and selection process are contained in booklets available from the *Foreign and Commonwealth Office* (see below).

## THE BRITISH COUNCIL

The British Council promotes Britain abroad; and provides access to British ideas, talents and experience through education and training, books and periodicals, the English language, the arts, sciences and technology. It is an independent, non-political body managed by a Director General working to a Board of Management. With a presence in 109 countries, it provides a network of contacts between government departments, universities and professional and business organisations in Britain and around the world. Its work helps to promote a climate for international co-operation in all its fields of activity, and its range of contacts enables it to act as a catalyst for British and foreign interests. Staffing levels are, at the time of writing, being reviewed; but most are employed overseas.

The five principal activities are:

(1) Helping people to study, train or make professional contacts in Britain; and enabling British specialists to teach, advise or establish joint projects abroad.

Thousands of people visit the UK every year under Council auspices, on individual study visits, attachments to educational institutions, courses or international conferences. Many are involved in the government's Technical Co-operation Training Programme, which the Council administers on contract for the Overseas Development Administration. Other programmes are handled on behalf of the Foreign and Commonwealth Office, UN agencies, the World Bank, the European Union and other funding bodies.

The Council also sends teaching and other staff to work overseas. For information on these appointments, contact Overseas Educational Appointments Department, The British Council, Medlock Street, Manchester M15 4AA. Further details are given under *The British Council* in chapter on *Teaching*.

(2) Teaching English and promoting its use.

The Council manages its own network of English language teaching and resource centres throughout the non-English-speaking world. Teachers are recruited on fixed-term contracts: the absolute minimum qualification required is a Cambridge/RSA Diploma (DELTA) or equivalent. For information contact the Central Management of Direct Teaching, The British Council, 10 Spring Gardens, London SW1A 2BN.

(3) Providing library and information services.

Working overseas in close co-operation with the local British Mission, the Council provides an information service which handles enquiries about British education and English language teaching, books, culture and qualifications. The service is provided from the network of libraries and resource centres mentioned above, in the major centres of population in the countries in which the Council has a presence.

(4) Promoting British education, science and technology.

Through its network of contacts in higher education, research institutions and government ministries, the Council enables co-operation between individuals and institutions and encourages and promotes the use of British services and products.

(5) Making British arts and literature more widely known.

Council assistance enables the promotion of high-quality British drama, dance and music, as well as a range of exhibitions which tour the world regularly, with significant and growing amounts of sponsorship from the business world both in the United Kingdom and abroad.

**Recruitment for posts overseas**
Recruitment exercises are publicised in the press, notably *The Guardian* plus relevant specialist journals such as the *Library Association Record* and *New Scientist*. Essential criteria are a good first degree and three years' work experience; a further degree plus experience of working overseas for an extended period are highly desirable. Ability and interest in foreign language learning is essential, though language training is provided when necessary. The British Council is an equal opportunity employer.

Further details can be obtained from the Recruitment Unit, Personnel Department, The British Council, 10 Spring Gardens, London SW1A 2BN.

# BRITISH GEOLOGICAL SURVEY

The Survey is concerned with geological mapping and resource investigations in Great Britain and its continental shelf and in developing countries overseas. The overseas component is administered by the Survey's International Division as part of the Overseas Development Administration's aid programme as well as other international programmes. Scientific staff of BGS have the opportunity of serving overseas either as members of geological teams working on specific technical assistance projects or on secondment as members of geological survey departments overseas.

The work of the International and Marketing Division is administered through Regional Units dealing with Africa, Middle East and South Pacific, Asia, Europe, and other areas. Much of the work overseas involves BGS specialists in the fields of hydrogeology, geophysics, geochemistry, engineering geology, etc.

Further details on employment and career prospects can be obtained from the Establishment Officer, *British Geological Survey,* Keyworth, Nottingham NG12 5GG; tel 0115-936 3100; fax 0115-936200.

# Military Service

## British Armed Forces

### ARMY

Europe has been transformed since 1989: the Warsaw Pact has been dismantled and Germany has been united. These factors have in turn had an effect on the shape, function and size of the British Army. The new Army will be smaller, even more highly trained, flexible, more mobile, and will be better prepared to operate as part of a multinational force.

The reduction in overall numbers has not meant a halt to recruiting. In 1997 the British Army sought over 700 new officers, approximately three-quarters of them graduates. New officers, both male and female, are always needed to bring youthful drive, enthusiasm and energy into the Army, as well as contemporary educational and technical skills.

British Army officers are employed worldwide, including Germany, Belize, Cyprus, the Falkland Islands and Gibraltar.

### Eligibility

The following points should be noted before an application is made:

*Marital Status* — Women and men, both single and married, are eligible to apply. Employment within or in support of the Armed Forces is in accordance with the conditions of the Equal Opportunities Act.

*Nationality* — An applicant must be, and must have been at all times in his or her life, a UK citizen, a Commonwealth subject, or a citizen of the Republic of Ireland; must have been born within the Commonwealth or the Republic of Ireland; and both parents must have been born within the UK, the Common-wealth or the Republic of Ireland.

*Political Bias* — No one, while a member of the Armed Forces, may take part in any political activity.

*Age* — The minimum age for entry into the Armed Forces is school leaving age, i.e. 16½. Parents' consent is needed for entrants under 18. The upper age limit is 25.

*Health* — All applicants must pass a strict health examination. Applicants for some branches may be refused on the grounds of their height, hearing or eyesight.

### Obtaining a Commission

Officers are commissioned at the Royal Military Academy, Sandhurst. All officers, graduates, non-graduates, men and women, those hoping for a Regular Commission, and those hoping for a Short Service Commission, undertake the same Commissioning Course which lasts 44 weeks. Details of the two types of commission in the British Army are:

The Regular Commission — open to both graduates and non-graduates and to both male and female applicants. All applicants must be aged over 17 years 9 months and under 25 on entry to the Royal Military Academy, Sandhurst, for officer training. In the case of the Technical Corps an upper age limit of 27 may be considered. Passes are required in five separate approved GCSE examinations

(A-C grades), including English Language and Mathematics, as well as either a science subject or a foreign language. Passes are also required in two A-levels at grades A-E. Regular Commission officers have the opportunity to serve up to the age of 55.

The Short Service Commission — open to graduates and non-graduates and to male and female applicants. All applicants must be aged over 17 years 9 months and under 25 on entry to the Royal Military Academy, Sandhurst, for officer training. In the case of the technical corps an upper age limit of 27 may be considered. Passes are required in five separate approved GCSE examinations (A-C grades), including English Language and Mathematics. The Short Service Commission officer serves a minimum of three and up to a maximum of eight years.

Professional Arms — Short Service and Regular commissions are granted to appropriately qualified personnel to serve in the Royal Army Chaplains' Department, Royal Army Medical Corps, Royal Army Veterinary Corps, Royal Army Dental Corps and the Army Legal Corps. Commissioned entry into these departments is via a four-week course at Sandhurst. Medical, legal and dental cadetships are available.

In addition to the two long-term types of commission, there is a temporary commission — the Short Service Limited Commission (GAP Year Scheme). The GAP Year Commission is open to school leavers before they take up a firm place at university to read for a degree. They must first pass the Regular Commissions Board selection. Successful candidates complete a three-week course at the Royal Military Academy, Sandhurst. Then they serve for between 4-18 months. They are required to give six weeks' notice if they wish to terminate their service. They have no reserve liability and no subsequent obligation to serve in the Army.

**Army Sponsorship**
The Army has several sponsorship schemes to sponsor young people while at school, sixth form college and university. Details are as follows:

Undergraduate Cadetships — open to men and women aged 17½-23 who are at, or about to go to, university. An undergraduate cadet is commissioned as 2nd Lieutenant on probation. Cadets agree to serve for five years on completion of Sandhurst training.

Undergraduate Bursaries — open to men and women aged 17½-23 who are at or about to go to university. A bursar is not commissioned but does sign an agreement to serve for three years on completion of training at Sandhurst.

Scholarship Scheme — Army scholarships are awarded to boys and girls aged 16-16½, to enable them to take the A-levels necessary for Sandhurst entrance.

Welbeck College — boys and girls aged 16-17½ with GCSEs in English, Maths, Physics, and preferably other science subjects, can take science A-levels at the Army Sixth Form College, Welbeck, to qualify to enter Sandhurst. They will mainly be commissioned into one of the technical corps.

**Non-Commissioned Service**
(a) Technical, Arms and Corps Apprentices — various technical apprentice colleges offer one-year courses for boys and girls aged 16 years to 17 years, six months on entry. Basic military training, education, general subjects, and many specialist employments are taught.

(b) Adult Entry — unqualified men and women aged 17-25 (sometimes up to 30) may enter one of the 135 employments in the Army.

**Length of Service**
Entry into the ranks is on the terms of an open engagement. Enlistment is for a minimum of three years, three months. Apprentices serve for a minimum of three years from their 18th birthday. Entrants under the age of 17½ are allowed to leave the Army within the first 6 months if they find themselves unsuited to Army life. A full career in the ranks is reckoned as 22 years, but 12 months' notice can be given at any time so long as the initial period of enlistment has been served.

**Further Details**
*Army Officer: The Career*, a booklet available from your local Army Careers Office, listed in the telephone book under 'ARMY' — for information on non-commissioned service. Or telephone the Army Answering Service on 0345-300111 for an information pack.

## WOMEN IN THE BRITISH ARMY

Since the abolition of the Women's Royal Army Corps (WRAC) in 1992 women who serve as commissioned officers or as non-commissioned soldiers are employed in all Regiments and Corps of the British Army. Women cannot presently be commissioned into the Household Cavalry, the Royal Armoured Corps and the Infantry, however, women are attached to these Units for up to three years at a time. Men and women are trained together at all stages including officer training at Sandhurst.

Women apply for commissioned service, both Short Service and Regular Commissions, and for non-commissioned service, in the same way as men apply. All terms of service, training, pay and promotion rules are identical. Likewise, entry requirements are identical to those for male applicants. Details can be obtained from local Army Careers Offices (for non-commissioned officers). Or telephone the Army Answering Service on 0345-300111 for an information pack.

## ROYAL NAVY

The Royal Navy provides extensive opportunities to serve both in ships and shore establishments situated all over the world. After a period of reduction, the Navy has stabilised at approximately 38,600 men and women of which 7,300 are of commissioned rank. The Navy is now actively recruiting at all levels of entry.

**Commissioned Service**
Scholarships and reserved places in the warfare, supply and aircrew branches are available to young men aged 15-17 with five GCSE passes or equivalent. All branches are open to graduate entry and university sponsorships are offered. For those interested in engineering, the Navy has an engineering sponsorship scheme at Southampton University. Currently, the navy has three types of commission open to all branches: Full Career Commission, offering the chance to serve to the age of 50; Medium Career Commission, where entrants serve for 16 years; and Short Service Commissions, which are initially for eight years. Only Medium and Short careers are initially open to aircrew candidates. The commission structure is to be changed in 1997, with all new entrants joining on a 12-year initial commission with opportunities to transfer to longer periods of service at a later stage. The age limits on entry differ depending on branch and commission, but range between 17 and 34. The Navy requires approximately 370 commissioned officers each year.

Doctors and dentists all enter on Short Career Commissions, and age limits vary.

All Naval officers go to the Britannia Royal Naval College, Dartmouth for basic officer training.

**Non-Commissioned Service**

Educational qualifications are not required for entry into most branches in the Royal Navy, but all applicants must pass a recruiting test and medical. Male and female applicants for Junior and Adult Entry in non-technical branches must be between the ages of 16 and 32.

Applicants for Artificer Apprentice entry (Engineering Technicians), male and female, must be between the ages of 16 and 27 and possess acceptable grades at GCSE or equivalent in Maths, English Language, and Physics (or a suitable physics-based science subject).

Applicants for Medical Technician must have acceptable grades at GCSE or equivalent in at least five subjects. For some Medical Technician specialisations, A levels or SCE passes at Higher Grades are required as part of the total number of subjects. Applicants must be between the ages of 17½ and 32, and pass a selection board.

Entry is also open to fully qualified Medical Technicians subject to Service requirements.

Applicants for Communication Technician must have acceptable grades at GCSE in at least two subjects, one of which must be English Language, and pass aptitude tests and a selection board.

For further information and how to apply to the Royal Navy and the Royal Marines see *Methods of Application* below.


# ROYAL MARINES

The Royal Marines are an autonomous military corps in the Royal Navy, and provide Britain's only commando forces. Special training for jungle, desert, snow and mountain warfare is given in Malaysia, Borneo, the Arctic, Norway, Canada and Scotland. The Royal Marines total 7,000 officers and men.

**Commissioned Service**

Full and Short Service Careers are offered. A limited number of sponsorships for undergraduates are also available. Entry age is limited depending on commission and whether the candidate is a graduate but ages range from 17½ to 25. Initial training lasts 15 months and minimum periods of service are comparable with those of the RN.

**Non-Commissioned Service**

Applicants for Royal Marines General Duties (other ranks) do not require educational qualifications, but must be male and between the ages of 16 and 27 (16 and 27½ for junior entry). They must pass a recruiting test, medical and the Potential Recruits Course.

Applicants for Royal Marines Musician and Bugler do not require educational qualifications, but must be between the ages of 16 and 27, male or female. They must pass a recruiting test, medical, and music assessment and audition. Selected candidates may apply for a bursary to attend an approved college music course.

**Length of Service**

For the RN there are three types of commission: Full Career (Pensionable), Medium Career, and Short Career. The RM have just two, Short and Full Career Commissions. The minimum period of service is the same for most commissions but is dependent on the branch and training undertaken and varies between three and six and a half years.

Royal Navy Ratings and Royal Marines other ranks are entered for 22 years from age 18 or date of entry, whichever is later. This service is pensionable. All personnel have the right to claim discharge on giving 18 months' notice at any time after completion of 2½ years' service — 3½ years for Artificer Apprentices, Medical and Communication Technicians — from the age of 18, or after completion of the standard initial training period, whichever is later.

**Methods of Application — Royal Navy and Royal Marines**
For further information, enquirers should contact their nearest Armed Forces Careers Office, Jobcentre or Careers Service. Those wishing to apply for a Royal Navy or Royal Marines commission should write to: *The Officer Enquiry Section,* Room 043, Victory Building, HM Naval Base, Portsmouth, PO1 3LS. Students and graduates may contact the *Graduate Liaison Officer,* The Royal Navy, at the address above, tel 01705-727746, fax 01705-727251.

# WOMEN'S ROYAL NAVAL SERVICE

The WRNS is an integral part of the Royal Navy, whose members (known as 'Wrens') serve in naval establishments, ships (there were 700 WRNS on 41 warships in 1997), and shore bases and air stations in Britain and abroad.

**Commissioned Service**
The direct entry scheme is open to candidates aged 20½-26½, with degrees; diplomas in social science; teacher training; professional, secretarial or catering qualifications and experience. Training courses are given at the Royal Naval College at Dartmouth, and service is in the following branches: secretarial; administrative; quarters and catering; communications; and computers.

**Non-Commissioned Service**
WRNS ratings must be between 17 and 28 on entry. Following five weeks of general training at HMS *Raleigh* at Torpoint, East Cornwall, specialised training there or elsewhere is given. These include: technical, secretarial, supply, communications and weapons analysis. Other posts include education and training support, dental surgery and hygienist assistant, telephonist.

**Length of Service**
Commissions are all for eight years, with options to leave after five years, or to transfer to a permanent commission. Non-commissioned WRNS entrants join for a 15-day probationary period, during which they may claim their release if they do not feel suited. They subsequently enter on a nine year engagement which commences either from age 18 or from date of entry, whichever is later.

**Further Details**
The *Directorate of Naval Recruiting,* Old Admiralty Building, Spring Gardens, London SW1A 2BE.

*Queen Alexandra's Royal Naval Nursing Service*
Registered General Nurses with at least two years' nursing experience, and preferably an extra qualification, may enter direct as an officer on a five year short-term commission. The maximum age on entry is 33.

Girls aged 18-28, with GCSEs may train for RGN training, five passes are required (English Language compulsory).

For further details, contact the Directorate of Naval Recruiting, Old Admiralty Building, Spring Gardens, London SW1A 2BE.

# ROYAL AIR FORCE

Although the number of RAF bases abroad has been reduced, there are still opportunities for overseas service. The Women's Royal Air Force is not a separate force and so is not listed by itself. The RAF is an equal opportunities employer.

**Commissioned Service**

University cadetships are available to applicants aged under 23, who have a university place or at least good prospects of one. The scheme is designed to help entrants obtain a degree by providing generous sponsorship.

Direct Entry — entry into commissioned service is via the RAF College at Cranwell. There are 15 Officer specialisations, including Pilot, Navigator, ATC and Fighter Control. Men and women aged over 17½, with two A-levels and five GCSE level passes, can be considered for Officer Training. The upper age limit varies with branch and can be up to 38; however, applicants for Pilot must be under 24 at start of training.

Professionally qualified men and women up to age 30 may enter via a shortened courses at RAF College Cranwell into the Medical, Dental, Chaplains and Legal branches.

The leaflet *Officer — Careers in the Royal Air Force* contains detailed information about conditions of entry at officer level in the Royal Air Force, available from RAF Careers Information Offices. Another leaflet, *Officer — Royal Air Force Sponsorship,* gives details of sponsorship arrangements. Students and graduates may contact the *Senior Careers Liaison Officer,* Royal Air Force, RAF C10, Norwich, 22 Uthank Road, Norwich NR2 1AH.

**Non-Commissioned Service**

(a) Non-Commissioned Aircrew — opportunities exist for NCO aircrew in one of the following areas: Air Loadmaster, Air Engineer and Air Electronics Operator. Applicants must usually be between 17½ and 26 with 3 GCSEs at grade C, including Mathematics and English Language. Also required is a background in a science subject.

(b) Ground Airmen and Airwomen — men and women aged 16½-39 can be considered for vacancies which arise in the following jobs: aircraft engineering, air electronic engineering, general engineering, ground electronic engineering, mechanical transport, security, air traffic control, general service, telecommunications, aerospace systems operating, surface and safety, photography, medical, dental, accounting and secretarial, supply and movements, catering, and other support trades.

**Length of Service**

Commissions are of two types — permanent commissions can last until the age of 55, but may be terminated at the age of 38 or after 16 years service if you enter after the age of 21, whichever is the later. Short service commissions are for 3-6 years for ground branches, and 12 years, with an option of leaving earlier, for aircrew. Fixed engagements for non-commissioned service are normally for nine years.

Further details can be obtained by writing to your nearest RAF Careers Information Office, address in the telephone directory under RAF.

# Ancillary Services

## NURSING AND WELFARE

Whichever service the student or registered general nurse chooses to join, prospects of an overseas posting are good. There are service hospitals wherever large numbers of servicemen and their families are based, and nurses are constantly in demand.

*Queen Alexandra's Royal Army Nursing Corps*
Men and women aged 21-38 holding the minimum of RN qualification, can apply for a Short Service Commission in the QARANC. This is an eight year commission, of which a minimum of three years are spent on the Active List and the balance on the Regular Army Reserve of Officers. A full career within the Corps is available to those accepted for conversion to a Regular Commission.

RNs who have proof of admission to Part I of the UKCC Register but have not as yet gained a year's post-registration experience, may apply for an 'S' type engagement for two years, with an opportunity after one year to apply and be considered for a commission. Direct entry is also available for ENs who have proof of admission to Part II of the UKCC Register.

Untrained men and women aged at least 17 who pass the Army Entrance Test to the required standard, may train as Health Care Assistants. Minimum service is for three years, which can be extended to a full career of up to 22 years. Student nurses are also trained within QARANC. All training and courses conform to affiliated civilian standards.

For further details of medical employment in RAF hospitals and units (as well as other support trades) see the leaflet *Support Trades in the Royal Air Force* available from RAF Careers Sevice Offices.

*Princess Mary's Royal Air Force Nursing Service*
Registered General Nurses aged 21-27 may apply for a Staff Nurse post in the PMRAFNS. If you are between ages 23-35 with a minimum of two years' post-registration experience, preferably with an insight into ward management, and normally a second nursing certificate, you are eligible to apply for a four year short service commission as a Nursing Officer. Limited opportunities for further service are open to suitable candidates.

For further information contact the *Director of Nursing Services (RAF),* Headquarters Personnel and Training Command, RAF Innsworth, Gloucester GL3 1EZ.

*Soldiers', Sailors' and Airmen's Families Association — Community Health and Social Service*
The SSAFA Community Health Service provides health care for Service families posted overseas. SSAFA recruits experienced United Kingdom-based civilian Health Visitors, Midwives, Community Psychiatric Nurses, Pharmacists, Practice Managers, and Practice Nurses to work with Service families. There are well-established Health Promotion and In-service Training Departments.

The SSAFA Social Work Service employs qualified and experienced Social Workers to work with servicemen and their families both overseas and in the United Kingdom.

For further details contact: Support Manager Community Health, or the Director of Social Work, SSAFA, 19 Queen Elizabeth Street, London SE1 2LP.

# Foreign Armed Forces

National armed forces are usually open only to citizens of that country. However, some countries welcome others into their ranks. A few countries even insist on foreign residents being prepared to do military service. So some British and American citizens do enroll in the armed forces of other countries.

The Middle East states are among the countries prominent in recruiting well trained personnel for their armed forces. The following company is involved in recruiting service and training personnel:

*Support Services, Short Bros. plc.,* Bournemouth International Airport, Christchurch, Dorset BH23 6EB – deals with all aspects of aircraft and communications maintenance and servicing. There are also vacancies for technical instructors in the fields of aircraft maintenance and telecommunications. Positions are in Oman, The United Arab Emirates, and Kuwait.

## FRENCH FOREIGN LEGION

The French Foreign Legion, immortalised by Beau Geste and Laurel and Hardy, was created in 1831 and is a semi-autonomous unit under the French Ministry of Defence. Although the legionnaire is idealised in fiction and the recruitment leaflets, it can in real life be very lonely and austere, and the chances of getting out before the end of the five-year contract are slim.

### Entry Requirements

Applicants should be aged between 18 and 40 (average is 24). 17 year-olds, perhaps with some difficulty, must get written consent from their parents. They should also be physically fit. Beyond this, the only requirement is complete loyalty to the legion, whose motto *legio patria nostra* (the legion is our country) demands that soldiers should renounce or forget their family, friends, home country and other loyalties. On the negative side, intellectual ability and knowledge of the French language are not required; colour, creed, nationality and social class have no bearing; and few questions are asked about identity or background.

Enlistment can only take place in France at one of the 23 Foreign Legion information centres. Any gendarmerie in France can direct you to the nearest centre. The obligatory medical, psychological and professional tests are held at Aubagne, near Marseille.

### Service

Contracts are initially for five years, starting with 16 weeks' training at Castelnaudary. Following the training course, soldiers will be classified as specialist combatant, technician or corporal, with promotion prospects to officer status. Service is one of the parachute, infantry, cavalry or mixed regiments in Corsica or the south of France; during the first five years it is also possible to serve for two years in one of the regiments stationed in Tahiti, Mayotte, Djibouti and French Guiana. Special training can be given in a variety of trades, including telecommunications, mechanics and building.

At the end of five years, contracts can be renewed for up to three years at a time, pensionable after a total of 15 years' service, or to obtain a 10-year residence warrant.

### Further Details

Contact: *Le Chef du Poste d'Information de la Légion Etrangère (PILE),* Fort de Nogent, F-94120 Fontenay-Sous-Bois, France. Write, or telephone +1-48 77 49 68. English is spoken. An English-language leaflet *Foreign Legion* and booklet *The Foreign Legion* is published. The enlistment procedure is unorthodox: 'Applicants must come to France at their own expense (we suggest Calais because it is the closest port) and contact the gendarmerie (open from 7am to 6pm) who will give the exact address, phone number and a transport ticket to the nearest legion recruiting office in Lille.'

# Other Services

## THE POLICE

Opportunities for British Policemen and Policewomen do occasionally arise in a few Commonwealth member states, although these have been reduced in recent years. There are no formal foreign exchange schemes available to Police Officers, but a small number are seconded abroad each year from the Metropolitan and other Constabularies. Police positions overseas are sometimes advertised in *The Police Review*, available on subscription from *The Police Review Publishing Company*, South Quay Plaza 2, 183 Marsh Wall, London E14 9FZ.

The Service Recruitment and Selection Centre of the Metropolitan Police (address below) advises that at any one time some 20 fairly senior Officers will be seconded abroad from this country. The Metropolitan Police also advise that much of this recruitment takes place by word of mouth, but serving Officers interested in the general prospects of contracts with overseas forces might like to contact the *Recruitment Branch,* of the *Overseas Development Administration* at 94 Victoria Street, London SW1E 5JL.

**The Metropolitan Police**
All Officers recruited to the Metropolitan Police Service must meet certain minimum entry standards. They must be physically fit, 18½ or older, a British or Commonwealth citizen permanently resident in the UK, and have good eyesight. They must have experience of living or working in London, possess excellent communication skills and be of good character.

Prospective police officers take a series of written tests and must also pass a rigorous physical fitness test and appear in front of a selection board. If appointed, they will begin their careers with a two year probationary period. The first 16 weeks of this are spent on integrated training, based at the Metropolitan Police Training Centre at the Peel Centre, Hendon, North London.

Further information about recruitment to the Met is available from the *Metropolitan Police Service,* Recruitment and Selection Centre, 26 Aybrook Street, London W1M 3JL.

# Worldwide
# Employment

# EUROPE

The following are the main countries of western, southern and northern Europe which belong to the EU and European Economic Area. The chapter *Rules and Regulations* explains the significance of these groupings for jobseekers; and covers the history of the European Union. Switzerland is also included here: it has close cultural links with its neighbours (even if the regulations for those seeking work are not the same). The institutions of the European Union are explained with reference to employment at the beginning of the chapter *International Organisations*.

This division of Europe into 'West' and 'East' is important in one major respect. In the countries of central and eastern Europe which are not yet EU members there has been a rapid process of economic change which has only recently allowed significant numbers of international workers to find employment. These tend to be in specialised areas relating to the transition from a centrally planned economy to the free market and to a more open society, which has brought new problems (and new opportunities) in its wake. Simply, there is a much longer history — so far as the readers of this Directory will be concerned — of living and working in the countries of Western Europe which are included below.

There are close historical links between them too. Since the war, they have followed more or less the same path of economic development. Now, the same changes are coming the the 'East', but more rapidly; and older affinities — between the countries of Central (or 'Middle') Europe for example — are beginning to reassert themselves. Germany will have a great role to play in this transition to a less divided continent. There will be new alignments and groupings too: among the countries of Scandinavia or the Mediterranean which have their own common interests. The EU, as it grows, will certainly become more decentralised; and a new dividing line between north and south may eventually reflect more accurately these changing economic and cultural realities.

# Austria

Austrian Embassy: 18 Belgrave Mews West, London SW1X 8HU, tel 0171-235 3731
Austrian Embassy, 3524 International Court, NW, Washington, DC 20008, tel 202-895-6700
Currency: 1 Schilling (S) = 100 groschen
Rate of Exchange: £1 = S 16.5; $1 = S 10.8

Austria is a full member of the EU, which makes it easier for other EU citizens (like the British and Irish) to find employment. No work permit is required. For more on immigration and working in EU countries, see the beginning of the *Rules and Regulations* chapter, and these general rules hold for each Member State. This is also good news for the Austrian tourist industry in particular, which can recruit more English-speaking staff to deal with its visitors who speak this language — particularly for skiing. The competition in hotel and tourism work is from East Europeans who work hard, and for less pay.

The future of the Austrian economy has much to do with Eastern Europe. Like Poland, the Czech Republic, or Hungary it regards itself as a Central European country, at the crossroads of east and west. It has a small economy, but with strong trading and cultural links with its neighbours; and enjoys a low inflation rate, and relatively low unemployment.

In fact, Austria is one of the most prosperous countries in the world. Manufacturing, including mining, accounts for nearly 30% of Gross Domestic Product (GDP). Agriculture in Austria, a bit like the Austrians, is rather self-sufficient, and meets 90% of its food needs. In its social life, coffee shops are a national institution (if rather expensive) and nightlife is quiet rather than boisterous. 'Early to bed, early to rise' could have been an Austrian saying. Work relations are quite formal and businesslike; and dressing smartly is important if you want to make a good impression. So is a working knowledge of German.

## GENERAL FACTS

### Population and Geography
The population is just over eight million. The landscape is famously scenic, with the high Alpine mountains of the Tyrol, the lakes of Carinthia, the River Danube (which flows through the capital Vienna), and the forests of Styria. Vienna has a population of 1.6 million. This is a landlocked country bordered by Switzerland, Liechtenstein, Germany, the Czech Republic, the Slovak Republic, Hungary, Slovenia and Italy, and is predominantly Alpine. Its geographical location means it will play a central role in the EU's expansion to the east.

### Climate
Be prepared for cold weather in winter. This is a moderate continental climate, and summers can be hot.

### Government
'Austria is a democratic republic. Legislative power is in the hands of the people.' So begins the Federal Constitution, which has its origins in the anti-fascists parties which proclaimed Austria's independence after its liberation (or defeat) in 1945. The head of state is the President; and there is a bicameral parliament — or 'federal assembly' — made up of the *Nationalrat* and *Bundesrat*. The former

is elected every four years. To the latter, Austria's nine provinces and their parliaments send representatives.

### Religion, Sport and Culture
It is 78% Roman Catholic and 5% Protestant. Soccer, motor sports, and cycling are important, but Austria leads the way in Alpine skiing and the various other winter sports, like tobogganing, whose international competitions it often hosts. Three million Austrians belong to sports or health and fitness clubs. Architecture, painting, and music are Austria's great cultural achievements; the annual Salzburg festival focuses mainly on work by Mozart and Richard Strauss. The ornate and formal baroque style of architecture to be found in this city and Vienna is regarded as representative of the Austrian national character. The twilight of the Austro-Hungarian Empire was also a time of great artistic and cultural activity, with writers like Robert Musil, the composer Arnold Schönberg, and psychologist Sigmund Freud among the leading lights.

## FACTORS INFLUENCING EMPLOYMENT

### Immigration
Visas are not required by US citizens for stays of up to 90 days. EU citizens can stay for up to six months. Only one type of entry visa is issued, and it is not stated if the purpose is for business or tourism. Work permits are required by Americans. The Austrian Embassy states that the permit can only be applied for by the future employer in Austria, and prior to the prospective employee's intended departure. Once the offer of work is secured, the employer obtains the work permit from the *Arbeitsamt* (employment agency — see below) which then forwards it to the *Austrian Consulate-General,* 31 East 69th Street, New York, NY 10021, tel 212-944-6880; and the employee then sends the work permit application, together with his or her passport, a completed application form for the issuing of a visa, and the fee, to the Consulate-General. The special visa will then be issued upon approval. In the case of short-term student exchange schemes (see below) the relevant documents are issued by the agency concerned. For British nationals there as a simpler procedure; and you have six months to look for an employer who will support your application for a residence permit. *EURES* (see *Getting the Job*) is your contact in the UK; you should approach your local Jobcentre. The equivalent employment services in Austria are the eight state-run *Arbeitmarktservice* offices (which will expect you to speak German).

In addition to work permits, foreign nationals (and Austrians as well) who intend to set up business, require a permit from the head of the provincial government (*Landeshauptmann*). For certain trades and professions a licence must be obtained, or proof of qualifications given.

All aliens are required to register with the police within 24 hours of arrival. After ten years' residence in Austria, aliens may apply for Austrian nationality.

### Embassies and Consulates
British Embassy, Jaurèsgasse 12, A-1030 Vienna; tel 1-7131575.
  *Consular Section,* Jaurèsgasse 10, A-1030 Vienna; tel 1-7146117-8.
American Embassy, Boltzmanngasse 16, 1091, A-Vienna; 1-31339.
  *US Consulate,* 4th Floor, Gartenbaupromenade 2, A-1010 Vienna; tel 1-31339.

### Tourist Offices
Austrian National Tourist Office, 30 George Street, London W1R 0AL; tel 0171-629 0461.
Austrian National Tourist Office, PO Box 1142, Times Square, New York, NY 10108-1142.

**Newspapers**

Austrian newspapers can be consulted in the reading room of the Austrian Institute, 28 Rutland Gate, London SW7 1PQ.

Advertisements can be placed in the daily *Die Presse* through *Powers International*, 517-523, Fulham Road, London SW6 1HD, tel 0171-385 8855 (which represents a wide range of newspapers and magazines worldwide).

## SPECIFIC CONTACTS

**Employment Service**

The Austrian Embassy cannot help in finding employment. Information can be obtained from Jobcentres in Britain; or from the relevant regional employment office (*Landesarbeitsamt*) in Austria. These Landesarbeitsamt addresses are:

| | |
|---|---|
| Permayerstrasse 10, A-7001 Eisenstadt | (for Burgenland) |
| Kumpfgasse 25, A-9010 Klagenfurt | (for Carinthia) |
| Hohenstaufengasse 2, A-1013 Vienna | (for Lower Austria) |
| Gruberstrasse 67-69, A-4010 Linz | (for Upper Austria) |
| Auerspergstrasse 67-69, A-5020 Salzburg | (for Salzburg) |
| Babenbergerstrasse 33, A-8021 Graz | (for Styria) |
| Schoepfstrasse 5, A-6010 Innsbruck | (for Tyrol) |
| Rheinstrasse 32, A-6901 Bregenz | (for Vorarlberg) |
| Weihburggasse 30, A-1010 Vienna | (for Vienna). |

Enquiries and applications may be addressed to any one of these offices as Austria has a nationwide computerised system of vacancy notification. These should be typed in German and contain the following details: name and address; date of birth; education; profession; type of present employment; knowledge of foreign languages; length of intended stay; type of job required; and where in Austria. British Jobcentres can advise on the procedure. The employment service may not help enquiries from outside the EU or EEA though. For US and other non-EU citizens, permission to work in Austria can be hard to obtain, and immigration is not encouraged.

**Au Pairs**

If you are looking for au pair work you are advised to contact *Auslands-Sozialdienst*, Johannesgasse 16, A-1010 Vienna, tel 1-2225-129795; or the *Austrian Committee for the International Exchange of Students (ÖKISTA)*, Garnisongasse 7, A-1090 Vienna, tel 1-2224-0148; which are both well established and respectable agencies. Many agencies in the UK also place au pairs in Austria; see the chapter *Au Pairs and Domestic* or the directory *Summer Jobs Abroad* (Vacation Work) for some of these.

Au pairs must be over 18 and have their own private health insurance. An application for a special work permit (*Beschäftigungsbewilligung*) should be submitted to a Landesarbeitsamt, together with an au pair agreement signed by the au pair and the host family. Positions lasting more than six months also require a residence permit. Both permits can be obtained after arriving in Austria.

**International Agencies**

An exception to the rigid work permit and visa requirements is made in the case of the international agencies in the Vienna city area. The Consular Section of the British Embassy (see above) advises that these organisations may employ foreign staff, accountants and computer programmers. Details can be obtained direct from *The Division of Personnel*, UNIDO (United Nations Industrial Development Organization), Vienna International Centre, PO Box 300, A-1400 Vienna, tel 1-211310, fax 1-232156; the personnel department of *UNRWA*, (United Nations Relief and Works Agency for Palestine Refugees in the Near

East, same address, fax 1-2307487; or the *United Nations Office* in Vienna (see *United Nations* chapter).

**Teachers**
Teachers in the Austrian State School System have civil servant status and therefore have to be Austrian citizens (this may change to bring it into line with recent European Court rulings. A limited programme for the exchange of teachers is run by the *Central Bureau for Educational Visits and Exchanges* (see *Teaching* chapter).

American language students can spend eight months (October-May) working as English-teaching assistants in Austrian schools. Applications should be sent before March to the *Austrian-American Educational Commission (Fulbright Commission),* Schmidgasse 14, A-1082 Vienna.

The English-teaching market in Austria is relatively small, and the emphasis is on business English and in-company teaching. The *Austrian Institute,* 28 Rutland Gate, London SW7 1PQ, can supply a list of language schools. *Berlitz* and *inlingua* both have schools in Austria (see *Teaching* chapter). *SPIDI (Spracheninstitut der Industrie),* Lothringerstrasse 12, A-1031 Vienna, hires part-time staff with a BA and several years' TEFL experience. A local interview is essential.

**Other Opportunities**
*Catro,* Trautsongasse 6, A-1080 Vienna, tel 1-430143, fax 1-4083008; *EFS Personalberatung,* Ungargasse 59-61, A-1030 Vienna, fax 1-7167610; and *Preng and Associates,* Nussdorfer Strasse 38, A-1090 Vienna, tel 1-3109584, fax 1-3100348: are all international management recruitment and search consultancies in Austria.

## SHORT TERM WORK

Although the Austrian authorities have made it very difficult for foreign temporary workers to work legally, this is much easier for EU citizens.

**Seasonal Work**
Austria's hotels need extra staff to cover both the summer and winter tourist seasons. For hotel work the best single area is the Tyrol, particularly in resorts around Innsbruck. Names of individual hotels can be found in the Vacation Work book *Summer Jobs Abroad.* Campsite companies such as *Canvas Holidays* and *Eurocamps* can also offer jobs over the summer: see *Transport, Tourism and Hospitality* chapter for details. Also see *Working in Ski Resorts* (Vacation Work) for more contacts.

**Ski Resorts**
Austria ranks second to France as the most popular destination for British skiers; and there are good chances of finding work for English-speakers. Competent ski instructors with some German may find work at the height of the season when there is a shortage of instructors. Others can try hotel, restaurant and chalet work.

**Voluntary Work**
Organisations offering workcamp are to be found in *Voluntary Work.* Austrian organisations who may be contacted directly include: *SCI Internationale Freiwilligendienste,* Schottengasse 3a/1/4/59, A-1010 Vienna (general workcamps); and *Oesterreichischer Bauorden,* PO Box 149, Hörnesgasse 3, A-1031 Vienna (construction and renovation camps).

## BRITISH COMPANIES
### with branches, affiliates or subsidiaries in Austria
(see appendix for numerical classification code)

Further information on British companies with Austrian links may be obtained from the *Austrian Trade Commission* 45 Princess Gate, Exhibition Road, London SW7 2QA; tel 0171-584 4411; fax 0171-584 2565.

BP Austria AG                    35
(London EC2Y 9BU)
Schwarzenbergplatz 13/3
A-1041 Vienna

British Airways                   3
(London TW6 2JA)
Kärntner Ring 10
A-1010 Vienna

British Bookshop                 38
Blackwell & Hadwiger GmbH
Weihburggasse 8
A-1010 Vienna

Cadbury Schweppes               16
(London W2 2EX)
PO Box 12
Halleinstrasse
A-5411 Oberalm

C&A Modes GmbH                   9
(London W1A 2AX)
Landstrasse Hauptstrasse 101
A-1030-Vienna

Castrol GmbH                     35
(Swindon SN3 1RA)
Schwarzenbergplatz 6
A-1030 Vienna

EMI Columbia GmbH               10
(W1R 9AH)
Webgasse 43
A-1060 Vienna

Ernst & Young Case Technology   14
(London SE1 7EU)
Praterstrasse 70
A-1020 Vienna

Gestetner GmbH                   30
(Northampton NN4 0BD)
Siemensstrasse 160
A-1210 Vienna

Glaxo Pharmaceuticals GmbH       8
(Bolton BL2 6PU)
Julius Meinl gasse 2a
A-1160 Vienna

Hoover Austria GmbH             18
(Bolton BL2 6PU)
Föstergasse 6
A-1025 Vienna

ICI Austria GmbH                10
(London SW1P 3JF)
Schwarzenbergplatz 7
A-1037 Vienna

ICL International Computers     10
Ltd
(London SW15 1SW)
12 Meidlinger Hauptstrasse 51
A-1120 Vienna

Johnson Matthey & Co            28
(Royston SG8 5HE)
Sandwirtgasse 10
A-1061 Vienna

London Rubber Co Products       42
(Hoddesdon)
2 Josefinengasse 10
A-1021 Vienna

Metal Box Group                 28
(Reading RG1 2JH)
Stelrade Radiatoren

Mothercare GmbH                  9
(Watford WD2 5SH)
Mariahilferstrasse 20
A-1070 Vienna

Österreichische Unilever GmbH    8
(London EC4P 4BQ)
Schenkenstrasse 8-10
A-1011 Vienna

Rank Xerox Austria GmbH         10
(Woking GU21 1ZZ)
Trieste Strasse 70
A-1100 Vienna

Reuters Ltd                     38
(London EC4P 4AJ)
Zweigniederlassung Wien
Börsegasse 11
A-1010 Vienna

Shell Austria AG      35
(London SE1 7NA)
Rennweg 12
1030 Vienna

Sun Alliance Versicherungs AG   23
(Horsham RH12 1BT)
Universitätsstrasse 5
Vienna

Thorn EMI Licht GmbH     10
(London W1A 2AY)
Erzherzog-Karlstrasse 57
A-1220 Vienna

Wellcome Austria Pharma   8
GmbH
(London NW1 2BP)
Inzersdorferstrasse 64
A-1010 Vienna

Wiggins Teape GmbH     33
(Basingstoke RG21 2EE)
Glanzinggasse 20
1190 Vienna

## AMERICAN COMPANIES
### with branches, affiliates or subsidiaries in Austria

American companies operating in Austria are comprehensively listed in the annual *US List*, published by the *American Chamber of Commerce in Austria*, Porzellangasse 35, A-1090 Vienna. Price: AS 500, plus postage: AS 50 (surface), AS 120 (airmail). ACCA also publishes a *List of Members* and *Austria in the USA* at the same price as *US List*.

# Belgium

Belgian Embassy, 103 Eaton Square, London SW1W 9AB, tel 0171-471 3700
Belgian Embassy, 3330 Garfield St., NW, Washington DC 20008, tel 202-333-6900
Currency: 1 Belgian Franc (BF) = 100 centimes
Rate of exchange: £1 = BF 48; $1 = BF 31

Belgium is the seat of the EU, NATO, and over 1,000 other international organisations which regularly recruit English-speaking personnel. Short-term, au pair, or seasonal work is also a realistic proposition; for long-term workers from the UK, a weekend at home presents little problem. Brussels has a large and diverse expatriate community. Although there is still a shortage of skilled labour in some economic sectors, high unemployment means considerable competition for jobs which do not require specialist expertise. A knowledge of French or Dutch may be required. Belgium is an 'international' country at a major European crossroads, which is proud of its affiliation to the EU. English is quite widely spoken, especially in the Flemish-speaking north and west. The economy is especially dependent on export earnings. *Newcomer* magazine, Ackroyd Publications S.A., 329 Avenue Molière, B-1060 Brussels, tel 2-343-99-09, fax 2-343-98-22, is an interesting and detailed guide for expatriate newcomers to Belgium.

## GENERAL FACTS

### Population
Belgium's population is almost exactly ten million. With a total area of 11,783 square miles, Belgium has, after the Netherlands, the second highest population density in Europe — 848 per square mile.

The landscape is a mainly flat and rolling, rising above 300m only in the Ardennes in the east. Over half the land area is farmland; and industry accounts for a considerable part of land use.

### Climate
The climate of most of Belgium is similar to that in the south-east of England. A more continental climate (with colder winters and drier summers) is found in the Ardennes and Luxembourg.

### Government
Belgium is a constitutional monarchy. The central legislative system consists of two chambers — the Chamber of Representatives and the Senate. Members of the Chamber of Representatives are elected every four years. Senators also serve four-year terms.

Belgium is also a federal state, with largely autonomous regions in Flanders, Wallonia, and Brussels, which control over half of the national budget. This federal structure may in part explain the enthusiasm for a European federal state in this linguistically divided country.

There are two lower tiers of government: ten provinces which are administratively divided into 589 *communes* or communal councils. The consitutional revisions which came into effect in 1995 allowed representation for its main language communities for the first time.

## Cities
Belgium is more urbanised than most European countries. Over 30% of the population is concentrated in five main urban areas: Brussels (which has a population of nearly one million); Antwerp (480,000); Ghent (230,000); Charleroi (210,000); and Liege (200,000). Antwerp at the mouth of the Schelde river is one of the world's major ports.

## Rural Life
Farmland accounts for just under half of the total land area, but less than 3% of the labour force is employed in agriculture. This figure also covers employees in forestry (a further 20% of the land area) and the fisheries on the North Sea coast.

## Religion, Sport and Culture
Belgium is overwhelmingly Roman Catholic, although religious freedom is oberved. Traditionally, the country's most popular sport has been cycling. Second comes football: many clubs are still semi-professional; golf, tennis, and basketball are also played; and there is the Belgian Grand Prix every year for Formula 1 fans. The national Belgian football team known as the 'Red Devils' has had some international success in the past but did not qualify for the 1996 European Cup.

The history of Belgian art is long, containing such names as Van Eyck, Breughel, Rubens and Magritte, many of whose paintings can be seen in the Brussels Museum of Ancient Arts. While the major cultural institutions are concentrated in Brussels, all the larger Belgian cities have art galleries, theatres and concert halls. There is jazz and avant-garde theatre; and the Belgian National Tourist office can be contacted for details of the many festivals. Antwerp was a European Cultural capital in 1993; other cultural and historic centres like Bruges, as well as battlefield sites and spas, are popular tourist attractions.

# FACTORS INFLUENCING EMPLOYMENT

## Immigration
The Belgian Embassy, although unable to assist in finding work, issues some general information for those wishing to settle in Belgium.

Although work permits are no longer required, all Britons intending to take up employment in Belgium must register their address within eight days of arrival at the town hall (French *maison communale*/Dutch *stadhuis*) of the district in which they are staying. The *maison communale* can issue a temporary residence permit, but a permanent residence permit can only be issued later on approval by the Aliens Police. Belgium is part of the 'borderless' region in the EU created by the Schengen Agreement.

US citizens may remain in Belgium for a three-month period without a visa. Work permits must be obtained before arriving in Belgium if this is the reason for your travel. People wishing to take up a temporary residence should apply to the Belgian Embassy.

## Language
The main linguistic divide in Belgium is between the Flemings and the Walloons, speaking Dutch and French respectively. For its first 164 years Belgium was a highly centralised state; but in 1971 legislation created a federal structure which could embrace Flemish, French and German speakers. The division between these language communities as one of the main political issues in the country. The Dutch-speaking part in the north and west contains 57% of the total population, compared with only 33% in the French-speaking area. Brussels itself is bilingual; and the fourth area is the small German-speaking Eupen-Malmédy region on the German frontier.

## Cost and Standard of Living

Although Belgium has a scarcity of raw materials, and imports are therefore high, Belgium and Luxembourg (with which it is linked under the Belgo-Luxembourg Economic Union — BLEU) export between 60% and 70% of their industrial production (the average for the 'developed' OECD countries is 25%). It is also highly integrated into the EU. More than three-quarters of trade is with other EU states. Together with its strategic position in Europe, this important trading role gives Belgium an economic and diplomatic profile in world affairs which is out of proportion to its size and population. The standard of living is relatively high.

## Way of Life

Belgian cuisine is similar to that of France, but each region has its own specialities and traditions. Local beers are renowned throughout the world; and the majority of cafés have licences to serve spirits. There are no licensing hours; and a lively restaurant and night life in most Belgian towns despite the sometimes dour image of the country. Belgium is one of the few countries in Europe that does not have an accommodation shortage; but prices, especially in Brussels,can be high. Ceramics, chocolate, lace, and jewellery are traditional products. Flemish-speakers in the north may prefer you to speak English to them rather than French. *Newcomer* magazine (see above) has a listing of expatriate clubs and societies and information about accommodation, as well as what to do and where to go, for English-speakers living in Belgium.

## Health and Welfare

Belgium has a comprehensive welfare system. Workers pay compulsory contributions out of their earnings. This covers sickness, disablement and unemployment; pensions; maternity and family allowances; and almost complete medical coverage. Employees who have completed a trial period are entitled to their full salary for one month in case of illness or accident; and then are entitled to disability payments. Any employee's contract is legally suspended during a period of illness and cannot be terminated for six months. After this period, it can be terminated provided the employee is payed an indemnity equivalent to six months' salary. Women are entitled to 15 weeks' maternity leave.

## Education

Education is free; and mainly run regionally by the French-speaking community and government of Flanders. Foreign schools offer education along British and American lines for all ages. School is compulsory for all children between the ages of six and 18; and crèches and nursery schools (from 18 months to two years) are available for working mothers. There are kindergartens for children from 2½ to six. Apart from the state schools there are a large number of private schools too, mainly Catholic.

Belgium has universities in each of its major cities. These are state-financed or subsidised, and entrance requirements are high. Many now offer courses taught in the English language. Undergraduate courses are generally longer than in British universities, usually four years.

## National Service

National Service is compulsory only for Belgian citizens.

## Embassies and Consulates

British Embassy, Rue d'Arlon 85, B-1040 Brussels; tel 2-287-62-11.
US Embassy, Boulevard du Régent 27, B-1000 Brussels; tel 2-508-21-11.

## Tourist Offices

Belgian Tourist Office, 5th Floor, 29 Princes Street, London W1R 7RG; tel 0171-629 3977.

Belgian National Tourist Office, Suite 1501, 780 Third Avenue, New York NY 10019; tel 212-758-8130.

## CONDITIONS OF WORK

### Wages
There is a standard legal minimum wage for workers over 21. Monthly salaries for white-collar worker are determined by negotiation between employers and unions according to age and skills. As mentioned above, wage levels (and also the cost of living) in Belgium are relatively high.

### Hours
Standard working hours are 40 hours per week, eight hours per day; but a 12-hour shift system is allowed in certain circumstances. This kind of overtime must be compensated for by paid time off within three months of the work being performed. This does not apply to managerial, domestic and some other categories of staff.

### Holidays
There are ten legal holidays in Belgium: New Year's Day; Easter Monday; Labour Day (1 May); Ascension Day; Whit Monday; National Day (21 July); Assumption (15 August); All Saints' Day (1 November); Armistice Day (11 November); and Christmas Day. For most workers, the legal minimum holiday is four weeks, and an extra holiday allowance is paid. All workers are entitled to ten days' unpaid leave per year for urgent family reasons.

### Trade Unions
Most of the unions are affiliated to one of the three major political parties. Membership is voluntary, and workers will have several unions who may represent them.

Labour-management relations are highly organised, with permanent delegations representing both sides at local and national levels. Agreements are usually reached without the necessity for drastic action, but there are special Labour Courts to settle particularly tough cases.

### Taxation
'The tax system in Belgium is so complicated that tax regulations seem a deliberate plot to employ more accountants and fiscal experts.' So says *Newcomer* magazine. If you are based in the country, you will be taxed under the Belgian system (although non-Belgian residents hired by Belgian companies on a temporary basis may escape this). Income tax is deducted from wages at source and is progressive, ranging from 25% to 55%. There are allowances for dependants and many professional expenses. Most Belgians will recognise the description of their country as bureaucratic. It could also be described as the country of the tax-free Volvo.

## WORK AVAILABLE

### General
The Belgian economy depends on manufacturing and trade; and there is a high level of foreign investment. Belgium is a world leader in non-ferrous metallurgy, and also in industrial textiles. The food industry has expanded rapidly in recent years; and some companies in this sector hire graduates with languages from abroad. Other good prospects are in administration, finance, information technology and manufacturing, as well as English teaching and temporary work. A high level of language ability is often necessary in order to be able to compete with the locals, though. There are numerous subsidiaries of US and UK companies in

Belgium (see below). The EU and NATO are among the major employers of English-speakers (see the *International Organisations* chapter).

Further information on all aspects of living and working in Belgium can be found in *Live and Work in Belgium, The Netherlands and Luxembourg,* published by Vacation Work.

*Focus Career Services* is an association providing services to people looking for career opportunities or exploring career alternatives open to women and men of all nationalities. It provides information on education, training and job opportunities; publishes a bi-monthly newsletter; and organises workshops and seminars. It also publishes a guide to working in Belgium entitled *Getting Started ... Legally: The Focus Guide to Working in Belgium and Starting a Business* available at BF 500 from their office at: 23 Rue Lesbroussart, B-1050 Brussels, tel 2-646-65-30.

### Newspapers

The leading French language newspaper, *Le Soir,* is represented by *Agence Rossel,* 112 Rue Royale, 1000 Brussels; and in Britain by *Powers International,* 517-523 Fulham Road, London SW6 1HF, tel 0171-385 8855; they can also place advertisements in the largest Flemish daily *Het Laatste Nieuws* and other newspapers and specialist magazines. *Le Soir* has a special section on Tuesdays for jobseekers.

The Belgian employment services publish a bi-weekly newspaper for jobseekers called *Offre d'Emploi* in French and *De Werkzoeker* in Dutch. The *Office Nationale de l'Emploi* address is: Boulevard de l'Empereur 7, B-1000 Brussels. Here non-EU nationals will have to apply through their employer for a work permit. Advertisements can also be placed in the English language magazine *The Bulletin,* Av. Molière 329, B-1060 Brussels.

## SPECIFIC CONTACTS

### Employment Service

British citizens, once in Belgium, may use the services of one of the regional employment services which each have sub-regional offices. The Dutch-speaking service is *VDAB,* Keizerslaan 11, B-1000 Brussels; tel 2-506-15-11. The French-speaking *FOREM* can also send you a list of local offices: FOREM, Administration Centrale, Boulevard de l'Empereur 3-5, B-1000 Brussels. The Greater Brussels employment service, *ORBEM,* is at: Boulevard Anspach 65, B-1000 Brussels; tel 2-505-14-11.

### Consultants and Agencies

As well as some organisations listed in the section *Consultants and Agencies,* the following are among those that recruit personnel for positions in Belgium, mostly in Brussels. A fee is generally not paid to recruitment agencies. See the *Yellow Pages* telephone book Volume B, section 7485 for more, or the *Pink Pages* Volume 1B, section 9000:

*Focus Career Services,* Rue Lesbroussart 23, B-1050 Brussels, tel 2-646-65-30 — is a non-profit, member-based association providing services for people looking for new career opportunities open to all nationalitites. Career counselling and advice on job search are among their services.

*Personnel Management Services (PMS),* Avenue des Croix du Feu 231, B-1020 Brussels — recruits for a wide range of enterprises in the Brussels, Louvain, Antwerp area. PMS specialises in low and middle management assignments and support staff (secretarial and administrative). Appointments are initially for a fixed term, but may become permanent.

*Sobeir SA,* Avenue Louise 396, B-1050 Brussels, tel 2-640-12-20, fax 2-647-28-97 — provides staff for the hotel and restaurant industry. See under *Hospitality* in the *Transport, Tourism and Hospitality* chapter.

**Teachers**
The addresses of Belgian universities and language schools can be obtained from the Belgian Embassy; and the *Private Language Schools Federation* can be contacted for a list of its member schools: 868 Chaussée de Waterloo, B-1180 Brussels; fax 2-374-45-91.

## SHORT TERM WORK

Belgium can offer many temporary jobs, despite its unemployment problems. See *Summer Jobs Abroad* published annually by Vacation Work for more hotel and tourism opportunities. Britons are helped both by their right to work here without a work permit and their ability to make use of the Belgian employment service (T-Service) which has branches which specialise in finding short term work. These are:

 69 Boulevard Anspach, B-1000 Brussels, tel 02-511-23-85
 2 Kloosterstraat, B-2200 Herentals, tel 014-216-401
 23 Lange Klarenstraat, B-2000 Antwerp, tel 03-232-98-60
 49 Burgstraat, B-9000 Ghent, tel 09-224-09-20
 17 Spanjaardstraat, B-8000 Brugge, tel 050-440-470
 34 Martelarenlaan, bus 1, B-3500 Hasselt, tel 011-221-177
 156 Leuvensestraat, B-1801 Vilvoorde, tel 02-252-20-25
 68 Beheerstraat, B-8500 Kortrijk, tel 056-203-079
 86 de Merodelei, B-2300 Turnhout, tel 014-422-731
 22 Rue de la Province, B-4020 Liège, 041-422-731
 36B Rue de Montigny, B-6000 Charleroi, tel 071-317-445
 34 Klorenmarkt, B-2800 Mechelen, tel 015-423-848
 14 Rue Borgnet, B-5000 Namur, tel 081-745-28-71
 24 Rue Géneral Molitor, B-6700 Arlon, tel 063-226-645

There are also numerous temporary work agencies. These are two of the largest (and see the local Yellow or Pink Pages for more temping agencies):

*Manpower,* Rue du Luxembourg 13, B-1040 Brussels, tel 2-512-38-23 — seeks bilingual secretaries (English-French) with any other language spoken in the EU with experience and knowledge of WP, 5.2, Word/Win and/or Excel for prestigous appointments.
*Select Interim,* Avenue de la Joyeuse Entrée 1-5, B-1040 Brussels, tel 2-231-03-33 — recruits secretaries, typists, accountants and other employees.

Temping appointments tend to last up to six months, as after this period employees become eligible for full-time employee benefits amd holidays.

**Seasonal Work**
It is possible to find seasonal employment in the hotels, catering and tourism sectors. Those looking for jobs should write directly to individual hotels (a list can be obtained from the *Belgium Tourist Office* above or an up-to-date travel guide). Local employment services will also be able to help. Some voluntary organisations organise workcamps in the summer:

*Natuur 2000 (Flemish Youth Federation for the Study of Nature and Environmental Conservation),* Bervoetsraat 33, B-2000 Antwerp — organises conservation activities and nature-study and conservation camps in Dutch-speaking parts of Belgium. Age 15+. Food, accommodation, transport from Antwerp provided. The cost is from BF1,000.

**Other Work**
Many UK and North American organisations dealing with exchange schemes and au pairs operate in Belgium. See the chapters, *Getting the Job, Au Pair and Domestic,* and *Voluntary Work.* Belgium also offers a number of opportunities in its cities through the branches of the 'T-Service'. Management recruitment and search consultants include: *DPSC International,* 126 Avenue Milcamps, B-1040 Brussels, tel 2-732-11-40 or 732-10-90, fax 2-732-13-44, mainly for computing, communications and sales staff; and *Staff Selection and Services,* Avenue Brugman 32, B-1060 Brussels, tel 2-344-18-04, fax 2-344-76-06, specialising in banking.

## LIST OF BRITISH COMPANIES
with branches, affiliates or subsidiaries in Belgium
(see appendix for numerical classification code)

A copy of the Year Book of the *British Chamber of Commerce in Belgium* containing the names and addresses of its member firms can be obtained from the secretary of the Chamber at 30 rue Joseph II, B-1040 Brussels; payment in advance.

Antwerpse Diamantbank NW   4
(London W1)
Pelikaansstraat 54
B-2018 Antwerp

Arthur Anderson & Co.   1
(London WC2R 2AS)
Avenue des Arts 56
B-1040 Brussels

BAT Benelux SA   47
(London SW1H 0NL)
Rue de Koninck 38
B-1080 Brussels

BP Chemicals Belgium   8
(London EC2M 7BA)
Division of BP NV
Postbus 30
B-2050 Antwerp

BTI Ferodo SA   7
(Stockport SK23 0JP)
Avenue Reine Astrid 1
B-1420 Wautier Braine

Blackwood Hodge (Belgium)   6
(London EC1)
Steenweg op Leuven II
B-1940 St Stevens Woluwe

Barclays Bank International Ltd.   4
(London EC3)
Avenue Louise 65
B-1050 Brussels

Beecham SA & Beecham Pharma   8
(Middlesex TW8 9BD)
Rue de L'Intendant 59
B-1020 Brussels

Belgian Shell SA   35
(London SE1 7NA)
Cantersteen 47
B-1000 Brussels

Bowater Industries plc   33
(London SW1X 7NN)
New Orleansstraat 100
B-9000 Gent

British Airways plc   3
(London TT6 2JA)
Rue de Trône 98
B-1050 Brussels

British Steel Corporation   28
(London WC1E 6BB)
Rue de la Loi 15
B-1040 Brussels

Brouwerijen Alken Maes   16
(London W1)
Waarloosveld 10
B-2571 Waarloos

Castrol Oil NV   35
(Swindon SN3 1RE)
Helmstraat 107
B-2140 Borgerhout

Chloride Belgium NV   8
(Manchester M27 8LR)
Lusthovenlaan 9
B-2640 Mortsell

Christies Belgium Ltd   50
(London SW1Y 6QT)
Boulevard de Waterloo 33
B-1000 Brussels

Co-operative Movement in   13
Europe
Rue Guillaume Tell 59
B-1060 Brussels

Coopers & Lybrand   1
(London EC4A 4HT)
Marcel Thirty Court
Avenue Marcel Thirty 216
B-1200 Brussels

Deloitte Touche Ross   1
(London EC4A 3TR)
Berkenlaan 6
B-1831 Diegem

DHL International   17
(Hounslow T44 6JS)
Kosterstraat 210
B-1831 Machelen (Diegem)

Dow Corning Europe   8
(Reading RG1 4EX)
Rue Gén de Gaulle 62
B-1310 La Hulpe

Dow Jones Telerate Belgium SA   2
(London EC4A 1BR)
Avenue de Tervueren 273
B-1150 Brussels

Dunlop Belgium Ltd   42
(Birmingham B24 9QH)
Place du Rinsdelle 27
B-1040 Brussels

EMI (Belgium) SA   29
(London W1R 9AH)
Rue Emile Claus 49
B-1050 Brussels

The Economist Intelligence   14
Unit (Europe) SAl
(London W1A 1DW)
Avenue Louise 137
B-1050 Brussels

Ernst & Young   1
(London SE1 7EU)
Avenue Marcel Thirty 204
B-1200 Brussels

The Financial Times   38
Benelux Ltd
(London SE1 9HL)
Hertogsstraat 39
B-1000 Brussels

General Accident Fire   23
& Life Assurance Corp Ltd
(Perth PH2 0NH)
J De Hasquestraat 7
2000 Antwerp

Glaxo Belgium SA   35
(London W1X 6BP)
Boulevard du Triomphe 172
B-1160 Brussels

Habitat Designs (Belgium) Ltd   13
(London W1P 9LD)
Rue Saint-Lambert 198
B-1200 Brussels

Hightons SA   28
(London WC1 2EB)
Rue Ortelius 32
Brussels

Hoverspeed Ltd   48
(London SW1V 1JT)
Rue A. Dansaert 101
B-1000 Brussels

ICI (Europe)   46
(London SW1P 3JF)
Everslaan 45
B-3078 Eversberg

ICL International Computers   40
Ltd
(London SW15 1SU)
Bessenveldstraat 9
B-1920 Diegem

King & Co SA   10
(London W1N)
Rue de la Loi 26
B-1040 Brussels

Kraft-Jacobs-Suchard-Côte d'Or   16
SA-NV
(Cheltenham GLO 3AE)
Riverside Business Park
Blvd International 55
B-1070 Brussels

Laura Ashley Ltd   46
(Newtown SY1 5LQ)
Rue de Namur 81/83
B-1000 Brussels

Belgian Shell SA   35
(London SE1 7NA)
Cantersteen 47
B-1000 Brussels

Lloyds Bank International 4
(London EC4)
Avenue de Tervuner 2
B-1040 Brussels

Marks & Spencer Belgium SA 13
(London W1A 4DN)
Boulevard Emile Jacqmain 6
B-1000 Brussels

Nestlé Belgilux SA 16
(Croydon CR9 1NR)
Rue de Birmingham 221
B-1070 Brussels

Pan European Publishing Co 38
(Berkhamsted HP4 2AF)
Rue Verte 216
B-1210 Brussels

Pitney Bowes Belgium SA 30
(Harlow CM19 5BD)
Mercure Centre
Rue de la Fusée 100
B-1130 Brussels

Price Waterhouse 1
(London SE1 9SY)
Bvd de la Wolvwe 62
B-1200 Brussels

Procter & Gamble Company 11
(Newcastle upon Tyne)
1 Rue P Le Bon
B-1040 Brussels

Rank Xerox SA 30
(London NW1 3BH)
Wezembeekstraat 5
B-1930 Zaventem

Reader's Digest 38
Quai du Hainault 29
B-1080 Brussels

Reckitt & Colman SA 8
(London W4 2RW)
Allée de la Recherche 20
B-1070 Brussels

Renold Continental Ltd 39
(Manchester M22 5W1)
Allée Verte 1
B-1000 Brussels

Reuters Ltd 38
(London EC4P 4AJ)
Rue de Trèves 61
B-1040 Brussels

Rhône Poulenc Agro 8
(Ipswich IP1 1QH)
Boulevard Sylvain Dupuis 243
B-1070 Brussels

Rover (Belgium) SA-NV 7
(Birmingham B37 7HQ)
Lozenberg 11
B-1932 Sint-Stevens-Woluwe

NV Smith & Nephew (Belgium) 12
SA
(London WC2R 2BP)
Av du Four à Briques 3B
B-1140 Brussels

W H Smith (Belgium) SA 38
(Swindon SN3 3LD)
71-75 Bvd Adolphe Max
B-1000 Brussels

Townsend Car Ferries 48
(Dover CT17 9TJ)
Doverlaan 7
B-8380 Zeebrugge

Unilever Belgique 16
(London EC4P 4BQ)
Rue Montoyer 51
B-1040 Brussels

Vandemoortele   Coordination 16
Centre
(Hounslow)
Kennedypark 8
B-8500 Kortrijk

XP Express Parcel Systems 17
Rijksweg 22-26
B-2880 Borhem

## AMERICAN COMPANIES
### with branches, affiliates or subsidiaries in Belgium

These are given in the *AMCHAM Directory (Combined Membership Directory/ List of American Companies in Belgium)*, price BF 4,000, from the *American Chamber of Commerce in Belgium*, Avenue des Arts 50, bte 5, B-1000 Brussels. Payment should be made in advance, preferably by bank transfer, to bank account No. 310-0548586-40 with Banque Bruxelles Lambert to the American Chamber of Commerce in Belgium at the above address.

# Denmark

Royal Danish Embassy, 55 Sloane Street, London SW1X 9SR, tel 0171-333 0200 or 333 0265
Royal Danish Embassy, 3200 Whitehaven Street, NW, Washington DC 20008, tel 202-234-4300
Currency: 1 Danish krone (Dkr) = 100 øre
Rate of Exchange: £1 = Dkr 9; $1 = Dkr 6

Unemployment and language difficulties make it difficult to obtain work in Denmark from another country, and some knowledge of Danish is essential in most jobs. But there has been an upturn in the economy, and wages are high. There is work in offices and hotels, and in international companies. A useful booklet is *Working and Residence in Denmark* published by *Use It, Youth Information Copenhagen* at the Touristinformation office in Copenhagen (Rådhusstraede 13, DK-1466 Copenhagen K, tel 33 15 65 18), who advise that 'in our experience the foreigners who do find a job in Denmark do it by asking around, and looking up the employers on their own initiative and by a direct approach.' There are no Danish offices operating as labour exchanges or advisory bureaux for foreigners, but when in Denmark you can try the local labour exchange or *AF (Arbejdsformidlingen).* A list of addresses can be obtained from the State Employment Service *Arbejdsmarkedsstyrelsen*, AMS, Blegdamsvej 56, Postbox 2722, DK-2100 Copenhagen Ø, tel 35 28 81 00. Alternatively, the addresses of local offices can be found under *Arbejdsformidlingen* in the telephone directory.

## GENERAL FACTS

### Population
Denmark's total population is 5.2 million. It is the smallest of the Scandinavian countries (with the possible exception of Estonia) and covers 11,783 square miles. In addition to the Jutland peninsula — and its low-lying landscape of beech woods, small lakes and fjords — there are 483 islands, 100 of them inhabited. Population density is 850 per square mile. There are few mineral resources. Most of the land is in productive agricultural use.

### Climate
Denmark's climate is similar to that of Britain or neighbouring Germany, rather than the rest of Scandinavia. It is a maritime climate, but there is generally more sunshine in summer than in England, and winter temperatures tend to be lower.

### Government
Denmark is a constitutional monarchy and the oldest kingdom in Europe. The present Queen is Margrethe II. The *Folketing* is the legislative assembly; and the government is headed by a Prime Minister. Elections are every four years. Denmark entered the European Economic Community in 1973; and has a reputation (again like Britain) as a less than enthusiastic member of the EU. The Danes made history in 1992 by narrowly rejecting the Maastrict Treaty, although this decision was later overturned.

**Cities**
Copenhagen, the capital and the largest port in Scandinavia, has a population of 1,700,000 (and is famed for the Little Mermaid statue in the bay). It was a European Cultural Capital in 1996. Other cities (with much smaller populations) are Aarhus, with its old buildings and museum; Aalborg, the chief city of North Jutland — a gourmet's paradise with 120 restaurants; and Odense the picturesque town made famous by Hans Christian Andersen. Legoland near Esbjerg is a popular tourist attraction.

**Rural Life**
Farms tend to be small. There are about 69,000 today for mainly milk, cattle and pigs, but this number is decreasing as smaller units are amalgamated. Agriculture and fishing are the basis of Denmark's large food-processing industry; but even today only 16% of farms have any full-time employees. The rest are family-run. Also important to the Danish economy are forestry (forests cover 10% of the country's land area), and fruit and vegetable production. The country is almost entirely surrounded by water and fishing plays an important part in Danish life and culture, and is organised on a cooperative basis.

**Religion, Sport and Culture**
Most Danes belong to the established Evangelical-Lutheran church. The most popular sport in Denmark (as in most other European countries) is soccer: soccer players are another of its 'exports' to major European clubs. In 1992, the Danish national team won the European Championship, its first major honour. Also popular are walking, cycling, golf, angling, windsurfing, and tennis. Keeping fit has also recently become a national pastime. Danes are sometimes introverted but friendly. There is a lively social and nightlife scene in Copenhagen; but the national character is better expressed in small intimate gatherings around a fire or at a picnic, in an atmosphere said to be *hygge,* which means intimate or cosy. A former British ambassador to the country once said that the Danes reminded him of the Ashanti tribe of Ghana, with a society and political system based on consensus and general agreement. Danes are sociable, and are described by most visitors as easy-going and welcoming.

# FACTORS INFLUENCING EMPLOYMENT

**Immigration**
In Denmark, you must have a legal residence (and a work permit before you come if you are from outside the EU or Scandinavia). Immigration is not encouraged. But the EU agreement on free movement of labour still applies, so Britons are still allowed to look for work. All visitors intending to work in Denmark must register with the local civil register (*Folkeregistret*) within five days of arrival to receive a personal code number (*personnummer*); and residence permits are required for all stays of over three months. These must be applied for at the *Københavns Overpraesidium,* Hammerensgade 1, DK-1267 Copenhagen K, tel 33 12 23 80, or through the local police.

US tourist and business visitors may remain in Scandinavia (including Denmark) for up to 90 days without a visa. So you will not be able to stay so long if you have come from one of the other Scandinavian countries and stayed there. If you wish to stay longer than three months, you should make your application in the USA first.

**Language**
Not speaking Danish is a problem if you are looking for work on the spot. English is quite widely spoken, but prospective jobseekers are advised to learn some Danish before they leave. Once in Denmark, local education authorities can arrange cheap language classes with an English-speaking teacher when the

need arises. The Universities of Copenhagen and Aarhus hold courses in Danish for beginners and intermediate students.

### Cost and Standard of Living
Almost all fields of work are covered by agreements between employers and the trade unions, so people working in Denmark are assured of a fairly stable standard of living; visitors to the country will find prices high.

### Housing and Accommodation
Housing standards in Denmark are good, but it can be hard to find somewhere to live. And yet one of the conditions for the granting of residence permits is that the applicant must have a suitable dwelling. So it is better to arrange accommodation before you arrive. Rents are high too, even for a single room. Buying may not be the answer. Foreigners wishing to buy a house must apply for permission to the Ministry of Justice; and this is only given if the applicant intends to reside in Denmark permanently.

### Health and Welfare
Denmark was one of the first countries in the world to introduce a welfare state; and social security today is the largest single item of Danish national expenditure. Sickness and unemployment benefit are generally 90% of the wage. Foreigners qualify for social security benefits if they have contributed to the system for a year, during which they must have worked for six months. Other benefits, such as maternity and industrial injury compensation, are available on similar terms. Maternity leave is four weeks prior to the birth and up to 24 weeks after. Paternity leave is two weeks. Hospital treatment is generally provided free of charge to EU visitors. Doctors and dentists are generally paid; and then this money is refunded in part or in whole by local municipal offices. Holiday pay becomes an issue after a year of your contributions (through your employer) to the *feriepenge* (this is an additional 12½% of your salary which your employer pays; you need a certificate known as a *FerieKonto-kort*).

### Education
Most education, including university, is free, although there are some private schools. Kindergartens care for around three quarters of all children aged from three to six and education is compulsory from seven to 16. Denmark has five universities (at Copenhagen, Aarhus, Aalborg, Odense and Roskilde). There are a number of other specialised training institutions, and courses for vocational training at secondary and tertiary level. State grants are available to Danes and foreigners alike for higher education.

### National Service
Foreigners in Denmark are not liable for military service.

### Embassies and Consulates
British Embassy, Kastelsvej 36-40, DK-2100 Copenhagen Ø; tel 35 26 46 00.
There are consulates in Aabenraa, Aalborg, Aarhus, Esbjerg, Fredericia, Herning, Odense, Rønne (Bornholm), and Tørshavn (Faroe Islands).

US Embassy, Dag Hammerskjold's Alle 24, DK-2100 Copenhagen Ø; tel 31 42 31 44.

## CONDITIONS OF WORK

### Wages
Wages and working conditions are fixed by negotiation between worker and employer organisations. Conditions of work are generally good. It should be noted, also, that Danes are widely regarded as hard-working and industrious. In 1992, the total value of work (or GNP) was DKR 874 billion, or USD 27,200

million per inhabitant, the highest in the EU. The greatest single item of expenditure is housing.

### Hours

In Denmark, 37 hours and a five-day working week are the norm. Shops generally close early on Saturdays, except for the first Saturday of the month. Banks are open until 6pm on Thursday, 5pm other weekdays, and closed on Saturday.

### Holidays

All employees in Denmark are entitled to five weeks' paid holiday per year. In addition, the following public holidays are observed: New Year's Day; Maundy Thursday (April); Good Friday; Easter Monday; Common Prayer's Day (April or May); Ascension (16 May); Whit Monday (May); Constitution Day (5 June, half day); Christmas Eve; Christmas Day;, Boxing Day; and New Year's Eve (half day).

### Trade Unions

On taking up employment you will be requested to join a trade union; in most industries wages and conditions are negotiated by these unions with the employer. Union membership, while not obligatory, covers around 80% of the workforce. Most foreigners join a Danish union; the rules then require contributions to the Unemployment Funds (*arbejdsløshedskasser*). To become a member you must have had, or be going to have, five weeks of work. It is also possible to become a member of an unemployment fund (A-kasser) without joining a union.

### Taxation

Tax is deducted at source. A foreigner will be subject to unlimited liability upon arrival if he indicates his intention to become a Danish resident, or if his stay exceeds six months. You need a *skattekort*. Without this document the employer has to deduct 60% of your salary to cover income taxes (but this tax can be claimed back in June of the next calendar year). You can get your *skattekort* at *Københavns Skatteforvaltning* (Gyldenløvesgade 15, DK-1639 Copenhagen V; tel 33 66 33 66). You pay tax according to your income, how long you work in Denmark, and any bilateral agreements with your own country (which you should check on first). Sickness and unemployment insurance contributions are also deducted at source, but are calculated separately. Comprehensive information can be obtained from the Danish Embassy.

## WORK AVAILABLE

### General

It is worth re-emphasising that finding work in Denmark is no easy task; and British jobseekers are advised to check the current situation at a local Jobcentre through the *EURES* scheme (see *Getting the Job*). In fact, few vacancies in Denmark are advertised in Britain or the USA; or in the international employment press. Non-EU nationals really need to be posted there by their company or organisation. Otherwise, your job search will have to be 'creative' and on-the-spot; and the services of *Use It*, once you are there, are very helpful (see above). No foreigner is allowed to take up a post in the Danish Civil Service.

### Newspapers

Advertisements can be placed in *Berlingske Tidende* and national and regional dailies, through their UK agent *Frank L. Crane Ltd.,* 5-15 Cromer Street, Grays Inn Road, London WC1H 8LS; tel 0171-837 3330. *Powers International*, tel 0171-385 8855, represents the leading daily *Morgenavisen Jyllands-Posten.*

A leading publishing house is *Teknisk Forlag A/S,* Skelbaekgade 4, DK-1780 Copenhagen V, which produces a range of journals from engineering and electronics to chemistry and plastics.

# SPECIFIC CONTACTS

## Local Agencies

There are a number of employment agencies in Copenhagen that may be able to offer jobs in offices, factories, etc. to personal callers. Two of the largest are *Adia* at Amagertorv 7, DK-1160 Copenhagen K (also in Odense and Taastrup); and *Western Services* at Kobmagergade 54; alternatively, look up *Vikarbureaux* in the telephone book.

## Medical Staff

Medical personnel wishing to work in Danish hospitals should consult the weekly journal of the *Danish Medical Association* (available from the DMA, Trondhjemsgade 9, DK-2100 Copenhagen Ø; tel 31 38 55 00; fax 31 38 55 07) in which hospital medical posts are advertised. A list of hospitals and other medical institutions is available from the same source, as is the free booklet *Information for Doctors Migrating to Denmark.*

Regarding authorisation to work as a doctor in Denmark the *National Board of Health (Sundhedsstyrelsen,* 13 Amaliegade, DK-1012 Copenhagen K; tel 33 91 16 01) should be contacted after employment has been obtained but before work is taken up. A solid knowledge of the Danish language is usually needed. See the Sunday edition of *Berlingske Tidende* for medical and nursing vacancies (cited under *Newspapers* above).

# SHORT TERM WORK

## Seasonal Work

It is worth writing directly to hotels for jobs in the tourist industry. Casual workers are also needed to help harvest tomatoes, strawberries, cherries, and apples over the summer. One contact is *Astrup Fruitplantage* (Astrup, DK-8305 Samso; tel 86 59 13 38). The site is close to the beach. Also see *Landsbladet,* a farming journal published by *Landboforeningernes Ugeblad* at Vester Farimagsgade 6, DK-1606 Copenhagen V. Students looking for temporary work around Copenhagen can use a special branch of the national employment service known as the *Studenternes Arbejdsformidling.*

## Other Work

Voluntary work can be arranged through some of the international agencies mentioned in *Voluntary Work.* If you are already in the country, *Mellemfolkeligt Samvirke,* (Danish Association of International Cooperation, Meslgade 49, DK-8000 Aarhus), organises workcamps in the summer helping on socially useful projects in Denmark as well as Greenland and the Faeroe Islands. *Use It* (see above) is a useful source of information.

Many agencies also offer au pair work.

The Danish Chamber of Commerce, *Det Danske Handelskammer,* Børsen, DK-1217 Copenhagen K, tel 33 95 05 00, fax 33 32 52 16, can provide other useful advice and information about business in Denmark.

## BRITISH COMPANIES

### with branches, affiliates or subsidiaries in Denmark
### (see appendix for numerical classification code)

Albright & Wilson                    8
(London B68 0NN)
Siestavej 7,
DK-2600 Glostrup

Arthur Anderson & Co                 1
(London WC2R 2PS)
Grøningen 17
PO Box 17
DK-1012 Copenhagen K

Barclays Danmark                     4
(London EC3P 3AH)
Herstedøstervej 27/29
DK-2620 Albertslund

Baxenden Scandinavia A/S             8
(Accrington BB5 2SL)
Fulbyvej 4
Pedersborg 4180 Sorø

Beecham-Lamco A/S                    8
(Brentford TW11 9BD)
Transformervej 16
DK-2730 Herlev

Boeg-Thomsen A/S                    16
(London W3)
Nybyvej 11
DK-4390 Vipperod

British Airways                      3
(London TT6 2JA)
Vesterbrogade 2B
DK-1620 Copenhagen V

British Steel Dansk                 28
(London SE1 7SN)
Hans Edvard Teglere Vej 7
DK-2920 Charlottenlund

British Tobacco Co ApS              47
(Woking)
Strandvaeget 43
DK-2100 Copenhagen Ø

Castrol A/S                         35
(Swindon SN3 1RE)
Esplanaden 7
DK-1263 Copenhagen K

Coopers & Lybrand/K G Jensen         1
(London EC4A 4HT)
Lyngbyvej 16-28
PO Box 2709
DK-2100 Copenhagen

Courtaulds Danmark A/S               9
(London W1A 2BB)
Falkoner Alle 53
DK-2000 Copenhagen

A/S Dansk Shell                     35
(London SE1 7NA)
Kampmannsgade 2
DK-1604 Copenhagen

DEB Swarfega A/S                     8
(Derby)
Teglvaerksvej 6
DK-5620 Glamsbjerg

Deloitte Touche Ross                 1
(London EC4A 3TR)
H C Andersons Boulevard 2
DK-1012 Copenhagen K

DER A/S                             10
(London WC2H 6ED)
Gungevej 17
DK-2650 Hvidovre

DHL (Couriers)                      17
(Hounslow T44 6JS)
Ringager 2A 7
DK-2605 Brøndby

DOW Danmark A/S                      8
(Hounslow)
Nyhavn 63A
DK-1051 Copenhagen

Dunlop A/S                          42
(Birmingham B24 9QH)
Tagensvej 85b
DK-2200 Copenhagen N

EMI (Dansk-Engelsk) A/S             10
(London W1)
Hoffdingsvej
DK-2500 Valby

Ernst & Young                        1
(London SE1 7EV)
Tagensvej 86
DK-2200 Copenhagen N

European Plastic Machinery 37
Manufacturing A/S
(Brentford)
'Euromatic'
Krimsvej 29
DK-2300 Copenhagen S

Ferrymasters A/S 17
(London E11)
Fabriksparken 8
DK-2600 Glostrup

Fisons A/S 8
(Ipswich IP1 1QH)
Rosenkaeret 22A
DK-2860 Soborg

Flymo A/S 10
(Darlington)
Lundtoftevej 160
DK-2800 Lyngby

Hoover El-Udstyr ApS 10
(Perivale)
Gasvaerksvej 16
DK-1656 Copenhagen V

ICI Denmark A/S 8
(London SW1P 3JF)
Islands Brygge 41
DK-2300 Copenhagen S

International Computers Ltd 10
A/S
(London SW15 1SW)
Klampenborgvej 232
DK-2800 Lyngby

International Factors A/S 17
(Brighton BN1 3WX)
Bredgade 29
DK-1260 Copenhagen K

Johnson Matthey A/S 28
(Royston)
Norre Farumagsgade 33
DK-1364 Copenhagen

Leyland-DAB A/S 7
(London NW1)
Kajlstrupvej 71
DK-8600 Silkeborg

Lloyd's Register of Shipping A/S 23
(London EC3M 4BC)
Kronprinsessgade 26
DK-1264 Copenhagen

Max Factor & Co ApS 11
(Bournemouth)
Naerum Hovedgade 2
DK-2850 Naerum

Nordland Trading 43
(London W1P 0AA)
St Strandstraede 9
DK-1255 Copenhagen K

John Player A/S 47
(Bristol)
Ndr. Fasanvej 108
DK-2200 Copenhagen F

Price Waterhouse/Seier-Petersen 1
(London SE1 9SY)
Tuborg Boulevard 1 64
Copenhagen K

Radical Radar Aktieselskab 45
(London SE1 7SW)
Mitchellsgade 9
1568 Copenhagen V

Rank Xerox A/S 30
(London NW1 3BH)
Borupvang 5
DK-2750 Ballerup

Readers Digest Europe 38
(London EC4M 7NB)
Jagtvei 169B
Postboks 810,
DK-2100 Copenhagen Q

Reckitt & Colman A/S 16
(London W4 2RW)
Industrivej 14
DK-2600 Glostrup

Renold A/S 25.
(Manchester M22 5WL)
Skelmarksvej 6
DK-2600 Glostrup

Thorn EMI 10
(London W1R 9AH)
Fona A/S
Brogrenen 68
DK-2635 Ishoj

TNT Danmark A/S 17
(Northampton NN3 8RB)
Kirstinehøy 17
DK-2770 Kastrup

United Biscuits A/S                                16
(Middlesex TW7 5NN)
Sdr. Ringvej 41-45
DK-2600 Glostrup


Universal Air Express A/S                          17
Fuglebaekvej 2C
PO Box 109
Copenhagen

Whitbread & Co (Scandinavia)                       16
(London EC1Y 4SD)
Strandboulevarden 130
DK-100 Copenhagen Ol


Wiggins Teape (Danmark)                            33
(London E15 2NT)
Hovedgaden 49
2970 Horsolm

# Finland

Finnish Embassy, 38 Chesham Place, London SW1X 8HW, tel 0171-235 9531
Finnish Embassy, 3301 Massachusetts Avenue, NW, 20008 Washington DC, tel 202-298-5800
Currency: 1 Markka (Mk) = 100 Penniäl
Rate of Exchange: £1 = 7.2 Mk; $1 = 4.7 Mk

Finland has entered a new era, now that it has joined the European Union; and as the only EU country with a border with Russia is well placed to take advantage of trading links with that country. It has a highly industrialised economy, producing a wide range of industrial goods. Agriculture is also important. In most food production Finland is virtually self-sufficient, despite a climate which allows for a very short growing season. Engineering is a major industry; and timber, paper, furniture, and other wood-related products are manufactured. Tourism is relatively not so important.

Finns tend to be rather reserved and introverted people who appreciate deeds rather than words. Conventions in work and business are rather more formal than in the UK or United States; and if you do not enjoy long periods of silence in a conversation, this may not be the place to be. Finns are also thoughtful. This was the only country to notify the editor of its 'Foreigners' Crisis Centres', set up 'to help foreigners in crisis situations'. These are in Helsinki and Turku.

Riding and hiking, fishing and watersports are all popular, as are cross-country skiing, golf (including a variety called snow golf) and — especially — tennis. One little-known Finnish leisure activity is gold-panning. A much better-known institution is the sauna — a place to relax in the company of friends or family. Food has both western (French) and eastern (Russian) influences; one local speciality is smoked reindeer meat. There are ambivalent attitudes towards excessive drinking which is both common — especially in winter — and strictly licensed.

The landscape is flat and forested, interspersed with many lakes and rivers. The forests recede to an Arctic tundra in the far north. The population of just over five million is low compared to the land area, and much of this is concentrated in the capital, Helsinki, which has 500,000 inhabitants; other towns are Turku, Tampere, and Oulu. The religion is mainly Lutheran, with other Protestant churches, Finnish Orthodox, Roman Catholic and others. Nature, Finnish traditions, and the language, all play an important part in national life.

## FACTORS INFLUENCING EMPLOYMENT

### Immigration
US and Canadian citizens may remain in Scandinavia (including Finland) for a total of three months without a visa, although this is required if you wish to work in the country, along with a Labour Permit. This will only be granted for a specific job, and a letter of recommendation from the prospective employer must be included with the application. Applications should be addressed to the *Finnish Embassy* (see above), from where they will be forwarded to the relevant authorities in Finland. Processing of applications takes up to six weeks. The Finnish Embassy does not provide assistance finding work, but may supply

(along with the National Tourist Board) the invaluable publication entitled *Are you planning to move to Finland?* with comprehensive information on residence, working, self-employment, housing, education, recognition of qualifications, social security, and health. It also contains a list of the twenty-seven or so Employment Offices (*työvoimatoimisto*) which have an international labour adviser or Euro adviser.

Residence permits are required by EU citizens living or working in Finland for longer than three months, but not a work permit. These can be obtained from local police stations, on production of a passport, photo, and employment cotract (*työsopimus*) or similar document.

## Language
Finland has two official languages: Finnish, spoken by 94% of the population, and Swedish, spoken by 6%. A tiny minority speaks the Lapp language Same. Finnish is not an Indo-European language, like most of the others spoken in Europe, but Finno-Ugric, like Hungarian. There are no less than thirteen case endings. Some interest in learning the language by foreign visitors is appreciated (but not expected). English is taught as the first foreign language, and German is also widely understood.

## Embassies and Consulates
British Embassy, Itäinen Puistotie 17, FIN-00140 Helsinki; tel 0-661-293.
There are also British Consulates in Jyväskylä, Kotka, Kuopio, Mariehamn, Oulu, Pori, Tampere, Turku and Vaasa.

US Embassy, Itäinen Puistotie 14B, FIN-00140 Helsinki; tel 0-171-931.

## Tourist Offices
Finnish Tourist Board, 30-35 Pall Mall, London SW1Y 5LP; tel 0171-839 4048 or 930 5871 (trade only).
Finnish Tourist Board, 655 Third Avenue, New York, NY 10017; tel 212-949-1333.


## WORK AVAILABLE

### General
Finland has significant shipbuilding, engineering and textile industries. Scope for foreign workers is limited because of the small size of the economy, and the fact that Finnish is an unusually difficult language. A knowledge of Swedish or German is an asset, and professionally qualified persons interested in working in Finland should approach recruitment agencies in that field.

### Newspapers
*Frank L. Crane Ltd.,* 5-15 Cromer Street, Grays Inn Road, London WC1H 8LS, tel 0171-837 3330, represents *Turun Sanomat* (Turku) and *Aamulehti* (Tampere) in Britain. *Powers International,* 517-523 Fulham Road, London SW6 1HD, tel 0171-385 8855, represents the national daily *Helsingin Sanomat.*


## SPECIFIC CONTACTS

*Työmarkkinat* published in Finnish and Swedish and available from employment offices is the fortnightly publication that gives information on vacancies and adult training opportunities.

### Teaching
There is a steady demand for English teachers with degrees and relevant training and it is possible to obtain a list of language schools from the Finnish Embassy in London or Washington. A key English-teaching organisation in Finland is the

*Federation of Finnish-British Societies,* Puistokatu 1 b A, FIN-00140 Helsinki. The following organisation in the UK recruits for its Finnish language school:

*Linguarama,* Oceanic House, 89 High Street, Alton, Hants GU34 1LG — runs a school in Helsinki. Address in Finland is: *Linguarama Suomi Oy,* Annankatu 26, FIN-00100 Helsinki.

There may be opportunities for suitably qualified teachers at the summer universities, which are run to help secondary school students prepare for university examinations. The *Summer High School Association in Finland* address is: Fabianinkatu 4 B, FIN-00171 Helsinki, tel 0-666-121; and the *Finnish Association of Summer Universities* is at: Hämeenkatu 26 B, FIN-33200 Tampere; tel 31-147-626.

## SHORT TERM WORK

Apart from the *Finnish Family Programme,* organised by the *Centre for International Mobility,* Hakaniemenkatu 2, Helsinki, tel 0-774-77-033, enabling young people aged 18-23 whose mother tongue is English, French or German to spend the summer months teaching the language to a Finnish family, opportunities for temporary work are mainly those available through the organisations mentioned in *Voluntary Work*; there is the scheme organised by the *International Farm Experience Programme* (see *Agriculture and the Environment*).

The Centre for International Mobility also offers a wide range of practical training placements on its *International Trainee Exchange Programme* for students or recent graduates, in agriculture, the environment, the service industries, social work, and commerce and retail. Information concerning its programme may also be obtained from the *Central Bureau* in Britain (see *Working Exchanges* in the *Getting the Job* chapter). The *Monastery of Valamo,* 7850 Uusi-Valamo, is an Orthodox religious community which needs helpers from time to time in its kitchen and garden, and to 'collect brushwood, mushrooms and berries in the forest.' It offers board and accommodation in return.

If you do not speak Finnish, some knowledge of a Scandinavian language or German is normally required for most types of paid work; and the authorities are strict in enforcing the regulations that state that no-one from outside the EU and EEA should take on a job that a local could do.

**Other Contacts**
*The Familia Club,* Il Linja, FIN-00530 Helsinki, tel 90-738-628 — is an international friendship society promoting activities like get-togethers and language clubs in Finland; and also distributes information on Finnish society and customs, as well as facts on various other countries.

*Crisis Prevention Center for Foreigners,* Simononkatu 12 B 13, FIN-00100, Helsinki, tel 0-685-2828, and the *Support Centre for Foreigners* in Turku, Yliopitonkatu 24 A 6, FIN-20100 Turku, tel 21-233-3422 — help foreigners all over Finland in crisis situations, especially with social and psychological problems. Also, see *Live and Work in Scandinavia* (Vacation Work) for more about living and working in Finland.

### BRITISH COMPANIES

with branches, affiliates or subsidiaries in Finland
(see appendix for numerical classification code)

| | | |
|---|---|---|
| Albright & Wilson Oy<br>(Birmingham B68 0NN)<br>Lönrotkatu 25A<br>Helsinki | 8 | British Airways<br>(London TW6 2JA)<br>Keskuskatu 7<br>FIN-00100 Helsinki | 3 |

British Oxygen Group        8
(Surrey GU20 6HJ)
Suomen Viggo Oy, Helsinki

Commercial Union        23
(London EC3P 3DQ)
PO Box 126
FIN-00121 Helsinki 12

Coopers & Lybrand Oy        1
(London EC4A 4HT)
Keskuskatu 3
00100 Helsinki

English China Clays        16
(St Austell PL25 4DJ)
PO Box 17
FIN-00101 Helsinki

EMI Finland        29
(London W1R 9AH)
Arinatie 6E
FIN-00371 Helsinki

GKN Hardy Spicer Ab        22
(Birmingham B24 0RB)
Tulppatie 10-12
PL 11
FIN-00881 Helsinki

Glaxo Pharmaceuticals Oy        8
(London W1X 6BP)
Ahventie 4 B
FIN-02171 Espool

Hambros Bank Ltd        4
(London EC3N 4HA)
Aleksanterinkatu 48 B
FIN-00100 Helsinki 10

Hamworthy Finland Oy        26
(Poole BH17 0LA)
Sirrikuja 3
FIN-00940 Helsinki

Hoover Oy        18
(Bolton BL2 6PU)
Orionintie 18
FIN-02200 Espool

ICI Pharma Oy        8
(London SW1P 3JF)
Halsuantie 4
FIN-00420 Helsinki

ICL Finland Oy        10
(London SW15 1SW)
Porkkalankatu 5
FIN-00120 Helsinki 12

KPMG Business Consulting        14
(London EC4V 3PD)
Mannerheimintie 20B
FIN-00101 Helsinki

Lloyds Register of Shipping        23
(London EC3A 3BP)
Hämeenkatu 30D
FIN-20700 Turku

PA Consulting Group        14
(London SW1 W9SR)
Kaupintie 11Al
FIN-00441 Helsinki

Rank Xerox Oy        20
(London NW1 3BH)
Sinimaentie 8
FIN-02631 Espool

Rhône-Poulenc Agro        8
(Ipswich IP1 1QH)
Lauppakartanonkatu 7
FIN-00931 Helsinki

Oy Shell Ab        35
(London SW1 7NA)
Neilikkatu 17
FIN-01301 Vantaa

Scandinavian Media Sources        2
(London W1M 8AN)
PO Box 16
FIN-00381 Helsinki

Spirax Oy        25
(Cheltenham GL51 9NQ)
Valimotie 13
FIN-00381 Helsinki

Suomen Unilever Oy        16
(London EC4P 4BQ)
Lönnrotinkatu 20
FIN-00120 Helsinki

Thorn EMI plc        45
(London W1A 2AY)
Arinatie 65
FIN-00371 Helsinki

Vickers Systems Oy        25
(London SW1P 4RA)
Virkat 10
FIN-01511 Vantaa

Other commercial information about Finland can be supplied by the *Finnish Foreign Trade Association*, (Arkadiankatu 2, FIN-001000, Helsinki; tel 0-69591).

# France

French Embassy, 58 Knightsbridge, London SW1X 7JT, tel 0171-201 1000
French Embassy, 4101 Reservoir Road, NW, Washington DC 20007, tel 202-944-6000
Currency: 1 Franc (Fr) = 100 centimes
Rate of Exchange: £1 = Fr 8; $1 = Fr 5

Although unemployment remains high, particularly among less skilled workers, France is becoming more and more popular as a place to work for young British and American professionals. The building of the Channel Tunnel has improved communications; and there is a large English-speaking expatriate community in Paris, as well as in the south and east of the country. Air, road and rail communications are good, and the standard of living generally high. Most young Britons consider France first, when they are thinking of short-term or seasonal work abroad for the first time, as there are strong historical ties between the two countries (even though the relationship has at times been stormy). Au pair and summer work prospects are good; grape-picking is the traditional agricultural occupation; and many Britons also choose to spend their retirement in France, or buy a second home there; in the region around Calais or Normandy, or in the south (Provence and the Dordogne). English is not always spoken but most educated people speak some; and French is commonly taught as a second language in British and American schools; so most English-speaking people find that they can get by. It may take a longer time to get used to the culture, though, where eating and socialising play an important part. British and American people do not talk quite so much about food! Dressing neatly, and being a little more formal than in Britain in America, are an important part of working life, in France as in many other continental European countries.

## GENERAL FACTS

### Population

France's population is about 57,700,000. Bounded by Italy, Switzerland and Spain in the south, and Gemany, Luxembourg and Belgium to the north and east (with the Atlantic Ocean to the west) France covers 220,668 square miles. The only countries in Europe which are larger are Russia and Ukraine. The average population density is 262 per square mile.

### Climate

France has all three European subdivisions of climate, ranging from continental (in the east), to maritime (in the west), and mediterranean (in the south). The wettest parts are the Central Plateau, the Juras, the Alps, the Pyrenees and the coastal Brittany area. The Paris Basin and the Mediterranean coast are the driest. The climate of the south-east of the country along the Mediterranean coast, and in the lee of the Maritime Alps, is probably the most pleasant. Winters in the north can be cold and dreary.

### Government

France is a Republic headed by a President who is elected every seven years, and is both head of state and, in the influence he wields over the Prime Minister, effectively the head of the government too. The Prime Minister chooses his ministers but this decision is then ratified by the President. The Parliament is bicameral, consisting of the National Assembly and the Senate. Major political groupings are the Socialists and the Gaullists (RPR) with a dwindling and largely unreconstructed Communist party, and a surprisingly popular anti-immigrant party, the National Front. Referenda are occasionally used in national decision-making, as when, in 1992, France narrowly accepted the Maastricht Treaty on European Union.

Administratively, the country is divided into 22 regions, and 96 departments (*départements*) which in turn are divided into 324 local areas, or *arrondissements.* The name of the smallest unit shows the origins of this administrative set-up in the French Revolution: it is the *commune,* of which there are about 36,500. One of the regions is the island of Corsica, birthplace of Napoleon and still considered very much part of France. So are the various overseas possessions like Guadeloupe, French Guiana, Réunion, Tahiti, and New Caledonia.

**Rural Life**
For many British people with an idyllic view of its peasant life, France is the countryside. In fact, rural life is becoming less important in national affairs, as the Common Agricultural Policy and intensive farming methods have hit the smaller French farmer and accelerated the drift to the cities. Historically, France has always been an agricultural country, to which the Industrial Revolution came relatively late. Her richest natural resources are her fertile farmlands and forests. France is a large wheat producer, with barley, oats, rice, and grapes for wine production; beef and dairy production and fisheries are also important.

**Religion, Sport and Culture**
Most French people are baptised into the Roman Catholic Church, but not so many go to church regularly. There is a minority of about 800,000 Protestants, and other evangelical and non-Christian (especially Jewish) faiths are represented. There are two million or so Muslims among the large North African Arab community (Morocco, Tunisia, and Algeria), most of whom were born in the country and are French citizens.

Sport has come to be an important part of national life, with considerable achievements in athletics, soccer and rugby. Horse-racing and other spectator sports are also popular. Cycling is widely followed; and the annual *Tour de France* is a national preoccupation in summer. Many French people also enjoy hiking, as well as more 'exotic' outdoor sports like mountaineering and windsurfing. Skiing is another favoured pastime, with an exodus in winter to the Alps and the Pyrenees matching the annual migration to the beaches of the south in August (when much of the country closes down). One traditional activity (played more usually in the south) is *boules* or *pétanque.*

The French are proud of their great achievements in culture, philosophy and the arts, and their architectural heritage. There is a tendency to see these not just as national achievements, but as universal; and the arts in France are strongly supported by the state. Popular and experimental art-forms are also encouraged, another consequence of the habit among the French of seeing themselves as the flag-bearers of a universal culture. The internationally renowned French film industry is another achievement of which they can be justly proud.

# FACTORS INFLUENCING EMPLOYMENT

**Immigration**
EU nationals intending to stay in France for more than three months can only do so if they have an offer of employment. The residence permit (*carte de séjour*) is only issued on production of a *déclaration d'engagement,* signed by the prospective employer. This should be done soon after arrival, and after you have obtained a job, at the *Commissariat de Police,* or *Mairie;* or, in Paris, at

the *Préfecture de Police.* You will then receive a *carte de séjour* or residence permit. Persons wishing to set up their own business in France should apply to the same authorities for a *carte de commerçant.*

Enquiries about visas, work permits etc., should be addressed to the *French Consulate General,* Service des Visas, 6a Cromwell Place, London SW7 2EW, tel 0171-838 2000 or at the French Consulate in Scotland: 11 Randolph Crescent, Edinburgh EH3 7TT, tel 0171-338 2000. Enquiries for Northern Ireland should be addressed to London. The telephone number of the Consular Section in Washington is 944-6200; there are consulates in Atlanta, Boston, Chicago, Detroit, Houston, Los Angeles, Miami, New Orleans, New York, and San Francisco. US citizens do not require a visa to visit. Those wishing to work (including voluntary work) should have a work permit arranged in advance. Your employer will do this through the *Office des Migrations Internationales* (44 rue Bargue, F-75732 Paris). Those with an international student card and a definite job offer may also be eligible for a temporary permit. The French Embassy in Washington will advise on these procedures.

## Language
The French are very proud of their language and their achievements in literature. It is seen as an international language, too; and there is some resistence to the idea that English may have superseded it in areas like diplomacy, science, and commerce as the main medium of international communication. Written English and grammar tend to be taught in French schools, but the spoken language is not taught well; so there are opportunities for English teachers in the many private schools which exist to remedy this situation. Basque is also spoken by some in in the south-west of the country; and Breton in Brittany by a few. The dialect of the south of France has its origin in a language different to French — the Langue d'Oc — and may be difficult to understand.

## Cost and Standard of Living
France has the fourth largest economy in the world; and in its general standard of living ranks higher than Britain (although not the USA). This relative affluence does not extend to all areas of society, though, and there are areas of 'exclusion' and unemployment in the suburbs of towns and in the countryside which are a major cause of concern. There is almost the same consensus abroad as in France that French food is the best in the world. The way of life is relaxed, and there is an enjoyment of the good things of life which is not matched in Britain or America. Like work, the French tend to take their leisure seriously too. Consumer goods and services (like restaurants) tend to be a more important item of expenditure than housing.

## Housing and Accommodation
Many French people do not like to invest money in property, and have a strong preference for rented accommodation. All the same, more than half of French families own their accommodation. All kinds of rented property are available for expatriate workers; and prices vary enormously depending on where you are. Paris and the Côte d'Azur are the most expensive.

## Health and Welfare
The various social security schemes cover almost everyone in France: wage earners, salaried staff, and self-employed people, and their families (including those foreign nationals who have paid their contributions).

The system is financed by contributions by the employer and employee. Reciprocal arrangments are also available for British and other EU nationals (see the *Rules and Regulations* chapter in *The General Approach*). These cover: national insurance; pensions (amounts dependent on salaries and length of insurance); death, maternity, family and housing allowances; and industrial accident insurance.

Medical treatment and medicines are available to EU citizens under the same conditions as for French nationals. North Americans will have to have paid their contributions to receive these benefits.

### Education

The French attach great importance to education, and are leaders in science and knowledge – based industries like information technology. Schooling is free and compulsory from the ages of six to 16; and nursery schools and crèches are widely available; there is only a small private sector (which includes international schools in areas where there are expatriate communities). Primary education lasts from six to 11. The first stage of secondary education lasts a further four years. Students usually stay on to take the *baccalauréat* exam which is necessary for university entry. French universities only require a modest payment for tuition charges; and are open to foreigners with the equivalent exam; but they are sometimes overcrowded and of variable quality. The reform of higher education is a major political problem which no party as yet has been able to solve. There are also the more prestigious *grandes écoles,* — which are part of the same system, and originally founded by Napoleon as military colleges — for which additional preparatory study is necessary. There is then a *concours* or competitive exam.

### National Service

In 1996, President Chirac announced proposals to abolish compulsory national military service.

### Embassies and Consulates

British Embassy, 35 rue du Faubourg St. Honoré, F-75383 Paris, Cedex 08; tel 1-42 66 91 42.

British Consulate General, 16 rue d'Anjou, F-75008 Paris; tel 1-42 66 38 10

British Consulate General, 353 boulevard du President Wilson, F-33073 Bordeaux; tel 556 42 34 13.

British Consulate General, 11 square Dutilleul, F-59800 Lille; tel 220 57 87 90.

British Consulate General, 24 rue Childebert, F-69002 Lyon; tel 478 37 59 67.

British Consulate General, 24 avenue du Prado, F-13006 Marseille; tel 491 53 43 32.

There are also British Consulates in Biarritz, Boulogne, Calais, Cherbourg, Dunkirk, Le Havre, Nantes, Nice, St. Malo-Dinard, Toulouse, and in French overseas territories.

US Embassy, 2 avenue Gabriel, F-75008 Paris, Cedex 08; tel 1-42 96 12 02. Consulates in Bordeaux, Lyon, Marseille, Martinique, and Strasbourg.

### Tourist Offices

French Government Tourist Office, 178 Piccadilly, London W1V 0AL; tel 0891-244123 (France Information Line).

French Government Tourist Office, 444 Madison Avenue, New York, NY 10020-2451; tel 212-838-7800.

### Telephones

For all calls within France a zero is dialled before the nine digit number which is now standard, except for Paris numbers beginning with 1. From France, international calls begin 00, as in Britain.

## CONDITIONS OF WORK

### Wages

Salaries in Paris are generally higher than in the rest of the country. The national hourly minimum wage (known as the SMIC — *Salaire Minimum Interprofessionel de Croissance*) is regularly reviewed to keep up with inflation.

Almost all workers in France are paid monthly. A sympathetic employer will direct you to a bank which can open an account for you. Otherwise this can be a time-consuming process.

## Hours
The normal working week is around 39 hours, and there are legal provisions limiting overtime to a basic nine hours. The length of the average working week has decreased markedly in recent years. The traditional working day lasts from 8.30 or 9.00 to 6.00 or 6.30 with a long lunch break, although a shorter day is becoming more common.

## Holidays
There are 11 public holidays annually; and most workers are entitled to five weeks in addition. There have been moves in industry to curtail the annual 'August madness' by staggering summer holidays. These have been only partially successful. The public holidays are: New Year's Day; Easter Monday; Labour Day (1 May); Victory in Europe Day (8 May); Ascension (16 May); Whit Monday (May); Bastille Day (14 July); Assumption (15 August); All Saints (1 November); Armistice Day (11 November); Christmas Day. There is an interesting French expression 'faire le pont', which means bridging the time between one of these holidays and the weekend by taking another day or two's unofficial holiday.

## Safety and Compensation
Hygiene and Security Committees are obligatory in large firms; and there are regular inspections. In addition, those working in France can expect an annual (and free) medical check-up.

Contributions for sickness and injury benefits come under social security (and the various taxes for social security, unemployment etc., as well as your social security number, should be detailed separately on your pay-slip). Compensation for industrial accidents usually carries the full cost of medical expenses, rehabilitation and retraining. Unemployment does not come under this social security heading, but under a separate scheme run by UNEDIC (*Union Nationale pour l'Emploi dans l'Industrie et le Commerce*).

## Trade Unions
The influence of organised labour has declined rapidly since the 70s and 80s; and now lies mainly in the public sector. They are not organised according to different areas of employment, as in Britain or America, but in groupings with political affiliations: socialist, communist, Christian, and independent. A committee of these will in practice negotiate wages and conditions in a particular workplace; and non-union staff have this right too.

## Taxation
France does not operate a PAYE (Pay As You Earn) scheme; and so the employee not the employer fills out his or her annual tax declaration form. In theory, tax is assessed on your earnings in one year and then payed the next, although in practice deductions begin straightaway (and can be adjusted later). Indirect taxes are a main source of French government revenue, and Value Added Tax is levied in some areas — like food — which are not taxed in Britain. The tax year runs from January to December; and returns must be filed before 1 March, on the basis of predicted income for the year. Taxes are paid in instalments, either three times per year, or monthly.

# WORK AVAILABLE

## General
France has a modern, developed economy; there are few areas where work is not available to qualified experienced personnel. One of these is teaching and

government service, where exams in the French language mean that only the most linguistically competent can qualify. French employers value training; and generally expect recruits to have specific professional qualifications for whatever job they are taken on to do. The general workplace atmosphere tends to be more formal and sometimes more hierarchical than in Britain or America. There are two definite categories of employee: blue-collar workers (known as *le personnel*) and white collar staff known as *cadres*, or sometimes (confusingly) as *staff*. It is also worth noting that a high standard of presentation in letters and CVs as well as in personal appearance are expected in prospective new recruits. Include International Reply Coupons in your letters of enquiry; or better send a fax.

**Newspapers**
Advertisements can be placed in the daily *Le Figaro* (which has an 'Economie' section) by *Mercury Publicity* in London, tel 0171-831 6631. The *International Herald Tribune* newspaper is published in Paris and has a worldwide circulation. Advertisements can be placed through offices at 63 Kingsway, London WC2; or 850 3rd Ave., New York NY 10022. *France-USA Contacts (FUSAC)* is a newsletter which contains work opportunities and can carry 'situations wanted' ads. It is distributed free in Paris but there will be a charge to send it abroad: *France-USA Contacts,* 3 rue Larochelle, F-75014 Paris; tel 1-45 38 56 57; fax 1-45 38 98 94.


# SPECIFIC CONTACTS

**Employment Service**
The official labour exchange in France is the *Agence Nationale pour l'Emploi,* which has over 600 branches in the main French towns. They handle all types of work, but special engineering departments exist in the offices in Paris, Lyon and Marseille. Their main office at *ANPE, Le Galilée, 4 rue Galilée, F-93198 Noisy-le-Grand (tel 1-49 31 74 00) can supply the addresses of the regional labour exchange branches. Your dealings with them will be in French, as with all French officialdom, unless you happen to find a sympathetic and English-speaking advisor. There is a regional branch of *EURES*, the European Employment Service in Britain, which assists with work in northern France at: *EURES Crossborder Kent,* Shorncliffe Road, Folkestone, Kent CT20 2NA; tel 01303-220580; fax 01303-220476.

**Local Agencies**
There are a number of private employment agencies in France that may be able to offer jobs in industry or office work, including *Ecco Interim* with offices throughout the UK and much of Europe as well as France (and the United States). Their head office at St. John's Hill, Clapham, London SW11 1TR, tel 0171-978 7733 (or in the US at 902 Broadway, New York, NY 10010, tel 212-995-2400) may send you a list of these offices. They deal with supervisory, secretarial, and general industrial and commercial positions. Another large agency is *Manpower,* 7-9 rue Jacques Bingen, F-75017 Paris, tel 1-44 15 40 40. Some temporary agencies may not be particularly helpful to those who do not already have a French social security number, which is hard to obtain without already having a job.

Two bilingual recruitment agencies for experienced secretaries are *Sheila Burgess International* (62 rue St Lazare, F-75009, Paris, tel 1-44 63 02 57, fax 1-44 63 02 59; also at 4 Cromwell Place, London SW7, tel 0171-584 6446) and *TM International* (36-38 rue des Mathurins, F-75008 Paris; tel 1-47 42 71 00; fax 1-47 42 18 87).

**Agricultural and Seasonal Work**
See *Work Your Way Around the World* (Vacation Work) in the chapter on France for the definitive guide to finding farming work. The *vendange* or grape harvest is best known but there are many others. You should certainly visit the local ANPE office in the wine-growing and other regions if you are looking for work there. These are listed in *Work Your Way Around the World* (or you can contact the *Agence National de l'Emploi* at the address above) although they are said not always to be particularly helpful. It is also possible to make arrangements in advance through *SESAME,* 9-11 square Gabriel Fauré, F-75017 Paris (tel 1-40 54 07 08). Another central recruitment office is *Jeunesse et Réconstruction,* 10 rue de Trévise, F-75009 Paris (tel 1-47 70 15 88). Both these organisations favour personal callers who speak good French.

**Au Pairs**
Apart from agencies listed in the *Au Pair* chapter, au pair positions are arranged throughout France by:

> *Accueil familial des jeunes Etrangers,* 23 rue du Cherche-Midi, F-75006 Paris
> *L'ARCHE,* 7 rue Bargue, F-75015 Paris
> *CONTACTS,* 55 rue Nationale, F-37000 Tours
> *Inter-Séjours,* 179 rue de Courcelles, F-75017 Paris
> *Service Social de l'Institut Catholique,* 21 rue d'Assas, F-75270 Paris Cedex 6

**Medical Staff**
The *Association Médicale Française,* 37 rue de Bellefond, F-75441 Paris Cedex 09, tel 1-45 96 34 52; fax 1-45 96 34 50, may be able to provide information on areas where doctors are needed. The nurses' association in France is *ANFIIDE,* BP 2332, F-45023 Orléans Cedex.

**Teachers**
Teachers of English are permanently needed in every region and department of France, if not in every *commune*, as the country struggles to reconcile its own international role in an increasingly English-speaking world with its attachment to French language and culture. In other words, there is a great desire, and a reluctance, to know how to use this language which many may have learnt imperfectly at school; learners range from children to business executives, at all levels of proficiency in the language. Going there and visiting some private language schools is one way. Alternatively, write to some of the larger international language school chains (see the *Teaching* chapter for details).

Information on the French education system and other openings for teachers can be obtained from *French Embassy Cultural Section,* 23 Cromwell Road, London SW7 2EL, tel 0171-838 2055 (ask for the leaflet *Teaching Posts in France*); or from the *Central Bureau for Educational Visits and Exchanges* (see *Working Exchanges*).

**Tourism**
A lot is spoken about EuroDisneyland (now DisneyLand Paris) but dressing up in Mickey Mouse costumes and observing the stern Disney dress code may not be your idea of fun. If it is, you can write enclosing your CV to: *DisneyLand Paris,* Service de Recrutement-Casting, B.P. 110, Marne-la-Vallée, F-77777 Cedex 4, France. Tour operators offering work opportunities in France are included in the chapter *Transport, Tourism and Hospitality.* In addition, there is a wide variety of tourism and hotel work which can be found 'on-the-spot' (see *Work Your Way Around the World). Working Holidays* (Central Bureau) has a comprehensive list of tourism and voluntary organisations in France, as well as au pair agencies; and there is *Summer Jobs Abroad* published by Vacation Work.

## Voluntary Work

There are also some opportunities in this area for construction and archaeological work. The International Secretariat of *Les Compagnons Bâtisseurs*, 5 rue des Immeubles industriels, F-75011 Paris, is one contact for the former (also at: Maison de la Solidarité, 6 avenue Charles de Gaulle, F-81100 Castres). The *Direction du Patrimoine, Sous-Direction de l'Archéologie*, a department of the Ministry of Culture at 4 rue d'Aboukir, F-75002 Paris, tel 1-40 16 73 00, has a list of excavations throughout France requiring volunteers; and can tell you about the Services Archéologiques of many French departments which organise digs. US citizens should remember that they need a work visa to do voluntary work in France. The local branch of the international voluntary and workcamp organisation *Service Civil International* is at 2 rue Eugène Fournière, F-75018 Paris. Other organisations are mentioned in the chapter *Voluntary Work.*

## Management Consultants

*Daniel Porte Consultants,* 102 Terrasse Boieldieu, La Défense 8, F-92000 Paris — specialising in accountancy.

*Drouot-l'Hermine Consultants,* 33 rue Miromesnil, F-75008 Paris — mainly for banking and accountancy.

*Oberthur Consultants,* 49 rue Saint-Roch, F-75001 Paris — for a range of management and staff level positions.

## Useful publications

In addition to the above, *Live and Work in France,* published by Vacation Work, gives a great deal of detail on all aspects of life in France. A directory of graduate opportunities is *Bac — que faire aprés?* available from *ONISEP,* 50 rue Albert, F-75635 Paris Cedex 13, which concentrates on matching higher education courses to specific potential employers.

BRITISH COMPANIES
with branches, affiliates or subsidiaries in France
(see appendix for numerical classification code)

The *Franco-British Chamber of Commerce and Industry,* 110 rue de Longchamps, F-75116 Paris, publishes a *Year Book,* which contains a full list of members of the Chamber, many of which are branches, subsidiaries or agents of British-based companies. The Year Book costs £50 (postage included).

| | | | |
|---|---|---|---|
| Arthur Anderson & Co<br>(London WC2R 2PS)<br>Tour Gan Cedex 13<br>F-92082 Paris | 1 | British Steel France<br>(London SE1 7SN)<br>3 allée des Barbonniers<br>F-92692 Gennevilliers Cedex | 28 |
| Automotive Products France<br>177 rue des Fauvelles<br>F-92404 Courbevoie | 22 | British Telecom France SA<br>(London WC2R 3HL)<br>Immeuble Jean Monnet<br>F-92061 Paris-la-Défense Cedex | 45 |
| Barclays Bank International<br>(London EC3P 3AH)<br>21 rue Lafitte<br>F-75009 Paris | 4 | British Tourist Authority<br>(London SW1A 1NF)<br>63 rue Pierre Charron<br>F-75008 Paris | 48 |
| British Airways<br>(London TW6 2JA)<br>Immeuble KUPKAA<br>18 rue Hoche<br>F-92980 Paris-la-Défense Cedex | 3 | Charterhouse SA<br>(London EC4M 7DH)<br>47 avenue George V<br>F-75008 Paris | 4 |

Commercial Union Assurance 23
(London EC3P 3DQ)
52 rue de la Victoire
F-75009 Paris

Cooper France SA 8
(Berkhamstead)
15 rue Sorins
F-92000 Nanterre

Courtalds Fibres SA 46
(Coventry CV6 5RZ)
Pont de Leu
F-62231 Coquelles

DHL International 17
(Hounslow T44 6JS)
BP 50252
Rue de la Belle Etoile
2.1 de patinet II
F-95957 Roissy

Courtaulds Fibres SA 46
(London W1)
Pont du Leu
F-62231 Coquelles

Ernst & Young 1
(London SE1 7EU)
HSD Castel Jacquet
Tow Manhattan
F-92095 Paris

Financial Times 38
(London)
42 rue de la Boétie
F-75008 Paris

Gestetner SA 30
(London W1M 2AP)
71 rue Cammille Groult
F-94400 Vitry-sur-Seine

Guardian Royal Exchange PLC 23
(London EC3V 3LS)
42 rue des Mathurins
F-75008 Paris

Habitat International 18
(London W1P 9LD)
1 place Royale
F-78230 Le Pecq

Hambros France Ltd 4
(London EC3N 4HJ)
16 place Vendôme
F-75001 Paris

ICI France SA 26
(London SW1P 3JF)
2 ave Louis Armand
F-92607 Asnières Cedex

ICL France SA 10
(London SW15 1SW)
24 ave de l'Europe
F-78140 Velizy-Villacoublay

International Herald Tribune 38
(London WC2E 9JH)
35 rue du Pont
F-92522 Neuilly-sur-Seine

JCB France 27
(Rochester)
BP 671
F-95200 Sarcelles Cedex

Johnson Matthey & CIE 28
(Royston)
13 rue de la Perdrix ZI
F-93290 Tremblay-en-France

Kraft Jacobs-Suchard 16
(Cheltenham GL50 3AE)
Cases Jacques Vabres
rue de St George
Dorques
F-34880 Laverune

Laboratoires Fisons SA 8
(Loughborough LE11 0BB)
BP 177,
Les 4 Chemin du Petit Bois
F-69130 Ecully

Laboratoires Glaxo Wellcome 8
(London W1X 6BP)
43 rue Vineuse
BP 166 16
F-75016 Paris

Laboratoires Fisons SA 8
(Leicester)
Tour PFA — la Défense 10
F-92076 Paris-la-Défense
Cedex 43

Legal & General Assurance 23
(London EC4N 4TP)
58 rue Victoire
F-75009 Paris

Lloyds Bank SA 4
(London EC4)
15 avenue d'Iéna
F-75783 Paris Cedex 16

Lucas France SA　26
(Birmingham)
11 rue Lord Byron
F-75008 Paris

Marks & Spencer (France) SA　13
(London W1A 1DN)
6-8 rue des Mathurins
BP 252-09
F-75424 Paris

Midland Bank SA　4
(London EC2P 2BZ)
20 bis avenue Rapp
F-75007 Paris

National Westminster Bank　4
(London)
18 place Vendôme
F-75001 Paris

Powell　Duffryn　Compagnie　35
Française
(Bracknell RG12 2AQ)
35 avenue de l'Europe
78143　Velizy-Villacoublay
Cedex

Rank Video Services France　36
(Brentford TW8 9PL)
1 rue Edouard Denis Baldus
F-71100 Chalon-sur-Saône

Rank-Xerox SA　22
(London)
3 rue Bellini
F-92806 Puteaux

Reckitt & Colman SA　18
(London W4 2RW)
15 rue Ampère
F-91301 Massy Cedex

Rowntree Mackintosh SA　16
(York)
Noisiel-Marne-la-Vallée
F-77422 Torcy

SAFAD (Alfred Dunhill)　47
(London SW1)
15 rue de la Paix
F-75002 Paris

Securicor France SA　43
(London E1 6JJ)
12 avenue des Cocquelicots
F-94380 Bonneuil-sur-Marne

WH Smith & Son SA　13
(Swindon SN3 SLD)
248 rue de Rivoli
F-75001 Paris

Standard Chartered Bank Ltd　4
(London EC4)
4 rue Ventadour
F-75001 Paris

Thorn EMI Computer Software　10
(London W1A 2AY)
101-109 rue Jean Jaurès
F-92300 Levallois-Perret

TNT International (Skypac)　17
(Northampton NN3 8RB)
rue Henri Becquerell
F-93600 Aulnay-sous-Bois

Trusthouse Hotels　20
(London WC1)
23 place Vendôme
F-75001 Paris

Weatherall Green & Smith　40
(London WC2A 1LT)
64 rue La Boétie
F-75008 Paris

Wimpey SA　6
(London W6)
72-78 Grande Rue
F-92312 Sèvres

## AMERICAN COMPANIES
### with branches, affiliates or subsidiaries in France

The *Guide to Doing Business in France* compiled by the American Chamber of Commerce and the Commercial Services of the American Embassy in France is published by the *American Chamber of Commerce in France,* 21 avenue George V, F-75008 Paris, and costs Fr 500 (Fr 550 postage and handling included). This guide includes a complete list of US Firms in France; US products and services represented in France; special sections on economic and political trends; investment climate; and useful addresses in France and the United States.

# Germany

German Embassy, 23 Belgrave Square, London SW1X 8PZ, tel 0171-824 1300
German Embassy, 4645 Reservoir Road, NW, Washington DC 20007-1998, 202-298-4000
Currency: 1 Deutschmark (DM) = 100 Pfennigs
Rate of Exchange: £1 = DM 2.3; $1 = DM 1.5

Germany is coming to terms with the reunification of former East and West Germany in 1990. The costs of reunification are not only a burden on German citizens, but also within Europe. Major reconstruction work has taken place in Berlin, which has become once again the capital. The country is taking a more active part in world affairs; and its position in central Europe means that it is well-placed to take advantage of commercial and trade opportunities in the east, where its cultural influence is also strong. It is also the major country in the EU leading the way to Economic and Monetary Union, along with France. Germany has undoubtedly become stronger; and leads the way in industries like vehicle manufacture and engineering; but many enterpises are locating new factories in countries where wage costs are lower; and there is relatively high unemployment. Germans are courteous and friendly, but there is far less 'service with a smile' than in the United States, or even Britain; and their directness is sometimes taken as rudeness. If you want to meet people you have to come forward and do it yourself. The work environment can also seem rather formal and bureaucratic at first. Team-working is the rule (as in many other countries nowadays); and this can be frustrating for those who prefer to work in a more individualistic way. Then there is 'Quiet Time' (1pm to 3pm and 10pm through to 7 am) which is taken very seriously. This is a time not to annoy the neighbours, who have the right to call the police if there are loud noises that bother them. There is no need to worry about any of this. This is just how things are. In the workplace, more informal dress is becoming common, but a neat appearance and — very important — punctuality is taken seriously. Stereotypes are inevitably inaccurate, but observers note a general difference in atmosphere between north and south. In the north, a more serious work ethic is evident, while those in the more Catholic southern part of the country take a more relaxed view of life (and there are more festivals, like the Munich Beer Festival, and the Shrove Tuesday Carnival).

## GENERAL FACTS

### Population
Germany's population numbers 82 million, of whom 6 million are classified as foreigners. The birth rate is ten per 1000 inhabitants, one of the lowest in the world. Germany covers 137,838 square miles; average population density throughout the country is 595 inhabitants per square mile, a little less than that of Britain.

### Climate
The climate is temperate with warm summers and cold winters. Annual precipitation varies, and is higher in the Alps. Winters can be severe, but in most parts of the country prolonged periods of frost and snow are rare.

## Government

Germany is a Federal Republic governed on a parliamentary basis. Its Constitution is based on the 1949 Basic Law. Until 1990, it was split into the liberal Federal Republic of Germany (FRG) in the west, and the communist German Democratic Republic (GDR) in the east. East Germany has now been completely absorbed into the Federal Republic's political system (and its national anthem is no longer heard at athletics and sporting events). The Federal Republic is headed by a President whose term of office lasts five years. The Chancellor is the head of the government; and may remain in office for a maximum of four years when the new *Bundestag* (the legislative body) is elected. The *Bundesrat* is the second chamber, whose members are appointed by the State Governments.

These regions (or *Länder*) also play an important part in political life. There are 16 of them: Bavaria; Baden-Württemberg — the two largest — Berlin; Brandenburg, Bremen; Hamburg; Hesse; Lower Saxony; Mecklenburg-Western Pomerania; North Rhine-Westphalia; Rhineland-Palatinate; Saarland; Saxony; Saxony-Anhalt; Schleswig-Holstein; and Thuringia. Berlin is the capital; and is scheduled to become the administrative capital in 2002.

## Cities

About one-third of the population lives in the 85 cities with over 100,000 inhabitants. These include Berlin with its rapidly growing population of around four million; Hamburg (2.8 million); Munich, with 1.2 million inhabitanst; and Cologne with around a million. Bonn, the former political and administrative capital of West Germany, has only 300,000.

## Rural Life

Germany has diverse landscapes, ranging from low and high mountain ranges, to uplands, hilly regions and lakelands, as well as wide, open lowlands. Land use is similary varied. The chief crops in terms of proceeds are milk, pork and beef, cereals, and sugarbeet. Wine, and fruit and vegetables, are also important in some regions. The number of agricultural workers is decreasing each year, and the number of small family farms is also diminishing. The collective farms of the east are now privately owned, or cooperatives. There is also a gradual population shift away from the large towns, particularly in the industrialised and overcrowded Ruhr Valley, which is turning some villages into small towns.

## Religion, Sport and Culture

'Freedom of faith and conscience' is guaranteed under the German Constitution. In the western part of the country 42% of Germans are Protestant and 43% Catholic. In the former East, 47% are Protestant and only 7% Catholic. There are the churches of immigrant groups (like the Greek Orthodox church); and other faiths include Islam, with around 1.7 million adherents (mainly Turkish residents) and Judaism. Before the Nazi genocide about 530,000 Jews lived in Germany. Today this community numbers around 40,000.

Sport is a favourite leisure activity; and football is the most popular. There are more than five million members of the German Football Federation and thousands of amateur clubs. Sports like gymnastics, rifleshooting, athletics, tennis, gold and swimming are also favoured. Horse-riding is also popular; and the fans who follow motor racing are many. Winter sports are enjoyed by some, and include skiing, ski-jumping, skating, ice-hockey, and tobogganing. Travel is also a popular leisure activity.

Germany has a tradition of decentralisation, which is embodied in the modern state. This makes for a wide and rich range of cultural diversity. Nightlife and is lively in the major cities; and Germans are fond of joining clubs, sports and otherwise.

# FACTORS INFLUENCING EMPLOYMENT

## Immigration

All aliens (including EU citizens) wishing to work or reside in Germany must register on arrival with the local registry office (*Meldestelle*). After answering some questions, you should receive your confirmation of residence. US citizens can remain in Germany for up to 90 days as tourists and no visa is required, but work permits must be obtained from outside the country.

German Embassies cannot help in finding employment, but can give information to intending workers and residents in Germany. The *Information Booklet for aliens working in the Federal Republic and emigrants returning to the Federal Republic* is obtainable from: Zimmer 202, 2. Stock, Grosse Bleichen 23, D-20354 Hamburg, tel 40-344-474, for a cover charge of DM20. The monthly publication *Germany: A Guide to Living and Working in Germany* (Rios Werbung GmbH, Eschersheimer Landstr. 69, D-60322 Frankfurt/Main; tel 69-590-805; fax 69-596-2227) is also useful, and the June '96 issue is recommended. This may also be obtained at the German Embassy. In the UK, there are also consulates in Manchester (tel 0161-237 5255) and Edinburgh (tel 0131-337 2323); and in the USA in Atlanta, Boston, Chicago, Detroit, Houston, Los Angeles, Miami, New York (tel 212-308-8700), San Francisco and Seattle.

## Language

English is widely spoken and French is also spoken, particularly in the Saarland. Danish is spoken by the small Danish minority in the north of Schleswig-Holstein. Regional dialects often differ markedly from standard German. Most English-speakers find German quite easy to pronounce, but find the grammar and word order more difficult.

## Cost and Standard of Living

Incomes have increased constantly in Germany thanks to its 'economic miracle' (*Wirtschaftswunder*); and a very broad middle class has emerged, as in the United States. Germany has enjoyed low inflation for many years, while salaries and the material standard of living have steadily increased. To an outsider, prices may appear quite high owing to the constant appreciation in the value of the Deutschmark, and inflation in the period after the unification of the country.

## Housing and Accommodation

Because of the enormous destruction of old houses during the Second World War, most of the present housing supply was built after 1945. In spite of substantial state subsidies for house-building, there is still a severe accommodation shortage at the lower end of the market, and repair and restoration is a major priority in the east. German house prices are very high by comparison with most of Europe. Although owner-occupation has increased — and it is not uncommon for Germans to build their own house — most people in cities live in rented accommodation. Finding this is not easy. Rented flats usually come with some kitchen appliances and efficient central heating.

## Health and Welfare

Germany's general social policy is to help an individual when in need through no fault of their own (e.g. through sickness, accident or old age), but not to allow any absolute claim on the state for subsistence. About 30% of the national budget goes on social security. Contributions from employer and employee are high — 38.6% of a worker's earnings at present for the old age pension fund, unemployment insurance and healthcare — but benefits are also high (up to 100% of earnings in case of sickness). Over 90% of the population are covered.

Insurance distinctions are made between manual workers (*Arbeiter*) and office staff (*Angestellte*). The *Arbeiter* is compulsorily insured, while above a certain (quite high) level of income *Angestellte* may choose whether or not to insure themselves, in which case the employer makes only a limited contribution.

The contributions cover maternity and unemployment benefits, death payments, old age and disability pensions, children's allowances, widows' and orphans' pensions, all medical and most dental treatment, and supplementary benefits in all cases of need.

### Education
There are a few private schools, but most children go to free state schools, starting with voluntary kindergarten at three or four. About 80% of all three to six year-olds attend kindergarten. Education is compulsory from the age of six when children enter primary school (*Grundschule*) — for four years — and then move on to a *Gymnasium* (grammar school), *Hauptschule* (intermediate school) — which may lead on to a course of vocational training — or a *Realschule* (general secondary school). *Gymnasium* pupils often stay on until they are 18 or 19, then continue with higher education. Pupils from the *Realschule* generally continue their studies at a *Fachschule* or technical college to learn a skill or trade. This is regarded as a preparation for a medium-level career in business or administration; and around a third of school students achieve this qualification.

### National Service
All German males have to serve 15 months' military national service, or in an alternative civilian service. Foreigners are exempt.

### Embassies and Consulates
British Embassy, Friedrich-Ebert Allee 77, D-53113 Bonn; tel 228-91670.
Consulates in Berlin, Bremen, Düsseldorf, Frankfurt/Main, Hamburg, Hannover, Kiel, Munich, Nuremburg and Stuttgart.
American Embassy, Deichmanns Av 29, D-53170 Bonn; tel 228-3391.
Consulates in Berlin, Franfurt/Main, Hamburg, Leipzig, Munich, and Stuttgart.

### Tourist Offices
German National Tourist Office, Nightingale House, 65 Curzon Street, London W1Y 8NE; tel 0171-489 3080.
German National Tourist Office, 52nd Floor, 122 East 42nd Street, New York, NY 10168; tel 212-661-7200.

## CONDITIONS OF WORK

### Hours
Most contracts are now for a five-day, 38-hour week. It is an objective of German trade unions to reduce this still further to 35 hours. Legislation provides that the regular working time may not exceed eight hours a day. Professional and self-employed people work longer hours.

### Holidays
Most employees (70%) receive six weeks paid leave; and 99% of employees covered by an agreement between unions and an employer receive four weeks or more. The statutory minimum is 18 days or three weeks paid holiday per year. The following are public holidays: New Year's Day; Epiphany (6 Jan); Good Friday; Easter Monday; Labour Day (1 May); Ascension Day (16 May); Whit Monday; Corpus Christi (not in Protestant areas); German Unity Day (3 October); Reformation Day (31 Oct — in Protestant areas); All Saints' Day (1 November — again not in Protestant areas); Christmas Day; and Boxing Day. Immaculate Conception (15 Aug) is also a holiday in some Catholic areas.

### Safety and Compensation
Special labour courts protect employees against unfair dismissal, and safeguard holiday rights, etc. Accident insurance is paid by all employers, who contribute

to an industrial injury society. This covers retraining and rehabilitation, medical treatment, daily cash allowances and pensions for those totally incapacitated, or for the widows and orphans of men killed at work.

## Trade Unions
In Germany there is free collective bargaining between employers and unions; these are both known as the 'social partners', each defending their own interests, and with a responsibility for society as a whole. The unions in Germany are 'unitary' in the sense that each represents all the workers in a particular sector of industry, and have no formal party or religious ties.

## Taxation
All German employees are divided into six income tax brackets, based on age, marital status and number of dependants. Single persons with no children (Class 1) are taxed at the highest rate. Very low income groups pay no tax at all. After the personal allowance is taken out (currently DM 5617 in the highest tax bracket and DM 11 in the lowest) income tax starts at 19%, and goes up to 53% at the highest rate.

# WORK AVAILABLE

## General
Today, there is as much demand as ever for skilled foreign workers; and your English language skills will be an advantage in an economy which depends heavily on trade. Construction is a sector where British and Irish citizens have traditionally worked. There are agencies (which advertise in the tabloid press, often giving just a telephone number) which deal with this kind of work. Legitimate ones should ask you for proof of E111 and E101 documents, and also ask for your Department of Trade and Industry Certificate of Experience or the European Union EC2/GN.

There are also vacancies in information technology; and at the upper management levels. Management consultants in Germany advertise their services in the Saturday papers; and can be looked up under *Personalberatung* in the Yellow Pages. Your first contact should be with the personnel department of the prospective employer; and a detailed CV with copies of letters of recommendation, citations etc. is also recommended.

The Germans are widely acknowledged as the world leaders in engineering, in particular in the automotive field. Much of Germany's industrial prowess stems from the excellent education and training of its workers. More junior positions are likely to be filled by local staff; and the more menial jobs tend to be done by guest workers (*Gastarbeiter*) from former Yugoslavia, Poland, Turkey, Greece and other countries, who now number about four million. Skilled office workers may find employment if they speak German. For temporary and seasonal jobs in tourism or agriculture and au pair work, see below.

## Newspapers
German dailies are published on a regional basis.
*Die Welt, Welt am Sonntag, Hamburger Abendblatt, Berliner Morgenpost* and *B.Z.* are among the papers published by the *Axel Springer Publishing Group*, whose UK office is at 2 Princeton Court, 53-55 Felsham Road, London SW15 1BY; tel 0181-789 4929.

Many German newspapers, including the major local dailies *Kölnische Rundschau, Hannoversche Allgemeine Zeitung, Süddeutsche Zeitung.* and the *Westdeutsche Allgemeine,* are represented by *Powers International,* 517-523 Fulham Road, London SW6 1HF, tel 0171-385 8855. Generally, the Saturday editions are the most promising for situations vacant advertisements. Small ads can also be placed in the British Chamber of Commerce's magazine and bulletin:

enquiries should be addressed to the BCCG Secretariat, Heumarkt 14, D-5000 Köln 1.

## SPECIFIC CONTACTS

### Employment Service
Since permanent employment agencies are a government monopoly, the most important contact is the Federal Employment Institute Central Placement Office *Zentralstelle für Arbeitsvermittlung (ZAV),* Feuerbachstrasse 42-46, D-6000 Frankfurt am Main 1 (International Department); tel 069-71110; fax 069-711-1540. This office handles enquiries for all types of work. Enquiries should include an International Reply Coupon and the following detailed information: your full name, address, date and place of birth, marital and family status, and whether you intend enter Germany alone or with other members of your family; professional or vocational training, qualifications and experience; present employer and occupation; knowledge of the German language; type of employment you are looking for; and the length of your intended stay in Germany.

If you want to work in a particular town in Germany, you can write to the labour exchange (*Arbeitsamt*) in that town, but you must include all the above information in your enquiry. The head office is the *Bundesanstalt für Arbeit,* Regensburgerstrasse 104, D-90237 Nürnberg. Local *Arbeitsamter* addresses are available from the ZAV in Frankfurt.

### Au Pairs
Apart from the agencies listed in the chapter *Au pair and Domestic,* and the help offered by the *Zentralstelle für Arbeitsvermittlung* (above) which handles au pair work for minimum stays of nine months, there are two main agencies in Germany itself that are officially allowed to offer au pair positions, preferably for one year (absolute minimum six months).

These are: the Catholic organisation *IN VIA, Deutscher Verband Katholischer Mädchensozialarbeit e.V.,* Ludwigstrasse 36, D-79104 Freiburg, with branches in 14 other towns (and a Centre with au pair placement service in England: German Catholic Social Centre, Lioba House, 40 Exeter Road, London NW2 4SB, tel 0171-4528566); and the *Verein für Internationale Jugendarbeit e.V.,* Adenauerallee 37, D-5300 Bonn, which has branches in 16 cities; and an office in England at 39 Craven Road, London W2 3BX; tel 0171-723 0216.

### Construction and Building
One of the side-effects of reunification has been a large programme of building and renovation work in Berlin and elsewhere, and opportunities for skilled craftsmen like builders, plasterers, carpenters, electricians, plumbers, etc. The best way to find well-paid jobs in eastern or western Germany is to be introduced directly to the employer, rather than using the services of the middlemen who operate from Dutch border towns and may rip you off (see above). Some knowledge of German is often expected. The *Construction* column of the 'Jobs' section of *Overseas Jobs Express,* Shoreham Airport, Sussex BN43 5FF, tel 01273-440220 or 440540, fax 01273-440229, is one source of jobs and addresses for some of the more reputable agencies.

### Doctors
Because of legal restrictions, arrangements for employment for doctors and medical staff are possible only through the *Zentralstelle für Arbeitsvermittlung,* in Frankfurt (see above). Vacancies are to be found in the weekly *Deutsches Ärzte-Verlag* available from the publishers at Dieselstrasse 2, D-50859 Köln.

### Teachers
Organisations which recruit English teachers for Germany from the UK include *inlingua* and *International House* (see *Teaching*).Others which may supply

information about international schools are also listed; and the British Council can supply further information about its own recruiting. Some of these international schools are:

*Frankfurt International School,* An der Waldlust 15, D-61441 Oberursel.
*ISF International School,* Friedberger Landstrasse 358, D-60389 Frankfurt.
*Munich International School (MIS),* Schloss Buchhof, D-82319 Starnberg.

Exchange positions for Language Assistants or teachers in the German school system are arranged by the *Central Bureau for Educational Visits and Exchanges* (see *Teaching*). Positions as *Lektors* in German universities can sometimes be obtained by direct application to the university.

### Other Opportunities
Opportunities in Germany are also referred to in the chapters of *Specific Careers,* including *Computer Services, Secretarial, Translating and Interpreting, Transport, Tourism and Hospitality,* and *Voluntary Work.* Recruitment consultancies with assignments in Germany are: *Berry Wilson Associates,* 43 Portland Place, London W1N 4LL, tel 0171-636 9575; and *Binder Hamlyn Fry,* 20 Old Bailey, London EC4M 7BH, tel 0171-489 9000.

## SHORT TERM WORK

### Seasonal Work
Seasonal opportunities in Germany are mainly in tourism and agriculture. Work can be found in hotels and restaurants in the Bavarian Alps and the Black Forest in the summer and over the winter skiing seasons. Summer jobs can also be found in resorts along the North Sea and Baltic coasts; in spa and health resorts; and the major cities. The chapter on tourism gives advice on how to obtain this sort of job. Addresses of individual hotels can be found in *Summer Jobs Abroad,* published annually by Vacation Work. In addition the agency *Alpotels,* PO Box 388, London SW1X 8LX, can arrange hotel work.

Fruit-picking jobs have become difficult to find in recent years because of the presence of workers from other countries who are a cheaper source of labour. It is necessary to know precisely when and where harvesting is going to take place. The grape harvest, for instance, tends to begin in October, slightly later than in France, and continues into November. Vineyards can be found along the Rhine, Mosel, Saar, Ruwer, and Nahe valleys. Other kinds of fruit are picked earlier in the summer. There is a particular concentration of fruit farms in the Altland, a region along the south bank of the Elbe to the west of Hamburg.
The Central Placement Office of the ZAF may also be contacted (see above) for details of temporary work during the holidays.

### Other Work
See the relevant chapters in the *Specific Careers* section for information on how to find temporary, voluntary, domestic and office work. Again, the ZAF should be contacted (see above). In Germany, there are relatively few private employment agencies, although branches of *Adia, Echo, Interim* and *Manpower* can be found in larger cities and are worth visiting. The headquarters of the *Ecco Employment Agency* in Britain are at: 7-11 St. John's Hill, Clapham, London SW11 1TR, tel 0171-978 7733; and in the United States at: *Echo Staffing Services Inc.,* 902 Broadway, New York, NY 10010, tel 212-995-2400.
Jobseekers who are already in Germany should also look out for the mobile temporary employment offices that are set up where there is a special need for temporary workers, for trade fairs or the wine or beer festivals. These offices are called *Service-Vermittlung.*

## Opportunities for US Citizens

A number of working exchanges, like those run by *AIESEC* and *AIPT,* are detailed under the *Working Exchanges* heading in *Getting the Job.* You may also write to *CDS International Inc., 330* Seventh Avenue, New York, NY 10001, which specialises in arranging career training, fellowships, and internships in Germany for young Americans. A knowledge of German, and business or technical experience or training, are required.

## Useful publications

Vacation Work's *Live and Work in Germany* goes into great detail about all aspects of employment in Germany. University students about to graduate can consult *Absolventenjahrbuch* (Directory of Graduate Opportunities in Germany), published in three volumes in German, namely: *Maschinenwesen/Chemie, Wirtschaft/Informatik* and *Elektrotechnik/Informatik. Absolventenjahrbuch* is available in the UK from Newpoint Publishing, Windsor Court, East Grinstead, West Sussex RH19 1XA.

BRITISH COMPANIES
with branches, affiliates or subsidiaries in Germany
(see appendix for numerical classification code)

The *German-British Chamber of Industry and Commerce* may be contacted in the UK for further information about business in Britain and Germany at 16 Buckingham Gate, London SW1E 6LB, tel 0171-233 5656. The *British Chamber of Commerce in Germany*, Rossmarkt 12, D-6000 Frankfurt am Main, tel 069-283401, may also be contacted.

| | | | |
|---|---|---|---|
| AIB Electronik GmbH<br>(Cardiff CF4 7YS)<br>Klöcknerstr 4<br>D-59368 Werne | 10 | Beecham-Wülfing GmbH<br>(Brentford 1TW 9BD)<br>Stresemannallee 6<br>D-4040 Neuss 1 | 8 |
| Acorn Computers Ltd<br>(Cambridge CB2 4VY)<br>Anzingerstr 1<br>D-8000 München 60 | 27 | Boosey & Hawkes Ltd<br>(London W1R 8JH)<br>Prinz-Albert-Str 26<br>D-5300 Bonn 1 | 29 |
| Allen Bradley GmbH<br>(Rockwell)<br>Düsselberger Strasse 15<br>D-42781 Haan | 10 | British Airways<br>(London TW6 2JA)<br>Kurfürstendamm 178-179<br>D-1000 Berlin 15 | 3 |
| BAT Deutschland<br>(London SW1H 0NL)<br>Alsterufer 4<br>D-20354 Hamburg | 47 | British Steel Deutschland<br>(London SE1 7SN)<br>Postfach 10 06 42<br>D-70005 Stuttgart | 28 |
| Balkan & Black Sea Shipping<br>Co Ltd<br>(London EC3M 5EQ)<br>Kanalstr 42a<br>D-2000 Hamburg 76 | 17 | British Telecom Deutschland<br>(London WC2R 3HL)<br>Bockenheimer Landstr 42<br>D-6000 Frankfurt am Main 1 | 45 |
| Barclays Bank plc<br>(London EC3P 3AH)<br>Bockenheimer Landstr 38-40<br>D-6000 Frankfurt am Main 17 | 4 | Cadbury Schweppes Ltd<br>(London W2 2EX)<br>Sonninstr 28<br>D-2000 Hamburg 1 | 16 |

Cannon Rubber GmbH 42
(London N17 9LH)
Romerstrasse 20
D-53840 Troisdorf 1

Courtaulds Ltd 46
(Derby DE 21 7BP)
Fuerstenwall 25
D-4000 Düsseldorf 1

Croda International Ltd 8
(Goole DN14 9AA)
Herrenpfad 38
D-4054 Nettetal-Kaldenkirchen

Das Beste aus Reader's Digest 38
(London EC4M 7NB)
Freiligrathstr 11
D-40479 Düsseldorf

Deutsche ICI GmbH 8
(London SW1P 3JF)

DHL Worldwide Express GmbH 17
(Hounslow T44 6JS)
Langer Kornweg 34b
D-6092 Kelsterbach
Frankfurt

Dunlop Ltd 42
(London LE12 9EQ)
Dunlopstr 2
Postf. 1342
D-63403 Hanau

Economist Intelligence Unit 38
(London W1A 1DW)
Friedrichstr 34
D-6000 Frankfurt 1

Ferranti GmbH 10
(Dalkeith)
Taunusstr 52
D-6200 Wiesbaden

Robert Fleming & Co Ltd 4
(London EC2R 7DR)
Friedrich-Ebert-Anlage 2-14
D-6000 Frankfurt 1

Ford-Werke AG 7
(Dagenham CN13 3BW)
Henry Ford Str 1
D-50735 Köln

GKN Automotive 25
(Redditch B98 0TL)
Alte Lohmarer Str 59
D-5200 Siegburg

Glaxo GmbH 8
(London W1X 6BP)
Ballindamm 33
D-2000 Hamburg 1

Ilford Ltd 36
(Ilford)
Dornhofstr 100
D-6078 Neu Isenburg

International Computers Ltd 10
(London SW15 1SW)
Marienstr 10
8500 Nürnberg

KPMG Deutsche Treuhand 1
Gruppe
(London EC4V 3PD)
Louise-Dumont-Strasse 25
Postfach 101930
D-4000 Düsseldorf 1

Marconi Messtechnik 10
(Stevenage SG1 4QB)
Landsbergerstr 65
Postfach 1929
D-8034 Germering

Midland Bank/Trinkhaus 4
Burkhardt
(London EC2P 2BX)
PO Box 1108
Konigsallee 21-23
D-4000 Düsseldorf 1

Morgan Grenfell GmbH 4
(London EC2P 2AX)
Bockenheimer Landstrasse 42
D-60323 Frankfurt am Main 1

National Westminster Bank AG 4
(London)
Feldbergstrasse 35
D-6000 Frankfurt am Main 1

Negretti & Zambra GmbH 3
(Aylesbury HP19 3AL)
Stadtring 88
D-6120 Michelstadt 1

Oxford Instruments 10
(Oxford OX2 0DX)
Postfach 4509
D-65035 Wiesbaden

PA Consulting Group 10
(London SW1)
Wiesenau 27-29
D-6000 Frankfurt am Main 1

Price Waterhouse GmbH 1
(London SE1 9SY)
Warburgstr 28
D-2000 Hamburg 36

Rank Xerox GmbH 30
(London NW1 3BH)
Emmanuel Leutze Str 20
D-4000 Düsseldorf 11

Schitag Ernst & Young 1
(London SE1 7EU)
Jagerstrasse 26
D-7000 Stuttgart 1

Securicor (Deutschland) GmbH 43
(London E1 6JJ)
Alter Markt 7
D-4000 Düsseldorf-Gerresheim
12

Thomas Cook & Sons Ltd 48
(Peterborough)
Postfach 10 18 41
D-40009 Düsseldorf

Thorn-EMI 29
(London W1R 9AH)
Maarweg 149
D-5000 Köln 30

TI International GmbH 28
(London W1Y 7PN)
Josephsburgstr 33
D-8000 München 80

TNT Express Deutschland 17
(Northapton NN3 8RB)
Welserstrasse 10D
D-5000 Köln

Trust House Forte Ltd 20
(London WC1)
Neue Mainzer Str 22
D-6000 Frankfurt am Main 1

Vickers Systems GmbH 26
(London SW1P 4RA)
Fröling Str 41
D-6380 Bad Homburg

## AMERICAN COMPANIES
### with branches, affiliates or subsidiaries in West Germany

These are listed in the *Membership Directory and Yearbook of the American Chamber of Commerce in Germany* available from the publishers: ACC Verlag & Services GmbH, Budapester Strasse 31, D-1000 Berlin 30. The *American Chamber of Commerce in Germany* is at: Rossmarkt 12, D-6000 Frankfurt am Main 1, tel 069-283401.

# Greece

Greek Embassy, 1A Holland Park, London W11 3TP, tel 0171-734 5997
Greek Embassy, 2211 Massachusetts Avenue, NW, Washington DC 20008, tel 202-939-5800
Currency: The unit of currency is the Drachma (Dr)
Rate of exchange: £1 = Dr 370; $1 = Dr 243

Greece is an integral part of the EU; and was its first Balkans member. Its historic links with Britain, and the Greek community in the United States, as well as the congenial climate and scenery which attract countless tourists each year, have made it a popular place for working travellers, and others working in industry and commerce. It is a growing, although still relatively small, export market for Britain; and expanding sectors for exports include telecommunications, sound recording equipment, clothing, power generation machinery, and professional and scientific instruments, according to a recent report. Iron and steel, beverages, and cars are top of the list of its production. So there is more to the Greek economy than just tourism. Negative factors include high unemployment, and inflation which is traditionally high (although efforts have been made to reduce it in recent years). But it still seems unlikely to be able to meet the Maastricht criteria which will enable it to participate in Economic and Monetary Union. There are opportunities in tourism, au pair and English teaching, as well as for consultants in civil engineering, financial, and other technical areas. The Greek-owned merchant fleet — the largest in the world — is partly run from London — and makes heavy use of its financial services. Its profile as a tourist desination means that those who find work there often do so on the spot, or have visited Greece before.

## GENERAL FACTS

### Population, Cities and Climate
The population of Greece numbers 10,300,000, spread over 50,960 square miles, and is relatively diffuse. Although the metropolitan area of Athens has a total of four million inhabitants, there are few other large cities, the main ones being Piraeus near Athens (200,000); Patras on the Gulf of Corinth (150,000); and Thessaloniki in the north with 400,000 citizens. The many islands stretch almost to the coast of Turkey in the east, are bounded by Crete in the south, and lie along the Ionian coast in the west. The mainland is bisected by the Gulf of Corinth. To the south, the Pelopponese has a picturesque coastline; there is a fertile central plain in Thessaly, with mountains to the west, south and north. This northern region of Macedonia has some cultural as well as geographical differences from the rest of Greece. There are pine-covered uplands, craggy, scrub-covered foothills, and farmland; and the landscape is greenest in spring. The climate is mediterranean, and mild in winter; but with summers that can be very hot, especially in Athens.

### The Government
Greece has had a rather unstable political history; and there are deeply felt divisions between right and left, with a 'natural' majority for the Pasok socialist party which has been whittled away in recent years. Six years after the *coup*

*d'état* of 1967, there was a referendum to decide whether Greece should be a republic. 77.2% voted in favour. But President Papadopoulos's government collapsed in 1974 and elections had to be held in November of that year, leading to the new Constitution of 1975, under which the President became the Head of State. He is elected to a five-year term of office. The Chamber of Deputies is elected by universal suffrage every four years.

**Rural Life**
Farming remains a vital part of Greece's economy, although there is a move towards mechanisation and away from the countryside, which has left large tracts of land deserted. Tourism has had this effect in some of the islands, replacing agriculture with a more profitable source of income for the locals. In 1960, agriculture accounted for 91% of all exports; by the mid-seventies this had dropped to 36%; and the number continues to fall. The agrarian sector today comprises 30% of total exports and 17% of Greece's GDP. Wheat, sugar-beet, olives, raisins and figs are the main agricultural products. The principal agriculture-based industries are canned fruit, cigarettes, leather, paper and viniculture. Much of the cultivation is still small-scale and traditional. The landscape often does not favour mechanisation and large-scale cultivation; and in some areas peasant life continues as it has always done.

**Religion, Sport and Culture**
The Greek Orthodox Church plays an important part in Greek life; and claims 98% of the population. There are also Muslim, Roman Catholic and Jewish minorities. Interference with — and proselytising from — the Church are forbidden under the Constitution; and complete religious freedom is observed.

Ancient rather than modern Greeks were famous for their athletic achievements. There are many tennis clubs and watersports centres; and fishing is popular with the locals. Hill-walking is also popular with Athenians getting away from it all; and the many festivals throughout the country are enjoyed by residents and visitors alike. Greeks enjoy food, especially seafood; and bars are more for men than women, although this is changing. Tourism means that nightlife on the islands (and in Athens) is lively and international. Nightclubs featuring Greek Bazouki music are also popular.

**Holidays**
There are eleven public holidays a year: New Year's Day; Epiphany (6 January); Shrove Monday (26 February); Independence Day (25 March); The Greek Orthodox Easter (two days); May Day; Holy Spirit Day (June); Assumption (15 August); *Ohi* day, celebrating the defiant stand against Italy in 1940 (28 October); Christmas Day; and Boxing Day.

# FACTORS INFLUENCING EMPLOYMENT

**Immigration**
The Consular Section of the British Embassy in Athens (see below) issues a free leaflet called *Notes on Greece for British Passport Holders.* Although nationals of EU (and EEA) countries do not require work permits to work in Greece, a residence permit is required for stays of over three months. Applications for this must be made within three months of arrival to the *Aliens Department Office*, 173 Alexandras Avenue, GR-15 522 Athens (tel 646-8103); or to the other Aliens Department offices in Amarousio, Piraeus, Glyfada, Elefsina and Lavrio. You should take your passport, a letter from your employer, and a medical certificate issued by the local hospital. You may also apply to the nearest police station. This means you need to find found employment within three months of entering Greece if you wish to stay.

US citizens can stay for up to three months without a visa. If a US citizen wishes to remain in Greece for longer, he or she has to obtain a permit by applying to the Aliens Bureau of the *Athens Police General Directorate* at 175 Alexandras Avenue, Athens. This may involve some communications with the USA — or a return trip — as you should receive a 'letter of hire' in your home country first; and it is necessary to get your passport stamped at the nearest Greek Consulate in your home country showing you have done this. Work permits must be obtained before entering the country to work.

## Language
Greek is not a difficult language to learn. Knowing the alphabet is the first step. There are two branches of modern Greek. *Katharevousa*, a formal revival of the classical language is rapidly losing ground to *Demotiki*, the more usual spoken language. Those connected to tourism or trade will speak at least some English, German, Italian or French.

## Health, Welfare and Education
A state social insurance system exists, including voluntary staff insurance for salaried people, and sickness and old age pension benefits for nearly everyone. Nursery, primary and secondary education is free for children between the ages of six and 15. For higher education there are six universities, one polytechnic and some other university-level independent institutions.

UK citizens requiring emergency medical treatment should contact the Social Insurance Foundation, known as IKA (*Idrima Kinonikon Asfaliseon*), 64 Pireos Street, GR-104 36 Athens, and submit form E111 (see *Rules and Regulations*). Local offices of the IKA are called 'Ipokatastimata' or 'Parartimata'. The costs of medical and dental treatment should then be refunded. US citizens should certainly be insured; and this is a good idea for British citizens, too, as there are often long waits at the public hospitals.

## Trade Unions
Trade union activity is generally regulated by the Associations Act of 1914: the Constitution guarantees union liberty. The National Body is the Greek General Confederation of Labour.

## Embassies and Consulates
British Embassy, Odos Ploutarchou 1, GR-10 675 Athens; tel 723-6211-9.
Consulates are in Crete, Corfu, Patras, Rhodes, Salonika, Samos, Skyros and Volos.
American Embassy, Leoforos Vasilissis Sophia 91, GR-10 660 Athens; tel 721-2951 or 721-8401. There is a US Consulate in Thessaloniki.

## Tourist Offices
National Tourist Organisation of Greece (GNTO), 4 Conduit Street, London W1R ODJ; tel 0171-734 5997.
National Tourist Organisation of Greece, Olympic Tower, 645 5th Avenue, New York, NY 10022; tel 212-421-5777.

# WORK AVAILABLE

Greece is among the the least industrialised countries in the EU, with 20% of the workforce involved in agriculture. Tourism is another major sector. The performance of the Greek economy has been disappointing since 1981, with slow growth and inflation often in double figures.

The major areas of interest to English-speakers wishing to work in Greece are shipping and financial services (see above), tourism, and English teaching. Shipping and shipping-related insurance companies are generally based in Piraeus, with offices in London or New York; a number of them are mentioned below under *British Companies*. In addition, there are some public sector projects in which British and US companies are involved. These include: the new Athens Airport; the Athens and Thessaloniki metros; a natural gas project; modernisation of railway and road communications; mobile phone communications; and power generation projects. There is an outpost of the EU in Athens, the *European Centre for the Development of Vocational Training* (see the *International Organisations* chapter).

### English Teaching

Greece means teaching in the sun and (outside Athens) a relaxing way of life; it is an attractive option for newly qualified English language teachers; and ads for Greece regularly appear in the Tuesday *Guardian* in Britain, and the *Times Educational Supplement* in the UK, especially over the summer, as the academic year begins in mid-September. American jobseekers may also wish to refer to these publications. Contracts generally run from September to May or from June to September. Work can also be found by visiting language schools in person; addresses appear in the *Blue Guide* (the Greek equivalent of the Yellow Pages); or in the local English-language daily the *Athens News*: Lekka Street 23-25, GR-10 672 Athens; tel 01-322-4253. Although wages tend to be modest, you can live well on relatively little money in Greece. Time will be more important; and you should check out the conditions of service to see how many hours you will be required to teach, or if time-consuming travelling is involved. Further information can be found in the excellent *Teaching English Abroad* published by Vacation Work.

The names of some well-known language schools (known as *frontisterion* in Greek) are given below. Many are also members of the *Pan-Hellenic Association of Language School Owners (PALSO)*, 2 Lykavitou Street, GR-10-671 Kolonaki, Athens, which, like the schools themselves, is probably best contacted on the spot.

*Athens College,* PO Box 65005, GR-15410 Psychico, Athens, tel 671-4621 or 671-4628, fax 647-8156 — hires teachers with an MA or MEd in ESL and at least 3 years' certified teaching experience. Contracts are for 3 years. Interviews are sometimes held in the UK or USA.

*Homer Association,* 52 Academias St., GR-10 677 Athens, tel 362-2887, fax 362-1833 — is the major language school chain in Greece, with 110 schools and over 2,000 teachers. BA or teaching certificate with experience of TEFL required. Interviews are only held locally. Advertises in Athens newspapers.

*Strategakis Schools of Languages,* 24 Proxenou Koromila St., GR-54 622 Thessaloniki, tel 31-264276, fax 31-228848 — is a major chain with over 100 schools. Regularly advertises posts in the UK and also recruits through UK agencies. A degree is required, but TEFL qualifications are not essential. Contracts are for one year. Interviews are held in the UK.

*Teachers in Greece (TIG),* Taxilou 79, Zographou, GR-15 771 Athens, tel 779-2587, fax 777-6722 — recruits teachers for schools all over Greece. Approximately 25 teaching hours a week. Enquiries can also be made to: *Teachers in Greece,* 13 Mill Hams Street, Christchurch, Dorset, UK; tel 01202-471362.

## SHORT TERM WORK

There are few 'organised' ways of finding a temporary job in Greece, and certainly none which will guarantee that an individual will earn enough in a couple of weeks to cover the cost of getting there and back. Jobs tend to be found simply by approaching a potential employer and asking for work.

### Au Pairs

There is a steady demand for au pairs and mother's helps in Greece with wealthy families. Drawbacks include problems in arranging satisfactory placings from outside the country and families who speak nothing but Greek. Apart from agencies mentioned in the chapter *Au pair and Domestic. Galentina's European Childcare Consultancy,* PO Box 51181, GR-14 510 Kifissia, tel 1-806-1005, is active in placing EU citizens, South Africans and Australians as au pairs; and receives applications in March/April for summer placements.

## Seasonal Work

The chapter *Transport, Tourism and Hospitality* lists British travel companies that need staff for the summer (in particular Eurocamps, Mark Warner and Thomson Holidays) and some large hotels needing staff are listed in the book *Summer Jobs Abroad* (Vacation Work).

A number of British expatriates manage to live all the year round in Greece combining fruit-picking with building and bar work or English teaching. Anyone prepared to travel to Greece on the off-chance of finding work should go in March or April, when hotel owners are preparing for the annual tourist invasion. Jobs can be found cleaning and decorating hotels and bars that have been closed all winter. Boats and cruise ships also need staff. There are the yacht agencies around Piraeus;, and the phone numbers of the agencies for cruise ships can be found under *Krouazieres* in the telephone directory.

Work can be also be found picking grapes, olives, and oranges, but again it is necessary to be on the spot. The best regions to look for work are on the Peloponnese (especially around Navplion), and the islands of Crete and Rhodes. Vineyards in Greece are generally far smaller and more widely dispersed than in, say, France: in practice this means that not many workers are needed; and this harvest may only offer a few days' work if a job is found. Prospects are better in both the olive harvest, which starts in late October, and the orange harvest, which begins in November and continues until April. You will be competing with migrants from eastern Europe — particularly Albania — for this work, so wages will not be high.

There are many other harvests that may provide work at various times of the year, from apricots to potatoes. Greece is a country of personal contacts, and the easiest way of discovering what is being grown locally at any time is to find a sympathetic stall-holder at the vegetable market.

## Other Work

There are also some employment agencies in Athens that can help to find temporary work around the year. *Pioneer Tours,* 11 Nikis Street (off Syntagma Square), GR-10 557 Athens, tel 322-4231, finds both governess and mother's help positions with Greek families and jobs in hotels and field work charging a non-refundable fee of about £20. *Interiom,* 24-26 Halkokondili Street, GR-10 432 Athens, tel 523-9470, may also offer help with various kinds of short-term work.

**BRITISH FIRMS**
with branches, affiliates or subsidiaries in Greece
(see appendix for numerical classification code)

The *British Hellenic Chamber of Commerce*, 25 Vas. Sofias Avenue, GR-106 74 Athens, tel 721-0361 or 721-0493, fax 721-8751, publishes a *Directory of Members* (some of which are British-run companies in Greece).

Arthur Andersen-S. Panzopoulos 1
& Co
(London WC2R 2PS)
377 Syngrou Avenue
GR-175 64 Athens

Barclays Bank International Ltd 4
(London EC3P 3AH)
15 Louizis Riankour St
GR-115 23 Athens

BP of Greece 35
(London EC2M 7BA)
268 Kifissias Ave
GR-152 10 Athens Halandri

British Airways 3
(London TW6 2JA)
10 Othonos Street
GR-105 57 Athens

Commercial Union Assurance 23
Co Ltd
(London EC3P 3DQ)
2-4 Sina Street
GR-106 72 Athens

Coopers & Lybrand 1
(London EC4A 4HT)
Abacus House
9 Semitelou Street
GR-115 28 Athens

Deloitte Touche Ross 1
(London EC4A 3TR)
250-4 Kifisslas Avenue
GR-152 71 Halandri-Athens

DHL International Hellas Ltd 4
(Hounslow T44 6JS)
44 Alimou Alinos
GR-174 55 Athens

Ernst & Young OE 1
(London SE1 7EU)
Tower of Athens
2 Messogion Street
GR-115 27 Athens

General Accident Fire & Life 23
Assurance
5-7 Christou Lada Street
GR-105 61 Athens

Glaxo AEBE 16
(London W1X 6BP)
226 Leof. Ionias Avenue
GR-111 44 Athens

Group 4 Securitas SA 43
(Broadway WR12 7LJ)
15 Omirou Street
GR-106 72 Athens

Hellas Can SA 31
(Reading)
135 Solonos Street
GR-176 75 Kallithea
Athens

Horizon Travel Tours Co Ltd 48
Nikis 14
GR-105 57 Athens

ICI Hellas SA 8
(London SW1P 3JF)
231 Syngrou Avenue
GR-171 21 Athens

ICL Hellas SA 10
(London SW15 1SW)
20 El. Venizelou Street
GR-176 6 Kallithea, Athens

International Paint Ltd (Hellas) 25
SA
4-6 Efplias Street
GR-185 37 Piraeus

KPMG Peat Marwick Kyriacou 1
(London EC4V 3PD)
15 Mesoghian Ave
GR-115 10 Athens

Legal & General Assurance 23
Society Ltd
(London EC4N 4TP)
115 Syngrou Avenue
GR-117 45 Athens

Lloyds Register of Shipping 23
(London EC3 A3BP)
87 Akti Miaouli
GR-185 38 Piraeus

Lucas Service Hellas SA 26
(Birmingham B19 2XF)
PO Box 1195
GR-101 10 Athens

Midland Bank Group 4
(London EC2P 2BX)
1A Sekeri Street
GR-106 71 Athens

Morgan Grenfell Ltd 4
(London EC2P 2AX)
19-20 Kolonaki Square
GR-106 73 Athens

National Westminster Bank Ltd 4
(London EC2 2BP)
Korai 5
GR-105 64 Athens

Oxford University Press 38
(Oxford OX2)
9 Amerikis Street
2nd Floor
GR-106 72 Athens

P&O Containers Ltd 17
Beagle House
Braham Street
London E1 8EP

Price Waterhouse & Co 1
(London SE1 9SY)
PO Box 14018
GR-115 10 Athens

Rank Xerox Greece SA 30
(London NW1 3BH)
154 Syngrou Avenue
GR-176 71 Athens

Reckitt & Colman 8
(London W4 2RW)
KLM National Road
Athene Lamia 14565
Kryoneri
Attica

Reuters News Agency (Hellas) 38
SA
(London EC4P 4AJ)
Vouchourestiou 15
GR-106 71 Athens

Royal Bank of Scotland plc 4
(Edinburgh EH2 2YE)
61 Akti Miaoull
GR-185 10 Piraeus

Shell Company Hellas 35
(London SE1 7NA)
2 El Venizelou Street
GR-176 76 Kallithea,
Athens

Star Express Co Ltd 17
110 Vouliagmenis Ave
Hellinikon
GR-167 77 Athens

Thorn-EMI Greece SA 29
(London W1A 2AY)
Heracliou 127
GR-111 42 Rizopolis
Athens

TNT Skypac 17
(Northampton NN3 8RB)
40 Vouliagmenis Avenue
Hellinikon
GR-164 52 Athens

Travel Trade Gazette 38
(London SE18 6QH)
6-10 Charilaol
Trikoupi Street
GR-106 79 Athens

Willis Faber Hellas SA 23
(London EC3P 3AY)
44 Ermou Street
GR-105 63 Athens

## AMERICAN FIRMS
with branches, affiliates or subsidiaries in Greece

The *American-Hellenic Chamber of Commerce*, 16 Kanari Str., Kolonaki, Athens GR-106 74 (tel 362-3231-3 or 361-1892; fax 361-0170 or 362-0995), with a branch office in Thessaloniki, publishes an *Annual Business Directory* which is a full listing of American companies in Greece and their representatives or agents. The cost is $150 plus postage and handling. There is also a bi-monthly magazine *Greek-America Trade*, $100 annual subscription, plus postage and handling.

# Ireland

Irish Embassy, 17 Grosvenor Place, London SW1X 7HR, tel 0171-235 2171
Irish Embassy, 2234 Massachusetts Ave., NW, Washington DC 20008, tel 202-462-3939
Currency: The unit of currency is the Irish Pound (Punt)
Rate of Exchange: £1 = I£ 0.98; $1 = I£ 1.57

The Republic of Ireland (Irish name 'Eire') is as an attractive place to live and work; and a country where the language and culture may already be familiar. Increased prosperity as a result of EU membership has been accompanied by social and political change. Emigration is no longer the only route for qualified Irish workers; and there is a reverse trend today as graduates return home, bringing with them new skills. Dublin is now a more cosmopolitan (and also more expensive) city; and social mores are changing, with the birth-rate down and the number of women participating in the workforce increasing. Foreign investment and EU support enabled the Irish economy to grow three times faster than the EU average in 1996. But unemployment is still relatively high; and this means job opportunities are comparatively limited. Ireland has itself a highly experienced and qualified workforce from which recruitment usually takes place. There are some opportunities in the new growth industries like information technology, in particular for US staff, and some short-term opportunities which are described below.

## GENERAL FACTS

### Population, Cities and Climate
The population of Ireland numbers 3,550,000.The capital city, Dublin, has a total of some 916,000 (in the Greater Dublin area), and the only other large city is Cork, which has 174,000 inhabitants. Limerick, Waterford, Galway and Dundalk are the other principal towns.

The landscape of Ireland consists of a central plain surrounded by isolated groups of mountains and rolling hills. The climate is similar to that of Britain, although it is wetter; and slightly warmer in the south-west.

### Government
Following seven centuries of English rule and intermittent uprisings, the constitution of the Irish Free State was adopted in December 1922. Northern Ireland, with its Protestant majority, remained part of the UK; and the future of this province remains a dominant political issue, in Ireland as well as in the UK. Successive Irish governments have favoured the peaceful unification of all of Ireland; but negotiations between the two governments (and the nationalist and unionist communities in the North) have been hampered by disagreement over this border and its status. In 1985, the Anglo-Irish Agreement was signed, giving the Republic a say in the affairs of Northern Ireland. The outcome of negotiations currently could lead to some kind of transitional constitutional arrangement.

### Religion, Sport and Culture
Although freedom of worship is practised in the Republic, 94% of the people are Roman Catholic, with a small Protestant or Anglican minority. The Irish

have a distinct predilection for rugby and soccer, but developed their own national sports in the nineteenth century as an alternative to these 'English' games. Hurling and Gaelic football (which has its counterpart in Australian Rules Football) are extremely popular.

Ireland has its own distinct cultural heritage, nowhere more so than in its literature. Irish writers include Jonathan Swift, Oliver Goldsmith, George Bernard Shaw, Oscar Wilde, James Joyce, W.B. Yeats, and Seamus Heaney; and a preoccupation with language is a thread which unites them all. Ireland is both a more relaxed and talkative country than Britain or the United States; and its pubs are the traditional place for meeting and socialising (as well as being another Irish export).

## Holidays
There are nine national holidays: New Year's Day; St Patrick's Day (18 March); Good Friday; Easter Monday; June Bank Holiday; August Bank Holiday; October Bank Holiday; Christmas Day; and Boxing Day.

# FACTORS INFLUENCING EMPLOYMENT

## Immigration
Persons born in an EU Member State, or those with at least one Irish-born parent or grandparent, are free to live in the country without restriction. Those who do not come under these categories should consult the *Department of Justice,* at 72 St Stephen's Green, Dublin 2, tel 678-9711.

EU citizens do not require permits to work here. Citizens of other countries may only be employed where the Ministry of Labour has issued the relevant work permits to prospective employers in Ireland. The Irish authorities state that the need to protect employment opportunities for EU citizens is a key factor in determining whether or not work permits are issued.

US citizens may remain in the country for up to 90 days without a visa. Work permits must be arranged before coming to Ireland to take up employment. Otherwise, after three months, a residence permit must be obtained from the Department of Justice (see above) for which a letter from your employer detailing the nature and period of your employment must be obtained.

## Language
Ireland is unique in having a first official language that almost no-one speaks. English predominates almost everywhere, outside a few isolated areas in the west (the 'Gaeltacht').

## Health, Welfare and Education
The state social insurance system, funded partly by both employees' and employers' contributions, and partly by general taxation, provides a comprehensive welfare system, including unemployment benefits.

Those on low incomes, and pensioners; are entitled to a full range of hospital and treatment services. Those on higher earnings are liable to pay hospital consultant fees.

School attendance is compulsory for children between the ages of six and 15; and primary education is provided free in national schools. Secondary education only became free in the 1960s; which galvanised some of the economic and social change mentioned above; today Ireland has one of the best educated populations in Europe; and more than 50% go on to third level education. There are universities in Dublin (three), Cork, Limerick, and Galway.

## Trade Unions
The Irish Trade Unions Congress was established in 1984. Freedom to form a trade association or union is guaranteed under the Constitution. More than half of the workforce belong to unions and the Irish Congress of Trade Unions

accounts for over 90% of the total membership. There are also a small number of licensed employers' organisations.

**National Service**
Military service is voluntary.

**Embassies**
British Embassy, 33 Merrion Road, Dublin 4; tel 269-5211.
US Embassy, 42 Elgin Road, Ballsbridge, Dublin; tel 668-7122.

**Tourist Offices**
Irish Tourist Board/Bord Fáilte, 150-151 New Bond Street, London W1Y OAQ; tel 0171-493 3201.
Irish Tourist Board, 345 Park Avenue, New York, NY 10154; tel 212-418-0800.

**Newspapers**
The Irish authorities advise prospective foreign workers to consult the national newspapers:

*Irish Independent,* 90 Middle Abbey Street, Dublin 1.
*Irish Press,* Parnell House, Burgh Quay, Dublin 2.
*The Irish Times,* 11-15 D'Olier Street, Dublin 2.

## CONDITIONS OF WORK

These are mainly determined in the contract of employment. There is no minimum wage; but legal minimums in particular categories are laid down through Joint Labour Committees (JLCs). A limit is set on a normal working week for those on non-shift work of 48 hours, plus ten hours unlicensed overtime. In practice, there is normally a 39-hour working week. Safety legislation now includes all places of work; and there is an inspectorate run by the Health and Safety Authority, a tripartite organisation representing workers, employers, and the state. Most employees are entitled by law to three weeks' annual holiday.

## WORK AVAILABLE

**General**
Many large enterprises are foreign-owned; and it may be worth approaching subsidiaries of UK and US-owned companies. There is, however, a surplus of qualified professionals in most areas. Those looking for short-term work can usually find something, but wages may not be high.

## SPECIFIC CONTACTS

British people interested in working in Ireland should ask their local Jobcentre for the publication *Working in the Republic of Ireland.* If already in Ireland consult the vacancy boards at the nearest *FAS Employment Services Office.* FAS is Ireland's Training and Employment Authority. The main office is at 27-33 Upper Baggot Street, Dublin 4; tel 668-5777; fax 668-2691. Lists of recruitment agencies in various fields can be obtained by writing to the *Employment Agencies Section,* Department of Enterprise and Employment, Davitt House, 65a Adelaide Road, Dublin 2, tel 66-1444, fax 676-9047. The *Irish Youth Council,* Montague Street, Dublin 1, can supply a youth information booklet on working in Ireland.
    The main source of seasonal work is the tourist industry; and the largest demand is in the southwestern counties of Cork and Kerry. For a list of hotels

contact the Irish Tourist Board (see above).Those seeking a longer term job may well have to settle for seasonal work before using the creative job search to find what they are looking for.

Apart from FAS, there are a number of private employment agencies listed in the Irish *Golden Pages* with whom one may register in addition to FAS (or addresses available from the Department of Enterprise and Employment cited above).

## Au Pairs

Au pairs must be aged 17-27 and must study English while in Ireland. The main source of au pair placements is through language schools. Evidently English-speakers do not qualify as au pairs in Ireland.

*Langtrain International,* Torquay Road, Foxrock, Dublin 18, tel 289-3876 – can place au pairs in Ireland for a minimum of six months. Age limits 18-24. EEA nationals only.

## Medical Staff

*Health Professionals Abroad* (Vacation Work) has a list of some of these recruitment agencies in Ireland. Information on medical (and other) agencies can be obtained by writing to the *Employment Agencies Section*, Department of Enterprise and Employment, Davitt House, 65a Adelaide Road, Dublin 2, tel 1-66-1444, fax 1-67-69047.

## Voluntary Work

*Conservation Volunteers Ireland,* PO Box 3836, Ballsbridge, Dublin 4, tel/fax 1-668-1844 — arranges and coordinates environmental working holidays. No previous experience needed but a knowledge of English essential. Unpaid volunteers work eight hours per day on projects to conserve Ireland's national and cultural heritage.

*Voluntary Services International,* 30 Mountjoy Square, Dublin 1, tel 1-855-1011 — organises placements for community work for international teams. It also places volunteers on workcamps throughout Europe, Africa, Asia and North America through Service Civil International (whose local branch you should contact first if you do not live in Ireland).

## Opportunities for US Citizens

There is a scheme which allows American students to work legally in the Irish Republic for four months at any time of the year — *Work In Ireland* — run by CIEE, 205 East 42nd Street, New York, NY 10017. Once you arrive in Ireland, the CIEE's co-sponsoring organisation, USIT (Union of Students in Ireland Travel Service) at 19 Aston Quay, Dublin 2 will advise on how to find work.

BRITISH FIRMS
with branches, affiliates or subsidiaries in Ireland
(see appendix for numerical classification code)

The *Industrial Development Authority of Ireland* publishes a list of *UK Companies in Ireland,* available free from IDA, 150 New Bond Street, London W1Y 9FE. (They also hold a useful list of American subsidiaries).

Admiral Customer Solutions Ltd   10
(Camberley GU15 3JT)
Avoca Court
Blackrock
Co Dublin

Barclays International                        4
Financial Services (Ireland)
(London EC3P 3AH)
47/48 St Stephen's Green.
Dublin 2

Bioglan (Irl) Ltd                            8
(Hitchin SG4 OTW)
Baldoyle Industrial Estate
Dublin 13

BP Nutrition                                16
(London EC2M 7BA)
Westport
Co Mayo

Brian Colquhoun & Partners      22
(London W1Y 0AP)
16 Upper Fitzwilliam Street
Dublin 2

Cadbury (Irl) Ltd                         16
(London W2 2EX)
Malahide Road
Coolock, Dublin 17

Chivers & Sons Ltd                     16
(Edinburgh EH3 6AJ)
Malahide Road
Coolock
Dublin 5

Continental Administration Co   10
Ltd
(London W1N 5F1)
Unit 1
Waterford Industrial Park
Cork Road
Waterford

Coopers & Lybrand                        1
(London EC4A 4HT)
PO Box 1283
Fitzwilliam House
Wilton Place
Dublin 2

Craig Gardner                               1
(London SE1 9SY)
Gardner House
Wilton Place
Dublin 2

David Ball (Irl) Ltd                      36
(Cambridge CB3 8HN)
Blackrock Road
Cork

DCS International Ltd                  10
(Leamington Spa CV32 3QJ)
122 Lower Baggott Street
Dublin 2

Dolphin Packaging Ltd               31
(Poole BH15 3BT)
Greenore
Co Louth

Eagle Star International               4
Financial Services Ltd
(Cheltenham GL53 7LQ)
Frascati Rd
Blackrock, Co Dublin

Evode Industries Ltd                    8
(Stafford ST16 3EH)
16 Upper Fitzwilliam Street
Dublin 2

Gilbeys of Ireland Ltd               16
(London NW1 4PP)
Nangor Road
Dublin 12

Grand Metropolitan                     4
Finance Ltd
(London)
La Touche House
IFSC
Dublin 2

Glaxo Labs (Irl.) Ltd                   8
(London W1X 6BP)
Grange Road
Rathfarnham
Dublin 16

Grants of Ireland                        22
(London EC1P 1AR)
Clonmell
Co Tipperary

Guinness Enterprises                    3
(London W111 9HB)
West Block
IFSC
Dublin 1

Harrington & Goodlass Wall     32
(Slough SL2 5DS)
Shandon Works
Commons Road
Cork

HB Birds Eye Ltd                        16
(London EC4 4BQ)
Whitehall Road
Rathfarnham
Dublin 14

Hoskyns Insight Ltd                    10
(London W1V 7DN)
83 Lower Leeson Street
Dublin 2

Kerridge Computer Systems 10
(Newbury RG13 1HT)
Anglesey House
Carysfort Avenue
Blackrock
Co Dublin

Irish Industrial Gases Ltd 39
(Windlesham GU20 6HJ)
PO Box 201
Bluebell
Dublin 12

Johnson Matthey Ltd 28
(Royston SG8 5HE)
101 Grafton St
Dublin 2

Kudos Partnership 10
(Woking GU22 9LQ)
3 Sandyford Office Park
Blackthorn Avenue
Sandyford
Dublin 18

Lafferty Group Ltd 38
(London SE1 1YT)
IDA Enterprise Centre
Pearse Street
Dublin 2

Laura Ashley (Ir) Ltd 9
(Newtown SY17 5LQ)
60 Grafton St
Dublin 2

Midland Montagu 4
(Horsham RH12 1BT)
Sun Alliance House
17 Dawson St
Dublin 2

Rank Xerox (Ireland) Ltd 30
(London NW1 3BH)
Unit 75, Lagan Rd
Dublin Ind Estate
Glasnevin, Dublin 11

Reckitts (Ir) Ltd 18
(London W4 2RW)
Belgard Road
Tallaght
Dublin 24

Reliance Precision Mfg (Ir) Ltd 2
(Huddersfield HD4 6SF)
Parnell Street, Bandon
Co Cork

Smith & Nephew-Southalls (Ir) 12
Ltd
(London WC2R 3BP)
Kill o'the Grange
Dun Laoghaire
Co Dublin

SmithKline Beecham 16
(Brentford TW9)
Dungarvan
Co Waterford

Thomson Financial Services (Ir.) 2
(London EC3N 1DC)
Park House
195 North Circular Road
Dublin 7

TNT Express 17
(Northampton NN3 8RB)
9-11 Ekland Devell
Coolock Ind. Estate
Dublin 17

Trebor (Dublin) Ltd 16
(Woodford Green IG8 8EX)
Moeran Road
Walkinstown
Dublin 12

Turner Grain (Irl.) Ltd 27
(Ipswich)
Sandyford Industrial Estate
Foxrock, Dublin 18

Ulster Bank Ltd 4
(Natwest Bank)
(London EC2N 1HQ)
33 College Green
Dublin 2

Unilever Ireland Ltd 8
(London EC4P 4BQ)
Harcourt Centre
33-39 Harcourt Road
Dublin 2

W & E Products Ltd 11
(Bury B10 0QG)
Kilbride
Arklow
County Wicklow

Wiggins Teape (Stationery) Ltd   33
(Basingstoke RG21 2EE)
Gateway House
East Wall Road
Dublin 3

William Blake Ltd   16
(Leeds L59 7RZ)
Units 1 & 2, Stag Ind. Estate
Ballybogan Road
Finglas
Dublin 11

## AMERICAN COMPANIES
with branches, affiliates or subsidiaries in Ireland

A list of American companies is contained in the *American Business Directory,* available from the *American Chamber of Commerce in Ireland*, 20 College Green, Dublin 2. Cost I£30 (Europe) or $60 (USA) post-paid. The *Industrial Development Authority of Ireland* also publishes a list of *US Companies in Ireland,* available free from IDA, 150 New Bond Street, London W1Y 9FE.

# Italy

Italian Embassy, 14 Three Kings Yard, London W1 2EH, tel 0171-312 2200
Italian Embassy, 1601 Fuller Street, NW, Washington DC 20009, tel 202-328-5500
Currency: the unit of currency is the lira
Rate of Exchange: £1 = 2370 lire; $1 = 1550 lire

Italy has had residents British and American for many years, attracted by the culture and the climate; and a people who are usually warmer and friendlier than those of northern European countries. Historic ties between Italy and Britain and the USA, where there are Italian expatriate communities as well, mean that Italian food, and art, and cinema, may already in part be familiar. A cultural difference lies in the expression of emotion, which is a virtue in Italy and may not come so easily to Britons and North Americans. This is a Catholic country with strong secular (and republican) traditions. Eating well is another Italian pastime; and there are many regional dishes as well as over 200 major wine regions. In Italy, there is an emphasis on consumption; and consumer goods, like cars and clothes, are likely to be major items in the average Italian budget; housing is a relatively less important item of expenditure. There is an emphasis in Italian industry on design.

This is also a favoured destination for the independently wealthy. But work in Italy is hard to find unless you speak the language. Engineers are sometimes required for large-scale projects. Growth areas are electronics, telecommunications, aviation and computing; and the smaller companies — of which there are many in Italy — are more likely to recruit someone they know. There is a steady demand for au pairs, secretaries and teachers of English, as well as in tourism and hotel work. A 'creative approach' is called for if you want to live and work in Italy.

## GENERAL FACTS

### Population and Geography
Italy's population is 56,800,000. The country extends over 117,578 square miles, including the islands of Sicily, Sardinia, Elba and others; and the Vatican City which, like San Marino, is an independent state (once memorably described as a 'country with a roof'). The average population density throughout the country is 483 per square mile, but this is unevenly distributed, the industrial North being the most populated. The predominantly agricultural South has the highest birth-rate and lowest death-rate, but the population has increased little. Many move north or emigrate in search of greater prosperity and employment. *Meridionale* is the name given in Italy to the South, which comprises 40% of its land area, 35% of its population, but only 20% of its wealth.

There are about 1.5 million immigrants in the country, mainly from North and sub-Saharan Africa, but also the Philippines, China, South America, Albania and former Yugoslavia.

### Climate
There is a great difference in climate between North and South. Winter is much drier and warmer in the South than in the northern and central areas. The hottest and driest month is July; and the rainiest is November.

## Government

Italy is a democratic republic. The President is elected by an electoral college to serve for seven years; the Chamber of Deputies and the Senate are elected by a combination of proportional representation and the 'British' first-past-the-post system to legislate and to advise the Council of Ministers. This has administrative powers and is headed by the Prime Minister. Regional rivalries, and a fragmentation of Italian politics in recent years, mean that governments are often an unstable coalition. There is a doubt about the legitimacy of the state in Italian political life which can explain the traditional strength of the now reformed communist party (PDS); and the rise of neo-fascist groupings like the National Alliance (which now describes itself as democratic); and a party led by media tycoon Silvio Berlusconi (Forza Italia). In recent years the national identity itself has been challenged by strong regional political movements which hark back to the days when Italy was a patchwork of different states, chief among which is the Northern League, a kind of independence movement for the North.

These regional interests are presently represented by 20 regions, with their own administrative structures; and supervised by a government commission. These are divided into provinces, which are responsible for health and similar matters; and are managed by elected councils. The unit of administration at local level is the commune.

The Italian judiciary also deserves comment, in that suspects may be held for months or years without trial. This is not a country to be arrested in.

## Cities

Rome, the capital, has about 2,700,000 inhabitants; there are in all 48 cities with populations above 100,000. Milan (1,300,000), Turin (900,000) and Genoa (700,000) form the 'industrial triangle' of the North; Florence Venice, Bologna, and Naples — the third largest Italian city, with a population of over a million — and many other smaller towns such as Cremona and Pisa are famous around the world for their cultural or historical attractions.

## Rural Life

The Italian population is more evenly distributed between town and country than in most European countries. About 50% of Italians live in small towns and villages, the majority of these in the South. Rapid industrialisation has meant that just 7% of the population is now directly engaged in agriculture. The principal crops are sugar beet, wheat, maize, tomatoes and grapes. Italy is a world leader in wine production.

## Religion, Sport and Culture

95% of Italians are baptised into the Roman Catholic faith. Catholicism has a great influence on Italian life, but not all Italians are observant Catholics. The secular constitution guarantees freedom of religion; and there are Protestant and other minorities.

Popular sports in Italy include football (which is a national obsession); fishing; golf; shooting, horse racing and jumping; motor racing; bowls (*bocce* — the only truly indigenous sport); cycling; and yachting. Rugby has grown in popularity in recent years. All winter sports are popular in the Alpine regions. There are no less than three daily newspapers devoted to sport; and Italians abroad tend to miss the latest football results.

The annual absolute number of visits made to the cinema is second only to the United States. Opera, theatre and music flourish in all forms. Italy has played a major role in history of art and architecture, and has many galleries, particularly in Rome, Florence and Venice, which display its art treasures.

# FACTORS INFLUENCING EMPLOYMENT

## Immigration
The *Italian Consulate General*, 38 Eaton Place, London SW1 8AN, tel 0171-235 9371 — or the Embassy and the various consulates in the USA, see below — will advise on entry requirements for nationals who require a visa to enter Italy. US and EU citizens do not require a visa for stays up to three months.

All visitors who are not tourists are required to register with the police within three days of arrival. Registration entitles you to a stay of the same validity as your visa; or, in the case of EU citizens, three months in which to look for work. For a longer stay, a residence permit is required, available from the *questura* (police station) of the area of intended residence. Work permits for US citizens must be arranged from abroad.

## Language
Dialects are spoken in the different regions of Italy which may differ markedly from standard Italian. German, French and Slovenian are also spoken in the regions bordering these language areas. German and French are the main second languages spoken, along with English. Prospective workers here are strongly advised to learn Italian, as English is not widely spoken by older people — although the young are enthusiastic learners (and those connected with tourism for example).

## Cost and Standard of Living
It has both very poor and very wealthy areas. The industrial region of Lombardy around Milan is reckoned to be the wealthiest in the EU. It should be remembered that Italy has overtaken Britain in terms of its Gross Domestic Product; and the standard of living is noticeably higher, in Lombardy or Tuscany, than Britain. The cost of living is about 10% higher than in the UK. Road and rail transport are relatively cheap, making travel easy. A toll is payable on Italy's motorway (or *autostrada*) network.

## Housing and Accommodation
Recent building programmes have concentrated on blocks of flats; in Rome there is now a surplus; but Naples and the South are generally still short of accommodation. Rents are highest in cities, and higher in the North.

## Health and Welfare
Contributory medical insurance (administered by *USL — Unità Sanitaria Locali*) now covers the whole of the working population, including foreigners; but private medical services continue. The number of state hospitals is widely reckoned to be insufficient, and some are run by the Church. Healthcare costs and contributions are a matter of intense public debate in Italy. A system of prescription charges (known as tickets) was instituted for doctors several years ago, although the chronically ill and some other groups are exempt from such charges. The Italian state social assurance scheme which covers all other benefits is run by the *INPS — Instituto Nazionale di Previdenza Soziale,* and employers tend to pay a disproportionate share of the contributions.

## Education
Schooling is compulsory and free (apart from registration fees) for all children aged between six and 14; and lessons are usually held in the morning. From the age of three, a child can go to a crèche or nursery school. Elementary schools take pupils between six and 11. The next step for most is a middle school (*scuola media*), providing a three-year general course, and the possibilty to stay on to take the final school leaving certificate (*maturità*). The more specialist *liceo* schools lead more directly to this certificate which grants entry to university; or students may choose one of the many technical institutes for a diploma in subjects ranging from agriculture to zoology; and this is in itself a professional

qualification, while the *liceo* merely prepares for university. There are 39 state universities and a small number of private ones. The many private schools in Italy are incorporated into the state system so far as the curriculum and exams are concerned.

There are also English-medium and international schools in those areas where there are English-speaking expatriate communities.

### National Service
Military service of 12-18 months is compulsory for all Italian males. Conscientious objection is a civil crime, so many Italians emigrate to avoid it. Foreigners are exempt.

### Embassies and Consulates
British Embassy, Via XX Settembre 80A, I-00187 Rome; tel 6-482 5551 or 482 5441.

There are consulates in Bari, Brindisi, Cagliari, Florence, Genoa, Messina, Milan, Naples, Palermo, Trieste, Turin and Venice.

US Embassy, via Veneto 119A, I-00187 Rome; tel 6-46741.

### Tourist Offices
Italian State Tourist Office (ENIT), 1 Princes Street, London W1R 8AY; tel 0171-408 1254.

Italian State Tourist Office (ENIT), Suite 1565, 630 5th Avenue, New York, NY 10111; tel 212-245-4822.

## CONDITIONS OF WORK

### Wages
Salaries for professional and managerial staff are considerably higher than in Britain, but less skilled workers are worse off. Minimum wages are set down by law for certain types of work. When evaluating the income of Italians as a whole, it is necessary to bear in mind that there remains a sizeable black economy; and many, in particular the self-employed, manage to evade paying taxes altogether. It is also common for low-paid workers to have two or three jobs.

Women are paid more or less the same rate as men for the same work. There is still some prejudice against career women, however, and relatively few have made it into the higher ranks of business and government.

### Hours
Anything between a 36 and 39-hour week has become standard. The two-hour lunch break for siesta is common practice in the South, so the working day may last until 7pm. In the North, nine-to-five working is usual. The statutory limits are eight hours in one day, and 48 hours in any one week.

### Holidays
Most employees receive between 25 and 30 days' holiday a year. In addition, there are the following public holidays: New Year's Day; Epiphany (6 January); Easter Monday; Liberation Day (25 April); Labour Day (1 May); Ascension Day (15 August); All Saints' Day (1 November); National Unity Day (5 November); Conception Day (8 December); Christmas Day; and Boxing Day.

### Trade Unions
The four major unions are organised according to their political affiliations, not trades or sectors; and are grouped together as the General Conference of Labour, along with several smaller unions. Total union membership is large but declining.

### Taxation
Taxes are imposed by the Treasury, the Ministry of Finance, the Minister of the Budget, and by the regions, provinces and communes. Income tax is progressive

and relatively low compared to other European countries. Those intending to work should go to the local tax office, the *Intendenza di Finanza*, and obtain a tax number (*codice fiscale*).

## WORK AVAILABLE

### General
The northern third of the country is wealthy, while the South (*Meridionale*) is relatively underdeveloped. Many British people now live or have second homes in the central rural regions of Tuscany and Umbria, while Americans tend to find Rome and the cities of the North more congenial. There are many regional industries, such as wool textiles in Prato, silk in Como, or shoes in Verona. But the large companies — like Fiat, Benetton, and Pirelli, are located in the North (see the introduction above for more on work opportunities). Italian language skills are a must. Job applicants should note that the postal service is sometimes slow; enquiries are best made by telephone or fax.

### Newspapers
The agency *Powers International,* 517-523 Fulham Road, London SW6 1HD, tel 0171-385 8855, represents some Italian newspapers, including *Il Giornale* and many regional daily newspapers.

## SPECIFIC CONTACTS

### Employment Service
The state-run *Ufficio di Collocaménto* is the only legal recruitment agency for permanent work, and is best dealt with in Italian. Temporary work agencies may also be found in the larger cities by looking in the Italian Yellow Pages. Few of these agencies is likely to be able to help non-Italian speakers though. Management consultancies with British and US links are: *Programma Aziendale SAS,* Viale Enrico Martini 9, I-20139 Milan, Italy, tel 2-5696360, fax 2-5696731 (engineering, electronics and manufacturing); and *Eurosearch Consultants,* Via Cusani 8, I-20121 Milan, tel 2-8052018, fax 2-8052062.

### Teachers
Italy has many English, American and international schools and colleges, that have a steady demand for teachers. And there are many opportunities for English language teachers in Italy, mainly because the standard of language teaching there is poor. The *British Council* at Palazzo del Drago, Via 4 Fontane 20, I-00184 Rome, will be able to offer useful advice. Addresses of schools are given under *Scuole de Lingua* in the Italian Yellow Pages.

Teachers of English are frequently required by the four British College schools in southern Italy. Applications should be addressed to the Director of Studies, British College, Via Luigi Rizzo 18, I-95131 Catania. *Connor Language Services,* Via M. Macchi 42, I-20214 Milan, tel 2-66987016, keeps a register of teachers, and are notified of vacancies throughout the year.

Other schools include:

*British Institute of Florence,* Palazzo Feroni, Via Tornabuoni 2, Florence — hires teachers on 2-year contracts, who must have RSA Dip. and 2 years' experience (preferably ESP, English for Specialised Purposes). Interviews usually held in Florence. There are 50 other schools affiliated to the British Institute.

*International House* has schools in Livorno and Turin for the qualified — RSA Diploma and 2 years' experience are essential. Enquire through International House in London (see the *Teaching* chapter).

Posts in Italian state schools are not open to foreigners, except in conjunction with the *Central Bureau for Educational Visits and Exchanges* (see the section on *Working Exchanges* in the chapter *Getting the Job*). However, there are a number of one-year posts for assistants in English faculties of Italian universities. Applications should be made direct to the university.

## SHORT TERM WORK

English-speaking people should look for temporary jobs where their language is a positive advantage, such as in hotels or offices, public and international relations (with the many companies which depend on trade), bilingual secretarial and English teaching work.

### Seasonal Work

Over the summer Italy's tourist industry can offer employment both in the cities (such as Rome, Florence and Venice) and in the coastal resorts along the Italian Riviera and the Adriatic; and to the south of Naples. Many of the camping holiday organisers in the chapter on tourism operate in Italy. Details of specific vacancies in Italian hotels can be found in *Summer Jobs Abroad* (Vacation Work). Jobs can also be found in ski resorts in the Alps, the Dolomites, the Apennines north of Florence, and in the region to the northeast of Turin.

Italy is the world's largest producer of wine, but work on the grape harvest is traditionally done by the locals, amd more recently by immigrants from east of the Adriatic. The comparatively high wages (sometimes 50% more than for the equivalent job in France, and a welcome which is reportedly more hospitable) still make this sort of work worth looking for by independent travellers. September or early October are the right time. Vineyards can be found all over Italy, but chances of employment are greater in the North.

### Other Work

Most types of casual work can only be found by people who are already on the spot and who can visit employment agencies and follow up newspaper advertisements. Domestic jobs in Italy and au pair positions for 2-12 months can be found through the agency *Au Pairs — Italy,* 46 The Rise, Sevenoaks, Kent TN13 1RJ (send SAE for details). Other au pair agencies are given in the chapter, *Au Pairs and Domestic.*

### LIST OF BRITISH COMPANIES
with branches, affiliates or subsidiaries in Italy
(see appendix for numerical classification code)

The *British Chamber of Commerce for Italy*, Via Agnello 8, I-20121 Milan, publishes a trade directory which contains not only a list of members, but also an 'alphabetical list of British firms present in the Italian market'.

APV Italia 27
(Crawley RH10 2QB)
Via Molise 9
I-20098 San Guiliano Milanese
MI

Arthur Andersen & Co Ltd 1
(London WC2R 2PS)
Via della Moscova 3
I-20121 Milan

Automotive Products Lockeed 22
SpA
Corso Marconi 160
I-17014 Cairo Montenotte (SV)

Avdel Srl 10
(Welwyn Garden City)
Via Manin 350/21
I-20099 Sesto S Giovanni (MI)

BP Italia Spa 35
(London EC2M 7BA)
Piazza di Spagna 15
I-00187 Rome

Barclays Bank SpA 4
(London EC2M 7BA)
Via Moscova 18
I-2021 Milan

Beecham Italia SpA 11
(Brentford TW8 9PD)
Via Pirelli 19
I-20124 Milan

Brit European Transport Ltd 17
(Stoke on Trent)
Via Salomone 61
I-20138 Milan

British Airways 3
(London TW6 2JA)
Via Bissolati 76
I-00187 Rome

British Tourist Authority 48
(London SW1A 1NF)
Corso Vittorio Emanuele II 337
I-00186 Rome

Cable & Wireless Italia 45
(London WC1X 8RC)
Via Archimede 207
I-00197 Rome

Castrol Italiana SpA 35
(Swindon SN3 1RE)
Via Aosta 4/A
I-20155 Milan

Clarkson Italiana SpA 26
(Nuneaton)
Via I Nievo 41
I-20145 Milan

Coats Viyella plc 46
(London W1X 2DD)
Via Emilio Greco
I-02100 Rieti

Commercial Union Assurance 23
(London EC3P 3DQ)
Viale Abruzzi 94
I-21131 Milan

Coopers & Lybrand 1
(London EC4A 4HT
Via Vittor Pisani 20
I-20124 Milan

Creditwest SpA 4
(National Westminster Bank)
(London EC2N 1HQ)
Via Ludovisi 23
I-00187 Rome

Croda Italiana SpA 8
(Goole DN14 9AA)
Via P. Grocco 917
I-27036 Mortara (PV)

Deloitte Haskins & Sells Snc 1
Via Falinia 495
I-00191 Rome

DHL International SARL 17
(Hounslow TA4 6JS)
Viala Milano Fiori
Strada 5
Pal U/3

English China Clays Int SpA 6
(St Austell PL25 4DJ)
Vialeg
Da Verrazano 29/B
I-54036 Marina di Carrera

Ernst & Whinney Sas 1
(London SE1 7EU)
Via Abbruzzi 25
I-00187 Rome

Ferodo Italiana SpA 22
(Stockport SK23 0JP)
Corso Inghilterra 2
I-12084 Mondovi (CN)

Ferranti International 45
(London SW1)
Viale dell'Industria 4
I-00040 Pomezia

Flexibox SpA   31
(Manchester M17 1SS)
Viale Spagna 106
I-20093 Cologna Monzese (MI)

Foseco Srl   8
(Birmingham B7 5JE)
Ravello 5/7
I-20010 Vermezzo (MI)

Gestetner Italia SpA   38
(Northampton NN4 0BD)
Via Appia Nuova 892
I-00178 Rome

ICI Italia   8
(London SW1P 3JF)
Viale Isonzo 25
I-20135 Milan

ICL Italia International   10
Computers SpA
(London SW15 1SW)
Centro Direzionale Milanofiori
Palazzo E1
I-20090 Assago (MI)

Italia Forte Hotels   20
(London WC1 6TT)
Via G. Fara 39
I-20124 Milan

KPMG Peat Marwick Fides   1
(London EC4V 3PD)
Via Vittor Pisani 25
I-20156 Milan

Letraset Italia Srl   38
(London SE1 8XJ)
Via Riccione 8
I-20156 Milan

Lloyd Italico SpA   23
(London EC3 4BS)
Via Serra 3
I-16100 Genoa

Marconi Italiana SpA   45
(Stevenage SG1 2BA)
Via Campo nell' Elba 3/5
I-00138 Rome

PA Personnel Services Srl   14
(London SW1X 7LA)
Via Turati 40
I-20121 Milan

Price Waterhouse   1
(London SE1 9SY)
Corso Europa 2
I-20122 Milan

Prudential Assicurazioni SpA   23
(Reading RG1 3ES)
Via C Celso 6
I-00161 Rome

Racal Systems Elettronica   22
(Newbridge EH28 8LP)
Strada 2, Palazzo C4
I-20090 Assago, Milan

Rank Xerox Ltd   30
(London NW1 3BH)
Via Andrea Costa 17
I-20131 Milan

Reconta Ernst & Young   1
(London SE1 7EU)
Via Torino 68
I-20123 Milan

Thorn EMI Italiana SpA   29
(London W1A 2AY)
Via Godames 89
I-20151 Milan

Unilever Italia SpA   8
(London EC4P 4BQ)
Via Nino Bonnet
I-20154 Rome

Travel Trade Gazette   48
(London SE18 6QH)
Via A Nota 6
10/22, Turin

## AMERICAN COMPANIES
### with branches, affiliates and subsidiaries in Italy

American business concerns in Italy (and Italian companies in the United States) are fully listed in the *Italian-American Business Directory,* published by the *American Chamber of Commerce in Italy*, Via Cantu 1, I-20123 Milan; price in other countries to non-members Lire 175,000 inclusive.

# Luxembourg

Luxembourg Embassy, 27 Wilton Crescent, London SW1X 8SD, tel 0171-434 2800
Luxembourg Embassy for USA and Canada, 2200 Massachusetts Ave., NW, Washington DC 20008, tel 202-265-4171-2
Currency: 1 Luxembourg Franc = 100 centimes
Rate of Exchange: £1 = LF 48; $1 = LF 32

Luxembourg covers just under a thousand square miles; and on most maps even a shortened version of its name — LUX — scarcely fits within its borders. The total population is only 385,000, which means that the Grand Duchy does not offer unlimited job opportunities. But there are some. One quarter of Luxembourg's population is foreign; and Luxembourg is a member of the European Union and as such is subject to EU regulations concerning free movement of labour. EU citizens intending to stay for more than three months should visit the police, the *Bureau des Etrangers,* 9 rue Chimay, L-1333 Luxembourg, tel 479-6252, to complete all the formalities and obtain an Identity Card for Foreign Nationals. Others must obtain a work permit from an approved employer and submit this before departure.

General information including a list of *Useful Addresses for New Residents* is available from the *Luxembourg Embassy* (please include an SAE)

## Language

The native tongue is *Letzeburgesch* (or 'Luxembourgeois' or 'Luxembourgish') which is spoken in all walks of life. Luxemburgers tend also to speak French and German, and English is widely understood. In fact, in a recent survey, they were found to be Europe's best language learners. The Embassy advises that 'a good knowledge of French and German' is needed to work in Luxembourg, and this proves a barrier to many English-speaking people. Jobs are obtained 'through personal or commercial relationships,' they say.

French is the official government and administrative language. German, on the other hand, is the language of the press and the church.

## Embassies

British Embassy, 14 boulevard Roosevelt, L-2450 Luxembourg; tel 229-8645-6.
US Embassy, 22 boulevard E. Servais, L-2535 Luxembourg; tel 460-123.

## Tourist Offices

Luxembourg Tourist Office, 122 Regent Street, London W1R 5FE; tel 0171-434 2800.
Luxembourg National Tourist Office, 2200 Massachussetts Avenue, NW, Washington, DC 20008; tel 212-935-8888.

## Newspapers

Adverts can be placed direct in:

*Luxembourg News*, 34 avenue Victor Hugo, L-1750 Luxembourg; and
*Luxembourger Wort*, 2 rue Christophe Plantin, L-2988 Luxembourg.

## Labour Force

Luxembourg has a highly developed economy and high standard of living. Its most important industries include: banking and finance, manufacturing, and media and communications. Jobs in these sectors, and also in international organisations and tourism (Luxembourg has 250 hotels) are most accessible to British and North American jobseekers (especially if they speak French and German). The major sector is not agriculture, or industry, but services.

**Work Available**
The best prospects for professionals are in IT for banking or administration. The European Parliament is based in Luxembourg and has a recruitment service (see the *International Organisations* chapter). The National Employment Office (*Administration de l'Emploi*, 38a rue Philippe II, L-2010 Luxembourg; tel 476-8551) can provide information on job prospects. You can write to *NARIC* at the same address for information on comparability of qualifications.

## SHORT TERM WORK

Luxembourg does offer some opportunities for short-term work. An employment agency that deals with temporary work is *Manpower-Aide Temporaire*, 19 rue Glesener, L-1631 Luxembourg, tel 482-323. The Embassy holds a list of the twenty or so employment agencies in Luxembourg.

**Seasonal Work**
Over a million tourists visit Luxembourg each year, most for business or for short-stays. Hotels and conference work provide many job openings. There is no central agency for this, but you may be able to get a temporary job by writing directly — a booklet *Hotels, Auberges, Restaurants, Pensions* is available from the Luxembourg Embassy on receipt of an A4 SAE.

Further information on opportunities in Luxembourg can be found in *Live and Work in Belgium, The Netherlands and Luxembourg,* published by Vacation Work. *Living in Luxembourg* is published by Insight Publications, 109 avenue Fond'Roy, 1180 Brussels, Belgium.

BRITISH AND AMERICAN FIRMS
in Luxembourg

A comprehensive list of both UK and American companies with Luxembourg connections can be obtained from the Luxembourg Embassy. Please enclose a large SAE. The *British Chamber of Commerce* is at: BP 2740, L-1027, Luxembourg; tel 435-853; fax 438-326.

# The Netherlands

Royal Netherlands Embassy, 38 Hyde Park Gate, London SW7 5DP, tel 0171-584 5040
Royal Netherlands Embassy, 4200 Wisconsin Avenue, NW, Washington DC, 20016
Unit of currency: 1 Dutch florin or Guilder (Dfl) = 100 cents
Exchange rate: £1 = Dfl 2.6; $1 = Dfl 1.7

The prospects for work and residence in The Netherlands are good for those who are qualified and willing to adapt to this liberal and fast-moving society. The Dutch authorities stress that immigration is not encouraged and permanent residence is only rarely granted to non-EU citizens, in view of the very high population density and shortage of housing and work. This view is contradicted somewhat by the many US and UK citizens who do actually live in the country. Culturally, The Netherlands can seem like home to many English-speaking people; the widespread use of English in everyday life contributes to this impression. But this is not the only language which Dutch people speak. Their knowledge of other languages is only one aspect of life in a trading nation which has always valued its contacts with other countries. Economically it depends on them. More than any other country in this book, Holland could be described as cosmopolitan. Some Dutch people themselves are uneasy about this international identity and are less tolerant of foreigners. It is also a racially mixed society in which the children of immigrants have full Dutch citizenship.

## GENERAL FACTS

### Population
The Netherlands has a population of 15.4 million. The country covers 15,900 square miles, over half of which is below sea level, and the population density is approximately 969 per square mile, one of the highest in the world.

### Climate
The Netherlands' climate is very similar to that of England, but noticeably windier. Winters are mild and summers cool. The average highest temperature in Amsterdam in January is 5°C; the average in July is 21°C. There are 65 days of frost in an average year.

### Government
The Netherlands is a constitutional monarchy. The head of state is Queen Beatrix. Legislative power rests with Parliament, of which there are two chambers. The Prime Minister exercises executive power through a Council of Ministers, drawn from the 150-strong lower chamber (akin to the UK's House of Commons) elected every four years on the basis of proportional representation. The upper chamber has 75 members who are elected by the Provincial Councils. Suffrage extends to all citizens aged 18 and over.

The Netherlands is divided into 12 provinces and 850 municipalities — governed by a mayor, aldermen and a council — which have the right to pass local regulations.

## Cities
The Hague, also known as Den Haag and 's Gravenhage, is the seat of government and has a population of 680,000. Amsterdam the capital has 700,000 or more; and Rotterdam, the world's largest port, more than one million inhabitants. There are 17 other towns with more than 100,000 inhabitants.

## Rural Life
Flowers and dairy products form part of a world-famous agricultural/horticultural industry which accounts for roughly a quarter of all Dutch exports. The Netherlands is highly urbanised; and just 2% of the population live in villages with less than 5,000 inhabitants. As a result, the Dutch value their leisure time; and Groningen, Friesland and Flevoland have developed many outdoor recreational facilities. The Dutch government has also taken steps to clean up the environment, which has suffered severely from the expansion of agriculture and industry in recent years.

## Religion, Sport and Culture
The Dutch constitution guarantees freedom of religion and that all sections of society, whether religious or secularist, are represented in national institutions. One-third of the population are Roman Catholics (mostly concentrated in the south) and one-fifth belong to the Dutch Reformed Church.

Sport plays an extremely important part in Dutch life; one third of the population belongs to a sports club of one sort or another. Angling and cycling are the two most popular pastimes, and tennis is second only to football in terms of the number of official participants. In the winter, and especially in Friesland in the north, skating tops the bill. Weather permitting, 17,000 competitors participate in the annual *Elfstedentocht* (Tour of the Eleven Towns) along 125 miles of frozen canals in Friesland. One of the lesser known consequences of global warming and mild winters has been to reduce the number of occasions on which this race can take place; only fifteen times so far.

The Netherlands has a wealth of museums (over 1,000 at the last count) and art galleries. The larger towns all have a full programme of concerts, opera, ballet and theatre, and there is a flourishing cultural and nightlife. Amsterdam has acquired the reputation of being not only one of Europe's top tourist attractions but also a leading venue for young, alternative travellers.

# FACTORS INFLUENCING EMPLOYMENT
## Immigration
Despite the warnings of the Dutch Embassy, The Netherlands is a member of the EU and as such UK citizens have the right to work there. If you enter The Netherlands with the intention of staying for over three months, you should report to the aliens police (*vreemdelingenpolitie*) within eight days of arrival. A residence permit (*verblijfsvergunning*) will normally be granted to persons with a definite job offer or adequate funds to support themselves. Permits can be refused on grounds of public health or public security.

US citizens may remain in The Netherlands for up to three months without a visa. Applications for work permits (once you have been offered a job) should be made well in advance at a Dutch consulate-general outside the country.

The Dutch Ministry of Justice has set up a helpline for English speakers with information about immigration regulations on 70-370-3533 or 370-3544. And they can send some publications on immigration: *Ministerie van Justitie,* Postbus 3016, NL-2500 GC Den Haag; tel 70-370-3124 or 370-3144.

## Language
The Dutch have an education system which values foreign languages; and English is understood almost everywhere. German comes second, and French third as far as other foreign languages go. It is possible to get by with only a knowledge

of English, but if you intend to stay for any length of time it is essential to try to learn Dutch, which has something in common with both English and German. Frisian, the country's second language, is spoken by 250,000 people in the northern province of Friesland, and is the European language which is closest to English.

## Cost and Standard of Living
Consumer prices for food and other goods are slightly higher than those in Britain. Wages tend to be quite a lot higher (30% is one estimate) and this is a relatively egalitarian society, although there are pockets of poverty in the cities.

## Housing and Accommodation
The Netherlands has a fairly permanent housing shortage, owing to the growth in population. Rented property, especially in the Randstad area (the almost continuous conurbation which includes Amsterdam, Rotterdam and The Hague), is higher than in the UK, although house prices are comparable. More than half of all Dutch homes are of post-war constructions; and about half are owner-occupied.

## Health and Welfare
Payment for medical treatment is arranged through health insurance schemes, both public and private. Taxpayers make no fewer than eight social security payments, including contributions towards unemployment and disablement benefits, pensions and family allowances. UK citizens need their E111 certificate to get free health treatment. US citizens should take out insurance. For further information on your health rights in The Netherlands you can contact *ANOZ Verzekeringen,* Sectie Buitenland, Postbus 85315, NL-3508 AH Utrecht; tel 30-256-5450.

## Education
Education is for the most part free and compulsory from six to 16; part-time education is also compulsory for a further year. Nursery and childcare provisions are also widely available. Nearly two-thirds of children attend private schools (subsidised by the state) which are mostly denominational. There are three types of secondary school: the *gymnasium* (grammar school) which leads to university; vocational schools which give special technical or trade training; and general schools which tread a line between the two. There are five state universities; a free municipal university at Amsterdam; an agricultural university at Wageningen; and a Catholic university at Nijmegen.

## National Service
All Dutch men between the ages of 18 and 25 must do military service for 14-17 months. Foreign nationals are not liable.

## Embassies and Consulates
British Embassy, Lange Voorhout 10, NL-2514 ED Den Haag; tel 70-364-5800.
Consulate of the United States of America, Museumplein 19, Amsterdam; tel 70-575-5309.

## Tourist Offices
Netherlands Board of Tourism, PO Box 523, London SW1E 6NT; tel 0891-200277.
Netherlands Board of Tourism, 21st Floor, 355 Lexington Avenue, New York, NY 10017; tel 212-370-7360.

# CONDITIONS OF WORK

## Wages
There is a statutory minimum monthly wage; and all wage contracts are reviewed at six-month intervals, and adjusted in accordance with the cost of living index.

The Minister of Social Affairs is empowered to disallow wage agreements deemed to be contrary to the national interest. Wages are competitive with anywhere in Western Europe.

## Working Conditions

The official working week is approximately 39 hours, although in reality it can be longer. The maximum working hours are restricted by law to 8½ hours a day, or 48 hours per week. Employers must obtain a permit for overtime from the Labour Inspection Board. The usual holiday entitlement is 23 working days; the minimum is 20. In addition, there are public holidays on: New Year's Day; Good Friday; Easter Monday; Queen's Day (30 April); National Liberation Day (5 May); Ascension Day; Whit Monday; Christmas Day; and Boxing Day.

## Trade Unions

Trade union membership is not compulsory but 40% of the Dutch workforce still belongs to a recognised organisation. There are three main unions, as well as a number of groups which cover agricultural and retail trades. Dutch trade unions are not regarded as militant and do not normally strike to achieve their goals.

## Taxation

To encourage foreign investment the Dutch government has set up what is known as the '35 per cent rule', which allows foreigners to qualify for taxation on only 65% of their gross salary. There are five separate tariff bands and after allowances have been made there is a progressive scale of taxation that ranges from 35.7% (plus 25.55% national insurance premiums) to 60% on the excess. Further information about tax can be obtained from the local tax authority in The Netherlands, or *Rijksbelastingen* (The Tax Authority), Stationplein 75, NL-2515 BX Den Haag; tel 70-330-4000. Form E101 should be obtained by self-employed people in Britain before moving to The Netherlands (see *Rules and Regulations*).

## WORK AVAILABLE

### General

The Netherlands has a highly developed and diverse economy; its major industries include petrochemicals, engineering, agriculture, information technology, transportation and publishing. The Dutch are the largest foreign investors in the USA, ahead of the British. The discovery of huge natural gas reserves, and to a lesser extent, oil, in the provinces of Groningen and Drenthe has also greatly improved The Netherlands' already excellent economic prospects. Most British and American people will find temporary work through employment agencies; the press and word of mouth are important ways of finding work.

## SPECIFIC CONTACTS

Dutch job centres (*gewestelijk arbeidsbureaux*) are found in every major city and town, and can offer job placements and advice on employment in The Netherlands. A full list of centres is available from the *Centraal Bureau voor de Arbeidsvoorziening,* Visseringlaan 26, Postbus 5814, NL-2280 AK Rijswijk; tel 70-313-0911. A consultancy in Holland offering a database of services in English, English-speaking counsellors, careers workshops, and a job advice booklet, is *ACCESS,* Societeit de Witte, Plein 24, NL-2511 CS Den Haag; tel 70-346-2525.

### Newspapers

There are several national newspapers. *De Telegraaf,* the highest circulation daily, is represented by the largest agency of its kind in Britain, *Powers International,* 517-523 Fulham Road, London SW6 1HD, tel 0171-385 8855; *Het*

*Parool, Trouw* and *de Volkskrant* are represented by *Frank L. Crane Ltd.,* 5-15 Cromer Street, Grays Inn Road, London WC1H 8LS, tel 0171-837 3330.

## Medicine and Nursing

Information on existing vacancies in Dutch hospitals can be obtained from *Geneeskundige Vereniging tot Bevordering van het Ziekenhuiswezen,* Postbus 9696, NL-3506 GR Utrecht. On obtaining an appointment a licence must be secured. Applications should be sent to the *Ministry of Welfare, Health and Culture, Public Health Section,* Dr. Reijersstraat 10, Leidschendam. *BNA International,* 3rd Floor, 443 Oxford Street, London W1R 2NA, recruits nurses for work in The Netherlands.

# SHORT TERM WORK

Dutch employers are accustomed to taking on British and Irish people for temporary jobs and to using the services of employment agencies like *Randstad, ASB, Unique* and *Manpower.* Addresses can be found under *Uitzendbureaux* in the local equivalent of the Yellow Pages, the *Gouden Gids.* Language is not normally a problem, but some knowledge of Dutch could pay dividends in influencing potential employers in your favour. Applications for short-term work can be addressed to: National Office of the Employment Afd: 1AB, EURES, PO Box 415, NL-2280 AK Rijswijk, The Netherlands; or contact the local 'arbeids' bureau. An on-the-spot job search is a good idea. Young people in Britain (18-28) with two years relevant experience in agriculture/horticulture who are looking for 3-12 month placements in The Netherlands can contact: *IFPA,* National Federation of Young Farmers Clubs, YFC, Stoneleigh Park, Kenilworth, Warwickshire CV8 2LJ; tel 01293-696584.

## Seasonal Work

The Netherlands has a comparatively long tourist season, as the bulb fields attract tourists and workers from April onwards. The most important single region for bulbs is between Leiden and Haarlem. The centre has shifted from Hillegom to Noordwijk and essential requirements to get a job are a tent and a bicycle. Conditions can be poor, especially in the smaller places, but food, accommodation and even beer are often provided free. An alternative to bulbs is tomato picking, centred in Westland around the villages of Naaldwijk, Westerlee, De Lier and Maasdijk. Tourism attracts more than five million visitors every year. The best areas for finding work are Amsterdam, the coastal resorts of Scheveningen and Zandvoort, and the island of Texel.

## Teaching

The Dutch place such a high value on knowing English that some have suggested that English should be the main language of instruction in schools. It is already widely used in Dutch universities; and Holland actually sends its own English teachers abroad. The implication is clear — this is not a country where you can easily find TEFL jobs. In general, the demand is for high level university and college teachers. Dutch schools do not need to recruit abroad — they generally rely on local expatriates who are often part-timers. *The British Council in The Netherlands,* Keizersgracht 343, NL-1016 EH Amsterdam, tel 20-622-3644, can provide information on schools and work prospects in Amsterdam.

## Au Pairs

The Dutch authorites have only recently officially recognised arrangements for au pairs. As a result, the demand is relatively small and comes mainly from expatriate families in Amsterdam, Rotterdam and The Hague. Wages are high and working conditions good. Au pairs must be aged 18-30 and be prepared to commit themselves for six months. The Association of Dutch Au Pair Agencies (tel 50-422-949) provides information on placements. Further agencies are:

*Au Pair International,* Bieslookstraat 31, NL-9731 HH Groningen.

*Exis (Au Pairs for Europe),* Postbus 15344, NL-1001 MH Amsterdam. They publish a guide to being an au pair in The Netherlands.

**Other Work**
The many private employment agencies *(uitzendbureaux)* are the best source of unskilled and temporary jobs (see above). There are 125 in Amsterdam alone. *The Federation of Recruitment and Employment Services Ltd.* (36-38 Mortimer Street, London W1N 7RB; tel 0171-323 4300) can provide details of UK employment agencies that offer work in The Netherlands.

**Opportunities for US Citizens**
There are few legal ways of working in The Netherlands, unless you find an employer who will apply for a work permit. The best chances are in the oil industry or working for US-based companies. Working exchanges are possible through organisations such as *IAESTE* and *AIPT (see Working Exchanges* in *Getting the Job).* Voluntary work opportunities can be found in the *Voluntary Work* chapter. The branch in Holland of the voluntary and workcamp organisation Service Civil International is *MVB,* Bastiaansestraat 56, 1054 SP Amsterdam.

*Lever and Vile,* Maliesingel 27A, NL-3581 BH Utrecht, tel 30-369-136, fax 30-369-199 — is a management consultancy specialising in sales and marketing with an associated office in the USA: *Vick and Associates,* Suite 1001, 3325 Landershire Lane, Plano, TX 75023; tel 214-612-8245; fax 214-612-1924.

BRITISH COMPANIES
with branches or subsidiaries operating in The Netherlands
(see appendix for numerical classification)

A list of over 400 companies is contained in the publication *Britain in the Netherlands,* available at A60 (including postage) from the *Netherlands-British Chamber of Commerce,* The Dutch House, 307-308 High Holborn, London WC1V 7LS; tel 0171-405 1356.

Accles en Pollock BV    27
(Warley B69 2DF)
Broekdijk 1
NL-7122 LD
Aalten

J C Bamford    39
(Uttoxeter ST14 5JP)
Bamfordweg 1
NL-6235 NS Ulestraten

Barclays Bank plc    4
(London EC3P 3AH)
Weteringschans 109
NL-1017 AD Amsterdam

Beecham Nederland BV    8
(Brentford TW8 9BD)
Sportlaan 198
PO Box 69
NL-1185 TH Amstelveen

British Airways    3
(London TW6 2JA)
Stadhouderskade 4
NL-1054 ES Amsterdam

BP Nederland BV    35
(London EC2M 7BA)
Neptunstraat
NL-2132 JA Hoofddorp

British Tourist Authority    48
(London SW1A 1NF)
Aurora Gebouw 5e
Stadhouderskade 2
NL-1054 ES Amsterdam

Cadbury Schweppes    16
Investments
(London W2 2EX)
Strawinskylaan 1725
NL-1077 XX Amsterdam

Calligen Europa BV    37
(Accrington BB5 2BS)
Konijnenberg 59
NL-4825 BC Breda

Coopers & Lybrand Dijker 14
van Dien
(London EC4A 4HT)
PO Box 4200
NL-1009 AE Amsterdam

Elsevier Science Ltd (OPMA) 38
(London OX5 1GB)
Postbus 211
NL-1000 AE Amsterdam

Equity & Law Levensverzekering 4
(London WC2)
Korte Voorhout 20
NL-2501 CZ The Hague

George Jowitt & Sons (Holland) 22
BV
(Sheffield S18 6PN)
Industrieweg 157-159
NL-5683 CC Best

Gestetner BV 30
(Northampton NN4 0BD)
Weesperstraat 140
NL-1112 AP Diemen

Habitat Designs 18
(Amsterdam) Ltd
(London W1P 9LD)
Stadhouderskade 106
NL-1073 AX Amsterdam

Hamworthy Engineering Ltd 39
(Poole BH17 0LA)
Hoofdweg 234
NL-3071 NE Rotterdam

ICI (Holland) BV 46
(London SW1P 3JE)
Het Kwadrant 1
NL-3606 KA Maarssen

ICL Nederland BV 10
(London SW15 1SW)
Postbus 4000
NI-3600 KA Maarssen

John Brown Engineers & 6
Constructors BV
(Clydebank G81 1YA)
Evoragroen 15
NL-2719 EZ Zoetermeer

KPMG 4
(London EC4V 3PD)
KPMG Gebouw Berg
PO Box 72001
NL-1007 TB Amsterdam

Lansing Benelux BV 39
(Basingstoke RG21 6XJ)
Haarlemmerstraat 39
PO Box 140
NL-2180 AC Hillegom

Lloyds Bank International Ltd 4
(London EC3P 3BS)
Hirsch Bldg
Leidseplein 29
NL-1017 PS Amsterdam

Marks & Spencer 13
(London W1 ADN)
Kalcerskade 66/72
NL-1012 PG Amsterdam

Merrill Lynch NV 4
(Chesterfield S43 2BU)
Strawinskylaan 941
NL-1077 XX Amsterdam

Midland Bank Ltd 4
(London EC2P 2BX)
Postbus 22681
NL-100 DD Amsterdam Z.O.

Moret Ernst & Young 1
(London SE1 7EU)
PO Box 488
NL-3000 AL Rotterdam

National Westminster Bank plc 4
F van Lanschot Bankiers NV
Hooge Steenweg 27-31
NL-5211 JN 's-Hertogenbosch

Oxford Instruments Benelux BV 22
(Oxford OX2 0DX)
Avelingen West 42
NL-4202 MS Gorinchem

PA Personnel Services 34
(London SW1W 9SR)
Sophialaan 1a
NL-2514 JP The Hague

Plessey Fabrieken BV 10
(Swindon SN2 5A1)
Van de Mortelstraat 6
NL-2200 AA Noordwijk

Price Waterhouse 1
(London SE1 9SY)
Atrium Bldgs
Strawinskylaan 3127
NL-1077 ZX Groningen

Renold Continental Ltd          22
(Manchester M22 5W1)
Kabelweg 42
PO Box 8019
NL-1042 AC Amsterdam

Reuters Nederland BV            38
(London EC4P 4AJ)
Hobbemastraat 20
NL-1071 ZC Amsterdam

Rover Nederland BV               7
(Birmingham B37 7HQ)
Sportlaan 1
PO Box 271
NL-4131 NN Vianen

Shell International Petroleum    35
(London SE1 7NA)
Carel van Bylandtlaan 30
PO Box 162
NL-2501 AN The Hague

Trusthouse Hotels Ltd           20
(London WC1 6TT)
Apollolaan 2
NL-1077 BA Amsterdam

Nederlands Unilever              8
Bedrijven BV
(London EC4P 4BQ)
Burg s'Jacobplein 1
PO Box 760
NL-3000 DK Rotterdam

Wellcome Pharmaceuticals BV      8
(London NW1 2BP)
Kobaltweg 61
NL-3503 RM Utrecht

## AMERICAN COMPANIES
with branches, affiliates or subsidiaries in The Netherlands

The *Netherlands-American Trade Directory* offers a complete picture of the American presence in The Netherlands and the Dutch presence in the United States; available from the *American Chamber of Commerce in The Netherlands,* De Ruyterkade 5, 1013 AA Amsterdam; tel 20-523-6600. *The Hague Chamber of Commerce and Industry*, Konigskade 30, 2596 AA Den Haag, tel 703-287-100, is also a source of information about Dutch and international companies.

# Norway

**Royal Norwegian Embassy, 25 Belgrave Square, London SW1X 8QD, tel 0171-235 7151**
**Embassy of Norway, 2720 34th St., NW, Washington DC 20008, tel 202-333-6000**
**Currency: 1 Norwegian Krone (NKr) = 100 øre**
**Rate of Exchange: £1 = NKr 10; $1 = NKr 6.6**

Norway is reckoned by the United Nations to have the highest quality of life in Europe, as well as one of the highest per capita incomes. The nation's wealth largely stems from the vast oil and gas reserves beneath its continental shelf in the North Sea (which it shares to a large extent with Britain). It is a country of high mountains and fjords stretching into the Arctic Circle; and covers 324,000 square miles, of which 69% is mountains and wasteland, 27% is forests, and 3% is cultivated. Its population is only 4,300,000; and 480,000 or so live in its largest city and capital Oslo. Fishing is on the decline; but it has established a large number of fish farms, making it the world's largest exporter of salmon. Heavy engineering is on the decline; and Norway maintains a large merchant fleet. Recent years have seen the emergence of advanced technological industries.

Norway is cold in winter, and sometimes hot in summer; but the climate of coastal areas is moderated by the Gulf Stream. The people can be reserved; and dress formally in a work or business environment. Punctuality is an important Norwegian virtue. The cost of living is also high in Norway; but for those who can afford them there are restaurants, discotheques, and clubs where folk music is played, in Oslo and cities like Bergen, Stavanger and Trondheim. Fishing and skiing are popular pastimes; swimming is possible in the summer months in its coast and inland waters. English is widely spoken. Norway is a member of the European Economic Area (EEA) but not the EU. This means in practice that EU jobseekers have much the same rights as in other European Union countries.

## FACTORS INFLUENCING EMPLOYMENT

### Immigration
US, Canadian and EU citizens may remain in Scandinavia (including Norway) for up to 90 days without a visa. Britons require a residence but not a work permit to work, and must apply after three months to the police for a residence permit (*oppholdstillatelse*). Work permits must be obtained by North Americans in all cases. Because of concerns about immigration, the Norwegian government imposed a ban on aliens seeking employment and residence in Norway from February 1975 which remains in force for the non-EEA countries today. The purpose of the ban was also to improve conditions for foreigners already resident in Norway, and to develop a positive programme for their educational, housing, social and cultural needs.

Among the exemptions from the ban are foreign diplomatic representatives and consular staff, sailors on Norwegian vessels, and workers on mobile drilling rigs on the Norwegian continental shelf. Of the people normally required to obtain a work permit, the ban is waived for: au pairs; trainees admitted under existing agreements with other countries; scientists; and a limited quota of specialists and skilled workers employed in work that is considered essential and cannot be done by a Norwegian citizen or resident.

Even those entitled to exemption from the ban are still subject to the following conditions: initial work permits will only be granted for a specific job with a specific employer at a specific place; applications for work permits must be filed in the applicant's native country or country of permanent residence; the employer must file a definite job offer on the approved form; and the employer must provide or arrange suitable accommodation for at least a year; applicants must be physically fit and literate in their native language — in Norwegian too, for certain types of work.

A leaflet explaining these conditions is available from the Norwegian Embassy in Washington.

### Language
There are two official forms of Norwegian in use; the older *Bokmaal* which is the principal language, and the newer *Nynorsk* (Neo-Norwegian), based on Norwegian dialects and developed following Norwegian independence from Denmark in 1814. Lapp is spoken by the Sami people in the north.

### Embassies and Consulates
British Embassy, Thomas Heftyesgate 8, N-0244 Oslo 2; tel 22-55-24-00.
There are also consulates in Aalesund, Bergen, Harstad, Haugesund, Kristiansand
   (N), Kristiansund (S), Stavanger, Tromsø and Trondheim.

US Embassy, Drammensveien 18, N-0244 Oslo 2; tel 22-44-85-50.

### Tourist Offices
Norwegian National Tourist Office, Charles House, 5-11 Lower Regent Street,
   London SW1Y 4LR; tel 0171-839 6255
Scandinavian Tourist Board, 18th Floor, 655 Third Avenue, New York, NY
   10017-5617.

### Newspapers
Oslo's leading daily *Dagbladet* is represented by *Frank L. Crane Ltd.,* 5-15 Cromer Street, Grays Inn Road, London WC1H 8LS; tel 0171-837 3330.

Vacancies for teachers, engineers, lawyers, etc., are advertised daily in *Norsk Lysingblad,* Postboks 177, N-8501 Narvik, which has an international subscription rate.

Engineers and other technical staff can place advertisements in *Teknisk Ukeblad,* Postboks 2476 Solli, N-0202 Oslo 2.

## SPECIFIC CONTACTS

### Employment Service
Private employment bureaux are prohibited by law, so the principal contacts are official government employment offices, run by the Directorate of Labour, *Arbeidsdirektoratet,* Holbergs Plass 7, Postboks 8127, Dep., 0032 Oslo 1, which can supply information on work and residence permit requirements. A useful English-language leaflet *Looking for Work in Norway* can be supplied by the Euroadviser there. There is a special department of the Norwegian Employment Service for foreigners at Trondheimsveien 2, Oslo 1. Other offices can be found in the Yellow Pages.

There are more contacts, and information about living and working in Norway, in *Live and Work in Scandinavia* published by Vacation Work.

### Nurses
Under the ICN (International Council of Nurses) Nursing Abroad Scheme, the *Royal College of Nursing,* 20 Cavendish Square, London W1M 0AB can arrange employment in Norway for RCN members only.

**Oil and Gas Exploration**
Norway is among the world's top half-dozen oil and gas producers; as a result, there is a high demand for skilled personnel in the Norwegian oil industry, centred on Stavanger. Applications may be made through recruitment agencies listed in the chapter *Oil, Mining and Engineering.* The Norwegian state oil company, *Statoil,* has an office at 10 Piccadilly, London W1V 9LA. Addresses of other oil companies are given below, under *Opportunities for US citizens* and *British Companies in Norway.* The *Oil & Gas* and *Engineering* columns of *Overseas Jobs Express* 'Jobs' section is a recommended source for this kind of work.

**Teaching**
The need for English teachers is limited, because most Norwegians who want to, learn it at school. A useful leaflet, *Information for Foreign Teachers Seeking Positions in the Norwegian School System,* is issued free by the Norwegian Ministry of Education and Research, Postboks 8119, Dep 0032, Oslo 1.
   A number of foreign teachers have been able to find temporary and part-time employment within one of the Norwegian voluntary adult education organisations: *Friundervisning i Oslo,* Postboks 496 Sentrum, N-0105 Oslo 1; or *Arbeidernes Opplysningsforbund,* Postboks 8703 Youngstorget, N-0028 Oslo 1. Non-EEA teachers still have to conform to the current immigration restrictions.

# SHORT TERM WORK

Paid temporary work has become difficult to obtain in recent years. Because of the decline of the fishing industry there is no likelihood of finding work in fish factories. But people who plan ahead may still be able to obtain well-paid casual work; when accepting a job remember that the cost of living is high; and check whether food and accommodation are provided. There are many private employment agencies (like *Manpower, Top Temp,* and *Norsk Personnel*) in the main cities; and ads appear for all kinds of temporary work in the main daily paper *Aften Posten* which is represented in the UK for advertising purposes by *Powers International,* 517-523 Fulham Road, London SW6 1HD, tel 0171-385 8855.
   There is one short-term scheme which may be of interest to non-EEA citizens looking for temporary work. The Immigration Ministry (*Utlendingskirektoratet*), Tolke og informasjonsavdelingen, Postboks 8108 Dep., N-0032 Oslo, publishes a booklet, *Work Permits and Residence Permits in Norway,* which states that temporary work permits will be issued for up to three months between 15 May and 30 October, where an employer has advertised a vacancy and been unable to find a Norwegian citizen or resident to fill it. The prospective employer also has to obtain statements from the local employment service and the local police authority that there is no objection to granting a summer employment permit, which is then forwarded to the applicant. Provided that you do not require a visa to enter Norway, it is possible to obtain the work permit from the police authority in Norway, subject to the above restrictions.

**Seasonal Work**
Norway's tourist hotels need a number of English-speaking staff over the summer: the greatest density of hotels can be found along the south coast around Kristiansand, and inland along the fjords north of Bergen. *The Directory of Summer Jobs Abroad* (Vacation Work) lists many hotels which recruit English-speaking staff.
   *Atlantis Youth Exchange,* Rolf Hofmosgate 18, oppg. 1, N-0655 Oslo 6, tel 22-67-00-43 — arranges individual stays for young foreigners from any country aged 18-30 as working guests on Norwegian farms and as au pairs as part of its *Working Guest* programme. These are at any time of the year. Free board and

lodging plus a weekly allowance (minimum NKr 600) are provided. All applicants must be able to communicate in English. Applications should include a reference, two photographs, and a medical certificate. There is a registration fee of NKr 880. Atlantis was established in 1987 by the Norwegian Youth Council to promote international understanding and youth exchanges.

There are also opportunities for short-term voluntary work (see *Voluntary Work*).

**Opportunities for US citizens**
It is worth knowing that workers on oil rigs and those looking for summer work may apply for a work permit from within Norway. Many major US oil and gas companies are represented in Norway; some addresses are given below:

*Amoco Norway Oil Co.*, Bergelandsgaten 25, N-4012 Stavanger.
*Chevron Petroleum Norge*, Mollergaten 24, Oslo, Akershus.
*Conoco Norway Inc.*, Postboks 488, N-4001 Stavanger.
*Marathon Petroleum Company*, Tolleodgaten 27, Oslo, Akershus.
*Phillips Petroleum*, Akersgate 45, Oslo, Akershus.
*Tenneco Oil Company*, N-4301 Sandnes, Rogaland.
*Texaco Norway*, Postboks 1680 Vika, Oslo, Akershus.

BRITISH COMPANIES
with branches, affiliates or subsidiaries in Norway
(see appendix for numerical classification code)

| | | | |
|---|---|---|---|
| Aker Offshore Construction<br>Postboks 369<br>N-4001 Stavanger | 35 | Castrol Norge A/S<br>(Swindon SN3 1RE)<br>Drammensveien 175<br>N-0212 Oslo 2 | 35 |
| Avesta Sheffield<br>(Sheffield S9 1TR)<br>Postboks 254<br>Holmlia<br>N-1203 Oslo 1 | 39 | Chloride A/S<br>(London SW1W 0AU)<br>Ostre Akervei 203<br>N-0975 Oslo 9 | 8 |
| BP Norge A/S<br>(London EC2M 7BA)<br>Arbinsgate 11<br>N-0235 Oslo 1 | 35 | Deloitte Touche Ross<br>(London EC4A 3TR)<br>Majorstua<br>Postboks 5945<br>N-0308 Oslo 1 | 14 |
| BP Petroleum Development Ltd<br>(London EC2 79B)<br>Forusbeen 35<br>PO Box 197<br>N-4033 Forus | 35 | Det Beste A/S<br>(London EC4M 7NB)<br>Postboks 1160<br>Sentrum<br>N-0107 Oslo 1 | 18 |
| British Airways<br>(London TT6 2JA)<br>Karl Johans gate 16B<br>N-0105 Oslo 1 | 3 | Duracell Norge A/S<br>(Crawley RH10 1FQ)<br>Postboks 45<br>Økern<br>N-0508 Oslo 1 | 8 |
| British Steel Norge A/S<br>(London SE1 7SN)<br>PO Box 2145<br>Grünerlokka<br>N-0505 Oslo 5 | 28 | Gillette Norge A/S<br>(Aylesbury HPA 3ED)<br>Rolf Hofmos gate 24<br>N-0605 Oslo 1 | 11 |

Glaxo Wellcome A/S 8
(London W1X 6BP)
Postboks 4312
Torshov
N-0402 Oslo 1

Hamworthy Engineering Ltd 25
(Poole BH17 0LA)
Stromsveien 312
N-1081 Olso 10

ICI Norden AB 37
(London SW1P 3JF)
Drammensveien 126Al
N-0277 Oslo 1

International Lighting Systems 10
Drammensveien 130
N-0277 Oslo 1

KPMG A/S 14
(London EC4V 3PD)
Postboks 6780
St. Olavs plass
N-0130 Oslo 1

LRC Norge A/S 42
(London EC1)
Sandakerveien 33C
N-0402 Oslo 1

Magnetic Reading Systems 49
Postboks 98
N-2007 Kjeller

Mobil Exploration Norway Inc 35
(London)
Postboks 501
N-4001 Stavanger

Mobil Oil A/S 35
(Milton Keynes MK8 1ES)
Postboks 6462
Etterstad
N-0605 Oslo 1

Newage Norge A/S 25
(Stamford PE9 2NB)
Stalfjaera 12
N-0975 Oslo 9

Normarc (Norsk Marconi) A/S 45
(Stevenage SG1 2BA)
Postboks 50
Manglerud 0612
Oslo 6

Norske Shell A/S 35
(London SE1 7NA)
Postboks 1154
Sentrum
N-0107 Oslo 1

PA International 14
Consultants A/S
(London SW1W 9SR)
Vika Atrium
Munkedamsveien 45
N-0250 Oslo 2

P&O Ferrymasters A/S 17
(Dover CT17 9TJ)
Skuteviksboder 1-2
N-5035 Bergen-Sandviken

Price Waterhouse A/S 1
(London SE1 9SY)
Holbergsgt 21
N-0166 Oslo 1

Rentokil Norge A/S 8
(East Grinstead RH19 2JY)
Postboks 24
økern
N-0508 Oslo 1

Reuters Norge A/S 38
(London EC4P 4AG)
Stortovet 10
N-0155 Oslo 1

Richards Scandinavia 8
(Essex CM20 2RQ)
Nye Vakasvei 64
Postboks 124
N-1364 Hvalstad

Rhône-Poulenc Rorer A/S 8
(Ipswich IP1 1QH)
Postboks 33
N-1345 Østeras

Schlumberger Norge A/S 35
(Felixstowe IP11 8ER)
Postboks 129
N-4051 Sola

Storeys Decor of Lancaster A/S 9
(Lancaster LA3 3DA)
Hvamsvingen 7
N-2013 Skjetten

Tate & Lyle Norge A/S 16
(London EC3R 6DQ
Tollbugate 8
N-0105 Oslo 8

Thorn Norge A/S 18
Bryngsengveien 2
N-0667 Oslo 1

Zanda A/S                    6
(Reigate RH2 0SJ)
Bjerkas Ind. omrade
N-3470 Slemmestad


## AMERICAN COMPANIES
with branches, affiliates or subsidiaries in Norway

*The Norwegian-American Chamber of Commerce*, 800 3rd Ave., New York, NY 10022, publishes a *Membership Directory* containing a list of 1,000 companies involved in American-Norwegian trade, for sale to non-members.

# Portugal

Portuguese Embassy, 11 Belgrave Square, London SW1X 8PP, tel 0171-235 5331
Portuguese Embassy, 2125 Kalorama Road, NW, Washington DC, tel 202-328-8610
Currency: The unit of currency is the Escudo (Esc or $). 1 Escudo is 100 centavos
Exchange Rate: £1 = Esc 242; $1 = Esc 158

Portugal, with a population of 9.9 million, has been an independent state since the 12th century when the first King of Portugal fought his way down the coast and extended his tiny kingdom of Portuçale. It covers an area of 36,390 square miles; it includes the two archipelagos in the Atlantic Ocean: the Azores and Madeira; and is divided into several provinces. Portugal has a traditionally agrarian economy which has industrialised extensively in recent years, and is less developed in the south. There are major infrastructure projects to improve the road network and the metro in the capital Lisbon. Portugal has friendly ties with Britain and links which go back to the Middle Ages. Port wine is named after the country; and Madeira (from the island) is another famous variety; wine production continues to be important today, as is agriculture; but there is a much bigger industrial sector which is dominated by textiles. English is not widely spoken except among those who have dealings with English-speaking people. Most Portuguese are Roman Catholics. Religion plays an important part in national life, especially in the country areas. The southern coast — the Algarve — is popular with tourists, and has a mainly British expatriate community. Job opportunities here are in tourism.

## FACTORS INFLUENCING EMPLOYMENT

### Immigration

Portugal is a full member of the EU; and EU citizens do not require work permits. If you intend to work for more than three months you should apply for a residence permit, an *Autorizaçâo de Residência* and will also need to apply for an identity card (*Bilhete de identidad*). Application forms are available at British consulates (see below). A detailed booklet entitled *Working in Portugal* published by the Overseas Placing Unit (c/o Mayfield Court, 56 West Street, Sheffield S1 4RE) is available from Jobcentres in the UK. A leaflet entitled *Some Hints on Taking Up Residence and Living Conditions in Portugal* is available from the British Embassy in Lisbon (see below).

US citizens may remain in Portugal for up to 60 days without a visa. Work permits must be obtained before entering the country; and after arrival the contract and documents including a medical certificate must be taken to the *Serviço de Estrangeiros e Fronteiras,* Avenida António Augusto Aguiar 20, tel 1-52-33-24 or 52-33-95, in Lisbon; or the offices in Oporto, Coimbra, Faro, Madeira and the Azores.

### Health and Welfare

The national health sytem is run by the *Ministério de Saúde.* UK visitors are advised to take their E111 and E101 forms; and others not paying national insurance contributions in the country are advised to take out private medical insurance. Social security benefits cover healthcare, pensions, sickness, unemployment, and maternity/paternity benefits. The local offices for such matters are the regional social security offices, *Centros Regionais de Segurança Social (CRSS)*.

**Taxes**
If you pay income tax you will need a fiscal number (*Cartão de Contribuinte*) obtainable at the local tax office on presentation of your passport. There is also a local municipal tax (*Contribuição Autárquica*) details of which are available at the town hall (*câmera municipal*).

**Embassies and Consulates**
British Embassy, 33 Rua de São Bernardo, P-1200 Lisbon; 1-396-11-91/11-47/ 31-81.
There are also British Consulates in Oporto, Madeira, the Azores and Portimão.

US Embassy, Avenida das Forças Armadas, P-1600 Lisbon; tel 1-726-66-00/66-59/86-70.
There are Consulates General in Boston, Honolulu, Houston, Los Angeles, Miami, Newark, New Bedford, New York (tel 212-246-4580), Philadelphia, Providence, San Francisco and Waterbury.

**Tourist Office**
ICEP/Investment Trade and Tourism of Portugal, 2nd Floor, 22-25a Sackville Street, London W1X 2LY; tel 0171-494 1441.

## SPECIFIC CONTACTS

The major industries in the Portuguese economy are textiles, pottery, shipbuilding, oil products, paper, glassware and tourism. Portugal is the world leader in cork production (in Alentejo). In spite of the rapid progress made in recent years, working opportunities in Portugal are not regarded as good. Portugal is one of the poorest countries in the EU (a very nice country to be poor in, some say though); and salaries are also low, although English teachers are paid more than the locals. Portuguese enterprises traditionally do not hire foreign workers; and the most likely job openings are in tourism and teaching, or in infrastructure projects. A dam which will be the largest in the Iberian peninsula is being built to improve agriculture at Alqueva in the Alentejo region, for instance. *Expo '98* is a huge international exhibition on the theme of the oceans, past, present and future backed by one billion of investment which will attract visitors and bring many employment opportunities in construction, engineering and for those with language and PR skills. Development of the site in Lisbon will continue after the exhibition is over.

**Newspapers**
The major newspapers include *Diário de Notícias, Correio da Manhã, Público* and *Jornal de Notícias*. Most newspapers can be contacted through *Powers International;* tel 0171-385 8855. Advertisements can be placed direct in English language publications like: *Anglo-Portuguese News (APN),* Av. de São Pedro 14 D, P-2756 Monte Estoril, Lisboa; and *Algarve News,* PO Box 13, P-8400 Lagos; and appear in international publications like *The European, International Herald Tribune,* and *Overseas Jobs Express* (see the *Getting the Job* chapter).

**Tourism**
Several British tour operators require staff to work in Portugal. *Thomson* is one (see *Transport Tourism and Hospitality*); and *Unijet Travel,* Sandrocks, Rocky Lane, Haywards Heath, West Sussex RH16 4RH, also employs a range of staff based in the main resort towns. The minimum age for reps is usually 21, and knowledge of at least one foreign language is required. A full list of companies

that operate in Portugal is available from the national tourist office in Britain. No address for the tourist office in America is available; but in Canada *ICEP/ Portuguese National Tourist Office* is at: Suite 1005, 60 Bloor Street W, Toronto, Ontario M4W 3B8; tel 416-921-7376.

## Teaching

There are several international schools for expatriates in Portugal. Enquiries about teaching posts can be made to the relevant organisations in the UK or USA (see *Teaching* chapter).

The British Council, Rua São Marĉeal, P-1294 Lisbon, provides a list of approved EFL schools in Portugal. Positions in English-language schools can be found through *International House* which has several affiliated schools here; and the market for English language teachers is described as 'buoyant' with many vacancies advertised before the new academic year in July and August.

Some addresses of other language schools are given below:

*American Language Institute,* Av. Duque de Loulé 22-1°, P-1000 Lisbon — hires US teachers with a degree. Interviews can be arranged in the US.

*American Language Institute,* Rua Joŝe Falcão 15, 5°, P-4000 Oporto — recruits full-time teachers for one-year contracts through the annual TESOL convention held in the USA by TESOL Inc. (see *Teaching* chapter).

*Cambridge Schools,* Avenida da Libertade 173, P-1200 Lisbon, tel 1-352-74-74 — employ around 100 teachers a year.

*Linguacultura,* Largo Padre Francisco Nunes Silva, Santarem — is a small group of schools. TEFL Certificate and one year's teaching experience required.

## Voluntary Work

Some of the major workcamp organisations listed in the *Voluntary Work* chapter run projects in Portugal. Agencies in Portugal which accept North American and other volunteers include:

*ATEJ (Associação de Turismo Estudentil e Juvenil),* Apartado 4586, P-4009 Oporto — places a small number of volunteers on farms, archaeological digs, projects with the handicapped, etc., and au pairs.

*Turicoop,* Rua Pascoal-Melo, 15-1°DTO, P-1100 Lisbon — runs nature conservancy and archaeological projects and workcamps as well as placing au pairs.

## Other contacts

The professional association you may belong to, Chambers of Commerce in Portugal, and the *Portuguese-British Chamber of Commerce,* Rua da Estrela 8, P-1200 Lisbon, and Rua Sá da Bandeira, 782-2-E/F, P-4000, Oporto, will not act as employment agencies but may offer general advice on job prospects; or may know which companies currently have vacancies. The employment agency *Manpower* has branches in Lisbon, Oporto, the Algarve, and in the Azores.

The Hispanic and Luso Brazilian Council, Canning House, 2 Belgrave Square, London SW1X 8PJ, tel 0171-235 2303, publishes a 12-page guide, *Notes on Employment, Travel and Opportunities in Portugal for Foreigners and Students.* The embassies in the UK and USA can supply other useful information.

## Useful Publications

Vacation Work publishes *Live & Work in Spain & Portugal,* which contains detailed information on all aspects of employment in Portugal.

## LIST OF BRITISH COMPANIES
with branches, affiliates and subsidiaries in Portugal
(see appendix for numerical classification code)

Arthur Anderson 1
(London WC2R 2PS)
Amoreiras Torrel 1
15 Piso
P-1000 Lisbon

Barclays Bank International Ltd 4
(London EC2M 7BA)
Avenida da Republica 50-3rd
Floor
P-1000 Lisbon

Building Design Partnership 6
(London W1A 4WD)
Sitio do Castelo 1-1
P-2750 Cascais

Beecham Portuguesa Produtos 11
(Brentford TW8 9BD)
Rua Sebstio e Silva 56
P-2745 Queluz

Berec Portoguesa Lda 7
(Stanley DH9 9QF)
Rua Gonçalves Zarco 6 6/J
P-1400 Lisbon

BP Portuguesa 8
(London EC2Y 9BU)
Praça Marqués de Pombal 13
P-1200 Lisbon

Cockburn Smithes & Cia Lda 16
(London EC1P 1AR)
Rua Corados 13
P-4400 Vila Nova de Gaia

Commercial Union Assurance 23
Co Ltd
(London EC3P 3DQ)
Av da Liberdade 38-4
P-1200 Lisbon

Companhia de Seguros 23
(Eagle Star)
(Cheltenham GL53 7LQ)
Rua de Outubro 70-6°/8°
P-1000 Lisbon

Coopers & Lybrand Ltd 1
(London EC4A 4HT)
PO Box 1910
P-1004 Lisbon

Deloitte Touche Ross 1
(London SE1 7EV)
Rua Silva Carvalho 234-4°
P-1200 Lisbon

DHL International 17
(Hounslow T44 6JS)
Aeroporto de Lisboa
Rua de Edificio 121 R/C
P-1700 Lisbon

Ernst & Whinney 1
(London SE1 7EU)
Av António Augusto de Aguiar
19-4°
P-1000 Lisbon

Fastecnica Electfonica e Téc- 41
nica Ltd
(Cable & Wireless, London
WC1X 8RC)
Praça Prof Santos Andra 5
P-1500 Lisbon

Glaxo Farmacêutica SA 8
(London W1X 6BP)
Rua S Sebastio da Pedreiro 82-1°
P-1000 Lisbon

Hoover Electrica Portuguesa Lda 10
(Glamorgan CF48 4BP)
Rua D Estefania 90
P-1000 Lisbon

ICI Portuguesa SARL 8
(London SW1P 3JF)
Avenida Duque D'Avila 120
P-1000 Lisbon

ICL Computadores Lda 10
(London SW15 1SW)
Av Estados Unidos da América
57-A/B
P-1700 Lisbon

Industrias de Alimentacão 16
(H.J.Heinz)
(Heyes UB4 8AL)
Av da Republica 52-7°
P-1000 Lisbon

James Rawes & Cia Lda 4
(London)
Rua Bernardino Costa 47
P-1200 Lisbon

Laing Portuguesa Lda 6
(London NW7 2ER)
Rua Augusto dos Santos 2-2
P-1000 Lisbon

Laboratórios Wellcome de 8
Portugal Lda
(London NW1 2BP)
Rua Visconde Seabra 4-4°-A
P-1700 Lisbon

Lloyds Bank plc 4
(London EC3P 3BS)
Avenida da Liberdade 222
P-1200 Lisbon

Lloyd's Register of Shipping 23
(London EC3A 3BP)
Av D Carlos 1, 44-6°
P-1200 Lisbon

Metal Box of Portugal 17
(Reading RG1 2JH)
Av Conselheiro Fernando
de Sousa 19-5
P-1000 Lisbon

PA Consultores 14
(London SW1X 7LA)
Rua Castilho 211-5
P-1000 Lisbon

Price Waterhouse & Co 1
(London SE1 9SY)
Avenida da Eng.
Duarte Pachecol
P-1000 Lisbon

Rank Xerox Portugal Lda 20
(London NW1 3BH)
Rua Pedro Nunes 16
P-1058 Lisboa

Reckitt Portuguesa Lda 16
(London W4 2RW)
Rua S Sebastio
da Pedreira 122-1°
P-1000 Lisbon

Reuters Portuguesa Lda 38
(London EC4P 4AJ)
Praça da Alegria 58-1
P-1200 Lisbon

Rhône Poulenc de Portugal Lda 8
(Birmingham B30 3JW)
Rua António Enes 25-2
P-1000 Lisbon

Rover Group Portugal 7
(Birmingham B37 7HQ)
Rua Vasco da Gama
P-2685 Sacavém

Royal Exchange Assurance 23
(London EC3N 1RE)
Avenida Marquês de Tomar
Apartado 1234
P-1000 Lisbon

Shell Portuguesa SA ·35
(London SE1 7NA)
Av da Liberdade 249
P-1250 Lisbon

# Spain

Spanish Embassy, 24 Belgrave Square, London SW1X 8SB, tel 0171-235 5555-7
Spanish Embassy, 2375 Pennsylvania Avenue, NW, Washington, DC 20037, tel 202-452-0100 or 782-2340
Currency: 1 Peseta (Pta) = 100 centimos
Rate of Exchange: £1 = 198 Ptas; $1 = 130 Ptas

Spain is described as a 'major industrialised country with a strong agricultural sector'. Since joining the EU in 1986, it has undergone rapid economic expansion and social change. Unemployment is still very high, although inflation is down. The economy and administration have also been reformed.

Spain used to be a centralised country, but power is being devolved to the regions, among which are Catalonia, the Basque Country and the Canary Islands. Spanish people are welcoming; and are generally international in their outlook. Agriculture remains important; and food and drink — especially wine — are enjoyed and understood. There are many regional delicacies. The evening — as in Italy — often starts with a leisurely stroll through the main streets, when the latest fashions are on display. Cafés and restaurants are plentiful and cheap. The nightlife in towns is lively, and tourists join in in Madrid, Barcelona and the Balearic Islands (Ibiza, Mallorca, and Menorca). Festivals and an enjoyment of life are also an important part of the Spanish way of life.

A traditional area for employment is tourism. The programme of privatisation means there will be opportunities for consultants in finance and restructuring. There is expansion in the electronics, information technology, and industrial design areas. Traditional heavy industries (along with agriculture and fishing) are however declining. The transition to democracy and away from a highly centralised economy has brought prosperity to many.

Spanish is universally spoken, although six regions use and teach their own languages besides Spanish. These are Catalan, Galician and Basque. English is widely spoken; but a knowledge of Spanish is needed by more long-term visitors.

## GENERAL FACTS

### Population and Geography

Spain has an area of 189,950 square miles and a population of 39.2 million. Its capital Madrid has three million inhabitants. Barcelona (capital of Catalonia), Valencia, and Seville are other major cities. With the exception of Switzerland, this is the most mountainous country in Europe with a vast central plateau where Madrid is located. The Mediterranean coastal area runs from the French frontier in the north-east down to the Straits of Gibraltar. There are two Spanish enclaves (Ceuta and Melilla) on the north African mainland (as Gibraltar is a kind of British enclave in Spain).

### Climate

The climate varies from temperate in the north and the Mediterranean islands, to dry and hot in the south, to sub-tropical (in the Canary Islands). Madrid can be very cold in winter.

**Government**

Spain is a constitutional monarchy, with 17 regions which each have their own parliaments and presidents (and account for a quarter of all public spending). The Basque country and Catalonia have their own police and tax-raising powers, as well as nationalist movements which seek independence from the rest of Spain.

## FACTORS INFLUENCING EMPLOYMENT

**Immigration**

EU citizens wishing to work in Spain do not require a work permit. Those intending to work should contact the nearest police station in order to obtain a residence permit (known as a *residencia*) and need to take a contract of employment, three photos and a passport in order to extend their stay beyond three months.

US citizens can stay in Spain for 90 days without a visa. Work permits must be obtained from outside Spain, and you will need to submit a copy of your contract, medical certificates and authenticated copies of your qualifications in duplicate. Anyone intending to live in Spain needs to acquire this Residence Entry Visa (*visado especial*) from the nearest Spanish consulate-general. There are some categories of employment where a work permit is not needed. Visas for tourism are not required.

The *Spanish Labour Office* in London (20 Peel Street, London W8 7PD, tel 0171-221 0098) has information on working and health care in Spain.

**Embassies and Consulates**

British Embassy, Calle de Fernando el Santo 16, E-28010 Madrid; tel 1-319-0200. There are consulates in Seville, Alicante, Barcelona, Tarragona, Bilbao, Lanzarote, Las Palmas, Santa Cruz de Tenerife, Málaga, Palma, Ibiza, Santander, Menorca and Vigo.

US Embassy, Serrano 75, E-28006 Madrid; tel 1-577-4000. 1

The Consular Section of the British Embassy in Madrid issues a leaflet, *Settling in Spain.*

**Tourist Offices**

Spanish National Tourist Office, 57-58 St James's Street, London SW1A 1LD; tel 0171-499 0901.

Spanish National Tourist Office, 666 Fifth Avenue, New York, NY 10022; tel 212-265-8822.

## WORK AVAILABLE

**General**

Career prospects are good for those who are willing to learn Spanish and are prepared remain in Spain for some time. It has never been easier to set up your own business in Spain: most popular are language schools, and enterprises catering for English-speaking expatriates in tourism.

**Newspapers**

Advertisements can be placed direct in:

*ABC,* Serrano 61, Madrid.
*El Pais,* Miguel Yuste 40, Madrid.
*La Vanguardia,* Pelayo 28, Barcelona, 1.

## SPECIFIC CONTACTS

**Employment Service**

General enquiries on working in Spain should be addressed to the *Ministerio de Trabajo,* Departamento de Extranjeros, Agustin Bethencourt 4, Madrid.

Enquiries about vacancies — although most unlikely to produce a job offer — can be sent to the *Centro Nacional de Colocación,* General Pardinas 5, Madrid; or to the *Delegación Provincial de Trabajo* in the provincial capitals. All such enquiries should be in Spanish and include an International Reply Coupon.

## Consultants and Agencies

*English Educational Services,* Alcala 20-2°, E-28014 Madrid, tel 532-9734, fax 531-5298, assesses and recommends qualified teachers to private schools all over Spain. Interviews are held regularly in London and occasionally in Dublin for client schools in Spain; from time to time primary and secondary school teachers are also helped to find jobs in equivalent schools in Spain. Most candidates have as a minimum qualification the Cambridge/RSA Certificate. In addition to recruiting teachers, EES also offers advice and guidance. Teachers should send their C.V. to the above address, together with an International Reply Coupon to ensure a reply.

*HRM International SA,* Felipe IV 10, E-28014 Madrid — is an executive search consultancy specialising in the selection and location of high level managers for the Spanish, Portuguese and Latin American markets. Interested applicants who speak fluent Spanish should send their CV.

## Teaching

As in the other Mediterranean countries, there is a considerable demand for English language teachers who speak English as a first language. (See *Teaching English Abroad* for more information and language school addresses; or ads under *Idiomas* in the newspapers mentioned above, for current vacancies). A list of the 350 members of the national federation of English language schools (FECEI) can be obtained from the Spanish Labour Office in London (see above). The lengthy procedures above make it more difficult for American citizens to find English teaching work.

*Centro de Idiomas Liverpool,* Libreros, 11-1°, Alcalá de Henares, 28801 Madrid, tel 1-881-3184 — recruits teachers for nine-month contracts for varied types of classes and in-company work. Minimum requirements: Cert.TEFL, driving licence, smart appearance.

*Centros Europeos,* C/Principe 12, 6 A, E-28012 Madrid — needs English and also French teachers for small groups of mainly adult students.

*English American College,* Calle Obispo Hurtado 21-1A, E-18002 Granada — recruits graduates with TEFL or similar qualifications for one year contracts to teach English at the college. The minimum age is 21 years. Enquiries should be directed to the Director of Studies.

*The National Association of British Schools,* International Primary School, Rosa Jardon 3, E-28016 Madrid — can be approached by qualified teachers wanting to work in British primary or secondary schools.

*Mangold Institute,* Avenida Marques de Sotelo 5, Pasaje Rex, E-46002 Valencia, tel 352-7714 — needs experienced EFL teachers and secretarial staff. Other languages taught are French, German, Italian and Russian, as well as computing and secretarial skills.

International language school chains present in Spain include: *Berlitz; International House;* and *inlingua.*

The *Spanish Institute* at 102 Eaton Square, London SW1, will supply a list of language schools to which applications can be made. The *British Council* is at Paseo del General Martinez, Campos 31, E-28010 Madrid and Calle Amigó 83, E-08021 Barcelona.

**Other Opportunities**
Detailed information on all aspects of employment in Spain can be found in the Vacation Work book, *Live and Work in Spain and Portugal*. Another source of information dealing with job opportunities in Spain is the *Hispanic and Luso-Brazilian Council*, Canning House, 2 Belgrave Square, London SW1X 8PJ. The council produces a leaflet, *Spain: A Guide to Work and Opportunities for Young People*. The relevant chapters in the *Specific Careers* section of this book should also be consulted.

## SHORT TERM WORK

Although Spain has a high rate of unemployment, especially among the young (which means that many young Spanish people go abroad to work), opportunities do exist for British people, and Americans who can get a work permit. Tourism is the major area; but these jobs are generally not well paid. British expatriates and others in your 'creative job search' may also help. Around eight million people from the UK alone go on holiday to Spain every year, which gives an idea of the scale of the industry and the opportunities which exist in everything from casual hotel and bar work through to working for a travel agency. There are many visitors from Germany, Holland, France and other countries, so some knowledge of these languages will help.

**Au Pairs**
Au pair and mother's help positions are generally available with more affluent households. You should expect at least Ptas 25,000 per month pocket money; and ask about opportunities for learning Spanish. UK-based organisations which deal with Spain include: *Anglo Au Pair Agency* (tel 0181-858 1750); *Avalon Agency* (tel 01483-563 640); *Helping Hands* (tel 01702-602067); and *Students Abroad* (tel 01462-438909).

*Canary Islands Bureau,* Urb Santiago Edf 4-5°, Santa Cruz de Tenerife, Canary Islands — will arrange au pair placements in the Canaries for 3 to 12 months, ages 18-27. Some childcare experience necessary.

*Relaciones Culturales Internacionales,* Calle Ferraz 82, Madrid E-28008, tel 541-7103, fax 559-1181 — charges an annual subscription fee which entitles you to make use of the broad range of services on offer, including one or more au pair placements per year, English teachers and camp counsellors.

**Seasonal Work**
Many Spanish hoteliers are happy to employ English-speakers to deal with their often English-speaking guests. Jobs in the tourist industry can be found by contacting hotels and campsites before the start of the summer. See *Summer Jobs Abroad* (Vacation Work) for lists of these. A more direct approach is to call in on potential employers, especially those along the Costa Brava and Costa Blanca, the Costa del Sol, and the Balearics. You can expect to work long hours in the peak summer season; year-round rsorts like Tenerife, Gran Canaria and Lanzarote offer a range of casual work.

If you have the necessary language and tourism skills, you can arrange a job with a tour company operating in Spain (see chapter, *Travel, Tourism and Hospitality*). Seasonal farm jobs such as orange or grape picking are mainly done by Spanish workers and migrants.

**Voluntary Work**
Work on many archaeological and conservation projects in Spain is coordinated by the *Instituto de la Juventud,* José Ortega y Gasset 71, E-28006 Madrid; they publish a handbook, *Campos de Trabajo,* giving details of over 100 projects throughout the country; and see the *Voluntary Work* chapter.

## BRITISH FIRMS
with branches, affiliates or subsidiaries in Spain
(see appendix for numerical classification code)

The *British Chamber of Commerce*, Pl. Santa Barbara, 10-1°, E-28004 Madrid, publishes a *List of British Companies in Spain*. The *Spanish Chamber of Commerce in Britain* is at 5 Cavendish Square, London W1M 0DP. The *Consejo Superior de Cámaras Oficiales de Comercio, Industria y Navegación de España*, Calle Claudio Coello 19, 1°, E-28001 Madrid, is another source of commercial information and advice.

APV Baker Iberica SA                     25
(Crawley)
Miguel Yuste 19
E-28037 Madrid

Blackwood Hodge (España) SA      25
(London W1)
Velazquez 75
Madrid 6

BP Española de Petroleos SA        35
(London EC2M 7BA)
Cea Bermudez 66, 3
Madrid 3

Brent Ibérica SA                          35
(Brentford)
Ctra Ajalvir Torrejón
E-28864 Madrid

British Airways SA                          3
(London TW6 2JA)
Serrano 60-5°
E-28001 Madrid

British Steel Corporation              28
Spain Ltd
(London SE1 7SN)
Serrano Jover 5,5
E-28015 Madrid 15

British Tourist Authority              48
(London SW1A 1NF)
Torre de Madrid, Planta 6a
Plaza de España
E-28008 Madrid

Cadbury Schweppes España SA     16
(London W2 2EX)
Sor Angela de la Cruz 3
E-28020 Madrid

Commercial Union                        23
Assurance Co Ltd
(London EC3P 3DQ)
Paseo de la Castellana 91
Planta 11
E-28046 Madrid

Coopers & Lybrand                         1
(London EC4A 4HT)
Edificio Torre Rioja
Posario Pino 14-16
E-28020 Madrid

Cory Hermanosos SA                    17
(London W1)
León Castillo 421
E-35008 Las Palmas
Canary Islands

Deloitte Touche Ross SA                 1
(London EC4A 3TR)
Torre Picasso, Planta 38
Plaza Pablo Ruiz Picasso
E-28020 Madrid

Ernst & Young SA                           1
(London SE1 7EU)
Torre Picasso
Plaza Pablo Ruiz Picasso
E-28020 Madrid

Expandite Asociada Iberica SA       6
(Kingston upon Thames)
Avda General Peron 4,3 b
Madrid 20

Ferodo Española SA                        7
(Stockport SK23 0JP)
Grupo TN
Progreso 384
E-08912 Barcelona

Flexibox de España SA                   25
(Manchester M17 1SS)
Ronda de los Tejares 19
E-14008 Cordoba

Formica Española SA                     18
(London W1)
Txomin Egileor 54
E-48960 Galdakaol

Guardian Assurance 23
(London EC3V 3LS)
Avenida Diagonal 523-3°
E-08029 Barcelona

Habitat SA 13
(London W1P 9LD)
Avenida Diagonal 514
E-08006 Barcelona

ICI España SA 8
(London SW1P 3JF)
Ctra Hostalric-Tosa
E-08490 Fogars de Tordera

Jones Lang Wootton España 40
(London EC4N 4YY)
Serrano 21-5°
E-28001 Madrid

Knight Frank & Rutley 40
(London W1R 0AH)
Valázquez 76
E-28001 Madrid

KPMG Peat Marwick 1
(London EC4V 3PD)
Edificio Torre Europa
Paseo de la Castellana 95
E-26046 Madrid

Laboratorios Beecham SA 8
(Brentford TW8 9BD)
Travera de Gradia 9
E-08021 Barcelona

Lloyds Bank 4
(London EC3P 3BS)
Calle Serrano 90
E-28006 Madrid

Lucas Service España SA 25
(Birmingham B19 2XF)
Poligono Industrial de Coslada
Avda de Fuentemar 23
Coslada, Madrid

Marks & Spencer 13
(London W1 ADN)
L1 LLA Block Edeniea
Barcelona

Marston Iberica SA 25
(Liverpool)
Talleronde Aldél
Sopelana, Vizcaya

Mather & Platt Española SA 25
(Manchester)
Tuset 23-25
Barcelona

Midland Bank 4
(London EC2P 2BX)
Calle de José Ortega y Gassett,
29-1
Edificio Beatriz
E-28006 Madrid

National Westminster Bank plc 4
(London EC2P 2BP)
Principe de Vergara 25
E-28002 Madrid

Perkins Hispania SA 25
(Peterborough)
Hermosilla 1 17
Madrid 9

Phoenix Assurance Co 13
(London EC4)
Ronda Universidad 20
Barcelona 7

Plessey Semiconductors 10
(Swindon SN2 5A1)
Plaza de Colon 2
Torres de Colon
Torre 18b
E-28046 Madrid

Price Waterhouse & Co 1
(London SE1 9SY)
Edificio Price Waterhouse
Paseo de la Castellana 43
E-26046 Madrid

Pritchard Española SA 24
(London W1)
Paseo de la Castellena 43
E-28046 Madrid

Professional Management 40
Services
(John Laing, London NW7 2ER)
Orense 16-2H
E-28020 Madrid

Rhône-Poulenc 8
(Ipswich IP1 1QH)
Avda Leganés 62
Algorćon
E-28925 Madrid

Rio Tinto Minera SA 8
(London SW1)
Zurbano 76
E-28010 Madrid

Rank Video Services Iberia 36
(London EC3P 3DQ)
Poligono Industriell
El Rasol
San Agustin
E-28750 Madrid


Rover España SA 7
(Birmingham B37 7HQ)
Mar Mediterráneo 2
San Fernando de Henares
E-28850 Madrid


Royal Insurance España 23
(Liverpool L69 3HG)
Po. de la Castellana 60
E-28046 Madrid

Sandeman Roomate 16
Hermanos y Cia
(Harlow)
Lealas 26
Jerez de la Fontera, Cadiz

Shell Española SA 35
(London SE1 7NA)
Rio Bullaque 2
E-28034 Madrid

Unilever España 16
(London EC4P 4BQ)
Apartado 36156
E-28080 Madrid

Wimpey Espãnola SA 40
(London W6 7EN)
Orense 20
Madrid 20

# Sweden

Swedish Embassy, 11 Montagu Place, London W1H 2AL, tel 0171-917 6400
Swedish Embassy, 1501 M Street, NW, Washington, DC 20005, tel 202-467-2600
Currency: 1 Swedish krona (plural kronor) (Kr) = 100 öre
Rate of Exchange: £1 = Kr 10.3; $1 = Kr 6.7

Sweden shares land borders with Finland and Norway, with a long Baltic Coast to the east. Half of the country is forested; and most of the many thousands of lakes are situated in the southern central area. It covers 173,732 square miles; and the population is 8,750,000, of which 700,000 live in Stockholm, the capital. Other large cities are Göteborg (known in English as Gothenburg), Malmö, and Uppsala. It is a constitutional monarchy and government is exercised by a Council of State, composed of the Prime Minister and 19 Ministers.

Sweden is now a member both of the European Economic Area (see *Rules and Regulations*) and the European Union. It has one of Europe's most advanced economies, with a highly developed health care and social security system; and unemployment is traditionally low (although structural changes in the economy, and the contraction of the public sector, mean that at the time of writing this is around 8%, four times higher than the figure for 1990). Immigration, at least from the non-Nordic countries, is not encouraged, although Sweden has a liberal policy in relation to refugees. The role of women and equal opportunities are important; employers must take measures to promote equality at work. In work life smart dress is expected, and punctuality is important. Outside work, Swedes are more relaxed, in their dress and behaviour. English is quite widely spoken; and there is a lively nightlife, with pubs, cafés and discos in Stockholm. There are strict licensing laws; and smoking in prohibited on public transport and in most public buildings. In food, the emphasis is on healthy, simple eating (the most famous expression of this being the Scandinavian cold table, or *Smörgasbord*). The liqueur traditionally drunk with this is *snapps*.

The extensive forests contribute to the production of wood-based products like paper and furniture, which account for 20% of exports. Many industries have recently been privatised. Engineering, motor vehicle manufacture, mining, steel and chemical industries, as well as agriculture, are all important. In October 1991, for the first time since the 1930s, Sweden elected a conservative-led government; and there is a lively political debate about the conflicting claims of the welfare state and the need to reduce public debt.

## Immigration

US, Canadian and EU citizens may currently remain for up to 90 days in Scandinavia (including Sweden) without a visa. Only EEA citizens (including the EU and Britain) can settle in Sweden without a residence permit. Aliens from other countries seeking temporary or permanent employment or residence in Sweden need to obtain either a work or residence permit (usually both) prior to arrival in Sweden. Both must be applied for at the nearest Swedish consular office. The work permit application must be accompanied by a written offer of employment, including details of working hours, pay, duration of employment and accommodation arrangements.

Work permit applications are usually assessed with reference to the state of the labour market by the National Labour Market Board (AMS) and the local county labour boards. The permits are then generally valid for one year, renewable by the Immigration Board, usually for special assignments or workers with limited-term contracts. Under recently introduced provisions, an immigrant can acquire Swedish citizenship after five years' residence.

For general information on immigration, write to the National Immigration Board (*Statens Invandrarverk*), Box 6113, S-600 06 Norrköping. Once in Sweden, you can turn for advice to the immigration bureaux (*invandrarbyraer*) that have been set up in about 125 communities all over Sweden.

**Embassies and Consulates**
British Embassy, Skarpögatan 6, S-115 93 Stockholm; tel 8-671-9000.
Consulates also in Göteborg, Lulea, Malmö and Sundsvall.

US Embassy, Strandvägen 101, S-115 27 Stockholm; tel 8-783-5300.

**Tourist Offices**
Swedish Travel and Tourism Council, 11 Montagu Place, London W1H 2AL; tel 0171-917 6400.
Swedish Travel and Tourism Council, 18th Floor, 655 Third Avenue, New York, NY 10017; tel 212-949-2274.

## WORK AVAILABLE

**General**
Sweden's industries have traditionally been based on its natural resources, notably its forests and iron ore (for engineering, the automotive industries, aircraft and weapons manufacture). A newer trend is towards higher-tech industries like electronics, pharmaceuticals and telecommunications. Work permits (for non-EU/EEA citizens) are short-term; and the chances of working in Sweden on a long-term basis are rather limited. Swedish workers themselves are highly trained, and English is widely spoken. The best opportunities are in international companies, of which the country has a disproportionately large number: some 2,700 or so have their headquarters in Sweden.

**Newspapers**
In the UK, advertisements in the leading dailies *Sydsvenska Dagbladet* and *Göteborgs Posten* can be placed through *Frank L. Crane Ltd.,* 5-15 Grays Inn Road, London WC1H 8LS; tel 0171-837 3330.

## SPECIFIC CONTACTS

**Employment Service**
There used to be a monopoly on employment services held by the AMS; private employment agencies are now permitted, but employers are still required to register vacancies with the public Employment Service; those intending to work in Sweden may write to the Swedish Labour Market Board (*Arbetmarknadsstyrelsen*), S-171 99 Solna, for general information on the employment scene. Once in Sweden, the local Employment Service offices are the first contacts when changing jobs.

**Medical Staff**
Information on registration requirements for foreign doctors and nurses are available from the *Swedish Board of Health and Welfare,* RT-enheten, S-106 30 Stockholm. However, the Board advises that the possibilities for foreign medical personnel to work in Sweden are extremely limited due to the lack of resources to provide the necessary complementary training. Vacancies are advertised in

*Läkartidningen (Swedish Medical Journal),* PO Box 5603, S-114 86 Stockholm; tel 08-790-330; fax 08-207-619.

**Teachers**
*International Language Services,* 36 Fowlers Road, Salisbury, Wilts SP1 2QU, tel 01722-331011, annually recruits British teachers to teach English on the various programmes run by the Folk University. Most of the work involves adult classes, but teachers may also be required to assist in Swedish state schools. See the *Teaching* chapter for further information.

**Other Opportunities**
Reference to other opportunities in Sweden will be found under *Getting the Job,* especially the section *Agencies and Consultants,* and in the various chapters of the section on *Specific Careers*; and see *Live and Work in Scandinavia* (Vacation Work) for more employment opportunities and information about living and working in Sweden

## SHORT TERM WORK

An exception the the strict immigration requirements for non-EU citizens is made for foreign students under 30 looking for jobs lasting for up to three months between May 15th and October 15th. Even they, however, need to find jobs and arrange work permits before entering the country, and possibilities are limited by the general requirement that they speak some Swedish.

**Seasonal Work**
Opportunities for seasonal work are limited. People who are already in Sweden may be able to find 'informal' farm jobs picking fruit and vegetables, especially in the agricultural area of Skane in the South. Swedish employers are generally reluctant to apply for work permits, since these are not often granted by the authorities.

See the relevant chapter in *Specific Careers* for details of organisations offering voluntary work in Sweden. The Swedish partner organisation (for workcamps) of Service Civil International is *IAL,* Barnängsgatan 23, S-11 641 Stockholm.

LIST OF BRITISH COMPANIES
with branches, affiliates or subsidiaries in Sweden
(see appendix for numerical classification code)

A list of British business organisations and their subsidiaries can be obtained from the *British-Swedish Chamber of Commerce in Sweden,* Nybrogatan 75, S-114 40 Stockholm. The *Federation of Swedish Commerce and Trade,* PO Box 5512, Grevgatan 34, S-114 85, Stockholm, tel 8-666-110, fax 8-662-7457, can also offer commercial advice and information.

Albright & Wilson Scandinavia 8
AB
(Birmingham B68 0NN)
Hälleflundreg 12
S-426 58 Vätra Frölunda

Atlantic Cargo Sevices AB 17
Box 2531
S-403 17 Göteborg

Atlantica Insurance Co Ltd 23
(London)
Box 2251
S-403 14 Göteborg

Barclays International 4
(London EC3P 3AH)
PO Box 7154
S-103 88 Stockholm

Bristol Babcock AB 25
(Kidderminster DY11 7QP)
Fallhammargatan 2Al
S-721 33 Västeras

British Airways 3
(London TW6 2JA)
Norrmalmstorg 1
S-111 46 Stockholm

British Steel Svenska AB        28
(London SE1 7SN)
Sjöporten 4
S-417 64 Göteborg

British Timken Scandinavian     25
Liaison Office
(Northampton NN5 6UL)
Virvelvindsgatan 6
Box 8819
S-402 71 Göteborg

Castrol AB                      35
(Swindon SN3 1RE)
Box 45168
S-104 30 Stockholm 35

Commercial Union Assurance      23
(London EC3P 3DQ)
Kungsgata 29
S-511 56 Stockholm

DHL International AB             17
(Hounslow T44 6JS)
Sveav 170
Stockholm

Foseco AB                        8
(Tamworth B78 3TL)
Hökedalen 3007
S-668 92 Ed

Gestetner AB                    30
(Northampton NN4 0BD)
Box 8334
S-163 08 Spanga

GKN Nordiska Kardan             28
(Smethwick B66 2RT)
Box 149
S-662 24 Amall

Glaxo Wellcome AB                8
(London W1X 6BP)
Box 263
Idrottsvägen 14
S-431 23 Mölndall
S-Försakring 1

Motor Union Assuransfirma AB    23
(London EC3V 3LS)
Sibyllegatan 32
Box 5071
S-102 42 Stockholm

Hamworthy Sweden AB             39
(David Brown Hydraulics)
(Poole BH17 0LA)
Box 115
S-162 12 Vällingby

P&O Ferrymasters AB              7
(Dover CT17 9TJ)
Box 8978
S-402 74 Göteborg

ICL Holding AB                  10
(London SW15 1SU)
Box 40
S-164 93 Kista

Ilford Anitec AB                36
(Knusford WA16 7JL)
Ödegärdet 58
Box 55066
S-400 53 Göteborg

International Färg AB            32
(London NW1)
Box 44
S-424 21 Angered

Johnson Matthey AB              22
Victor Hasselblads 8
S-421 31 Västra Frölunda

Lloyds Register of Shipping     23
(London EC3)
Första Langgatan 28B
32 Göteborg

Ogilvy & Mather Direct           2
Sergels Torg 12
S-10392 Stockholm

P&O Ferrymasters AB              7
(Dover CT17 9TJ)
Box 8978
S-402 74 Göteborg

Pilkington Floatglas AB         19
(St Helens WA10 3TT)
Box 530
S-301 80 Halmstad

Racal Health & Safety AB        10
(Wembley HA0 1QJ)
Girovägen 13
S-175 62 Järfälla

Rank Xerox AB                   30
(London NW1 3BH)
Domnarvsg 11
S-163 87 Sparga

Rentokil Svenska AB              8
(East Grinstead RH19 2JY)
Landskronavägen 28
Box 5025
S-250 05 Helsingborg

Reuters Svenska 38
(London EC4P 4AJ)
Sveavägen 17
Box 1732
S-111 87 Stockholm

Rhône-Poulenc Sverige 8
(Ipswich IP1 1QH)
Box 4189
S-102 64 Stockholm

Schenker Transport AB 17
(London EC1N 8QJ)
Box 90119
S-120 21 Stockholm

Sotheby's Scandinavia AB 4
(London W1A 2AA)
Arsenalsgatan 6
S-111 47 Stockholm

Stanley Svenska AB 26
(Sheffield S3 9PD)
Box 1054
S-436 22 Askim

Svenska Dunlop AB 28
(Birmingham B35 7AL)
Metalastik Sweden
Box 9020
S-151 09 Södertälje

Svenska GEC AB 10
(London WD2 3LS)
Box 6770
S-113 85 Stockholm

Svenska Unilever AB 8
(London EC4P 4BQ)
Box 5881
S-102 48 Stockholm

Thorn Svenska AB 10
Box 1362
S-171 26 Solna

Trusthouse Hotels 20
(London WC1)
Sibyllegatan 81
S-114 43 Stockholm

Wellcome Sverige AB 8
(London NW1 2BP)
Kanalvägan 17
Box 528
S-183 25 Täby

Wormald Fire Systems Ltd 25
(Manchester M40 2WL)
Box 5044
S-121 05 Johanneshov

Zanda AB 6
(Reigate RH2 0SJ)
Box 100
S-313 02 Sennan

# Switzerland

Swiss Embassy, 16-18 Montagu Place, London W1H 2BQ, tel 0171-723 0701
Swiss Embassy, 2900 Cathedral Ave., NW, 20008 Washington DC, tel 202-745-7900
Currency: 1 Swiss Franc (SFr) = 100 rappen or centimes
Rate of Exchange: £1 = SFr 2.08; $1 = SFr 1.30

Switzerland is a confederation of 24 cantons, which have some degree of autonomy, including the right to levy taxes. Legislative power is exercised by the bicameral Federal Assembly: a Council of State representing the cantons; and the National Council which is elected every four years. Referendums are another important part of lawmaking. The postal abbreviation CH stands for Confoederatio Helvetica (Swiss Confederation in Latin).

Switzerland has been internationally recognised as a neutral state since 1815 and therefore does not enter into military alliances with other states. It is not a member of the EU or EEA; and the Swiss are reluctant to give up what they see as their consitutional rights to enter into this larger political unit. But it is a member of the organisation which was the forerunner of the EEA, EFTA, the European Free Trade Association.

Switzerland has the highest mountains in Europe, green mountain pastures (or 'alps') and many waterfalls and lakes. It has seven million inhabitants; and the population is divided between Roman Catholic and Protestant, as well as the various different language groups. It has a mixed economy, with many small craft industries (of which watchmaking is probably the most famous). There is a substantial chemical industry; and agriculture is important (although half its food is imported). Banking dominates the service sector; and Swiss banks are known for their discretion. Wages are high, as is the cost of living.

Tourism plays an increasingly important part in the economy; and this is where many job opportunities lie. There are also openings in information technology and some of its international organisations. The Alps cause the climate to be varied (and rather unpredictable). Mountaineering, hiking, and winter sports are all popular, as well as the main sport, which is soccer. Food, and the way of life in its different cantons, is also varied, with cheeses, meat dishes, and cakes and pastries which are specialities in its villages, towns and cities (chief among which are Bern, Zurich, and Basel). Restaurants and the nightlife are cosmopolitan. Switzerland is another country which dresses well, even at work, and where business cards are important. Bern is the capital.

The national public holidays are: New Year's Day (1,2 Jan); Good Friday; Easter Monday; Labour Day (1 May); Ascension Day; Whit Monday; National Day (1 Aug); Christmas Day; and Boxing Day.

## Immigration

US, Canadian and EU citizens may remain in Switzerland for up to three months without a visa.

It is very difficult at present to obtain work and residence permits, as the current policy of the Swiss authorities is to limit the number of foreigners settling in their country. There is an annual quota based on skills and qualifications.

All foreigners must have a work permit to enter Switzerland to take up employment, and for this it is necessary to have a definite job offer of employment. The future employer must apply to the Aliens Police of the canton where the applicant wants to work. The cantonal authorities will decide each case on its merits, and successful applicants will receive a combined work and residence permit (known as an *Assurance of Residence Permit* or *assurance d'autorisation de séjour* (French) or *Aufenthaltsbewilligung* (German)). This must usually be posted to an address outside the country, and is presented to the immigration authorities on arrival; the only other formality is a medical examination at the point of entry. Those who enter Switzerland as tourists, visitors or on business and then look for work will not be granted a permit while they are in the country.

Temporary work permits are available in limited numbers for seasonal work, mainly in the hotel and catering trades (see below). Students on exchange schemes or wishing to train (for a maximum of six months) in a Swiss enterprise, or gain experience with machines and production procedures used in Swiss firms, are also subject to quota limitations.

Swiss Embassies and Consulates can offer no assistance or information on the subject of employment. There is no consular involvement in the issuing of work and residence permits. Enquiries about employment addressed to any consulate will be answered with the circular *Note for Persons wishing to take up Employment in Switzerland*, which explains the reasons for the virtual ban on foreign workers.

The British Embassy's Consular Section (address below) issues a free note on *Employment for British Subjects* which says that work applicants should have a good knowledge of German, French or Italian, and that males should normally be under 45 and females under 40 years of age. The leaflet also contains a number of useful addresses in the areas of nursing, teaching, hotels, agriculture, au pairing, medicine and printing.

## Embassies and Consulates
British Embassy, Thunstrasse 50, CH-3005 Bern 15; tel 31-352-5021-6.
There are consulates in Geneva, Montreux, Zürich and Lugano.
US Embassy, Jubiläeumstrasse 93, CH-3005 Bern; tel 31-357-7011.
There are consulates in Geneva and Zürich.

## Tourist Offices
Swiss National Tourist Office, Swiss Centre, Swiss Court, London W1V 8EE; tel 0171-734 1921.
Swiss National Tourist Office, 608 Fifth Avenue, New York, NY 10020; tel 212-757-5944.

## British Residents' Association
Although unable to help in any way with employment, the *British Residents' Association of Switzerland* is a useful contact for advice and information. The Association's *Handbook* contains information on Swiss taxation, law and social security; and lists various clubs, schools and contact points for British residents. For further information contact the Honorary Secretary, British Residents Association, Ponfilet 74, 1093 La Conversion, Vaud.

## Languages
Switzerland has a variety of languages within its small area. Most educated people speak two or three fluently. 65% of the population speak Swiss German — Schweizer Tytsch — as their first language (which is almost incomprehensible to most German speakers, although the Swiss can also speak and write standard German (Hochdeutsch); 18.4% speak French; and 9.8% Italian. A further 1% speak dialects of a local language — Romansch — which bears little resemblance to German, French or Italian, but some to Latin. And many Swiss speak excellent English.

## WORK AVAILABLE

### General

Switzerland is well-known for banking and financial services. Other major employers of international workers are the many international organisations and multinational companies based in Geneva, and the headquarters of various multinationals based in the country. Immigrant workers are to be found in most types of employment; many unskilled workers come from Spain, Portugal and Yugoslavia.

### Newspapers

*Powers International,* 517-523 Fulham Road, London SW6 1HD, are agents for the most important Swiss newspapers, including *Tages Anzeiger, Basler-Zeitung, La Suisse* and *Tribune de Genève.*

### Labour Force

The Swiss labour force includes around a million foreign workers, 200,000 of whom are 'frontier commuters' living in neighbouring countries and commuting to Switzerland. It is worth noting that unemployment is projected at 3% for the year 2000. Presently it is between 3% and and 4% which in Swiss terms is high, but is extremely low for Europe.

## SPECIFIC CONTACTS

### Healthcare

Qualified nurses with a good working knowledge of either French or German can apply to work in Swiss hospitals through the *Schweizerische Vermittlungs- und Beratungsstelle für Personal des Gesundheitswesen AG (SVAP)* (Swiss Employment and Information Office for Medical Personnel), Schaffhauserstrasse 21, Postfach 51, CH-8042 Zürich. This office is affiliated to the Swiss Hospital Federation *VESKA,* Swiss Association of Graduate Nurses and Male Nurses *SBK,* Swiss Association of Laboratory Technicians, Swiss Society of Radiographers and Swiss Midwives Association.

Under the ICN (International Council of Nurses) Nursing Abroad Scheme, the *Royal College of Nursing,* 20 Cavendish Square, London W1M 0AB, tel 0171-409333, fax 0171-355 1379, can arrange employment in Switzerland for RCN members only.

*BNA International,* 3rd Floor, 443 Oxford Street, London W1R 2NA, recruits nurses for hospitals throughout the French-speaking part of Switzerland; the majority are at the University Hospital in Lausanne. RGNs should have a minimum of six months' post-registration experience. Contracts are for a year.

### International Organisations

United Nations organisations like *UNCTAD* (UN Conference on Trade and Development); *UNITAR* (UN Institute for Training and Research); and *UNHCR* (UN High Commissioner for Refugees) are based in Geneva. See the *United Nations* chapter. Administration, information technology, finance, language, legal, or other skills will be required.

### Teaching

The *Swiss Federation of Private Schools,* Service Scolaire, rue de Mont-Blanc, PO Box 1488, CH-1211 Geneva 1 will send (for five International Reply Coupons airmail, ten IRCs airmail) a full list and details of schools to which English-speaking teachers may apply. This should be direct to the school.

### Other Opportunities

*Elan Computing,* Rue San Maurice 2, CH-2001 Neuchâtel, tel 38-214-840, fax 38-214-842 — specialises in computing and data processing, as well as telecommunications.

*PS-Management AG,* Gubelstrasse 19, CH-6300 Zug — is a recruitment agency for management and professional appointments, with offices in Aarau, Basel, Bellinzona, Bern, Chur, Luzern, Olten, Solothurn, Sursee and Zug.

Other opportunites for work will be found in the earlier sections of the directory. Particularly in the following: *Au Pair and Domestic, Banking and Accountancy, Getting the Job* and *Voluntary Work.*

## SHORT TERM WORK

The Swiss authorities recognise the need for temporary workers and therefore issue a work permit known as *Permis A* or *Saisonbewilligung* which is valid for nine months in one year. Each canton has a strict quota of nine-month permits. There is also a four-month permit, for which the employer has to pay about £250. Once you have a work permit you enjoy similar rights to Swiss workers including the possibility of obtaining unemployment benefit after six months, assuming that you have paid contributions, a minimum wage which is set at around £850, and accident insurance (although foreign workers should take out their own health insurance).

### Agricultural
Swiss farms also offer temporary jobs over the summer. Informal jobs may be found on farms in the summer picking anything from cherries to hazelnuts; the area along the Rhône between Martigny and Saxon is especially recommended.

The grape harvest (*vendange*) in the French-speaking cantons of Vaud and Valais usually starts in mid-October, later than in France. Work should be arranged well in advance by contacting vineyard owners, who will then arrange work permits.

Young people with some French or German who are interested in gaining experience of farm work can visit the *Landdienst-Zentralstelle (Central Office for Voluntary Farm Work),* Postfach 728, Mühlegasse 13, CH-8025 Zürich, tel 1-261-4432, who can arrange a place on a farm between March and October. Minimum daily pocket money of SFr 20 is paid. The postal address is: *Landdienstzentralstelle,* Postfach 6331, CH-8023 Zürich.

### Au Pairs
The two major au pair agencies in Switzerland are: *Verein der Freundinnen Junger Mädchen* (FJM), Zähringerstrasse 36, CH-8001 Zürich, tel 1-252-3840 (known as *Amies de la Jeune Fille* in French); and *Pro Filia,* 51 rue de Carouge, CH-1205 Geneva, tel 22-3298462, also at Beckenhofstrasse 16, CH-8035 Zürich, tel 1-363-5501.

### Tourism
Switzerland has a healthy tourist industry over both the summer and winter seasons which needs to import many temporary workers from abroad, as the many hotel vacancies in *Summer Jobs Abroad* attest. This work is normally more than adequately paid, but the hours can be long and hard.

Hotel work can be found in the many hotels listed in *Summer Jobs Abroad* (Vacation Work) — for the summer and winter seasons. Also see *Transport, Tourism and Hospitality.* More information about hotel work can be obtained from the *Swiss Hoteliers Association (Schweizer Hotelier-Verein),* Monbijoustrasse 130, CH-301 Bern, tel 31-370-4333). *Village Camps,* c/o Chalet Seneca, CH-1854 Leysin, tel 25-342-338, organises American-style camps for children from the international and business communities, and requires all types of staff; priority is given to those who also speak German, French, or Italian.

### Work Exchanges
Under an agreement between the UK and Switzerland 400 British trainees can work in Switzerland each year and vice versa. Under this agreement, persons

aged 18-30 who have completed their studies or occupational training and who wish to broaden their professional and linguistic skills will be granted a work and residence permit for one year, which may be extended for a further six months in special cases. Employment may only be taken within the occupation for which the applicant has been trained. Initial enquiries in the UK should be made to the Department of Employment, or through your Jobcentre.

A similar agreement exists with the USA, for 150 American trainees (age 21-30) to go to Switzerland each year. The relevant agency in the USA is AIPT (see *Working Exchanges* in the *Getting the Job* chapter).

**Other Work**
Other opportunities are largely limited to voluntary work. Enquiries in the UK should be made to IVS. US residents can contact SCI (see *Voluntary Work*) for information on workcamps. Also see *Working in Tourism* and *Working in Ski Resorts* published by Vacation Work.

BRITISH FIRMS
with branches, affiliates or subsidiaries in Switzerland

A list of British concerns operating in Switzerland is not included here, as many of the companies are simply registered in the country for tax purposes and are not actively engaged in business there. The *British-Swiss Chamber of Commerce in Switzerland*, Freiestrasse 155, CH-8032 Zürich, has various publications, including a Members' handbook. The Chamber should be contacted directly for an up-to-date list of their publications and prices.

# United Kingdom

British Embassy, 3100 Massachusetts Ave., NW, Washington DC 20008, tel 202-462-1340
British High Commission, 80 Elgin Street, Ottawa, K1P 5K7, tel 613-237-1530
Currency: £1 (Pound Sterling) = 100 pence (p)
Rate of Exchange: £1 = US$1.65; £1 = CAN$2.1

The United Kingdom has long attracted workers from other countries, from the Commonwealth in particular, and more recently the EU. There has been a growth in foreign investment in recent years, particularly US and Japanese companies who see low labour costs, a skilled workforce, and Britain's participation in the larger market of the EU as advantages; and unemployment — though high — is lower than in many other European countries. The UK, with its diverse regions and cultural heritage, is a fascinating place to visit and to live for anyone from another English-speaking country; and is popular with visitors from many parts of the world. Language will not be a problem for the North American readers of this book but the culture may be. It is true that the British are a little more reserved; but they are not necessarily any more formal. Britain is a country which is still coming to terms with its diminished world role, and its political destiny in Europe; and these tensions have led to a rise in nationalist sentiments in Scotland and Wales, and, in their more complicated manifestations, in Northern Ireland (where the Protestant community still regards itself as British). Britons may prefer to be identified as English, Scots, Welsh, or Northern Irish (and Irish citizens may serve in its armed forces). These are where the deeper national affiliations lie. Service is not so often 'with a smile'; but Britons in the world of work are surprisingly informal. Nightlife and socialising centres around the many pubs, which look inwards, not out like continental cafés, a little like the British national character; and there are many international restaurants in all the major towns and cities. Tourism is one of the growing industries; manufacturing and agriculture are in (relative) decline. It is in the large service sector and new technologies that employment opportunities are to be most often found; with a wide variety of other openings at all levels for those who speak the language and understand the culture.

## GENERAL FACTS

### Population
The UK's population of 58,200,000 increases annually by 0.28%; emigration narrowly exceeds immigration. There are sizeable minorities from the Commonwealth countries, in particular India, Pakistan, and the West Indies. The average population density throughout the country is 618 per square mile. Population distribution is relatively even, if the mountainous areas of Scotland and Wales and the disproportionately large population of London are excluded.

### Climate
The climate is temperate, with some variation between north and south. The average winter temperature in the South is 4°C, summer 18°C; in summer temperatures may reach 30°C or more. The North of England, and Scotland are somewhat cooler. Rainfall is higher in the west and north.

## Government

The UK is a constitutional monarchy. The monarch is Head of State, and the temporal head of the Church of England, both of which are largely symbolic roles. The two Houses of Parliament are the House of Lords — which at present is unelected — and the elected House of Commons.

The United Kingdom is made up of four separate countries — England, Scotland, Wales and Northern Ireland. The term 'England' and 'English' are strictly only applicable to England, and should not be used for the entire United Kingdom. The term Great Britain or Britain includes England, Scotland and Wales. The constitutional arrangements for Northern Ireland, the Isle of Man, and the Channel Islands (which are geographically closer to France), are separate from those for the rest of the country.

## Cities

London, the capital, has about seven million inhabitants; other major cities include Birmingham (one million); Manchester (900,000), Leeds (700,000), Glasgow (700,000), Sheffield (500,000), Bradford (450,000), Liverpool (450,000), Edinburgh (capital of Scotland — 430,000) and Bristol (370,000).

## Rural Life

The UK is highly urbanised. A mere 8.5% of the population live in the countryside although three-quarters of the land area is either cultivated or used for pasture. Farming is highly mechanised and only 1% of the labour force is engaged in agriculture.

## Religion, Sport and Culture

Religion does not play a major part in the lives of most people — 86% of the population are nominally Christian, of whom 15% belong to the Roman Catholic faith, 57% to the established Anglican church, and the rest to various reformed churches. There are also Muslim, Jewish, Hindu and Sikh minorities. Catholics are most observant, although there has been a revival of the evangelical churches in recent years.

Britons have a well-known obsession with sport, and invented many popular varieties, such as soccer, cricket and rugby. Other popular sports include fishing, golf, horse racing, athletics, bowls and sailing. Skiing is only possible in the Scottish Highlands when weather permits; otherwise British people travel abroad. Another recreational activity which is popular is gardening.

Britons are great readers, of newspapers if not of books. Outsiders will find a cosmopolitan atmosphere in the major urban centres; theatre and music are particularly well-supported, with a growth in the popularity of the cinema among younger people. Britain is also famous for its youth culture; and a long list of internationally successful pop groups have been British.

# FACTORS INFLUENCING EMPLOYMENT

## Immigration

US citizens may enter and remain in the UK for up to six months without a visa. Work permits should be obtained through a British employer prior to arriving in the country. Further information is given below.

Citizens of a number of Commonwealth countries, including Australia, Canada, New Zealand and South Africa, may enter the UK without a visa and remain for up to six months or more. Patriality — a grandparent born in Britain or Ireland — will give you the right to live and work in Britain.

## Work permits

EU citizens do not require work permits, unless they wish to work in the Channel Islands or the Isle of Man. Also exempt are: Gibraltarians; Commonwealth citizens given leave to enter or to remain in the UK on the basis of patriality (see above); spouses and dependent children of work permit holders or anyone who does not need a work permit (provided that the endorsement in their passport places no restriction on their employment in the UK).

Anyone who is not an EU citizen is subject to work and residence permit regulations. Since 1 October 1991, there has been a two-tier arrangement for the issue of work permits:

*Tier One:* includes jobs at board level, jobs essential to inward investment, and jobs requiring skills in extremely short supply in the EU. Posts in Tier One are not subject to a resident labour test (i.e. the employer does not need to show that there are no suitable local workers available).

*Tier Two:* comprises jobs that would not qualify for inclusion in Tier One; and the employer will be required to demonstrate that he/she has advertised the post. Where the overseas national is already in the UK, the application will be treated as a Tier Two application; and the employer will be required to test the resident labour market.

## Students
Students from the USA, Commonwealth and some other countries on courses at recognised educational institutions may work in the UK under certain conditions. Once you have found a job, ask your employer to fill in form WP1 (obtainable from a Jobcentre) and then return it, along with your passport, police registration certificate (if you have one), and a letter from your college stating that your employment will not interfere with your studies. If further information is needed, employers can make enquiries to the *Employment Department,* Overseas Labour Section, Caxton House, Tothill Street, London SW1H 9NF; or, in Northern Ireland, to the *Department of Economic Affairs, Work Permits Branch (ES2),* Netherleigh, Massey Avenue, Belfast T4 2JP.

Somewhat different regulations apply in the case of training and work experience. Permission for work experience is usually granted for up to 12 months, to persons aged between 18 and 35. Once you have found an employer, you should obtain form WP2 or OW22, along with an explanatory leaflet OW21 from a Jobcentre and ask the employer to return it to the Department of Employment (see above).

Once your training or education has ended, it is generally impossible to arrange employment without leaving the country first. Potential employers are only likely to apply for a work permit if they feel that the British *Home Office* can be persuaded that your employment is going to be of benefit to the British economy and where no EU citizen can be found to do the job. Precise categories of workers who will be considered for work permits are laid out in the leaflet WP1/5 (notes) — *Guide for employers: work permit applications* obtainable from Jobcentres. Work permits are not granted for crafts, manual, secretarial, clerical or similar levels, or for resident domestic work, e.g. nannies and housekeepers.

## Languages
English is spoken universally throughout the United Kingdom, with regional variations. Differences are mainly a matter of pronunciation. In addition, some Celtic languages are still spoken in the UK. About 20% of the population of Wales is bilingual in Welsh and English; 32,000 only speak Welsh. In remote areas of Scotland, Gaelic is spoken by about 90,000 people. And a number of Asian languages are spoken in the United Kingdom by immigrants and their children, such as Hindi, Urdu, Punjabi, Bengali, Gujarati, and Cantonese.

## Cost and Standard of Living
US citizens usually find the cost of living high in the UK, depending on the current exchange rate with the dollar. Basic items such as food, public transport

and gasoline (known as 'petrol' in the UK) are far more expensive. House buying — which is a national preoccupation — is a major item of expenditure.

## Health and Welfare

Most workers are obliged to pay a fixed proportion of their earnings in National Insurance (NI) contributions. If you come to Britain to work, you should apply for a National Insurance number as soon as possible from a *Department of Social Security* (DSS) Office in your town (see Yellow Pages). You will need to give this number to employers, or at least have applied for one. Once you have paid enough of the right type of NI contributions you can claim Sickness Benefit, Maternity Allowance, Job Seeker's Allowance (unemployment benefit), State Retirement Pension, etc. EU citizens will generally already be entitled to these, either directly or through reciprocal arrangements with their countries; and there are agreements with Australia, Canada, New Zealand and the USA, which make it possible for citizens of those countries to qualify for a limited pension after paying one year's NI contributions. A complete list of these countries with reciprocal social security agreements is given in the chapter *Rules and Regulations.*

## Education

Free schooling is available to all children aged between five and 18; it is compulsory from six to 16. But there are too few nursery schools and kindergartens. Only 50% of 3-5 year olds go to nursery school in the UK, one of the lowest figures in Europe. From the age of five onwards a variety of possibilities present themselves, including state-funded Primary Schools (age 5-11), or private Preparatory Schools (up to age 13). The majority (90%) of children then go on to centrally funded state schools (11-16 or 11-18). At age 16, children can either leave school, with or without qualifications (GCSEs — General Certificate of Secondary Education); or go on to specialise in three subjects or more, taking 'A' (Advanced) Level examinations at 17 or 18. The minimum entrance qualification for university is two A levels. An alternative to purely academic A levels are National Vocational Qualifications (NVQs).

Alongside the underfunded state schools, are many partially state-aided or entirely independent private schools which may also accept overseas pupils.

Foreigners should also be aware that there are some international schools catering for different nationalities, some of which offer the International Baccalaureat, providing a more rounded education than the British A-Level system (which calls for early specialisation in three subjects).

British institutions of higher learning attract a growing number of foreign students every year. In spite of difficult economic circumstances, the UK has some of the most respected universities in the world, including its elite institutions Oxford and Cambridge which receive more state funding. A relatively low percentage of the population goes on to higher education though.

## National Service

There is no compulsory military service in the United Kingdom.

## Embassies and Consulates

US Embassy, 5 Grosvenor Square, London W1A 1AE; tel 0171-499 9000.
Canadian High Commission, Macdonald House, 1 Grosvenor Square, London W1X 0AB.

## Tourist Offices

British Tourist Authority, 7th Floor, 551 5th Avenue, New York, NY 10176-0799.
British Tourist Authority, Suite 450, 111 Avenue Road, Toronto, Ontario K1P 5K7; tel 613-237-1530.

## Hours and Wages

A particular feature of the United Kingdom economy is the large number of low-paid, part-time jobs which are available. These at least leave some opportunities open to foreign workers willing to accept a subsistence wage. There is no national legal minimum wage.

Legal safeguards at the time of writing fall short of EU standards; and the UK does not accept much EU employment legislation. The UK has specifically refused to agree to a limit of 48 hours per week, which is a part of the Social Chapter of the Maastricht Treaty on European Union; and Britons work more overtime than any other EU workers.

## Holidays

Most workers receive four weeks' paid holiday per year. The public holidays are known as Bank Holidays. These are: 1 January; 2 January (Scotland only); Good Friday; Easter Monday; May Bank Holiday (1st Monday in May); Spring Bank Holiday (last Monday in May); Summer Bank Holiday (last Monday in August); Christmas Day; and Boxing Day.

## Safety and Compensation

All businesses are obliged to have accident insurance to cover liability for an accident to one of their employees. They also have to report accidents to the authorities. The precise details of the rules and regulations can be obtained from the: *Health & Safety Executive,* Library and Information Services, Baynards House, 1 Chepstow Place, Westbourne Grove, London W2 4TF.

## Trade Unions

In the 1980s legislation severely curtailed the powers of trade unions, and there is a declining membership. It now stands at nine million and is falling. Unions represent different sectors or trades; and are generally members of the Trades Union Congress (TUC).

## Taxation

Foreigners who work in the United Kingdom are usually liable for UK income tax. Those from countries which have double taxation treaties with the UK may not be liable, if they remain for less than six months in any tax year (April 6 to April 5), and are paying taxes abroad. Details are given in the booklet, IR6 *Double Taxation Relief,* available from the British Inland Revenue (see *Rules and Regulations* for addresses).

Unless you are self-employed or have your own company, tax will be deducted from your salary on a Pay As You Earn (PAYE) basis. There is a tax-free allowance  which is revised annually), and a graduated or progressive system. PAYE means you will often find that you are entitled to a tax rebate at the end of the tax year. As from the tax-year 1997-8 there is a new system based on self-assessment, which means it is advisable to keep all pay-slips and details of your income throughout the year; and even those on PAYE will have to keep records, as they may be randomly asked to fill out a self-assessment form. A local tax inquiry office will advise you on the necessary procedure (see *Inland Revenue — Inspector of Taxes* in the Yellow Pages).

Value Added Tax (VAT) is payable on goods and services, with some exceptions, including food. Non-EU residents can reclaim VAT paid on goods (but not services) by presenting their passport and having VAT form 407 filled in by the retailer. This is presented to Customs & Excise on leaving the UK, for stamping. The form is then returned to the retailer for your refund. Further information on this scheme is available from *Europe Tax Free Shopping,* Europa House, 266 Upper Richmond Road, London SW15 6TQ.

## WORK AVAILABLE

### General

There is no shortage of opportunities for professionals in Britain, provided that they can obtain a work permit. The best chances lie in areas where a high level of training is required, such as medicine, the oil industry, management consultancy, scientific research, social work, and higher education.

The option of being transferred to the UK by a company based abroad is generally restricted to senior staff who come to the UK for 'career development', on the understanding that they will be transferred to another country in due course. The British Home Office expects junior staff to be hired in the UK. Marrying an EU citizen, or participating in a recognised work exchange or working holiday scheme, are the only ways round such restrictions.

### Newspapers

The quality press, namely *The Times, Guardian, Independent* and *Daily Telegraph*, are some of the most respected newspapers in the world, and are the best source of job vacancies. Their addresses are given in the chapter *Journalism*.

Local and free newspapers are a good source of job offers and accommodation. In London, the free magazine *TNT*, which appears on Mondays, is a source of job advertisements for accountants, au pairs and nannies, computer programmers, nurses, etc., as well as for temporary employment agencies, travel agencies and firms which will deal with your tax affairs. These are aimed at its mainly Australasian readership. The address is: *TNT Magazine,* 14-15 Child's Place, Earls Court, London SW5 9RX; tel 0171-373 3377; fax 0171-373 9457; e-mail enquiries@gtntmag.co.uk.

## SPECIFIC CONTACTS

### Employment Service

Job vacancies are advertised on noticeboards at Jobcentres which are to be found in most British towns. Anyone is free to look at the noticeboards and enquire about the jobs on offer. Jobcentres have specific leaflets for EU and non-EU citizens looking for work, explaining work permit regulations, in particular WP1/5 for non-EU citizens. The addresses and telephone numbers of Jobcentres can be found under 'Employment Service' in the telephone book.

### Employment Agencies

In addition to the government employment service, there are many temporary and permanent work agencies. There is no legal restriction on so-called 'temping' agencies arranging permanent posts as well. Names to look for include *Reed, Brook Street Bureau, Alfred Marks,* and *Manpower.* The names and details of many UK management consultants are given in the chapter *Getting The Job* and under *Specific Careers.* While recruitment consultants in the UK are happy to receive speculative applications from North Americans or Australasians, the regulations on work permits mean that only those who have suitable specialised qualifications are likely to attract the attention of these consultants, agencies, or potential employers.

### Medical Staff

Jobs in medicine and nursing may be short or long term. There is a shortage of doctors and nurses. The latter will find agencies in *TNT Magazine* (address above under *Newspapers*). Doctors may find current vacancies in the *British Medical Journal*; and employment agencies are increasingly used to fill these vacancies, too, in National Health Service hospitals. See the *Medicine and Nursing* chapter; and also *Health Professionals Abroad* (Vacation Work) under *United Kingdom* for a summary of useful information.

**Teachers**

There is a shortage of teachers in certain subjects at secondary school level (mainly mathematics and sciences). British Local Education Authorities are often keen to recruit trained teachers from abroad who speak English, for either temporary 'supply' teaching or permanent work. Agencies dealing with this kind of work advertise regularly in *TNT Magazine* (see above). Work permit restrictions tend to exclude Americans. *Pro Tem Personnel,* 87 New Bond Street, London W1Y 9LA, tel 0171-491 1045, can find work in any subject area at primary or secondary level for teachers with work permits.

Exceptions to work permit restrictions can be made where a teacher is required for a school where a foreign curriculum is taught, e.g. the US curriculum. These 'American' schools in the UK fall into different categories: those that are run by the Department of Defense; those which were started by Americans and take American pupils, but are not controlled by the US government; and international schools which follow a largely US curriculum. The following organisations will give information on these three categories:

*Department of Defense Dependent Schools,* Teacher Recruitment Section, Hoffman Building I, 2461 Eisenhower Ave., Alexandria, Virginia 22331-1100; tel 703-325-0885.

*Office of Overseas Schools,* SA-29, Room 245, US Department of State, Washington DC 20522-2902; tel 703-875-7800.

*International Schools Services,* PO Box 5910, Princeton, New Jersey 08540; tel 609-4520-990.

Work exchange programmes for US teachers can be arranged by: Teacher Education Branch, Division of International Services and Improvement, *International Education Programmes,* US Department of Education, Washington DC 20202; or *Fulbright Teacher Exchange Program,* E/ASX, USIA, 301 4th Street, SW, Washington DC 20547; tel 202-619-2555. The *British Information Services* office, at 845 3rd Ave., New York, NY 10022, issues a free leaflet, *Teaching in Britain.*

During the summer there are numerous English-language summer schools who will employ English-speakers with (or sometimes without) teaching experience. In some cases courses are residential.

*EF Language Travel,* 1-3 Farman Street, Hove, Sussex BN3 1AL.

*Nord-Anglia International Ltd.,* 10 Eden Place, Cheadle, Stockport, Cheshire SK8 1AT.

*TASIS England American School,* Coldharbour Lane, Thorpe, Surrey KY20 8TE — is of special interest to American EFL teachers who want to teach in England for eight weeks. Only suitably qualified Americans are eligible for work permits.

## SHORT TERM WORK

The numerous temping agencies are the best source of this kind of work; and you may consult Jobcentre notice-boards (see above).

**Agricultural**

Between May and October, thousands of casual workers are recruited by farms in England and Scotland to pick fruit (strawberries, raspberries, apples, pears), vegetables (tomatoes, courgettes, potatoes, lettuces, etc.) and hops (used for making beer). Some of the largest fruit growers in the UK are traditionally allowed to recruit fruit pickers from outside the EU. Instead of having to obtain work permits, such foreign 'volunteers' are issued with Entrance Authorisation

Cards which satisfy Immigration Control, provided they are used only for working on the issuing farm camp. Farm camps are international affairs, with workers mainly from eastern European countries. This scheme has attracted some bad publicity lately, though, and not all operators may be reputable. Some charge a fee for 'English lessons'. The amount of money you can earn depends on how fast you pick!

The main recruitment organisations are *Concordia,* Heversham House, 20/22 Boundary Road, Hove, East Sussex BN3 4ET, which recruits pickers for over 150 camps between May and October; and *Harvesting Opportunity Permit Scheme (GB),* YFC Centre, NAC, Stoneleigh Park, Kenilworth, Warwickshire CV8 2LG, which finds work on farms between May and November for 4-13 weeks. It is also possible to contact farms directly, although they may ask you to go through Concordia or HOPS. The following are some of the Home Office recognised farms:

Gagie House, by Dundee, Angus DD4 0PR, Scotland
Fridaybridge Agricultural Camp, March Road, Wisbech, Cambridgeshire
Hickman & Co. Ltd., Leverington, Wisbech, Cambridgeshire PE13 5DR
R. & J.M. Place, Church Farm, Tunstead, Norwich, Norfolk NR12 8RQ
International Farm Camp, Hall Road, Tiptree, Colchester, Essex CO5 0QS
Lentran Fruit Farms (Lentran, Inverness-shire), c/o Perimeter Farms Ltd., Yeld
   Lane, Kelsall, Cheshire CW6 0JD
Leroch Farm Camp, Alyth, Blairgowrie, Perthshire PH11 8NZ.

The Australian-linked temping agency *Bligh* (131-135 Earls Court Road, London SW5) has an agricultural section which places people on farms throughout Britain, as well as operating placement services for nannies, secretaries, etc.

**Au Pairs and Nannies**
Strictly speaking, North Americans and Australasians cannot be au pairs in the UK, since they do not need to learn English. Nevertheless, there are a few organisations which will arrange au pair or mother's help positions in the UK for English-speakers (see below). It should be noted that the UK only recognised the existence of male au pairs in 1992, and there may still be problems at the port of entry.

*Au Pair/Homestay Abroad,* 1015 15th Street NW, Washington DC 20005 — arranges au pair positions for full-time US students aged 18-26, which may last from 6 to 12 months. The programme fee of $1,200-$1,400 does not include travel or passport fees. Further information can be found under *Au Pair/Homestay Abroad* in the chapter *Au Pair and Domestic.*

*Australian Au Pair Connection,* 404 Glenferrie Road, Kooyong, 3144 Victoria, Australia — can place nannies, au pairs, mother's helps and housekeepers in the UK for six months or more. Summer placements are also possible.

**Tourism**
It has been estimated that one worker in ten is involved in this industry; and there is always some demand for staff such as waiters, dishwashers, chambermaids, barmen/maids, etc. In some cases, employers are willing to hire foreigners 'off the books'. Wages in the hotels and catering industry are often low. Board and lodging may be included in the terms of employment.

If you are applying from abroad, it is advisable to send a detailed CV and photo to the hotel of your choice several months in advance. Addresses can be found in the Vacation Work publication *Summer Jobs in Britain* or by asking for lists of hotels from British Tourist Boards abroad (see above). If you are in London, contact the *Jobcentre,* 3 Denmark Street, London WC2, which deals exclusively with hotel and catering staff, or specialised private employment agencies (see *TNT Magazine* or the Yellow Pages).

**Voluntary Work**
Foreign visitors may be surprised to learn that there is widespread poverty and deprivation in the UK, in particular in the inner cities. There is both a need for voluntary workers, and a ready supply of local volunteers, so it is advisable to make arrangements in advance. Some names of organisations which accept North American citizens are given below:

*AFS Intercultural Programs, 313 East 43rd Street, New York, NY 10017,* runs a summer programme combining home stays and conservation camps.

*American Youth Hostels,* PO Box 36713, Washington DC 20013-7613, can supply information on possible employment in British Youth Hostels during the Easter to October season; unpaid voluntary positions are available for up to three weeks, or longer-term posts which pay pocket money, as well as offering board and lodging.

*Community Service Volunteers,* 237 Pentonville Road, London N1 9NJ, runs an overseas programme in which foreign volunteers aged 18-35 are placed in projects with disabled people. During the 10-16 week long projects, food, accommodation, pocket money and travel expenses from the point of entry are paid.

*Winant Clayton Volunteers,* 109 East 50th Street, New York, NY 10022, will place US citizens wishing to spend 6-10 weeks of the summer volunteering their time to work in youth clubs, camps, homes for the elderly, etc. Contact them before the end of January.

**Working Exchanges**
As the UK is a member of most international work exchange organisations, there is a good likelihood of finding a placement here. Organisations to contact include *IAESTE* and *AIESEC*; see *Working Exchanges* (in *Getting The Job*) and *Agriculture, Conservation and Forestry* for further information.

*Future Farmers of America* runs a *Work Experience Program* in the UK for young agriculturalists (19-24) with a strong background in production agriculture. Placements last from 3-12 months; the programme fee is a minimum of $2,400.

**Working Holidays**
US students can work in the UK for up to six months at any time of the year, through the *Work in Britain* programme, run by *CIEE*, Work Abroad, 205 East 42nd St., New York, NY 10017. The co-operating organisation in the UK, *BUNAC*, 16 Bowling Green Lane, London EC1R 0BD, provides orientation and information about where to look for work. A similar programme for Canadian students is run by *Student Work Abroad Program (SWAP),* 243 College Street, 5th Floor, Toronto, Ontario M5T 2Y1. Canadians may also come to Britain as Working Holiday Makers (see below) in which case they do not benefit from the services of BUNAC.

Some Commonwealth citizens between the ages of 17 and 27 with no dependants can come to the United Kingdom as a 'Working Holiday Maker' to take up employment. As such they can work full-time for a part of their stay or part-time for the whole length of their stay. Before leaving their home country they may apply to the British Embassy for an entry certificate which takes the form of an endorsement in their passport. The total period which can be spent in the UK as a working holiday maker is two years, whether aggregated or in one continuous spell. It is also possible to obtain working holiday status at the port of entry, providing you can show a letter offering employment or sufficient funds for maintenance, and a return ticket. This will normally be for one year in the first instance.

## LIST OF AMERICAN COMPANIES
with branches, affiliates or subsidiaries in the United Kingdom

The *American Chamber of Commerce (UK)* publishes the *Anglo-American Trade Directory* which contains the names of 20,000 companies with trans-Atlantic links.

# Central & Eastern Europe

The 1990s have seen a major realignment in the map of Europe. No longer is there a simple division between East and West. Countries such as Poland, the Czech and Slovak Republics, and Hungary see themselves as Central European. The three Baltic States to the north are keen to identify themselves with the 'West'. The former Yugoslavian countries, Serbia and Montenegro, Croatia, Bosnia-Herzegovina and F.Y.R. Macedonia, along with Albania, see themselves as belonging to the South-East. Slovenia has close historic ties with Austria and Italy. There are states which come more directly under Russian influence, like Belarus and Ukraine (although the latter also has some real independence from Russia). The Russian Federation itself stretches far into Central Asia, and to the Pacific coast.

The former Soviet Union was an artificial state; and its disappearance has seen the rise of competing nationalisms (not least in Russia itself). These tensions are expressed less acutely in the Central European countries which have moved more easily to a market economy; and aspire to membership of the European Union in the near future. The history of Eastern Europe is a story of shifting borders. Each state has its own minority communities (like the Russians of the Trans-Dneister Republic, who seceded from Moldova, which seceded in its turn from the part of former Soviet Union which is now Ukraine). Some of these divisions will not last. Others are more stable. Poland, for example, has its postwar borders which are much further to the west than the historic Polish state, but has no claims on its lost teritories in Lithuania, Belarus or Ukraine. There is a desire in these countries simply for economic (and social) development; and to avoid the conflicts which could arise between the patchwork of ethnic communities and nationalisms left behind by the collapse of the Soviet Union, and of Yugoslavia. In Russia itself, economic reform and reconstruction is a greater priority than nationalism, although there is a kind of nostalgia for communism, and the influence which the Soviet Union and its Tsarist forerunner used to wield in neighbouring countries. There are Russian minorities, too, in many of these countries in Eastern Europe and Central Asia. Russia is still the most influential country in the region.

So far as democracy and economic development are concerned, there is also a gradation from east to west (as there is in the kinds of nationalism which are expressed). Poland, the Czech Republic, Hungary, and Slovenia have developed closer economic ties with the European Union; Croatia and the Baltic States are not far behind. Prosperity has come to Russia itself, at least to certain sections of the population, although democracy is not so firmly established. Less successful have been the Slovak Republic, Serbia, F.Y.R. Macedonia, Bulgaria, and Romania. Ukraine and Belarus are relatively poor and underdeveloped, as are the countries of Central Asia — Kazakhstan, Turkmenistan, Kyrgyzstan and Tajikistan. Along with Uzbekistan, Armenia and Georgia, south of the Caucasus Mountains, they have found the transition from the centralised Soviet system to a diverse market economy most difficult (although there are substantial natural resources, like minerals and oil in many of these).

It should be emphasised that they now all regard themselves as independent and sovereign states. This process of economic development and reconstruction is the background against which work in these countries should be seen. There are many new opportunities for international workers — in everything from consultancy to volunteer work — and also a challenge: to live in a country whose history and way of life are often very different from the experience of most western Europeans or North Americans. Again, there is an alignment from west to east: the countries of central Europe are those where there is the broadest range of job opportunities; and a less pronounced economic and cultural difference.

From the point of view of those interested in working there, these countries have certain features in common. Expatriate workers can be roughly divided into those who are sent by large companies, and are paid at international rates; and those who work for local organisations, and are paid at the local rate. There are some areas of work — such as English teaching — which fall between these two categories. Many are volunteers; some will even pay for this privilege.

Others do valuable work in training and consultancy, in helping to put the local economy back on its feet; or looking after the casualties of social change, the poor and underprivileged, where provision is often inadequate. The growth in future will be in the 'middle' range of jobs, teaching, secretarial, retail, technical, and managerial positions, as these economies develop.

In the wider jobs market, the main area is infrastructure: roads, railways, airports; telecommunications; financial services; and administration. Manufacturing industry and distribution are being developed, often in collaboration with foreign companies, as are service industries like food distribution and retailing. There are opportunities in oil, mining, gas, and engineering, airlines and road transport, and all the other areas where there are partnerships between 'western' and local firms.

Challenging conditions (where accommodation is often cramped, and bureaucracy a major problem) mean that volunteers, as well as other workers, will often be of a more adventurous nature. Experts are needed in consultancy and development who should have real experience and understanding of their field, as well as the right qualifications. There are openings, too, for those who are more entrepreneurial; who know how to make new contacts and develop new ideas; and who can start a business and make it grow.

These countries of Central and Eastern Europe — and the territory covered by the Commonwealth of Independent States (CIS), which replaced the Soviet Union, and has now been succeeded by the Russian Federation — are all open for business; and open to a wide variety of international jobseekers. Preparation, perseverance, and practical knowledge, will all be required.

### Immigration
The procedures for immigration and visas may be subject to change; you are advised to check with the embassy concerned. There may be restrictions on the import and export of local and international currency; and the embassy or consulate will advise on procedures for this. Companies which offer a visa service and travel and trade services in the region are: *Overseas Business Travel Ltd.*, 8 Minories, London EC3N 1BJ, tel 0171-702 2468, fax 0171-488 1199; and *Rossia Consultants Ltd.*, tel/fax 0181-340 4131.

### Language
English is often spoken in the business community, and by young people; but some knowledge of the local language will be an asset. A rival to English as a second language is German; French can sometimes be used. Russian is universally spoken in the countries of the former Soviet Union or CIS; and is widely spoken elsewhere, although it is no longer generally taught in Central and Eastern Europe or the Baltic States.

### Newspapers
Agencies in the UK which represent a wide variety of newspapers and other publications are: *Frank L. Crane Ltd.*, 5-15 Cromer Street, Grays Inn Road, London WC1H 8LS, tel 0171-837 3330; *Mercury Publicity,* 16 John Street,

London WC1N 2DL, tel 0171-831 6631; and *Powers International,* 515-523 Fulham Road, London SW6 1HD, tel 0171-385 8855. There are English-language publications like *The Warsaw Voice* and *The Budapest Sun* in many countries, aimed at the local business and expatriate communities. *New Markets Monthly* — for 'traders and investors in the newly emerging markets of Eastern Europe and Asia' — is a source of news about UK and US companies investing in the region, with special reports on particular countries: *NMM,* Paper Mews Place, 290 High Street, Dorking, Surrey RH4 1QT. A subscription is currently £55 within the UK; and $160 overseas.

**Other Contacts**
Other contacts may be found in the *Voluntary Work, Teaching,* and other chapters of the *Specific Careers* section. The Commercial Department of your embassy in that country, or embassies and tourist offices in your own, are useful sources of up-to-date information. The *East European Trade Council,* Suite 10, Westminster Palace Gardens, Artillery Row, London SW1P 1RL, tel 0171-222 7622 is an advisory group attached to the Department of Trade and Industry promoting trade opportunities and offering business advice with an extensive library on eastern Europe.

# The Baltic States

The three Baltic republics — Estonia, Latvia and Lithuania — are situated between Russia and the Baltic Sea. Their recent history was marked by Russian occupation in the 19th century; and again in 1944. Each is now keen to assert its own national identity. They are culturally very different; although each one has a Russian minority population; and lives still in the shadow of its larger neighbour. They are also looking to a 'European' future; and aspire to membership of the European Union.

These are, in a sense, the most European of the states formerly belonging to the Soviet Union. Russian is spoken by all except the very young; but the locals prefer to speak English or German to foreigners. The Estonian language belongs, like Finnish, to the Finno-Ugric family of languages (and has even more case endings: 14). Latvian and Lithuanian belong to the Baltic group, and stand in some relation to the Slavonic and Germanic families. Language is a political issue, and is seen as an expression of national identity. Many Russian settlers are now having to master the local tongue to find employment or get a work permit.

Other cultural influences have been Danish, Swedish, Polish, and especially Hanseatic German: the architecture in the coastal towns can be reminiscent of Germany or Holland. The Baltic States are similar in their weather, too, with a mix of continental and maritime climates, and prevailing westerly winds.

There are religious as well as cultural and linguistic differences between them too. Estonia and Latvia are predominately Lutheran, whereas Lithuania is mainly Roman Catholic. There are also many Protestant, Russian Orthodox and Evangelical Reform churches, as well as a number of synagogues.

See *Estonia, Latvia* and *Lithuania* below.

# Bulgaria

**Bulgarian Embassy, 186-188 Queen's Gate, London SW7 5HL, tel 0171-584 9400/9433**
**Bulgarian Embassy, 1621 22nd Street, NW, Washington, DC 20008, tel 202-387-7969**

**Currency: 1 Lev (BGL) = 100 stotinki**
**Exchange Rate: £1 = BGL 330; $1 = BGL 210**

Bulgaria is located on the Black Sea Coast, between Romania to the north and Greece and Turkey to the South. Serbia and F.Y.R. Macedonia are its western neighbours. The population is 8,500,000 in an area of 43,000 square miles. The capital Sofia in the west has 1,200,000 inhabitants. The Balkan and the Rhodope Mountains stretch across the country to the Black Sea coast with its sandy beaches; the climate is never extreme, with warm summers, and snow on the mountains in winter. The economy is traditionally agricultural; and Bulgaria is famous for its exported wine. Food-processing and packaging are important; there are heavy industries like engineering as well as newer ones like biotechnology. But the transition to a market economy has been slow. There is high inflation; and increasingly high unemployment.

Handshaking is the common form of greeting; and as in much of the region small gifts from one's own country are appreciated. There is one social convention which may nor come so easily. In Bulgaria, nodding your head means 'no' and shaking your head means 'yes'.

**Immigration**
British and North America passport holders require a visa to enter Bulgaria, which authorised travel agents like *Balkantourist,* Boulevard Vitosha 1, 1040 Sofia, tel 2-43-331, can arrange; or these may be obtained at the border. A letter of invitation is required. Longer-term residents require a residence and work permit; and those working or looking for work in Bulgaria should register at the local police station. Enquiries about work and residence permits should be made to a Bulgarian consulate or embassy abroad.

**Embassies**
British Embassy, Boulevard Vassil Levski 65-67, Sofia 1000; tel 2-885-361-2 or 885-325.
US Embassy, Saborna Street 1, Unit 1335, Sofia; tel 2-884-801.

**Tourist Offices**
Balkan Holidays, Sofia House, 19 Conduit Street, London W1R 9TD; tel 0171-491 4499.
Balkan Holidays (USA) Ltd., Suite 508, 41 East 42nd Street, New York, NY 10017; tel 212-573-5530.

## SPECIFIC CONTACTS

The Bulgaria Desk of the *Department of Trade and Industry*, Bay 756, Kingsgate House, 66-74 Victoria Street, London SW1H, can provide an information pack (for commercial or business purposes) which contains a list of UK companies with Bulgarian links. The *British-Bulgarian Chamber of Commerce* is at the Embassy address in London (above), tel 0171-584 8333. *The Bulgarian Chamber of Commerce and Industry,* Suborna Street 11A, 1040 Sofia, tel 2-872-631 can provide commercial advice and information.

**Teaching**
The *Central Bureau* (see *Teaching* chapter) recruits a number of teachers for foreign language secondary schools in Bulgaria in a programme run by the Bulgarian Ministry of Science, Education, and Technology.

**Tourism**
*Crystal Holidays,* Crystal House, The Courtyard, Arlington Road, Surbiton, Surrey KT6 6BW, tel 0181-241 5111 — requires a small number of representatives for skiing holidays in Borovets and Pamperova. Previous experience and

fluent Bulgarian are desirable. For voluntary work contacts see this chapter in *Specific Careers*.

# Czech Republic

**Czech Embassy, 26-30 Kensington Palace Gardens, London W8 4QY, tel 0171-243 1115**
**Czech Embassy, 3900 Spring of Freedon Street, NW, Washington DC 20008, tel 202-363-6315-6**
**Currency: 1 Koruna (Kc) = 100 hellers**
**Exchange Rate: £1 = Kcs 43; $1 = Kcs 27**

The Czech Republic covers 31,000 square miles. The population is 10,300,000, and there are German, Slovak, Hungarian, Ukrainian and Polish minorities. Bohemia in the west is mountainous; and there are hills and a rich agricultural plain in Moravia in the east. One third of its territory is covered with forests, which are popular places for hiking or climbing. South Bohemia is picturesque, with castles and palaces, and medieval towns. The climate is colder in winter and warmer in summer than in Britain, the average in January being 0°C and in July 20°C. Prague, the capital, is a historic city on the banks of the River Vltava; and other major towns are Brno, Ostrava, and Plzen. The official language is Czech; but German and English are also spoken.

The Republic of Czechoslovakia was declared in October 1918, made up of the former Austro-Hungarian possessions of Bohemia, Moravia and Slovakia. In 1938 the country was taken over by Nazi Germany following the Munich Agreement. After World War II, the communists seized power and remained in power up until the bloodless 'Velvet Revolution' of November 1989. In 1992 it was decided that the country would split into independent Czech and Slovak Republics.

Czechoslovakia had one of the healthiest economies in the former Warsaw Pact; production fell and inflation rose from 1991 onwards, but there has been a return to prosperity and stability in the new Czech Rupublic, which is less hampered by a dependence on heavy engineering than its Slovak neighbour. Unemployment is very low by international standards, around 3% at the time of writing. Germany is now its main trading partner.

For those who wish to look for work in the Czech Republic, there are opportunities in English teaching and voluntary work. Workers who are posted there from abroad include lawyers, bankers, economists, diplomats and journalists (see relevant chapters).

**Immigration**
British and US passport holders do not require a visa to enter the Czech Republic and may remain for up to 30 days before they need to apply for a residence permit. Work permits are arranged by the employer at local Employment Offices, and a photocopy of your passport and qualifications/diplomas are required. Long-term Czech residence applications must include this permit and should be made to the Czech Embassy abroad. Those working or looking for work in the Czech Republic must register within three local days at the local police station, where they may obtain an Identity Card for Foreigners. Enquiries about work and residence permits should be made to a Czech consulate or embassy abroad.

**Embassies**
British Embassy, Thunovská 14, 125 50 Prague; tel 2-24 51 04 39.
US Embassy, Trziste 15, 125 48 Prague; tel 2-24 51 08 47.

**Tourist Offices**
Czech Tourist Centre, 78 Finchley Road, London NW3 6BP.

Czech Centre, 95 Great Portland Street, London W1; tel 0171-243 7981-2.
Czech Centre, 1109-1111 Madison Avenue, New York, NY 10028.

## SPECIFIC CONTACTS

**Teaching**
The English-language teaching industry is booming in the Czech Republic, with many private schools; there is also some demand for teachers in other subjects, from primary school level up to universities and other institutions of higher education. Salaries here are usually only adequate to cover local living expenses; but it is usually possible to teach private classes. Free accommodation and medical insurance are sometimes provided. The following organisations can be contacted for work (and see under 'Jazykové Školy' in the telephone directory):

The *Academic Information Agency (AIA)*, Dům zahraničnich styků, MŠMT ČR, Senovážné Náměstì 26, 111 21 Prague 1, tel 2-24 22 96 98 — recruits qualified staff for primary and secondary schools. Applicants are sent a questionnaire which is then circulated among schools who contact teachers directly when they are needed. Qualifications are necessary. Contracts are usually for one year; and include free accommodation.

*Angličtina Expres,* Vodičkova 39, Pasaz Svetozor, (Galerie), Praha 1, 110 00, tel 2-26 15 26 — was the first private language school to be licensed, in 1990. Requires teachers for classes in Prague, Brno, Jabonlec, Liberec, Hradec, Kralove, Olomouc, Sokolov and Ostrava. Caters for all levels of students, in particular business English.

*The International Placement Group,* Jezkova 9, 130 00 Prague 3 (London office: 72 Bond Street, London W1Y 9DD) — recruits EFL teachers to work in Central and Eastern European cities including Prague, Brno, Bratislava, and Warsaw; and offers competitive pay-scales and assistance with accommodation.

**Voluntary Work**
There is a great demand for voluntary workers, particularly for environmental projects. Prospective volunteers should take note of the escalating cost of living when considering their allowance. Free accommodation is a minimum requirement. Below are some of the organisations who send volunteers to the Czech Republic:

*Education for Democracy USA,* PO Box 40514, Mobile, Alabama 36640-0514; and *Education for Democracy UK,* 3 Arnellan House, 144-146 Slough Lane, London NW9 8XJ — aim to provide primary and supplementary conversational English teaching. Volunteers are asked to supply their own instruction materials.

*INEX* Senovázné námestì 24, 116 47 Prague, tel 2-24 10 23 90 — needs volunteers to take part in international workcamps contributing to the environment and historical conservation in July and August. Volunteers pay for their own travel and insurance.

For other organisations arranging voluntary work see the *Voluntary Work* chapter.

**Other Contacts**
The Commercial Department of the British Embassy, Prague, has prepared a list of *British Companies in the Czech Republic* which can be obtained from the Embassy address above. The *Czech Chamber of Commerce and Industry* is at: Argentinská 38, 170 05 Prague 7; tel 2-66 79 48 80; fax 2-87 53 48.

# Estonia

**Estonian Embassy, 16 Hyde Park Gate, London SW7 5DG, tel 0171-589 3428**
**Estonian Embassy, 2131 Massachussets Avenue, NW, Washington DC, tel 202-588-0101**
**Currency: 1 Kroon (EEK) = 100 sents**
**Exchange Rate: £1 = 19 kroons; $1 = 12 kroons**

Estonia is the most northerly of the Baltic States, with linguistic and cultural ties to Finland, its neighbour to the north. The population is 1.5 million, and nearly a third of these live in the capital Tallinn. Other big towns are Pärnu, Tartu and Narva, which straddles the border with Russia. It covers 17,600 square miles. The landscape is not unlike that of Finland, with forests, lakes and islands. There are few raw materials; and it relies mostly on imported commodities to produce finished goods. Agriculture and increasingly tourism are important. Privatisation was quite a rapid process in Estonia; and the cost of living is high. The currency is tied in value to the Deutschmark.

### Immigration
A work and residence permit are needed; but visas are not required by UK and US citizens to enter the country. These permits may be applied for in advance, or on arrival to the Department of Citizenship and Immigration (*Kodakonsus ja Migratsiooniamet*), Lai 38-40, 0101 Tallinn; tel 2-664-333. Documents needed include an invitation to live in Estonia from a private individual or organisation; proof of income or funds; and the completed application form; as well as your written contract or work agreement.

### Embassies
British Embassy, Kentmanni 20, 0100 Tallinn 0100; tel 3726-313-353 or 313-461-2.
US Embassy, Kentmanni 20, 0001 Tallinn; tel 2-312-021 or 2-312-024.

## SPECIFIC CONTACTS

For managers and businesses the immediate opportunities are in retail and the re-equipment and management assistance for the core Estonian industries of wood and textiles. *The Chamber of Commerce and Industry in Estonia,* Toom-Kooli Street 17, 0001 Tallinn, tel 2-444-929, can supply information about businesses operating in Estonia.

### Teaching
There are many new private language schools springing up. The Estonian Embassy has details of these; and the *Teachers' Training Centre* which is a part of the Ministry of Culture and Education offer posts in secondary schools in collaboration with local State School Boards.

# Hungary

**Hungarian Embassy (Consular Section), 35 Eaton Place, London SW1X 8BY, tel 0171-235 4048**
**Hungarian Embassy, 3910 Shoemaker St, NW, Washington DC 20008, tel 202-362-6730**
**Currency: 1 Forint (Ft) = 100 fillér**
**Exchange rate: £1 = Ft 243; $1 = Ft 155**

Hungary occupies an area of 36,000 square miles. The population of 10,245,000 is largely made up of Hungarian-speaking Magyars (92%) with small German and Gypsy minorities. The language belongs, like Finnish, to the Finno-Ugric family. German is also widely spoken. Most of the country is flat; there are several ranges of hills, chiefly in the north and west; and the country forms part of the catchment area of the River Danube on whose banks the capital Budapest is situated. Budapest has 1,930,000 inhabitants. Other cities are Győr, Pécs, Szeged, Debrecen and Miskolc. Summers can be very hot, with the temperature frequently reaching 30°C, while during winter the average is around 0°C.

Hungary's recent history is not dissimilar to that of most of Eastern Europe — domination by the Soviet Union, followed by democratic reforms in 1989. The last Soviet troops left Hungary in June 1991. A striking feature of the Hungarian economy was the early adoption in 1968 of some free market reforms, which provided much of the inspiration for change in other Warsaw Pact countries. Integration with the world economy has gone further than in some of its neighbours; foreign investment is high. It is a member of the Organisation for Economic Cooperation and Development (OECD); and has already adopted many European Union regulations in preparation for entry into the EU. Agriculture is still a major activity, accounting for 6% of Gross Domestic Product (GDP); and food products are currently 20% of exports. Industrial production started to grow again in 1992, following a severe contraction in 1989-1991. Inflation has been brought under control; and Hungary is part of the Deutschmark zone, so prices are often expressed in this currency. Opportunities are in English teaching; and in construction and investment projects, as well as for experts in industrial restructuring and finance. Pharmaceuticals, computers, telecommunications and mining are important industries.

**Immigration**
British and EU citizens do not require a visa to enter Hungary; and may remain generally for 90 days (for UK citizens this is six months). Work and residence permits should be arranged in advance by the Hungarian employer with the local authorities in Hungary. Foreigners wishing to stay for more than a year must obtain a residence permit from the police force in the town of residence within six months. In the case of Budapest this is: *BRFK Igazgatásrendészeti Főosztály Külföldieket Ellenőrző Osztály*, 6th District Varosligeti fasor. Addresses must be registered within 30 days of arrival. The form requesting a residence permit, two passport photos, a letter from the employer (in Hungarian) and medical certificate will be required. Another form needs to be completed in duplicate to register your address, including the signature of the landlord/landlady, a copy of the contract and details of rent paid. Certain high-level teachers and researchers, as well as executives and technical consultants sent to perform essential work for foreign companies with subsidiaries in Hungary, are exempted from work permit requirements.

**Newspapers**
*Powers International* can place advertisements in the national dailies *Magyar Hirlap* and *Nepszabadsag* (see above).

**Embassies**
British Embassy, Harmincad Utca 6, 1051 Budapest; tel 1-266-2888 or 1-226-1430.
US Embassy, Unit 1320, Szabadság tér 12, 1054 Budapest; tel 1-112-6450.

**Tourist Offices**
Hungarian Tourist Board, PO Box 4336, London SW18 4XE; tel/fax 0181-871 4009.
Hungarian Tourist Board, 150 East 58th Street, New York, NY 10155; tel 212-586-5230.

## SPECIFIC CONTACTS

There is a great demand for English teachers and voluntary workers; other types of work are mostly available to those who are posted to Hungary by international companies or organisations. Some knowledge of German, or making an effort to learn some Hungarian before starting work, will make life considerably easier on arrival.

### Teaching

Most people who go to teach English in Hungary report that students are eager to learn; and find it an excellent place to work. This is not always well-paid, however, and you should bear in mind that the cost of living is high, with rents in Budapest approaching those of London. Teaching posts can be found through the following organisations:

*Bell Language School,* Városmajor Secondary School, Budapest XII, Vársomajor u. 71, tel 1-212-4190 — recruits British teachers with a degree, Cambridge/RSA Certificates or Diplomas and several years' teaching experience. Contracts can range from a few weeks to several years depending on requirements. Enquiries can be made to the *Bell Educational Trust,* 1 Red Cross Lane, Cambridge CB2 2QX, or to Hungary.

*English Teachers' Association of Hungary,* Dózsa György út 104.II.15, 1068 Budapest, tel 1-132-8688 — will try to put prospective teachers in contact with primary and secondary schools. A TEFL qualification is desirable. Contracts last for at least one school year.

*International House Language School,* Bimbó út. 7, 1022 Budapest — employs 40 language instructors. Contracts are usually for one year. Minimum qualification: Cambridge/RSA Certificate. (grade B). Enquiries must be made to the London office in the first place (see *Teaching* chapter).

*Lingvarium Bt,* Frankel Leó út 114, Budapest II; tel 1-115-2123.

In addition, Hungarian embassies can provide useful information on job prospects and work permits for language teachers in Hungary.

### Voluntary Work

*Biokultúra Egyesület (The Hungarian Association of Organic Growers),* Rezeda u. 2, 1024 Budapest, tel/fax 1-285-2723 or 285-6540 — is a non-profit organisation founded as a club in 1983, which seeks to promote sustainable forms of agriculture and ecological awareness. Volunteers are required for work on organic farms for up to six months, and on placements of 1-2 weeks between April and October, in exchange for food and lodging, with free time included and the opportunity to learn about organic farming methods. No previous experience is required, only an interest in the association's objectives. Applications must speak German or English.

For other organisations arranging voluntary work see the *Voluntary Work* chapter for further details

# Latvia

Latvian Embassy, 45 Nottingham Place, London 1M 3FE, tel 0171-312 0040
Latvian Embassy, 4325 17th Street, NW, 20011 Washington DC, tel 202-726-8213-4
Currency: 1 Lat (LVL) = 100 santims
Exchange rate: £1 = Ls 0.8; $1 = Ls 0.5

Latvia covers 25,000 square miles and has a population totalling 2.6 million. It borders Estonia in the north, Lithuania in the south, the Russian Federation to the east, and Belarus to the south-east. The capital is Riga, with 850,000 inhabitants. Other towns are Liepaja, Daugavpils, Rezekne, Valmiera, Jurmala and Jelgava. The coastal plain is flat, but inland the landscape is hilly with forests, lakes and rivers. Pollution is a problem along the Baltic coast, but there are also wildlife areas. Key industries include the manufacture of railway rolling stock and light machinery, fertilisers, chemicals, and electronics. At present, more than 100 joint ventures have been established between Latvian and UK companies. Salaries are low: on average £120 a month.

**Immigration**
UK and US passport holders do not require a visa to visit the country. Residence and work payments may be arranged in the country; or before departure. For further information contact the Ministry of Welfare, Department of Employment, K. Valdemara iela 38, Riga.

**Embassies**
British Embassy, Alunana iela 5, 1010 Riga; tel 733-8126.
US Embassy, Raina bulvaris 7, 1050 Riga; tel 721-0005.

**Tourist Office**
National Tourist Board of Latvia, Pils Laukums 4, Riga 1050; tel 722-9945.

## SPECIFIC CONTACTS

The *Latvian Development Agency,* 2 Perses Street, Riga 1442, tel 728-3425, has published a report on *Development Potential* which summarises areas where Latvia needs inward investment. The *British-Latvian Chamber of Commerce,* Marlborough House, 68 High Street, Weybridge KT13 8BL, tel 01932-831150, has a database of contacts within Latvia and works closely with the Latvian Development Agency. Business information is available from *Latvian Chamber of Commerce,* Brivibas bulvaris 21, Riga 1442; tel 728-3424.

**Voluntary Work**
*International Exchange Centre,* 2 Republic Square, Riga 1010, tel 2-327-476 — requires camp counsellors for summer camps in Latvia and Lithuania from June to August. Accommodation and a small allowance is provided. The refundable registration fee is $50.
*Joint-Stock Company Minta,* Perkuno al. 4. 3000 Kaunas, tel 3707-202-560 — recruits volunteers for international work camps; also teachers paid 'by arrangement' for summer camps; and English-speaking au pairs.

# Lithuania

**Lithuanian Embassy, 84 Gloucester Place, London W1H 3HN, tel 0171-486 6401**
**Lithuanian Embassy, 2622 16th Street, NW, 20009 Washington DC, tel 202-234-5680 or 234-2639**
**Currency: 1 Litas 100 = centas**
**Exchange rate: £1 = 6.2 Litas; $1 = 4 Litas**

Lithuania is the largest of the Baltic States, with a population of 3.7 million. 600,000 live in Vilnius, the capital. Other cities are Klaipeda, Palanga and Kaunas. It borders on Latvia the north, Poland and the Russian enclave of Kaliningrad in the south-west, and Belarus to the south-east. There is a landscape of plains and low hills with over 2,800 lakes, most of which are in the east.

There is a great dependence on agriculture; the food industry is dominated by the production of milk, meat and fish. Textiles and knitwear, electrical, electronic, and optical goods are also produced; there is light rather than heavy industry; and the economy relies heavily on imported raw materials.

Other than the Russian Federation and Ukraine, Germany is its main trading partner. Lithuanian has many dialects; German and also Polish are spoken; English is used for international commerce and by those who work in tourism.

**Immigration**
UK and US passport holders do not require a visa to visit for up to 90 days.

**Embassies**
British Embassy, PO Box 863, Antakalnio 2, 2055 Vilnius; tel 2-222-070.
US Embassy, Akmenu 6, 2600, Vilnius; tel 2-223-031.

**Tourist Office**
Lithuanian State Tourism Department, Gedimino pr. 30/1, 2695 Vilnius; tel 2-226-706.

## SPECIFIC CONTACTS

The privatisation of industry has resulting in opportunities in re-equipping and management consultancy. The *Lithuanian Investment Agency* can supply information on privatisation: Sv. Jono St. 3, 2001 Vilnius, tel 2-624-671. The *Association of Lithuanian Chambers of Commerce and Industry,* Kudirkos 18, 2600 Vilnius, tel 2-222-630, can supply information on foreign companies investing in Lithuania.

**Teaching**
The British Council in Vilnius advises that information concerning the employment of English language teachers is provided by Mrs. A. Svilpiene, Ministry of Science and Education, A. Volano str. 2/7, 2691 Vilnius, tel 2-617-649.

**Voluntary Work**
*International Exchange Centre* — see *Latvia.*
*Joint-Stock Company Minta* — see *Latvia.*

# Poland

**Polish Embassy, 47 Portland Place, London W1N 3AG, tel 0171-580-4324 or 0171-580-4329**
**Polish Embassy, 2640 16th St, NW, Washington DC 20009, tel 202-234-3800-2**
**Currency: Zloty (Zl) = 100 groszy**
**Exchange Rate: £1 = Zl 4.4; $1 = Zl 2.8**

Poland occupies an area of 780,000 square miles, equivalent to about 87.5% of that of Germany. Thirty-five per cent of the population of 38,418,000 lives in the countryside. There are lakes and islands in Mazuria, forests to the east and along the border with Belarus; and the River Vistula flows through the centre of the country to the Baltic Coast in the north. The climate can be termed continental, with a long winter (when average temperatures are usually below 0°C) and a mild summer when the average is 18°C or more. Poland's borders have shifted westwards in the course of its history; and the capital Warsaw (with an estimated 1,700,000 residents) is now in the east; with the greatest economic growth taking place in the west, and along the German border. Kraków in the south is the historic and cultural capital of the country; and is a destination for international tourists. The nearby Tatra Mountains (part of the Carpathian Arc) are popular with hikers and skiers. Basketball and soccer are other popular sports, as are fishing, horse-racing and boating. Other cities are Szczecin, Poznań, Wrocław, Katowice, Łódź, Lublin, and Gdańsk. The religion is 95% Roman Catholic, with Orthodox, Jewish, and Muslim minorities.

English is the most commonly taught second language. German, French, and Russian are also spoken; some knowledge of Polish will be useful for those staying for a longer time in the country. Poland is a relaxed and easy-going place to be. Dress should be smart in the workplace, although it may be more informal outside. A short lunchbreak is common. Historical ties between Poland and Britain and the USA mean that nationals of these countries are made welcome and feel at home. Accommodation, as in other central and eastern European countries, is often cramped, and is getting more expensive.

Historically, Poland has had frequent boundary changes; for a time it was divided between Prussia, Russia, and the Austro-Hungarian Empire. Present-day Poland incorporates part of what was Germany; and has lost territory in Belarus, Ukraine, and Lithuania (with which for a time it formed one kingdom). Forty-five years of Russian domination came to an end in 1991; in economic and cultural terms Poland now looks to the west. In the 1980s and 90s, it suffered much greater economic disruption than Hungary or the Czech Republic. But industrial production has recovered; foreign investment is high; and many industries have now been privatised. Poland is now on course for membership of the European Union in the near future. The cost of living is also rising.

Agriculture is still of major importance, employing 27% of the labour force in 1989 (although this is likely to change with EU membership). Much of Polish industry still needs to be modernised if it is to have any hope of competing with more 'developed' economies; and the first wave of foreign workers living in the country, as elsewhere in the region, were often businessmen and consultants, developing trade or partnership links between Polish and international companies. Some parts, like Gdańsk and Silesia, are heaviliy industrialised; but Poland also has some largely unspoilt natural landscapes, including the last tract of primeval forest in Europe, the beautiful Białowieza National Park, home to the rare European bison.

### Immigration
British passport holders may enter and remain in Poland for up to six months without a visa. For US passport holders this is 90 days. Applications for work and residence permits should be made from outside the country.

### Newspapers
The English-language newspaper, *The Warsaw Voice,* is represented by *Frank L. Crane Ltd.,* 5/15 Cromer Street, Grays Inn Road, London WC1H 8LS, see above.

### Embassies
British Embassy, Aleja Róz No 1, 00-556 Warsaw; tel 2-628-1001.
US Embassy, Aleje Ujazdowskie 29-31, 00-540 Warsaw; tel 2-628-3041.

### Tourist Offices
Polish National Tourist Office, First Floor, Remo House, 310-312 Regent Street, London W1R 5AJ; tel 0171-5808811.
Polish National Tourist Office, Suite 1711, 275 Madison Avenue, New York, NY, 10016; tel 212-338-9412.

## SPECIFIC CONTACTS

Work opportunities in Poland are similar to those in Hungary and the Czech Republic, with openings for consultants and 'experts', and in English teaching and voluntary work. Speaking Polish and other language skills will be necessary for jobs at other levels, like secretarial work. Pay scales are low; and the cost of living is rising, so these are important factors to be borne in mind. It is advisable to obtain up-to-date information on exchange rates and the cost of living in order to ensure that you are being paid a living wage. Some international companies will pay an additional allowance to their expatriate workers.

**Teaching**
Enthusiasm for learning English — and in life in Britain or the United States — is intense. Demand for English teachers is such that almost anyone who can speak the language will find work. The main limitation is the salary; and appropriate qualifications will be an advantage here. There is also scope for private tuition. Some useful contacts are given below:

*American English School,* Ul. Kryniczna 12-14, Warsaw 03-934, tel 2-617-1112 — is looking for friendly and energetic English-speakers interested in teaching. Experience and qualifications are not prerequisites. A long-term commitment is desired. There are branches in Radom and Wolomin.

*International House,* Szkoła Języka Angielskego Toruń, Legionów 15; tel 25081.

*Poliglota,* ul. Kiełaśnicza 6, Wrocław; tel 343-7879.

*Program-Bell,* ul. Fredry 7, 61-701 Poznań, tel 061-536-972 — requires English teachers and volunteers to teach and organise activities on summer camps.

The Polish Ministry of Education recruits some English-speaking academics to help train teachers of English at foreign language training colleges, and in some elementary and secondary schools. Free accommodation and a basic salary are provided. Copies of diplomas and CV's should be sent to the Deputy Director, Department of Foreign Relations, Al. 1 Armii Wojska Polskiego 25, 00-918 Warsaw, Poland. The *Anglo-Polish Universities Association (APASS),* 93 Victoria Road, Leeds LS6 1DR, tel 0113-275-8121, recruits volunteers and paid teachers. For volunteers clear spoken English, but not necessarily teaching experience, is required.

For other organisations which recruit language teachers, see the *Teaching* chapter. The British Council in Warsaw can provide a list of local language schools.

**Voluntary Work**
For further information on workcamps in Poland, see the *Voluntary Work* chapter.

**Other contacts**
The *Polish Commercial Office,* 15 Devonshire Street, London W1N 2AR, and the *Polish Chamber of Commerce* (Krajowa Izba Gospodarcza), PO Box 361, Trebacka 4, 00-074 Warsaw, tel 22-260-221, can supply information about business and trade in Poland.

# Romania

Romanian Embassy, Arundel House, 4 Palace Green, London W8 4QD, tel 0171-937 9666-8
Romanian Embassy, 1607 23rd Street, NW, Washington, DC 20008, tel 202-332-4848 or 232-4747
Currency: 1 Leu (BGL) = 100 bani
Exchange Rate: £1 = 5000 Lei; $1 = 3200 Lei

Romania lies between the Black Sea in the south-east and Montenegro, Serbia and Hungary in the west, Moldova and Ukraine to the north, and Bulgaria to the south, covering an area of 92,000 square miles. The population is 22,800,000;

and its density is 247 per square mile. It is divided into four parts: mountainous and forested Transylvania and Moldavia in the north, which is separated by the Carpathian Mountains from the flat Danube plain of Wallachia in the south and east; and the Black Sea coast and Danube delta. The capital is Bucharest, with two million inhabitants. Business cards are widely used (as throughout Eastern Europe) and exchanges of presents are important for visitors. Romanian Orthodox is the majority religion, with Roman Catholic, Protestant, Muslim and Jewish minorities. Some Hungarian and German are spoken in the border areas, in addition to Romanian. Agriculture supports a third of the population; oil, natural gas and their products are important in the industrial sector. The state of the economy remains fragile, with high inflation and unemployment. Romania's largest trading partner is Russia.

**Immigration**
British passport holders require a visa to enter; but Americans may stay for up to 30 days without one. Business visa applications should also include the name of the sponsoring Romanian company. Those working or looking for work should register at the local police station; they require a residence and work permit. Enquiries about these should be made to a Bulgarian consulate or embassy abroad.

**Embassies**
British Embassy, Strada Jules Michelet 24, 70154 Bucharest; tel 1-312-035.
US Embassy, Strada Tudor Arghezi 7-9, Bucharest; tel 1-210-0149 or 1-210-4042.

**Tourist Offices**
Romanian National Tourist Office, 83A Marylebone High Street, London W1M 3DE; tel/fax 0171-224 3692.
Romanian National Tourist Office, Suite 210, 342 Madison Avenue, New York, NY 10173; tel 212-697-6971.

## SPECIFIC CONTACTS

The British Embassy in Bucharest publishes a 'Commercial Newsletter' quarterly, with details of UK companies investing in Romania. The *Ministry of Commerce,* Str. Apolodor 17, 70663 Bucharest, tel 1-141-141, or the *Chamber of Commerce and Industry,* Boulevard Nicolae Balcescu 22, 79502 Bucharest, tel 1-615-4703, may also offer advice and commercial information. The Romania Desk of the *Department of Trade and Industry,* Bay 835, Kingsgate House, 66-74 Victoria Street, London SW1H, can provide an information pack for commercial or business purposes; and holds lists of foreign trade organisations and UK business representatives and companies in Romania.

**Tourism**
*Crystal Holidays* (see *Bulgaria*) requires experienced representatives who speak Romanian to meet and look after skiers in Poiana Brasov and Sinaia.

**Voluntary Work**
*Romania Information Centre,* The University, Southampton, Hampshire, holds a register of voluntary work contacts in Romania.

# Russian Federation

Russian Embassy, 13 Kensington Palace Gardens, London W8 4QX, tel 0171-229 3628
Russian Embassy, 2650 Wisconsin Avenue, NW, Washington, DC 20007, tel 202-298-570
Currency: 1 Rouble (Rub) = 100 kopeks
Exchange Rate: £1 = Rub 8470; $1 = Rub 5400

The Russian Federation stretches from its borders with Finland, the Baltic States, Belarus and Ukraine in the west across the Ural mountains and through

Siberia to the port of Vladivostok in the east. It is about twice the size of the United States in land area (nearly seven million square miles) and has a low population density (22 per square mile), especially in Siberia. The capital Moscow has nine million inhabitants. Other major cities are St. Petersburg, Arkhangelsk, Nizhny Novgorod, Volgograd, Vorkuta, Yekaterinburg, Omsk, Novosibirsk, Irkutsk, Yakutsk, Khabarovsk,and Vladivostok. There is a patchwork of different republics which are all regarded as part of Russia: Adygheya; Bashkortostan; Buryatia; Chechnya; Chuvashia; Daghestan; Gorno-Altai; Ingushetia; Kabardino-Balkaria; Kalmykia; Karachayevo-Cherkess; Karelia; Khakassia; Komi; Mari El; Mordovia; Northern Ossetia; Sakha (Yakutia); Tatarstan; Tuva; and Udmurtia. European Russia extends from the North Polar Sea to the Black Sea in the south, and is bordered by the Ural Mountains in the east. Russian is universally spoken, with some English, French and German.

The religion is mainly Russian Orthodox, with Muslim, Buddhist and Jewish minorities. There is a range of natural resources; and rich farming land where private ownership is becoming more common. Oil and gas are major export earners, as well as coal and minerals including gold and diamonds, nickel, copper, and iron ore. The economic situation in Russia has improved; but the infrastructure of road and telephone communications remains poor. There is an extensive rail network, and air-routes which connect the more distant centres. Developing modern distribution and transport networks, and modernising manufacturing and the service industries, are some of the areas where international consultants are being recruited.

Many western companies have developed joint ventures with Russian partners. Business and work relations are often developed through personal contacts and trust; and not in more formal ways. Deficiencies in the legal system mean that investment is often a risk; and there are rules for personal safety which should be followed, as in all the countries of the former Soviet Union, such as keeping expensive valuables out of sight; and not calling too much attention to yourself as a foreigner.

Those arriving in these countries for the first time will need the services of a guide; and professional help from companies such as *Worldmark,* Alliance House, 12 Caxton Street, London SW1H 0QS, tel 0171-799 2307. Knowledge of the Russian language is a great advantage. Public transport — like the famous Moscow metro — is relatively cheap, if crowded. Theatre, concert and variety performances are plentiful; and there is a lively nightlife in Moscow and St. Petersburg. There is also a big difference between life in these cities and the provinces, where the pace of life is slower and there are not so many visitors from abroad.

### Immigration
British and US passport-holders need a visa; and a letter of invitation from a business or other organisation in Russia is required. Those working there should register with the local police; and obtain a residence and work permit. Enquiries should be made to the Russian Embassy. In Britain, the Consular Section is at: 5 Kensington Palace Gardens, London W8 4QS; tel 0171-229 3628.

### Embassies
British Embassy, Sofiyskaya Naberezhnaya 14, Moscow 72; tel 095-956-7200.
British Consulate General, Pl. Proletarskoy Diktatury 5, 193124, St. Petersburg; tel 812-325-6036.
US Embassy, Novinsky Bulvar 19-23, Moscow; tel 095-252-2451-9.
US Consulate general, ul. Furshtatskaya 15, St. Petersburg 191028; tel 812-275-1701 or 812-8504170.

### Tourist Offices
Intourist Travel Ltd., Intourist House, 219 Marsh Wall, Meridian gate II, Isle of Dogs, London E14 9PD; tel 0171-538 8600.

Intourist, Suite 603, 610 Fifth Avenue, New York, NY 10020; tel 212-757-3884.

## SPECIFIC CONTACTS

The Commercial Department of the British Embassy in Moscow produces a *Business Directory* with British commercial representations in Russia and former Soviet Union and British companies operating in Russia. Personnel agencies are *Alpha Training and Recruitment,* 5 Proezd Serova, Floor 3, Room 12, Moscow 101958, tel/fax 243-3742, for English language training and those with office skills; and *Meteor Personnel,* ul. Nizhnyaya Krasnoselskaya, Dom 3, Office 12, Moscow, tel 261-0139. Two management consultancies are: *Human Factors (Russia) Ltd.,* Denisovski pereulok 23, 107005 Moscow, tel 261-3566; and *Moscovy Management International,* Petrovsky Blvr. 25, Moscow 103051, tel 925-4846.

The Russia Desk of the *Department of Trade and Industry,* Kingsgate House, 66-74 Victoria Street, London SW1H, can supply information for commercial or business purposes; and holds lists of UK business representatives and companies in Russia.

### Voluntary Work

*International Ecological Camp,* 665718 Bratski-18, Irkutsk Region, PO Box 52, Russia — organises workcamps and voluntary projects in Siberia. About 80 workcamp volunteers are involved, each one lasting for 2-3 weeks. Volunteers who speak fluent Russian to lead the workcamps and English teachers are also required. Registration fees are payable.

# Slovak Republic

Slovak Embassy, 25 Kensington Palace Gardens, London W8 4QY, tel 0171-2430803
Slovak Embassy, Suite 250, 2201 Wisconsin Avenue, NW, Washington DC 20007, tel 202-965-5160-1
Currency: 1 Koruna (Sk) = 100 hellers
Exchange Rate: £1 = Sk 49; $1 = Sk 31

The Slovak Republic covers 17,000 square miles. The population is 15,300,000; and the capital Bratislava has 440,000 inhabitants. The other major city is Košice, with 240,000 inhabitants. The northern area is hilly, as it approaches the Carpathian Mountains; and southern and eastern parts of the country are low-lying and agricultural; the River Danube connects the country with Vienna, to the west and the Black Sea to the east. There are cold winters and mild summers. There are some mineral and gas resources; and also a large chemical industry. Agriculture is particularly important for exports; two of these are beer and timber; and Slovakia is making efforts to develop its tourism, in particular winter sports which, like hiking and hunting, are also popular with the locals. Its main international vocation since independence in 1992 is — like its central European neighbours — the membership of organisations such as the EU and Nato which can confirm its independent status and help with economic development. It is developing new trading links with EU countries, especially Germany; these links also continue with traditional trading partners like Poland, Ukraine, and Hungary. Privatisation is the watchword in the Slovakian economy; and experts are needed in the financial services field. It is also aiming to develop its traditional craft-based industries and to be less dependent on heavy industry. There are opportunities in trade and development, and English-teaching and voluntary work.

**Immigration**

EU and North American passport holders do not require a visa for the Slovak Republic. Foreigners may work only after they have been granted residence and work permits. Applications should be submitted to the Embassy in the country of origin, and accompanied by a provisional work permit from the local labour office in Slovakia; a letter from the employer; a doctor's certificate; the 'Crime and Criminal Proceedings Register from the Slovak Republic'; and five photographs. These documents must be in Slovak or with an authorised Slovak translation. The procedure takes up to 60 days. Enquiries about work and residence permits should be made to an embassy or consulate abroad.

**Embassies**

British Embassy, Grösslingova 35, 811 09 Bratislava; tel 7-364-420.

US Embassy, Hviezdoslavovo námestie 4, 811 02 Bratislava; tel 7-330-861.

**Tourist Offices**

Slovakia Travel Service, Suite 3601, 10 East 40th Street, New York, NY 10016; tel 212-213-3865 or 212-213-3862.

# SPECIFIC CONTACTS

**Teaching**

The *Slovak Academic Information Agency* recruits qualified staff for primary and secondary schools. Applicants are sent a questionnaire which is then circulated among schools who contact teachers directly when they are needed. The address for the Slovak Republic is: Na Vŕšku 2, 81100 Bratislava; tel 7-533-5221. Language shools which employ native English-language speakers include: *The English Club*, Pri Suchom mlyne 36, 81104 Bratislava, tel 7-372-411; *Eurolingua*, Drieňoná 16, 82101 Bratislava, tel 7-233-137; *ILC*, Sokolská 1, Brno, tel 5-412-40-493; and *Aspekt*, Piaristická 8, 94901 Nitra, tel 87-32-218.

**Voluntary Work**

*Inex Slovakia*, Prazská 11, 81413 Bratislava, tel 7-486-249 — recruits volunteers for workcamps aimed at promoting international understanding and cooperation mainly in environmental and historical conservation. The working language is English.

**Other Contacts**

*Slovak National Agency for Foreign Investment and Development*, Sládkovičova 175, 811 06 Bratislava; tel 7-533-5175; fax 7-533-5022.

# Canada

Canadian High Commission, Macdonald House, 1 Grosvenor Square, London W1X 0AA, tel 0171-258 6582
Canada Centre (Canada House), 62-65 Trafalgar Square, London WC2N 5DT, tel 0171-930 8540
Canadian Embassy, 501 Pennsylvania Avenue, NW, 20001 Washington DC, tel 202-596-1600
Currency: $ (Canadian) 1 = 100 cents
Rate of Exchange: £1 = CAN$2.1; US$1 = CAN$1.4

Since the war, Canada has accepted over five million immigrants, more than a million of them coming from Britain and Ireland. But the unacceptably high level of unemployment in recent years has necessitated strict controls; the flow of incomers is now limited to those possessing skills and qualifications in major demand. The attractions of Canada are many. According to a United Nations ranking, taking into account factors such as life expectancy, education, and adjusted real incomes, it ranks number one in the world as a place to live and work.

## GENERAL FACTS

### Population
Canada's population is nearly 29 million; and is expected to exceed 30 million by the year 2000.

Canada is bounded to the west by the Pacific Ocean, to the east by the Atlantic, and to the south by the 'Lower 48' of the USA. With a land area of 3,851,809 square miles, it is the world's second largest country (after Russia). Overall population density is 7.5 per square mile. However, the population is unevenly distributed and all except the Maritime provinces (Nova Scotia, New Brunswick and Prince Edward Island) have large, almost uninhabited areas. Eighty per cent of the total population is concentrated in the four provinces of Quebec, Ontario, Alberta and British Columbia. By contrast, the Yukon and Northwest Territories contain 0.3% of the population, yet cover one-third of Canada's total area.

### Climate
The climate varies widely, from severe Arctic conditions in the north to the more moderate climates of the temperate coastal regions, with extremes of heat and cold experienced in the central provinces. The Pacific coast has the highest rainfall and, inland, snow covers all regions during three to five of the winter months. In general, Canadian winters are cold but dry; springs short but dramatic; summers quite warm and sunny for two or three months; autumn usually clear and crisp.

### Government
Canada is a confederation of ten provinces (Ontario, Quebec, Nova Scotia, British Columbia, Alberta, Saskatchewan, Manitoba, New Brunswick, Prince Edward Island and Newfoundland) and two territories (Yukon and Northwest Territories). The Queen is the head of state of Canada, and is represented by a Governor-General nominated by the Canadian Prime Minister.

The federal government legislates over matters of national and general concern, including defence, external affairs, trade, the postal services, navigation and shipping. Provinces have jurisdiction over matters of local interest, including municipal institutions, the law relating to property and civil rights, health care and education. Federal legislative power is vested in the Parliament of Canada which consists of the Queen, an appointed upper house, the Senate, and a lower house, the House of Commons, elected by universal adult suffrage.

A consistent feature of Canadian politics is the strong separatist movement in the French-speaking province of Quebec. A referendum in October 1992 on the Charlottetown Accord which would have enshrined Quebec's special status in the constitution resulted in rejection by five of the ten provinces of Canada, including Quebec itself. The question of Quebec's remaining within the Canadian confederation is still an open one; with the electorate divided roughly half and half.

## Cities
The major cities are Toronto, with a population of 3.9 million; followed by Montreal (3.2 million); Vancouver (1.6 million); the capital Ottawa (920,000); Edmonton (840,000); Calgary (740,000); Quebec City (700,000); and Winnipeg (650,000). Altogether there are over 25 metropolitan areas with over 100,000 inhabitants.

## Rural Life
The post-war years have seen a continued drift to the cities; only 20% of the population now lives in the countryside. Agriculture is still Canada's most important primary industry: farmed land exceeds 174 million acres and there are 260,000 farms, all highly commercialised, mechanised and specialised, producing mainly wheat, other field crops, dairy products, livestock, fruit, vegetables, tobacco, honey, maple syrup and furs.

Forestry is another major rural occupation: forests cover 800 million acres; pulp and paper manufacture are the most important related industries.

## Mining and Petrochemicals
Canada is rich in mineral wealth with vast reserves of petroleum and natural gas, and is a major world producer of nickel, iron ore, copper and zinc. Exports of crude and fabricated mineral products account for nearly 25% of Canada's total exports.

## Religion, Sport and Culture
According to the most recent census, 44.6% of Canada's population is of British origin, 28.7% French, and the remaining 26.7% of other origins. The native peoples, Native Canadians and Inuit (Eskimos), are estimated to number approximately 323,000, or 1.4% of the population. There are 54 different Indian languages or dialects, plus Inuktitut, the language of the Inuit.

47% of Canadians are Catholics and 41% Protestants. 1.5% of the population is Jewish.

The USA exerts a strong cultural influence, especially in the cities near the US border. The arts in Canada have developed rapidly in recent decades and now exhibit a growing sense of Canadian identity. As well as theatre, ballet and music in the cities, there is a strong crafts movement in more isolated areas. In recent times, its films and television programmes, and especially animations, in English or French, have become more widely known.

The multicultural nature of Canadian society is recognised and supported by government policy. A Multicultural Directorate was established in 1971 and provides assistance to a wide range of activities organised by various cultural groups.

Canadians spend a lot of their free time out of doors. Most provinces have set aside vast areas for parks for the conservation of the environment and the enjoyment of visitors. Most of the national and provincial parks provide camping facilities and hiking trails. Skiing, swimming, ice skating, ice hockey, tennis and golf are amongst the most popular recreational activities; and sports facilities are generally excellent.

## FACTORS INFLUENCING EMPLOYMENT

### Immigration

Most of the immigration since the war has been to Ontario. Although British citizens do not require a visa to enter Canada, visitors cannot change their status from visitor to worker while in the country. Persons who wish to work in Canada must obtain the appropriate documentation prior to entering Canada/leaving the UK/USA.

Under current regulations, the flow of migrants is tied closely to labour market demands. There are two ways for permanent residence, known as landed immigrant status, to be obtained: through sponsorship, or by independent application. Sponsored applicants must be dependent relatives (i.e. spouses, retired parents, or unmarried children) of Canadian citizens or residents.

Applicants in the independent category are assessed according to several factors, including age, education, knowledge of English and French, training and occupation. Under current immigration regulations, persons in certain occupations are able to meet the selection criteria without arranged employment; others require a job offer which has been certified by employment officials in Canada as a position for which no qualified Canadians are available. In some cases the presence of relatives — brother, sister, uncle or aunt — can assist a person's application.

In addition to the sponsored (Assisted Relative) and independent (Independent Applicant) categories, Canada is encouraging applications from those with proven business ability and substantial capital to invest.

The Canadian High Commission in London (address above) deals with all immigration matters for England, Scotland, Wales and Northern Ireland. For the province of Quebec the approval of Quebec House (address below) must be obtained before applying for a visa from the Canadian High Commission. *Brownstein & Brownstein, Attorneys,* 1310 Greene Avenue, Suite 750, Montreal, Quebec, H3Z 2B2, tel 001-514-939-9559, fax 001-514-939-2289 (from the UK) are specialists in this area, with associated offices in many countries around the world.

The *Immigration Department (Visa Section),* is at: 38 Grosvenor Street, London W1X 0AA, tel 0891-616-644, in Britain; and in the United States there is a *Canadian Consulate General,* 1251 Avenue of the Americas, New York, NY 10020-1175; tel 212-596-1600.

### Regulations for US Citizens

US citizens do not require a passport to enter Canada, merely proof of US citizenship (e.g. driving licence), and they may stay for up to 90 days as tourists. Employment Authorizations (or Student Authorizations for students) must be arranged from outside Canada. The prospective employer first informs the nearest Canada Employment Centre (CEC) about the job offer. If the CEC agrees that there are no suitable Canadian residents available to fill the job you may then apply for an Employment Authorization from the nearest Canadian diplomatic representative office.

### Language

Canada is officially bilingual in French and English; and all federal government publications and federal court decisions are published in both languages. French and English language radio and television are available throughout the country, and it is the intention to make state financed schooling available in both languages wherever numbers warrant. In Quebec, French is the official language.

## Cost and Standard of Living
British visitors to Canada find the standard of living high; many articles are much cheaper in terms of hours of work needed to buy them.

## Housing and Accommodation
Although there is no actual housing shortage in Canada, there is a shortage of low-cost housing; and it is for this reason that the Immigration Department recommends immigrants to have accommodation pre-arranged if possible. Government loans are available for home building and buying. 65% of homes are owner-occupied.

## Health and Welfare
Each provincial government has primary responsibility for health, and operates two insurance programmes — one for hospital treatment, one for medical care. There are also supplementary private insurance schemes, often operated through payroll deductions.

Family allowances are paid for all dependent children under 18. All persons aged 65 and over who have lived in Canada for at least ten years (regardless of citizenship) receive a monthly old age pension; if their income is limited, they receive an additional guaranteed income supplement. There is also a contributory pension scheme whereby employees pay up to 1.8 per cent of their income while working.

Social assistance is provided by a shared-cost programme to people in need. The federal government provides 50% of the cost to each province by agreement. There is also a separate unemployment insurance scheme, contributions for which are shared by workers and employers.

## Education
Education is compulsory for all children for about ten years in every province and is free up to the end of secondary school. The starting age is six and the minimum leaving age usually 16. Most schools are co-educational; and few people are privately educated. In some provinces, French-speaking pupils are entitled by law to receive instruction in French. In Quebec, the policy is to register the children of immigrants in French schools.

Higher education is provided by 68 universities and some 200 colleges; students may receive financial aid in the form of federal or provincial loans, repayable over a period of up to ten years.

## National Service
There is no military conscription in Canada.

## Embassies and Consulates
British High Commission, 80 Elgin St., Ottawa, Ontario K1P 5KL; tel 613-237 1530.
British Consulates in Montreal, Toronto, Vancouver, Halifax, Winnipeg, and St. John's.

US Embassy, 100 Wellington Street, Ottawa K1P 5TI; tel 613-238-5335.
US Consulates in Calgary, Halifax, Montreal, Quebec, Toronto, and Vancouver.

## Tourist Office
Canadian Tourist Office (see High Commission in London address above); tel 0171-258 6582.

## CONDITIONS OF WORK

### Wages

The only federal law governing wages is the Canada Labour (Standards) Code, which covers only government employees and workers in industries under federal jurisdiction. This Code, which also prohibits unequal pay and discrimination based on sex, race, colour or religion, is the basis for the different provincial laws covering all professions and workers. However, there are wide variations from province to province. Minimum wages vary from province to province, but do not fall below $5 an hour. The average yearly salary for a skilled worker is in the region of $40,000.

### Hours

For government employees and workers in industries under federal jurisdiction, the working week is five days of eight hours each. In general, hours above eight in a day or forty in a week must be paid at 150%, up to a maximum of 48 hours a week. The average working week in practice is 38 or 39 hours.

### Holidays

Annual paid holidays vary from two to four weeks. There are also ten national public holidays: New Year's Day; Good Friday; Easter Monday; Victoria Day (25 May, or the Monday immediately preceding); Canada Day (1 July); Labour Day (first Monday in September); Thanksgiving (second Monday in October); Remembrance Day (11 November); Christmas Day; and Boxing Day. The different provinces also observe local holidays.

### Safety and Compensation

Canadian industry is proud of its low injury rate, and is very safety-conscious. Many large firms conduct constant safety programmes, supplementing the minimum safety standards laid down in most provinces.

All employees in industries and workplaces covered by Workmen's Compensation Funds are entitled to free medical aid and payment of up to 75% of regular earnings. Benefits are also provided for the spouses of workers killed on the job.

### Trade Unions

Union membership represents about a third of the labour force. The collective bargaining system between employers and unions functions under the federal Industrial Relations and Disputes Investigation Act, and under labour relations acts in all provinces. The government has the ultimate duty of conciliation when parties are unable to reach an agreement. In some provinces, legislation forbids strikes by workers in essential services, such as by firemen, policemen and hospital employees.

### Taxation

Income tax is deducted on a PAYE basis, with allowances for dependent children, pension contributions etc. As examples of tax rates, a single man earning $25,000 would pay around $5,000 in tax. On the same salary, a married man with two children under 16 and a dependent wife would pay $4,000. Tax is paid in two parts — federal and provincial, so tax rates vary from province to province.

Municipal authorities also levy taxes, especially on corporate incomes. Some provinces have variable purchase taxes on consumer goods and services.

## WORK AVAILABLE

### General

The government offices in the UK and USA for the various provinces provide similar services to the diplomatic missions (addresses available from the High Commission or Embassy); they do not necessarily handle recruitment, but can provide prospective immigrants and job-seekers with specific information about the provinces they represent.

Members of the professions should ascertain whether their qualifications are acceptable in Canada, or whether they must attend further courses. Assessment of qualifications is carried out by the relevant professional associations in Canada, whose addresses can be obtained from any Canadian Consulate, High Commission or Embassy.

A list of the professional associations is also given in the *Canadian Almanac and Directory,* available in public reference libraries. This also gives the addresses of many potential employers, such as colleges, universities, law firms, insurance companies, libraries, publishers and broadcasting companies.

## Newspapers

Newspapers are available for reference at the *Canada Centre* in Trafalgar Square, London, whose library can be used by prior appointment. Local city and regional newspapers can be consulted at the offices of the provincial government offices, where information will be given on subscriptions and advertising.

A list of the names and addresses of the main newspapers is included in the free booklet *Teaching in Canada,* issued by the *Canadian Teachers' Federation,* 110 Argyle Street, Ottawa, Ontario K2P 1B4, although this service is intended only for the benefit of teachers seeking work in Canada. The *Globe and Mail,* Canada's only national newspaper, contains a daily employment and careers section, with a special supplement on Saturdays. Their UK address is: 1st Floor, The Quadrangle, 180 Wardour Street, London W1A 4YG.

Copies of *Canada News,* a monthly newspaper for tourists and migrants, are available from Canada House, London, or by subscription from: *Outbound Newspapers,* 1 Commercial Road, Eastbourne, East Sussex BN21 3XQ; tel 01323-412001.

# SPECIFIC CONTACTS

Landed immigrants can use the services of the Canada Manpower Centres, which display lists of vacancies in their 'job banks'. There are 400 Manpower Centres across the country. Addresses are available through the High Commissions. For more about living and working in Canada, and specific addresses and contacts, see *Live and Work in the USA and Canada* published by Vacation Work.

## Doctors

The *Canadian Medical Association,* Box 8650, Ottawa, Ontario K1G 0G8, publishes the *Canadian Medical Association Journal, Canadian Journal of Surgery, Canadian Association of Radiologists Journal* and the *Canadian Journal of Respiratory Therapy,* which have classified sections. The Association also issues a free leaflet *Medical Practice in Canada,* which gives information on registration and appointments and lists the addresses of the provincial Medical Associations and their respective registration requirements.

## Au Pairs and Nannies

Several of the organisations listed in the chapter *Au Pair and Domestic* offer posts in Canada on one-year contracts. These programmes are organised as part of what is called the Live-in Caregiver Program.

*Agence Dometier Agency,* 4640 Decarie Blvd., Suite 210, 210 Montreal, Quebec H2X 2H5 — places au pairs, nannies, governesses, nurses (paediatric/geriatric), butlers, chauffeurs and chefs with Canadian employers. Nationalities include Americans, Europeans and East Asians. Work can also be arranged in the USA, Europe and Singapore for Canadian residents. Minimum stay is one year.

Applicants should be high school graduates, with minimum six months' full time training in a relevant occupation. Fees are charged according to according to qualifications and background.

*Nannies Unlimited Inc.,* 350-604 1 St SW, Calgary, Alberta T2P 1M7, can place nannies in Calgary, Saskatchewan and the Northwest Territories.

## Engineers
The *Canadian Council of Professional Engineers,* 116 Albert Street, Suite 401, Ottawa, Ontario K1P 5G3, can advise on procedures used in evaluating foreign engineering education qualifications. For Quebec the address is *Ordre des Ingénieurs du Québec,* 2020 Université, 14th Floor, Montreal, Québec H3A 2A5.

## Hospital Staff
The *Grenfell Regional Health Services* operates and staffs two hospitals and 17 nursing stations and health centres. The staff consists of doctors, dentists, nurses, occupational therapists, physiotherapists and volunteers. Employment is for negotiable periods, preferably a minimum of two years. GRHS has short appointments for medical students in their clinical electives. Interested applicants should write to: *Grenfell Regional Health Services,* Charles Curtis Memorial Hospital, St. Anthony, Newfoundland AOK 4SO, Canada.

## Pharmacists
Licensing of foreign pharmacists is a provincial responsibility. Candidates are advised to contract first the *Pharmacy Examining Board of Canada,* Suite 603, 123 Edward Street, Toronto, Ontario M5G 1E2. For Quebec the address is *Ordre des Pharmaciens du Québec,* 266 Notre Dame Ouest, Montreal, Québec H2Y 1TS.

## Teachers
The *Canadian Teacher's Federation,* 110 Argyle Avenue, Ottawa, Ontario K2P 1B4, cannot help in finding work, but issues the free booklet *Teaching in Canada,* which includes a lot of useful information for immigrants, such as details of entry requirements, and a list of the provincial authorities, from whom permission to teach must be obtained before an apointment can be taken up.

The *Canadian Education Association,* 252 Bloor Street W, Suite 8-200, Toronto, Ontario M5S 1V5, issues the leaflet *Information for teachers thinking of coming to Canada,* but cannot otherwise assist in finding work.

Those teachers wishing to work in British Columbia, Manitoba, New Brunswick and the Northwest Territories may seek information from the following bodies:

Computerised Teacher Registry, British Columbia School Trustees' Association, 1155 West 8th Avenue, Vancouver, British Columbia, V6H 1C5.

Administration and Professional Certification Unit, PO Box 700, Russell, Manitoba R0J 1WO.

The Registrar, Department of Education, Government of the Northwest Territories, PO Box 1320, Yellowknife NT, X1A 2L9.

Teachers interested in appointments in private schools should contact the Executive Secretary, *Canadian Association of Independent Schools,* c/o Stanstead College, Dufferin Road, Stanstead, Quebec JOB 3E0.

## University Staff
Academic and administrative vacancies in the universities are advertised in the *CAUT Bulletin*, the news and information magazine published ten times during the academic year by the *Canadian Association of University Teachers.* Publication Office: 294 Albert Street, Suite 308, Ottawa, Ontario, Canada, K1P 6E6. (Subscription: Yearly, September-June).

University academic and administrative vacancies are also publicised in

*University Affairs,* the news magazine published ten times a year by the *Association of Universities and Colleges of Canada,* Publications Office, 151 Slater Street, Ottawa, Canada K1P 5N1. Lists of specific university departments and addresses are also available from AUCC Information.

**Other Opportunities**
Opportunities in Canada are also referred to throughout the *Specific Careers* section, covering a wide range of professions.

## SHORT TERM WORK

Foreigners looking for legal temporary work in Canada must either apply for specific jobs before they arrive and then wait for the employer to arrange a work permit or, in some cases, take part in an approved 'educational' scheme such as that offered by BUNAC. People looking for unauthorised work when in Canada risk exposure because they will not be able to provide a prospective employer with a Canadian social insurance number, which is required by law.

**Seasonal Work**
Students can obtain an Employment Authorization which will allow them to look for jobs in Canada and make use of the government's *Canada Employment Centres* from: *British Universities North America Club (BUNAC),* 16 Bowling Green Lane, London EC1R 0BD; tel 0171-251 3472. BUNAC'S *Work Canada Programme* allows students to work up to six months. BUNAC can also directly arrange for students to work on the tobacco harvest.

Students with a definite job offer from a Canadian employer may apply directly to the Canadian High Commission in London for an Employment Authorization which is valid for 20 weeks and not transferable to another job.

Non-students can apply for the various jobs listed in the section on Canada in *Summer Jobs Abroad* (Vacation Work); and there is useful information in *Work Your Way Around the World* (Vacation Work). Alternatively, they can try writing directly to hotels listed in tourist guides: those in resorts in the Rocky Mountains are especially recommended, as many of them can offer work on the winter skiing season (from November to May) as well as in the summer.

Students with Employment Authorizations can look for work picking fruit or tobacco in the Okanagan Valley in British Columbia, where a succession of harvests takes place, beginning with cherries in June and ending with apples in September and October. Jobs can be found through local Agricultural Employment Service offices, which specialise in helping people to find this sort of work. Another good area for fruit-picking is Southern Ontario.

**Opportunities for US citizens**
Information on work permits is given above under *Regulations for US Citizens.*

The *Council on International Educational Exchange,* Work Abroad, 205 East 42nd Street, New York, NY 10017, runs the *Work in Canada* scheme for students and those within one semester of graduating. If your application is accepted, you will receive a *Certificate of Participation* that authorises employment in Canada between 1 May and 31 October. There is a participation fee.

**Other Work**
It is possible to take part in various construction projects in Native Canadian communities around the year. These are arranged by *Frontiers Foundation,* 2615 Danforth Avenue, Suite 203, Toronto, Ontario M4C 1L6. Participants need to pay for their own travel expenses as far as Toronto, and must be free to work for at least three months. Expenses paid in Canada only. *Frontiers Foundation,* organises these construction and other projects in low-income rural communities across Canada.

## BRITISH FIRMS
with branches, affiliates or subsidiaries in Canada

The British High Commission in Ottawa (see above) can supply information about the many British companies operating in Canada.

The *Canada-United Kingdom Chamber of Commerce,* 3 Lower Regent Street, London SW1Y 4NZ, tel 0171-930 7711, can also supply commercial information. The *Canadian Chamber of Commerce* is at: Suite 1160, 55 Metcalfe Street, Ottawa, Ontario K1P 6N4, tel 613-238-4000; or, 1080 Beaver Hall Hill, Montréal, Québec H2A 1T2, tel 514-866-4334.

# United States of America

US Embassy, 24-31 Grosvenor Square, London W1A 2JB, tel 0171-499 9000
US Consulate General, 5 Upper Grosvenor Street, London W1A 2JB, tel 0171-499 6846
Currency: (US) $1 = 100 cents
Rate of Exchange: £1 = $1.65

The United States is still seen as the land of opportunity. Britons are no longer allowed to participate in the 'Green Card' lottery; but many thousands do emigrate or take up employment there through the conventional visa programme; and a parent born in one of the qualifying countries could still allow you to participate in this annual lottery. There has been a slight economic upturn in the mid-1990s; opportunities are very good for highly trained foreign workers, and are likely to remain so. In particular, the USA will need to import thousands of foreign scientists to make up for the shortfall at home. 'Exceptional ability' (which means a major and original achievment in science, academia, the arts, athletics, or business) is another category which could get you in.

## GENERAL FACTS

### Population
The resident population of the USA is over 260 million. The capital Washington has a population of 600,000, but 16 other cities have a population which is larger. The total land area is 3,536,855 square miles, including Alaska and Hawaii; and the country spans seven time zones.

The population density is about 73 per square mile, but distribution is uneven, with areas of desert and mountains, and the great expanses of Alaska, which are almost uninhabited. Most of the population lives within 50 miles of a coastal shoreline.

### Climate
The climate can be classed as continental, but varies from Arctic in Alaska to sub-tropical in Hawaii and Florida, the only states that get no frost. Average January temperatures are below freezing in all but the southern states, and in the northern mid-west states, the average is often below 0°F. Summer, on the other hand, can be unbearably hot, with average July temperatures rising into the 30s and up to 40°C.

Precipitation is about twice as high as in Britain on average, but most of this is accounted for by heavy snowfalls, rainstorms and hurricanes, rather than constant drizzle. In the desert areas, however (New Mexico, Arizona, Nevada), annual rainfall is only 2-3 inches.

### Government
The United States is a federal republic led by a President, who is elected by all citizens aged 18 and over, for a four-year term of office. No president may serve for more than two terms. The President, and the cabinet which he appoints, form the executive branch of the government.

Congress is the seat of the legislature, and consists of the Senate and the House of Representatives. Each state elects two senators, who serve a six-year term; and one-third of the membership is renewed every two years. There are only two major parties - Democrats and Republicans.

The USA is a confederation of states, each of which has its own governor and legislature (which takes different forms in different states). These have considerable autonomy and legislative power; they run their own courts and police forces; and levy their own taxes. They are further sub-divided into counties, which are responsible for local government.

### Cities

As the world's leading industrial power, the USA has built its economy on large industrial cities. 80% of the population live in urban areas, and there are 39 metropolitan areas with over a million inhabitants.

The major cities and conurbations are: New York (the world's second largest port after Rotterdam); Los Angeles; San Francisco; Chicago; Houston; Philadelphia; San Diego; and Detroit.

### Rural Life

Cultivated land covers 47% of America's total land area; forests another 32%. With a farming population of only six million, the USA still leads the world in both production and export of meat and agricultural produce. The size of some farms in the mid-west is enormous. About 50% of the country's farms cover 2000 acres or more.

### Religion, Sport and Culture

All major religious faiths are represented. The many denominations of the Protestant or Episcopalian church predominate; but Catholicism is stronger in some areas, such as the Mexican-influenced southwest. Industrial regions settled by immigrants from southern and eastern Europe also have large Catholic populations.

The USA is one of the few countries in the world where soccer is not a major sport; interest is growing and the World Cup was held there in 1994. The main sports are baseball, American football, ice-hockey, and basketball. Tennis and skiing are also popular, and there are facilities for golf, horse-racing, and almost every sporting activity.

Cultural facilities are of the highest standard, with cinemas, theatres, concert halls and galleries in all large towns and cities; America still leads the world in its popular culture: the movies, rock music, and television programmes which are familiar everywhere.

## FACTORS INFLUENCING EMPLOYMENT

### Immigration

The processing of United States visas involves a long and complicated ritual, and quite a large outlay in application and other fees. Numbers of immigrants are limited, which allow the Immigration Service to be very selective. Those wishing to enter the country solely for the purpose of employment must have a definite job offer (petitions must be filed by the prospective employer) and must obtain a certification from the US Department of Labor that there are no able, willing and qualified workers in the USA for that particular type of employment. Only workers with really valuable skills will be considered for work permits.

US immigration laws were comprehensively reformed by the Immigration Act of 1990. The total number of immigrants entering the US annually during rose as a result to about 650,000. Three categories of immigrants are now recognised:

*Family-sponsored immigrants:* 480,000 visas are issued per year to relatives of US citizens. This includes spouses, children and sons and daughters of US citizens. It also includes brothers and sisters of US citizens and their spouses and children, provided the US citizens are aged over 21; also parents of US citizens over 21.

*Employment-based immigrants:* a total of 140,000 immigrant visas are available divided into five main categories. Preferences one to three include persons of extraordinary ability, exceptional ability and highly skilled workers. Preference four covers ministers of religion, religious workers and employees of certain international organisations (10,000). Preference five is for those who can invest at least $500,000 in an enterprise.

*Diversity Transition Immigrants:* reserved for persons with a definite job offer coming from countries considered to have been previously adversely affected by the provisions of the immigration law.

It should be noted that every year a lottery is held for 55,000 immigrant visas, and a percentage of these are reserved for citizens of Northern Ireland and the Irish Republic. Britons with a parent from an eligible country may apply, but should bear in mind that the chances of obtaining a place by this method are about 200 to one (and even then you still need to find a job).

There are also various types of 'non-immigrant' visa, issued to people wishing to take up short-term work in the USA. These are only issued for the following categories: lecturers and performing artists; trainees and exchange visitors on approved programmes; intra-company transferees on short-term transfers; and other temporary workers fulfilling limited term contracts. Non-immigrant and tourist visas cannot be changed to immigrant visas once you are in the country, except in special circumstances, such as marriage to an American. Holders of exchange visitor visas are normally required to spend at least two years outside the US before being considered for an immigrant visa.

Good health is still a prerequisite, as is sound moral character. Those that are totally ineligible to receive visas are: narcotics addicts or traffickers; members of a totalitarian party; persons with mental deficiencies or contagious diseases; ex-convicts; offenders against public morals; illiterates; and anyone likely to become a public charge.

When considering emigration to the United States, the first step is to contact the Visa Branch at the US Consulate General, address above. Because of the strong possibility of an application being rejected or taking longer than expected, it is advisable not to make any definite plans until the visa is issued.

There is also a Visa Branch for Northern Irish citizens at: Queen's House, Queen Street, Belfast BT1 6EQ.

## Cost and Standard of Living
British visitors find the USA cheaper than home in many respects. Retail food prices, for instance, compare very favourably with UK prices, because so much is home-produced. Gasoline (petrol) is about half as cheap. Entertainment, apartment rents and certain luxury items tend to be more expensive, but because wages are two to three times higher, they are well within the reach of most of the population.

## Housing and Accommodation
On average, rents are somewhat higher than in Britain, but so too is the average size and quality of property. Housing of all kinds is generally readily available in the United States. There is relatively little public housing, the equivalent of council housing in the United Kingdom; and most people either own their own houses or rent privately-owned houses or flats. Average house prices vary enormously across the country.

## Health and Welfare
While there is no equivalent to the National Health Service in the USA, the Social Security Department provides, against contributions from an employee's wage (half paid by the employer), benefits for old age, disability, unemployment and injury.

Personal medical insurance is the responsibility of the individual, who must

insure him/herself privately. Many employers give advisory and financial assistance in this. Because medical fees are so high, insurance premiums are also high,
and can account for 5-10% of a week's pay packet. This is an inevitably
necessary expense.

## Education
State laws vary concerning the ages of compulsory school attendance, but the
highest minimum age is seven, and nearly all states set the upper age at 16
although obtaining a high school diploma usually requires attendance at school
until the age of 18. Public schools are free, but there are also a number of
private, fee-paying schools.

With over 2,500 universities and specialised training colleges, entrance to
higher education can be easier than in the UK. Each state controls at least one
university, which gives preference to state residents. University courses are
completed on the basis of credits, which offer students the chance to change
courses, even colleges, or drop out for a year or two, without damaging their
chance of obtaining a degree. On the whole, university courses last a minimum
period of four years. University tuition fees range from $5,000 to $20,000 a
year, but government loans are available.

## National Service
Although the draft was ended in 1973, the Selective Service System is still
functioning and requires all men aged 18-26 to register for possible call-up in
the case of a national emergency. This also applies to alien residents, who must
register with their local Selective Service Board within 60 days of arriving; or,
if application for residence is granted after arrival, within 60 days of registration
as a resident.

## British Embassy and Consulates
British Embassy, 3100 Massachusetts Ave. NW, Washington DC 20008; tel
202-462-1340.

Consulates in Atlanta, Boston, Chicago, Houston, Los Angeles (tel 310-477-
3322), San Francisco, Anchorage, Cleveland, Dallas, Kansas City, Miami,
New Orleans, Norfolk, Philadelphia, Portland, New York (tel 212-745-0200),
and Seattle.

# CONDITIONS OF WORK

## Wages
Minimum wages are laid down by state and federal laws; and equality of pay
for women is fast becoming a reality. In matters of employment, advertising
vacancies, etc., discrimination based on sex, age, colour, creed or national origin
is banned by law.

## Hours
The standard is a 40-hour, five-day week, but many offices get by with a 35 or
37½-hour week. Banks and shops keep longer hours than in Britain, and all-
night shops are common. Sunday work and shop-opening are generally forbidden,
but laws vary from state to state; and essential services are exempt.

## Holidays
Most employees are given at least two weeks' paid holiday a year. There are also
ten nationally observed public holidays: New Year's Day; Martin Luther Day
(15 Jan); President's Day (third Monday in February); Memorial Day (last
Monday in May); Independence Day (4 July); Labor Day (first Monday in
September); Columbus Day (second Monday in October); Veterans' Day (fourth
Monday in October); Thanksgiving (fourth Thursday in November); and Chri-
stmas Day. Other holidays vary from state to state but Lincoln's Birthday (12

February); St. Patrick's Day (17 March); and Arbor Day (26 April) are quite widely observed.

**Safety and Compensation**
Safety standards are set down by federal and state laws, and are rigidly enforced. Compensations are paid for injury, accident, death and disability. Very few benefits, even in the cases of permanent disability, are payable for an indefinite period, but short-term payments are quite adequate.

**Trade Unions**
A mere 15% of the American labour force are union members; most unions are affiliated to the American Federation of Labor and Congress of Industrial Organizations (AFL-CIO). Labor Courts exist to arbitrate between employers and employed.

**Taxation**
Federal and state income tax is deducted on a PAYE basis at fixed rates, and adjusted at the end of the tax year. Total tax deductions are generally less than 25% of the total income.

Sales tax (between 3% and 12%, varying from state to state) is payable on most goods and services. State variations make for big differences in the prices of many items, for instance, cigarettes, alcohol and cars.

## WORK AVAILABLE

**General**
Details of the types of work likely to qualify for a permit cannot be precisely defined, but the American Department of Labor has given advance certification for persons with advanced degrees in dietetics, nursing, pharmacy, physical therapy, or medicine and surgery. With the exception of medicine and surgery, the advanced degree requirement is sometimes waived if the applicant has a combination of a regular degree and specialised experience. This certification is also given to members of bona fide religious organisations, entering the United States to perform non-profit duties for such an organisation. The US Embassy is not in a position to help applicants to find work. They suggest contacting friends or relatives already resident in the United States.

**Newspapers**
See the main US newspapers under *Advertisements* in the *Getting the Job* chapter. The *New York Times,* has a large 'help wanted' section on Sundays, and is represented by *Powers International,* 517-523 Fulham Road, London SW6 1HD, tel 0171-385 8855. *Colin Turner* represents some major regional newspapers for advertising purposes in Britain (City Cloisters, 188-196 Old Street, London EC1V 9BX, tel 0171-490 5551), as well as *The Washington Post.* The very informative monthly newspaper for migrants *Going USA* — with many contacts for visa and removal specialists — is available free of charge at some travel agents in the UK; or by subscription from: *Outbound Newspapers Ltd.,* 1 Commercial Road, Eastbourne, East Sussex BN21 3XQ; tel 01323-412001. *Union Jack* is 'America's only national British newspaper with news for the expatriate community': PO Box 1823, La Mes, California 91944-1823; fax 619-466-1103.

## SPECIFIC CONTACTS

There are more specific addresses and contacts on all aspects of emigration to the United States in *Live and Work in the USA and Canada* published by Vacation Work.

**Au Pairs**
There are a number of agencies in the UK who can place au pairs in the USA. See chapter, *Au Pairs and Domestic* for details.

**Librarians**
The generally accepted qualification is a Master's degree from a school accredited by the *American Library Association,* 50 East Huron Street, Chicago, Illinois 60611, USA. In addition certain states may have additional requirements for employment in certain positions. These may need the holding of United States citizenship or the possession of qualifications in addition to a Master's degree. For example, school library positions often call for qualification as a teacher in the state. For further information write to the American Library Association at the above address.

**Nurses**
To practise professional nursing in the USA one must pass a licensing examination in one of the 50 states, the District of Columbia, Guam, American Samoa, Northern Mariana Islands or the Virgin Islands. Passing an examination given in the applicant's home country by the Commission on Graduates of Foreign Nursing Schools (CGFNS) is a requirement to sit for the National Council of State Boards of Nursing Licensure Examination (NCLEX). Obtaining a CGFNS Certificate, signifying a passing grade, is a requirement to obtain a non-immigrant occupational preference visa (H-1A) from the United States Immigration and Naturalization Service. Also, the CGFNS Certificate will be required in order to obtain an immigrant occupational (third) preference visa and a work permit from a US Labor Department regional office.
   Information and application forms may be secured by writing to:

*Commission on Graduates of Foreign Nursing Schools (CGFNS),* 3600 Market Street, Suite 400, Philadelphia, Pennsylvania 19104-2651.

Addresses of state boards of nursing are available from: *National Council of State Boards of Nursing,* 676 North St. Clair Street, Suite 550, Chicago, Illinois 60611-2921; tel 312-787-6555.

*BNA International,* 3rd Floor, 443 Oxford Road, London W1R 2NA, has vacancies in hospitals throughout the USA, the most popular areas being Boston, California, New York, New Jersey, and Florida. Contracts for all hospitals are for a minimum of one year; one-way tickets to the USA or subsidised accommodation are normally provided.

Further addresses of agencies can be found in the chapter *Medicine and Nursing.*

**University Staff**
Applications for university places are usually made direct. The *Directory of Postsecondary Institutions* is a complete list of American universities and institutes of higher education. It is available from the Superintendent of Documents, *US Government Printing Office,* Washington DC 20402.
   Lists of vacancies in university Modern Language Departments and English Departments are supplied by the *Modern Language Association Job Information Service,* 10 Astor Place, New York, NY 10003.
   Female, minority and disabled people can contact the *Affirmative Action Register,* 8356 Olive Blvd., St. Louis, Missouri 63132, which registers applicants and provides free lists of business, industrial, university and academic vacancies.

**Other Opportunities**
Opportunities in the USA are also referred to in each of the chapters of the *Specific Careers* section.

# SHORT TERM WORK

America presents a number of obstacles for foreigners looking for work there. Students have a definite advantage as they can obtain work visas as part of approved *Exchange Visitor Programs* with comparative ease: these enable them to look for work inside the country. Others wanting to work legally must first obtain an offer of a job, then wait several months while the employer applies for a *Temporary Worker Visa* for them. These temporary visas apply only for specific jobs; and cannot be transferred if you come across a better job when in America.

Below is a list of official 'program sponsors' for exchange visitors, organisations which are approved for the issue of the J-1 visas which apply to these:

*AIESEC/US*, 135 West 60th Street, 20th Floor, New York, NY 10020; tel 212-757-3774.
*American-Scandinavian Foundation*, 725 Park Avenue, New York, NY 10021; tel 212-879-9779.
*Association for International Practical Training*, AIESTE Trainee Program, 10400 Little Patuxent Parkway, Suite 250, Columbia, Maryland 21044-3510.
*CDS International*, 330 Seventh Avenue, New York, NY 10001; tel 212-760-1400
*Council of International Programs*, 1420 K Street, NW, Suite 800, Washington, DC 20005; tel 202-842-8424.
*Council on International Educational Exchange*, 205 East 42nd Street, New York, NY 10017; tel 212-661-1414.
*Interexchange*, 161 Sixth Avenue, Suite 902, New York, NY 10013; tel 212-924-0446.
*Minnesota Agricultural Student Trainee Program*, 199 Coffey Hall, University of Minnesota, 1420 Eckles Avenue, St. Paul, Minnesota 55108; tel 612-624-3740.
*Ohio International Agricultural Intern Program*, 113 Agricultural Administration Building, Ohio State University, 2120 Fyffe Road, Columbus, Ohio 43210-1099; tel 614-292-7720.
*Sister Cities International*, 120 South Payne Street, Alexandria, Virginia 22314; tel 703-836-3535.

Also see the annual *Peterson's Internships*, available through Vacation Work in Britain.

### Seasonal Work
An enormous range of summer jobs exists in America; also see Peterson's annual *Summer Jobs USA* (which, like the above, is available through Vacation Work) for more details. Their website is http:www.petersons.com. It should be consulted by anyone looking for this sort of work.

Organisations which place young British people on children's summer camps in America are included in the chapter *Voluntary Work.*

One such is *British Universities North America Club (BUNAC)*, 16 Bowling Green Lane, London EC1R 0BD, tel 0171-251 3472, which operates the *Work America Programme* that enables students to look for and take up any temporary work they want in America between June and October. Qualifying for the programme and the J-1 work and travel visa depends on having either a pre-arranged job, sponsorship or proof of adequate funds. Programme brochures are available from October onwards.

BRITISH FIRMS
with subsidiaries, parents, agents, distributors in the USA

*The Anglo-American Trade Directory* is published by the *American Chamber of Commerce United Kingdom,* 75 Brook Street, London W1Y 2EB and aims to list 'all British and American businesses having trade and/or investment relations with each other'. Other organisations which can provide commercial information are: *Chamber of Commerce of the USA,* 1615 H Street, NW, Washington, DC 20062, tel 202-659-6000; and *National Foreign Trade Council Inc.,* 1270 Avenue of the Americas, New York, NY 10020, tel 212-399-7128.

# Latin America

No one can deny that progress has been made in recent years towards greater political and economic stability in Latin America; but few countries in this region can offer the employment or education prospects to their own citizens which they would aspire to. Development is often hampered by high levels of debt, and an uneven distribution of wealth. There is also a general under-utilisation of human resources, so that on average only one-third of the population is economically active, compared with 50% in the more advanced economies. The distribution of work shows a fundamental imbalance. On the one hand, there is a large unskilled or semi-skilled workforce which is unable to find suitable employment, while on the other hand there is a constant demand for skilled technicians and managers.

Despite the efforts made by Latin American governments to combat illiteracy, and to expand the capacity of their educational systems, many countries are not yet in a position to prepare a sufficient number of students for the various professions. Much of this is attributable to the fact that many children leave school early, with a minimal level of skills. In spite of the assistance of international organisations, vocational training and the training of higher-level personnel also lags behind; training and development are areas where there is scope in Latin America for international jobseekers. But the skills still fall far short of requirements.

As with many other transitional regions, Latin America has to accept a considerable outflow of its own qualified personnel. In many cases, these engineers and scientists, doctors and skilled technicians pursue their training abroad, especially in the United States, and often pursue a career outside their country of origin as well. Confronted with this problem of immediate needs for special skills, governments have pursued supplementary policies to attract the expertise required, often through multilateral and/or bilateral technical co-operation programmes, organised by aid agencies, which place experts at the disposal of developing countries for a fixed period of time.

As far as permanent migration is concerned, it is clear that in the current economic climate Latin America can only accept a limited number of immigrants from wealthier countries, and in certain specialised areas, like consultancy, English language teaching, tourism, or voluntary and development work. Those who are interested should contact the relevant embassies; or the *Intergovernmental Committee for Migration* (see below) which is active in promoting the transfer of foreign experts to Latin America.

## Languages

Apart from the many native American languages, the almost universal language of Latin America is Spanish. The main exceptions are Brazil — where the official language is Portuguese — and the few former colonies and possessions of other European countries, where French, English and Dutch are spoken. English is not widely spoken, apart from the former British territories like Guyana and Belize, and among the middle class. If you are going to study Spanish or Portuguese, it is worth noting that there are significant variations between the European languages and their South American counterparts; this is something to take into consideration when you choose a language course.

**Politics and Culture**

While Latin America has a great deal to offer in terms of its cultural achievements in art and literature, and a lifestyle which is relaxed and friendly, there is a darker side: the ever-present problem of political instability, and human rights violations. In the 1980s, many of the former military dictatorships gave way to freely elected governments, but these democracies do not always have deep roots in civil society; and there is the possibility in many of these countries that the situation will deteriorate again. The eradication or persecution of indigenous populations and the widespread destruction of rainforests are also matters of concern to foreign workers.

Detailed information about political and environmental developments is available from pressure groups such as *Amnesty International, Friends of the Earth*, and *Survival International* (which can be found in your local telephone directory; and can be useful sources of supplementary information about Latin America).

# IMMIGRATION AND WORK PERMITS

Employment in all Latin American countries is subject to obtaining work and/or residence permits. In general, the procedure is based on your finding a job first, from within or outside the country; and then the employer applies for a work permit on your behalf. Residence permits will normally be issued on production of a valid work permit. For some countries, residence permits may be issued without a firm job offer, provided certain other criteria are fulfilled, e.g. financial viability, character references, health certificates and political testimonies. In most cases, residence permits must be obtained before arriving in the country.

In general, embassies and consulates abroad do not send out very detailed information. In compiling this directory, Peru, Mexico and Brazil were exceptions to this; certainly none of them is in any way involved in finding or offering employment. If pressed, most will send at least a circular describing the procedures involved, and refer enquirers to other addresses for further information. National tourist agencies may send more general information which is relevant.

# WORK AVAILABLE

**General**

Most Latin American countries are rich in raw materials; those in mainland South America generally maintain a trade surplus with the rest of the world. Certain countries have also made great progress in developing their industries, notably, Brazil, Chile, Argentina and Mexico. Prospects for future development appear to be improving, now that serious efforts are being made to reduce the crippling burden of debt. The general liberalisation of local economies should also increase demand for foreign workers.

There is a strong movement towards instituting free-trade areas on the lines of the European Union, which may eventually embrace the whole of North and South America. In 1992, Canada, the USA and Mexico negotiated the North American Free Trade Agreement (NAFTA) which has led to the abolition of many tariff and trade barriers between these countries. Trade barriers have been lifted between Venezuela, Colombia, Bolivia, Peru and Ecuador, to establish the Andean Common Market; as well as in Central America and the Caribbean.

Suitably qualified people with Spanish or Portuguese are in a good position to find translating or secretarial work in the more developed areas. Anyone with money to invest, or a good track record in business, will also generally be welcomed. For others, the most practical method of obtaining work in Latin

America is through an overseas posting from an international company. Sectors where there is a regular demand for foreign workers include petrochemicals in countries such as Ecuador, Venezuela and Colombia, and banking and finance wherever there are large foreign banks. Many Japanese and Far Eastern companies are moving production facilities to Latin America because of its low labour costs, especially to Mexico and Panama; so joining a Far Eastern concern could lead to a transfer to this area. Further opportunities for work in Latin America can be found in most chapters in the section *Specific Careers.*

## Newspapers

Argentina's principal English language daily, *The Buenos Aires Herald,* is represented by *Frank L. Crane Ltd.*, 5-15 Cromer Street, Grays Inn Road, London WC1H 8LS, tel 0171-837 3330; as are many Brazilian newspapers, magazines and journals, including *O'Estado de São Paulo* and *Jornal do Brasil.*

## Specific Contacts

Apart from the addresses quoted under separate countries below, the following organisations are involved in migration and employment in Latin America:

*Intergovernmental Committee for Migration (ICM),* 17 route des Morillons, 1211 Geneva 19, Switzerland — runs a programme for assisting in the emigration of European technical and professional workers to Latin American countries. ICM has offices throughout Latin America, and issues free booklets and fact sheets on aspects of life and work in all these countries (see *International Organisations* chapter).

*HRM International SA,* Felipe IV 10, 28014, Madrid, Spain — an executive search consultancy specialising in the selection and location of high level managers for the Spanish, Portuguese and Latin American markets. Interested applicants who speak fluent Spanish and/or Portuguese should send their CV.

## English Teaching and Tourism

For those without professional qualifications, opportunities are generally limited to teaching English or work in the travel industry. Unskilled or semi-skilled manual work is generally not open to foreign workers. There is a considerable demand for English teachers all over Latin America, but wages are low by international standards. Trying to obtain a permit for this kind of work is often impractical and unnecessary, unless you wish to work for an established organisation such as the British Council or USIA (see *Teaching* chapter). Berlitz run schools in Argentina, Colombia, Chile, Mexico, Puerto Rico, Venezuela and Brazil. Precise information is available from: *Latin American Division, Berlitz Language Centre,* Ejercito Nacional No 530 1er Piso, Col Polanco, 11550 Mexico DF.

The chances of working for a tour operator are good if you have the right languages and skills. UK travel companies operating in Latin America are featured in *Travel, Tourism and Hospitality.*

## Voluntary Work

If you are unwilling to risk a trip without pre-arranged work, volunteering is another possibility, but participation costs can be high. American residents have a range of opportunities open to them in this respect; major organisations in this area for Britons and Americans are included in *Voluntary Work.*

## Work Exchanges

Major work exchange organisations such as IAESTE and AIPT can sometimes arrange positions in Latin America. US students or those within six months of their final semester can work in Costa Rica and Jamaica between 1 May and 1 October through CIEE's *Work in Costa Rica* and *Work in Jamaica* schemes. In the case of Costa Rica, a knowledge of Spanish is required. See *Working Exchanges* in *Getting The Job.*

British students of Spanish in universities may apply for an assistantship in a Latin American school through the *Central Bureau for Educational Visits and Exchanges* in London (see *Working Exchanges*).

## Useful Publications

Further information on casual work in Latin America can be found in *Work Your Way Around the World* (Vacation Work). A general source of information on work opportunities is *Latin America — A Guide to Employment and Opportunities for Young People,* available from: *The Hispanic and Luso Brazilian Council,* Canning House, 2 Belgrave Square, London SW1X 8PJ; tel 0171-235 2303. Extensive listings of voluntary work opportunities are to be found in *International Directory of Voluntary Work* published by Vacation Work. Other *Canning House* publications available from the above address include *The British Bulletin of Publications on Latin America, the Caribbean, Portugal and Spain* published twice yearly; and the leaflets *Latin America: A guide to sources of information and material; and Language courses in Latin America.*

## Argentina

In spite of the war over the Falklands (or *Malvinas*) there are close links between Britain and Argentina, and a long-established British expatriate community. At one time, Argentina was the most prosperous and developed country in South America. Democracy has returned; and inflation has fallen, but Argentina's economic difficulties are far from over. Enquiries about visa requirements should be addressed to the *Argentine Consulate,* Trevor House, 100 Brompton Road, 5th Floor, London SW3 1ER, tel 0171-589 3104; or to the *Argentine Embassy,* 1600 New Hampshire Avenue, Washington DC 20009, tel 202-939-6400.

## Bolivia

Immigration is no longer encouraged. All enquiries should be made to *Consejo Nacional de Immigración,* Ministerio de Migración, Avenida Arce esq. Belisario Salinas, La Paz, Bolivia. General enquiries can be made to the *Bolivian Embassy and Consulate,* 106 Eaton Square, London SW1W 9AA, tel 0171-235 4248 or 235 4255 (visas); or the *Bolivian Embassy,* 3014 Massachusetts Avenue, NW Washington DC 20008, tel 202-483-4410-2.

## Brazil

To take up employment in Brazil, an application for a temporary, or permanent, work permit in favour of the visa applicant must be made by a prospective employer in Brazilian employer to the Ministry of Labour for permanent stay in the country. Application for a permanent visa, based on the establishment of commercial or industrial activities, requires transference of US$200,000. Details are set out in a circular issued by the *Brazilian Consulate-General,* 6 St. Alban's Street, London SW1Y 4SG, tel 0171-930 9055; or the *Brazilian Embassy,* 3006 Massachusetts Avenue, NW Washington DC 20008, tel 202-745-2700.

## Chile

Residence permits are required by all those who wish to work in Chile or stay more than 90 days for any purpose. Applications for residence permits will be considered individually by the *Chilean Embassy,* Consular Section, 12 Devonshire Street, London W1N 2DS, tel 0171-580 6392; 1732 Massachusetts Ave., NW, Washington DC 20036, tel 202-7851-746. Enquiries about employment, accompanied by information on your qualifications, experience and type of employment being sought, should be addressed to the *Servicio Nacional de Empleo,* Avenida Independencia 2, 3er Pabellón, Santiago, Chile.

## Colombia

Enquiries about immigration and work permits should be addressed to the *Colombian Consulate*, Suite 10, 140 Park Lane, London W1Y 3AA; tel 0171-495 4233 or 493 4565; *Embassy of Colombia*, 2118 Leroy Pl., NW Washington DC 20008, tel 202-387-8338. Procedures for obtaining visas are set out in the circular *Documentation Required when Applying for Residents' Visas*.

## Costa Rica

Sandwiched between Panama and Nicaragua, Costa Rica has become a popular destination for teachers, environmentalists and voluntary workers, because of its progressive social policies and good human rights record. The management of its rainforests is seen as exemplary by many. The *Costa Rican Consulate* is at: Flat 1, 14 Lancaster Gate, London W2 3LH, tel 0171-706 8844; 2114 S Street, NW, Washington DC 20008, tel 202-234-2945 or 338-6628 (consular section).

## Guyana

Information on immigration is obtainable from the Passport and Consular Section, *Guyana High Commission*, 3 Palace Court, Bayswater Road, London W2 4LP, tel 0171-229 7684; ask for the leaflet, *Notes on Conditions in the Republic of Guyana*. The *Guyanese Embassy* in the USA is at: 2490 Tracy Place, NW, Washington DC 20008; tel 202-265-6900-1. Although preference in employment is given to Guyanese nationals, non-nationals who possess certain skills can secure employment on a contract basis.

## Mexico

Industry is expanding rapidly in Mexico, and some North American firms are relocating some of their activities there. Wages tend to be one-tenth of those in the USA. Casual work opportunities are limited to teaching English or crewing on yachts. The English-language newspaper *Mexico City News* is useful for finding work. Information on immigration can be obtained from the *Mexican Embassy (Consular Section)*, 8 Halkin Street, London SW1X 7DW, tel 0171-235 6393; *Mexican Embassy*, 1911 Pennsylvania Avenue, NW, Washington DC 20006, tel 202-728-1600. The Embassy emphasises that it does not have information on firms or employment; and that immigration is not permitted except where firms require cetain specialist and professionals, in which case the firm itself applies to the immigration authorities in Mexico City.

## Paraguay

Opportunities for work and residence are good, and the requirements for establishing residence are minimal — a passport, health certificate and character references (an offer of work is not essential). The *Paraguay Embassy*, Consular Section, Braemar Lodge, Cornwall Gardens, London SW7 4AQ, tel 0171-937 1253 or 937 6629 (visa section); 2400 Massachusetts Avenue, NW, Washington DC 20008, tel 202-483-6960-2.

## Peru

An open market economy as well as other policies have stimulated foreign investment and thus created a demand for a wide variety of jobs for specialised foreign workers. A definite job offer is a pre-requisite to obtaining a work visa. Applications for work visas must be made by the employer through the *Ministry of the Interior*. Information and assistance can be offered by the *Peruvian Consulate General*, 52 Sloane Street, London SW1X 9SP, tel 0171-235 6867; 1700 Massachusetts Avenue, NW, Washington DC 20036, tel 202-833-9860.

## Uruguay

Residence permits are issued upon submission of a variety of documents testifying physical, mental, political and financial soundness. The details are set out in the circular *Formalities to be Complied with by Applicants for Permanent Residence in Uruguay*, available from either the *Uruguay Embassy*, 2nd Floor,

140 Brompton Road, London SW3 1HY, tel 0171-584 8192 or 589 8735 (visa section); or the *Uruguay Embassy*, 1919 F Street, NW, Washington DC 20006, tel 202-331-1313/6 or 3318142 (visa section).

**Venezuela**
Notwithstanding its substantial oil revenues, Venezuela is still an developing country in some respects. Immigration, even of high level technical and managerial personnel, is subject to quotas. Application for a work permit must in the first instance be made by the employer in Venezuela, and he must also act as sponsor for obtaining a residence permit. *The Venezuelan Embassy, Consular Section,* 56 Grafton Way, London W1P 5LB, tel 0171-387 6727, or 1099 30th Street, NW, Washington DC 20007, tel 202-342-2214, can offer little practical help or advice, and tend to refer enquiries to ICM (see above).

## EMBASSIES AND CONSULATES

British Embassy, Casilla de Correo 2050, Dr Luis Agote 2412/52, 1425 Buenos Aires, Argentina; tel 1-803-7070-1.
US Embassy, Unit 4334, Avenida Colombia 4300, 1425 Buenos Aires, Argentina; tel 1-774-7611 or 777-4533-4.

British Embassy, Avenida Arce 2732-2754, Casilla 694, La Paz, Bolivia; tel 2-357-424.
US Embassy, Avenida Arce 2780, Casilla 425, la Paz, Bolivia; tel 2-430-251.l

British Embassy, SES, Quadra 801, Conj. K, Lote 8 (Caixa Postal 07-0586), 70408-900 Brasilia, DF, Brazil; tel 61-225-2710.
British Consulate-General, Caixa Postal 669, 2° andar, Praia do Flamengo 284, 20001-970 Rio de Janeiro, RJ, Brazil; tel 21-552-1422. Consulates also in in Belém, Manáus, Recife, Salvador, Belo Horizonte, Pôrto Alegre, Rio Grande, São Paolo, Santos and Curitiba.
US Embassy, Lote 3, Unit 3500,Avenida das Naçôes, 70403-900, Brasilia, DF, Brasil; tel 61-321-7272.
Embassies also in Rio de Janeiro, São Paolo, Pôrto Alegre and Recife.

British Embassy, Casilla 72-Dor Casilla 16552, Avenida El Bosque Norte 0125, Santiago 9, Chile; tel 2-231-3737.
There are Consulates also in Antofagasta, Arica, Concepción, Punta Arenas and Valparaiso.
US Embassy, Avenida Andrés Bello 2800, Las Condes, Santiago, Chile; tel 2-232-2600.

British Embassy, Apdo Aéro 4508, Torre Propaganda Sancho, Calle 98, No 9-03, Piso 4, Santa Fe de Bogotá DC, Colombia; tel 1-218-5111.
There are Consulates in Barranquilla, Cali and Medellín.
US Embassy, Apdo Aéro 3831, Calle 38, No 8-61, Santa Fe de Bogotá DC, Colombia; tel 1-320-1300.

Apartado 815, Edificio Centro Colón 1007, San José, Costa Rica; tel 221-5566/5716/5816.
US Embassy, Pavas, San José, Costa Rica; tel 220-3939/3127.

Calle González Suárez 111, Casilla 314, Quito, Ecuador; tel 2-560-669 or 670-1.
There are Consulates in Guayaquil, Cuenca and Galápagos.
US Embassy, Avenida 12 Octubre y Patria, Quite, Ecuador; tel 2-562-890.

British Embassy, Edificio Financielo, Torre II, Nivel 7, 7a Avenida 5-10, Zona 4, Guatemala City, Guatemala; tel 2-321-601-2 or 321-604.

US Embassy, Avenida La Reforma 7-01, Zona 10, Guatemala City, Guatemala; tel 2-311-541.

British High Commission, 44 Main Street (PO Box 10849), Georgetown, Guyana; tel 2-65881 or 65884.
US Embassy, PO Box 10507, 99-100 Young and Duke Streets, Kingston, Georgetown, Guyana; tel 2-54900 or 57963.

British Embassy, Edificio Palmira, 3er Piso, Colonia Palmira, PO Box 290, Tegucigalpa, Honduras tel 325-429 or 320-612/8.
US Embassy, Avenido La Paz, Apdo 26-C, Tegucicalpa, Honduras; tel 323-120.

British Embassy, Lerma 71, Col. Cuauhtémoc, 06500 Mexico City DF, Mexico; tel 5-207-2089.
There are Consulates in Acapulco, Cancún, Ciudad Juarez, Guadalajara, Mérida, Monterrey, Tampico and Veracruz.
US Embassy, Paseo de la Reforma 305, Colonia Cuauhtámoc, 06500, Mexico City DF, Mexico; tel 5-211-0042.

Reparto 'Los Robles', Iera Etapa, Carretara de Masaya, Managua, Nicaragua; tel 2-780-014 or 780-887 or 674-050.
US Embassy, Apartado 327, Km 4.5, Carretera Sur, Managua, Nicaragua; tel 2-666-010.

British Embassy, Torre Banco Sur, Calle 53 (Apartado 889 Zona 1), Panama City 1, Panama; tel 2-690-866.
US Embassy, Apartado 6959, Avenida balboa, Entre Calle 37 y 38, Panama City 5, Panama; tel 2-271-777.

British Embassy, Calle Presidente Franco 76, Casilla de Correo 404, Asunción, Paraguay; tel 21-444-472 or 449-146 or 496-067.
US Embassy, Casilla 402, Avenida Mariscal López 1776, Asunción, Paraguay; tel 21-213-715.

British Embassy, Edificio El Pacifico Washington (Piso 12), Plaza Washington, Avenida Arequipa, PO Box 854, Lima 100, Peru; tel 1-433-5032.
There are Consulates in Arequipa, Piura, Trujillo, Iquitos and Cusco.
US Embassy, Avenida La Encalada Cuadra 17, Lima 33, Peru; tel 1-434-3000.

British Embassy, Calle Marco Bruto 1073, 11300 Montevideo, Uruguay; tel 2-623-630 or 623-650.
US Embassy, Lauro Muller 1776, Montevideo, Uruguay; tel 2-236-061.

British Embassy, Edificio Torre Las Mercedes, Piso 3, Avenida la Estancia, Chuao, Caracas 1060, Venezuela; tel 2-993-4111.
Consulates in Maracaibo and Mérida.
US Embassy, Suite F, Street Suapure, Colinas de Valle Arriba, Caracas, Venezuela; tel 2-977-2011. Consulate in Maracaibo.

# Australia

Australian High Commission, Australia House, Strand, London WC2B 4LU, tel 0171-379 4334
Australian Embassy, 1601 Massachusetts Avenue, NW, Washington DC 20036, tel 202-797-3000
Currency: 1 Australian Dollar ($) = 100 cents
Rate of Exchange: £1 = $1.9; US$1 = $1.3

Although some five million migrants have settled in Australia in the post-war period, the number of newly admitted immigrants has been drastically reduced in recent years, in view of the economic difficulties Australia is now facing. The majority of these, about 10,000 a year, are British; and the Australian government is still eager to encourage migrants with useful skills and training. Once area of expansion guaranteed to generate jobs into the next century is Australia's burgeoning tourist industry.

## GENERAL FACTS

### Population
Australia's total population is 17.7 million with a yearly increase of 2%, two-fifths of this through net migration. Spread over three million square miles, the average population density is very low: six per square mile. Distribution is very uneven, however, with only one person per square mile in Western Australia, and a mere 0.3 in the Northern Territory. Over ninety per cent of Australians are of European descent (75% or so from Britain and Ireland). Of the indigenous inhabitants, the aborigines, only 160,000 remain. Other major ethnic groups are mainly Asian: Chinese, Vietnamese, Indian, Iranian, etc.

### Climate
Because of its enormous area, Australia's climate varies considerably, ranging from tropical and sub-tropical in Queensland and other northern areas to temperate, cooler weather in the south. In the western and central regions desert conditions prevail.

In general, Australia is warm and sunny (Perth has a daily average of almost eight hours of sunshine); summer temperatures often exceed 38°C (100°F) and humidity is high in the northeast. Snow falls on the Australian Alps and in Tasmania.

Annual rainfall varies from 160 inches along the tropical northeast coast) to below five inches in the Lake Eyre region of northern South Australia. Annual rainfall in the capital cities is less extreme, varying between Darwin with 58.7 inches and Adelaide with 2.1 inches.

### Government
Australia is made up of six states — New South Wales, Victoria, Queensland, South Australia, Western Australia, and the island of Tasmania — and has a three-tier structure of Government. Matters of national concern are the responsibility of the Australian Parliament and Government. Six State Governments and legislatures have responsibilities within their own boundaries which

complement the activities of the national government. About 900 Local Government bodies are concerned with matters of a local or regional nature.

Close institutional links are retained with Britain and the Commonwealth (although there have been moves to change to a republican system of government). Queen Elizabeth II is also Queen of Australia and is represented by a Governor-General (at the national level) and six State Governors. The Governor-General is the Head of State and formally the Chief Executive. The six Governors perform a similar constitutional role in the States.

## Cities
The majority (65%) of the Australian population live in urban metropolitan areas, with a further 20% in provincial towns. Australian cities cover a much larger area than comparable European towns, as most Australians prefer to live in detached houses set in their own gardens rather than in flats or terraced houses. The suburbs of Sydney (the largest of Australia's cities, with 3.7 million inhabitants) stretch out to cover a radius of over 20 miles. Other capital cities have populations ranging from Melbourne's 3.1 million to Darwin with 80,000. Canberra, the national capital, has 330,000 inhabitants.

## Rural life
Only about 15% of Australians live in rural areas; some of these are farmers, while others are engaged in mining or development projects. Many aborigines also live on the land, but in reserves or settlements.

## Religion, Sport and Culture
Christianity is the majority faith with the Church of England claiming 24% of the faithful, and Roman Catholicism 26%.

Hot summers and a largely sandy coastline have made swimming Australia's favourite pastime, closely followed by yachting, power boat racing, surfing and other water sports. British settlers introduced traditional sports such as cricket, tennis, rugby and athletics — in all of which Australians have excelled. Other sports include Australian Rules football (a mixture of rugby and Gaelic football), squash, basketball, martial arts and skiing.

Australia has a strong and rapidly developing arts scene, which derives much of its potency from its Australian and not its European roots. A tradition of fine artists (Nolan, Drysdale, Boyd) and opera singers (Joan Sutherland), plus international success in literature (Patrick White's Nobel Prize and Peter Carey's Booker Prize for example) reveals vigour and originality in the arts. In particular, a new generation of Australian film makers have made their mark over recent years: the exploits of *Crocodile Dundee* and *Mad Max* are known to cinema audiences everywhere.

## Immigration
UK, US and Canadian citizens require visas in order to enter Australia as tourists, students, or workers. Enquiries should be made to the nearest High Commission or Embassy.

Current Australian immigration policy stems from the basic principle that employment opportunities must be available as a first priority to Australian citizens and migrants admitted for permanent settlement. During periods of high unemployment the quota of migrants must inevitably be reduced. Nevertheless, some 87,428 settlers arrived in 1994-95.

Eligibility for permanent settlement falls into five categories, including those with close family connections who must be sponsored by their relatives; people whose occupations are in the labour shortage category; those nominated by an Australian employer for a specific job under the Employment Nomination Scheme (ENS); and experienced business people with definite proposals and sufficient capital (at least $500,000) to establish viable enterprises which will aid Australia's economic development.

There are currently few opportunities for unskilled or semi-skilled workers. Details of occupations in current demand are available, together with the free leaflets on immigration and life in Australia are available from the Australian High Commission or Embassy.

Under the Government's Temporary Residence policy there is provision for people from overseas who are management, executive, professional, technical and specialist personnel to enter Australia for a specific employment period where it can be shown that the job cannot be filled by an existing resident. It is restricted to working for a sponsoring organisation, although you can change sponsors.

The Financial and Migrant Information Service of the *Commonwealth Bank of Australia,* 3rd Floor, 1 Kingsway, London WC2B 6DU, conducts special Information Days for approved migrants at venues in London, Manchester, Edinburgh and Glasgow. To obtain further details of these promotions as well as information on such aspects as housing, cost of living, taxation, health insurance, household expenses, transfer of capital and banking/investment facilities, contact the Bank at the above address.

Citizenship will normally be granted after at least two years' residence in Australia.

## Cost of Standard of Living
As an indication of the standard of living, latest figures show that the statistically average home in Australia has more than five rooms, with less than one person per room; 99% of all homes have gas or electricity, or both; 90% have television; and most own at least one radio, a refrigerator, a washing machine and a telephone.

## Housing
More than 60% of the Australian population live in the five major cities of Brisbane, Sydney, Melbourne, Adelaide and Perth. Most of the others also live in cities and towns along the coastal fringe. The cost of housing varies considerably from state to state and depends on such factors as proximity to facilities and the city centre. Prices for two-bedroom houses in Sydney's suburbs start from about $150,000. Housing is cheaper in Perth and Adelaide, while Melbourne and Brisbane are at least as expensive as Sydney. Rented accommodation is most expensive in city centres. A one-bedroom flat in a down-market area of Sydney will cost at least $120 a week. The Financial and Migrant Service of the Commonwealth Bank of Australia, (address above) issues a comprehensive *Cost of Living and Housing Survey,* free to prospective migrants to Australia.

## Health
Persons who are approved to live in Australia for a period more than six months are entitled to enrol for, and receive, basic hospital and medical cover under the National Health Insurance scheme, Medicare. Funded by a 1.25% income surcharge, Medicare covers hospital accommodation and treatment as well as 85% of the scheduled fee charged by general practitioners. Supplementary insurance for services not covered by Medicare such as dental and optical treatment or treatment in hospital as a private patient, is available from private health organisations.

## Education
Education is free in both primary and secondary schools, though some fee-paying schools exist, usually denominational, attended by one out of four children. Compulsory schooling ages are 6-15 in all states except Tasmania where the leaving age is 16. The school year begins in February. School education culminates with the examination for the High School Certificate, conducted in the sixth year of secondary school.

There are 21 universities and over 200 specialist or technical colleges. The Australian Government operates a number of student assistance schemes; grants are subject to a means test.

**Embassies and Consulates**
British High Commission, Commonwealth Avenue, Yarralumla, Canberra, ACT 2600; tel 6-270-6666.

US Embassy, Moonah, Canberra, ACT 2600; tel 6-270-5000.
Consulates in Brisbane, Melbourne, Perth and Sydney.

**Tourist Offices**
Australian Tourist Commission, Gemini House, 10-18 Putney Hill, London SW15 6AA; tel 0181-780 2227.
Australian Tourist Commission, Suite 1200, 2121 Avenue of the Stars, Los Angeles, CA 90067; tel 310-552-1988.

## CONDITIONS OF WORK

**Hours**
Hours of work are fixed by awards or legislation and are usually 35 or 38 hours per week, based on a five-day week, except for the retail trade (5½-day week) or those who work on a shift basis.

**Holidays**
Most employees receive four weeks' paid holiday per annum. In addition, there are eleven national public holidays — New Year's Day; Australia Day (26 Jan); Good Friday; Easter Monday; Anzac Day (25 April); May Day; Queen's Birthday (10 Jun); Labour Day (7 Oct); Christmas Day; Boxing Day.

**Safety and Compensation**
State and national laws protect workers by laying down strict conditions concerning standards of safety, sanitation, heat and lighting, applicable to all workplaces. Frequent inspections are carried out by officers of each State's Department of Labour and Industry. All employers are required to insure their workers against industrial accidents; compensation is paid either in weekly amounts or as a lump sum, based on the worker's normal earnings.

**Trade Unions**
Membership of unions is not compulsory in Australia but 55% of employees are union members. Unions are similar in structure to those in Britain, and biennial Congress of the Australian Council of Trade Unions fills the role of the TUC in Britain. Industrial disputes are settled by arbitration.

**Taxation**
All people in employment in Australia are now obliged to apply for a nine-digit tax file number. Income tax is deduced on PAYE basis, and adjusted at the end of the tax year (30 June). Deductions are allowed for dependants, life insurance schemes, etc. The first $5,400 is tax free. There is a 20% rate on the tax band between $5,400 to $20,700; followed by 38% on the next band up to $38,000; and 43% on the band up to $50,000. All additional income is taxed at 47%. Further details can be obtained from the Australian High Commission or from the Advisings section of the Sydney South Tax Office, GPO Box 5300, Sydney NSW 2001.

## WORK AVAILABLE

**General**
Australia has traditionally derived its wealth from its vast agricultural and mineral resources, but this has also made it vulnerable to fluctuations in

commodity prices. All aspects of Australian industry and services are highly developed. The demand is now for highly skilled workers such as teachers, medical staff, computers specialists, and engineers. Requirements change constantly, so it is worth checking with Australian information offices.

Prospective migrants are advised to contact the Chief Migration Officer at the Australian High Commission. The Migration Department can supply a free factsheet on the *Australian Labour Force* which contains details of minimum and basic wages, recent wage increases by geographical area and the latest information on job vacancies.

In many professions, eligibility for work in Australia depends on acceptance of British or US qualifications. Agreement has been reached on the mutual acceptance of many qualifications, but in some fields the membership of an Australian professional association, or the passing of additional examinations is a necessity.

Individual assessments of qualifications and employment prospects are referred back to the Commonwealth Department of Employment, Education and Training, whose *National Office of Overseas Skills Recognition (NOOSR)* decides what recommendation to make concerning would-be migrants or temporary residents. NOOSR stresses that would-be migrants should have their qualifications assessed (as far as possible) before travelling to Australia. Otherwise they may find that they cannot work.

In principle, it is not possible to move to Australia without a pre-arranged job; and new migrants are not allowed to draw state benefits until they have been in Australia for six months.

The Agents General for the Australian states can offer information on all aspects of life in their respective areas, but in general recruitment is confined to specific requests from employers. Their methods of recruitment usually centre on advertising campaigns in the national press. Their addresses in London are:

New South Wales, 75 King William Street, EC4
South Australia, 50 Strand, WC2N 5LW
Victoria, Victoria House, Melbourne Place, WC2B 4LG
Western Australia, 115 Strand, WC2R 0AJ.

### Newspapers
Regional newspapers can be consulted at the Agents General listed above, and at Australia House (which also holds the Australian Yellow Pages). A useful source of information in the UK is the monthly newspaper *Australian News,* available by subscription from *Outbound Newspapers,* 1 Commercial Road, Eastbourne, East Sussex BN21 3XQ, tel 01323-412001, which may also supply a number of guides, atlases, and employment guides. *TNT Magazine* also publishes a useful *Australia and New Zealand Travel Planner,* enquiries to: TNT Planners, 14-15 Childs Place, London SW5 9RX; it is available in tourist offices and travel agents. Agents for Australian newspapers are: *TNT Newsfast,* Unit 6, Spitfire Estate, Spitfire Way, Heston, Middlesex TW5 9NW, tel 0181-56,12345 or 6612113; and *F.A. Smyth and Associates Ltd.,* 23A Aylmer Parade, London N2 0PQ.

## SPECIFIC CONTACTS

Listings of professional bodies and relevant State authorities can be supplied by the High Commission (see above).

### Chiropodists
Overseas chiropody qualifications are not automatically recognised in Australia. All foreign-trained chiropodists must undertake at least the Stage II and perhaps also the Stage I examination.

Registration with a chiropody board is a prerequisite for practising as a chiropodist (known as a 'podiatrist' in Australia) in all Australian States. Enquiries should be made either to the *Migration Branch* of the Australian High Commission (address above); the *National Office of Overseas Skills Recognition*, PO Box 1407, Canberra City, Act 2601; or to the Executive Secretary, the *Australian Podiatry Council*, Suite 11, 96 Camberwell Road, Hawthorn, Victoria 3112, who will also make available a list of the State Registration Boards and of Podiatry Schools.

## Consultants and Agencies

*AB Secretarial Pty Ltd.,* 8b Borrack Square, Altona North, Victoria 3025 — offers temporary and permanent office staff placements in major oil, chemical, manufacturing, transport and meat industries, and professional and engineering companies.

*Centacom Staff Pty Ltd.,* 72 Pitt Street, Sydney 2000 — has a network of 44 city and local branches in Australia (there are branches in capital cities of every state). Placements are in secretarial, word processing, computer and accounting positions.

*Staffing Centre Personnel Services,* Suite 3403, 60 Margaret Street, Sydney 2000, and 155 Queen Street, Melbourne — places people with office or computer experience in full or temporary positions.

## Nursing

*The Royal Women's Hospital,* 132 Grattan Street, Carlton, Victoria 3053 — has a Staff Development Programme to whom nurses may apply. Applicants must have an appropriate visa for employment in Australia and be eligible for registration as a general nurse and midwife in Victoria. The two major areas of employment possibilities are the Operating Theatres and Special Care Nurseries of the hospital. The High Commission can provide a full list of Australian hospitals where enquiries concerning placements can be made. There are also a number of agencies offering more short-term nursing work.

The *Australian Nursing Federation* may be contacted at: 373-375 St George's Road, North Fitzroy, Vic 3182.

## Secretarial

The main agencies include *Centacom Staff, Drake Personnel, Western Staff Service, Select, Allstaff, Ecco, Lorraine Martin Personnel* and *Kelly.* Addresses are available from the Information Office, Australian High Commission.

## Other Opportunities

Opportunities in Australia are also referred to in the chapters in *Specific Careers. Live and Work in Australia and New Zealand* (Vacation Work) contains some valuable employment contacts and information about living and working in Australia.

# SHORT TERM WORK

There are some schemes that enable people to pre-arrange short term work in Australia; but many of the most interesting — and lucrative — jobs are available only for those who are prepared to make the journey to Australia and then look on the spot. Those aged between 18 and 25 who are not deterred by the cost of getting there can obtain a 'working holiday' visa that will enable them to work legally for up to six months.

## Official schemes

BUNAC's *Work Australia* programme is open to any citizen of the UK, Ireland, The Netherlands or Canada between the ages of 18 and 30 and is especially suitable for gap- and final-year students. Participants can take any job, anywhere in Australia. The benefits of going with BUNAC include help with booking flights and obtaining insurance, pick-up from the airport on arrival, guaranteed accommodation for the first two nights and comprehensive orientation to help with jobs, tax, health etc. Participants on the BUNAC North American programme can continue westwards from Los Angeles with a Hawaiian stopover en route to Australia. Proof of $2,000 in personal funds is a requirement of the programme, but the cost of the air fare can be taken out of this and stopovers can be made on the return route.

**Voluntary Work**
There are several *GAP* projects for school leavers, mainly for young people willing to stay an average of six months working on farms or conservation projects or helping in schools. See *Getting the Job* and *Voluntary Work* for details of these schemes.

There are two major voluntary work organisations:

*Australian Trust for Conservation Volunteers,* ATCV Headquarters, PO Box 423, Ballarat, 3353 Victoria, tel 6153-331-483 — places volunteers in ATCV workteams in Australia at any time of the year. Conservation work may be farm fencing, seed collection, tree planting, trail construction, etc. Volunteers must be over 17, physically fit and able to speak and understand English. Potential volunteers are offered a package costing $745 and lasting six weeks. This covers food, accommodation and travel expenses over that period but not travel to and from Australia. For further information contact the National Director, enclosing an IRC.

*Involvement Volunteers Association Inc.,* PO Box 218, Port Melbourne, Victoria 3207, tel 613-9646-5504 — is an international voluntary work organisation with offices in the USA and Germany involved in projects in Australia and other countries.

**Other Work**
The Australian Government's *Commonwealth Employment Service (CES)* can help those looking for work, when work is available: its branches notify each other of any vacancies by computer, and in some major cities there are branches which specialise in temporary work, known as *Templines.* These offices are most helpful to those looking for seasonal work on farms, and issue a booklet that gives the locations and dates of various harvests around the country. Two of the most important of these are the tobacco harvest, which begins in the Atherton Tablelands of Northern Queensland in late September, and around Myrtleford in central Victoria in late January; and the grape harvest, which takes place in February and March: two particular regions to head for are Griffith in New South Wales and the Barossa Valley in South Australia. There are also possibilities for working as ranch hands (roustabouts) in the outback, especially on sheep farms when shearing takes place in October and November or February and March. See the harvest Guide in the *Australia and New Zealand Travel Planner,* address above.

Temporary work is available in offices, shops, restaurants, bars, petrol stations etc. The CES may be able to help people find such work, as may private agencies such as *Bligh,* 428 George Street, Sydney 2000; tel 02-235-3699.

## BRITISH COMPANIES
with branches, affiliates or subsidiaries in Australia

At the time of publication, the *Australian British Business Directory* was not available from the *Australian British Chamber of Commerce* (Suite 10/16, 3rd Floor, Morley House, 314-322 Regent Street, London W1R 5AJ). They advise writing to the *Australian British Chamber,* Level 5, 520 Collins Street, Melbourne, VIV 3000.

*Who's Who in US Business in Australia,* with the names of 1400 businesses with US connections, is published annually by the *American Chamber of Commerce in Australia*, 50 Pitt Street, 3rd Floor, Sydney, NSW 2000, Australia.

# New Zealand

New Zealand High Commission, New Zealand House, Haymarket, London SW1Y 4TQ, tel 0171-930 8422
New Zealand Embassy, 37 Observatory Circle, NW, Washington DC 20008, tel 202-328-4800
Currency: NZ$1 = 100 cents
Rate of Exchange: £1 = NZ$2.3; US1$ = NZ$1.5

New Zealand has some of the world's most beautiful scenery, and still offers a quality of life that can hardly be matched by any other country, although the standard of living has fallen steadily since the late 1970s. New Zealand's current immigration policy is meant to attract migrants with the skills and experience required for the country's economic development. These laws have been altered to bring them into line with the points system already operating in Australia and Canada (see below).

## GENERAL FACTS

### Population
New Zealand comprises two large islands and some smaller islands covering 103,736 square miles. The total area is slightly larger than that of the UK; average population density is 35 per square mile. The total population of 3.6 million includes those of European and Maori descent, and immigrants from East Asia and the Pacific islands.

### Climate
While generally similar to that in Britain, there is a greater range from north to south; and New Zealand's average temperatures throughout the year are 3-4°C higher. The north is considerably warmer. Rainfall is heavier than in the UK, but unevenly distributed, with the Southern Alps receiving 480 inches and Central Otago a mere 16 inches. Unusual features of the landscape include geysers, volcanoes, glaciers, fjords and occasional earthquakes.

### Government
New Zealand is a parliamentary democracy; a Governor-General represents the Queen, but is politically insignificant. The House of Representatives has 97 members. The Parliament, headed by a Prime Minister, is elected by all citizens and permanent residents aged 18 and over.

### Cities
Eighty-four per cent of the population live in urban areas, and more than 1,600,000 inhabit the four main cities.

Auckland (910,600) is New Zealand's largest city: one-third of manufacturing employees work there in the developing secondary industries. Wellington (327,000), the capital, is famous for its fine harbour, and houses many national organisations.

Christchurch (310,000), the largest city in South Island, is a beautiful, open city, set in lush farmland and known for its parks, botanical gardens and sports grounds. Dunedin (110,000), was founded by Scotsmen; as well as being an important educational centre, is also the port for the agricultural area of Otago.

## Rural Life

Pasture and arable land accounts for 53% of New Zealand's land area; forests cover a further 27%. Both are essential to the country's economy. Although farms are large, not much manpower is required, due to the high level of mechanisation, so that a typical farm could be run by a farmer, his wife and an agricultural labourer only, with occasional extra help.

## Religion, Sport and Culture

There is complete religious freedom, and no state-aided church. The majority (24%) belong to the Church of England; the remainder include Presbyterians (18%), Catholics (15%) and Methodists (4%).

New Zealand is a modern country with its own distinctive culture, which includes an appreciation of the outdoor life. New Zealand is ideal for all kinds of sport, with facilities for rugby (the national game), cricket, soccer, tennis, skiing, sailing, etc.

# FACTORS INFLUENCING EMPLOYMENT

## Immigration

British citizens may enter New Zealand without a visa, and can remain for up to six months, given evidence of sufficient funds and a return ticket. Information for British visitors is contained in leaflet UK30 (see below). US and Canadian citizens may remain for up to 90 days without a visa. All visitors may extend their stays to 12 months by applying to the local Immigration Service office.

In spite of high unemployment, it is still possible for British citizens to obtain a temporary work permit from the Department of Labour if they find a job while in New Zealand as visitors, provided that they can show that they are not depriving a New Zealand resident of employment.

## Migrants

New Zealand went over to a points system for allocating places to migrants in November 1991. Prior to this, potential migrants had to arrange work before applying for a visa, a system which made it difficult to apply without going to New Zealand first.

Points are awarded on the basis of the applicant's qualifications, work experience and age. Further points are awarded to applicants with over NZ$100,000 in settlement funds; relatives in New Zealand; or an offer of skilled employment. The highest points are awarded to those with postgraduate degrees or degrees in science, technology or engineering. The preferred age range is between 18 and 45. A leaflet entitled *Applying for Residence* explains all these conditions.

Recognising that it is often difficult for prospective migrants to make contact with an employer there, the New Zealand High Commission in London operates an Immigration Placement Service with the Department of Labour in New Zealand. Migrants can complete a 'Personal History Card' to be circulated to employers who are interested in recruiting staff overseas.

## Entrepreneurs and Businessmen

Migrants who are applying for residence on the basis of their business skills will be assessed on their potential contribution to New Zealand and account will be taken of: their business record and skills; the amount of investment capital they have available (in addition to the funds required for personal establishment costs in New Zealand); and their intended business activities. Migrants and their families will also need to satisfy routine immigration, health, character and interview requirements.

In approving a residence application under the business skills category, the New Zealand authorities expect that migrants will move within a reasonable period of time and establish a base of family and business operations in New

Zealand. Residents who remain abroad for too long may have to go through the entire procedure again.

Applications for residence permits, and all enquiries about immigration, should be addressed to the *Migration Branch,* New Zealand House, Haymarket, London SW1Y 4TQ. Some of the many leaflets available on various aspects of living in New Zealand include:

| | |
|---|---|
| L34 | Education in New Zealand |
| L35 | Foreign Exchange and Banks |
| L38 | New Zealand Income Tax |
| L82 | Housing and Home Ownership in New Zealand |
| L84 | Social Security |
| L200 | Health Care in New Zealand |
| UK30 | Visiting New Zealand |

**Housing and Accommodation**
New Zealanders typically prefer to live in detached bungalows with large gardens. An average three-bedroomed house in one of the larger cities costs NZ$150,000. Prices are highest in Auckland and Wellington. Potential migrants are encouraged to build or buy their own house, but it is not a condition for acceptance. Additional points are awarded to those who have at least NZ$100,000 available in settlement funds. There is plentiful rented accommodation, starting from as little as $90 a week.

**Health and Welfare**
New Zealand's social security system is financed by taxation, and no special contributions are required. With one in three of New Zealanders on welfare benefits of some kind, and a huge budget deficit, the Government decided in 1992 to reduce benefits. Free hospital care has been abolished and patients must now pay NZ$50 a night for hospital stays (up to ten nights per year) as well as being means-tested for all kinds of treatment. Visits to doctors and prescriptions have also become more expensive.

**Education**
Education is compulsory between the ages of six and 16, and free from three (kindergarten) to 19 (except for private schools). Most children start co-educational primary school at five, and at 12 or 13 go on to secondary school, where a two-year general course is followed by one year's specialisation leading to the School Certificate examination.

University entrance is by examination or by a certificate of fitness issued by a recognised school; most students remain at school for one extra year after qualifying to obtain the Higher School Certificate, which entitles the holder to a university grant covering tuition fees and an annual allowance. There are universities in Auckland, Christchurch, Dunedin, Hamilton, Palmerston North, and Wellington; there are also 13 technical institutes and six teacher training colleges.

**National Service**
New Zealand has abolished compulsory military service, and maintains a purely voluntary defence system.

**Embassies and Consulates**
British High Commission, 44 Hill Street, Wellington 1; tel 4-472-6049.
British Consulate-General, 15th Floor, Faye Richwhite Building, 151 Queen Street, Auckland 1.
British Consulate, 2nd Floor Suite, 173 Cashel Street, Christchurch 1.

US Embassy, 29 Fitzherbert Terrace, Thorndon, Wellington; tel 4-472-2068.

# CONDITION OF WORK

## Wages

Although there is a minimum wage fixed by national legislation, each profession or industry also has sets of minimum wages which are usually higher. Wages for unskilled manual work generally do not fall below NZ$7 per hour. The average annual wage is around NZ$35,000. Since 1980, however, the real disposable income of most workers has fallen by 5%.

## Hours

Wages are based universally on the 40-hour, five-day week. In some industries, overtime is paid at up to 150% for the first three hours, and 200% for every hour thereafter, depending on workplace agreements.

## Holidays

Employees are legally entitled to at least three weeks' paid holiday per annum. In addition, there are the following public holidays; New Year's Day; 2 January; Waitangi Day (6 February); Good Friday; Easter Monday; Anzac Day (25 April); Queen's Birthday (first Monday in June); Labour Day (fourth Monday in October); Christmas Day; and Boxing Day. Each province also celebrates its own Anniversary Day.

## Safety and Compensation

Industrial awards lay down certain standards, but conditions are usually far above the minimum. Employers are obliged to insure their workers against industrial accidents resulting in temporary incapacity disablement or death.

## Trade Unions

Union membership is not obligatory under national legislation. Under the Labour Relations Act of 1987, only unions with at least 1,000 members can be legally registered, leading to the amalgamation of many smaller unions. All unions are represented by one collective organisation, the New Zealand Council of Trade Unions.

## Taxation

A direct tax on personal income is deducted on a PAYE basis and includes social security contributions. Allowances are made for dependants, life insurance premiums, school fees, charitable donations, etc. See Leaflet L38 for further details.

# WORK AVAILABLE

## General

The major problem facing the New Zealand economy, apart from worldwide recession, is the difficulty of establishing large-scale industries in a country with only 3.6 million inhabitants. Manufacturing industries have not grown at the rate that was expected in the 1980s; the government hopes that following drastic free market reforms and the end of chronic inflation, New Zealand's international competitiveness can be quickly restored.

New Zealand is very anxious to encourage qualified immigrants and business-people, partly because many highly qualified New Zealanders prefer to make their own careers abroad.

## Newspapers

Advertisements for insertion in the national and regional New Zealand press can be placed with the *New Zealand Press Association,* 85 Fleet Street, London EC4Y 1DY, which represents the major dailies (*New Zealand Herald, Evening Post, The Press, Otago Daily Times, The Dominion*). Subscriptions to New

Zealand newspapers can also be arranged through NZPA, who will also sell specimen copies on request.

The Saturday editions of the major New Zealand dailies are available for inspection at the Migration Branch on the first floor of New Zealand House. Also available from New Zealand House is leaflet L86 *Subscriptions to New Zealand Newspapers. TNT Magazine* publishes a useful travel guide (see *Australia, Newspapers*).

## SPECIFIC CONTACTS

### Accountants
An accountant wishing to practise in New Zealand must be a member of the New Zealand Society of Accountants. Under a reciprocal agreement, membership of the society is automatically granted to members of any of the main British Associations of Chartered Accountants; The Canadian Institute of Chartered Accountants (and Provincial Institutes); and the Institute of Chartered Accountants in Ireland.

There are good prospects for qualified accountants in New Zealand, both in public accountancy and in other fields. There are also excellent opportunities for young people (up to age 25) who are almost qualified and intend to complete their academic training in New Zealand.

Further information on prospects and eligibility for registration is available from the Executive Director, *New Zealand Society of Accountants,* 57 Willis Street, Box 11342, Wellington.

Advertisements can also be placed in the Society's official publication *The Accountants' Journal,* Print Advertising, Ground Floor, 214 Willis Street, PO Box 3016, Wellington.

### Chartered Secretaries
Information on registration can be obtained from the Executive Director, *New Zealand Institute of Chartered Secretaries and Administrators,* PO Box 444, Auckland 1.

### Doctors and Medical Staff
Doctors registered in the UK or Eire by virtue of a university degree obtained in either of these two countries are eligible for registration in New Zealand. Queries on eligibility should be addressed to the Secretary, *Medical Council of New Zealand,* PO Box 11-649, Wellington.

To ascertain eligibility for registration as specialists, doctors should contact the *Medical Council of New Zealand.* Actual recruitment is carried out by local health boards known as 'Crown Health Enterprises'.

Agencies also recruiting medical staff include:

Acorn Medical Staffing, PO Box 74-385, Auckland.
Drake Medox, 7th Floor, Southpac Towers, Cnr Queen and Customs Street, Auckland.
Med Staff Healthcare, 68 Shortland Street, Auckland.

### Engineers
Intending migrants can advertise in *New Zealand Engineering*, the monthly journal of the *Institution of Professional Engineers*, New Zealand. The publishers are Engineering Publications Co Ltd., PO Box 12241, Wellington.

### Public Service Appointments
The *State Services Commission,* PO Box 329, Wellington, is a convenient source of information on the functions of the New Zealand Public Service Departments. These departments occasionally need persons with high technical, scientific or managerial qualifications and experience. Enquiries should be directed to

individual departments as they each function as an employing organisation in their own right.

**Other Opportunities**
Opportunities in New Zealand are also referred to in many of the chapters of *Specific Careers.*

# SHORT TERM WORK

Opportunities for temporary work in New Zealand are very similar to those in Australia. For British citizens, there is a 'Working Holiday Scheme' enabling British citizens to travel to New Zealand for up to 12 months.

US students can spend up to six months working in New Zealand between 1 April and 31 October through the *Work in New Zealand* programme run by CIEE (see *Working Exchanges* in the *Getting the Job* chapter).

**Seasonal Work**
People already in the country may be able to get jobs over the English summer in hotels in New Zealand's expanding skiing resorts. Areas to head for include Mount Hutt and Coronet Peak in the Southern Alps on the South Island and Mount Ruapehu on the North Island. Jobs over the New Zealand summer may be found in Nelson and Christchurch on the South Island or Tauranga or the Bay of Islands on the North Island.

Casual fruit picking jobs may be found, from picking peaches and apricots around Kerikeri in December to picking kiwi fruit in May around the Bay of Plenty. It is also possible to stay on farms while doing some work in exchange for board and lodging. Farmers often look for casual workers at local youth hostels. The dates and locations of different harvests are covered in detail in the book *Work Your Way Around the World* (Vacation Work).

**Other Work**
*GAP Activity Projects* can arrange jobs lasting for six months on farms in the Christchurch area for school leavers (see *Getting the Job* for details). The *International Farm Experience Programme* (see the chapter *Agriculture and the Environment*) finds farm jobs lasting for six or eight months for UK, US and Canadian students of agriculture.

## BRITISH COMPANIES
with branches, affiliates or subsidiaries in New Zealand

The *New Zealand-United Kingdom Chamber of Commerce*, Suite 10/16, 3rd Floor, Morley House, 314-322 Regent Street, London W1R 5AJ publishes the *New Zealand British Business Directory.*

## AMERICAN COMPANIES
with branches, affiliates or subsidiaries in New Zealand

The *American Chamber of Commerce in New Zealand Directory* is published annually by the *American Chamber of Commerce*, PO Box 3408, Wellington, New Zealand.

# China

Embassy of the People's Republic of China, 49-51 Portland Place, London W1N 3AH tel 0171-636 9375
Embassy of the People's Republic of China, 2300 Connecticut Ave., NW, Washington DC 20008, tel 202-328-2500-2
Currency: 1 Yuan (Y) or Renminbi = 10 jiao = 100 fen
Exchange rate: £1 = Y13; $1 = Y6

China underwent rapid economic expansion during the late 1980s. Excessive imports and high inflation forced the government to slow economic growth from 1989. There are now moves towards liberalising the economy, allowing for greater foreign participation and cooperation. The suppression of the democracy movement in 1989, and the continued occupation of Tibet on the other hand, have done damage to China's prestige, but not to its international contacts. Growth is high (currently 10%) but China is really a series of interlocking economies, with areas of development, and other provinces lagging behind. China's policy-makers are concentrating on infrastructure development, in roads and other communications; and technology transfer, which means that larger UK and US companies setting up there often include consultancy and training for local staff as part of the deal. Other opportunities are in English-teaching. 150 million people in China are currently estimated to be learning English.

## GENERAL FACTS

### Population
China is the world's most populous country, and the third in land area, with an estimated population of 1.2 billion spread over 3,696,100 square miles. The average density of inhabitants is 325 per square mile, although 80% of the population is concentrated in the east, and especially the northeast.

### Climate
The climate varies greatly from region to region. While the whole of north China has harsh winters with cultivation only possible in the summer, the south is humid with mild winters and hot summers that last five to eight months. In the very south the climate is tropical and year-round cultivation is possible. Temperatures during winter vary from 10°C in the Yangtse Valley to freezing in Inner Mongolia. In the summer, the temperature reaches 35 or 40°C in some areas. Greatest rainfall is during the summer, except in the arid northwest and Tibet.

### Government
Under the Constitution of 1982, the National People's Congress (NPC) became the most powerful organ in the state hierarchy. Its 2,569 (in 1994) deputies are elected by each region for a five year term. The NPC elects the head of state, the President of the People's Republic of China, and the national Government — the State Council — to administer the country.

China is divided into 22 provinces, three municipalities (Beijing, Shanghai and Tianjin), and five autonomous regions including Tibet. The latter regions, forming 50-60% of the total land, are home largely to minority nationalities including at least 55 different ethnic groups, compared to the Han Chinese group which comprises 94% of the rest of the population.

## Cities
Shanghai is the largest city, with a population of 8 million, followed by Beijing 7 million, Tientsin (6 million), Shen-yang (4,500,000), Wuhan (4 million) and Canton (3,500,000).

## Rural Life
China consists largely of high mountain ranges, deserts and steppes. Only 10.3% of the country is under systematic cultivation, although a recent survey showed that the agricultural sector employed about 60% of China's labour force. This is changing; there is a drift to the cities and a more 'industrial' pattern of development in the countryside. The main crops are cereals, rice, tea and cotton. Most agricultural production is carried out on self-administered fields. The administrative functions of the people's communes were abolished by the new Constitution leaving them as mainly economic enterprises.

## Religion, Sport and Culture
Most Chinese are officially non-religious or atheists. The indigenous religion is a combination of Confucianism, Taoism and animism, mostly aimed at the preservation of traditional social values and the propitiation of numerous deities. There are also estimated to be 70 million Buddhists, 27 million Muslims and two million Christians. During the Cultural Revolution places of worship were ransacked; the 1982 Constitution granted the people freedom of religious activity, but under strict state control.

These is an ancient tradition of physical fitness in China, and every school and factory has its sports facilities. Fitness also forms part of a general awareness of civil defence. The younger generation is mainly interested in Western sports in which China has had international success, especially in swimming, football, table tennis and badminton. Older people prefer the traditional martial arts (*wushu*) such as *taijiquan* for which China is famous.

China's cultural heritage is very rich, with a literature going back over 2,500 years. The 20th century has seen a great spread of literacy; and modern works of a more popular nature have been added to the older literary tradition.

Calligraphy and painting are the two most respected art forms, evidence of which can be seen wherever you go in China. Dancing, singing, theatre and opera are all part of China's cultural scene, and Peking opera has gained worldwide fame.

# FACTORS INFLUENCING EMPLOYMENT

## Immigration
Although procedures tend to change constantly, tourist visas are easy to obtain from Chinese embassies. In the first place, you should request a visa application form from the nearest Chinese embassy. Tourists visas permit you to stay in China for the duration of your tour or visit; an extension may be granted within the country. It is usual to arrange a visa through the *China International Travel Service*, which is the official state travel agency. Enquiries about visas should be made well in advance.

Foreign workers, once informed that they have a job in China, will be requested to apply for a visa. They will be supplied with an interim visa which, on arrival in China, they take to the Public Security Office where they will be given a residence permit.

## Language
The official language of China is Mandarin (known as *putonghua* to the Chinese), a dialect originating in the north of the country. Although roughly 70% of the

population speak Mandarin, there are eight major dialects, of which Cantonese is the most important.

Chinese is a tonal language, which means that the intonation you use can change the meaning of a word; this makes it exceptionally demanding for speakers of western languages. The writing system is also extraordinarily complex, consisting of a system of some 60,000 characters or ideographs, of which about 7,000 are in current use. A system of romanisation, known as *pinyin,* is also widely used, especially in areas frequented by foreigners.

### Currency
There is a dual currency system in China. This was instigated in an attempt to prevent foreign currency leaving the country and to restrict the domestic purchase of consumer imports. *Renminbi (Rmb)* and *Foreign Exchange Certificates (FEC)* are both produced in units of Yuan. Renminbi is the local currency for Chinese use only. FECs are issued in exchange for foreign currency and are therefore only available to foreigners. No money of either sort may be taken out of the country; however, FECs may be exchanged back into hard currency on leaving, unlike *Renminbi.* Therefore, if you wish to save money to take home, it must be in the form of FECs. Most imported goods and Western luxury goods in general, such as film and foreign newspapers, as well as air tickets, cannot be bought with *Renminbi.* Although officially one FEC is equivalent of one *Renminbi,* due to their unequal purchasing power, there is a thriving black market.

Salaries are paid monthly, in cash. Sending money back home can be done through the Bank of China and some Units (see below) will arrange this directly for you. It is possible to open an account at the Bank of China, but this offers no advantages. Money can also be transferred to China fairly easily (at least in Beijing) by a bank draft to the Bank of China.

### Housing and Accommodation
There are two types of housing available for foreigners: at the place of work or in a hotel. Recent policy has been to try to house everyone at their place of work.

At the place of work, flats are usually provided which are comfortable enough, if a little spartan. Obviously a good deal will depend on where you are working — flats in the provinces can be very basic indeed; hot water and electricity will certainly be rationed. The main benefits of such housing are the proximity to work and the full involvement with it this implies. The disadvantages include never being able to get away from work (particularly important for teachers, who may be inundated with 'visitors').

Hotels offer the advantages of a larger foreign community with the chance to meet workers in different fields. Although foreign workers live in a special area, with their own flats, they can use the facilities of the rest of the hotel. These can include tennis courts, swimming pools and so on. There are also courses in Chinese, martial arts, calligraphy and various other traditional skills. Life here is undoubtedly more comfortable than in the place of work, but one can begin to feel cut off from the Chinese themselves.

### The Unit
The Unit is the administrative division of any workplace. Its responsibilities go far beyond mere work, however, and cover just about every aspect of its employees' lives. It is the Unit that employs, arranges housing, gives permission for marriages, study and travel. For foreign workers, almost as much as for Chinese colleagues, the Unit determines the quality of life.

Units vary from institute to institute, especially in their political colouring. Whilst most welcome foreigners sincerely and openly, there are still some which resent the privileges foreigners are given and they make no secret of this. Try not to antagonise your Unit. If they take against you they can very easily make your life extremely difficult. Conversely, they can be very helpful in arranging extra visas, travel permits and even interpreters.

The Unit will assign you an interpreter to help with day-to-day problems. How useful they prove depends on the luck of the draw; it is worth complaining if they are of no use since the post is a coveted one and can lead to study abroad. Most Units employing foreigners have a Foreign Affairs Office, and it is through this that most things are arranged. All problems should be directed through it. In the case of finding yourself up against a truly hostile Unit it is possible to appeal direct to the Ministry of Education and to arrange a transfer.

Each foreigner is issued with four cards by the Unit. These are:

(a) White card:    This enables you to buy goods with *Renminbi* and allows discounts on trains, planes and in hotels.
(b) Green Card:    Resident's permit, used mostly when travelling.
(c) Red Card:    Work permit
(d) Blue Card:    Medical card.

## Education

School in China begins at the age of seven. Six years in Primary School are followed by six years in Secondary School (three years at Junior Middle and three at Senior Middle). Higher education is open to students who can pass the strict Entrance Examination organised by the Ministry of Education every year in July.

Children of foreign workers, if of school age, would benefit by being in the cities or Beijing itself. Only Shanghai and Beijing have English speaking schools, run by diplomatic missions for the children of their staff and a few others. Space is limited and it is best to write to the embassy or consulate in advance. They take children up to 13 and charge at least $4,000 a year.

### Embassies and Consulates

British Embassy, 11 Guang Hua Lu, Jian Guo Men Wai, Beijing 100600; tel 1-532-1961/5 or 532-1930/1938-9.

British Consulate General, 244 Yong Fu Lu, Shanghai 20031; tel 21-433-0508 or 437-4569.

US Embassy, 3 Xiu Shui Bei Jie, Beijing 100600; tel 1-532-3831.
There are also US Consulates in Guangzhou, Chengdu, Shanghai and Shenyang.

### Tourist Offices

China National Tourist Office, 4 Glentworth Street, London NW1 5PG; tel 0171-935 9427.

China National Tourist Office, Suite 6413, 350 Fifth Avenue, New York, NY 10118; tel 212-760-9700.

China National Tourist Office (los Angeles), Suite 201, 333 West Broadway, Glendale, CA 91202; tel 818-545-7504-5.

## WORK AVAILABLE

Since the late 1970s, China has employed an increasing number of foreigners to aid its modernisation programme. Most of these have been in academic institutions, but recently they have been employed in other fields too, in the areas of trade and joint ventures. In 1988, there were only 2,000 foreigners in Beijing; but today the expatriate community will certainly be in the thousands. The policy on foreign consultants is administered by *The Foreign Experts Bureau* of the State Council (FEB) but actual recruitment and day-to-day affairs are handled by the *Bureau of Foreign Affairs* of the Ministry of Education (BFA). The BFA puts out a pamphlet outlining its requirements and policies entitled *Information for the Recruitment of Foreign Experts* that can be obtained from the BFA itself or local embassies. As a rule, they are interested in three types of personnel: genuine experts in particular fields, media people and teachers.

## General

There are a number of jobs which do not involve teaching, although this can be a useful skill whatever field you happen to be working in. It is never a bad idea to pack a few English teaching books before you go.

Most non-teaching jobs are presently in the media, although the market is expanding. All these jobs confer Foreign Expert (FE) status, the status given to most foreigners who work for the Chinese government (see below under *Teaching*); and therefore enjoy much the same terms and conditions. However, these FEs are expected to work a full year with just one month's holiday and they also usually work a longer day and a six-day week. The majority of jobs are in the capital and can begin at any time of the year. Anyone who thinks their skills could be useful to the country's modernisation programme should write to the *Bureau of Foreign Affairs* (see below under *Addresses*) enquiring about possible openings.

The *China International Publishing Group,* 24 Baiwanzhuang Street, Beijing, employs a number of FEs to work on its various publications. These include *China Today, China Pictorial* and *Beijing Review.* These are produced in English, German, Spanish and Japanese. The work consists of 'editing and polishing' literally translated copy and making it read properly; while it is sometimes interesting, wading through almost incomprehensible 'Chinglish' can become tedious.

Other potential employers include the daily English-language newspaper, the *China Daily,* the *Xinhua News Agency, Beijing Radio, and China Television.* All of these employ FEs as journalists and editors, but do not expect to be a roving reporter; the work is mainly correcting work written by Chinese staff.

## Teaching

There are literally thousands of higher education establishments in China, including universities, colleges, foreign language institutes, institutes of science and technology and so on. It is difficult to assess the relative status of these, but in general the universities are top of the pile. Nearly all of them hire foreigners, although the majority are taken on as language teachers. Each year there are nearly 700 posts, of which 400 are to teach English. Other disciplines include literature, history, law, economics and all the sciences and technology. There is also an increasing demand for management training and any discipline connected with business.

Non-language teaching posts are generally under the auspices of various agencies, such as the UN and the EU, but there are opportunities for the independent teacher too. To teach the hard sciences or the arts one really needs to be a true expert with the appropriate qualifications, and to be perceived as such by the Chinese.

Most teachers in China end up teaching English, regardless of their original brief. Although some do teach their own subject it is quite common to go believing you are to teach one subject and end up teaching another. The majority of teachers are contracted to teach 14 to 16 hours a week, but most spend between 10 and 12 hours in the classroom. To this can be added office hours and the occasional unofficial lecture or seminar; and everyone asks for help with translations, recordings, singing clubs and so on. These can be accepted at your discretion.

A large proportion of foreigners are employed in Beijing, but there are a great many opportunities elsewhere. Although there is no guarantee, it is possible to state a preference for an area when applying. The academic year begins in early September. The year is divided into two semesters, running from 1 September to 4 February, and 4 March to 31 July.

The Chinese Government classifies teachers either as Foreign Teachers (FT) or Foreign Experts (FE). These are degrees of status, conferred usually according to qualifications and experience, which bring different conditions and privileges set by the BFA.

*Foreign Teachers*: FTs are very much the poor relations of FEs in terms of pay, conditions and privileges; indeed, they are virtually volunteer workers. They are usually under 25 and/or without an MA, although there is flexibility here. Some go straight from university, but it is unlikely that non-graduates will be accepted unless they show true expertise in some area. FTs are recruited directly by institutions many of which are in the provinces, and by local education departments as well as by the Ministry of Education; all of these can be contacted through the Bureau of Foreign Affairs. Unlike Foreign Expert contracts, those of FTs are not standard and vary from institute to institute. This allows for a certain flexibility and it is worth negotiating over a number of points. It is quite possible, and normal practice, to change status once in China, especially if staying a second year; it is therefore inadvisable to sign a two-year contract as an FT.

Foreign Teachers are expected to pay their own return fare to China. They are funded by the hiring institutes and not, like the Foreign Experts, by central government. Consequently their salaries are considerably lower. An FT can expect in the range of 450 to 600 Yuan a month, which is just about enough to live on. (Note that a professor in China earns 350 Yuan per month.) An FT's salary is paid entirely in the local money, Renminbi, which cannot be exchanged for Foreign Exchange Certificates (FEC) or hard currency (see *Currency*, above). In effect, your stay in China as an FT could actually cost you money, but while the FT's life may not be as comfortable as that of an FE, it would be wrong to think of it as a misery. Most FTs are housed, rent-free, usually in a flat on campus. These flats are luxurious by Chinese standards but seem fairly spartan to Europeans (see the section *Housing and Accommodation* above).

*Foreign Experts*: FEs are paid according to qualifications and experience; salaries range from 800 to 1,200 Yuan a month. A single person can exchange 50% of this into Foreign Exchange Certificates but the figure drops for married couples, to 30% each. Since, in general the more FECs you have the better, if your spouse is working it is a good idea for them to acquire independent status so that they can exchange 50% too. This should be negotiated with the institute before leaving for China and confirmed in writing. Although FE contracts are standardised there is room for negotiation. You will not be expected to sign a definitive contract until at least two months into the first semester, to give both sides a trial period. By this time you should be well aware of what to ask for.

Foreign Experts are housed either on campus or, in the larger cities, in hotel complexes. As well as paying the rent and providing facilities, the Government will also pay for the full round trip airfare.

For those whose term of service is a year or longer, a spouse and children under 12 will be paid for if they accompany you for the full term, i.e. not just for a visit. It is possible to bring them out later, but this has to be negotiated with the hiring institute. Other privileges of the FE include: income tax exemption, free transport to and from work and free medical treatment.

In theory, FE language teachers should have at least three years' experience of teaching a language or literature in a university or college, or five years' experience of teaching in senior schools. Experience can count for more than qualifications and thus it is not strictly necessary to have a PGCE or Diploma in EFL and nor, for British applicants, is an MA mandatory (although it is preferred for American and Australian candidates). It is enough, for an FE, to have had some teaching experience and be over 25. However, having said this, the Chinese do greatly respect qualifications and they will certainly use them, as well as experience, to determine pay and conditions.

## Application

The Bureau of Foreign Affairs recruits Foreign Teachers and Foreign Experts through China's embassies abroad. There is no publicity or advertising, in the belief that China needs dedicated, genuinely interested workers who will, by definition, discover the opportunities for themselves.

The individual establishments send requests for FTs and FEs to the BFA in Beijing, which is then responsible for recruitment. The BFA in turn informs the various embassies around the world, which handle incoming applications. When an application is received by an embassy suitable applicants are invited for an interview; if this goes well, you may be offered a job there and then and asked to decide. It is at this stage that one should stress any preference as to job location. It is best to accept tentatively. The application is forwarded to the BFA in Beijing where it is matched to a request by an institute. The institute is then informed of this and contacts the applicant directly. There can be a considerable time lag between these two stages of the process and a wait of several months is not unknown. When you do receive notification of the job it is best to ask for more details, such as your status, salary and conditions. This is an important stage, especially for the FT, as it sets the terms of employment. Having accepted formally you may be asked to sign a provisional contract, but it is quite normal to have very little in writing before you go.

You will be requested to apply for a visa from the embassy, often another lengthy process. You will probably hear nothing else at this stage, until a few weeks, even days, before your departure.

Once in China, many issues, such as teaching hours, are open to negotiation. Usually a full contract will not be signed until after a two-month probationary period. Any disagreement can be referred to the BFA in Beijing, although a threat to do so is usually enough. Similarly, a threat to write to the papers or to resign should be sufficient, if desperate. In general, try to clarify as many details as you can before leaving. Make sure you have agreed all points before signing a contract. It becomes virtually impossible to negotiate after you have put your name to one. Similarly, having negotiated successfully over an issue, ask for it to be written down immediately before memories blur. Always try to talk to the highest authority, since one of the reasons for hedging is a fear of taking responsibility.

Applicants who do not receive a reply from an institute after three months can assume that the application has not been accepted. It is possible to apply at any time for the non-academic positions, while teaching jobs generally begin in September. Recruiting starts in January and it is advisable to begin early, both because this offers a wider choice and because it allows plenty of time for the lengthy bureaucracy to function. It is possible to apply later, indeed there are nearly always some last-minute posts available in July and August, but they could be anywhere.

Applications can be made either direct to the BFA or through the embassy. The latter is preferred since you have a contact in this country with whom to discuss things and negotiate. In the USA and UK the Chinese embassy has a special Education Section, where all enquiries should be sent (see below).

## SPECIFIC CONTACTS

### The British Council

The Council recruits up to 50 English language specialists to work on their ELT development projects in China. Minimum qualifications are an MA in an appropriate subject and several years' teaching experience, preferably overseas.

Project lecturers are employed by Chinese institutions on Foreign Expert conditions and receive a sterling subsidy. Advertisements are placed in the Education press each February/March for posts beginning the following September. Enquiries should be made direct to: The British Council, Overseas Educational Appointments Department, Medlock Street, Manchester M15 4AA. The British Council has also established links with Chinese teaching associations.

*China Educational Exchange,* 1251 Virginia Avenue, Harrisonburg, VA 22801 — sends teachers of English to China on two-year terms to work in colleges and universities; a month of Chinese language study at the start of each year is included. Teachers should have at least a BA degree, and preferably an MA or PhD. CEE also runs exchange programmes with China for doctors, nurses, agriculturalists, engineers and others. Room and board and a local stipend are paid. CEE is sponsored by agencies of the Mennonite Church in North America (see *Voluntary Work*). Volunteers need not be Mennonites but should have a Christian commitment and be active church members.

*China Teaching Program, Western Washington University,* Old Main 530, Bellingham, Washington 98225-9047 — is a training and placement service for people wishing to teach English as a Second Language in the People's Republic of China. Applicants from a variety of fields are accepted into the programme; the minimum requirement is an undergraduate degree. One short-term training session is conducted annually on the Western Washington University campus. Participants study Chinese language; TESL methodology; Chinese geography, history and culture; and preparation for living in China. Placement without attendance of the training session is also possible for qualified applicants. Teaching positions are negotiated for participants at a university in China. For further information or an application, contact the above.

*International Scientific & Information Services (ISIS),* 49 Thompson Hay Path, Setauket, NY 11733 — is a non-profit organisation which has been recruiting native English speakers to teach English in universities in China since 1983. Teachers are placed in several major cities in one-year, renewable positions beginning in September or February. Applicants should send a resume to ISIS. Those who pass the initial screening will be asked for letters of recommendation, biographical essay, diploma(s) and an interview (by phone or in person). If ISIS decides to recommend you for employment, your application will be forwarded to institution(s) of your choice for actual hiring decisions. In lieu of formal orientation, ISIS works closely with each individual that it recommends to China. There is no charge for this service.

*WorldTeach, Harvard Institute of International Development,* offers summer teaching positions in Shanghai; see chapter *Teaching* for further details.

Teaching positions for UK residents are also available through VSO (see *Voluntary Work*).

## ADDRESSES

Embassy of the People's Republic of China, Section of Education, 5 Birch Grove, Acton, London W3 9SW.
Embassy of the People's Republic of China, Education Division, 2300 Connecticut Ave., NW, Washington DC 20008.

China-Britain Trade Group, 5th Floor, Abford House, 15 Wilton Road, London SW1W 1LT; tel 0171-828 5176.
Great Britain-China Centre, 15 Belgrave Square, London SW1X 8PG; tel 0171-235 6696.

Society for Anglo-Chinese Understanding Ltd., 109 Promenade, Cheltenham, Gloucestershire GL50 1NW; tel 01242-226625.

## China

Bureau of Foreign Affairs of the Ministry of Education (BFA), Ministry of Education, Beijing 100806, People's Republic of China

The External Relations Secretary, Chief of Recruiting and Placement Division, Box 300, Beijing, PRC (for general enquiries)

The British Council, The British Embassy, Landmark Building, 8 North Dongsanhuan Road, Chaoyang District, Beijing 100006; tel 10-6501-1903.

China Daily, 2 Jintai Xilu, Beijing. Hong Kong Edition, 2-4 Floors Hing Wai Centre, 7 Tin Wan Praya Road, Aberdeen, Hong Kong; tel 287-39-889.

# Hong Kong

The success of Hong Kong as a leading manufacturing and commercial centre in Asia, and its strong links with the UK and other English-speaking countries, mean that opportunities for British and American citizens are likely to continue despite its return to China. In some areas, like construction, expatriates are likely to be replaced by local workers; and administration is no longer a route to employment in Hong Kong. Financial services, consultancy, and work for joint ventures and international companies are the main areas. As Hong Kong has a tradition which is different from the rest of China; and is the most likely destination for UK and US jobseekers, some specific information about this new Special Administrative Region of China is included here.

## GENERAL FACTS

### Geography

Hong Kong consists of 236 islands, and a part of the mainland coast east of the Pearl River estuary adjoining the Chinese province of Guandong (Kwangtung). Victoria, on Hong Kong Island, is the commercial centre. Topographically, Hong Kong is mostly steep hillside; and living conditions are crowded.

The climate is sub-tropical and monsoonal; the winter is cool and dry, and the summer, hot and humid. Most rain falls in the summer.

Hong Kong is one of the most densely populated areas in the world; the total population in 1991 was about 5,862,000; 99% of these are Chinese. Cantonese is spoken by the majority of the people, but several other dialects are also used. The English language is also spoken; and plays an important part in business life.

## History

The island of Hong Kong was ceded by China to Britain in 1841; Kowloon was acquired in 1860, and the New Territories were leased from China in 1898. Hong Kong was run by a British-appointed governor for 100 years until its return in June 1997 to China under the terms of the original lease. Under the Sino-British Joint Declaration, signed in 1985 by the British and Chinese governments, China guaranteed 'to preserve Hong Kong's unique economic position and way of life for 50 years after 1997,' with Hong Kong to exercise a degree of autonomy (except in such areas as defence and foreign affairs). Although the situation is at present far from clear, developments in the rest of China, and its transition to a semi-market economy, mean that it is in China's interest to preserve this important trading and financial asset and many of its institutions. Hong Kong seems likely to continue as an important manufacturing and commercial centre.

Before the handover to China in 1997, many of the wealthy and educated moved to other countries; this has created openings for many foreign professionals.

# Japan

Japanese Embassy, 101-104 Piccadilly, London W1V 9FN, tel 0171-465 6500
Japanese Embassy, 2520 Massachusetts Avenue NW, Washington DC 20008, tel 202-936-6700
The unit of currency is the yen (Y)
Rate of exchange: £1 = Y167; $1 = Y109

Japan has undergone massive development over the last 50 years; and is now the world's second industrial power after the United States. The economy has been affected by a slowdown; and there is now no longer full employment. Japanese industry is based on engineering and high-tech industries; nowadays much basic production has been moved to less expensive countries (like Britain) because of high labour costs in Japan itself.

Getting a job in Japan is not such an easy option, now that more and more foreigners are based there; but it can be rewarding, especially for those who are willing to stay for some time, and get to know its remarkable culture and (most important) its language, while also taking advantage of job opportunities ranging from English teaching to technical work. Although younger Japanese are less insular than their parents, they are far less westernised in the essentials of their culture than many might think. Certainly, it is important to prepare for a trip there; and to understand a little of its way of life before you go. It is one of the safest countries in the world to live; and also one of the most conservative; a desire to find out more about European or US customs which many Japanese people express is sometimes matched by a belief that westerners will never understand their culture; etiquette and behaviour are different;  and you need some patience and tolerance if you are going to understand Japan and its culture more deeply.

## GENERAL FACTS

### Population
Japan is one of the world's most crowded countries, with around 124 million inhabitants spread over 377,815 square kilometres. There are four large islands — Hokkaido, Honshu, Shikoku and Kyushu — and several hundred smaller ones. The average population density is high, varying from the sparsely populated island of Hokkaido in the north, to the crowded flat coastal strip of Honshu.

### Climate
Japan lies in the northeast corner of the Asian monsoon area, so the months of June and July are extremely wet and humid. Temperatures range from minus 5°C in Sapporo in winter to 35°C in Kagoshima in summer. In the winter months, snow is heavy in the island of Hokkaido and the north of Honshu, but is infrequent south of Tokyo.

### Government
Under the new constitution of 1947, Japan renounced war and the threat and use of force. The constitution also withdrew power from the emperor, who remains as a symbol of the state and the unity of the people. Legislative power now lies in the hands of the Diet, composed of the House of Representatives

and the House of Councillors. Representatives are elected for four years, councillors for six. The Prime Minister, who is nominated by the Diet, heads the 20-member Cabinet, which forms the executive branch of the government. The right-wing Liberal Democratic Party has governed Japan almost without interruption ever since; and presently holds the balance of power in a coalition government.

Regional government is based on 47 prefectures, which are divided into 3,262 local administrations - 644 cities (*shi*) 1,974 towns (*machi*) and 644 villages (*mura*).

### Cities

80% of Japan's population live in cities; well over half in the four metropolitan areas of Tokyo, Osaka, Nagoya and Kobe. The largest cities are Tokyo, the capital (11.6 million); Yokohama (4 million), Osaka (3 million), Nagoya (2,200,000); Sapporo (1,800,000); Kobe (1,500,000) and Kyoto (1,500,000). There are twelve other cities with over 500,000 inhabitants.

### Rural Life

Japan is a mountainous land, and only 13% of it is cultivated. The farming population numbers about 20 million, living on some five million farms. The main crop is rice, of which thirteen million tons are produced a year. Other crops include tea, tobacco, potatoes and wheat. Forests account for 67% of the land area. The other major primary industry is fishing, with a catch of 12,000,000 tons a year. Japan has the world's most lucrative fishing fleet.

### Labour Force

The labour force numbers 64 million, or 63% of the population aged 15 and over. The distribution is 8% in agriculture; 23.6% in manufacturing; 22.2% in trade; 25.9% in services. A severe shortage of workers developed during the late 1980s, but the slowdown of more recent times, when Japanese companies no longer guarantee employees a job for life, has changed the situation somewhat. There are still not enough university graduates available so far as large companies are concerned.

### Religion, Sport and Culture

Shintoism, the worship of nature and ancestors, is the traditional Japanese 'religion'. It was encouraged by the State prior to World War II in order to raise the fighting spirit of the people. It is not really a religion in the western sense, though; and most Japanese consider themselves to be adherents of both Shinto and Buddhism. All religions are tolerated; and Christianity is actively practised, but by just 1% of the population.

Most western sports are represented, including athletics, soccer, rugby, baseball, and skiing, with tennis and golf being the most popular and the most expensive. The traditional Japanese sports are *sumo* (wrestling), *kendo* (fencing), *kyudo* (archery), as well as the more familiar martial arts of *judo*, *karate* and *aikido*.

Literature, theatre, art and music are heavily influenced by western traditions; but traditional Japanese forms are still alive — such as *noh* and *kabuki* drama, *bunraku* puppet theatre, *haiku* poetry, and music played on the *shakuhachi* (a bamboo flute), *koto* or *shamisen* (stringed instruments). Other major traditional art forms are flower arranging (*ikebana* or *kado*), the tea ceremony (*chanoyu*) and calligraphy (*shodo*).

# FACTORS INFLUENCING EMPLOYMENT

### Immigration

Britons and US citizens require no visa to enter Japan and can stay as tourists for up to six months (UK) or three months (US citizens). It may be possible to extend a tourist visa by applying to one of the immigration offices at least ten days before its expiry.

Japanese embassies do not issue work permits. When you have obtained a job, your employer will go to the local immigration bureau in Japan to apply for a 'certificate of eligibility', which is in effect a work permit. Once it has been processed, the original will be sent to the employee, who can then obtain a working visa from any local Japanese embassy or consulate. If you are already in Japan, your employer will have to go through the same procedure, and you will then have to make your application from outside Japan. The most popular places to apply from are Korea and Taiwan. The work visa has to be collected from the same place, but it is possible to return to Japan while waiting for your papers to be processed.

Another type of visa which allows one to work is the cultural visa. These cater for those wishing to go to Japan to study but they also allow 15 to 20 hours' work per week (as long as you attend a minimum of 20 hours of classes a week too), which brings in enough money to live on. The cultural visa is restricted to those doing high-level academic research or studying Japanese culture at an advanced level. The rules may be applied less strictly within Japan itself, depending on which immigration bureau you deal with, but you will have to pay in advance for six months' tuition in a recognised subject.

Because of the need for unskilled labour and a total ban on immigration, the authorities tend to tolerate a number of illegal workers in Japan, most of them from poorer Asian countries. The penalties for working illegally are severe for the employer and for the worker, who is certain to be deported. The Japanese police do not spend a great deal of time looking for illegal western workers, but one has to bear in mind the possibility of being exploited by unscrupulous employers.

For information on visas and work permits, contact the *Japanese Embassy,* 101-104 Piccadilly, London W1X 9LB. General information about Japan is available from the *Japanese Information and Cultural Centre* at the same address.

## Language

Japanese syntax bears no resemblance to that of European languages; but the phonology or sound system is not as difficult as it might appear, and there is no hierarchy of tones as in Chinese. The writing system has been borrowed in its essentials from China, but uses far fewer symbols. Although most Japanese have studied English at school, very few can speak it beyond an elementary level; the Japanese way of teaching English concentrates on grammar and writing.

## Cost and Standard of Living

The cost of living is very high, but prices are stable. The major item of expenditure is rent. A tiny unfurnished flat in a city is likely to cost at least £130 per week. Food is also very expensive (about 50% more than in the UK). Public transport is relatively cheap. Looking for work can take time; and it would be unwise to go to Japan without some funds for you to get by. It may take some time with all these expenditures to begin to save some money.

## Housing and Accommodation

For newcomers, home ownership in a Japanese city is a virtual impossibility because of astronomical prices. Rented accomodation is available, but very expensive. Heavy deposits (non-returnable) are almost always paid when moving into rented accommodation; and an agreed percentage is returned when you move out. As contracts are for a limited duration, the deposit will have to be paid again every few years. This is known as 'key money' and usually adds up to six months' rent. Unless you speak fluent Japanese, you will need to take a Japanese friend or interpreter along with you when meeting the landlord. Employers may help with finding accommodation; and some have special apartment blocks for their employees, but otherwise estate agents' windows (*fudosan*) are the best place to look.

In big cities, many foreigners stay in *Gaijin Houses* (some of which advertise in the *Tokyo Journal, Kansai Time-Out,* etc.). While the cost may be reasonable (£15 a night) living conditions can be basic. They tend to get extremely full in the summer.

### Health and Welfare
Japan's social security system has made great progress since the war, and the Social Insurance Act of 1961 laid down programmes for health insurance, pension insurance, unemployment insurance and industrial accident insurance. Resident aliens are required to enrol with the local health insurance office (*kokuho*), unless they are covered by some other insurance scheme. Medical expenses tend to be high, but facilities are good in the cities. You will still have to pay a percentage of your treatment costs, depending on the scheme.

### Education
Education is free and compulsory between the ages of six and 15, but 95% of pupils stay on after the age of 15. Education is divided into five basic stages — kindergarten (up to the age of six), elementary school (six years); junior high school (three years); senior high school; and there are several technical colleges offering courses lasting up to four years. Japan has nine major universities — seven State-run (Tokyo, Kyoto, Sapporo, Sendai, Osaka, Kyushu and Nagoya), and two private (Keio and Waseda).

### National Service
In accordance with post-war treaties with the USA, Japan has been allowed to build up a self-defence force, which numbers around 250,000. Enlistment is purely voluntary, so aliens are not liable to conscription.

### Embassies and Consulates
British Embassy, 1 Ichiban-cho, Chiyoda-ku, Tokyo 102; tel 3-32-65-6511. Consulates in Fukuoka, Hiroshima, Nagoya and Osaka.

US Embassy, 10-5 Akasaka 1-chome, Minato-ku, Tokyo 107; tel 3-32-24-5000. Consulates in Fukuoka, Nagoya, Okinawa, Osaka, and Sapporo.

### Tourist Offices
Japan National Tourist Organisation, Heathcoat House, 20 Savile Row, London W1X 1AE; tel 0171-734 9638.
Japan Information and Cultural Centre, Lagayette Centre III, 1115 21st Street NW, Washington, DC 20036; tel 202-939-6949.

## CONDITIONS OF WORK

### Wages
There is little legislative control over wages, which nevertheless manage to keep up with the retail price index. The pattern of Japanese wage levels contains some unique features, such as the generous fringe benefits, which amount to an average of 20% of a worker's actual wage. Regular bonuses at six-monthly intervals can boost salary by a further 25%. Salary scales rise steeply with age and seniority; and skilled and qualified workers are highly paid, although wage differentials within companies are not so great as in Britain or the United States. Unskilled work is not well-paid, however.

### Hours
Since 1960, when the average working week was 44.7 hours, the five-day, 40-hour week has been slowly phased in. Most industries and offices now open only five days a week, and the average working week is already below 40 hours.

## Holidays

As with wages, the allocation of annual paid holidays is often based on length of service; but two weeks is usually the minimum. British people may find the length of holidays in a Japanese company far too short. In addition the following national public holidays are observed: New Year's Day; Coming of Age Day (15 January); National Foundation Day (11 February); Spring Equinox (21 March); Greenery Day (29 April); Constitution Memorial Day (3 May); Children's Day (5 May); Respect for the Aged Day (15 September); Autumnal Equinox (23 September); Health Sports Day (10 October); Culture Day (3 November); Labour Thanksgiving Day (November 23); Emperor's Birthday (23 December).

## Safety and Compensation

Worker's accident insurance is covered in the broad welfare programme. Enterprises with more than five employees are all compulsorily insured, with contributions shared by employers and employees. Smaller enterprises are required to provide their own insurance cover, with contributions paid entirely by the employers.

## Trade Unions

National unions are virtually unknown in Japan: the union structure is based on individual enterprises, rather than on trades or professions. About 16 million workers belong to unions, or 25% of the labour force. The main function of unions is to take part in the annual collective bargaining negotiations held each spring, the so-called 'spring offensive'.

## Taxation

Tax is deducted at source and, if necessary, adjusted at the end of the tax year. Basic taxes are very low — 6-9% — and include social security payments. Health insurance is paid separately by individual workers. Japanese citizens have to pay at least 10% of their income in local municipal taxes, but unless you intend to stay in Japan for more than a year you will probably not have to pay.

# WORK AVAILABLE

## General

Looking for work in Japan from abroad can be a difficult process and the Japanese embassy does not offer help. However, it is possible to apply directly to companies and schools.

Work is easier to find once you are there, and much recruiting (and business life in general) is based on personal links. Employment agencies are springing up, but on the whole the best method for seeking work is to read the English-language newspapers or contact companies or schools in person or by telephone. In larger cities, Gaijin Houses have noticeboards with advertisements; and they are often willing for you to use their phone number as a contact.

Given the international nature of Japanese business, there are opportunities for managerial, technical and professional staff as well as openings in the fields of finance and banking. Japanese companies and international firms operating in Japan are increasingly willing to take on foreigners as regular employees, as long as they can speak the language, or are willing to learn.

There is also a lot of scope for editorial work, as well as translation, where English, other European and some Middle Eastern languages can all be used to varying degrees. Advertising agencies, together with publishers of newspapers, magazines and books, require proof-readers, editors and so on. A specialist knowledge of legal or technical terminology, along with a high level of linguistic knowledge in one's own language are useful assets.

Non-teaching jobs tend to be scarce outside the big cities and you may need to do some teaching while looking around. Teaching business people and others privately is a possible source of useful contacts.

## Teaching

Teaching English is probably the most reliable full-time work to be found in Japan. There are also highly paid jobs in related subjects, such as linguistics or English literature. There is a great demand for English teachers in universities and colleges, government departments, big businesses and in language schools. Britons and Americans are at a disadvantage in seeking part-time or full-time work, as Canadians, Australians and New Zealanders aged 18-30 can use the 'working holiday scheme' which allows them to work for up to a year without a work permit. A further consideration is the fact that Japan has recently been flooded with highly qualified American English teachers; and it is now becoming difficult to find a good job without a masters degree in a relevant subject. It is therefore advisable to arrange a job before going out to Japan. If you are already there it is helpful to have a degree certificate or something similar; this will make it easier to obtain a work permit.

There are over 500 English schools in Tokyo alone and thousands more in the rest of Japan. Some of the bigger ones have representatives abroad to recruit teachers, but the majority do not; those that do may pay less than the going rate. If you are looking for work on the spot, the crucial point to remember is that you will need a sponsor in order to obtain a permit, and this will only be granted if a school can offer a full-time contract.

For those looking for work once in Japan, most hiring is done in March and September. The school and university year begins in April, and other terms start in September and January. There are a limited number of openings in Japanese high schools as teachers' assistants (see JET programme below), but these are highly sought after, as are the vacancies at Japanese universities and colleges, because of the high salaries and generous holidays.

Teaching can be very well paid, with hourly wages ranging from £15-£40. Salaried teaching in a language school tends to bring in less money than freelance work but usually involves less travel around town. Most schools will pay for your season ticket. Teachers' pay varies, depending on the quality of the school and its staff. Private lessons are usually very lucrative (Y6000 per hour), especially if you teach small groups of students who each contribute to the cost. The most effective way to make money is to organise a small school in your home, if you have enough space. It is possible to advertise by distributing leaflets in blocks of flats, but a more effective approach is to get to know some educated people and offer to teach them. If you ask around, you may be able to inherit some private students from someone who is leaving the country.

Besides the language schools, companies also organise classes for businessmen. These may take place within the company building or on school premises. Lessons are either very early in the morning or in the evening, to fit around working hours, and therefore involve some waiting around during the day.

Lessons tend to be conversational more than theoretical, since Japanese students receive very thorough English grammar instruction during their time at school. Enthusiasm and a friendly personality are more of an asset than an in-depth knowledge of English grammar.

*Making it in Japan* by Mark Gauthier, published in the USA and distributed in Europe by Vacation Work, includes extensive information about private schools and other organisations useful to the job seeker. As well as discussing teaching prospects, it gives advice on all types of work available and explains how to negotiate with employers. Vacation Work also publishes *Teaching English Abroad*, which has a useful chapter on Japan.

## Newspapers

*Powers International*, 517-523 Fulham Road, London SW6 1HD, tel 0171-385 8855, represents Japan's leading financial and business daily *Nihon Keizai*

*Shimbun* and the weekly trade and technical publications *Nikkei Ryutsu Shimbun* and *Nikkei Sangyo Shimbun.*

There are various English-language daily newspapers in Japan: the *Japan Times;* the *Daily Yomiuri;* the *Mainichi Daily News;* and the *Asahi Evening News.* The *Tokyo Journal* and *Kansai Time Out* (for the Osaka area) which appear monthly are good sources of jobs during the hiring season. Both *Nihon Keizai* (Japan Economic Journal) and *Toyo Keizai* (Tokyo Business Today) release certain editions in English and they both give information on Japanese business and industry.

## SPECIFIC CONTACTS

### English Teachers

Each year, hundreds of highly qualified graduates are recruited in Britain to work as teaching assistants for EFL by the Japanese Government, under its Japan Exchange and Teaching (JET) programme, for secondary schools, technical schools and local education authorities, and private companies. Contracts are for one year.

The Programme is open to UK citizens under the age of 35 holding a degree from a university or college of higher education. Teaching qualifications and experience are an advantage but not essential. Contracts begin in July. For recruitment, the period of application is usually from October to mid-December.

For more information and application forms contact the *JET Programme Desk,* Council on International Educational Exchange, 52 Poland Street, London W1V 4JQ.

A large number of US citizens and Canadians, and smaller numbers of Australians and New Zealanders, are also recruited each year. US applicants should contact the *Office of the JET Program,* Embassy of Japan, 2520 Massachusetts Avenue, NW, Washington DC 20008.

Teachers are also needed to teach the resident British and American children in Japan, for whom a number of special international schools exist. A list of these schools is available from Japanese Embassies (see above).

The *Overseas Educational Appointments Department,* The British Council, Medlock Street, Manchester M15 4AA, is notified of vacancies in Japanese state schools. For information on direct recruitment by the British Council in Japan contact the *Central Management of Direct Teaching, The British Council,* 10 Spring Gardens, London SW1A 2BN; tel 0171-389 4931. Vacancies in Japan are also advertised in the UK press. The minimum requirement is a Certificate (or preferably a Diploma) in TEFL (see the *Teaching* chapter).

*AEON Inter-Cultural USA,* 9301 Wilshire Boulevard, Suite 202, Beverly Hills, California 90210, tel 310-550-0940, http//www.aeonet.com — has one of the largest chains of English conversation schools in Japan with over 230 branch schools, 450 foreign teachers and 2,500 Japanese employees. AEON hires new teachers year round to fill one-year contracts. A four-year college/university degree in any major is required. AEON provides each teacher with their own fully furnished apartment at a subsidised rent, full sickness and accident insurance, 5-day 36-hour work-week, end of contract bonus, and return airfare. Teachers are recruited in the United States and Canada. To apply, please send a resumé and an essay entitled 'Why I want to Live and Work in Japan' to the address above, or to its other offices: *AEON Corporation,* 203 N. LaSalle Street 2100, Chicago, IL 60601, tel 312-251-0900; *AEON Corporation,* 230 Park Evenue 1000, New York, NY 10169, tel 212-808-3080.

*The Japan Association of Language Teachers (JALT),* Shamboru Dai 2 Kawasaki, 1-3-17 Kaizuka, Kawasaki-ku, Kawasaki 210 — runs a Job Information Centre for its members at its annual conference and publishes a monthly newsletter which lists jobs as well. Note that the address frequently changes.

*The Language Institute of Japan,* Asia Centre Nai, 4-14-1 Shiroyama, Odawara, Kanagawa, 250 Japan — recruits teachers to teach adults on residential courses. Other full-time opportunities are available and LIOJ also runs Summer Work-camps for the training of Japanese teachers of English. TEFL qualifications or similar are required, or a background in business, economics, law etc., together with experience. Applicants should apply to the Director, at the above address.

*Nova Group,* Knightsbridge House, 4th Floor, 197 Knightsbridge, London SW7 1RB — is the London office of one of the largest networks of language schools in Japan, with over 80 schools and 1,000 teachers. Teachers recruited in the UK receive sponsorship (work permit) and have accommodation arranged for them.

*YMCA Schools* – the YMCA and YWCA run numerous schools in Japan. Salaries are somewhat below average, but conditions are very good. US citizens can make enquiries to *OSCY (Overseas Service Corps of the YMCA),* Program Administrator, 909 4th Avenue, Seattle, Washington 98104, tel 206-382-5008.

Also see the *Teaching* chapter for organisations which recruit for language schools in Japan.

**Other Opportunities**
There are now employment agencies in Japan willing to find work for foreigners. One of these is *Borgnan Human Development Institute,* Daisan Taihei Building, 1-25-3 Igashi Ikebukuro, Toshima-ku, 170 Tokyo, which specialises in recruiting technical experts, engineers, business consultants, financial experts, technical writers, proofreaders and instructors.

*Cannon-Persona Recruitment Ltd.,* Aldemary House, 10-15 Queen Street, London EC4N 1TX, tel 0171-489 8141, fax 0171-236 5785 — is a bi-lingual and bi-cultural recruitment agency for Japanese and British or European candidates in the areas of administrative and clerical staff; sales, marketing and management; banking, finance and insurance; and data processing, engineering and technical personnel. *Persona* offices also in Tokyo, Los Angeles, New York, San Francisco, Düsseldorf, Sydney, Hong Kong, and other locations worldwide.

## SHORT TERM WORK

The high cost of travelling to Japan prevents most from looking for temporary work there. Even if a job can be found beforehand, it can easily take two months for a work permit application to be processed. But once you are in there, it is quite easy to pick up casual part-time employment, either as a main source of income, or to supplement another job. A general meeting point and grapevine for young people in Tokyo is a hostel called *Okubo House* at 1-11-32, Hyakunin-cho, Shinjuku-ku. Their notice boards advertise vacancies that might interest foreigners.

There is a wide variety of jobs on offer, as models, movie extras, waiter/waitresses, hosts/hostesses, shop assistants, in the media, and other jobs in clubs, bars and restaurants, etc. Hostessing involves chatting to and dancing with Japanese businessmen, whose English tends to be limited. Acting can be an attractive prospect, but is fun rather than good money. Both radio and television networks employ foreigners to help with language programmes. There are about 150 broadcasting companies in Japan, the most important being the *Nippon Television Network* (NTV), the *Tokyo Broadcasting System* (TBS) and *TV Asahi; Nippon Hoso Kyokai* (NHK) is the only state network. Westerners with fluent Japanese who can speak entertainingly are in great demand for television chat shows, but not many fall into this category.

Au pairs do not exist officially in Japan, although some European families make informal arrangements with young women from their home countries. Pocket money may be wholly inadequate as far as paying for leisure activities in Japan goes.

## BRITISH COMPANIES
### with branches, affiliates or subsidiaries in Japan

The *British Chamber of Commerce in Japan*, 3rd Floor, Kowa Building, No.16, 9-20 Akasaka 1-Chome, Minato-Ku, Tokyo 107, tel 03-35-93-8811, produces a list of members. Payment is by bank draft payable to the Chamber.

The *Japanese Chamber of Commerce and Industry in the UK* is at: Salisbury House, 29 Finsbury Circus, London EC2M 5QQ; tel 0171-628 0069.

## AMERICAN COMPANIES
### with branches, affiliates or subsidiaries in Japan

The *American Chamber of Commerce in Japan*, Toranomon Bldg. 5F, 3-25-2 Toranomon, Minato-ku, Tokyo 105, publishes a directory of 2,600 members representing 800 American companies in Japan, for Y10,000 ($100) plus $24 airmail, in addition to a number of publications on living and working in Japan, The ACCJ also provides a resume listing service for job hunters. Many ACCJ companies hire staff through this service. Their World Wide Web site is: http://www.accj.or.jp.

# Singapore

Singapore High Commission, 2 Wilton Crescent, London SW1X 8SA, tel 0171-235 8315 l
Embassy of Singapore, 3501 International Place, Washington DC 20008, tel 202-537-3100
Currency: Singapore S$1 = 100 cents
Rate of Exchange: £1 = S$2.2; US$1 = S$1.4

Singapore's economy has expanded rapidly in recent years, and now rivals Japan's in efficiency. The Singapore government actively encourages the recruitment of highly skilled workers from English-speaking countries to relieve the local labour shortage, through various special employment and residence schemes.

## GENERAL FACTS

Singapore consists of the island of Singapore and 57 islets inside its territorial waters. Singapore's total land area is about 641.4 square kilometres, 90% of which is occupied by the main island. Half of the land is built-up, with a further 3.3% farming land, and some 5% of forest. The island can be divided into three regions: the central hilly region; the relatively flat eastern region; and the western area of hills and valleys.

Singapore has a fairly uniform temperature, high humidity and abundant rainfall. Average daily temperature is 26.7°C.

The population consists of 76.3% Chinese, 15% Malay, 6.4% Indians, and 2.3% from other ethnic groups; 55% of the population is under 30.

The main religious faiths are Buddhism, Christianity, Islam, Taoism and Hinduism. The official languages are Malay, Chinese (Mandarin), Tamil and English. Malay is the national language, with English as the language of administration.

Singapore was acquired for Britain in 1819 by Sir Stamford Raffles. It was accorded British Crown Colony status after the Second World War, and was declared an independent Republic in December 1965. It has been ruled by the People's Action Party since 1959 as a virtual one-party state. All foreign publications, cassettes, films, and now the Internet, are subject to censorship. There are also draconian laws against any form of anti-social behaviour (e.g. up to S$1,000 fine for littering), with the result that this is one of the cleanest and safest cities in Asia. Drug traffickers may be sentenced to death.

## FACTORS INFLUENCING EMPLOYMENT

US and UK citizens may remain in Singapore for up to 90 days without a visa.

Aliens who come to Singapore on Social Visit Passes (i.e. as tourists) may take up work there provided they first obtain either a Work Permit issued by the Ministry of Labour, or an Employment Pass or Professional Visit Pass issued by the Immigration Department (address below). An Employment Pass is issued to any foreign worker who is not a permanent resident, and who holds a university degree or has a basic salary over S$1500 per month. Employment Passes are usually valid for a three-year period, application form available from: *The Immigration Department,* Pidemco Centre, 95 South Bridge Road, Singapore 0105; tel 65-530-1817.

Employmemt Pass holders who wish to reside permanently in Singapore may apply for an Entry Permit. There are a number of schemes whereby foreigners can obtain permanent resident status (Entry Permit). Under the Professional/ Technical Personnel and Skilled Workers Scheme, any person working in Singapore who is below 50 years of age, and who has professional or specialist or technical skills which would enable him to pursue his trade or profession in Singapore may apply for permanent residence.

Under the Economic Benefit Schemes, persons identified as having entrepreneurial skills and financial resources likely to benefit the Republic may also apply for permanent residence. Information on both schemes is available on request from the *Singapore Economic Development Board (EDB)*, Norfolk House, 30 Charles II Street, London SW1Y 4AE; or from *Singapore EDB*, 1350 Connecticut Avenue, NW, Suite 504, Washington DC 20036-1701. The Economic Development Board also has offices in New York, Boston, Chicago, Dallas, Los Angeles and San Francisco.

**Trade Unions**
There are mainly employee trade unions; a few employer unions; and a federation of employee trade unions, the National Trades Union Congress (NTUC).

**Embassies**
British High Commission, Tanglin Road, Singapore 1024; tel 473-9333.
US Embassy, 30 Hill Street, Singapore 0617; tel 338-0251.

**Tourist Offices**
Singapore Tourist Promotion Board, 1st Floor, Carrington House, 126-130 Regent Street, London W1R 5FE; tel 0171-437 0033.
Singapore Tourist Promotion Board, NBR, 12th Floor, 590 Fifth Avenue, New York, NY; tel 212-302-4861.

## WORK AVAILABLE

**General**
Singapore currently has the second highest per capita GNP after Japan.The economy has progressively diversified over the years. Trade and manufacturing (especially electronics) are the traditional mainstays of the economy. Financial and business services also play an increasingly important role in Singapore's prosperity. High-technology industries are expanding rapidly, while much basic manufacturing is being transferred to neighbouring areas of Malaysia and Indonesia.

**Newspapers**
Advertisements can be placed direct in the English language paper: *Straits Times*, 390 Kim Seng Road, Singapore 0923.

## SPECIFIC CONTACTS

**Employment Service**
The Ministry of Labour runs an employment service at 78 Prinsep Street, Singapore, in order to assist employers in securing workers and job-seekers in obtaining work. The Ministry of Labour address (where enquiries can also be made about work permits) is: 18 Havelock Road, 03-01, Singapore 0105; tel 65-538-3033.

The *International Manpower Division (IMD)* of the Singapore Government maintains a database of employers and potential workers. To get onto the database, ask for an application form from an overseas Singapore Economic Development Board office, or Singapore Embassy (addresses above). IMD also provides information on companies and current developments in Singapore.

**Employment Agencies**

*JAC Property & Employment Pte. Ltd.,* 14-10 Hong Leong Centre, 138 Robinson Road, Singapore 0104 — recruits qualified management, marketing and financial people.

*Skilltek Consultants,* 545 Orchard Road, 15-02/04 Far East Shopping Centre, Singapore 0923 — recruits engineers, surveyors, maintenance and construction staff and administrators.

*Tekniskill Ltd.,* 151 Chin Swee Road, 03-04 Manhattan House, Singapore 0316 — can place experienced and qualified personnel in industry, design, construction, petrochemicals, etc.

Worldwide recruitment agencies, such as *Adia, Ecco* and *Drake International* also have branches in Singapore, as do the international consultancies in banking and finance like *Ernst and Young,* 36 Robinson Road, 17-00 City House, Singapore 0106; fax 65-225-0465.

**Teaching**

Qualified and experienced teachers of all levels are in demand in Singapore, mainly for expatriate schools and in higher education. Agencies in the UK which can help find work in Singapore can be found in the *Teaching* chapter). Direct approaches can be made to the Director of Personnel, *National University of Singapore,* 10 Kent Ridge Crescent, Singapore 0511. Enquiries can also be made to any Singapore Economic Development Board office.

**Useful Contacts**

The Singapore *Economic Development Board* can be approached direct for information about job opportunities. The address is: 250 North Bridge Road 24-00, Raffles City Tower, Singapore 0617; tel 65-330-6836/6864/6867; fax 65-337-8552.

When you arrive in Singapore, an office set up by the government to assist new immigrants and integrate into Singapore society is: *Social Integration Management Service,* Prime Minister's Office, Public Service Division, 8 Shenton Way, 13-02 Treasury Building, Singapore 0106; tel 65-225-7392-5.

BRITISH FIRMS

with branches, affiliates or subsidiaries in Singapore

*Kompass South East Asia Ltd.,* 326C King George's Ave., Singapore 0820, publishes the *Directory of British Business in Singapore.* The *Singapore International Chamber of Commerce,* 10-001 John Hancock Tower, 6 Raffles Quay, Singapore 0104, tel 224-1255, fax 224-2785, may also be contacted for commercial information.

# South Korea

Embassy of the Republic of Korea, 4 Palace Gate, London W8 5NF, tel 0171-581 0247
Embassy of Korea, 2320 Massachusetts Avenue, NW, Washington DC 20008, tel 202-939-5600
Currency: Won (W)
Rate of Exchange: £1 = 1220 Won; $1 = 800 Won

Korea is one country split into two. It was a Japanese colony from 1910 to 1945. Then, the country was divided between Soviet and American zones of occupation. The communist North's attempt to conquer the South in 1950 was halted by United Nations intervention; and the country was partitioned. The economy of the North today is on the verge of collapse; and this remains one of the last outposts of the communist world. South Korea became a free market, and in recent years, a democratic country. Its economy has grown at a remarkable rate from the 1950s, but had started to run into difficulties by the late 1980s. High inflation rates, a problem of overstaffing and high labour costs in relation to some of the competing Asian economies, and also political instability as the country meets the challenge of possible reunification, are all clouds on the horizon of this country's new-found prosperity.

In 1988, Korea successfully hosted the Olympic Games; this, together with its new-found democracy (President Roh Tae Woo was elected through direct elections in December 1987), focused world attention on the country. At the time of writing, the problem of reunification with North Korea is no closer to resolution, however, and the integration of Korea with its northern neighbour continues to dominate political discussion.

Its unique culture is hardly known to outsiders, and is well worth discovering. In spite of their often tragic history, Korean people are generally friendly and helpful towards foreigners. The main stumbling block is language: English is not widely understood outside the capital, Seoul.

## GENERAL FACTS

The Republic of Korea (or South Korea), has a population of roughly 43,700,000 people, some 27% of whom are under 15. The country has a population density of 1,143 people per square mile. 75% live in urban areas, the largest of which is the capital Seoul, with 10,700,000, followed by Pusan with 3,900,000, and Taegu with 2,300,000.

The Republic covers a land area of 38,211 square miles. It is generally mountainous, with a rugged east coast. The climate is extreme, with long, cold winters and a short, very hot and humid summer.

The main language and ethnic group is Korean. The major religious faiths are Buddhism, Confucianism, Christianity (mainly reformed) and the indigenous Korean religions, Wonbulgyo and Chondokyo.

## FACTORS INFLUENCING EMPLOYMENT

### Immigration

US and Canadian citizens may visit Korea for up to 15 days without a visa, provided they have confirmed return tickets. For longer stays a visa is required.

UK and Irish citizens do not require visas to enter Korea as tourists or for business purposes, and may remain for up to 90 days. The length of your intended stay should be made clear to the immigration authorities on arrival, otherwise you will only receive a 15-day transit visa. Any foreigner who wishes to stay for more than 60 days for whatever purpose is required to apply for a residence certificate at the District Immigration Office in Korea (addresses available from Korean Embassies).

Any alien wishing to work in Korea must have a definite job offer before applying for a work permit. Applications should be addressed to the Korean Embassy (see above).

**Embassies and Consulates**
British Embassy, 4 Chung-Dong, Chung-Ku, Seoul 100; tel 2-735-7341-3.
British Consulate, 12th Floor, Yoochang Building, 25-2, 4-Ka, Chungang dong, Chung-Ku, Pusan; tel 51-463-0041.
US Embassy, 82 Sejong-Ro, Chongro-ku, Seoul 96205-0001.

**Trade Unions**
Trade union activity is strictly controlled by the government. Regional union organisation is banned, strikes are almost impossible, and unions are only allowed to operate individually on a single company basis.

## WORK AVAILABLE

**General**
Korea's major industries are textiles, electronics, shipbuilding and motor manufacture. The agrarian sector is very important, with 22% of the land under permanent cultivation; the main crops are rice, barley and vegetables (especially cabbages and garlic).

What concerns the economic planners at the moment is diversification in Korea's export-orientated economy. This requires the exploration and opening-up of more European markets (in particular those of Eastern Europe) and the absorption of more foreign technology, enabling the Republic to become as much a supplier of parts as of finished products.

Korean industry is dominated by huge, family-owned corporations, known as *chaebol,* some of which are now household names in the West, for example, Daewoo, Hyundai and Samsung. Prospects for foreign workers are not especially good, since Korean workers are well-educated, and very few foreigners can speak Korean. In addition, wages are considerably lower than in Japan or the West.

**Newspapers**
The two English language daily papers take advertisements direct: *The Korea Herald,* 11-3 3-ga, Hoehyou-dong, Jung-Gu, Seoul; *Korea Times,* 14 Junghak-dong, Jongo-gu, Seoul. Advertisements are also handled by *Bel-Air,* Bel-Air House, 10 Gainsborough Road, Woodford Bridge, Woodford Green, Essex IG8 8EE London EC1V 9BX; and *Marston Webb International,* 60 Madison Avenue, Suite 1204, New York, NY 10010, USA.

**Labour Force**
The labour force is divided as follows: 19% in agriculture; 27% in manufacturing; and 54% in services.

## SPECIFIC CONTACTS

The British Embassy in Seoul is not in a position to assist with finding employment in Korea, and suggests contacting the Korean Embassy. Lists of Korean firms trading abroad may be obtained from the *Korea Trade Centre,* Vincent

House, Vincent Square, London SW1P 2NB; or *Korean Traders Representative Club of New York,* 460 Park Ave., Suite 402, New York, NY 10022.

**Foreign companies**
A number of overseas companies have subsidiaries in Korea which employ overseas staff; some names are given below. Enquiries should be addressed to recruitment departments in the UK or USA:

Banks: Bankers Trust New York, Citicorp, Citibank.
Computers and components: IBM, Rockwell.
Pharmaceuticals and Chemicals: Janssen, Squibb, Johnson & Johnson, Pfizer, Cyanamid.

**Teaching**
There is considerable demand for English teachers, mostly in Seoul and Pusan. Much of the teaching is done by travellers on tourist visas, and this is generally tolerated by the authorities. Full-time jobs are sometimes advertised in the UK press or through agencies (see *Teaching* chapter). Salaries are somewhat lower than in neighbouring Japan, but there is also less competition for jobs.

Both *ILC* in the UK, and *TESOL Placement Bulletin* in the US have openings in Korea from time to time. If you have good qualifications it is worth contacting a Korean university or college (there are over 100). Addresses can be obtained from a Korean embassy.

Some names of well-known language schools are given below:

*ELS International,* 649-1 Yeoksam-Dong, Kangnam-ku, Seoul 135-080 — offers one-year contracts, with a competitive salary and return air fare. Interviews are held in the UK and USA. Contact the head office in Culver City, USA (see *Teaching* chapter).

*Jong-ro Foreign Language Institute,* Jong Ro Ku, Kong Pyong Dong, 55 Bungi, Seoul — is willing to hire walk-ins for part-time or full-time contracts. The majority of teachers are American. You may send a cassette or video of yourself in action if you are applying from abroad.

*Sogang Institute for English as an International Language,* Sogang University, CPO Box 1142, Seoul, 100-611 — prefers experienced teachers with an MA in a relevant subject. Recruitment through advertisements or direct application.

# Middle East and North Africa

In terms of the international jobs market, the oil-producing countries of the Middle East and North Africa occupy a position which is not unlike that of the now developed economies of East Asia. Sixty years ago, they were struggling economically, and there were few opportunities for development. The discovery and exploitation of oil, and the price rises in this essential commodity instituted by OPEC in the 1970s, changed everything; the revenue has been ploughed back into development, hospitals, universities, industry, and all the trappings of a consumer society. Oil has been able to provide the money to pay wages that are still relatively high, and sometimes among the highest in the world: and taxes are generally low.

As one would expect, the sudden flow of wealth has been followed by investment, as countries try to broaden the base of their economy and to create more long-term industries; but while there is money to invest in infrastructure like roads, airports, defence systems, irrigation, and so on, there is still a time lag in the training of local personnel to fill labour needs, particularly in managerial and skilled positions. Add to this the lack of ambition which seems to go hand in hand with an oil-rich society, and it is easy to see why there is so much demand for foreign workers in this part of the world.

A look at the Middle Eastern countries shows that the highest demand is in the Gulf States. Here, political considerations have ruled out too many contacts with Iran or Iraq. Syria is also something of a closed society; and Jordan is struggling with its own economic problems. Israel is in the process of cutting its dependence on blue-collar workers from abroad; and having to cope with an influx of often highly trained new citizens from Russia; there is the hope also that Palestinians who are not Israeli citizens will participate more in its relative economic success. The countries that belong to the Organisation of Petroleum Exporting Countries (OPEC), like Saudi Arabia, Bahrain, and the United Arab Emirates, are the traditional destinations for expatriate workers in the region.

The potential for political instability here is one drawback, although Gulf Arabs are hospitable. Some find the lifestyle for expatriates enjoyable, despite the strict rules on alcohol and anti-social behaviour (and an attitude to women which seems archaic to westerners but is seen as a part of traditional Muslim culture to the locals).

Sometimes visitors will be regarded as irreligious, even though Gulf Arabs themselves may not all be as highly moral or pious as they appear. Certainly, criticism of the local way of life or religion should generally be avoided; relations between men and women are such that women should conduct themselves in a brisk and businesslike manner at work; and will often have to show patience, and some firmness and assertiveness, to gain the respect of colleagues.

Conditions in the workplace, office buildings, hotels, and hospitals, tend to be up-to-date and well-apppointed, with all the latest technology. Ways of working and doing business may be less modern, though; and foreign workers will have to get used to a more laid-back approach to getting things done; and be careful when it comes to negotiating their terms and conditions (and make sure these are kept to). The Gulf States (chief among which is Saudi Arabia) are outwardly modern and advanced societies; but there is a more deeply rooted value system; and this cosmopolitan appearance is often only superficial. To understand these countries, you will have to find some sympathy and understanding for their Islamic inheritance and traditional values. Foreign travel, and the quite widespread use of English in business circles, have done little to change more enduring attitudes to human relations which, as in every country, have their positive and their negative side. Expatriates who are attracted by high wages and low or non-existent income taxes sometimes fail to consider this aspect of Middle Eastern life; and are affected by boredom and loneliness. Some local customs (like being woken up by the call to prayer at 4am) come as an unwelcome surprise; many others find they cannot get used to the climate, or to living without alcohol.

These points should be borne in mind; and preparation is important. It should also be made clear that the days of limitless oil wealth are over. Oil prices are now relatively not so high; governments are under pressure to reduce their dependence on foreign workers, and to train their own. Salaries are not quite what they used to be, either, in the boom years of the 1970s and early 80s.

As for the types of work being offered, the main needs are for professional and technical staff,especially in engineering and medicine. The range of vacancies is vast: accountants, IT professionals, doctors, nurses, all types of engineers, technicians and fitters, and anyone with qualifications relating to the petrochemical or construction industries may be able to find work in the Middle East. Many contracts  are offered for single men; the number of jobs open to women is correspondingly limited. Men in the Gulf States are often preferred even as secretaries and nurses. The same holds true in nursing, or for English-language teaching, although some of these jobs will be for women only.

An important aspect of employment patterns is that contracts tend to be large-scale, often between the government and a major international company. Recruitment procedures tend to be more formal as a result; and are often in the hands of the foreign companies themselves, or the international recruitment agencies which advertise regularly in the national and international press or specialist magazines in the particular field of work. This all helps to create expatriate communities which are insulated from the society in which they are based; which can provide a network of support — and on-site entertainments or sports facilities — but may also contribute to the feeling of isolation and boredom which some experience.

### Languages

The languages of the Middle East all belong to the Semitic group (except for Persian and Turkish) and are therefore related to each other. Arabic is the most common, and is spoken in Saudi Arabia, the Gulf States, Syria, Iraq, Lebanon, Jordan and North Africa. Within this area there are major linguistic variations — both written and spoken. The most noticeable dividing line is that between the Maghreb area (Morocco, Algeria, Tunisia and the western part of Libya) and countries to the east. The other major languages are Farsi (or Persian) and Hebrew (spoken only in Israel), both of which have certain similarities to Arabic.

A knowledge of the appropriate local language is useful, although one can often find people who speak one or other European language — for instance English in Egypt and the Gulf States; French in Syria, Lebanon, Morocco, Tunisia and Algeria; and Italian in Libya.

### Customs and Culture

In the Arab world more than in most countries, expatriate western workers are forced to accept that they are outsiders (see above). While no one expects foreign workers to become Muslims, it is necessary not to offend against codes of social behaviour or dress.

Many were European colonies in the past: their legal systems are more like western ones, and their tolerance of European lifestyles is greater. Jordan is a case in point, or Oman. The greatest difficulties arise in Saudi Arabia and some of the Gulf States where Islamic laws are applied to foreigners and locals alike. Needless to say, it is essential to know what is acceptable and what is not. In general, consuming alcohol, intimacy with others, even if unmarried, and certainly same-sex relationships, or even becoming aggressive towards local people, can be grounds for imprisonment and deportation, or worse.

This culture also rests on the Arabic language and its literature; which is something that few westerners have an opportunity to appreciate. The homeland of Arab classical music and dance is now to be found in Egypt. The previously lively cultural scene in Lebanon, with its large French-speaking Christian population, has greatly declined after the years of civil war. As far as the Gulf States are concerned, freedom of expression is very limited, and all films, books, etc. are subject to strict censorship.

# Saudi Arabia

Royal Saudi Arabian Embassy, 32 Charles Street, London W1X 7PM, tel 0171-917 3000
Royal Saudi Arabian Embassy, 601 New Hampshire Avenue, NW, Washington DC 20037, tel 202-342-3800
Currency: 1 Saudi riyal (SRl) = 100 halalah
Exchange rate: £1 = SRls 5.73; $1 = SRls 3.75

There are plentiful opportunities for citizens of English-speaking countries interested in professional, skilled and semi-skilled work in Saudi Arabia.

The USA and the UK are both traditionally seen as an ideal source of talented staff for recruitment to the Kingdom. English is the main language of commerce, and professional qualifications from English-speaking countries are highly respected. The country has close historical ties with Britain, which helped her gain independence during World War I, and with the USA, on whom she relies for military support.

Saudi Arabia's economic development began with the discovery of the first oilfield in Dammam in 1938. Initially, the Saudis had little control over the exploitation of their greatest natural resource, but with the formation of the Organisation of Petroleum Exporting Countries (OPEC) in 1973, and the consequent huge rises in the price of crude oil, the country began the process of turning itself into a modern, industrialised state. In addition to oil, Saudi Arabia has also started to produce gold, silver and copper.

Foreigners seeking work in the Kingdom must first obtain a work permit, which the employer or sponsor applies for in the country. When this has been obtained it is forwarded to the Saudi Arabian Embassy in your country (see above), who will then issue you with a visa. As soon as you arrive in Saudi Arabia you should register with your local embassy or consulate.

## Work Available

Saudi Arabia's continued development requires the presence of qualified and experienced foreign personnel, although government policy is aimed at reducing the number of expatriates in the long term. As the mainstay of the Kingdom's national economy, oil accounts for some 70% of Gross National Product and 90% of its exports. These days about 50% is exported in crude form, while the rest is refined or processed into other products.

Saudi Arabia has for a number of years been building up basic industries, including refining, steel and fertiliser plants. Most of this heavy industry is concentrated in Jubail, Jeddah and Yanbu. Other types of industry, such as building materials, chemicals, cement, electrical equipment, rubber and plastics are also expanding. Great emphasis is also placed on developing agriculture, which now accounts for 8% of GNP.

The outlook for jobs for expatriates is dependent on how much money the Saudi government feels it can afford to spend on new projects. The Kingdom had to borrow heavily to finance its part in the Gulf War of 1991, but a subsequent rise in oil prices has improved matters. The greatest source of international employment is construction, which employs nearly 20% of the entire Saudi workforce. One recent project has been the £10 billion Al-Yamamah airbase, planned to cover an area the size of London when it is completed. The project includes a 10 square-mile airfield and a town for 25,000 people. While details are kept secret, many of Britain's top construction firms are involved, and British Aerospace had up to 4,000 British workers there at one time.

Other areas where large contracts are currently being secured include: road construction and drainage, school and office construction, hospitals, air-conditioning, telecommunications systems, and street networks and water reservoirs.

A useful list of current tenders is published in the *Middle East Economic Digest,* available on subscription from *MEED,* 21 John Street, London WC1N 2BL. Other titles include *Meedmoney, The Advertisers' Guide to the Middle East,* and the *Finance Guide to the Middle East.* The British Embassy's Commercial Department, PO Box 94351, Riyadh 11693, may be able to offer general advice on working opportunities in Saudi Arabia; and the *Riyadh Chamber of Commerce and Information,* PO Box 596, Riyadh 11421, tel 1-404-0044, fax 1-402-1103, can offer commercial information and advice.

For general information on working in the Gulf, a recommended book is *Working in the Persian Gulf,* by Blythe Camenson (published by Desert Diamond Books, PO Box 9580, Coral Springs, Florida 33075, USA). It should, however, be made clear that the term 'Persian Gulf' is only used by Iranians and westerners. As far as Arabs are concerned the correct term is the 'Arabian Gulf'. English teachers can consult *Teaching Opportunities in the Middle East and North Africa* published by *AMIDEAST,* 1100 17th Street, NW, Washington DC; and see *Teaching English Abroad,* published by Vacation Work.

The *Saudi Arabian Information Agency,* in the UK is at: 18 Cavendish Square, London W1M 0AQ; tel 0171-6298803.

**Embassies and Consulates**
British Embassy, Al Hamra, PO Box 94351, Riyadh 11693; tel 1-488-0077.
There are consulates in Jeddah and Al Khobar.
US Embassy, PO Box 94309, Collector Road M, Diplomatic Quarter, Riyadh 11693; tel 1-488-3800.

**Newspapers**
Advertisements may be placed in the English language daily *Arab News,* Saudi Research and Marketing Building, Jeddah, PO Box 4556, Saudi Arabia.

## SPECIFIC CONTACTS

**Consultants and Agencies**
Many of the agencies mentioned in *Getting the Job* deal with posts in Saudi Arabia and other Middle Eastern countries. Agencies under *Computer Services* and *Oil, Mining and Engineering* are particularly likely to be involved in recruitment for the Middle East. Also see the relevant columns of vacancies in *Overseas Jobs Express,* Premier House, Shoreham Airport, West Sussex BN43 5FF; tel 01273-440220; fax 01273-440229; e-mail editor@oje1.demon.co.uk; http://www.overseasjobs.com.

**Construction and Engineering**
*CCL (Contracts Consultancy Limited),* 162-164 Upper Richmond Road, London SW15 2SL, tel 0181-333 4141 — offers positions to highly qualified engineers and professionals in a wide variety of locations including Saudi Arabia.

*Thomas Mining Associates,* PO Box 2023, Bournemouth BH4 8YR, tel 01202-751658, fax 01202-764448 — has vacancies for engineers and mining technicians in Saudi Arabia (See *Oil, Mining and Engineering*).

**Medicine and Nursing**

*Al Mouwasat Hospital,* PO Box 282, Damman 31411 — offers one and two-year contracts to doctors, head nurses and supervisors, and other administrative department heads. All certificates should be confirmed by the Saudi Arabian Embassy.

*Arabian Careers Ltd.,* 115 Shaftesbury Avenue, Cambridge Circus, London WC2H 8AD, tel 0171-379 7877, fax 0171-379 0885 — has vacancies for administrative and medical staff in Middle Eastern hopsitals, including Saudi Arabia.

*BNA International,* 3rd Floor, 443 Oxford Street, London W1R 2NA — recruits nurses for hospitals in Dhahran, Jeddah, Khamis Mushayt and Riyadh. RGNs must have a minimum of two years' post registration, with some opportunities for ENs with two years' post-enrolment experience as well as for midwives, lab technicians, radiographers etc. Contracts are for a year.

*HCA International,* One Park Plaza, PO Box 500, Nashville, Tennessee 37202 — manages the King Faisal Specialist Hospital & Research Centre for the Saudi Government. Staff requirements include physicians, surgeons, nurses, administrators, pharmacists, etc. There is an office in the UK at: St Christopher's House, St. Christopher's Place, London W1M.

For more medical recruitment agencies, see *Health Professionals Abroad* (Vacation Work).

**General**

*Anthony Moss & Associates,* 173 Drummond Street, London NW1 3JD — recruits for a range of professions in the Middle East, including banking, construction, oil and gas, CAD specialists, telecommunications, training, medical.

# Other Countries

## IMMIGRATION AND WORK PERMITS

Methods of obtaining the necessary work and residence permits vary, but the embassies are usually not involved in the procedure. The Consular Section which can arrange your visa is likely to be your first port of call. In every country in this part of the world, immigrants will have to overcome some bureaucratic procedures and time-consuming paperwork that has to be filled out (usually in triplicate) at each stage of the application. Most of the forms are printed in several languages; in some cases they must also be completed in Arabic, or accompanied by an official translation into Arabic.

A few guidelines are given below for each of the countries offering a significant amount of employment openings to international workers, along with the addresses of their embassies.

**Bahrain**

Generally considered the most cosmopolitan of Gulf States, many expatriates based in Saudi Arabia come here for relaxing weekends. This is a small country (only 500,000 population), so work opportunities are limited in this respect. Non-oil sectors of the economy include aluminium smelting, ship repair, building materials, iron and steel pelletising and light engineering, as well as food processing. Application for a work permit is made by the employer in Bahrain. The *Embassy of Bahrain* is at 98 Gloucester Road, London SW7 4AU, tel 0171-370 5132-3; and 3502 International Drive, NW, Washington DC 20008, tel 202-342-0741-2.

## Jordan

Ruled by the British-educated King Hussein, the Hashemite Kingdom of Jordan is too impoverished to offer many employment opportunities. Local English-language schools sometimes recruit teachers on the spot. One such school is *Yarmouk Cultural Centre,* PO Box 960312, Amman. There is a British Council office at: Rainbow Street (off First Circle), Jabal Amman (PO Box 634, Amman 11118, tel 6-636147). The *Jordanian Embassy* is at 6 Upper Phillimore Gardens, London W8 7HB, tel 0171-937 3685; and 3504 International Drive, NW, Washington, DC 20008, tel 202-966-2664.

## Kuwait

The number of jobs available in Kuwait following the Gulf War has not increased, partly because the Kuwaitis would like to reduce their dependence on foreign workers. Inquiries should be made to agencies or contractors, rather than embassies. Work permits are obtained in advance by the employer in Kuwait. *The Embassy of the State of Kuwait,* 45 Queen's Gate, London SW7 5HR, tel 0171-589 4533, suggests placing an advertisement in the classified section of a Kuwaiti newspaper through the *Arab Advertising Agency,* PO Box 2221, 13023 Safat, Kuwait. The *Embassy of Kuwait in the USA* is at: 2940 Tilden Street, NW, Washington DC 20008; tel 202-966-0702.

## Morocco

Work permits are necessary for employment in Morocco; they are generally only given to people who speak French and/or Arabic, and where no Moroccan is available to fill the post. Applications should be addressed to the *Ministère de l'Emploi,* Quartier Administratif, Rabat, Morocco.

Because of high unemployment among local professionals and graduates, the main (and not always well-paid) opportunities are in English teaching (see the *Teaching* chapter) or with tour operators (see *Transport, Tourism and Hospitality*). Students who want information about work camps may contact the following organisation: *UMAC (Union Marocaine des Associations des Chantiers),* 37 rue el Hind, Immeuble Ghandouri, appt 3, BP 455, Rabat RP, Maroc. The *Moroccan Embassy* is at 49 Queen's Gate Gardens, London SW7 5NE, tel 0171-581 5001 (the Consulate telephone number is 0171-724 0719); 1601 21st Street, NW, Washington DC 20009, tel 202-462-7979/82.

## Oman

The Gulf State of Oman has close historical links with Britain, which gave military assistance when the country was threatened by an internal rebellion in the early 1970s. By all accounts, it offers a comparatively good quality of life for expatriates. Advertisements for workers sometimes appear in the national and international recruitment press. The Embassy of Oman is sometimes involved in recruitment of workers from abroad. There are particularly good opportunities for teachers.

A prospective employer must first obtain a Labour Clearance from the Directorate General of Labour, *Ministry of Social Affairs & Labour,* PO Box 560, Muscat and a 'No Objection Certificate' from the Directorate General of Immigration, Oman. Upon arrival, a residence permit (valid for two years, renewable) must be obtained. Further details from the *Embassy of the Sultanate of Oman,* 167 Queen's Gate, London SW7 5HE, tel 0171-225 0001; 2535 Belmont Road, NW, Washington DC 20008, tel 202-387-1980-2.

**United Arab Emirates**

A union of seven small sheikhdoms, most of the UAE's wealth is generated by Abu Dhabi and Dubai. Without their extensive oil and gas reserves, the Emirates would otherwise still be economically dependent on pearl-diving, fishing and dates. Dubai is also a significant trading centre and developing its non-petroleum industries. In Abu Dhabi, employment opportunities are mainly in petrochemicals.

The *Embassy of the United Arab Emirates,* 30 Princes Gate, London SW7 1PT, tel 0171-581 1281 (the consulate tel is 0171-589 3434), and Suite 600, 3000 K Street, NW, Washington DC 20007, tel 202-338-6500, suggests that those considering employment in the UAE should write to the *Ministry of Labour,* PO Box 809, Abu Dhabi, but is otherwise unable to help. There is a *Dubai Commerce and Tourism Promotion Board,* 125 Pall Mall, London SW1Y 5EA; tel 0171-839 0580.

**Other Countries**

There is far less demand for foreign workers in the other countries of the Middle East and North Africa, but the embassies listed below may be able to provide information on procedures if necessary. In many cases, however, the reply will be that they are not involved in the issuing of work permits.

*Algerian Embassy,* 54 Holland Park, London W11 3RS; tel 0171-221 7800.
*Algerian Embassy,* 2118 Kalorama Road, NW, Washington, DC 20008; tel 202-265-2800.

*Egyptian Embassy,* 26 South Street, London W1Y 8EL; tel 0171-499 2401.
Egyptian Embassy, 3521 International Court, NW, Washington, DC 20008; tel 202-895-5400 or 966-6342 (Consular Section).

*Israeli Embassy,* 2 Palace Green, London W8 4QB; tel 0171-957 9500.
*Israeli Embassy,* 3514 International Drive, NW, Washington, DC 20008; tel 202-364-5500.

*Lebanese Embassy,* 21 Kensington Palace Gardens, London W8 4QN; tel 0171-727 6696.
*Lebanese Embassy,* 2560 28th Street, NW, Washington, DC 20008; tel 202-939-6300.

*Syrian Embassy,* 8 Belgrave Square, London SW1X 8PH; tel 0171-245 9012.
*Syrian Embassy,* 2215 Wyoming Avenue, NW, Washington, DC 20008; tel 202-232-6313.

*Tunisian Embassy,* 29 Prince's Gate, London SW7 1QG; tel 0171-584 8117.
*Tunisian Embassy,* 1515 Massachusetts Avenue, NW, Washington DC; tel 202-862-1850.

*Yemeni Embassy,* 57 Cromwell Road, London SW7 2ED; tel 0171-584 6607.
*Yemeni Embassy,* Suite 705, 2600 Virginia Avenue, NW, Washington, DC 20037; tel 202-965-4760-1.

# Africa

Work prospects for foreigners are limited in most of Africa. Much of the continent is heavily indebted. Civil wars, droughts, and disease have left their mark on economies which have generally been mismanaged since most African countries achieved independence. Corruption is endemic; and the economic situation leads to political instability, although democracy is making a tentative reappearance in some. The former colonial powers left behind their own democratic institutions; these have often failed to take root; and the map of Africa does not really correspond to the various ethnic and national affiliations. On the positive side, this colonial inheritance means there are many cultural links with western European and North American countries. Africans often speak English (or French); and have a close understanding of Britain and other European countries which is greater than in some Asian countries, for example. Emigration means that many are familiar with life in Europe or the USA at first — or second, or third — hand. While the formal jobs market may be fragmented (and dependent on the 'primary' areas of development and infrastructure) there are informal opportunities for those with the right skills; or the more adventurous who are willing to fund their own trip and living costs.

Macroeconomic structures, to lay the foundation for industrial and commercial development and the long process of nation-building, are linchpin of international work in sub-Saharan Africa. Environmentalists and agriculturalists; those working in related industries, like food-processing and distribution; as well as healthcare workers, engineers, and those who can train and act as advisers in these fields, are most in demand. The difficulties must not be overlooked, but there are also opportunities for work, for example in tourism, or the exploitation of mineral and energy resources, which are already sources of employment for international jobseekers in countries like the Gambia, Nigeria, Senegal, or Zimbabwe; there are likely to be jobs 'on-the-spot' for many of those experienced enough in the local conditions to try this approach to living and working in Africa. Otherwise, the international recruitment press, and publications like *African Business* (represented in the UK for advertising purposes by *HZI International Ltd.*, Africa House, 64-78 Kingsway, London WC2B 6AH, tel 0171-242 6346), can be sources of direct and indirect job opportunities in this region.

*Skillshare Africa* is a charity which recruits qualified volunteers and workers in construction, civil engineering. auto mechanics and other technical areas, in Botswana, Lesotho, Mozambique and Swaziland. (There is more about voluntary and development work in the *Voluntary Work* chapter). Other jobs and careers which involve working in Africa can be found in the chapters on the *United Nations, International Organisations, Teaching* and *Transport, Tourism and Hospitality*.

A knowledge of French will also be an advantage: there are many vacancies in the often more affluent French-speaking parts of West Africa, for instance, which are more often advertised for French citizens (so a look at the recruitment pages of the major French newspapers like *Le Monde* and *Le Figaro* can be one more way of finding some of these in countries which have strong French connections). Portuguese is also spoken in Angola and Mozambique. But English is the most widely known and fastest growing medium of communication in the domains of business and and international trade throughout Africa.

South Africa, with its greater expatriate population, and more developed economy, is a separate case; and is dealt with below.

# South Africa

South African High Commission, South Africa House, Trafalgar Square, London WC2N 5DP, tel 0171-930 4488
South African Embassy, 3051 Massachusetts Avenue, NW, Washington DC 20008, tel 202-232-4400
Currency: 1 Rand = 100 cents (R or ZAR)
Rate of Exchange: £1 = R7; $1 = R4.5

South Africa has made a successful transition to a majority democratic government which at present includes all sections of the population. This has led to the raising of sanctions; and increased trade and employment opportunities (although unemployment is a problem, especially at the unskilled end of the jobs market, across all sections of its ethnically and culturally diverse communities). At the southern end of the African continent, it has its largest economy. Agriculture is strong enough to make it self-sufficient in most food products, and an exporter of some, like fruit and wine. The foundation of its economy is mining, with valuable metals like chromium, manganese, vanadium and platinum, as well as gold and diamonds. There was a slowdown in the 1980s, in part due to sanctions (which were a factor in the transition to a democratic majority government) and the priorities are presently to ease its considerable foreign debt; and a Reconstruction and Development Programme (RDP) which is aimed at reducing some of its social inequalities. Manufacturing contributes 25% to its Gross National Product; trade 13.5%; mining 10%; and agriculture 4.3%

Britons still represent the largest group of immigrants to South Africa, with about 1,000 settling there every year. These range, according to the South African High Commission, from pensioners wishing to spend their retirement there to 'young professionals seeking to advance their careers'. A larger number of white South Africans are emigrating every year to countries like Australia and New Zealand. South Africa recently introduced stricter criteria for those seeking permanent residence, including a charge currently of £1,020 for residence permits for individuals.

## GENERAL FACTS

### Population
South Africa has a population of 41 million. In terms of migration, the majority of newcomers come from the UK, Europe and Zimbabwe. Some of its own citizens have emigrated to Britain and the USA more recently, though. The Republic covers 450,000 square miles (one-eighth the size of the USA) and is divided into nine regions: Western Cape; the Eastern Cape; the Northern Cape; KwaZulu/Natal; the Orange Free State; the North West; the Northern Transvaal; the Eastern Transvaal; and PWV (Pretoria and Witwatersrand Vereeniging).

### Climate and Geography
The country is divided into three main geographical regions: plateau, mountains, and the coastal belt. The vegetation is generally grassland, changing to bush in Northern Transvaal, and approaching dry, desert conditions in the north-west. The climate is broadly temperate, but the summer heat can be oppressive and exceed 30°C. Winter temperatures average 17-19°C; and during these months

the interior is renowned for its clear, sunny skies. The average daily sunshine varies from 7.5 to 9.5 hours.

## Cities

South Africa is comparatively urbanised; more than half of its people live in towns and cities. Those classified as black or coloured were until recently legally excluded from certain residential areas; and still live mainly in sprawling 'townships' such as Soweto, on the outskirts of the main cities.

## Religion, Sport & Culture

It is a predominantly Christian country (80%). The largest grouping is the Black Independent Church movement, while the largest of the established churches is the Dutch Reformed Church (*Nederduitse Gereformeerde Kerk*). An estimated five million people follow traditional religions to a greater or lesser extent; the other major religions are Hinduism, Islam and Judaism.

Sport could be said to be the other religion in South Africa. One major factor in bringing about political change in the 1970s and 80s was the severing of international sporting links, in cricket, rugby, and athletics in particular, which are especially popular among the white population. Soccer is mainly popular in the townships; and is the most widely played game in terms of participants. Other pastimes include tennis, golf and a host of water sports — in all of which South Africans have excelled.

South Africa possesses as rich a cultural mix as anywhere in the world. The major cities can offer theatres, cinemas, music, and other arts, and a cultural life which is a mixture of European and African influences.

# FACTORS INFLUENCING EMPLOYMENT

## Immigration

British, Irish and US citizens do not require a visa for holiday and business visits to South Africa. Temporary residence permits are available on arrival, granted for up to three months. This can be extended at the nearest Regional Office of the Department of Home Affairs, or the head office in Pretoria: Director-General for Home Affairs, Private Bag X114, Civitas, Struben Street, Pretoria 0001. Work, work-seekers and study permits must be obtained before entry. Work permits are only issued to individuals who are in possession of a firm written offer or contract of employment from a South African employer. Nowadays, the number of places are limited; and applicants must meet strict criteria. Details are available from the South African Embassy or High Commission from the Chief Migration Officer, but 'the overriding consideration in dealing with applications for work permits will be whether the employment offered cannot be filled by a person already in South Africa'.

*Citizenship:* A migrant can apply for citizenship after a five-year period of permanent residence; and no requirement exists for individuals to relinquish their original nationality or citizenship. New migrants are allowed to change their occupation within the first three years of residence only with permission from the department of Home Affairs. A holder of permanent residence who does not wish to become a South African citizen after the designated five-year period relinquishes the right to both.

## Languages

Several official languages exist side by side: Afrikaans; English; isiNdebele; Sesotho sa Leboa; Sesotho siSwati; Xitsonga; Setswana; Tshivenda; isiXhosa and isiZulu. The majority of South Africans speak English; and signposts, government literature and even telephone directories are generally printed in this language. In general, newspapers and the broadcasting media operate in separate languages, the main ones being English and Afrikaans.

## Cost and Standard of Living

Although prices are lower than in the UK or USA, so are the salaries. Costs vary from region to region; and in the case of fresh foodstuffs also differ according to the season. The previously disproportionately high standard of living of the white population, of mainly Dutch and British descent, has diminished somewhat; and there is a new black middle class. But all sections of society have suffered from an incomplete recovery from the recession of the 1980s and unfavourable exchange rates. Housing for expatriates, typically with swimming pools and tennis courts, is still luxurious by most standards. The excellent climate and superb scenery are major attractions.

## Health

The system of health care is presently under strain; and private insurance is recommended. One of the first priorities of the national Reconstruction and Development Programme (RDP) has been to bring together the various services as one national health system.

## Embassies and Consulates

British Embassy, 255 Hill Street, Arcadia, Pretoria, 0002; tel 12-461-7220.
There are Consulates also in Cape Town, Port Elizabeth, East London, Johannesburg, and Durban.

US Embassy, PO Box 9536, 877 Pretorius Street, Pretoria; tel 12-342-1048.
Consulates in Cape Town, Durban, and Johannesburg.

## Tourist Offices

South African Tourism Board (SATOUR), 5-6 Alt Grove, London SW19 4DZ; tel 0181-944 8080.
South African Tourist Board (SATOUR), Suite 2040, 500 Fifth Avenue, New York, NY; tel 212-730-2929 or 1-800-8225368. Office also in Los Angeles.

# CONDITIONS OF WORK

## Wages

A system of industrial councils oversees collective bargaining. Minimum wage levels differ from industry to industry and from region to region. By law a minimum of two weeks' sick leave is payable. Wages are generally lower than the UK or USA.

## Hours

The normal working week is 40 hours, and does not exceed 46 hours. Some industries shut down annually for three weeks from the middle of December.

# WORK AVAILABLE

## General

South Africa generally requires migrants with certain specific skills, in particular in computers, medicine, engineering (including petrochemicals), financial management, business consultancy, accountancy and sales. *SASTS,*, 8th Floor, JHI House, 5 Heerengracht, Cape Town 8000, tel 021-418-3794, fax 021-418-3795, e-mail sasts@iafrica.com — is developing exchange and work programmes for students and young people (in the UK in cooperation with its partner *BUNAC*).

## Newspapers

The monthly newspaper for potential migrants, *South Africa News,* is available from some travel agents in the UK, or by subscription from: *Outbound Newspapers*, 1 Commercial Road, Eastbourne, East Sussex BN21 3XQ. *Powers International* (517-523 Fulham Road, London SW6 1HD; tel 0171-385 8855) represents for advertising purposes in the UK the largest circulation newspaper, the *Sunday Times*. Advertisements in South African newspapers can also be placed through their offices in South Africa. *A&J Distribution*, 79-81 New Kings Road, Fulham, London SW6 4SQ, tel 0171-384 3771, distributes the *Sunday Times* (which has a recruitment section) and the *Financial Mail* in the UK. One of the major newspaper groups is *Argus South African Newspapers*, PO Box 56, 8000 Cape Town.

## SPECIFIC CONTACTS

### Employment Agencies
A selection of agencies is given below:

Kelly Personnel: Cuthberts Building, 102 Maitland Street, Bloemfontein; tel 47-9991

Drake SA: Kingsfield Place, Field Street, Durban; tel 304-4343

Rent-a-Student: 12 Regent Place, Westville; tel 86-2127

Drake Personnel: Shell House, Riebeeck Street, Cape Town; tel 25-3300

Canimploy Staff Services: 247 Lower Main Road, Cape Town; tel 47-8138

Staff Plan: Harland House, 17 Loveday Street, Johannesburg; tel 832-1546

Churchill Personnel Ltd. Sanlam Centre, Andries Street, Pretoria; tel 322-1130.

### Professional Organisations
Professional organisations are quick to point out they do not act as employment agencies. However, they can often prove a useful source of general information on career prospects and offer possible contacts to job hunters. A selection is given below:

Division of Veterinary Services, Private Bag X138, Pretoria 0001.

Financial Institutions, Accountant-General, Poynton Centre, Church Street West, Pretoria 0002.

The National Institute of SA Architects, PO Box 7322, Johannesburg 2000.

The South African Medical and Dental Council, PO Box 205, Pretoria 0001.

The South African Nursing Council, PO Box 1123, Pretoria 0001.

The Pharmaceutical Society of South Africa, Pharmacy House, PO Box 31360, Bloemfontein 2017.

### Other Opportunities
For opportunities in medical and healthcare work, see *Health Professionals Abroad* by Tim Ryder (Vacation Work). The S.A. JOBWEB Home Page on the Internet has links to vacancies and recruitment agencies in South Africa. See under *The Internet and the World Wide Web* in the chapter *The Creative Job Search*. General Information on South Africa, with listings of companies, commercial and development projects, trade fairs etc., may be supplied by the *Department of Trade and Industry*, South Africa Desk, Bay 448, Kingsgate House, 66-74 Victoria Street, London SW1E 6SW. Two quarterly magazines, *Opportunity Africa* and *Opportunity South Africa*, are published free of charge in the UK by Westoning House Ltd., tel 0171-336 7312.

The *United Nations Development Programme* (see the chapter *International Organisations*) has recently established a field office in South Africa, mail address: PO Box 6541, Pretoria 3001.

## IMMIGRATION AND WORK PERMITS

The procedures for immigration vary from one African country to another. The respective embassies in London (with the exception of those listed under *Government Agencies* in the *Getting the Job* chapter) are unlikely to get involved in either issuing/processing work permits or arranging work. Tourist offices may be able to offer useful information and advice about the country in question, for medical and travel purposes for instance. Applications generally involve a great deal of paperwork, and can take months to process.

## Namibia

For those who literally want to get away from it all, Namibia could be an ideal destination, with a population of 1.4 million spread out over an area four times the size of Great Britain. This very scenic and unspoilt land only gained its independence from South Africa in March 1990, after years of bitter struggle. The main economic activities are mining and agriculture, as well as tourism. Tourists from Britain and the USA do not require an entry visa for stays of up to three months; business visitors should provide a letter of introduction. Because of very high unemployment, the government has had to clamp down on foreign workers. It is now necessary for potential employers to look for local workers first; residence and work permits must be arranged in advance with the Ministry of Home Affairs. For further information contact: *Namibian High Commission* at 6 Chandos Street, London W1M 0LQ, tel 0171-636 6244; *Namibian Embassy*, 1605 New Hampshire Avenue, NW, Washington DC 20009, tel 202-986-0540.

## Nigeria

A brief circular from the Nigerian High Commission in London states bluntly: 'There are no employment opportunities in Nigeria'. The majority of jobs in Nigeria are for skilled personnel who are recruited by multinational companies or the government. These are usually in connection with the oil industry, which accounts for up to 90% of Nigeria's export earnings. English language teachers are often in short supply; jobs are usually available on the spot rather than through UK adverts. Enquiries to the *Nigerian High Commission* which is at 9 Northumberland Avenue, London WC2 5BX; Nigerian Embassy, 2201 M St., NW, Washington DC 20037.

## Zimbabwe

Zimbabwe has close economic ties with South Africa. Most of the population is reliant on agriculture; and the limited economy offers little in the way of employment. Mining (of nickel and gold) is also important. Harare and Bulawayo are the two major cities and provide the best work prospects, especially in the growing tourist industry. Other sources of jobs are through South African companies with branches in Zimbabwe. Immigration details are available from the *Zimbabwe High Commission*, 429 Strand, London WC2R 0SA, tel 0171-836 7755; or the *Zimbabwe Embassy*, 1608 New Hampshire Avenue, NW, Washington, DC 20009, tel 202-332-7100.

# Other Countries

The rest of Africa offers very few employment opportunities. The positions that are available tend to be with aid agencies and multinational organisations (see chapters on *Voluntary Work, United Nations* and *International Organisations* in particular). The Embassies and High Commissions listed below can provide information on immigration, but are unlikely to offer much advice on work prospects.

*Botswana High Commission*, 6 Stratford Place, London W1N 9AE; tel 0171-499 0031.
*Botswana Embassy*, Suite 7M, 3400 International Drive, NW, Washington, DC 20008; tel 202-244-4990-1.

*Ethiopian Embassy*, 17 Princes Gate, London SW7 1PZ; tel 0171-589 7212.

*Ethiopian Embassy,* Kalorama Road, NW, Washington, DC 20008; tel 202-234-2281-2.

*The Gambia High Commission,* 57 Kensington Court, London W8 5DG; tel 0171-937 6316-8.
*The Gambia Embassy,* Suite 1000, 1155 15th Street, NW, Washington, DC 20005; tel 202-785-1399 or 785-1379.

*Ghana High Commission,* 104 Highgate Hill, London N6 5HE; tel 0181-342 8686.
*Ghanaian Embassy,* 3512 International Drive, NW, Washington, DC 20008; tel 202-686-4520.

*Kenya High Commission,* 45 Portland Place, London W1N 3AS; tel 0171-636 2371 or 636 2375.
*Kenya Embassy,* 2249 R Street, NW, Washington, DC 20008; tel 202-387-6101.

*Senegal Embassy,* 11 Philllimore Gardens, London W8 7QG; tel 0171-9370 925-6.
*Senegal Embassy,* 2112 Wyoming Avenue, NW, Washington, DC 20008; tel 202-234-0540-1.

*Sudan Embassy,* 3 Cleveland Row, London SW1A 1DD; tel 0171-839 8080.
*Sudan Embassy,* 2210 Massachusetts Avenue, NW, Washington, DC 20008; tel 202-338-8565.

*Tanzania High Commission,* 43 Hertford Street, London W1Y 8DB; tel 0171-407 0566.
*Tanzanian Embassy,* 2139 R Street, NW, Washington, DC 20008; tel 202-939-6125.

*Zambian High Commission,* 2 Palace Gate, London W8 5NG; tel 0171-589 6655.
*Zambian Embassy,* 2419 Massachusetts Avenue, NW, Washington, DC 20008; tel 202-2659717-9.

# Appendix One
# Bibliography

See the inside back page for a full list of Vacation Work publications which may also provide useful further reading and contacts. A catalogue is available from Vacation Work, 9 Park End Street, Oxford OX1 1HJ, England, tel 01865-241978, fax 01865-790885. Vacation Work publications are distributed in the USA by Peterson's Guides, PO Box 2123, Princeton, NJ 08543-2123. Peterson's Education Center and Summer Options sector is on the Internet at http:www.petersons.com.

*A Mouthful of Air, Language and Languages, especially English,* Anthony Burgess, Hutchinson, 20 Vauxhall Bridge Road, London SW1V 2SA.

*A Year Between,* Central Bureau for Educational Visits and Exchanges, 10 Spring Gardens, London SW1A 2BN.

*AGCAS Careers Information Booklets,* CSU (Publications) Ltd., Armstrong House, Oxford Road, Manchester M1 7ED.

*And A Good Job Too,* David Mackintosh, Orion Publishing Group Ltd., Orion House, 5 Upper St Martin's Lane, London WC2H 9EA.

*Build Your own Rainbow, a Workbook for Career and Life Management,* Barrie Hopson and Mike Scally, Mercury Books, 125A The Broadway, Didcot, Oxfordshire OX11 8AW.

*Career Opportunities in the European Commission,* European Commission (UK address: 8 Storey's Gate, London SW1P 3AT).

*Careers Encyclopedia,* Audrey Segal and Katherine Lea (eds.), Cassell, Wellington House, 125 Strand, London WC2R 0BB; 387 Park Avenue South, New York, NY 10016-8810.

*CEPEC Recruitment Guide,* CEPEC Ltd., Princes House, 36 Jermyn Street, London SW1Y 6DN.

*Changing Your Job After 35,* G. Golzen and P. Plumbley, Kogan Page Ltd., 120 Pentonville Road, London N12 9JN.

*Directory of International Internships,* Office of Overseas Study, 108 International Center, Michigan State University, East Lansing, MI 48824.

*The Directory of Opportunities for Graduates,* Newpoint Publishing Company Ltd., Windsor Court, East Grinstead House, East Grinstead, West Sussex RH19 1XA.

*Discovering Germany,* Central Bureau for Educational Visits and Exchanges.

*The EARLS Guide to Language Schools in Europe,* Cassell, Wellington House, 125 Strand, London WC2R 0BB; 387 Park Avenue South, New York, NY 10016-8810.

*Great Answers to Tough Interview Questions,* Martin John Yate, Kogan Page Ltd.

*Guide to Careers in World Affairs,* Foreign Policy Association, 729 Seventh Avenue, New York, NY 10019.

*Home from Home — The Complete Guide to Homestays and Exchanges,* Central Bureau.

*How to Complete a Job Application Form,* University of London Careers Service (ULCS), 50 Gordon Square, London WC1H 0PQ.

*How To Find Temporary Work Abroad,* Nick Vandome, How To Books, Plymbridge House, Estover Road, Plymouth PL6 7PZ.

*How To Get a Job Abroad,* Roger Jones, How To Books.

*How to Get a Job in the Pacific Rim,* Robert Sanborn and Anderson Brandao, Surrey Books, 230 East Ohio Street, Suite 120, Chicago, Illinois 60611.

*How to pass Graduate Recruitment Tests,* Kogan Page Ltd.

*How to Write a Curriculum Vitae,* University of London Careers Service (ULCS).

*International Guide to Qualifications in Education,* Cassell.

*Internships USA,* Peterson's Guides, PO Box 2123, Princeton, NJ 08543-2123; Vacation Work Publications, Oxford (UK distributors).

*Job Hunting Made Easy,* John Bramham and David Cox, Kogan Page Ltd.

*Opportunities to Work in the European Community's Institutions,* by J. Goodman and C. Tobin, CSU (Publications) Ltd., Armstrong House, Oxford Road, Manchester M1 7ED.

*The Penguin Careers Guide,* Anna Alston and Anne Daniel, Penguin Books Ltd., 27 Wrights Lane, London W8 5TZ.

*Succeed at your job interview,* George Heariside, BBC Books, Woodlands, 80 Wood Lane, London W12 0TT.

*Summer Jobs Abroad,* Vacation Work Publications.

*Overseas Summer Jobs* Peterson's Guides; Princeton.

*Summer Jobs USA,* Peterson's Guides; Vacation Work Publications (UK distributors).

*Teaching English Abroad,* Vacation Work Publications; Peterson's Guides (USA distributors).

*Test Your Own Aptitude,* J. Barrett and G. Williams, Kogan Page Ltd.

*Volunteer Work,* Central Bureau for Educational Visits and Exchanges.

*What Color Is Your Parachute?,* Richard Nelson Bolles, Ten Speed Press, PO Box 7123, Berkeley, California 94707.

*Work, Study, Travel Abroad,* Council on International Educationall Exchange, 205 East 42nd Street, New York, NY 10017.

*Work Your Way Around the World,* Vacation Work Publications; Peterson's Guides (USA distributors).

*Working Abroad,* Godfrey Golzen, Kogan Page Ltd.

*Working Holidays,* Central Bureau for Educational Visits and Exchanges.

*Working in Tourism,* Vacation Work Publications.

*Working in the European Union,* W.H. Archer and A.J. Raban, CSU (Publications) Ltd.

*Working on Cruise Ships,* Vacation Work Publications.

*Writers' & Artists' Yearbook,* A.&C. Black Ltd., 35 Bedford Row, London WC1R 4JH.

*Yearbook of Recruitment and Employment Services,* Federation of Recruitment and Employment Services Ltd. (FRES), 36-38 Mortimer Street, London W1N 7RB.

# Appendix Two
# Worldwide Living Standards

The following table represents the average per capita Gross National Product in thirty-two of the countries cited in this book.

|  | US Dollars |
|---|---|
| Switzerland | 37,930 |
| Japan | 34,630 |
| Denmark | 27,970 |
| Norway | 26,390 |
| USA | 25,880 |
| Germany | 25,580 |
| Austria | 24,630 |
| Sweden | 23,530 |
| France | 23,420 |
| Belgium | 22,870 |
| Singapore | 22,500 |
| Netherlands | 22,010 |
| Canada | 19,510 |
| Italy | 19,300 |
| Finland | 18,850 |
| United Kingdom | 18,340 |
| Australia | 18,000 |
| Ireland | 13,530 |
| Spain | 13,440 |
| New Zealand | 13,350 |
| Portugal | 9,320 |
| South Korea | 8,260 |
| Greece | 7,700 |
| Saudi Arabia | 7,050 |
| Hungary | 3,840 |
| Czech Republic | 3,200 |
| South Africa | 3,040 |
| Russia | 2,650 |
| Poland | 2,410 |
| Ukraine | 1,910 |
| China | 0,530 |

(Source: *From Plan to Market — World Development Report 1996,* World Bank)

# Appendix Three
# Key to Company Classifications

1  Accounting and Auditing
2  Advertising and Public Relations
3  Airlines and Aerospace Products
4  Banking, Finance and Investment
5  Boats
6  Building materials
7  Cars, Caravans and other Vehicles
8  Chemicals and Pharmaceuticals
9  Clothing
10  Computers, Electrical and Electronic Equipment
11  Cosmetics and Toiletries
12  Dental, Medical and Optical Supplies
13  Department Stores
14  Executive and Management Consultants
15  Export and Import Trading
16  Foodstuffs and Beverages
17  Freight Storage and Transport
18  Furnishings and Domestic Appliances
19  Glassware and Tiles
20  Hotels and Restaurants
21  Hotel Supplies
22  Industrial Instruments and Precision Engineering
23  Insurance
24  Lawyers

25  Machinery and Industrial Equipment
26  Machine Tools
27  Mechanical Handling Equipment
28  Metal Products
29  Music and Musical Instruments
30  Office Equipment
31  Packaging
32  Paints
33  Paper Products
34  Personnel Agencies
35  Petrochemicals
36  Photographic Equipment
37  Plastics
38  Printing, Publishing and Graphics
39  Pumps and Hydraulic Equipment
40  Real Estate
41  Ropes and Cables
42  Rubber Goods
43  Security
44  Shoes
45  Telecommunications
46  Textiles
47  Tobacco and Tobacco Machinery
48  Tourist Agencies and Travel Services
49  Toy Manufacture
50  Watches and Jewellery

# Index to Organisations

412